NICHOLSON'S
HISTORIC
BRITAIN

WITHDRAWN

8/11/83 B+T $12.95

Robert Nicholson Publications

A Nicholson Guide

First published 1982

© **Robert Nicholson Publications Limited 1982**

Original cartography: Fairey Surveys Limited,
Maidenhead, to © design by Robert Nicholson
Publications Limited. Maps revised by Geographia
Limited, London.
Maps based upon the Ordnance Survey with the
sanction of Her Majesty's Stationery Office. Crown
copyright reserved.
Original black and white county maps by Geographia
Limited 1982.

Edited by Rosemarie McCabe

Drawings by Towler Cox

Robert Nicholson Publications Limited
17–21 Conway Street
London W1P 6JD

Typeset in England by
Rowland Phototypesetting Ltd
Bury St Edmunds, Suffolk

Printed in Great Britain by The Anchor Press Ltd
and bound by Wm Brendon & Son Ltd,
both of Tiptree, Essex

Colour section printed in Great Britain by
Balding & Mansell, Wisbech, Cambridgeshire

ISBN 0 905522 53 2

&CONTENTS&

HOW TO USE THIS GUIDE

Great Britain is divided into 13 regions, as shown on the diagrammatic map on P.5. Each region is made up of a number of counties and each county is highlighted by an individual map to which each place mentioned is keyed by number. This enables you to see at a glance how many places of interest are to be found in the area you're visiting. Every entry in the guide is listed alphabetically within its county section. When reading the descriptions, you may come across unfamiliar architectural terms or periods in history. So for easy reference, we have included a glossary, a summary of architectural terms and a family tree showing the reigns of British monarchs from William the Conqueror onwards.

Once you decide where to go, look for the map reference on the right-hand side of the entry. This gives its location on the colour touring maps at the front of the book and will show you how to get there. More specific directions are given in italics below. For example:

> 10. Leith Hall   11 M3
> *7m S of Huntly, B9002.*

Opening Hours: These are in italics at the end of the entry, but only if the place is open on limited days. *Most days* is four or more days a week, *certain days* three or less a week and *special days* less than once a week. If a building is open to the public every day throughout the year, no indication is given. For more details we suggest contacting the local tourist office which will have the current opening times.

Individual Counties: For the purpose of this guide the large counties of Sussex and Yorkshire are each treated as one county. London is the only region without a county map. We have regarded this as a special case for – as every Londoner knows – the best method of finding your way around the capital is with a detailed street map.

Map key

Motorway and junction number	Height above sea level in feet	
A road primary route	3000 and above	
A road	1000 – 3000	
B road	200 – 1000	
Other roads	0 – 200	
Main railway	·1334 Spot height	
Private railway	Built up area	
Canal	County boundaries	
River	8 Number of adjoining map	

Scale 1:1050 000

0 ————————————— 25 ————————————— 50 Miles

0 ————————————— 40 ————————————— 80 Kilometres

Orkney Islands

Shetland Islands

Hebrides

HIGHLANDS

LOWLANDS

Isle of Man

LAND OF RED ROSE

LAND OF WHITE ROSE

PEAK & PENNINES

WALES

SHAKESPEARE & HEART OF ENGLAND

EAST ANGLIA

HOME COUNTIES

LONDON

WEST COUNTRY

SOUTHERN COUNTIES

SOUTH-EAST ENGLAND

Isle of Wight

Channel Islands

Scilly Isles

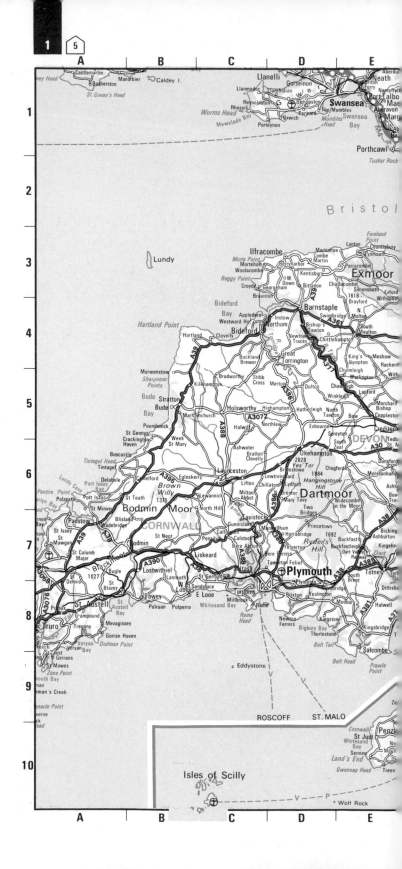

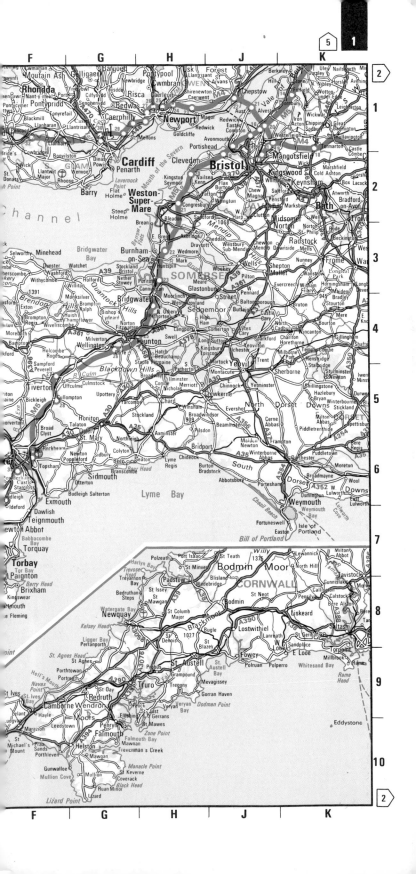

| | A | B | C | D | E |

Newchurch Whitney Eardisley King's Bodenham Wellington A4103 Malvern Link Kempsey Bishampton On Avo Harvington
1 castle Clyro Bredwardine Staunton-on-Wye Credenhill Withington WORCESTER Bosbury Great Malvern Pershore Defford A443 Evesham Mickle
Nantstephan Dorstone Blakemere Madley Vowchurch Hereford Mordiford Ledbury Longdon Eastnor Ashton under Hill Overbury Bredon Broadway Willersey Camp
Black Michaelchurch Escley Abbey Longtown Kilpeck Kings Caple Fownhope Much Marcle Dymock Stanton Bishop's Cleeve Cleeve Cloud Winchcombe Stanway
Mountains Talgarth Llangorse Tretower Llanthony Pontrilas St. Weonards Peterstow Ross-on-Wye Lea Gloucester Huntley Newent Hartpury Norton Churchdown Cheltenham Chedworth Nort

2 ngyr Gilwern Llanvihangel Crucorney Abergavenny Monmouth Whitchurch Goodrich Forest Mitcheldean Newnham Longhope A40 Staunton Coleford Cinderford Paradise Brimscombe Winstone GLOS A417 Cr Calmsden Bibury Barnsley
Brynmawr Blaenavon Llangattock Gobion Raglan Trelleck Coleford Parkend Blakeney Eastington Stroud Daglingworth Cirencester
Ebbw Vale Blaina Abercychan Usk Tintern Bream St. Briavels Sharpness Woodchester Uley Minchinhampton S. Cerney Poulton
Abertillery Pontypool Cwmbran Llantrisant Forest Hill Berkeley Dursley Horsley Avening A433 Kemble Cricklade

3 Bargoed Risca Newbridge Caerleon Shirenewton Caerwent Chepstow Vale Thornbury Wotton- under-Edge Leighterton Tetbury Charlton Ashton Keynes Purton Cricklade
nrydd Bedwas Coch Caerphilly St. Mellons Magor Redwick Redwick Aust Alveston Iron Acton Chipping Sodbury Great Badminton Great Somerford A429 Wootton Bassett Wroughton
Cardiff Penarth Clevedon Goldcliffe Avonmouth Westerleigh Pucklechurch Tormarton Castle Combe Chippenham Malmesbury Brinkworth Broad Hinton Mar

4 Dinas Powis Lavernock Point Flat Holme Kingston Seymour Nailsea Kenn Bristol A370 Mangotsfield Marshfield Cold Ashton Corsham Castle Combe Lyneham Calne Cherhill A4 W. Over Yatesbury 887
Weston- Super- Mare Steep Holme Congresbury Wrington Chew Magna Saltford Keynsham Kingswood Bath Box Bradford- on-Avon Melksham Bromham Bishops Cannings WILTS Devizes Ahington Barnes

5 water Bay Brean Bleadon Sandford Axbridge Cheddar W. Harp Clutton Midsomer Norton Wellow St. Philip Frome Trowbridge Steeple Ashton Bratton Lavington Market Lavington Urchfont Netheravon Upa
Burnham- on-Sea A39 Mark Wedmore Draycott Westbury- Sub-Mendip Mendip Downside Radstock Mells Nunney Longleat Park Warminster Westbury Heytesbury Chitterne Shrewton Salisbury Plain

6 Stockland Bristol Nether Stowey Cannington Huntspill Puriton Wookey Wells Shepton Mallet Evercreech Horningsham Maiden Bradley Longbridge Deverill A303 Codford Wylye Stapleford Great Wishford Wilton
Bridgwater Moorlinch Westonzoyland Glastonbury Street W. Pennard Pilton Nunney Friary 944 Stourton Mere E. Knoyle Hindon Dinton Quantock Hills

7 Bishop Lydeard Norton Fitzwarren Taunton Langport Somerton North Cadbury Sparkford Charlton Horethorne Wincanton Bourton Gillingham Shaftesbury Swallowcliffe Broad Chalke Comb Bisset
rton ngton Carfe Hatch Beauchamp Staple Fitzpaine Kingsbury Episcopi Martock Yeovil Milborne Port Henstridge Stalbridge Sturminster Newton Iwerne Minster Sixpenny Handley Cranborne Chase A354 Damerham
Blackdown Hills Broadway Combe St. Nicholas Ilminster Merriott Crewkerne Chinnock Montacute Yetminster Sherborne Shillingstone Hazlebury Bryan Winterbourne Stickland Blandford Forum Witchampton Verwood Cranborne

8 Upottery Yarcombe Chard Winsham Broadwindsor 909 Beaminster Evershot Cerne Abbas North Dorset Downs Milton Abbas Spettisbury Piddletrenthide Bere Regis Lytchett Minster Wimborne Minster Hurn
stock Stockland Axminster Pilsdon Maiden Newton Frampton Puddletown DORSET A35 Poole Bournemouth
aty Northleigh Colyton Bridport Winterborne Abbas Dorchester Moreton Wool Wareham Isle of Purbeck Poole Harbour Studland
Sidbury Beer Seaton Chideock Lyme Regis Burton Bradstock South Dorset Downs A352 W Broadmayne Lulworth Corfe Castle Swanage Bay Swanage Durlston Head

9 dmouth alterton Lyme Bay Abbotsbury Portesham Chesil Beach Osmington Weymouth Lulworth Cove Lulworth St. Alban's Head
Branscombe Beer Head Fortuneswell Easton Isle of Portland Weymouth Bay Bill of Portland

10 E n g l i s h

1 GUERNSEY JERSEY CHERBOURG

| | A | B | C | D | E |

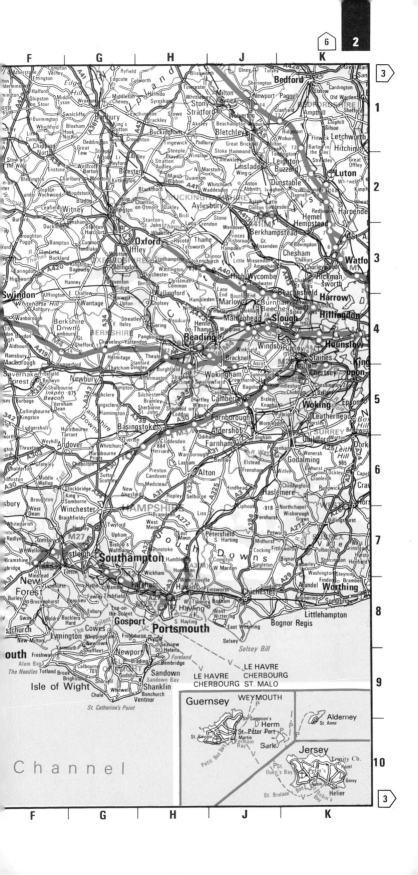

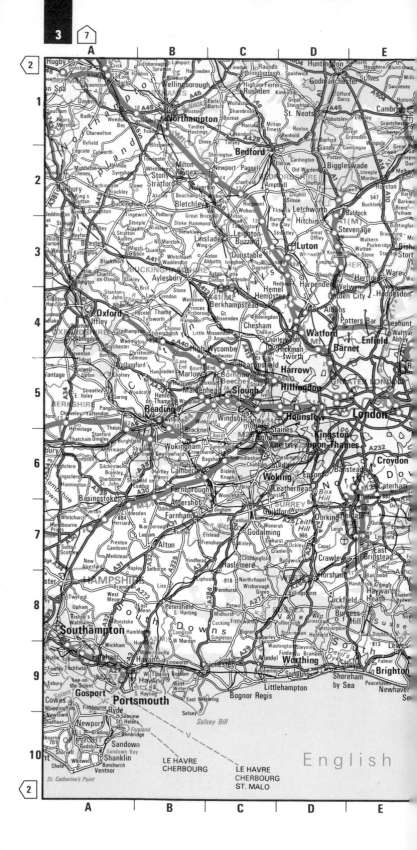

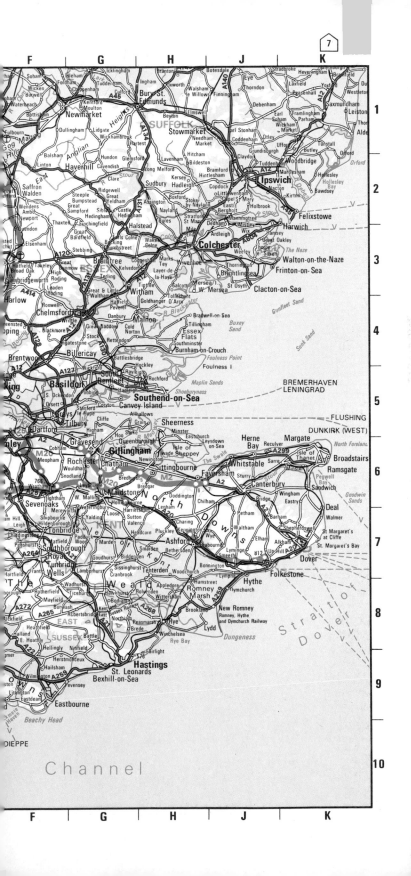

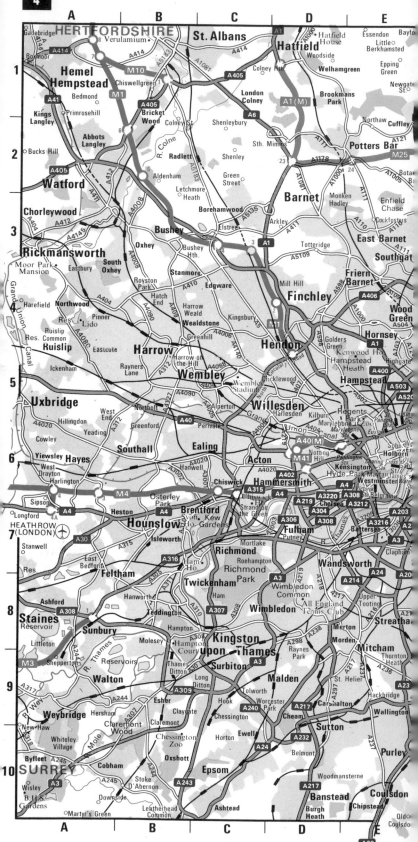

F G H J K

1

Hoddesdon
Hacketts
Gt. Parndon
Foster St.
Potter Street
High Laver
Little Laver
Magdalen Laver
A10 A1170
A414
Harlow
Broxbourne
Roydon Hamlet
Hastingwood
Fyfield
Wormley
Nazeing
Moreton
Appleby St.
Lower Nazeing
Epping Green
Thornwood Common
Bobbingworth
A414
off's Oak
Res.
Bumbles Green
Epping Upland
M11
North Weald Bassett
Shelley
A414

2

Cheshunt
A10
Waltham Cross
A121
Waltham Abbey
Upshire
B1393
Epping
A121
Ivychimneys
Theydon Bois
Coopersale Common
Toothill
Greensted
High Ongar
Chipping Ongar
A128
ESSEX
Fiddlers Hamlet
Stanford Rivers
Little End
Museum
Fortyhill
25
Lea
Valley
Park
Enfield Wash
High Beach
Epping
A104
Birch Hall
Stapleford Tawney
Kelvedon Hatch
A113
R. Roding

3

Enfield
A406
Pondets End Reservoirs
Sewardstonebury
Forest
A121
A1168
Abridge
Stapleford Abbotts
Bournebridge
Navestock
Navestock Side
Winchmore Hill
Edmonton
Chingford
Queen Elizabeth's Hunting Lodge
Buckhurst Hill
Chigwell
Lambourne End
Havering-atte-Bower
Noak Hill
South Weald
A1010
A1009
A110
A112

4

1080
A503
05
Tottenham
Walthamstow
Woodford
A406
M11
Wanstead
A123
Woodford Bridge
Grange Hill
Hainault
Chigwell Row
Mark's Gate
Collier Row
Gidea Park
Harold Hill
A12
A102(S)
Harold Wood
Squirrel's Heath
Romford
Aldborough Hatch
Barkingside
A12
A118
Emerson Park
Cranh
B1

5

A10
Hackney
Leyton
A116
A114
Ilford
A1083
Seven Kings
Newbury Park
Manor Park
A124
Becontree
Hornchurch
Rush Green
Elm Park
Upminster
Corbets Tey
A207
A104
Lea
A11
A102(M)
Forest Gate
Barking
A117
A124
Dagenham
A1020

6

A1200
Shoreditch
sbury
City of London
Spitalfields
A11
Stepney
Poplar
A102
E. Ham
W. Ham
Beckton
Creekmouth
R. Thames
Rainham
Belhus
Wennington
Liverpool St. Sta.
ard
A13
A1011
Blackwall Tunnel
A1020
Thamesmead
Belvedere
Purfleet
Aveley
Bankside
Rotherhithe Tunnel
Tower
thwark
Bermondsey
A102(M)
A1206
Woolwich
Plumstead
Abbey Wood
Erith

7

A2
A202
Deptford
A200
Maritime Museum
Greenwich
Charlton
A206
A209
Slade Green
Tunnel
A282
Stone
mherwell
New Cross
Blackheath Village
Kidbrooke
A207
Bexleyheath
Crayford
Dartford
A2214
Lewisham
A2213
Welling
A2
A226
Hither Green
A206
Bexley

8

Dulwich
South Circular Road
A2212
Palace
Eltham
New Eltham
A210
Crayford
Sidcup
A223
Coldblow
Darenth
Sydenham
rwood
A212
Catford
A21
Grove Park
Mottingham
A20
Foots Cray
North Cray
Wilmington
Hawley
Sutton at Hone
South Darenth
West
National Recreation Centre
A212
A20
A222
Chislehurst
Caves
Hextable
M25
Penge
A213
Beckenham
A222
Bromley
Petts Wood
St. Paul's Cray
Swanley
Horton Kirby

9

Sth. rwood
Selhurst
Addiscombe
A214
Eden Park
Bickley
A208
A224
St. Mary Cray
Swanley
Farningham
M20
Croydon
A232
Hayes
West Wickham
Bromley Common
Orpington
Crockenhill
Roman Villa
Lullingstone Castle
R. Darent
Eynsford Castle
Eynsford
KENT
A232
A21
Keston
Farnborough
Chelsfield
Well Hill
Braids Hatch
South Croydon
Addington
B268
New Addington
A233
Green St. Green
Pratts Bottom
West Kingsdown

10

Selsdon
Sanderstead
Leaves Green
Downe
Badger's Mount
Shoreham
Hamsey Green
Farleigh
Knockholt Pound
Halstead
A225
Kemsing
yteleafe
A22
Warlingham
Biggin Hill
Cudham
Westerham Hill
Knockholt
Chevening Park
Chevening
Otford
Heaverham

F G H J K

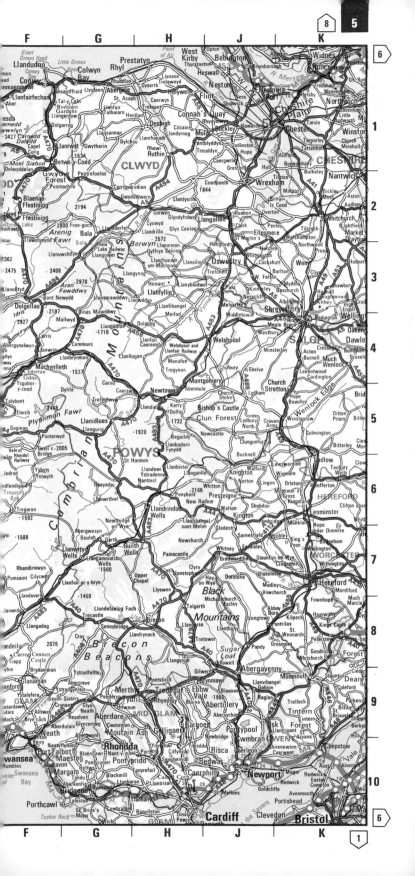

A B C D E

5

1

Formby Ormskirk Burscough Standish Horwich Bolton Radcliffe Royton Marsden
Skelmersdale Wigan Farnworth Middleton Oldham Mossley 1908
Crosby Maghull Kirkby Ramford Billinge Leigh Failsworth Ashton-under-Lyne
Bootle Knowsley St. Helen's Newton-le-Willows Salford Manchester Hollingworth 20
Wallasey Birkenhead Liverpool Warrington Sale Altrincham Stockport Hyde Glossop
Hoylake Upton Widnes Runcorn Lymm Gt. Budworth Wilmslow Marple Kinder 2088
West Kirby Bebington Bromborough Alderley Edge Bollington Whaley Bridge New Mills
Heswall Neston Ellesmere Port Frodsham Weaverham Knutsford Macclesfield Buxton
Holywell Flint Northwich Chelford Alderley Macclesfield Forest
Cheshire Plain Davenham Middlewich Holmes Chapel Congleton Longnor
Connah's Quay Cilcain Llandyrnog Mold Buckley Hawarden Tarvin Winsford Sandbach Mow Cop Biddulph Leek
Broughton Chester Tarporley Church Minshull Crewe Alsager Kidsgrove Endon Stones
Caergwrle Gresford Holt Tattenhall Burwardsley Aldford Bulkeley Nantwich Audlem Stoke-on-Trent Cellarhead
Coedpoeth 1844 Wrexham Malpas Bickley Moss Aston Audlem Newcastle-under-Lyme Cheadle Kingsley Mayf
Llantysilio Ruabon Bangor Is Coed Overton Woore Whitmore Ellastone
Llangollen Chirk Penley Tilstock Whitchurch Lightfield Adderley Stone Hilderstone Uttoxeter
Glyn Ceiriog Ellesmere St. Martin's Welshampton Northwood Prees Market Drayton Standon Sandon Stafford Blithfield Hoar Cross Abbots
Oswestry Cockshutt Burlton Wem Hodnet Eccleshall Woodseaves Gnosall Haughton Rugeley Cannock Chase Lichfield
Welshpool Montgomery Abermule Minsterley Acton Burnell Cressage Ironbridge Bridge Albrighton Codsall Brownhills Aldrid
Church Stretton Shelve Leebotwood Cardington Much Wenlock Morville Wombourn Claverley Sedgley Dudley Walsall Wednesbury West Bromwich
Bishop's Castle Clun Forest Wenlock Edge Hope Bowdler Winstanstow Ditton Priors Billingsley Bridgnorth Severn Valley Railway Amblecote Warley Bir
Newcastle Clun Craven Arms Culmington Bitterley Cleobury Mortimer Clows Top Kidderminster Stourbridge Hagley Halesowen So
Knighton Leintwardine Wigmore Ludlow Tenbury Wells Bewdley Stourport on Severn Hartlebury Bromsgrove Redditch
Presteigne Shobdon Orleton Wooferton Astley Holt Heath Martley Droitwich Worcester
Kington Pembridge Monkland Leominster Hope under Dinmore Bromyard Whitbourne Great Witley Dormston Inkberrow Abbots Morton Feckenham Alces
Weobley Dilwyn Pencombe Bodenham Wellington Withington Crowle Worcester Spetchley Bishampton Evesham
Madley Vowchurch Hereford Mordiford Ledbury Bosbury Great Malvern Kempsey Pershore Defford Ashton under Hill Overbury Broadway
Black Mountains Llanthony Dorstone Kilpeck Fownhope Much Marcle Eastnor Welland Tewkesbury Bredon Bishop's Cleeve Cleeve Hill Winchcombe
Sugar Loaf Pandy Grosmont Petertow-on-Wye Ross-on-Wye Lea Forest of Dean Newent Staunton Hartpury Gloucester Cheltenham
Abergavenny Monmouth Llanvihangel Gobion Goodrich Whitchurch Mitcheldean Cinderford Huntley Churchdown A40
Ebbw Vale Blaenavon Coleford Dean Newnham Frampton

5

A B C D E

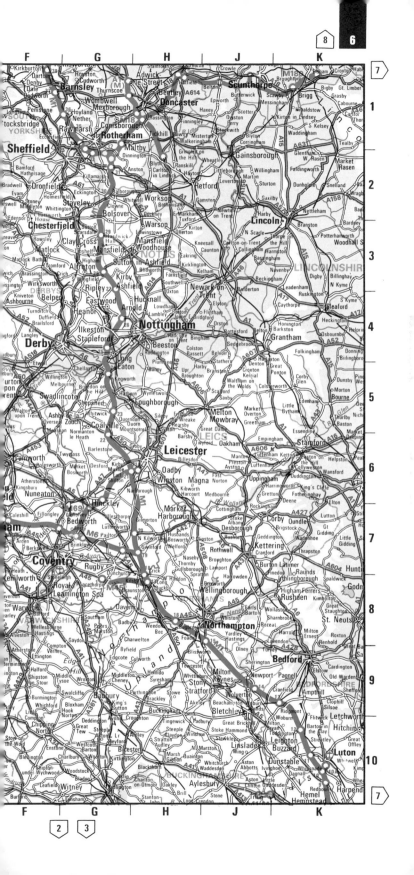

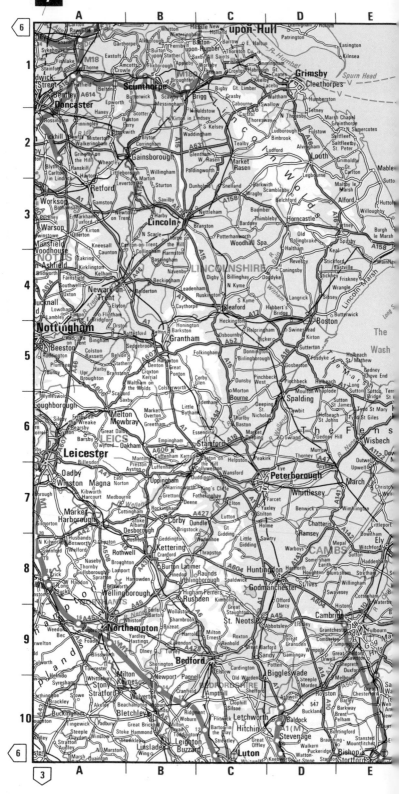

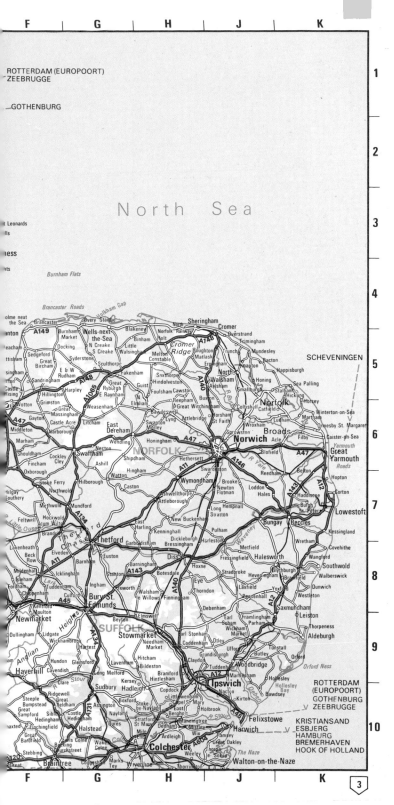

8 9

A B C D E

1

2

3

4

5

6

7

8

9

10

Point of Ayre
Bride
Jurby
Andreas
Ramsey
Ramsey Bay
Ballaugh
Sulby
Maughold Head
Kirk Michael
Snaefell 2034
Peel
St John's
Patrick
Crosby
Glenmaye
Foxdale
Dalby 1585
St Marks
Isle of Man
Onchan
Clay Head
Bradda Head
Douglas
Port Erin
Colby
Ballasalla
Cregneish
Derbyhaven
Port St Mary
Castletown

Headheads
Eastgate
Stanhope
Durham
gate
Wolsingham
Frosterley
Brandon
Tow Law
Crook
Spennymoor
DURHAM
Newbiggin
St Helen Auckland
Bishop Auckland
Shildo
Teesdale
Eggleston
Woodland
West Auckland
Fell
Romaldkirk
Staindrop
Heighington
Forest
Barnard Castle
Winston
Gainford
Darlington
Bowes
Caldwell
Stainmore
Barningham
Ravensworth
Scotch Corn
R Greta
Winton
Kirkby Stephen
Brough
Marrick
Richmond
Catterick Camp
Nateby
Ravenstonedale
Reeth
Marsk
Patrick Brompton
ebay
Thwaite
Feetham
Muker
Castle Bolton
Redmire
Leyburn
Langstrothdale Chase
Hardrow
Wensleydale
Askrigg
W. Witton
E. Witton
Lowgill
Hawes
Bainbridge
Aysgarth
Carlton
Horsehouse
Healey
Sedbergh
Dent
Buckden
Middlesmoor
Kirkby Malzeard
Oxenholme
Middleton
Kettlewell
Ramsgill
Studley Roya
Ingleborough
Horton in Ribblesdale
Great Whernside
Conistone
Grassington
Pateley Bridge
Barbon
Ingleton
Arncliffe
Hebden
Summer Bridge
Kirkby Lonsdale
Clapham
Stainforth
Burnsall
Appletreewick
Melling
Austwick
Kirkby Malham
Linton
Blubberhouses
Hornby
Wray
Giggleswick
Airton
Rylstone
Fewsto
High Bentham
Wigglesworth
Hetton
Gargrave
Addingham
Ilkley
Slaidburn
Newton
Gisburn
Skipton
Silsden
Otley
Marshaw
Bolton-by-Bowland
Embsay
Thornton-in-Craven
Menston
Chipping
Hellifield
Earby
Aireyle Railway
Guiseley
Shipley
Whalley
Chatburn
Foulridge
Cowling
Haworth
Pudse
Longridge
Ribchester
Pendle Hill
Colne
Trawden
Keighley
Keighley and Worth Valley Railway
Bingley
Grimsargh
Clitheroe
Barrowford
Nelson
Bradford
Preston
Blackburn
Padiham
Brierfield
Oxenhope
Haslingden
Accrington
Burnley
Hebden Bridge
Queensbury
Halifax
Darwen
Rawtenstall
Bacup
Todmorden
Walsden
Sowerby Bridge
Elland
Mirfield
Chorley
Ramsbottom
Littleborough
Rippenden
Huddersfield
Edgworth
Tottington
Rochdale
Milnrow
Slaithwaite
Bolton
Bury
Marsden
Meltham
Kirkb
Standish
Radcliffe
Royton
Mossley
Wigan
Norwich
Middleton
Oldham
Holmfirth
Farnworth
Failsworth
Ashton-under-Lyne
Dunford Bridge
Leigh
Manchester
Hollingworth
Bleaklow Hill
St. Helens
Salford
Stretford
Stockport
Glossop
Kinder Scout
Warrington
Sale
Cheadle
Marple
Altrincham
Hazel Grove
New Mills
Liverpool
Widnes
Lymm
Wilmslow
Alderley Edge
Bollington
Whaley Bridge
Buxton
Runcorn
Knutsford
Nether
Prestbury
Dove Holes
Tideswell
Frodsham
Macclesfield
Northwich
Macclesfield Forest
Bakewell
Chester
Winsford
Congleton
Longnor
Matlo
Crewe
Biddulph
Leek
Wrexham
Nantwich
Audlem
Endon
Stoke-on-Trent
Newcastle-under-Lyme
Cheadle

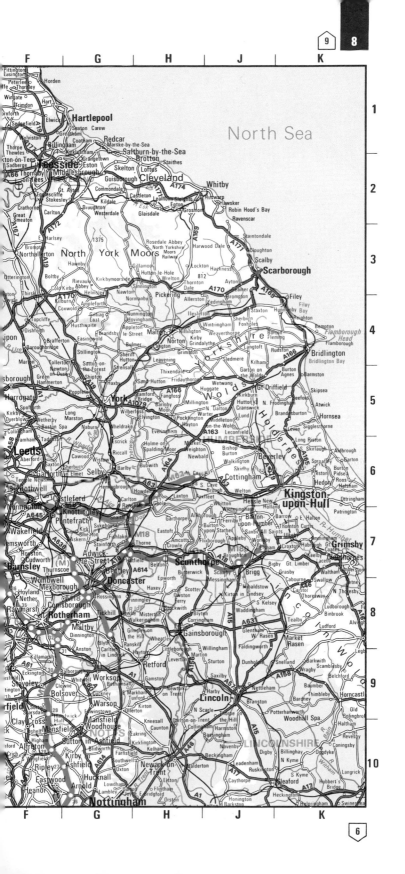

	A	B	C	D	E

1

Forth, Braehead, Carlops, Carnwath, West Linton, Temple, Leadburn, Heriot, Fountainhall, Oxton, Westruther, Lauder, Preston, Duns, Swinton, Whitsome, Norham

Dolphinton, Romannobridge, Eddleston, Heriot, Stow, Lauder, Greenlaw, Gordon, Polwarth, Merse, Leitholm, Cornhill on Tweed

Libberton, Newbigging, Lyne Church, Peebles, Innerleithen, Walkerburn, Galashiels, Earlston, Stichill, Eccles, Coldstream, Birgham, Carham, Branxton

BORDERS

Biggar, Broughton, Drumelzier, Traquair, Clovenfords, Melrose, St Boswell's, Maxton, Roxburgh, Kelso, Sprouston, Yetholm, Akeld

Coulter, Lamington, Broad Law, Cappercleuch, 2756, Yarrow, Selkirk, Eildon Hills, Ancrum, Lanten, Crailing, Morebattle, The C...2681

2

Abington, Crawford, Ettrickbridge End, Ashkirk, Ettrick Forest, Denholm, Bedrule, Jedburgh, Hownam, Cheviot Hills

Moffat, Beattock, Davington, Holm, Teviothead, 1996, B6399, Kielder, Redesdale, Rochester, Otterburn

3

St Ann's, Johnstonebridge, Boreland, Kirkstile, Langholm, Newcastleton, Kielder Forest, Falstone, Greenhaugh, West Woodburn, Ridsd...

Parkgate, Templand, Corrie Common, Bellingham, Redesmouth, Birtley, NORTHU...

4

Lochmaben, Lockerbie, Bankshill, Waterbeck, Middlebie, Canonbie, Rowanburn, R Lyne, Chipchase Castle, Simonburn, Humshaugh, Chollerford, Wark

Tinwald, Hightae, Collin, Ecclefechan, Eaglesfield, Kirtlebridge, Longtown, R Irthing, Gilsland, Greenhead, Henshaw, Newbrough, Haltwhistle, Hexham

Dalton, Mouswald, Bankend, Ruthwell, Caerlaverock Castle, Annan, Gretna, Smithfield, Walton, Low Row, Lambley, Whitfield, Catton, Allendale Town

5

Cummertrees, Bowness-on-Solway, Drumburgh, Scaleby, Irthington, Castle Carrock, Staggford, Kirkbean, Kirkbride, Solway Plain, Carlisle, Wetheral, Cumwhitton, Knarsdale, Alston

6

Silloth, Beckfoot, Mawbray, Allonby, Maryport, Dulton, Thursby, Dalston, Ainstable, High Hesket, Croglin, Leadgate, Nenthead, Allenheads, Garrigill, Westgate

Wigton, Rosley, Caldbeck, Sebergham, Lazonby, Kirkoswald, Glassonby, Melmerby, St John's Chapel

7

Flimby, Clifton, Brigham, Cockermouth, Bassenthwaite Lake, Skiddaw 3053, Greystoke, Penruddock, Penrith, Cross Fell 2930, High Force, Dufton 2591, Middleton-in-Teesdale, Mickle Fell 2591

Workington, High Lorton, Lamplugh, Loweswater, Braithwaite, Keswick, Dockray, Pooley Bridge, Lowther, Hackthorpe, Bolton, Murton, Hilton, Lune Forest

8

Whitehaven, Arlecdon, Kirkland, Buttermere, Grange, Thirlmere, Patterdale, Bampton, Crosby Ravensworth, Warcop, Brough, Stainmore

Ennerdale Wr, Egremont, Lake District, Sca Fell Pikes 3210, Helvellyn 3118, Haweswater Resr, Shap, Orton, A685, Tebay, Ravenstonedale

9

Beckermet, Haile, Calder Bridge, Gosforth, Wast Water, Boot, Ambleside, Skelwith Bridge, Troutbeck, Staveley, Grayrigg, 2220, Soulby, Winton, Kirkby Stephen, Nateby

Seascale, Drigg, Old Man 2635, Hawkshead, Windermere, Bowness Ferry, Kendal, Lowgill, Sedbergh, Dent, Langstrothdale Chase

Ravenglass, Ravenglass and Eskdale Railway, 1881, Coniston, Torver, Winster, Crosthwaite, Oxenholme, Middleton, Hawes, Ingleborough 2419

10

Bootle, 1969, Whitbeck, Silecroft, Kirksanton, Millom, Ulverston, Grizebeck, Greenodd, Lindale, Cartmel, Holme, Burton, Kirkby Lonsdale, Ingleton, Clapham, Austwick, Stainforth

Dalton-in-Furness, Bardsea, Grange-over-Sands, Flookburgh, Carnforth, Melling, Hornby, Wray, High Bentham, Giggleswick, Settle, Kirkby Malham

Barrow-in-Furness, Vickerstown, Aldingham, Bolton-le-Sands, Hest Bank, Morecambe Bay, Morecambe, Heysham, Lancaster, Clougha Pike 1836, Forest of Bowland, Wigglesworth

Isle of Walney, Hilpsford Point, Glasson, Dolphinholme, Marshaw

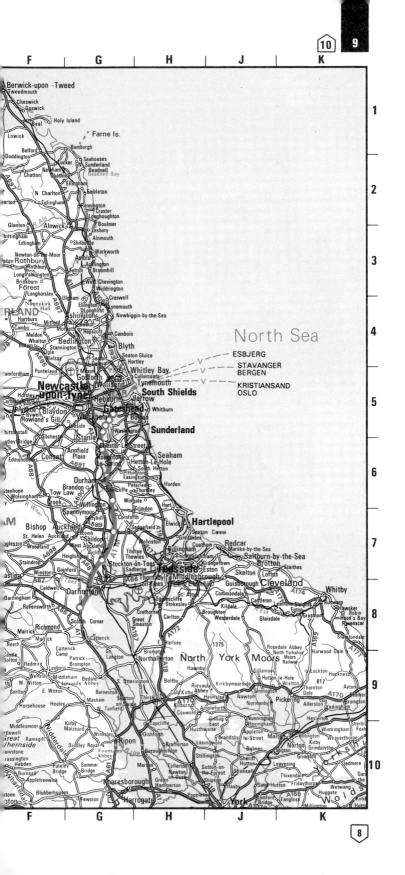

A B C D E

1

Staffa · Little Colonsay
Iona · Fionnphort · Bunessan · Ross of Mull
Ben More 3171
Mull · Lochdonhead
Duart Pt. · Dunstaffnage Castle · Connel
Loch Scridain · Loch Spelve
Lochbuie
Kerrera · Oban
Taynuilt
Kilbride · Lorn
Kilninver · A816
Kilchren
Loch na Keal
Croggan
Seil · Balvicar
Luing · Kilmelford · L. Avich
Cullipool · Loch Awe
Loch Feochan
Melfort · Kilchren

2

Rubh 'a 'Geadha
Kiloran Bay
Lunga
Scarba
Gulf of Corryvreckan
Shuna
Ardfern · Loch Craignish
Ford · Crarae Forest Gdn
Kilmartin · Kilmichael Glassary · Minard
Crinan · Cairnbaan · Lochgair · A83 · B8000
Kiloran
Colonsay · Scalasaig
Garvard
Oronsay

3

Ardlussa
Loch Tarbert
Lagg
Keillmore
Castle Sween · Loch Sween
Tayvallich · Lochgilphead
Kilmichael of Inverlussa · Inverlussa · Otter Ferry
Achahoish · Auchenbreck · Kilfinan
Jura
Paps of Jura · A846
Pt. of Knap
Kilmory · L. Caolisport
Tighnabruaich · Kames · B
Tarbert · Kyles of
Ardnave Pt. · An Clachan
Gortantaoid · Bunnahabhainn
Sanaigmore · Gruinart
Loch Gorm · Port Askaig
Ballygrant
Feolin Ferry
Craighouse
West Tarbert
Kilberry · Kilberry Hd. · Inchmarnock
Ardlamont

4

Machir Bay · Bruichladdich · Kilchoman
Kilchiaran · Indaal
Bridgend
Bowmore
Islay
Port Charlotte · A846
Ardtalla
W L · Kilberry · Tarbert
Whitehouse · Skipness
Clachan · Skipness Pt.
McArthur's Head
Ardpatrick Pt.
Claonaig · Cock of Arran
Rinns of Islay
Rubha na Faing
A847
Lochranza

5

Portnahaven
Laggan Bay
The Oa
Lower Killeyan
Mull of Oa · Rubha nan Leacan
Ardbeg · Lagavulin
Port Ellen
Gigha I
Ardminish · Achamore
Killean
Cara I
Glenacardoch Point
Muasdale
Grogport
Tayinloan
Dippen
Glenbarr · 1490
Carradale Pt.
STRAT
Arran · 2868
Pirnmill · Corr
Dougarie · Goat
Saddell · Drumadoon
Blackwaterfoot · Brodick
Lamlas

6

Machrihanish Bay
Kilkenzie
Campbeltown
Machrihanish
Campbeltown Loch
Kilm
Pla

7

Rathlin Island
Carskiey · Southend
Sanda I
Mull of Kintyre
Macharioch
Giant's Causeway · Benbane Head
Portballintrae · Bush
Carrickarade I.
Fair Head
Ballintoy · Ballycastle · Ballycastle Bay
Ballyvoy
Ailsa Craig
North Channel

8

Bushmills
Ballyrashane · Moss-side · Moyarget 1695
Ballybogy · Dervock · Armoy
Balnamore · Stranocum · 1676
Cushendun
Ballymoney · Waterfoot · Trostan 1817 · Cushendall · Red Bay
Bendooragh
Cullycapple · Dunloy 689 · Clogh Mills · Garron Point
Garvagh · Kilrea · Rasharkin
Newtown Crommelin 1439 · Carnlough
Clogh · 1179
Carnlough Bay
Milleur
Martinstown · Glenarm

9

Upperlands
Portglenone · Cullybackey
Ahoghill · Gracehill · Broughshane · 1446
1259 · Ballygalley
The Maiden
Gulladuff · Bellaghy
Grange Corner · Ballymena
1563
Larne · Island Magee
Portmuck
bermore · Lough · Castledawson
Ahoghill · Kells · Seminary · Connor · 1163 · Glynn
Glenoe · Ballynure · Glynn
Kirkc
Lesw
Moneymore

10

Randalstown
Toome · M22
Antrim · M2 · Ballyclare
Deaghl · Straid 1034
Ballycarry · Whitehead
Eden · Carrickfergus
Portpatrick
Money
Logan B.
Ballyronan
Muckamore · Templepatrick
Antrim
Newtownabbey · Greenisland · Belfast Lough
Moneymore
stown · Lough Neagh
Belfast · Holywood · Bangor · Groomsport · Copeland Island
Gartree · Crumlin · Divis · 662 · Conlig · Donaghadee
hoge · Newtownards
A52

A B C D E

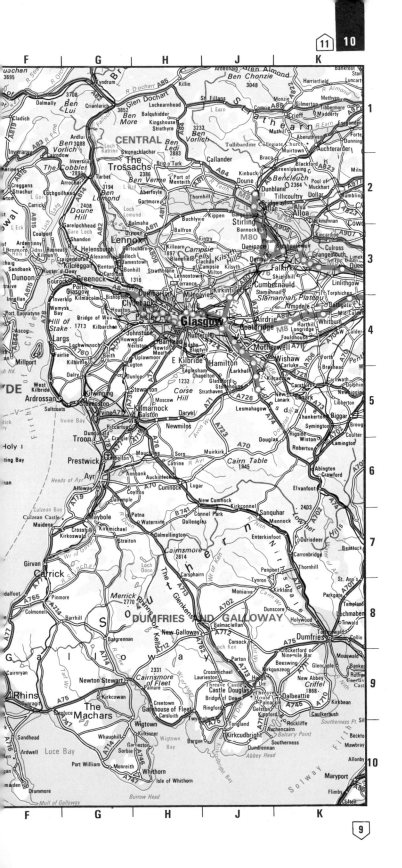

L M N O P

1
Guildtown, Fowlis, Muirhead, Liff, Dundee, Monifieth, Carnoustie, Buddon Ness, Inchcape or Bell Rock, Broughty Ferry, Newport-on-Tay, Tayport, Inchture, Balbeggie, New Scone, Kinfauns, Glencarse, Wormit, Leuchars, St. Andrews Bay, St. Andrews, Newburgh, Bridge of Earn, Abernethy, Luthrie, Kilman, Strathkinness, Auchtermuchty, FIFE, Cupar, Pitscottie, Ceres, Peat Inn, Dunino, Boarhills, Kingsbarns, Fife Ness

2
Falkland, Lomond Hills, 1713, Ladybank, Kirkton of Largo, Largo Ward, Kellie Castle, Crail, Kilrenny, Kinross, Leslie, Markinch, Fife, Anstruther, Pittenweem, Glenrothes, Leven, Elie, St. Monance, Earlsferry, Isle of May, Methil, Buckhaven, Lochgelly, Kirkcaldy, Ore

3
Dunfermline, Kinghorn, Burntisland, Bass Rock, North Berwick, Tantallon Castle, Inverkeithing, Dirleton, Gullane, Whitekirk, Dunbar, Rosyth, Dalmeny, Aberlady, Direm, Athelstaneford, W. Barns, Kirkliston, Leith, Portobello, Cockenzie, Prestonpans, East Linton, Stenton, St. Abb's Head, Musselburgh, Tranent, Haddington, Cockburnspath

4
Edinburgh, Dalkeith, Ormiston, Fencaitland, Gifford, Garvald, St. Abb's, Eyemouth, Currie, Lasswade, Newtongrange, Pathhead, Saltoun, Humbie, Lammermuir Hills, Grantshouses, Coldingham, Reston, Burnmouth, Loanhead, Fala, 1755, Preston, Abbey St. Bathans, Cranshaws, Ayton, Penicuik, 1899, Temple, Heriot, Westruther, Duns, Chirnside, Fouldin, Berwick-upon-Tweed, Tweedmouth

5
Oxton, Lauderdale, Polwarth, Swinton, Norham, Cheswick, Goswick, Romannobridge, Eddleston, Fountainhall, Lauder, Greenlaw, Leitholm, Cornhill, Ancroft, Peebles, Stow, Gordon, Eccles, Coldstream, Birgham, Crookham, Lowick, Belford, Innerleithen, Walkerburn, Galashiels, Earlston, Stichill, Carham, Sprouston, Branxton, Doddington, Clovenfords, Traquair, Merse, Kelso, Kilham

6
BORDERS, Yarrow, Melrose, Eildon, St. Boswell's, Roxburgh, Kirknewton Town, Akeld, Wooler, Chatton, Broad Law, A708, Selkirk, Midlem, Maxton, Nisbet, Linton, Yetholm, Ettrickbridge End, Ashkirk, Ancrum, Lanton, Eckford, Crailing, Morebattle, The Cheviot, 2681, Wooperton, Ettrick Forest, Denholm, Bedrule, Jedburgh, Oxnam, Hownam

7
Moffat, Ramseycleuch, Hawick, Kirkton, Bonchester Bridge, Cheviot Hills, Glanton, Whittingham, Edlingham, Davington, Hott Hill, Teviothead, 1996, Alwinton, Harbottle, Thropton, Rothbury, Holm, Redesdale, Netherton, Hepple, Longframlington, Brinkburn, Longhorsley, Kirkstile, Kielder, Rochester, Otterburn, Elsdon, Nunnyk, Newton, Johnstonebridge, Boreland, Corrie Common, Langholm, Newcastleton, Kielder Forest, North Tyne, Falstone, NORTHUMBERLAND, Greenhaugh, West Woodburn, Hartburn, Cambo, Meldon, Whalto, Bellingham, Redesmouth, Kirkwhelpington

8
Lockerbie, Bankshill, Waterbeck, Middlebie, Canonbie, Rowanburn, Birtley, Ecclefechan, Eaglesfield, Kirtlebridge, R. Lyne, Chipchase Castle, Simonburn, Humshaugh, Stamfordham, Chollerton, Annan, Longtown, Liddesdale, Gilsland, Nithing, Chollerford, Wall, Acomb, Horsley, Prudhoe, Bywell, Rowlands

9
Cummertrees, Gretna, Scaleby, Irthington, Smithfield, Walton, Low Row, Haltwhistle, Haydon Bridge, Hexham, Riding Mill, Corbridge, Bowness-on-Solway, Drumburgh, Low Crosby, Brampton, Greenhead, Henshaw, Whitfield, Catton, Allendale Town, Whittonstall, Shotley Bridge, Solway Plain, Kirkbride, Carlisle, Haytton, Castle Carrock, Knarsdale, Lambley, Blanchland, Edmondbyers

10
Dalton, Thursby, Wetheral, Cumwhitton, Staggyford, Carr Shield, Allenheads, Sinhope, Wolsingham, Aspatria, Wigton, Dalston, Ainstable, Croglin, Leadgate, Nenthead, Westgate, Eastgate, Rosley, High Hesket, Kirkoswald, Garrigill, B6218, Mealsgate, Caldbeck, Lazonby, Glassonby, Gamblesby, Melmerby, St. John's Chapel, Frosterley, Torpenhow, Ireby, Uldale, Newmarket, Plumpton Wall, Great Salkerd, Langwathby, 2930, Cross Fell, R. Wear, DURHAM, Bothel, Inglewood Forest

CUMBRIA, Bassenthwaite, Greystoke, Penrith, Skiddaw, Bisho

L M N O P

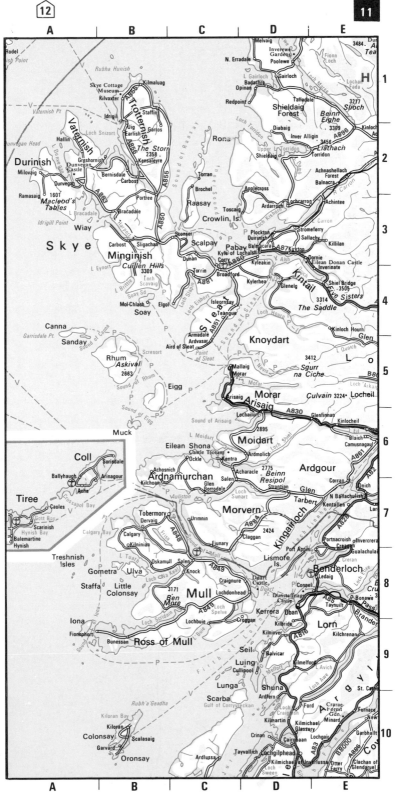

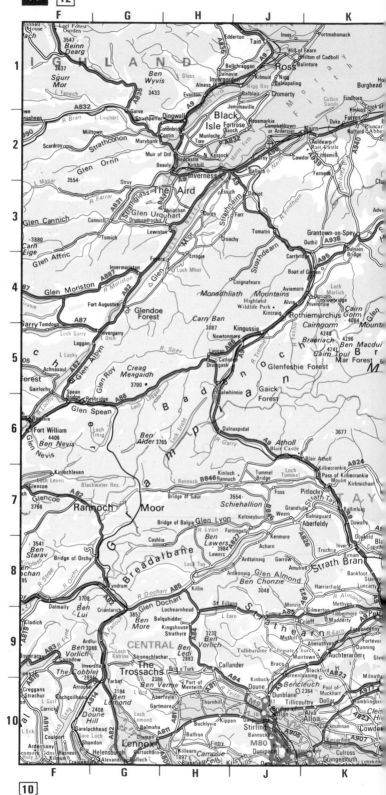

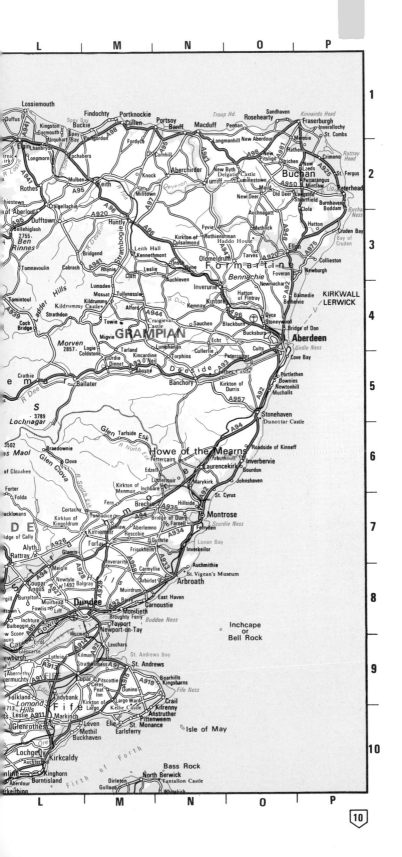

Lossiemouth
Findochty Portknockie
Duffus   Buckie   Cullen   Portsoy   Macduff   Penman   Rosehearty   Sandhaven   Kinnairds Head
Kingston Spey Bay   Banff   Longmanhill New Aberdour   Fraserburgh   Inverallochy
Garmouth   Portgordon   Fordyce   Troup Hd.   St. Combs
Urquhart Bay   Cornhill   New   Rathen   Crimono   Rattray
Elgin Lhanbryde   Fochabers   A941   New   Pitsligo   Strichen   A952   Head
Longmorn   Aberchirder   New Byth   Leeds   St. Fergus
R Lossie   Mulben   Knock   Delgatie Castle   Cuminestowo   Maud   Buchan
Rothes   Keith   Turriff   Old Deer Longside   Peterhead
Milltown   New Deer   Stuartfield   Buchanness
chiestown   A95   Deveron   Auchnagatt   Clola   Boddam
of Aberlour   Craigellachie   A920   Huntly   Fyvie   Methlick   Hatton   Bay of
Bellehiglash   Dufftown   Kirkton of   Rothienorman   Tarves   Ellon   Cruden
2755   Culsalmond   Haddo House   A920   Newburgh
Ben   Bridgend   Oldmeldrum   Formartine   Collieston
Rinnes   Rhynie   Leith Hall   Insch   Newburgh
Tomnavoulin   Cabrach   Kennethmont   Leslie   Bennachie   Foveran
Clatt   Auchleven   Balmedie
Hills   Lumsden   Inverurie   Hatton   Belhelvie
Tomintoul   Mossat Tullynessle   of Fintray   KIRKWALL
Kildrummy   Kemnay   Oyce   Stoneywood   LERWICK
A939   Kildrummy Castle   Alford   Kintore   Blackburn   Bridge of Don
Strathdon   A944   Sauchen   Echt   Aberdeen
Cock   Towie   Craigievar   Bucksburn
Bridge   Migvie   Castle   Cults   Girdle Ness
GRAMPIAN   Lumphanan   Cullerlie   Petercutter   Cove Bay
Morven   Logie   Tarland   Kincardine   Torphins   Portlethen
2857   Coldstone   Urdie O'Neil   Downies
Crathie   Dinnet   Aboyne   Deeside   Kirkton of   Newtonhill
R Dee   Ballater   Banchory   Durris   Muchalls
em   Stonehaven
S   Dunottar Castle
3789
Lochnagar   Glen Tarfside Esk
3502   Braedownie   Howe of the Mearns   Roadside of Kinneff
as Maol   Glen Clova   Fettercairn   Arbuthnott   Inverbervie
of Glenshee   Clova   Edzell   Laurencekirk   Gourdon
Forter   Kirkton of   Littlemoor   Johnshaven
Folda   Menmuir Inchbare   Marykirk
acklmuns   Fern   Brechin   St. Cyrus
DE   Cortachy   Hillside   Montrose
Kirkton of   Tanladice   Bridge of Dun   Scurdie Ness
dge of Cally   Kingoldrum   Aberlemno   Farnell
Alyth   Kirriemuir   Rescobie   Guthrie   Ferryden
Rattray   Forfar   Lunan Bay
Meigle   Glamis   Friockheim   Inverkeilor
Coupar   Newtyle   Inverarity   Auchmithie
Angus   W 1492 Balgray   Carmyllie   St. Vigean's Museum
rgill   Burrelton   Muirhead   Airbirlot   Arbroath
town's   Fowlis   Liff   Muirdrum
Balbeggie   Inchture   East Haven
w Scone   Wormit   Barry   Carnoustie
aus   Dundee   Monifieth
ewburgh   Carse   Broughty Ferry   Buddon Ness
Errol   Tayport
bernethy   Newport-on-Tay   Inchcape
ermuchty   Leuchars   or
Falkland   St. Andrews Bay   Bell Rock
Luthrie   Kilmany
Abernethy   Strathkinness   St. Andrews
Cupar   Pitscottie   Boarhills
Lomond   Ceres   Kingsbarns
713   Hills   Ladybank   Peat   Dunino   Fife Ness
Leslie A911   Kirkton of   Inn   Largo Ward
Markinch   Largo   Kellie Castle   Crail
Glenrothes   Leven   Elie   Kilrenny
Methil   Earlsferry   St. Monance   Anstruther
Buckhaven   Pittenweem
Ore   Isle of May
Lochgel   Kirkcaldy
Auchtertool
nline   Kinghorn   Bass Rock
Aberdour   Burntisland   North Berwick
rkeithing   Dirleton   Tantallon Castle
Firth   of   Forth   Gullane   Whitekirk

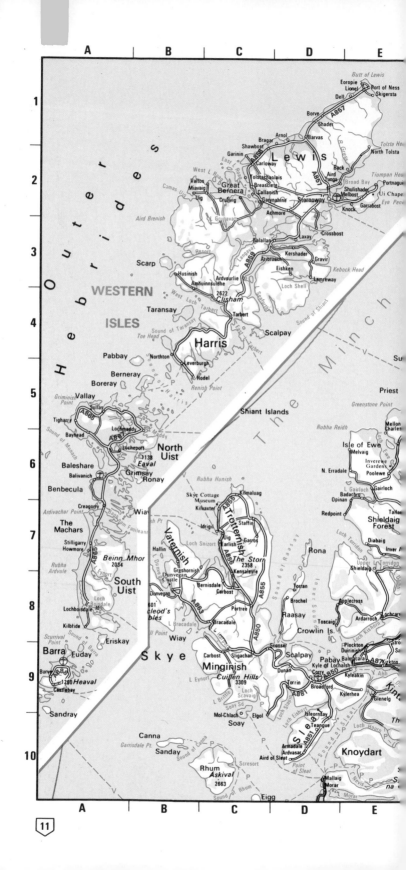

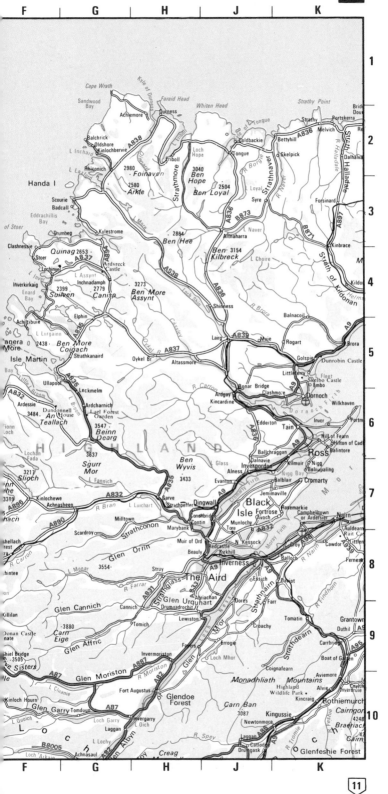

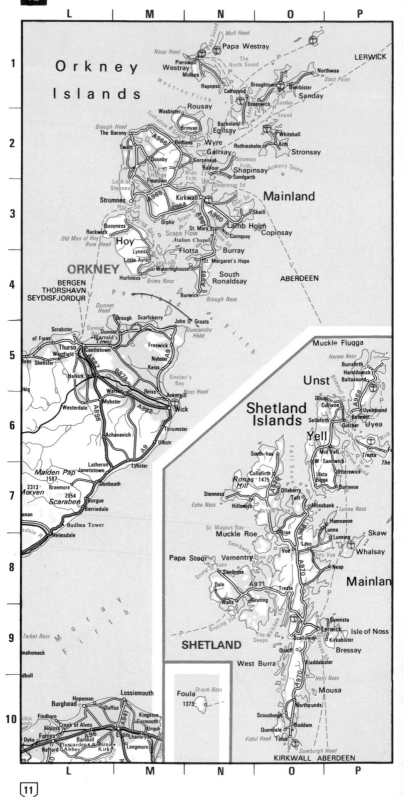

O r k n e y

I s l a n d s

Orkney Islands

Mull Head
Noup Head
Papa Westray
Pierowall
Westray
Midbea
Rapness
Calfsound
Northwaa
Start Point
LERWICK
The North Sound
Broughtown
Overbister
Sanday
Braeswick
Wasbister
Rousay
Eday Sound
Sanday Sound
Egilsay
Brinyan
Backaland
Whitehall
Stronsay
Brough Head
The Barony
Redland
Wyre
Aith
Rothiesholm
Twatt
Gairsay
Stronsay
Firth
Dounby
Gorseness
Balfour
Shapinsay
Sandgarth
Auskerry Sound
Wide Firth
Finstown
Shapinsay Sd
Loch of Stennes
Kirkwall
Mainland
Stromness
A965
A964
A960
Skaill
Deer Sd
Orphir
St. Mary's
Lamb Holm
Quoyness
Scapa
Copinsay
Hoy Sd
Rackwick
Cornquoy
Old Man of Hoy
Rora Head
Hoy
Scapa Flow
Holm Sd
Italian Chapel
Burray
Lyness
Flotta
ORKNEY
Little Ayre
Longhope
Waterinhouse
St. Margaret's Hope
South
Ronaldsay
ABERDEEN
BERGEN
Hurliness
Brims Ness
THORSHAVN
SEYDISFJORDUR
Burwick
Brough Ness
Dunnet
Head
Pentland Firth
Scarfskerry
Duncansby
John O'Groats
Head
Brough
of Foras
Scrabster
Dunnet
Harrald's
Tower
Freswick
Reay
Thurso
Castletown
Nybster
Westfield
Keiss
Shebster
Halkirk
A882
B874
Reiss
Sinclair's
Bay
Noss Head
Ackergill
Watten
A9
Wick
A896
Mybster
Westerdale
A892
Achavanich
Thrumster
Ulbstr
Latheron
Lybster
Maiden Pap
1587·
Janetstown
Dunbeath
2313·
Braemore
Morven
2054·
Borgue
Scaraben
Berriedale
Badbea Tower
Helmsdale
Tarbat Ness
Moray
Firth
mahomack
SHETLAND
dboll
Lossiemouth
Hopeman
Burghead
Duffus
Kingston
Garmouth
Findhorn
Crook of Alves
Urquh
Elgin
Hanbrigg
Kinloss
Forres
Barnhill
Birnie
Kirk
Longmorn
Dyke
Pluscarden
Abbey
Rafford

Shetland Islands

Muckle Flugga
Herma Ness
Burrafirth
Haroldswick
Baltasound
Unst
Gloup
Cullivoe
Uyeasound
Belmont
Uyea
Sellafirth
Gutcher
Yell
South-haa
Mid Yell
Sandwick
Otterswick
Collafirth
W Sandwick
Ronas
Hill
1475
Ulsta
Bigga
Burravoe
Stenness
Ollaberry
Taft
Esha Ness
Hillswick
Sullom Voe
Mossbank
Lunna Ness
St. Magnus Bay
Hamnavoe
Skaw
Muckle Roe
Brae
Lunna
Swarbacks
Minn
Laxo
Lunning
Whalsay
Voe
Papa Stour
Vementry
Bury Voe
Neap
Sound of Papa
Sandness
Mainlan
Dale
A971
Tresta
Walls
Gruting
Gunnista
SHETLAND
Gruting Voe
Scalloway
Lerwick
Isle of Noss
The
Deeps
Quarff
Kirkabister
Bressay
Fladdabister
West Burra
Helli Ness
Mousa
Foula
Strem Ness
1373·
Northpunds
Scousburgh
Boddam
Quendale
Toiob
Fitful Head
Sumburgh Head
KIRKWALL ABERDEEN

INTRODUCTION

All over Britain the landscape is engraved with symbols of her cultural evolution. Thousands of years of history have left behind a treasure trove of relics which enables us to trace the development of our modern civilisation.

It is a fact that Britain hasn't been invaded since 1066, which has helped to protect its architectural heritage. The richness of this heritage plus that ancient institution which shaped the course of history – the monarchy – draws millions of tourists to Britain every year. This book is not only for the many visitors from abroad, but also for everyone who wants to discover more of this fascinating country either on a Sunday afternoon's drive, a holiday, or a weekend away from it all. The fun of exploring Britain is chancing upon that tiny church behind the trees and discovering that it was built by the Saxons. Or recalling the gripping associations of Jamaica Inn over a picnic on Bodmin Moor, then hiking over to mournful Dozmary Pool where the grisly hand which held King Arthur's sword and sank with it forever into the murky depths, appears more real than legend allows.

The archaeology section, glossary and family tree in the front of this book will help you to trace the development of history and recognise the heirlooms of the centuries. Stonehenge remains one of the most important prehistoric monuments in the world. The massive blue-stones were uprooted from their bed in South Wales and erected on the windswept Wiltshire plains nearly 2,000 years ago. How and why remains a mystery: despite all our scientific knowledge, Stonehenge has withheld its secret from us. We owe majestic London to the Romans who established it as England's capital. Further evidence of their influence can be traced in the straight Roman roads and in Hadrian's Wall, one of Britain's most ancient monuments. Norman fortresses still glower over the hilltops jealously guarding their territory, while intricately decorated medieval cathedrals such as Wells and Lincoln still grace our cities.

But Britain's architecture hasn't totally escaped the ravages of history. After the Dissolution of the Monasteries, Henry VIII seized many of the most beautiful church buildings and laid them open to the sky. The Tudors, however, did have the foresight to build their black-and-white timber-framed houses sturdy enough to charm us in the 20thC. The Civil Wars and the Great Fire of London in 1666 destroyed much, but the development of the British Empire in the 18th and 19thC created a prosperity reflected in the elegant homes and budding new towns. A new fashion led to the development of the spa town and Bath became the social centre of the country. Under the patronage of the Prince Regent, Brighton was crowned with his pleasure dome – the Royal Pavilion – and with the coming of the railways small fishing villages grew into holiday resorts almost overnight.

Rural Britain's face was changed dramatically during the Industrial Revolution. Because of the location of natural resources such as coal, South Wales and the North developed rapidly into smoky, industrial areas. East Anglia thankfully made the most of the fertile soil of the Fens, and Kent with its orchards became known as 'the garden of England'. While factories came more and more to dominate the skyline, bombs from the World Wars shook to the ground ancient buildings that were the pride of places like London and Coventry.

Nicholson's Historic Britain will guide you through the huddled stone villages of Cornwall to the whisky-tippling towns of Scotland. You might choose to stop at Petworth House with its magnificent collection of paintings and Grinling Gibbons carvings, and afterwards, take the family for a ride on the steam-driven merry-go-round at nearby Hollycombe Steam Fair and Museum. Ancient forests, open moorlands and gardens aren't forgotten for they are as much a part of our heritage as any abbey ruin. And don't ignore the Boots Factory, Nottingham, or Fylingdale's Nuclear Early Warning System. One day they, too, might be regarded with nostalgic affection – as we tramp along the ancient Pennine Way it is worth remembering that history is still being created today.

ARCHAEOLOGY

PREHISTORIC

Palaeolithic (Old Stone Age) from 500,000 BC
Britain was barely habitable during this period, because of the southern extension of the Polar ice-cap and its effect on the climate. Few traces of early man survive.

Mesolithic (Middle Stone Age) from 20,000 to 4,000 BC
Until about 6,000 BC Britain was still joined to Europe by a land-bridge. No permanent dwellings apparently survive, but seasonal camping sites are frequently indicated by finds of small worked flints and tools.

Neolithic (New Stone Age) from 4,000 to 1,500 BC
Immigration of peoples from Europe introduced agriculture and the domestication of animals, and the first monuments that are visible today were built during this period. *Causewayed camps* were probably used as assembly or religious places. *Long barrows* were constructed for the burial of the dead. *Long cairns*, barrows built of stone, were probably used as vaults for a family or social group. *Henges*, the mysterious circular monuments, sometimes set with stones, are believed to have had some religious significance. *Flint mines*, essential for the manufacture of tools, were made by digging through chalk and mining out the flint layers below.

Bronze Age from 1800 to 400 BC
The Bronze Age saw the first application of primitive metal technology. The best known Bronze Age civilisation of Britain was the Wessex Culture, centred on Wiltshire and Dorset. Some of the finest *henges*, including Avebury and Stonehenge, belong to this period. *Stone circles, avenues, rows*, and single *standing stones*, probably usually of religious significance, can be seen frequently in remote areas. *Round barrows* and *round cairns* replaced the long varieties of the Neolithic, some cairns having chambers and entrance passages. *Settlements* of round stone huts with associated enclosures are typical of the Bronze and later periods.

Iron Age from 500 BC to AD 50
The most impressive monuments of this period are the *hill forts*, often having complex multiple defences and elaborate entrances, occupying hilltops and similar defensible sites. *Settlements of huts* within enclosures, and their associated *field-systems*, survive in places, and were often occupied well into the Roman period. Some of the carved *hill-figures* cut into the chalk downs are Iron Age in date. Underground structures, called *fogous*, are found in Cornwall and are like the *souterrains* found in Scotland and Ireland; their purpose is still unknown.

ROMAN

From AD43 to the early 5thC.
Britain was conquered by the Romans under the emperor Claudius in AD 43. Military monuments include complex *frontier works*, of which Hadrian's Wall is the best example; *fortresses* for a legion of 6,000 men, and *forts* for an auxiliary unit of 500 or 1,000 – both built to a standard pattern, with headquarters, barracks, granaries, workshops, officers' quarters, and a hospital; temporary *marching camps* built on campaign; *siege-works* and *camps* built to drill the soldiers in constructing earthworks; and *signal-stations*. In the civil zone can be seen the impressive remains of *town walls* and *gates*, often incorporated in later structures; *villas*, usually with fine mosaic pavements, architectural detail, and elaborate central heating; *roads*, frequently followed by modern roads or surviving as country lanes; *canals*; *theatres* and *amphitheatres*; magnificent public *bath-houses*. More humble monuments also survive: *workshops, potteries*, and the outline of *field systems*.

DARK AGES

Saxon and Celtic from the 5th to the 11thC AD
Following the collapse of Roman control and the settlement of Saxon colonists from the Continent, England and Wales evolved into Saxon and Celtic areas, with the Saxons dominant in the east and north and the Celts surviving in the west and south west. Visible Saxon monuments include massive *linear earthworks*, which probably marked frontiers rather than served for defence. Defensive strongholds, known as *burhs* were built by Alfred and his son against the Danes. Burial *barrows* and Christian *churches* and *crosses*, were erected. Celtic monuments that survive are *defensive* and *monastic* sites, and carved Christian *stones* and *crosses*. Iron Age *hill forts* were sometimes reoccupied at this period, both by Celts and Saxons. Invading Vikings reached many parts of Britain, and their *settlements* and *forts* have survived in coastal Scotland and on the Isle of Man.

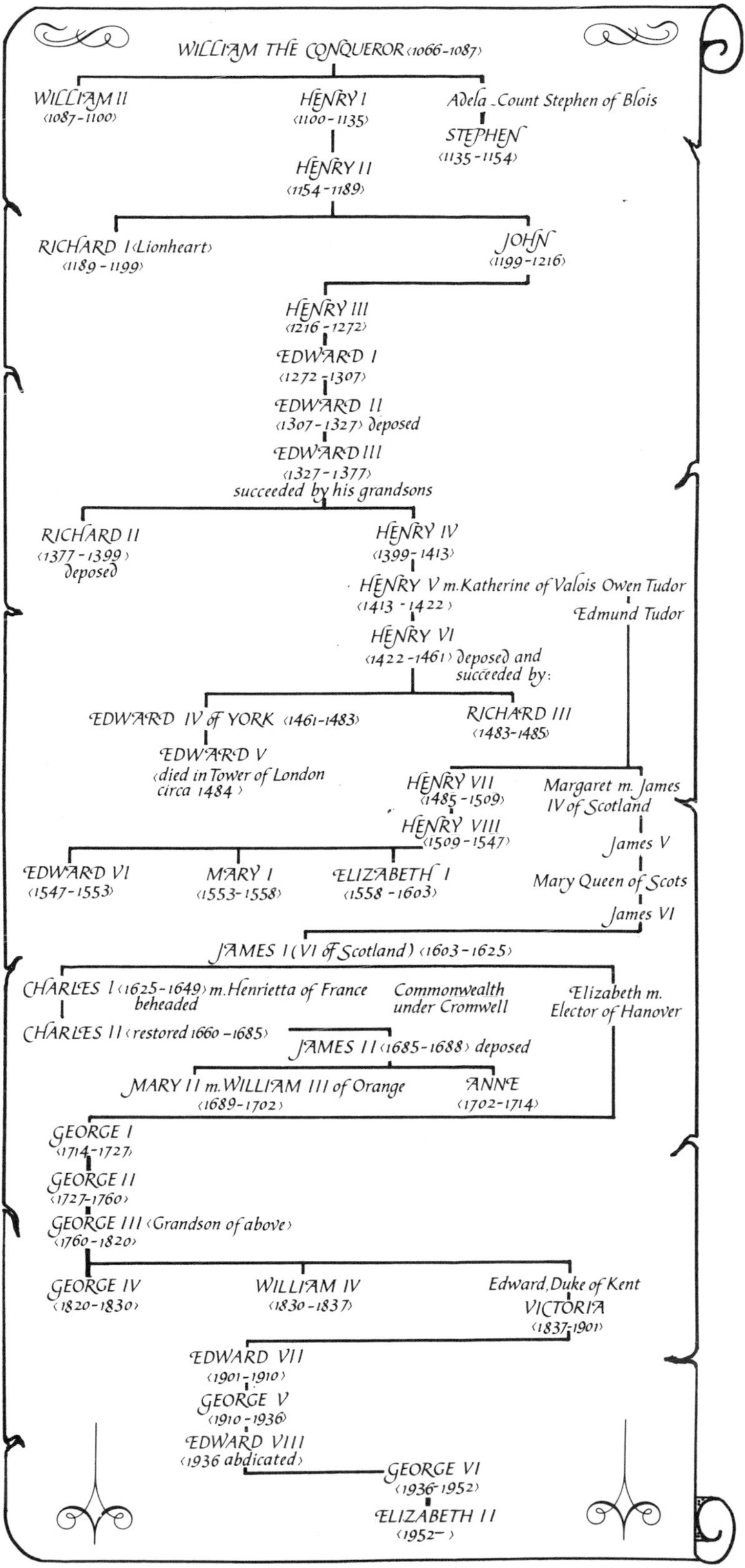

WILLIAM THE CONQUEROR (1066-1087)

WILLIAM II (1087-1100)

HENRY I (1100-1135)

Adela _ Count Stephen of Blois

STEPHEN (1135-1154)

HENRY II (1154-1189)

RICHARD I (Lionheart) (1189-1199)

JOHN (1199-1216)

HENRY III (1216-1272)

EDWARD I (1272-1307)

EDWARD II (1307-1327) deposed

EDWARD III (1327-1377) succeeded by his grandsons

RICHARD II (1377-1399) deposed

HENRY IV (1399-1413)

HENRY V m. Katherine of Valois Owen Tudor (1413-1422)

Edmund Tudor

HENRY VI (1422-1461) deposed and succeeded by:

EDWARD IV of YORK (1461-1483)

RICHARD III (1483-1485)

EDWARD V (died in Tower of London circa 1484)

HENRY VII (1485-1509)

Margaret m. James IV of Scotland

HENRY VIII (1509-1547)

James V

EDWARD VI (1547-1553)

MARY I (1553-1558)

ELIZABETH I (1558-1603)

Mary Queen of Scots

James VI

JAMES I (VI of Scotland) (1603-1625)

CHARLES I (1625-1649) m. Henrietta of France beheaded

Commonwealth under Cromwell

Elizabeth m. Elector of Hanover

CHARLES II (restored 1660-1685)

JAMES II (1685-1688) deposed

MARY II m. WILLIAM III of Orange (1689-1702)

ANNE (1702-1714)

GEORGE I (1714-1727)

GEORGE II (1727-1760)

GEORGE III (Grandson of above) (1760-1820)

GEORGE IV (1820-1830)

WILLIAM IV (1830-1837)

Edward, Duke of Kent

VICTORIA (1837-1901)

EDWARD VII (1901-1910)

GEORGE V (1910-1936)

EDWARD VIII (1936 abdicated)

GEORGE VI (1936-1952)

ELIZABETH II (1952-)

GLOSSARY

AMBULATORY: A place for walking; arcade; especially in an aisle or around east end of church, behind the altar.

APSE: Large semi-circular or polygonal recess, arched or dome-roofed, particularly at end of church.

ARCADE: Series of arches supporting a wall or roof.

BAILEY OR WARD: Fortified enclosure; the courtyard of a castle. In more complex castles, the space between the outer and inner walls is known as the outer bailey, and between the inner walls and the keep as the inner bailey.

BARBICAN: An outer defence, often a tower, defending the entrance to a castle.

BAROQUE: Literally 'irregularly shaped', an Italian style popular in 17thC Europe, characterised by extravagance and lavish ornament.

BARROW: A burial mound made of earth.

BAS-RELIEF: Carving which projects from the material from which it is formed.

BASTION: A projection from the outer wall of a castle or fortification.

BEAKER PEOPLE: People who came to Britain from the Low Countries c2000BC, named after the drinking vessels they made.

BENCH ENDS: See PEW.

BOSSES: Ornamental projection at intersecting points of ribs of a vault, and sometimes of beams in open wooden ceilings.

BROCH: Prehistoric circular stone tower with passages and chambers in its thick walls, found in northern Scotland and adjacent islands.

BUTTRESS: A mass of stone or brickwork built against a wall to give it additional support.

CAIRN: Burial mound like a barrow, but made of stone-rubble rather than earth.

CAMBER: A slight rise or convex curve in an otherwise horizontal member, such as a beam.

CAPSTONE: The horizontal slab covering a stone-built chamber.

CHAMBER: Tomb of stone, timber or turf, with access to the open, containing the dead in a long barrow.

CHANCEL: East end of church where altar is placed.

CHANTRY: Endowment within a church for priests to say mass for the soul of the founder.

CHAPTER HOUSE: Building attached to a church used for meetings of the clergy or governing body.

CHINOISERIE: Style imitating Chinese arts and building, usually a manifestation of European 18thC Rococo.

CLASSICAL: Style inspired by ancient Greek or Roman buildings.

CLERESTORY: Upper storey of the nave above the aisle roofs, with a series of windows.

CLOISTERS: Covered walk attached to a monastery, often around an open space with a wall on one side and a colonnade or windows on the other.

CORBELS: Bracket projecting from a wall, intended to support something.

CORNICE: Projecting ornamental moulding crowning a building, especially the uppermost member of an entablature.

CRENELLATED: Furnished with battlements or loopholes.

CRINKLE-CRANKLE WALL: Continuously curving or serpentine wall.

CROCKET: Small ornament, usually a curled leaf or bud, decorating the edge of pinnacles, gables, etc.

CRYPT: Underground cell or burial chamber beneath the chancel of a church.

CUP-AND-RING MARKS: Series of small hollows and incised circles cut into the face of a stone slab, made by long barrow builders and probably a feature of their religion.

CUPOLA: A small domed roof; a small domed turret built on a roof or the inside of a dome.

CURTAIN WALL: The outer wall of a castle, connecting towers and gatehouse.

DECORATED: Second stage of English Gothic (14thC) with increasing decoration and geometrical tracery.

DONJON: Keep.

DORMER: Window standing upright from the slope of a roof.

EARLY ENGLISH: First stage of English Gothic (13thC) characterised by pointed arches, lancet windows and simple tracery.

EARTHWORK: Concentric rings of ditches dug in prehistoric times around hilltop settlements as a protection.

ELIZABETHAN: Architecture of the reign of Queen Elizabeth I (1558–1603), often a mixture of Renaissance principles and Gothic elements.

FACADE: The front or main face of a building.

FAN-VAULTING: A vault composed of inverted concave cones overlaid with numerous ribs of the same curve and length, radiating at equal angles from one springer, producing a fan-like pattern.

FLUTING: Semi-circular grooves on the shaft of a column for decoration.

FOLLY: An architectural joke – a structure built solely for decorative effect.

GABEL: Triangular upper part of wall at end of ridged roof.

GALILEE: Vestibule or chapel enclosing a porch or entrance to a church.

GARGOYLE: Rain-water spout, usually in form of grotesque human or animal mouth protruding from gutter of a medieval building to carry water clear of the wall.

GATE-HOUSE: Entrance building of a castle.

GEORGIAN AND REGENCY: Period covering the reigns of the four Georges (1714–1830) which brought a return to the beauty of form and proportion. Regency decoration emerged towards the end of the period.

GOTHIC: Style of medieval architecture, particularly in churches, characterised by the use of the pointed arch and the vault. Subdivided into the Early English, Decorated and Perpendicular styles.

GOTHIC REVIVAL: Fanciful revival of the Gothic style in the late 18thC and 19thC, also known as Gothick or 'Strawberry Hill Gothick'.

HA-HA: Wide, sunken ditch, bounding park or garden.

HALF-TIMBERED: Having walls with timber frame and brick or plaster filling.

HAMMER-BEAM ROOF: A timber bracket that supports a trussed roof eliminating the need for a tie-beam.

HILL FORT: Fortified residential area occupying hilltops and similar defensible sites, typical of the Iron Age.

HUT CIRCLE: Ring of stones or earth, indicating site of prehistoric hut.

JACOBEAN: Architectural style predominant in the reign of James I (1603–25) often mixing the late Gothic and the Classical styles.

KEEP: The massive inner tower and defensive stronghold of a Norman castle.

KING POST: Roof with an upright post joining the ridge and the centre of the tie-beam.

LADY CHAPEL: Chapel dedicated to the Virgin Mary, usually east of the high altar.

LANCET: Tall, narrow, pointed windows.

LAVATORIUM: Place for washing in.

LECTERN: Reading desk or singing-desk in church, especially that for the lessons.

LINENFOLD PANELLING: Form of decorative, carved panelling, resembling a fold or scroll of linen.

LINTEL: Horizontal length of timber or stone over door or other aperture, carrying weight of the wall.

LOGGIA: Covered colonnade or arcade open on at least one side.

LONG-AND-SHORT WORK: Saxon stonework alternating tall quoins with flat slabs.

LYCH GATE OR LICH GATE: Covered gateway at entrance of churchyard where coffin awaits clergyman's arrival.

MAUSOLEUM: Magnificent, elaborate tomb.

MENHIR: Tall, upright, usually prehistoric monumental stone.

MIDDLE AGES: Period from c1000 to 1400, or more broadly c600 to 1500.

MISERICORD: Bracket on the underside of a hinged choir stall seat, often carved, serving, when the seat was turned up, to give support during periods of standing.

MOTTE: Steep mound forming the site of a castle, surrounded by a deep ditch and usually surmounted by the keep. It was generally accompanied by one or more baileys, hence the term motte-and-bailey castle.

MULLION: Vertical bar dividing a bay window.

NAVE: The main body or central aisle of a church excluding the transept and chancel.

NEO-CLASSICAL: Mid 18thC revival of Classical style, continuing well into the 19thC, characterised by vast frontages of extreme regularity crowned by domes and cupolas.

OGHAM SCRIPT: Ancient British and Irish alphabet of 20 characters formed by parallel strokes on either side of or across a continuous line.

ORIEL WINDOW: Bay window supported by corbels, projecting from an upper floor.

OVERMANTLE: Ornamental shelves over a mantle.

PALLADIAN: Italian style introduced to England by Inigo Jones in 1615 and revived in the early 18thC. Characteristic houses are symmetrical and often have wings and a pedimented central block.

PALLISADE: Fence of stakes around a castle or defensive position.

PANTILE: Roof tile with an S-shaped transverse section.

PARAPET: Low wall for protecting any sudden drop, as on the sides of a bridge, or in front of a roof.

PARGETTING: Plasterwork carved with ornamental patterns.

PEDIMENT: Triangular gable in Grecian style crowning front of building, especially over portico.

PELE OR PEEL TOWER: Square fortified tower house, generally built in the border counties of England and Scotland in the 16thC.

PERPENDICULAR: Third period of English Gothic architecture (15th–16thC) preceding the Tudor age, characterised by elegant vertical tracery in large windows and a return to comparative simplicity.

PEW: Fixed wooden seat in a church, partially enclosed to the aisles with bench-ends.

PIER: Square column or vertical support, also the area of wall between windows.

PINNACLE: Small ornamental turret used to terminate a buttress, gable, etc, especially found in Gothic architecture.

PISCINA: Shallow basin with a drain in which Communion or Mass vessels are washed.

PORTCULLIS: Strong, gridded defensive entrance gate in a medieval castle, lowered to block gateway.

PORTICO: Covered colonnade supported by columns, forming an entrance to a building.

QUEEN ANNE: Architecture of the reigns of William and Mary, and Queen Anne (1689–1714), which saw the rise of English Baroque.

REFORMATION: 16thC movement for reform of doctrines and practices of Roman Catholic Church ending in establishment of Reformed or Protestant churches.

REREDOS: Ornamental screen of wood or stone covering wall at back of altar.

RETRO CHOIR: Area behind the high altar in a major church.

REVETTED: Faced with masonry, especially in a fortification.

ROCOCO: Elegant style of decoration prevalent in 18thC Europe, characterised by use of natural forms, plants and animals in plasterwork, chimney-pieces, furniture, etc.

ROOD-SCREEN: Wooden or stone carved screen at west end of chancel, separating nave and choir.

ROSE WINDOW: Circular window typical of Gothic architecture, traceried to resemble a rose.

ROTUNDA: Circular building, often with a domed roof.

SEDILIA: A series of usually three seats for use of the clergy, on the south wall of the chancel, often decorated.

STALLS: Fixed seats in choir or chancel of a church, for the use of the clergy and choir. Often canopied and elaborately carved with misericords.

STUCCO: Plaster or cement used on the face of buildings to represent stonework.

TENON: Projecting piece of wood made for insertion into corresponding cavity, especially mortice, in another piece.

TESSELLATED: Decorating floor or wall mosaic made up of small blocks of stone, marble or tile, embedded in cement.

TIE-BEAM: The main beam which connects the bottom ends of a pitched-roof.

TIMBER-FRAMED: A form of building in which walls and partitions are made of wood, and filled in with plaster, brickwork, wattle and daub etc, characteristic of the 15th–18thC.

TITHE BARN: Structure built to hold tithes paid in kind, eg. annual product of land.

TRACERY: Ornamental carving of mullions and transoms in head of Gothic window.

TRANSEPT: The transverse area of a cruciform church.

TRIFORIUM: Gallery or arcade above arches of nave and choir of church.

TUDOR: Period extending from 1485–1603, but often used to mean the first half of the 16thC. Brick is a characteristic material.

TURRET: Small tower connected with main building, of round or polygonal plan.

TYMPANIUM: The space between a lintel and the arch above it.

UNDERCROFT: A vaulted, underground room, often found in monasteries.

VAULT: An arched roof or a series of arches whose joints radiate from the central point or line. Also an underground chamber for burial or storage.

VICTORIAN: Architecture of the reigns of William IV and Queen Victoria (1830–1901), including Gothic Revival and Greek Revival.

WAGGON ROOF: Roof formed by closely set rafters with curved braces but no tie-beams, so-called for its resemblance to the covered roof of a wagon.

WAINSCOT: Wood panelling, particularly in lower part of room wall.

WATTLE AND DAUB: Primitive interlacing of rods and twigs roughly plastered with clay or mud and straw.

THE WEST COUNTRY

England's rocky south-west peninsula is an example of how tremendous variety can exist within overall coherence. The unity is provided by the basic, unchanging elements of the landscape: rough moor, narrow combe, the wild Atlantic sea. Contrast comes in the form of thrilling smugglers' coves in Cornwall, cheerful hurly-burly ports in Devon, urbane stone villages in Somerset and the straggling hamlets of lonely heathlands – Dartmoor and Exmoor.

Amid all this variety there is another, more exclusively physical principle of unity – the unity that comes from being a remote peninsula at England's south-western end. This has given it a certain separateness from England's usual scene, and made it a region with a certain strangeness, and a distinct quality of high romance. It is said that the Isles of Scilly were once joined to Cornwall and that both were the core of the fabulous lost kingdom of Lyonnesse, where noble King Arthur held sway over the brave and pure of heart. Nowhere is the myth more prevalent than in this region where it's traditionally believed that at Tintagel Arthur was born, at Cadbury he held Camelot's court and at Glastonbury he is buried.

The basis for a separate Celtic identity was to remain long after Arthur: the River Tamar remained the border of a Cornish kingdom which England did not subdue until the 9thC, and even now there is a sense in which Cornwall may be regarded as a distinct, almost separate part of England. The Celtic heritage, reflected in the Cornish language (which itself did not finally die out until the 18thC), is still evident in place names.

As time went on, the south-west was often to become a centre of rebellion against the central authority in London: it rose several times against Henry VII, against the Prayer Book of Edward VI in 1549, and most tragically, in 1685 when Monmouth's enthusiastic but pitifully ill-armed band of rebels went down on the bogs of Sedgemoor. Gradually, as the ties with England became stronger, economic and social benefits were accrued. These are expressed in the growth of such industries as the china clay of Cornwall, the textile manufacture of Devon, and in the development of tourism that gave rise to Devon's elegant Torquay or Avon's genteel Weston-super-Mare.

All four counties in this region of England have their own distinct individuality and appeal, but perhaps Cornwall has the most idiosyncratic qualities. You do not visit Cornwall for rich churches or magnificent country houses, although there are some of both. Cornwall is rough villages tucked into hills near the sea-cliffs, lonely pack-horse lanes fragrant with primrose and foxglove, black rocks and cliffs battered by the sea, and ancient towns where pre-Christian customs still linger. It offers a compelling landscape in its many ancient stone circles, Celtic crosses and holy wells, in the patchwork system of small solid-hedged fields, and in the strange industrial landscapes produced by the workings of china clay and tin.

Devon veers from the savage wildness of the moors, into which the narrow stream-haunted combes or valleys are cut, to the rich red sand country of the lowlands, where many of the exquisitely pretty villages do actually resemble their counterparts on chocolate boxes. There is also a certain homespun warmth in the Devon scene – as expressed in its small churches. These are rarely elaborately decorated, but often detailed by beautiful wood carvings, locally crafted. In many parts Devon is among the most beautiful of English counties, with steeply banked lanes full of ferns and bluebells, stretching over craggy Dartmoor or the gorselands of Exmoor.

Somerset is the most fully English, the most urbane of these counties, a land of strong, sweet pasture and shining stone. The country houses – exemplified by Montacute – rival those of neighbouring Dorset, and the profusion of church towers, powerful expression of the Christian tradition that produced Wells and Glastonbury, are among the glories of English civilisation. But romance, again, is never far away, whether you are dreaming of Arthur at Camelot, searching for the Grail at Glastonbury, or when the winter bleakness of Sedgemoor reminds you of the grim season when Alfred was hiding here, fearing that all England was lost to the Danes.

Avon is a new county, product of the 1974 local government reorganisation that changed 1,000 years of continuity in English county life. Although it has yet to find a fresh identity, its great strength is the possession of two of England's most attractive cities – Bath, that supreme product of 18thC leisured civilisation, and Bristol, a fascinating blend of ancient dignity with modern liveliness. The Avon countryside, with its steep green hills and striking stone villages, also abounds in historic sites – many of which date back to the Roman occupation.

A patchwork, or a finely-constructed tapestry, even if this region is not quite the lost kingdom of Lyonnesse, it is surely as beautiful and historically significant a corner of England as you could hope to find.

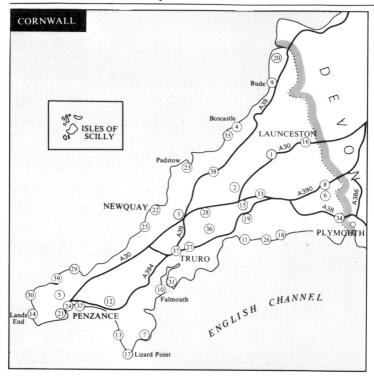

CORNWALL

CORNWALL

1. Altarnun
1 B6

7m SW of Launceston. A wild, upland parish on
the north east edge of Bodmin Moor, it
straggles down a slope to a bubbling stream,
Penpont Water, which is crossed by an
ancient pack-horse bridge and
stepping-stones. Looming above the village
are the dark hills of Bray Down and Hendra
Down. The impressive and sombre early
16thC church is known as the 'Cathedral of
the Moor', because of its size. Its 109-ft-high
tower, topped by strong pinnacles, is one of
the highest in Cornwall. The imposing
interior has a fine Norman font with bearded
faces at its corners, a good rood-screen
enclosing the 17thC communion rails and a
magnificent collection of bench-ends, the
work of an early 16thC local craftsman,
Robert Daye.

2. Blisland
2 B7

Beautiful little granite village, one of the few
in Cornwall centred around a village green – a
handsome specimen with gnarled, old
sycamore trees and surrounded by ancient
stone cottages. Blisland's greatest glory is the
Church of St Protus and St Hyacinth,
basically Norman but with 15th and 16thC
additions. A pleasant slate-and-granite
building, it's remarkably beautiful inside. This
is due to an exquisite restoration by F. C.
Eden in 1896, with a huge, painted
rood-screen and richly carved woodwork on
the barrel roofs as well as a grand Jacobean
pulpit Eden embellished with cherubs and
flowers carved from limewood.
The area around Blisland, on the western
fringe of Bodmin Moor, has much of interest:
several hoary old manor houses, now mainly
farms, and many strange pre-Christian stone
circles and monoliths in remote corners of the
dark moors.

3. Bodmin
2 B7

Officially Cornwall's county town, and in the
Middle Ages the largest. Bodmin has now
been overtaken in size by many others and
most Cornishmen regard Truro as their
capital. The town has a commanding position
over the Fowey and Camel estuaries and the
area has been heavily populated since the Iron
Age. But Bodmin really began to grow as a
religious centre (the very name means 'abode
for monks'), for it was here that the virtuous
Irish saint, St Petroc, founded a missionary
priory in the 6thC. The medieval priory has
vanished, as has the great 13thC Franciscan
friary, but Bodmin still possesses the largest
parish church in the county, a fine 15thC
Perpendicular example.
Bodmin's failure to grow great really dates
from the Tudor period when it became a
noted centre for rebellion against the Crown:
it rose against taxes in 1496, for the
Pretender, Perkin Warbeck in 1497, and
against the new Protestant prayer book of
Edward VI in 1549. In those years of lost
causes the town gibbets seem to have been
seldom unoccupied. Public executions took
place in the town square, Mount Folly, until
1862. The 19thC assize courts and old
Bodmin gaol still have an air of grimness,
although the latter has a rather different
function now, being in use as a night-club.
Bodmin today is a straggling town with few
fine buildings, although the prevailing
buff-grey stone can be attractive. It is,
however, a good centre for exploring Bodmin
Moor, and has a couple of good museums – a
railway museum of the Great Western
Railway and a museum of the history of the
Duke of Cornwall's Light Infantry, housed in
the barracks where the regiment was once
stationed.

Bodmin Moor

Though Cornwall has no moorlands to match
those of Devon, Bodmin Moor is the nearest
comparison. Wonderful walking and riding

country, the great heights, such as Brown Willy at 1,375ft, are comparable with those of Dartmoor in their rugged grandeur. Ancient man displayed here his strange love for high and windy places, and the moor is littered with hut-circles, stone circles and menhirs. **Dozmary Pool**, a mournful lake set in the bleak heights, is said to be the one into which King Arthur's magic sword, Excalibur, was thrown. A hand rose from the pool, caught the sword and waved it three times before it disappeared into the bottomless depths. In the Middle Ages the moor was a great centre for tin-mining, and you may still see many rakes – furrows used in a sort of open-cast mining – dating from that time. Tin-mining has ceased, but there is still china clay mining here: a particularly striking cone of spoil is visible near the A30 on Menacrin Downs.

Another interesting spot is **Jamaica Inn**, on which Daphne du Maurier based her famous novel. Thrillingly set in the lonely heart of the moor, the 18thC building itself, dour and slated, is disappointing. But its immensely romantic associations with smugglers, stage-coaches and ghosts, for which it became notorious, make it a popular place. **King Arthur's Hall** *below Garrow Tor* is a rectangular enclosure once lined with huge granite slabs, which is thought to have been built around 2,000BC as a shelter for livestock.

Crowned with rough grass rather than gorse or heather, and with few really striking peaks, Bodmin Moor can seem a rather bleak place. But surrounding it are many interesting villages such as Blisland, Altartun and St Neot, noted for its beautiful wild ponies. Few lanes enter its heart and it is crossed by only one major road, the A30. The whole area will be far more appreciated by those prepared to leave the car and exercise the walking boots.

4. Boscastle   1 B6

Quaint seaspot, where two forest streams meet the tide in an incredibly narrow harbour. The Normans built a castle here and parts of the ancient grey church are also Norman. Certainly the most unusual and macabre feature of Boscastle is the **Museum of Witchcraft and Black Magic**, an astonishingly comprehensive museum of the occult for such a small place – and stronger on black than on white magic. There is the skeleton of a 16thC witch, Ursula Kemp, who was executed in 1589, many working materials for witches such as flying-ointment and magic powder used against enemies, and the thigh bone of an ancient Tibetan sorcerer. On the walls are several paintings by the master of 20thC diabolism, Aleister Crowley, who turns up so regularly in the memoirs of foreign visitors to the Paris of the Belle Epoque.

Boscastle

5. Chysauster Ancient Village   1 F9

Gulval. A fascinating place because it has the remains of what is the first recognisable village settlement in England. The village was lived in from about 100BC to the 3rdC and although the houses now lack roofs and much of their walls, the shape of the village main street is still plain. These people farmed and probably smelted tin, and to protect themselves from the elements, built their houses with walls up to 15ft thick. Above their settlement, on the hill's crest is an Iron Age fort.

6. Cotehele House   1 C7

2m W of Calstock. Many people consider this the best preserved late medieval manor house in Britain. Not large, but certainly magnificent, there's no timbering, pillaring or whitewash to disturb the brown-stone solidity of an exterior that was built to last. The present house is late 15th and early 16thC but incorporates some 14thC remains of an earlier house. It was the home from the 15thC of the Edgcumbe family, but in 1947 they presented it to the National Trust. Much of the present house (and the family's fortunes) was built up by Richard Edgcumbe, who led local rebellion against Richard III in 1483 but survived to become one of Henry VII's trusted ambassadors. In the woods below the house stands a chapel which he built to mark the spot where he once escaped arrest from Richard's men: he threw his cap and a large stone into the river, and hearing the splash and seeing the cap afloat, the soldiers concluded he was drowned and rode off! The rich furniture, tapestries and armour in the house were collected by Richard Edgcumbe and his successors. In the chapel stands a clock that has been there since 1489. More than 1,000 acres of grounds contain gardens, ponds and a medieval dovecote, all merging exquisitely into the lovely natural setting. Woodlands drop down to the shining River Tamar where there's a manorial water-mill, a cider press and a charming little quay. *Open most days, summer; grounds daily, all year.*

7. Coverack   1 G10

Charming and unsophisticated little village on the east coast of the Lizard peninsula, full of whitened stone houses under thatch. Some modern housing and a few tourists have little disturbed its ancient atmosphere of fishing and smuggling. Smuggling was immensely prevalent here in the 19thC, and one despairing excise man complained that no less than 7,000 ankers of brandy had been run ashore in the previous 12 months (an anker was about 10 gallons). The village has a great tradition of lifeboat heroism, which was often needed, for three miles to the north east lie the dreaded black rocks of the Manacles. The nearby church of St Keverne has an octagon spire which once acted as a landmark to ships trying to avoid the Manacles. However, more than 400 men who drowned are buried in its churchyard.

8. Dupath Well-Chapel   1 C7

Nr Callington, 1m S of A390. According to legend, this holy well was built in memory of two amorous knights who fought a duel over a lady, and killed each other instead. It's the best preserved well-chapel in Cornwall, and stands among a simple group of farm-buildings, enclosed by great walls of granite and containing a crystal-clear spring. The chapel certainly dates from at least the early 16thC, and perhaps from a century before that. It was a baptistry for the surrounding mountain lands during the medieval period, and is also thought to have been the scene of ancient pagan fertility rites, before Cornwall was converted to Christianity during the Dark Ages. The most striking feature of this small chapel is at the west end, where the roof carries an ornate stone belfry which is built in such a way that, standing on the rising ground just in front of it, you get a beautiful view eastwards across the valley to the sweeping hills beyond.

9. Ebbingford Manor   1 B5

Bude. One of England's most ancient manor houses, set like a little jewel in the heart of the modern town centre. Much of the house is thought to date from the 12thC, but it was extensively altered in the 16thC. Especially notable here is the exquisite little walled garden, an oasis of peace. *Open most days, summer.*

10. Falmouth 1 G10

These days a fairly undistinguished seaside resort, and certainly not an ancient town, but it has a memorable past as well as a truly beautiful natural setting. Its harbour is among the most sweeping in Britain, and is claimed to be the third largest natural harbour in the world. Surprisingly its career as a port began very late: Sir Walter Raleigh came here in the 1590s, when there was just a tiny village, a manor house and isolated Pendennis Castle, and he tried to persuade the authorities that it would make a good port. Partly because of the rivalry of other ports like Truro and Penryn the idea was long getting off the ground, and the first quay was not built until 1670. From 1688 it became the great port for the mail packets from abroad which brought great prosperity. When this function was transferred to Southampton, the port became less significant, but from the 19thC the railway brought summer visitors, attracted by the most equable climate in Britain. Falmouth remains Cornwall's most densely populated town, and for one that was essentially planned, it seems a bit of a historical jumble. The parish Church of King Charles the Martyr was built in the 1660s, and is Perpendicular outside with a classical interior.

Custom House Quay, Falmouth

10. Falmouth, Pendennis Castle 1 G10

Pendennis Point. Part of the great chain of castles that Henry VIII built from 1538 onwards to guard against a French invasion, Pendennis Castle remains one of the most magnificent, perhaps because of its splendid setting on the headland overshadowing the town. It is approached by way of the headland road called Castle Drive, which rises and falls memorably among bushes and trees which cling to the cliff, occasionally parting to give a spectacular view. The castle was started in 1540 and built quite quickly: Henry VIII was responsible for the round castle and his daughter, Elizabeth, later added the outer defensive walls.

The castle is interesting as it is exceptionally well preserved, with complete portcullis remaining. The main octagonal room in the tower has walls 16ft thick! Reproduction 18thC furniture brings the governor's lodging to life. A small museum contains fine collections of arms, armour and cannons. Within the Elizabethan walls are several former barracks: one built in 1901 is now used as a youth hostel. The whole place gives an impression of strength and defiance, and it is appropriate to reflect that during the Civil War it withstood a five-month-long Roundhead siege, under the 70-year-old Sir John Arundell, and was the last castle to hold out for the King except for Raglan in Wales, which held out two days longer.

11. Fowey 1 B8

Bright, breezy port town, with an atmosphere given to it by many centuries of marine activity. It was an important port west of Bristol from the early Middle Ages, when the town was spelt Fawi (it is even now pronounced 'Foy').

This congested town with its delightful narrow streets is easy to explore. Most of the main buildings lie where the centre of the town meets Fore Street, its winding main street. Place House is an Elizabethan and Victorian manor house, long the home of the Treffry family. The beautiful largely 14thC church, also used until the 17thC as the town hall, has a particularly splendid and high 16thC tower, elaborately decorated with ornaments in bands. See, too, the more modern town hall, the 17thC almshouses, the town quay, and remains of Broadgate, one of the medieval gates to the town.

Castle Dore *2½m N of town,* an Iron-Age earthwork, also has the 6thC Castle Dore stone, thought to mark the home of King Mark in the medieval myth of Tristram and Iseult.

Fowey

12. Godolphin Court 1 G10

Godolphin Cross, 5m NW of Helston. One of the grand manor houses of Cornwall, once the seat of the Godolphin family who kept popping up in history in unexpected and enterprising lights. The most famous Godolphin was Sidney, Lord High Treasurer to Queen Anne in the early 18thC and political ally of the great Marlborough. Among others were a poet killed in the Civil War and, in the 16thC, one of the first Cornish landlords to patronise tin-mining. The family died out entirely in the 18thC, but Godolphin Court remains a carefully-tended family home.

Fanned by cypresses as you approach, the house is richly and mysteriously set in dark woods, giving it an air of both grandeur and melancholy. It was first erected in the late 15thC and is partly Tudor, but the grand, long, colonnaded front is 17thC and there is an 18thC Great Hall. The gardens are a haven of peace. *Open certain days, summer.*

13. Gunwalloe 1 G10

A beautiful coastal spot which seems to breathe romantic old Cornwall, truly one of the high spots of the west coast of the Lizard peninsula. The A3083 comes down a high hill to a wide, shallow combe which has no other building but an ancient church: there is a small village, however, on a nearby hill. The church, strangely, is actually on the beach, hunched up against a small headland called Castle Mound, with the stone in its nave turning green from algae produced by the damp sea air. It was built in the 14th and 15th C. Outside is a small graveyard around an ancient cross. Round a corner is a church tower, quite detached. On Castle Mound are the remains of an ancient earthwork.

The sea in front of the cove is full of sunk ships and treasure, including the contents of the St Andrew, an early 16thC ship carrying rich treasure for the King of Portugal. In the 19thC a dam was built with the aim of pumping the water out and discovering these hidden riches, but it was wrecked in a storm. The sea retains its treasure, but if you are lucky you may well find a gold coin on the beach, either on the ample sand or on the surrounding great grey stones, laden with pebbles.

14. Land's End 1 E10

The area has great symbolic significance as

the westernmost point of England, although the granite cliffs are not as dramatic as others nearby and the area is now over-touristic. Amid the car parks and ice-creams it's difficult to feel that this peninsula was the last land of the Celts, but come at dawn or dusk and its remoteness will evoke a poignant sense of its ancient and significant past. Look out from the rocky cliffs across the foaming sea towards the 19thC Longships Lighthouse, 120ft high and solitary on its rock, or beyond that, strain your eyes towards the Isles of Scilly which can sometimes just be seen on fine days. Even if the 'first and last house' is a souvenir shop this is, after all, the end of England.

Isles of Scilly 1 C10
Beautiful islands, aptly if poetically described by Swinburne as 'a small sweet world of wave-encompassed wonder'. And the visitor, even if he is at first dismayed by the lack of spectacular cliffs or thick woods, will surely agree when he has savoured the beautiful sandy beaches and the friendly charm of the villages. There are 150 small islands, most uninhabited, lying to the south west of Land's End, reached by sea or helicopter from Penzance, 38 miles away.
The islands have had an eventful history and were, strangely enough, probably more heavily populated in prehistoric times than they are now. Certainly more islands were inhabited than the present five. These 'Islands of the Blest', which some say are part of the lost kingdom of Lyonnesse, were popular as burial places with Bronze Age warriors, and of 250 Bronze Age chamber tombs in England and Wales, about 50 are in the Scillies. The Romans used Scilly as a place of banishment, while in the Civil War the islands were so Royalist that they held out for the King two years after the war on the mainland was ended. The great developers of the Scillies were the 19thC feudal landlords, the Dorrien-Smiths, who still lease the island of Tresco from the Duchy of Cornwall. It was they who introduced the growing of early flowers for the London market, which replaced smuggling as the mainstay of the local economy.
The various islands have different charms. St Agnes is the most westerly inhabited island, a craggy place with its mysterious ancient tombs and ancient lighthouse (built in 1680 and almost the oldest in Britain). St Mary's is the largest island with the only 'town', Hugh Town – a village by mainland standards. There are many low, ancient granite-built houses and the island is dominated by Star Castle, now a hotel, built on the orders of Elizabeth I in 1593. St Mary's also has many prehistoric graves. Tresco is probably the most beautiful island, dominated by 'The Abbey', the large 19thC house of the Dorrien-Smiths, which stands on the site of a Saxon abbey built on the orders of King Athelstan. *View from outside only*. There are two 17thC castles: King Charles's Castle, consisting of Civil War additions to a Tudor building, and Cromwell's Castle, in a better state of repair. Tresco is noted for its sandy beaches and for some of the few trees to be found in the Scillies – luxuriant and sub-tropical.

Hugh Town, St Mary's, Isles of Scilly

15. Lanhydrock 1 B7
2½m SE of Bodmin, B3268. Originally an early 17thC house, obstinately built in the Tudor and Gothic style when the fashion had changed to the Renaissance style. A softly appealing building of warm, brown-stone, it has large, mullioned windows and a battlemented roof crowning its long wings. Much of the present house was rebuilt in the late 19thC, to become the epitome of the solid comfort of the late Victorian age. The outstanding room, which dates from the 17thC, is the gallery. It has a magnificent, very long plaster ceiling, with panels vividly illustrating the Creation and the books of Genesis from the Bible. Over the two fireplaces are more scenes, from the book of Samuel. The attached church is attractive, as are the formal gardens, shrub gardens and beech avenue leading to the road at Respryn Bridge. *Open summer; gardens open daily, all year.*

16. Launceston 1 C6
A fine market town which still remains in its medieval plan and narrow streets. The looming ruins of a Norman motte-and-bailey castle and a medieval gate are reminders that Launceston once guarded the main route from Devon into Cornwall. The castle owes its survival to the fact that it was taken and retaken so often in the Civil War, and became in such poor condition that it wasn't thought worth the trouble to blow it up entirely, as happened to most castles under Cromwell. The other great building of the town is the 16thC Church of St Mary Magdalene, of dazzling decoration and one of Cornwall's most beautiful. Not a stone of the exterior is without carving, either of figures or foliage. Look out for the beautiful vision of the Magdalene under the east window, surrounded by 12 surpliced minstrels, most delicately carved in the granite.
Launceston is a very ancient town which was important in the Dark Ages when the Saxons clashed with the Cornish Celts. Naturally it is rich in buildings of most periods, while the town skyline, with the castle coming in and out of view, lends the place an air of grandeur. Idle wandering is fun, but don't miss the White Hart Hotel with its genuine Norman doorway in The Square, and Castle Street which has some particularly fine Georgian houses.

17. Lizard Point and Peninsula 1 G10
The southernmost peninsula of England, almost an island but joined to the mainland by a small isthmus near Helston. While Land's End is the furthest west that England extends, Lizard Point is the furthest south. It is a high, bleak tableland, with the wild moorland of the Goonhilly Downs at its centre and ringed round with high cliffs. Speckling the area are beautiful small coves, like Kynance, which the walker of the lonely hills will happily chance upon.
Lizard Town is a fairly hideous settlement, but the Lizard Point is fine for spotting great ships at sea. Off this coast are jagged rocks of great danger, and many vessels have come to grief near here. In Pistol Meadow, a little west of Lizard Point, 200 bodies were buried after they were found on the rocks at low tide in the mid 18thC. One of the great Cornish lighthouses on a rock guards the approach to the Lizard Point. The first lighthouse on this site was built in 1619 – and the present one substantially dates from the mid 18thC, but was given a powerful lighting system in 1900. It is visible 20 miles out at sea.

18. Looe 1 B8
Not a town for those who detest crowds, it's more notable for its natural setting than for its actual character. Nestling among high wooded valleys and lonely mudflats, for centuries Looe has been a fishing village, but

is now rather spoiled by tourism. The name is Celtic (it means 'inlet of the sea' and is the same as the Scottish loch), and there was a Celtic settlement, probably a monastery, on the hills above, the ruins of which can still be seen.

Until 1883 East and West Looe were separate towns facing each other across the river, and the new guildhall *Fore Street*, built in 1877, was the symbol of their union. The old 16thC guildhall, now housing a small museum, is prettier. St Nicholas's Church was also once used as the guildhall. Its tower contained a 'Scold's Cage' in which nagging women were placed – and, according to the vicar, it proved 'most effective'. East Looe quay has some very fine Victorian warehouses and some of the higher streets, with their old houses, are reached by romantic flights of steps. Besides its historic interest, Looe has all the accoutrements of the modern touristy seaside town, from slot machines in the amusement arcades to the sandy beaches. But it is also the British centre for shark fishing, has fine walks over the estuary at low tide, lovely views over the estuary from the bridge connecting the two towns built in 1855, good angling, and a bird sanctuary on Looe Island.
Of particular interest is the **Cornish Museum** *Lower St, East Looe*. Fascinating, entertaining and grisly, it emphasises the strange associations of a region that still bears the strong impress of Celtic folkways. It specialises in exhibitions of folklore and crafts. *Open summer*.

19. Lostwithiel 1 B7
Elegant and historic town, more important in the Middle Ages when it was the capital of the Duchy for a time. It is still small and on the medieval grid plan. Especially in the main street you'll find a wide range of buildings of all historic periods, from the medieval Duchy Palace, to the guildhall of 1740, to the rather forbidding Methodist chapel of 1900. St Bartholomew's Church, with its famous 13thC lantern spire and beautiful Early English window is an impressive building. But Lostwithiel's most outstanding building is the great castle of **Restormel** *1½m NW of town*, the best-preserved medieval castle in Cornwall. Its large circular shell keep on a mound on a hill falling steeply down to the Fowey, makes it also one of the most romantic. Parts of it may date from c1100, but most of what you see today is 13thC. The remains of many of the rooms can be seen clearly, such as the Great Hall, the kitchen with its great fireplace and the lord's bedchamber.

20. Morwenstow, Church of St Morwenna 1 B5
Lonely with only the wild Atlantic for company this tiny, windswept hamlet with just a church, a vicarage and an ancient farm is the northernmost parish in Cornwall. It's very ancient, most of the present building being Norman, but some remains, including the remarkable font, shaped like a sort of bent egg-cup, are possibly Saxon. Notice the fine Norman carving and the 16thC bench-ends. This coast was remarkable for wrecks, and in the churchyard are many pathetic graves of dead sailors.
The nearby vicarage is a remarkable fantasy, with chimneys in the form of miniatures of church towers. It was the work of a remarkable but well-loved eccentric, Robert Hawker, who was vicar here from 1834 to 1875. He enlivened his days by writing poems (including the ballad 'Song of the Western Men'), inventing the harvest service, meditating long hours in his hut on the cliff-top, and wearing odd clothes like a brimless hat. In old age he married an immigrant Polish woman much younger than himself. Having spent most of his Sundays in the pulpit railing against Catholicism, under

her influence he was received into the Roman Catholic church on his deathbed! The south window of the church is a memorial to Hawker.

21. Mousehole 1 F10
Attractive fishing village near Penzance, once a great centre of the pilchard-fishing industry. Now very small it is full of picturesque cottages and has a particularly charming harbour, with colour-washed and grey-granite houses jostling each other on the quayside above two piers enclosing the half-moon shaped cove. The village should be pronounced 'Mowsal'. Since the 19thC it has been a haunt of artists painting harbour scenes and is now very touristic. But before that it was an isolated place and one of the last strongholds of the Cornish language in the 18thC. In the church lies Dolly Pentreath who died in 1777, a beggar who claimed to be the last Cornish native speaker and would speak it for a shilling. Some experts, however, think that Zennor was the last place where Cornish was spoken.

22. Newquay 1 G8
Cornwall's largest and most popular seaside resort, with miles of wonderful sandy beaches, it was only a small fishing village until the end of the 19thC and has very little of historic interest. Despite it being the site of an Iron Age settlement, almost the only old building is the Huer's House of 1875 – 'huers' would watch for the pilchard shoals and shout out to the village if they saw one. Some historically noteworthy places can be found in the vicinity, however. In the eastern suburb of St Columb Minor is a parish church with an exceptionally fine pinnacled tower, and some attractive old cottages.
The Elizabethan manor house of **Trerice** *3m SE of Newquay* has unusual curly gables and contains plaster ceilings and contemporary fireplaces. *Open summer*.
Near Newquay is **Bedruthan Steps**, a magnificent beach with a jumble of inhumanly impressive dark rocks said to be stepping stones used by the giant Bedruthan. Most impressive of all is the line of 200-ft-high stacks, which at high water stand proudly in the surf. Look out for Queen Bess rock at the north end, with an outline uncannily resembling Queen Elizabeth I.
Guide to GB–gal. 7

23. Padstow 1 A7
Lovable place of narrow streets and old stone cottages with gardens profuse with fuchsias. The town is very ancient, and there seems already to have been a settlement here, called Lodenek, when St Petroc, the celebrated Irish missionary, arrived in his coracle to found a monastery. The fine Elizabethan manor house, Prideaux Place, is said to stand on the site of the monastery.
Padstow was an important religious centre in the Middle Ages, and was a favourite stopping place for Irish pilgrims on their way to continental shrines. It also became an important fishing and boat-building centre. Look out for Abbey House on the north quay – a strange, rather crude building of the 15thC which may have been a meeting place for merchants. Raleigh's Court House on the south quay is where Sir Walter Raleigh received his visitors when he was Warden of Cornwall and there are many pretty houses around the harbour. Largely in the Decorated style, the Church of St Petroc has a fine Elizabethan pulpit as well as a handsome font.

24. Penzance 1 F10
The great Cornish resort town of the Regency period and the Victorian age, it remains a favourite place to enjoy the winter sunshine and tropical vegetation. It has an ancient history, having been granted a market in 1332 and harbour rights in 1512, but it is curiously short on historic buildings. Apart from the

rather grand Regency and Victorian promenade, and Chapel Street with its Georgian houses, the town is chiefly notable for the pleasant beaches and the extraordinary number of car parks.

Being staunchly Royalist, Penzance was plundered by the Roundheads during the Civil War, which partly accounts for its lack of historic heritage.

Most of the development took place in the later 19thC after the arrival of the railway, which allowed increased tourism and the rise of market gardening, early flowers being dispatched to London. The 1836 pillared market hall (now Lloyds Bank) is impressive, there are a number of good museums, and the Morrab municipal gardens are beautiful.

25. Perranporth   1 G9
In the 19thC a tin-mining village and now a typical Cornish resort with nice sandy beaches and excellent surfing and golfing. It is historically notable for St Piran's 'lost church', a little chapel built in the 6th–7thC and almost the earliest Christian building in Britain. Submerged for centuries under the drifting sands, it was only rediscovered in 1835 and unfortunately encased in 1910 in an extraordinary and very ugly concrete shell for protection. The building itself, although fabulously ancient, is rather crude, but the magnificent sand-dune country in which it's situated, gives it chilling associations: periodically the shifting sands reveal skeletons from its cemetery. Three skeletons were found under the altar when the church was excavated, all with their heads cut off and laid beside them – perhaps Christian martyrs killed by a pagan chief. There is an ancient Celtic cross near the church, and nearby St Piran's Round, a large hollow, is the impressive site of an Iron-Age camp.

26. Polperro   1 J9
The very epitome of a picturesque Cornish village, with lime-washed cottages in narrow, steep streets running down to the harbour. To an even greater extent than most Cornish fishing villages it was noted for smuggling, and the Preventive Service was primarily created in the early 1800s to deal with Polperro. The resident excise men were forced to live in a boat in the harbour because no Polperro householder would take them in! Many of the old cottages still have secret hiding places for contraband, and there is an entertaining smugglers' museum. Close by is a house whose front is patterned with sea shells, the patient artistry of a retired fisherman.

27. Probus, Church of St Probus   1 A8
The 16thC church tower is one of the most handsome in England, and certainly the finest, as well as the tallest, in Cornwall. Lofty and yet elegantly streamlined, it's covered in elaborate carving but without any suggestion of fussiness. It is carved in granite and covered in lichen-green, and the roof is battlemented and pinnacled – the whole thing reminiscent of the great church towers of France. The church itself doesn't quite match the splendour of the tower, but it has a spacious interior, and if it is a little plain, there are interesting brasses and wall-monuments.

28. Roche Rock Chapel   1 B8
Roche, 9m N of St Austell, B3274. Lonely and ancient chapel on the top of a group of high crags, Roche Rocks, which remain impressive in spite of lying in the midst of the man-made crags created by the china clay industry. The Chapel of St Michael was built in 1409 – exactly why no-one knows but perhaps as part of a hermit's cell. It came in time to be known as the Hermit's Cell, because a member of a local landowning family, the Tregarricks, fell victim to leprosy and was public-spirited enough to shut himself away here in the hope that he would not spread the disease. His

daughter, Gundred, brought him food and water until his death and then took possession of the cell herself, in case she were contaminated. She was later canonised. The chapel is now roofless but has windows and a buttress and can be reached by means of an iron-runged ladder cut into the rock. From the top you receive a magnificent view over the pleasant village of Roche, with its cricket pitch and ancient church.

29. St Ives   1 F9
Once a great pilchard port of Cornwall, but when this trade declined in the 1880s the Victorian artists, attracted by its Mediterranean-like sunlight and beauty, began to come here in droves. Even now the harbour is rarely free from easels, while the fine Penwith Gallery houses many of the paintings and sculptures of local artists. Among famous residents have been Whistler, Sickert, Bernard Leach and Barbara Hepworth. Her house is now a museum where you may see a display of her sculptures. The novelist, Virginia Woolf, spent childhood holidays here, and drew much inspiration for her great novel, 'To the Lighthouse'.

All steep, cobbled, corkscrew streets and tiny alleys, with granite cottages and colour-washed chapels, the town has never become spoilt.

St Ives is an ancient place, having been founded in the Dark Ages by the Irish missionary saint, St Ia. It has been a traditional centre of Nonconformism, both political and religious: in 1497 it declared for Perkin Warbeck, the rebel against Henry VII, was strongly for Parliament in the Civil War, and received visits from John Wesley, founder of Methodism, 27 times. His influence is seen today in street names like Salubrious Street, Teetotal Street and Virgin Street. The mainly 15thC parish church has a good waggon-roof and contains a magnificent Madonna and Child by Barbara Hepworth. For sun and sea worshippers there are sandy beaches and beautiful coastal walks.

30. St-Just-in-Roseland   1 H9
The ancient country church here is outstandingly beautiful not so much for itself but for its setting. It also contains one of the country's most exquisite graveyards. Through the ancient lych-gate you look down onto the church tower and to the graves cascading down among the beautiful tropical shrubs and 19thC trees to the calm waters of the local creek. After this approach, the church itself is slightly disappointing, although its chancel dates from 1261, the tower is 14thC and it has a 15thC font. The village is pretty and there is usually a collection of modern boats moored in the harbour as well as remains of some picturesque old wrecks.

31. St Mawes   1 A9
Beautifully situated at the entrance to the Carrick Roads, this is one of the affluent towns of south Cornwall, its old cottages now often occupied by the wealthy retired. St Mawes has an ancient holy well *nr Victory Inn* where St Mawe, a Welsh saint of the Dark Ages who founded the settlement, often used to meditate. But the greatest sight at St Mawes is the Tudor fortress, St Mawes Castle, built by Henry VIII in the 1540s as part of his great network of south coast castles. The castle is built in a series of entwining circles, giving an aesthetically pleasing as well as an impressive effect. Rumour has it that the castle represented a Tudor rose in plan, as a compliment to Henry. The interior is well preserved and the gardens contain many unusual sub-tropical plants.

32. St Michael's Mount   1 F10
Penzance. Fairy-tale castle, one of the truly great monuments of Cornwall. Looking across the narrow water from Marazion, the magical, ethereal view is perhaps more impressive than

the actual buildings of the castle: some of them are very ancient, but additions and changes were being made up until the 20thC, which ruined some of the character.
The island of St Michael, which seems once to have been joined to the mainland, was originally the home of Celtic saints. Legend also says that it is a fragment of the lost kingdom of Lyonnesse, famous through the legends of King Arthur. There was a Celtic monastery here, and the walls of the present refectory have been there since its successor was built in the 12thC. The chapel is 14thC, but much restored. In the 15thC the buildings were annexed by the Crown, and then passed to various noble families. Inside, there's a collection of armour, pictures and furniture. At high tide the castle must be reached by boat, but it's more atmospheric to walk across the causeway at low tide and up a steep cobbled pathway to where the great battlemented pile of masonry awaits you. *Open most days, summer; certain days, winter.*

St Michael's Mount, Penzance

33. St Neot Church   1 B7
This church is chiefly notable for its most magnificent collection of stained glass from the late 15thC and early 16thC: it is one of the finest collections that in England escaped the hammers of the Puritans. The church is interesting throughout, with a noble west tower rising to a battlemented and pinnacled roof. There is a magnificent granite vaulted porch roof, delicately-carved roof timbers inside and a beautiful early 17thC tomb-chest. St Neot seems to have been quite extraordinary, even by the standards of Dark Ages saints: he is commemorated in a window in the north aisle. Tradition claims that he was little more than a foot high and liked to spend hours meditating, immersed to the neck in his holy well (the holy well still remains). Although St Neot probably lived as early as the 6thC, he is also said to have been the elder brother of King Alfred, who died in AD900, and to have founded Oxford University.

34. Saltash, Royal Albert Bridge   1 K8
One of the great feats of the heroic Victorian age of English engineering, it was built to carry the Great Western Railway across the Tamar from Devon into Cornwall. The crowning masterpiece of Isambard Kingdom Brunel, the bridge was completed in 1859, the year he died. It was acknowledged as a marvel of engineering at the time – a great iron bridge that combined the principles of suspension and arched bridges supported on giant granite piers. There is also an elegant modern bridge here, opened in 1961.

35. Tintagel   1 A6
A name that more than any other in England is redolent of high romance – this is the legendary birthplace of the greatest of British

Tintagel Post Office

heroes, King Arthur. The actual village of Tintagel is rather dull and disappointing although the Old Post Office is an interesting 14thC building, and there is also a rather commonplace museum of sorcery. But the ruin-strewn cliffs which legend connects with Arthur are romantic and impressive indeed. There is a great crag, just half-joined to the mainland, on which the proud ruin of the ancient Norman castle stands topping the cliffs.
The island also has the remains of an ancient Celtic monastery of the 6thC and abandoned at the time of the Norman Conquest. Just on the mainland is old Tintagel church, part Norman and part Saxon, strangely isolated on the bare headland. Come here on a stormy day of the grey and beating Atlantic and you can easily imagine the noble knights who once walked these cliffs, and heroic King Arthur facing the evil Mordred, inspired by the love of Guinevere and the loyalty of Bedwyr, faithful unto death.

36. Treffry Aqueduct   1 B8
Between St Blazey and Luxlilian. Both aqueduct and viaduct, this magnificently impressive structure was the 1839 work of a local engineer, Joseph Treffry who, 20 years before, was pioneering some of the methods used by Brunel on his great railway viaducts. A succession of gigantic, granite piers carried the water channel and narrow-gauge line 100ft above the narrow valley, to create a dual impression of immense strength and ethereal delicacy.

37. Truro   1 A8
Although Bodmin is the official county town of Cornwall, Truro is generally regarded as its real capital as it is the largest town and has the cathedral. Truro's origins date back to a manor founded by William the Conqueror. Since the Middle Ages it has been a pleasant, well-kept town, important but not over-large, comfortably nestling in its bowl of hills. Well planned, it has some very fine Georgian streets. In Walsingham Crescent are some elegant Victorian survivals, and from the Victorian age, too, came Boscawen Park with its many rare sub-tropical plants. The superb viaduct carrying the railway into Truro over its 28 great granite arches is a more modern structure, built in 1908.

37. Truro Cathedral   1 A8
A late Victorian cathedral that demonstrates the Victorian Gothic at its most masterly and dignified. The cathedral, which incorporates the 16thC Church of St Mary, was built by J. L. Pearson from 1880 to 1910, and is a late Victorian interpretation of the Early English and Normandy Gothic styles. Its great spire, 250ft high, is the dominating feature of the Truro skyline, giving the town an impressiveness it lacked before (the coming of the cathedral had, in fact, been in response to public agitation for this civic dignity). Inside, the various vistas and vaults are carefully planned, and the granite and Bath stone in which it is built give a cool effect. Among highlights are the carved Bath stone reredos and the attractive baptistry, while the glass and embroideries give a richness and colour that the building might otherwise lack.

38. Wadebridge Bridge   1 H8
A great highlight among the medieval bridges of Britain, this magnificent erection still stands as firmly as in 1468, the year it was completed. It is 320ft long, has 14 arches, and almost all the east side is original although there has been some later widening. The money for the bridge was raised by a public-spirited 15thC vicar, Thomas Lovibond, who endowed the ferry over the river to be too dangerous. It is said that great packs of wool were used to make a firm base for the great piers of the bridge, in the sandy river bed.

🐚 DEVON 🐚

1. A la Ronde   1 F6
2m N of Exmouth, A377. One of the most
unusual and interesting private homes in
England, A la Ronde is the personal
expression of two remarkable sisters, the
Misses Parminster, who had the house built in
1798. Gripped by the romantic movement
they had travelled extensively in Europe, and
were great collectors of curiosities such as
shells and dolls. These interests are reflected
in the house they built: the curious 16-sided
cottage is a copy of San Vitale in Ravenna and
with its prettily decorated windows, tall brick
chimneys and balcony at the top of the house,
the whole thing has an air of elaborate fantasy.
The gallery on the upper floor is intricately
decorated with thousands of sea shells (stuck
on patiently during many a winter evening),
while there are also charming feather pictures
and other relics of the sisters' collections.
Nearby is a chapel the sisters also built, with
attached almshouses for 'four spinsters over
50 years of age and of approved character'.
Open summer.

2. Arlington Court   1 D4
7m NE of Barnstaple, off A39. Not
architecturally of very great distinction,
although there is a rather grand central hall,
this is a 19thC house built in the 1820s for the
local landowners, the Chichesters. But the
house is outstanding both for its exquisite
park and gardens, and its many fine
collections: that of 19thC vehicles (coaches,
broughams, gigs and victorias galore) is the
most comprehensive. Many of the other
collections were gathered together by Miss
Rosalie Chichester, who lived here alone for
40 years and left the house to the National
Trust when she died in 1949. Her love of
small and curious things is evident in her
delicately kept rooms – full of pewter,
porcelain, paintings, snuffboxes, models of
ships and many other objets d'art. The

National Trust has made few changes to her
loved home, and her presence is still felt
strongly.
The park is full of many unusual wild animals:
peacocks (which have a disconcerting habit of
trying to wander in through the door), rare
Jacob's sheep, Shetland ponies and ducks on
the lake. Miss Chichester, as well as her work
in the house, also decided to make a nature
reserve in her park. The whole creation is set
by the River Yeo and beautifully bordered by
rhododendrons. The church is full of
Chichester monuments, including one to
Rosalie Chichester by John Piper. *Open
summer; gardens and park daily, all year.*

3. Bickleigh Castle   1 F5
A fascinating example of how castle buildings
have changed and adapted through the ages, it
consists of a massive, medieval, sandstone
gatehouse on the banks of a river, closed
round with exquisite 18thC wrought-iron
gates and grouped around with Tudor
buildings. See the armoury, guard room,
Great Hall and fascinating museum. Nearby
is an ancient Norman chapel thought to be the
oldest complete building in Devon. *Open most
days, summer.*

4. Bicton Gardens and Countryside
Museum   1 F6
3½m N of Budleigh Salterton, A376. There is
much to see here, ranging from exquisite
formal 18thC gardens to one of the most
comprehensive museums of the countryside to
be found anywhere. The gardens were laid
out by the magnificently rich 18thC Devon
landowner, Lord Rolle (who also built the
great house), to the designs of André Le
Nôtre, who had planned the classic gardens at
Versailles. With watercourses, terraces and
parterres they are quite splendid and later
additions include American gardens, a
pinetum of 1840 and a charming 19thC

greenhouse. A miniature railway runs through the grounds. The Countryside Museum is rich in exhibitions of rural crafts and industries, and has an unrivalled collection of agricultural implements and machines. *Open summer.*

5. Bideford
1 C4

Once one of the great ports of Devon and the setting for Charles Kingsley's romantic novel, 'Westward Ho', it is now a sleepy but agreeable market town. The pretty tree-shaded quay still welcomes the occasional small ship but its greatest days as a port were in the 16thC when it was patronised by the great sea-dog family, the Grenvilles. The cannons round the bandstand in Victoria Park are said to have come from Armada galleons. Bideford has many preserved medieval streets, and fine merchants' houses, but few exciting monuments. The Municipal Buildings contain a small local history museum.

The greatest attraction of the town is medieval Bideford Bridge, an ethereal 15thC poem in 24 arches all of unequal width. It was widened in 1925, and restored and widened in 1968, but the basic structure remains the same as the one built in 1460, when the townsfolk decided to replace their ancient wooden bridge with a glittering new one of stone.

6. Brixham
1 F8

Once the premier fishing port of Britain, where 300 trawlers plied regularly in 1850, it remains a shadow of its former glory – but with its associations with Francis Drake and other famous seamen, it retains a distinct nautical air. This quaint little harbour town set snugly in the hills was the one into which Drake sailed with the first prize captured from the Spanish Armada, the ship Capitana. And here in 1688 William of Orange first set foot on English soil reportedly declaring: 'Mine goot people, I mean you goot, I am here for your goot, for all your goots'. There is a rather pompous statue to mark the spot, showing him between two guns as a big-booted civilian carrying his hat in his hand.

There is a good deal to see in Brixham. The harbour has a replica of Drake's Golden Hind and in Middle Street is a good maritime museum. Brixham Cavern is said to have been a home of prehistoric man, and Berry Head may have been the site of a Romano–Celtic port. The church is 500 years old and has many interesting possessions, including a Crusader's tomb and an altar cross from Jerusalem. A 19thC vicar here, Henry Lyte, wrote the famous hymn 'Abide with me'.

7. Broadhembury
1 G5

5m N of Ottery St Mary. One of the prettiest of Devon's many exquisite villages with ancient thatched cottages and houses standing among the many beautiful trees, or near the stream that runs past the churchyard gate. The village has a superb parish church of the 14th and 15thC, with an elegant tower and carved porch as well as a richly decorated 15thC Perpendicular font. The Priest's House is 15thC or earlier. Crowning the village is **Hembury Camp**, *Black Down*, the best prehistoric earthwork in Devon which was a neolithic settlement of c3,000 BC.

8. Buckland Abbey
1 C8

11m N of Plymouth, 6m S of Tavistock. A great abbey church of the Middle Ages turned into a stately home – a most uncommon conversion. The church was founded by Cistercians in the 13thC, but after the Reformation, was first bought by Sir Richard Grenville and then Sir Francis Drake, in 1581, when much captured Spanish gold and his circumnavigation of the world had enriched him. Drake's descendants owned the house until 1947, when it passed to the National Trust. The house is still topped by the ancient church tower, and there is a

beautiful drawing room which Drake had panelled himself. Most of the building is now a naval and folk museum with Drake relics, including his legendary drum and model ships. There is a beautiful garden, and, nearby, a huge early 14thC tithe barn with a magnificent timber roof. *Open summer; certain days, winter.*

9. Castle Drogo
1 E5

2m NE of Chagford, 1m S of A30. The English country house is one of the great architectural glories and social heritages of the country, and Castle Drogo leaves its mark as the very last one to be built, presumably for ever. These houses were originally built for noblemen, but in the 19thC increasingly for wealthy industrialists and merchants. Castle Drogo was built by Sir Edwin Lutyens between 1911 and 1930 for a super-rich grocer, Julius Drewe, and was acquired by the National Trust in 1974. A romantic conception in granite, rising sheer from the moorland and perched on a rocky outcrop for all the world like a medieval fortress, it is a fitting end to a great tradition that lasted 400 years. The house was intended for comfortable living, and has attractive paintings, tapestries and furniture. *Open summer.*

Castle Drogo

10. Clovelly
1 C4

Those with a sweet tooth will recognise the pretty, cobbled main street from the lids of chocolate boxes and, indeed, this is one of the most perfect villages in England. It is unique in that no traffic can enter the village itself, and perhaps no English village so delectably combines the disparate charms of woods and sea. Since its discovery by enthusiastic writers like Kingsley and Dickens in the mid 19thC, the place has become no more spoilt than tourism has made inevitable, and the roses and fuchsias blooming in cottage gardens are as luxuriant as ever. There is a good church, mainly 15thC and with elaborate 17thC memorials to the Cary family, lords of the manor.

11. Compton Castle
1 F7

1m N of Marldon, off A381. Its setting in rich Devonshire countryside is truly superb. One of the finest of the fortified manor houses of the West Country, its stupendous facade was built in 1500, about the same time as Dartmouth Castle and presumably also in response to the French threat. These walls protect an earlier house, probably built in about 1420. Parts of this older house survive today including the restored medieval Great Hall, and also parts of the medieval kitchen quarters. The castle has long been the home of the Gilbert family, which included Sir Humphrey Gilbert, the Elizabethan seadog who discovered Newfoundland in 1583. *Open certain days, summer, or by arrangement.*

12. Dartington Hall
1 E5

Nr Totnes. A fascinating combination of medieval splendour and modern social conscience, there has been an estate here since the 9thC. The magnificent Hall itself was built in the late 14thC by John Holland, brother of Richard II and Duke of Exeter, who had been virtually exiled to the West Country owing to the violent tendencies which had involved him in two murders: he was eventually executed. The house was built on a massive scale with a huge Great Hall and many lesser rooms, but over the centuries it fell into ruin.

In 1925 the estate was bought by two rich and idealistic Americans, Dorothy and Leonard Elmhirst, influenced by progressive ideas, including the teachings of Gandhi. They set up a trust both to encourage education for adults and children, and to reconstruct the crafts and industries of rural life. The whole enterprise still flourishes mightily today, and activities range from the manufacture of tweeds, to the experimental school, to the many arts courses. The restored house remains magnificent and is always open for cultural and creative activities. The grounds, with their Irish yews and many exotic shrubs, are especially lovely in springtime.

13. Dartmoor

The grandest, wildest and largest stretch of unspoilt moorland in the south of England, magnificent walking and riding country and full of historic interest. It is well over 1,000ft high in most parts and from its heights sparkling streams cut their way through rich valleys in which Dartmoor farms nestle, often housed in great granite buildings dating from medieval times. On the edges of the moor are many pleasant country towns and villages: Totnes and Tavistock, Lydford and Okehampton.

Like many high lands, Dartmoor was comparatively more populated in prehistoric times, when lowlands were often swampy and unhealthy, than it is now. There are many Bronze Age antiquities, including stone hut circles at Grimspound and Legis Tor, and stone avenues at Merrivale and Trowlesworthy Warren. In the 12thC the great tin-mining boom began and the moor became a centre of virtually independent tin-miners. Mining lingered on until the early 20thC and many old workings can still be seen, for instance at Grimspound, which also has the most impressive of the prehistoric settlements.

The moor at its bleakest can be experienced at Princetown, with its forbidding prison of Dartmoor almost like some huge Lancashire mill on the moor. The prison was originally built on the suggestion of Sir Thomas Tyrwhitt, owner of granite quarries and friend of the Prince Regent, for French prisoners from the Napoleonic wars. It was they who built roads and opened up the moor generally – and they slept in hammocks slung between pairs of cast-iron pillars. The place became a domestic prison after 1850. The ugly and joyless town itself, not much enlivened by the grand house Tyrwhitt built, provides an authentically grim setting for Dartmoor. Walks on the east side of the moor, which is gentler and, in summer, beautiful and fragrant with the heather, give you the moor at its most human and accommodating.

14. Dartmouth   1 F8

The mouth of the River Dart is still dominated by its two castles, and the town which in the Middle Ages was one of Devon's greatest ports, retains its defence and maritime traditions. The Royal Naval College, which was originated on board HMS Britannia in 1863 and was housed in its present heavy building in 1905, constitutes, together with tourism, the chief mainstay of the town today. There are beautiful Elizabethan houses near the old quay and the Butterwalk, where dairy produce was once sold, is a row of 17thC houses, many of which are supported on granite pillars. St Saviour's, largely 14th and 15thC, is among Devon's most attractive churches. In a shed at the entrance to Coronation Park you can see the first ever really effective steam engine, invented by locally-born Thomas Newcomen in 1706.

Dartmouth's most outstanding monument is the great castle built in the late 15thC. Though partly ruined, it remains in superb condition and should be visited for a lesson in coastal defence. There is also a more minor castle built as part of Henry VIII's ring of coastal defences.

Dartmouth Castle

15. Exeter   1 F6

Long the great city of England's west, this was the Isca Dumnoniorum of the Romans, parts of whose splendid walls can still be seen in Rougemont Gardens, West Street and Southernhay. In Saxon times it was already an important town. A cathedral came in 1050 and the Normans added the castle after a long siege in 1068. In the Middle Ages, shipping and the cloth trade both flourished, while in Elizabethan times the seadogs often sailed from here. The first floor of quaint Mol's Coffee House, *The Close*, is where Drake, Raleigh, Hawkins, Frobisher and Gilbert used to knock back a toddy or two as they conducted their meetings. It's now an art shop.

Exeter has had its share of violence and bloody insurrections. After the Prayer Book Rebellion of 1549, for instance, the vicar of St Thomas's was hanged in his vestments and his body left dangling for four years from his own church tower, as a warning to the Catholics of the west. But on the whole, this has been a peaceful and prosperous town, loyal to the Crown – or *semper fidelis*, as Elizabeth I put it. In May 1942 German bombers flattened most of the old centre, which has been rebuilt largely in worthy, if somewhat unimaginative, red-brick. The most attractive areas of Exeter are the Cathedral Close and the Quay. The Close area has many medieval buildings, including Bishop's Palace and, nearby, the Church of St Mary Arches, perhaps the best-preserved Norman church in Devon. The High Street has Exeter guildhall, 'the oldest Municipal Hall and Criminal Court in the Kingdom', as the plaque claims; it was rebuilt in 1330 on Norman and possibly Saxon foundations. The magnificent arched front, built in 1593, marvellously expresses the confidence and ebullience of Elizabethan Devon, while inside there is fine 15thC roofwork and panelling, and some pleasant portraits.

Now largely destroyed, medieval Rougemont Castle once dominated the town and the preserved Norman gate tower demonstrates how impressive it must have been. Attractive Rougemont Gardens are on the slopes of the old moat. The Quay is a rather beautiful area of riverside with its fine Customs House of 1681, pretty 18thC Collaton Crescent, and the outstanding Maritime Museum, opened in 1969.

15. Exeter Cathedral   1 F6

Especially noted for the unparalleled richness of its superb interior, the glory of Exeter, like St Pauls, remains to us by a miraculous survival of the bombs of the Second World War. The cathedral was first built in 1050 and rebuilt by the Normans in the early 12thC. But around 1260 it was demolished, except for the two Norman transept towers that remain today. The new building appeared gradually over the next century, and has been remarkably little altered since.

The splendour of the interior is breathtaking: looking down the great nave, the Purbeck marble columns on either side support with immense dignity the vaulting of the roof, the longest unbroken stretch of 13thC Gothic vaulting in the world. The 14thC west front is adorned with fine stone figure carving, and among other highlights is the magnificent 14thC oak Bishop's Throne, more than 60ft high, and made entirely without the use of a single nail (a fact which allowed it to be quickly taken apart and hidden when Cromwellian troops were entering the building during the Civil War). Note, too, the exquisite 14thC minstrels' gallery and the chantry chapels. The cathedral is enriched with modern art, as well as medieval, for in the chapter house you may see Ken Carter's individual and striking figures showing the story of creation from Genesis to the Resurrection. Don't miss the 15thC astrological clock.

16. Exmouth   1 F6
An ancient town – the Danes destroyed it, it was a medieval port, it had a Cromwellian fort – but all this has left no trace today. Exmouth began to grow mightily from the late 18thC as a centre for sea bathing, and this era has certainly left its reminders in the form of the many fine marine villas dotted around. The town's outstanding building is Holy Trinity Church, built in the early 19thC and refurbished in the 20thC. A vast, light-filled, clerestoried church, the rich tracery inside is as attractive as the high richly-pinnacled tower of its exterior.

17. Lundy Island   1 B3
Delightfully wild, Lundy is mainly inhabited by puffins, ponies and seals, although there are also about 40 people. It is composed of very hard granite (which was used for building the Thames Embankment in the late 19thC), and is mainly a high plateau with cliffs, varieties of wild flowers and coarse grass among which the many animals wander. The main historic buildings consist of the ruins of a probably 13thC castle, in use during the many centuries when Lundy was a pirate stronghold. There is also an ancient ruined chapel and a granite church of 1889, both dedicated to St Helen. In the 19thC the island passed into the ownership of private families but in 1969 it passed to the National Trust. The best way to reach the island is by boat from Ilfracombe.

18. Lydford   1 D6
Set deep in the eerie enchantment of its dark wooded gorge on the edge of wild Dartmoor, this is a small, grey village of ancient foundation. In the Middle Ages it was the headquarters of the tin-miners who virtually ruled Dartmoor as an independent country. Lydford Castle, their prison, is now a ruin (it was built in 1195), but still retains much of the grim atmosphere of the days when 'Lydford Law' was famous for its cruelty and injustice – the tin-miners would often execute first and examine the evidence later. Near the gorge is Gibbet Hill, scene of many a 'Lydford Law' hanging. Here, too, Lady Howard was burned as a witch after she had murdered four husbands in succession, and highwaymen were left in an iron cage until they died of starvation.
Lydford Gorge offers a spectacularly beautiful walk through overhanging woods beside the

Lydford Castle

cascading river. If you can muster up the energy afterwards, visit the ancient church with its fine modern screen and carved bench-ends.

19. Lynton and Lynmouth   1 E3
Two villages on the north Devon coast, the one on a cliff directly above the other, and linked to it by a cliff railway. They were largely cut off by surrounding Exmoor until the early 19thC, when they suffered for the surrounding wild and beautiful scenery by being turned into resorts. Most of the Romantic poets, including Wordsworth, Coleridge and Southey knew and loved this spot. Shelley came here with his 16-year-old bride, to escape family and social disapproval, but his revolutionary sentiments so annoyed the natives that he was forced to escape in a small boat to Wales.
The place is beautiful, but the surrounding waters can make it dangerous, too – Lynmouth was almost wiped out by a freak high tide in 1607, and in August 1952 disaster struck again when the river turned into a torrent three miles long and took the lives of 34 people. The town, therefore, has few remaining old buildings (Rock House and Manor House are two pre-Victorian survivors) and rather too much ugly modern building, while Lynton has largely the exuberant but endearing architecture of a typical Victorian resort. But people come here largely for Exmoor at its most darkly romantic. You'll never feel this more strongly than at the unique Valley of the Rocks, a great ridge of shaly pinnacles rising straight from the sea and enclosing a little hidden valley on whose slopes the mountain goats climb.

20. Plymouth   1 D8
The largest city of the west after Bristol, it is certainly a highly historic town – but as we see it today, it has something of the nature of the modern upstart. German bombers smashed its centre even more comprehensively than Exeter's, and while the rebuilding has been much more ambitious, it is even more uninspired.
Several outlying parts are much more ancient than its centre anyway: at Mount Batten there was an Iron Age trading post, and at Stoke a considerable Saxon settlement. It is only in the 13thC that we hear of a port at Plymouth itself, but then the town grew fast. A major naval base was established in 1295, and it was the great Elizabethan seadogs that confirmed its naval glory – it was to Plymouth's natural harbour that Drake returned from his navigation of the world in 1580, his lady sovereign waiting before him, and it was on The Hoe (still with one of the greatest harbour views in England) in 1588 that Drake made the Armada wait until he had finished his game of bowls. The Pilgrim Fathers set sail in 1620 from the spot still known as Mayflower Steps. In 1689 William III decided to build the Royal Dockyard in the lonely marshes that were to become Devonport, and Plymouth's position as premier Navy town was confirmed.
The best of the older parts is The Barbican, an area of narrow, cobbled alleys around which Plymouth originally developed in the 12thC. Here there are several genuine Elizabethan merchants' houses (including period-furnished and open-to-inspection 32 New Street), the Customs Houses of 1586 and 1810, the Mayflower Steps and several excellent hostelries.
From the Hoe, Smeaton Tower, the restored Eddystone lighthouse and premier beacon of Britain, is visible, while at the eastern end of the Hoe is Charles II's great mass of stonework, the Citadel. Perhaps the grandest building in the city is the Royal William Victualling Yard, a naval supply centre built by Sir John Rennie from 1826 to 1835. HM Dockyard can be visited with permission, if

suitable precautions are taken and you are British, and the fleet may often be seen in Plymouth Sound.

21. Powderham Castle 1 F6
Kenton, 8m SW of Exeter, off A379. The ancestral home of the earls of Devon, it was built originally in 1390, extensively damaged in the Civil War, and restored in the 18thC and 19thC. Perhaps because of this it does not have quite the raw splendour of certain other south-coast castles, but it is certainly powerful enough. It has a large park well stocked with deer and some fine furniture. Each year there's a special historic exhibition on a different theme, and in July, Powderham hosts a historic vehicle gathering. *Open most days, summer.*

Powderham Castle

22. Saltram House 1 D8
2m W of Plympton, 3½m NE of Plymouth. One of the finest and grandest 18thC houses in Devon, built around a Tudor core and with early 19thC additions by Foulston, the great architect of Regency Plymouth. It is furnished with utmost splendour, with two Robert Adam rooms. Its fine picture collection is enriched by several examples of Reynolds, who was a friend of the family of rich Devon gentry, the Parkers, for whom the house was built. There are magnificent grounds including an orangery, and many quiet walks in the woods lining the Plym estuary. *Open most days, summer; grounds daily, all year.*

23. Tavistock 1 D7
Tavistock grew round a 10thC Benedictine abbey, some ruins of which remain, and was the birthplace of Sir Francis Drake. Tin-mining flourished in the Middle Ages, then cloth, then in the 19thC, copper-mining. The great Consols Mine was one of the biggest in the world and 'safe as Consols' became a common term in the world of stocks and shares. Most of the mines are now gone, but you'll get a haunting reminder of lost industries if you walk along the overgrown towpath of the Tavistock Canal towards the abandoned port of Morwellham, where a new

museum of industrial archaeology is bringing some life back to what was once the mining industry's great port. Tavistock's 15thC church is simple but attractive and has a William Morris window.

24. Torquay 1 F7
The Cannes of the English south-west, beautiful with shady trees and sub-tropical shrubs. It first began to grow during the Napoleonic Wars when it became a centre for officers' wives from the warships anchored in Torbay: at the end of the war, the prisoner Napoleon, on his way to lonely exile at St Helen, gazed on Torquay from the deck of the Bellerophon.
Later in the century French and Russian royalty patronised the town, and it became the most glamorous and chic of English watering places. There are not many individual buildings of great architectural merit, but Torquay has been grandly planned for the well-to-do, and you can see it – sample the magnificent cream facade of Hesketh Crescent of 1846 (now the Osborne Hotel), for splendour. Some of the oldest buildings are part of Torre Abbey: a 14thC gatehouse, a barn where Spanish prisoners were locked up after the Armada, parts of an ancient church and the 18thC mansion of the Cary's built into the older buildings of the abbey. Torquay is particularly notable for Victorian churches, including St John's by G. E. Street with glass by Morris and Burne-Jones.
Kent's Cavern added to the attraction of Torquay when it was discovered in the mid 19thC. Both prehistoric human bones and those of Ice Age beasts were discovered, some of which still remain. Visit it for the magnificent display of red, green and white stalactites and stalagmites.

25. Totnes 1 E7
Rich farming and retirement country, Totnes is an ancient town founded by the Saxons, the centre of which is markedly more attractive than its dreary modern suburbs. Narrow Fore Street is one of Devon's outstanding ancient streets, with many interesting old buildings including an Elizabethan merchant's house, now a museum. Dividing this street from the High Street is the restored 15thC East Gate. Some of the smartest modern antique shops, craft shops and boutiques in Devon are to be found here, many of them in the Butterwalk. Though neither as old nor as impressive as Dartmouth's, it's pretty all the same with arcades and slate-built houses. Totnes is the starting-point for steamer trips up the lovely River Dart, country denied to the motor car.

🎗 SOMERSET 🎗

1. Bridgwater 1 G4
Town of tragic associations, for it proclaimed the Duke of Monmouth, Charles II's ill-fated illegitimate son, king, and it was here that he and his followers spent their last night before being routed by James II's forces at Sedgemoor. If you're drinking at the Sedgemoor Inn, look for the sharpening stone on the mantlepiece; it may well have been used by the King's men for extra-sharp battling blades. In Bridgwater is a house where Judge Jeffreys stayed during the trials in which he condemned so many of Monmouth's courageous and ill-armed band to death.
Bridgwater was long the chief inland port of Somerset and has a long and varied industrial history, but it is full of fine buildings, both ancient and modern. Castle Street, running down to the West Quay, is all early 17thC, and is among the finest streets of that date in the

West Country. King's Square is on the site of the 13thC castle which was destroyed after the Civil War.
St Mary's Church, begun in the 13thC, has many outstanding features, including a remarkably slender 175ft spire of Ham stone, a magnificent 15thC oak pulpit, fine 15th and 16thC screens, and a notable 16thC altar painting. If you climb the tower in the cool evening, you will only be following in Monmouth's footsteps 300 years ago; the scene will be just as lovely, if less troubled.

2. Brympton d'Evercy 1 J5
2m W of Yeovil, off A30. Grand mansion house, with a frontage that is part Tudor and part 17thC. There are fine state rooms and extensive grounds, including a vineyard. Among special features of interest are a Priests' House Museum and the I Zingari Cricket Club Collection, England's premier cricket club. *Open most days, summer.*

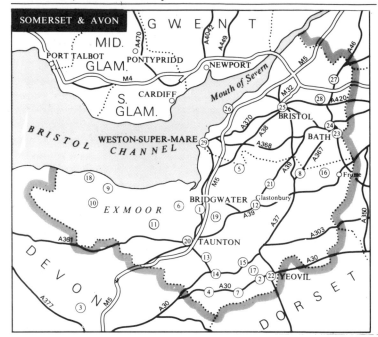

SOMERSET & AVON

3. **Cadbury Castle** 1 J4
North Cadbury. The steep, grassy hill that is
thought to be the site of King Arthur's
Camelot. The wonderful view over the broad,
green vale of Somerset could certainly set up
many an Arthurian dream. It's not difficult to
imagine the glittering court that included
Lancelot, Kay, Merlin, Bedwyr, Tristan and
Guinevere, gathered during the heroic days
when the Romans had left and the Saxon
English not yet claimed the island that was to
bear their name. The story, like most legends,
may well be based on truth, for traces of a
timbered hall of the late 5thC have been
found here, while thorough excavations have
revealed that the site was defended in those
times as well as in the neolithic, Iron-Age,
Roman and Anglo-Saxon periods. There is
not an enormous amount to see now, except
for impressive earth ramparts.

4. **Chard** 1 G5
Perching at 400ft above the surrounding low,
grassy country, this is an ancient town whose
main street probably follows the Roman plan.
Most of the best buildings are concentrated in
this mile-long street, including 17thC
almshouses, remains of the 17thC grammar
school, part of an Elizabethan manor house
and the pillared guildhall. Judge Jeffreys
hanged a dozen men at a single gibbet here
after Monmouth's rebellion, which no doubt
his lordship considered a very minor day's
work. The 15thC parish church is a little
dreary, and much of the rest of the town is
industrial. The Chard Canal of 1835 was one
of the last English canals to be built, and had
only 25 rather profitless years in full business.

5. **Cheddar** 1 H3
Most famous, of course, for the spectacular
and fossil-encrusted gorge cut into the
limestone of the Mendips. But we must also
remember that Cheddar was royal hunting
country for both the Saxon and Norman
kings, and extensive excavations have revealed
the remains of a magnificent royal hall.
Cheddar cheese did indeed originate here
around the 12thC, and until the 18thC the
name was only used for cheese that came from
Cheddar itself. This has obviously long ceased
to be true. The town itself is rather drab, but

follow up your visit to the spectacular caves,
with the museum which contains a
12,000-year-old skeleton. *Open summer.*

6. **Coleridge Cottage** 1 G3
W end of Nether Stowey, nr Bridgwater. The
small house where the great poet lived from
1797 to 1800 for a cost of £7 per year, and
experienced the serenest times of his
madness-haunted life, can still be visited.
While he was here he spent much time with
his friends, William and Dorothy
Wordsworth, who lived nearby at Alfoxden,
and planned with them 'Lyrical Ballads', the
publication of which in 1798 was to
revolutionise English poetry. Charles Lamb,
too, came down from London as often as he
could to see them. Here Coleridge wrote the
'Ancient Mariner' (planned on a walk on the
nearby Quantock Hills) and the
opium-inspired 'Kubla Khan'. The northern
accents and brown complexions of this literary
community proved too much for the locals,
whose suspicions increased when they were
spotted taking nocturnal walks with
note-books. Rumours spread that they were
French spies. An inspector was called and
servants summoned to give evidence – but
eventually they were patronisingly dismissed
as harmless cranks. *Open most days, summer.*

7. **Crewkerne** 1 H5
Pleasant and ancient town of Saxon
foundation which manufactured the sails for
Nelson's ship, the Victory. Crewkerne
suffered for its support of Monmouth's
rebellion in 1685, but survived to triumph
over James II when it welcomed William of
Orange on his arrival in 1688. It has an
interesting 15thC Ham stone church, and the
17thC grammar school where Captain Hardy,
in whose arms Nelson died, was educated, is
now a church hall.

8. **Downside Abbey Church** 1 J3
One of the great modern Benedictine
foundations in England, the monastery was
founded in 1814 by English Benedictine
monks fleeing the French Revolution, who
now had a renewed welcome in their own
country. In 1899 it became an abbey. The
church, which was finally completed in 1935,
is a memorable mixture of 19th and 20thC

work. It has cathedral-sized dimensions and a tower 166ft high, the cold, white, stone pillars of the nave contrasting with the warmth of the chapels. Meditating monks convey an atmosphere of great spirituality, oddly blending with the worldly grandeur that created the fashionable Roman Catholic public school next door.

9. Dunster 1 F3
Olde Worlde Somerset town of serene beauty. Still rather medieval and feudal in its atmosphere (in the park archery contests are still held) it has many historic buildings besides the romantic castle. The Luttrell Arms is a mainly 17thC hostelry and has some medieval parts: it was originally a house of the Abbot of Cleeve. The octagonal yarn market was built in the 16thC when Dunster was an important cloth town. The 15thC Church of St George is one of Somerset's most magnificent, with fine 15thC roofs, a rood-screen claimed to be the longest in England, many interesting monuments, an exquisite walled garden outside the north door, and a medieval dovecote and tithe barn. But notwithstanding all this interest, it is **Dunster Castle** that is the town's great sight. The earliest parts of this splendid castle, romantically perched on a hill overlooking the town, are from 1070. But ever since 1376 it has been the home of the Luttrell family, and it has more the atmosphere of a home than a fortress. It was, though, the last point in Somerset to hold out for Charles I during the Civil War, only falling after a five-month siege in 1646. Richly decorated, it is mainly 16th to 19thC. See the magnificent late 17thC staircase, the splendid plaster ceiling in the dining-room of the same date and the beautiful 17thC leather panels in the banqueting hall, illustrating the story of Antony and Cleopatra. *Open most days, summer; certain days, winter.*

10. Exmoor
Not England's largest, highest or wildest moorland but surely its most beautiful, with graceful horizons richly crowned with the heather and the thorn. Exmoor lies partly in Devon, but is largely in Somerset. Stand on its heights and look down to where Porlock's vale fronts the Bristol Channel, beyond which the misty coast of Wales may sometimes be visible. Or wander down into some secret valley through which a fierce stream runs, and discover the heart of the moor, little disturbed by modern life.
There is much to see around the moorland, especially for those prepared to park the car and don the walking boots. One of Exmoor's greatest associations, of course, is its connections with R. D. Blackmore's 'Lorna Doone', and the Doones were, in fact, a family of 17thC Exmoor bandits. Doone Valley is not really as wild or romantic as you might hope, but there are still traces of the real Doone settlement to which they would return to carouse after their daring raids. At Oare Church you can see the window through which Carver Doone shot Lorna at her wedding.
Exmoor has several pretty villages including Exford, the unofficial centre of stag-hunting (Exmoor was royal hunting country from Anglo-Saxon times to 1818), and Culbone, with its tiny, exquisite, largely Norman church remotely situated in a hidden glade. Tarr Steps is a famous antiquity, the site of a medieval packhorse bridge crossing the Barle below Winsford Hill. No-one knows when they were built, but they may be prehistoric. Nearby is the probably Celtic Caractacus Stone and many Bronze Age earthworks. Simonsbath House is a 17thC mansion, later the home of John Knight, the ironmaster. It was he who built the eerie Pinkworthy Pond, *Challacombe*, over 1,500ft high and near the moor's highest point, where you can experience Exmoor at its most misty and mysterious.

11. Gaulden Manor 1 G4
Tolland, 9m NW of Taunton. A highly attractive small red sandstone manor house, the earliest parts of which date from the 12thC. The house was long the Somerset seat of the Dorset Turberville family, immortalised by Thomas Hardy in 'Tess of the D'Urbervilles', and, although it is quite grand, it's welcoming and homely. Among outstanding features are the magnificent plaster ceiling of the impressive Great Hall and the fine antique furniture. *Open certain days, summer.*

12. Glastonbury 1 H3
The scene of one of the most poignant and enduring of medieval legends. It is said that under the waters of a spring on its great hill, the Tor, the pilgrim Joseph of Arimathea buried the chalice used to perform the miracle of the Last Supper, and that on the site of the great abbey that flourished here from the 9thC, he built England's first church and converted the country's first Christians. This gave rise to Glastonbury's reputation as a place of pilgrimage in the Middle Ages, a fame given a further twist by the tradition that Arthur and Guinevere were reburied in the abbey church.
The medieval abbey was the richest monastery in England after Westminster, and around it grew a rich town. Nothing but fragments remain of the great abbey church, and there are only two intact buildings – the kitchens and the 14thC Abbot's Barn. But the site of the abbey on the Tor is still grandly impressive, with one of Somerset's best views. As you stand among the ruins, remember the tragic last act in the history of this great abbey when the last abbot, refusing to accept the Dissolution of the Monasteries ordered by Henry VIII, was hanged here in 1539 at his own splendid gateway.
There are a number of other interesting things to see in Glastonbury, which flourished as a cloth town after the abbey was gone and is now known for its sheepskin products. Notice St John's Church with its splendid 15thC tower and stained glass, the 15thC court-house once used by the abbey which is now a museum, and the 15thC George Inn where medieval pilgrims once stayed.

Glastonbury Abbey

13. Hatch Court 1 H4
Hatch Beauchamp. Fine Palladian-style mansion, nobly built in Bath stone in 1755, it is exceptionally beautifully set among rolling Somerset views and a deer park. The interior is rich, with fine furniture and pictures, and a china room. One special feature of interest is the small but interesting Canadian military museum. *Open certain days, summer.*

14. Ilminster 1 H5
Pleasant small town, only just now becoming industrial, with many ancient thatched cottages, a basically Elizabethan grammar school, a fine Ham stone central square and the George Hotel which was the first hotel in which Queen Victoria ever stayed – she was then seven months old.
Ilminster's most superb feature is undoubtedly its mainly 15thC church, whose central tower soars magnificently over the little town. Lovely clear glass lets in the sun to shine on the splendid monuments; many are to the local Wadham family whose money built the church and members of which

founded Wadham College, Oxford. Besides the exceptional tombs and brasses, there is also a fine 18thC brass chandelier.

15. Martock Church   1 H4
With perhaps the finest interior of any of Somerset's splendid churches, the great tie-beam roof is its most overwhelming feature. The Ham stone here gives a uniquely rich effect which the lavish decoration only complements. The building is mainly 15thC, but there are earlier remnants, and the roof is of 1513.

16. Mells   1 K3
Among the finest of Somerset's stone villages, it is full of pleasant cottages and has a good 15thC church with one of Somerset's distinguished towers. The Elizabethan manor house was long the home of the Horner family. John Horner is thought to be the Jack Horner of the nursery rhyme. To save Glastonbury Abbey from the Dissolution, it's said that the abbot sent Henry VIII a gift of the title deeds of Mells Manor, hidden in a pie. His gift-bearer and steward, John Horner, removed 'the plum' and kept the deeds for himself. But there's no real evidence and the rhyme didn't appear until the 18thC. This century Katherine Horner married Raymond Asquith, and the Asquiths still own the house.

The famous intellectual priest and detective-story writer, Ronald Knox, lived at Mells and said mass in the manor chapel. The village, close to Downside Abbey, became a great centre for intellectual and society 20thC Catholics, including Evelyn Waugh. The graveyard is populated by the famous, too, including First World War poet Siegfrid Sassoon.

17. Montacute House   1 J4
Montacute. Among the grandest of Elizabethan houses in England, it was built in Ham stone for the rich family of lawyer-politicians, the Phelipses, one of whose members prosecuted at the trial of Guy Fawkes in 1605. In the early 1920s it became for a while the country home of Lord Curzon, former Viceroy of India, and was redecorated for him by the fashionable demi-mondaine, Elinor Glyn.

Impressive rather than beautiful, it is tall and symmetrical, with large windows. But its interior is very rich with fine, panelled rooms, elaborate fireplaces and a good collection of 16th and 17thC paintings which came to it from the National Gallery. The immaculate gardens contain fine lawns and well-kept yew trees, with pretty summer-houses completing a perfect Elizabethan picture. *Open most days, summer.*

18. Porlock   1 F3
Cheerful hillside village which will always be famous as the home of the ill-timed 'person' whose arrival destroyed the composition of one of England's greatest poems – 'Kubla Khan'. It is exceptionally beautifully situated between wild Exmoor and the sea, at the head of the lovely Vale of Porlock which stretches east towards the resort of Minehead. Thatched buildings and pretty Doveray Court, a 15thC manor, survive among much sadly undistinguished modern building. An

enchanting spot near the village is Porlock Weir, a hidden quay with attractive whitewashed cottages and pleasant pubs. From here you can walk through bluebell woods towards Culbone which claims the smallest complete church in England.

19. Sedgemoor
Now fen-farmland, but in prehistoric times covered by the sea, and for long centuries a marshy expanse of sedges, reeds and rushes. Famous as the scene of the proverbial burnt cakes, it was to these lonely marshes, around AD878, that King Alfred retired when all England seemed lost to the Danes. Here he rallied the English before the decisive Battle of Ethandune, probably fought nearby. Sedgemoor stamped the history books again in 1685, when Monmouth's army of rebels met defeat at the hands of James II's well-equipped force. A memorial marks the battlefield *nr Weston Zoyland* and dents on the buttress of the south wall of nearby Chedzoy's church are said to be where Monmouth's men sharpened their weapons.

Nowadays the moor is rich with cattle and scattered with willow beds which provide material for local basket-making industries. This 25-miles of moor still remains some of the flattest country in the world, and on dark winter days, when it is often half-flooded, it's as lonely and mysterious as ever it must have looked to Alfred.

20. Taunton   1 G3
One of the great agricultural marketing towns of the west, farmers from the surrounding Blackdown, Brendon and Quantock Hills have been bringing their produce here for generations. Taunton is said to have been given its first charter by Ine, a king of the West Saxons, cAD710.

As a proud merchant town of the outlying west, it became a centre for political rebellion and Nonconformism: in 1497 it proclaimed Perkin Warbeck king, in the Civil War it was strongly for Parliament and withstood a siege, but it suffered most cruelly when in 1685 it lent support to Monmouth's rebellion. The day after the battle James II's officer, Colonel Kirke, sat drinking in the White Hart Inn looking out onto the market place where 30 men he had just hanged still dangled. Three months after this Judge Jeffreys arrived, and in the Great Hall of Taunton Castle, condemned 200 men to the gallows and transported hundreds more to slavery in the West Indies. The Tudor House restaurant, a 16thC dwelling, was at the time the home of the local member of Parliament who entertained Jeffreys to a meal there – a thought which must occasionally disturb present-day diners.

Taunton's outstanding feature is the beautiful red sandstone tower of its great church, St Mary Magdalene, built in the 15thC and rebuilt, because unsafe, in 1858.

The first castle was probably built in the 8thC; the present castle, partly Norman but much altered, is now a local museum, although the Great Hall can still seem to echo with Jeffreys' vituperative tongue. St James's is another church with a fine Somerset tower, the Municipal Offices contain the remains of the 16thC grammar school buildings, Gray's Almshouses in East Street are of 1635, and the Market House of 1770 is now a pub in the middle of the main traffic junction. Here you can sample Taunton's best-known product – cider – a result of the fertile soil and warm climate of the Vale.

21. Wells   1 J3
Tiny, cheese-making town, looking with dedication towards its great cathedral. Other historic buildings include some ancient pubs: the City Arms was the city jail until the 19thC, and in the courtyard of the Crown, the 17thC Quaker and founder of Pennsylvania, William

Culbone Church, Porlock

Penn, is said to have preached to an audience of 2,000 and to have been arrested for his pains. The 15thC Church of St Cuthbert is meritorious, and nearby is the ancient guildhall. Close to the cathedral are many old houses, medieval, Tudor and Georgian, all basking in the atmosphere of cathedral peace and dignity.

21. Wells Cathedral

One of the first attempts at English Gothic architecture, built mainly between the 12th and 14thC. Wells had first become the seat of a bishopric in 909, when it was simply the best available town in Somerset. It became one of the richest sees in England – a great jewel in the portfolio of ecclesiastical offices that Cardinal Wolsey amassed in the early 16thC. Particularly notable is the remarkable array of 12th and 13thC sculptures on the west front, the wonderful inverted scissor arches that support the central tower, the marvellously vaulted chapter house, the choir's 14thC east window, the Lady chapel and its windows and the beautiful 15th and 16thC cloisters. A great attraction is the astronomical clock of 1390, one of the oldest working clocks in the world, on the face of which knights joust on the hour. Among the important group of ecclesiastical buildings in the precincts are the Vicar's Close, consisting of 14thC houses, and the 15thC deanery, next to a good museum of local history. Across the green is that grand medieval building, the 13thC **Bishop's Palace**, a real handsome home for a feudal-style bishop, complete with the episcopal swans. From their Victorian ancestors who were taught by the Bishop's daughter, the swans have inherited the trick of ringing a bell for food. *Bishop's Palace open certain days, summer.*

Wells Cathedral

22. Yeovil   1 J5

The great growth-point of busy modern Somerset, its old centre suffered from bad fires in 1499, 1623 and 1640, as well as from a severe pasting from German bombers during the Second World War. Yeovil is, therefore, rather short on ancient remains, although it was founded by the Romans. It is worth visiting for its ruggedly impressive 14thC Ham stone Church of St John the Baptist, whose windows admit such a flood of light that it is known as 'The Lantern of the West'. Also of interest are Abbey Farm with its medieval tithe barn, on the western edge of the town, Newton Surmaville, an early 17thC manor house, and some pleasant Georgian and Victorian building, though now rather eclipsed by masses of modern concrete, metal, brick and glass.

AVON

23. American Museum in Britain   1 K2

Claverton Manor, 3¾m SE of Bath. One of the most comprehensive museums of early American life to be found anywhere in the world outside the United States. Appropriately furnished period rooms recreate the various phases of New World civilization, showing scenes as varied as the classical dignity of Washington's 18thC home, Mount Vernon, to the homeliness of the New England general country store. *Open most days, summer.*

24. Bath   1 K2

The Romans knew the value of these waters, and they called the place 'Aquae Sulis' (Waters of the Sun). The emergent spa attracted visitors from all over Roman Britain and even some from abroad. The remains of the Roman baths can be visited today. Bath never entirely ceased to be a spa town, but conditions in Tudor and Stuart times were squalid. It was only under the benevolent patronage of Beau Nash, the great arbiter of late 18thC fashion, that it rose to be the queen of English watering places and one of the most important spas in the world.

Much of Bath was built in the 18th and early 19thC, and it remains today one of the most attractive Georgian cities in England. Basically it was the work of only a few architects, including the two John Woods and William Pulteney who built those matchless terraces, crescents and squares, all exquisitely varied in the same basic Bath stone. Royal Crescent is superbly grand, while Pulteney Street is held by some to be the finest street in Europe. Adams's Pulteney Bridge is a creation to match those straddling the waters of Venice. And today you can still visit the Pump Rooms of 1785, enjoy coffee and a string orchestra, and imagine the days when to a Jane Austen heroine, six weeks' stay in Bath was an intrepid adventure into the tricky waters of society. Prior Park, *1m SE of centre*, is a fine Palladian house of 1735 and Bath has many beautiful public gardens of which Victoria Park, near Royal Crescent, is outstanding. The towpath of the Kennet and Avon Canal, which begins on the eastern edge of the city, is wonderful for walks.

24. Bath Abbey   1 K2

There was a Saxon abbey on the site of present Bath Abbey, and Edgar, of the house of Wessex, was crowned first king of all England here in AD973. The present structure was begun in 1499 and there has been 17th and 19thC restoration. The building is notable for the fine stone vaulting of the choir, chancel and nave, the large Perpendicular windows, Prior Bird's Chantry, an elegant carved corner, and the 614 tablets commemorating those who lived and died in Bath during its heyday as a spa. Outside, the fine west front is exquisitely carved with ascending and descending angels on Jacob's ladder.

24. Bath Museums   1 K2

Bath is unrivalled among English cities of its size for the quality and variety of its museums. **The Bath Museum of Costume** *Assembly Rooms*, built in 1771 but badly bombed in 1942, has a most comprehensive collection of historical costumes, including Byron's Albanian dress. **The Holburne of Menstrie Museum** *Great Pulteney Street*, is housed in a beautiful Palladian building and has magnificent collections of silver and porcelain as well as paintings by Gainsborough, Reynolds and Stubbs. **The City Art Gallery**

Queen's Road, as well as a magnificent collection of English artists, holds pre-Conquest coins from the local mint, Bristol glass and Chinese ceramics. **The Roman Museum** *Abbey Churchyard*, holds relics from the baths as well as other Roman finds, and is conveniently situated next to the baths themselves.

24. Bath, Roman Baths 1 K2
In Roman times this was one of the greatest bath establishments in the world, and the remains today provide an impressive monument to the Roman genius. The great main pool is open to the sky, and its lead floor and some of the paving remain from Roman times. Details of Roman plumbing, the heavy lead lining to all baths and some mosaic floors are all clearly visible, to make this one of the most impressive remaining Roman monuments in Western Europe. It's all the more arresting when you remember the baths were lost for centuries and only rediscovered in 1879.

25. Bristol 1 J2
Great city, as important in medieval Britain as it is today. Bristol was granted county status as early as 1373 and is now the centre of the county of Avon. Of all the cities in the west, it was the most heavily bombed, and since then there has been much unsuitable modern building. But even so, Bristol remains a city of great charm and character, as busy with business as it is distinguished as a cultural centre.
There was a Roman port at Sea Mills, but Bristol was neither a Roman nor a Saxon city. During the Middle Ages, however, it became one of the most important ports in England. The cathedral was founded in 1140, and as the centuries passed Bristol became a beautiful city, enriched by buildings put up on the wealth of men in the tobacco, wine, chocolate and, ashamedly, slave trades. The Royal Portbury Dock, opened by the Queen in 1977, is the latest expression of Bristol's trading tradition, but you can still relive its great days at the now quiet, ancient port where the Cabots sailed for America in 1497. There's a lot to see in Bristol, bomb damage notwithstanding. **Bristol Cathedral** is partly early 14thC, and the renowned chapter house is Norman, although the nave and western towers were built by G. E. Street in the 1860s in one of his authentic but rather uninspired moods. **St Mary Redcliffe**, dating from the 13thC, is one of the great religious buildings of England, with its fabulous Decorated doorway to the north porch, tall clerestory, flying buttresses and magnificent spire. The old heart of Bristol has lost much, but there are still delightful narrow streets and

Avon Gorge

timber-framed houses as well as the Theatre Royal, opened in 1766 and the oldest British theatre now in use.
Clifton, Bristol's most famous suburb, is an 18thC spa almost as magnificent as Bath: sample Royal York Crescent and The Paragon for Regency architecture at its grandest. Brunel's wonderful **Avon Suspension Bridge** built in 1830 high above the gorge, in its lightness and delicacy looks as if it has just been elegantly thrown across the chasm.

26. Clevedon Court 1 H2
Clevedon, off B3130. A well-preserved, beautiful, medieval manor house, dating from the early 14thC although altered in the 16th and 17thC. The beautiful terraced gardens are 18thC. Among features of interest are the celebrated pottery and glass collections, largely built up by the enthusiastic amateur, Sir Edmund Elton, 8th Baronet. Don't miss the unusual upstairs chapel with its fine windows. Thackeray was staying here while writing 'Vanity Fair' and he renames it 'Castlewood' in his 'Pendennis'. *Open certain days, summer.*
Clevedon today is a pleasant resort town and has a romantically sited headland church where Arthur Hallam, a member of the Elton family of Clevedon Court, is buried. As his bereaved friend the poet Tennyson put it in the commemorative poem 'In Memoriam', he lies 'by the pleasant shore and in the hearing of the wave'.

27. Dodington House 1 K1
Chipping Sodbury. Classic 18thC house, it was the work of James Wyatt, better known for his destructive restorations. Grand if heavy, the huge double staircase hall and unusual fireplaces are its most notable features. The vast 700-acre park was landscaped by Capability Brown with few concessions to expense, as the owner, Codrington of Dodington, had made a fortune out of the slave trade of the West Indies. The children will love it here as there is a vast amount to do: a splendid carriage museum, nature trails, a narrow-gauge railway and a fine model aviation collection. *Open summer.*

28. Dyrham Park 1 K2
12m E of Bristol, 2m S of Tormarton. Fine late 17thC house renowned for its lovely sweeping setting and well-stocked deer-park. It is built in Bath stone and has warm, panelled rooms containing paintings by Murillo and Dutch masters. It was built for William Blathwayt, Secretary of State to William III. His uncle, Thomas Povey, was a great patron of the arts, so the house has strong connections with Pepys, Evelyn and other 17thC men of letters. *Open most days, summer.*

29. Weston-super-Mare 1 H2
Famous as the resort town where at low tide the sands seem literally to go on for ever. It was only a small collection of fishermen's huts in 1819 when Mrs Thrale, Dr Johnson's literary friend, visited it and could find but two books in the whole place – The Bible and 'Paradise Lost'. Where 100 fishermen lived then, a town of 19,000 existed in 1900, a figure now more than doubled. Like many rapidly-grown resort towns it is not architecturally distinguished in general, but it has the magnificent late Victorian Church of All Saints by G. F. Bodley with additions by F. C. Eden. The museum in the Boulevard includes finds from the Iron Age fort at Worlebury Hill, *N of town,* and nearby Kewstoke has a good medieval church.

THE SOUTHERN COUNTIES

The Southern Counties form a region of intriguing variety. Each county has a strong sense of local identity, yet a regional integrity is equally discernable, unfolding a richly-woven tapestry of fields, manors and gardens, with prosperous towns crowned by their ancient cathedrals and abbey churches: Salisbury, Winchester, Portsmouth, Malmesbury and Sherborne. The area formed the core of the ancient kingdom of Wessex, greatest of Anglo-Saxon political organisations in the 9th and 10thC; in the 19thC, the great writer Thomas Hardy could still think of an area called 'Wessex', because the sense of region still seemed so strong. In those intervening years local traditions were established and man tamed the wild landscape, making it domesticated.

Essentially, the area is agricultural. Though it has its large towns, in most cases they do not really seem to be the natural centres of their surrounding areas, but lately-grown outcrops serving some special purpose – the resort like Bournemouth, the railway town like Swindon, the modern light-industrial town like Basingstoke. It is not here, but in the small market towns and in the ancient villages that the true heart of this region is to be found. Many of these small towns have been holding a weekly market for close on 1,000 years, and, as you walk their streets among people in comfortable tweeds and with country burrs, you can still imagine the world which Thomas Hardy painted with such vividness 100 years ago.

The coast, with its great inlets and harbours such as Poole Harbour or Southampton Water, is rich in sights and vistas, many with historical associations. Facing the coast of France, the nation with which England can trace centuries of enmity, great castles and other military installations (many of them built by Henry VIII) give a powerful focus to the sweeping coastline. Some coastal areas, isolated by their position, have been 'islands' historically, either in fact or metaphor – The Isle of Portland, The Isle of Purbeck, The Isle of Wight. Others, like the great ports of Southampton and Portsmouth, have used their position to gain profit from trade with the world beyond. The lush interior has generally been more peaceful, as we can see from the stone manor houses of Dorset gracefully set among their farmed acres, but it can be lonely and desolate too, as on the vastness of Salisbury Plain. Here it's the army which has left its military impact on the landscape, blasting up hearthlands to train recruits and test weapons.

The counties that make up this southern region each have a marked individuality, and of none of them is this more true than Dorset. There is something remote from the rest of England about Dorset, expressed equally by the local stonework, the strongly preserved regional dialect and the novel place names. Where else but in Dorset would you see a signpost to three such strangely named villages as Mappowder, Folly and Plush? And where else would you find three small places so mysterious and interestingly individual? The diversity of Dorset is inherent, too, in the great heathlands that stretch across it while it is also characterised by rich downlands and dignified seaside resorts like Lyme Regis and Weymouth, which give its ebullient and amazingly varied coastline such charm.

Wiltshire is the most rural, the most undisturbed of the counties, with its quiet market towns set in the shadow of vast Salisbury Plain. Here on the high downlands you can feel the touch of ancient man at its most insistent, because this is the country of the white horses cut into the chalk turf, and the great monuments, like Stonehenge and Avebury, which prehistoric engineers raised with the aid only of soaring human imaginations and simple tools.

To many people, Hampshire may seem less interesting, and this will be so especially if they know only its busy main roads which pass through such blasted areas as the army heathlands around Aldershot. Yet one turn off the main road and into the country lane, and the ancient life of this region is all around you, especially in the abundance of fascinating villages, set in valleys of rivers like the Itchen and the Test. Here is the intimate, detailed, local world of timber and plaster, yew-clad churchyard, and winding lane. And if Hampshire has its souless modern centres, it has, too, its delightful towns – places like Titchfield and Lyndhurst – which were the focus of the busy rural life Jane Austen immortalised in her novels. And in the New Forest, Hampshire has an area where primitive wildness is just tamed enough to refresh the soul of modern man.

In modern times the Isle of Wight has been subject to very intensive holiday developments, and it is one of the parts of the region whose traditional character is most threatened by modern encroachments. But its history is as long as any part of England, and vividly evident in Roman and prehistoric remains, old thatched cottages and Victorian villas frequented by 19thC literati. The Isle of Wight remains as picturesque as it was to the Victorians who first developed it as a holiday island, and they have left lovers of Victorian architecture with an added bonus.

DORSET& WILTSHIRE

DORSET

1. Abbotsbury   2 C9

Pretty village of thatch and stone, with a
collection of historic buildings of great
interest. There was a great Benedictine
monastery here in medieval times, and one
reminder of it is the noble, stone-buttressed
tithe barn which the monks built in the 15thC.
Fragments of the monastery are to be seen to
the south of the present parish church, a
mainly 15th and 16thC building, with a fine
early 17thC canopied pulpit and a plastered
chancel ceiling of 1638. Stark and castle-like,
15thC St Catherine's Chapel stands high on a
hill and is worth the climb for its buttresses
and gargoyles.
The remains of an Iron Age fort are to be seen
outside the town *Wears Hill* and there are
splendid panoramic views of the coast from
White Hill. Near the Bridport Road are
wonderful sub-tropical gardens where
camellias and hydrangeas grow in profusion.
Open summer.

1. Abbotsbury Swannery   2 C9

1½m S of village. One of the finest and most
ancient swanneries in the world, famous since
1393 when it was started by the monks on a
lagoon formed from Chesil Bank, the huge
coastal sandbank of this area. Swans were
once considered a great delicacy and graced
the tables of the monastery at the village.
Today a safe breeding ground and home, the
swannery now houses over a thousand swans
as well as many examples of geese and ducks.
Open summer.

2. Athelhampton House   2 C8

5m NE of Dorchester, ½m E of Puddletown, A35.
Surrounded by walls and courts and almost
encircled by the river, this is one of the finest
essentially medieval houses remaining in
England. It was the home of the Martyns,
whose symbol was the chained ape and whose
strange family motto: 'He who looks at
Martyn's ape, Martyn's ape shall look at him',
suggests some long-forgotten comic episode
in the family's history. The Martyns died out
in the late 16thC, but the house has been
immaculately kept and is beautifully
furnished. What remains of the original work,
especially the magnificent Great Hall with its
gallery and open timber roof, still potently
suggests the style in which they lived. The
delightful 10 acres of formal and landscaped
gardens merit a visit in their own right. *Open
certain days, summer.*

3. Badbury Rings   2 D8

3m NW of Wimborne, nr Sturminster Marshall.
Huge Iron Age fortification, standing
menacingly on the chalk upland overlooking
the River Stour, consisting of three concentric
rings of trenches and banks enclosing a dark
wood. Although there are many traces of
earlier occupation, the present fort dates
largely from the 1stC BC, and became a focus
for Roman roads.
Legend has it that King Arthur fought his last
battle against the invading Saxons and
received his death-wound here, ever
afterwards to haunt the wood in the form of a

raven. Be that as it may, the Rings still hold a dark mystery, especially at dusk when nobody is about.

4. Bere Regis, Church of St John the Baptist 2 D8
Bere Regis. Once an important medieval centre, this modern village is now rather ugly, but its chief glory is its fine church, originally late Norman. It has been rebuilt many times, most notably by Henry VII's chief tax-gatherer, Cardinal Morton, who retained the medieval arcades and grotesque carvings, and added the beautiful battlemented tower. He also built the wide nave which is spanned by an elaborate timber roof with huge carvings of the 12 apostles and heraldic imagery celebrating Morton's place in history.
Later the manor passed to the family of Turberville (the marble tomb where Tess Turberville slept is said to have inspired Hardy to his 'Tess of the D'Urbervilles'). Despite some tasteless restoration in the 19thC this remains one of Dorset's best church interiors.

5. Bournemouth 2 E8
The doyen of English seaside resorts, with a quiet and dignified style of its own, Bournemouth is almost entirely a creation of the 19thC, for until then it was a wilderness of wild moorland. In 1810 Lewis Tregonwell and his wife came here and were so enchanted by its beauty that they built a holiday house: later, he planted the coast and valley with the pines for which Bournemouth became famous, and a resort grew up which the Victorians loved. Robert Louis Stevenson came here for his health, Keble, the great theologian, died here, and writer George MacDonald as well as naturalist W. H. Hudson and politician Gladstone were familiar figures in its streets.
The Victorians beautified the town with many exquisite parks and gardens, often decorating the steeply rising cliffs, and the town has many fine Victorian buildings. The mother Church of St Peter, built by G. E. Street and with a nobly elegant spire, is especially notable. Here the heart of the poet Shelly lies buried. St Stephen's is worth visiting and Bournemouth also has a fine group of churches.

6. Bovington Camp 2 D9
6m N of Lulworth, 5m W of Wareham. An area of wild heathland south of the River Piddle is planted with windy conifers and traversed by the tanks of the Royal Armoured Corps. Their headquarters at Bovington house the regimental tank museum, a unique collection of over 130 vehicles demonstrating every phase of tank development from 1900. Lawrence of Arabia was stationed at Bovington during his last years as a private soldier: the telegram he sent just minutes before his death in a motor-cycle accident read: 'One mile north Bovington Camp'. His home at **Clouds Hill**, a gamekeeper's cottage in the middle of the heath which he rented in 1923, is now kept by the National Trust very much as he left it, containing his furniture and his gramophone with its huge amplifier horn. The Greek inscription he placed over the door, still remaining, means 'nothing matters'. *Open certain days, summer.*

7. Bridport 2 B8
Retaining its Georgian ambience, this straggling brick town is one of the finest in Dorset. Since medieval times Bridport has been the great centre for the making of twine, ropes and cord, largely for the Royal Navy, and for hundreds of years the colloquial expression 'Bridport dagger' meant 'the hangman's noose'. The elegant Georgian streets were built purposely wide for the handling of ropes and the town has many old inns and a most handsome 18thC arcaded town hall. The adjoining harbour of West Bay is homely and peaceful.

8. Cerne Abbas 2 C8
Highly attractive village with some of the loveliest stone work in all Dorset, it was once the site of a famous leather industry and a medieval Benedictine abbey. The remains of the abbey, a handsome gatehouse with oriel windows and a guest house, are very fine, and the 14thC tithe barn of the abbey, now partly a house, also survives.
The church, mainly 15thC, is one of Dorset's most beautiful with a magnificent brown-yellow tower of c1500 ornamented with grotesque gargoyles. Other features include a 13thC chancel and a lovely interior full of light and space and adorned with 14thC wall-paintings, the whole having been most sensitively restored in the 1960s. Opposite, note the row of overhung Tudor cottages with outside carving and the attractive Georgian house on the corner.

8. Cerne Abbas Giant 2 C8
¼m N of village, off A352. One of Britain's most uninhibited ancient monuments, this great, naked figure cut in the turf and chalk is 180ft tall, half the size of the dome of St Paul's. It is thought to have been cut during Roman or slightly earlier times, perhaps representing some powerful god. But there are those who feel that fertility rites at this spot were much more ancient, and even now courting couples are known to ceremoniously climb up to this spot to wish for a fruitful union.

9. Charmouth 2 B8
4m E of Lyme Regis. Jane Austen in the early 19thC loved this charming seaside resort spending hours 'sitting in unwearied contemplation' surveying its 'sweet retired bay'. Although the motor car has destroyed some of its peacefulness, the place is still full of ancient thatched houses and exquisite Regency bow-fronts.
The most historic building is the Queen's Arms, where Catherine of Aragon stayed in 1501 shortly after her arrival in England to wed the future King Henry VIII. Charles II also spent the night here in 1651 when he was looking for a ship to take him across to the Continent after his escape from Cromwell's men at the Battle of Worcester. The room where he slept can still be seen – and note the large chimney, which is said to have served as a hiding place.

10. Christchurch 2 E8
Chiefly famous of course for its great church after which the town is named, this is a pleasant and tranquil town in its own right, with the remains of a Norman castle and a good museum housed in a pleasant Georgian building. The pretty suburb of Mudeford still retains the atmosphere of the ancient fishing village it once was.
The church was begun in the late 11thC by Flambard, a careerist who rose from superintendent of the royal kitchen to bishop, and it became an Augustinian priory in about 1150. Of the priory buildings only the church now remains. The church is thought to be the longest parish church in England, measuring 312ft, and much of the most impressive work we see today is Norman: note in particular the spacious nave with its seven massive arcades and the fine turret in the north transept. The choir and towers date from the 15thC, the magnificently carved stone reredos is 14thC, but perhaps most beautiful of all are the chantries, of which the Salisbury Chantry, built of hard, shining Caen Stone, is perhaps the most notable. The whole is truly one of England's great churches, and one can surely understand why the town, which until the 12thC was known as Twynham, changed its name to that of its most outstanding feature.

11. Corfe Castle 2 D9
Historic focus of the lovely Isle of Purbeck and a ruined castle of spectacular

impressiveness, the views from the Arne Road in the north or from Kingston to the south are truly romantic. The existing buildings range from the time of William the Conqueror to the 14thC, but it is thought that the Saxon kings had a castle here from the 9thC.

Here, the young Saxon King Edward the Martyr was murdered in AD978 by a dagger in the back as he was drinking wine, at the instigation of his stepmother. This dastardly deed may have been the origin of the 'wicked stepmother' tradition of fairy tales. Here, too, King John starved to death 22 French nobles who supported his nephew Arthur's claim to the throne: indeed, the whole history of the castle is a long series of blood, treason and revenge. After the Civil War the castle was the scene of a spirited defence for the Royalists by Lady Bankes and her family and was destroyed after one of her servants turned traitor.

Nowadays, the gaunt ruins of the crumbling keep and the strangely tilted watch-towers stand like skeletons over the modern, perhaps over-touristic village of Corfe, and retain a grim dignity which few other castles can match.

Corfe Castle

12. **Dorchester** 2 C8

The historic county town of Dorset, Dorchester is today a busy administrative and business centre but retains the unhurried air of the country. It's not hard to picture it as it was at the end of the 19thC when Thomas Hardy, who loved the town, made it the 'Casterbridge' of his novels. The actual site of Dorchester was probably unoccupied until Roman times and there was a Norman castle (now gone). But a series of fires in the 17th and 18thC destroyed most of the town and now cheerful, rather undistinguished Georgian building predominates, interspersed with Victorian chapels and modern shops. Many historical events took place here, including some famous trials. The 'Bloody Assizes' of Judge Jeffreys, when he indiscriminately sentenced to public hanging and mutilation men who had fought in Monmouth's rising of 1685, were largely held here, and in 1834 the town was the scene of the trial of the Tolpuddle Martyrs, agricultural labourers persecuted for having formed an early trade union. The old Shire Hall, where the Martyrs were tried, was purchased as a memorial by the Trades Union Congress. *Open weekdays.* St Peter's Church is mainly 15thC and was restored by a local architect in the 19thC with the young Thomas Hardy as his assistant: in 'The Mayor of Casterbridge' Hardy refers to it as 'a grizzled church whose massive square tower rose unbroken into the darkening sky'.

12. **Dorchester, Maiden Castle** 2 C8

1½m SW of town. Perhaps the most impressive pre-Roman hill fort in Britain and one of the largest earthwork fortifications in Europe. There was a fort here from the Iron Age, although most of the ramparts you can see now were erected by invaders from Brittany in the 1stC BC. The whole place is still visible: the ramparts and earthworks, the elaborate entrance defences, remains of an earlier neolithic camp and the foundations of a Romano–British temple of the 4thC. Maiden Castle was stormed by the Romans in AD43, and dramatic evidence of this has been found in the form of many dead bodies, one with a catapult bone up his spine. Many of the finds can be seen in the Dorset County Museum in Dorchester.

12. **Dorset County Museum** 2 C8

High St, Dorchester. One of the best of the county museums, it is noted for its variety of exhibits: items from the Iron Age fort at Maiden Castle, many Roman finds, interesting fossils and traps for catching poachers of the 18th and early 19thC. The Thomas Hardy Memorial Collection includes notebooks, manuscripts and personal items, much of it housed in a reconstruction of Hardy's study at his house at Max Gate, on the outskirts of the town. *Open weekdays.*

13. **Forde Abbey** 2 A8

1m E of Chard Junction, 7m W of Crewkerne. Originally an abbey for 12 Cistercian monks built in 1142–8, Forde Abbey is now largely a Tudor and mid 17thC house, but with much interesting medieval work remaining. It has exquisite informal gardens, very large and with many beautiful lakes, but art lovers from all over the world come to see its most treasured possessions – magnificent tapestry copies of Raphael's cartoons of the Acts of the Apostles. They were made in Mortlake by Brussels weavers brought over by Charles I in the mid 17thC to teach English workers. *Open certain days, summer.*

14. **Hardy's Cottage** 2 C8

Higher Bockhampton, 3m E of Dorchester, off A35. Hardy is the great poet of the south of England and in particular, 'untamed and untamable wild' Wessex where his life was mainly spent. Dorset towns turn up very thinly disguised in his novels: Casterbridge is Dorchester, Shottesford Forum is Blandford Forum, and the Kingsbere where 'Tess of the D'Urbervilles' was located is Bere Regis. Many of the places associated with Hardy are within a few miles of each other. The modest thatched house where Hardy was born in 1840, smothered in greenery and set in a pretty garden, is now in the care of the National Trust: nearby is an obelisk erected to Hardy by 'a few American admirers'. At Lower Bockhampton nearby Hardy went to school, his later home where he died was at Max Gate just outside Dorchester, and his heart is buried in the churchyard at Stinsford. *Cottage open by arrangement; gardens open summer.*

Hardy's Cottage

15. **Lyme Regis** 2 A8

A queen of seaside resorts, Lyme still retains with pride the royal suffix Regis (meaning 'of the King') it first won in the reign of Edward I in the 13thC. Already an important port and cloth town Edward chose it as a base for his wars against the French. Lyme Regis became a resort very early, in the 18thC, and it was from the Cobb, an old 14thC breakwater and harbour built for fishermen, that Louisa Musgrove had her traumatic fall in 'Persuasion'.

Lyme has seen several dramatic historical events besides this fictional episode: the first skirmish between the Armada and the defending fleet of Drake took place in its bay in 1588, in 1644 the town withstood a two-month-long siege for Parliament, and in 1685 the ill-fated Duke of Monmouth and his followers landed on its beach to raise rebellion against James II (12 of his followers were to be hanged by the Cobb).

The wide bay encircled by hills between which the town nestles is still an exceptionally beautiful spot, and the town itself has some places of interest. The town museum houses some relics of the Monmouth rebellion, as well as good fossils, and is in the 19thC town hall. *Open summer*. St Michael's Church, mainly 15thC, contains a carved 17thC pulpit and the Peek Memorial Chapel, converted from a stable in 1844, is a Victorian building of exuberance and charm.

Lyme Regis

16. Mappowder, Folly and Plush   2 C8
N of Piddeltrenthide on Sherborne rd. Three pretty villages strung along the road, with the sort of improbable names, gathered together on the one signpost, that you would surely only find in Dorset.

Mappowder, its name a corruption of the 'maple-dre' that appears in the Domesday Book, has a cluster of picturesque cottages around the fine Church of SS Peter and Paul with its lovely 15thC windows. Nearby was the home of the Dorset writer, T. F. Powys, one of a trio of writing brothers (the others being John Cooper and Llewellyn), who painted a strange and powerful picture of the Dorset scene in their now sadly half-forgotten books. Folly is a tiny place squeezed between two hills, each of which has the remains of a prehistoric camp, while Plush, whose name is a corruption of an old Dorset word meaning 'shallow water', has a fine old inn, 'The Brace and Pheasants', and also a small local industry growing orchids for export. These three tiny places, indeed, express something of the very essence of Dorset.

17. Milton Abbas and Milton Abbey 2 D8
A collection of historical buildings and sites in a small area: a large 18thC Gothic mansion, a medieval abbey church and what is generally considered to be the first integrally planned village in Britain. A monastery and abbey were founded here in the 10thC, but the original abbey church was destroyed by lightning in 1307. What remains is mainly 14th and 15thC, and this splendid church is in beautiful condition, with Ham stone vaulted crossing, a lofty reredos and the 19thC addition of a stained glass window by Pugin.

In 1771 the property which until the Reformation had belonged to the abbey was bought by Joseph Damer, later Earl of Dorchester, whom Horace Walpole described as: 'the most arrogant and proud of men, with no foundation but great wealth and a match with the Duke of Dorset's daughter'. Damer built himself the present mansion (now a school), using Wyatt as architect, and incorporated into it the old Abbot's Hall of 1498 which retains its fine hammer-beam

roof. And with utmost callousness, he had the old village of Milton Abbas rased (thereby making much of its population homeless), and built a new village, neatly planned and more in line with his splendid tastes. It has been little interfered with and remains a work of art. *Abbey Church open most days, summer.*

Milton Abbey

18. Parnham House   2 B8
1m S of Beaminster, 6m S of Crewkerne. One of the great Tudor houses in Dorset, altered in 1753 and later romanticised by Nash in 1810. It was a seat of the Strode and Oglander families for 500 years, but since 1896 has had several owners. In 1976 Parnham was bought by John Makepeace, one of the world's leading designers of furniture. He converted the old stable block to provide his own furniture workshops and another section houses the John Makepeace School for Craftsmen in Wood.

John Makepeace has done much restoration to the house and now provides the setting for some of his furniture. The Tudor Great Hall with its Minstrel's Gallery is a splendid room and the Drawing Room has been restored to its former glory.

The 14 acres of gardens surrounding the house were laid out mainly in 1910; on the south front are three terraces with much topiary and spring-fed water channels ending in cascades. There are also magnificent trees and formal gardens. *Open certain days, summer.*

Parnham House

Piddles and Puddles
Dorset is full of towns and villages which incorporate 'piddle' and 'puddle' in their name. They are all named after the River Piddle – Pidele at the time of the Domesday Book – but the prudish Victorians preferred Puddle and for a long time there was controversy as to what each village should be called, with endless parish meetings and letters of protest to the County Council. After all, as it was often pointed out, the Piddle is hardly a puddle but a fine stream flowing through chalk hills and some of the prettiest villages in Dorset!

Many of these villages are not to be missed: Piddletrenthide has a remarkably fine church with some 12thC work; Affpuddle also has a good church dating back to the early 13thC and splendidly set among tall yews; Piddlehinton is a pretty greystone flint and thatch village; and Tolpuddle is of course a place of pilgrimage to all trade unionists.

19. Poole   2 E8
Magnificently sited around a great natural harbour more than 100 miles round, Poole has a distinct maritime air. Much of its shore is still undeveloped and full of secret inlets and islands that were once the haunt of smugglers. Poole is an ancient town, and in

the medieval period supplanted Wareham as the county's chief port. It is now by far the largest town in Dorset with many seaside activities and industries.

The history of the port has been adventurous: Queen Elizabeth I encouraged the buccaneers of Poole to rob French and Spanish ships, in 1747 smugglers were bold enough to raid the Customs House and to depart with a cargo of tea, and in the 19thC the Newfoundland trade was largely built up from Poole. Much of Poole is modern, but there are some interesting old buildings. The distinguished guildhall of 1761, is now a museum, and the Maritime Museum is also worth a visit. St James's is an unusually dignified early 19thC church, and Scaplen's Court, *Sarum St*, has splendid timbered roofs and oak mullions from the 15thC, while parts of it date from the 12thC. It is now a museum specialising in local archaeology and has interesting displays. Crazily-paved Blue Boar Lane has some beautiful 19thC cottages and you mustn't miss the Poole Pottery on the quayside, where the secrets of this traditional industry are revealed. *Open most days.*

20. Portland (Isle of) 2 C9

Portland is in fact joined to the mainland by the Chesil Bank, but it is an island in a deeper sense: the inhabitants, locked in their dramatic, almost treeless limestone landscape, have developed ways and customs all their own. In the Middle Ages the islanders lived by smuggling, fishing and breeding a peculiar breed of sheep, allowed their women the same property rights as men, and were famed for their aptitude with slings using ammunition from the Chesil Bank. Thomas Hardy regarded them as having 'strange beliefs and singular customs' and it is thought that the origin of these people differs from that of the mainlanders.

Portland is famous for its magnificent limestone, from which many of the great buildings of England are built including St Paul's Cathedral. In 1847 the government built a prison to house convict workers in the quarries: these unfortunates also built the Verne Fortress above Fortuneswell and the breakwaters on the huge naval harbour, also developed in the 19thC.

Portland Castle is a blockhouse built by Henry VIII and still remains impressive, while the Church of St George, *Weston Rd*, surrounded by a forest of fantastic gravestones, is a fine 18thC church but badly in need of restoration. Portland is not beautiful but it retains an air of isolation and past suffering, expressed in the bare quarry-pitted landscape, which makes it a quite unique place to visit.

21. Purbeck (Isle of) 2 9E

Actually a part of the mainland and with even less right to be called an island than Portland. But it has been something of an 'island' historically: the sandy heathlands to the north were marshy and almost impassable, so the area developed a life and customs of its own. The houses are distinguished by the local, Purbeck limestone and the large fields on the hills are divided by the characteristic drystone walls, making the whole area a study in grey and green.

Purbeck is an excellent centre for a holiday incorporating places of historic interest: here are the interesting, old towns of Wareham and Swanage, the magnificent ruins of Corfe Castle and many delightful villages such as Worth Matravers or Kimmeridge. The popular centres of Poole and Bournemouth, as well as the Isle of Portland are nearby, while Purbeck also has one of the most spectacular coastlines in Britain, including such well-known features as Lulworth Cove and Durdle Door.

22. Shaftesbury 2 D7

Perched on a hill-top and with a magnificent setting, Shaftesbury is a town of great historic interest but in its present-day buildings is perhaps a little disappointing. The town grew around a Benedictine abbey, founded in AD888 by Alfred the Great. Excavations have unearthed what may well be the relics of St Edward, hidden at the Dissolution, and the ruins, *Park Walk*, incorporate a museum where the finds can be seen. *Open summer.*

In medieval times Shaftesbury was distinguished by no less than 12 churches, but only one, St Peter's, remains, and that in rather poor condition. There is little else to show for the town's long history except a few fine 18thC houses, a Georgian hotel in the market place and a museum of button-making for which Shaftesbury was once famous. This lack of historic buildings is compensated for scenically; Gold Hill, the steep and cobbled lane at the centre of the town, down which the town cascades along its ancient wall, is justifiably the most photographed street in Dorset, while the view from Park Hill across the sweet vales to Bulbarrow Hill is breathtaking.

The Abbey Ruins Museum, *Park Walk*, contains fascinating ruins of one of the greatest and richest of medieval Dorset abbeys, destroyed at the Dissolution. It grew up from the Benedictine nunnery founded by Alfred the Great cAD880, with his daughter Ethelgiva as first abbess. There was an immense church connected to the abbey in medieval times and the ruins you can see today, *W of Market Place*, with great stones and fine tiles, are still impressive. The museum also has models of the church and the town before 1539. *Open summer.*

23. Sherborne 2 C7

Exceptionally fine country town, with a compact, attractive town centre distinguished by a great number of medieval and other historic buildings. It was a cathedral city from the early 8thC until 1075 and in the later medieval period had an important monastery. It was the monks who began the town's educational tradition, expressed today in its many private schools.

Sherborne School for boys was founded in 1550 and took over many of the old monastery buildings – the chapel, for instance, was the old Abbot's Hall. There are 15thC almshouses just south west of the abbey, a good museum of local history and several streets of pretty houses of which Long Street, Hound Street, Newland and The Green are notable.

A range of shops in Half Moon Street dates from the early 16thC, the timber-framed Conservative Club is also partly 16thC, and Lord Digby's School, in Newland, is a dignified house of 1720. One interesting structure is the Conduit, a stone hexagon to the east of the abbey churchyard, which was once a medieval monks' washhouse. *Museum open most days.*

St John's Almshouse, Sherborne

23. Sherborne Abbey Church 2 C7

Sherborne. Golden-stoned and noted for its rich detail, this is one of the greatest ecclesiastical buildings in southern England. Basically 12thC although with many later additions, the finest feature of the abbey is the

15thC fan-vaulted roof covering the entire length. Much of the west wall is Saxon and the transepts and the north and south nave walls are from the 12thC. Under an exquisite early English arch is the entrance to the Lady chapel, part of which is modern: a handsome reredos of black and white engraved glass by Lawrence Whistler is behind the choir. There are fragments of three abbots' tombs in the 15thC presbytery, the earliest of Abbot Clement who died in 1160, plus other tombs and monuments. A brass in the abbey records that two 9thC Saxon kings, Ethelbald and Ethelbert, were buried here.

23. Sherborne Castles   2 C7

E of centre. Sherborne, rather confusingly, has two famous castles, the Old and the New, but the older is merely a picturesque ruin, and it is the New that is normally meant when people speak of Sherborne Castle. The Old was built between 1107 and 1139 and destroyed under Cromwell and the New was built by Sir Walter Raleigh in the 1590s after his attempts to modernise the old castle failed. He lived here for 15 years. The story goes that while Sir Walter was enjoying a relaxing puff of newly-discovered tobacco, a servant drenched him with water – he thought he was on fire! The artificial lake between the two castles and the lovely grounds of the New are the work of Capability Brown in the 18thC. Neither castle is particularly beautiful or spectacular in itself, but the whole conception and the historical associations make them interesting. *Open certain days, summer.*

24. Studland   2 E9

Set on a soft, dreamy coastline with trees, dunes, beeches and green valleys, this village is exceptionally beautiful. Much of the red-brick building is old and very attractive and the Church of St Nicholas of Myra is the finest and most unspoilt Norman church in Dorset. Built on Anglo-Saxon foundations and beautifully positioned among ancient yews, its fine rounded arches and fan-vaulting are especially notable, the corbels around the nave are quaint, and there are interesting traces of Norman wall-painting.
To the north west is the great moor stretching almost to Wareham, part of the wide heathlands of Dorset. An enjoyable walk leads to the stupendous Agglestone, a huge mass of ironstone 17ft high and thought to weigh about 400 tons.

25. Swanage   2 E9

Pleasant, quiet seaside resort, snuggled peacefully in a sandy, cliff-lined bay, belying its long, eventful history. Swanage was originally an Anglo-Saxon port often raided by the Danes, and King Alfred won a great victory over a Danish fleet here in AD877, rather oddly commemorated today by a column on the sea front topped with cannon balls captured at the Crimea.
Many of the historic monuments of the town, often Victorian in date, have a faint air of the ludicrous: there is a clock-tower without a clock which was once a memorial to the Duke of Wellington on London Bridge, and the town hall has a facade designed by a pupil of Wren which was transported from the Mercers' Hall in Cheapside, London. Near the town hall, too, is a tiny stone lock-up, 8ft by 10ft, ventilated by holes, unblushingly proclaiming it was, 'Erected For the Prevention of Vice and Immorality By the Friends of Religion and good Order. AD1803'.
The atmosphere of 19thC seaside bathos is, however, rather dispersed by the area of fine older houses around the Mill Pond and by St Mary's Church, which though mostly Victorian has a tower that may originally have been a Saxon fort. Swanage is also an excellent centre for seaside walks and for exploring the beauties of the Isle of Purbeck.

26. Sydling St Nicholas   2 C8

3m SW of Cerne Abbas. Lying in the heart of a valley between soft downs, narrow streams flow along and under the long, thin streets of the village, past houses of yellow stone and sleek wheat reed thatch. The church is splendid, bristling with gargoyles and full of grandiose 19thC monuments. Basically 15thC in date, it has a huge font which may have been carved from a Roman capital and the 'Sydling Cup', the 400 year old chalice, has also survived.
Built like a fortress, the 16thC stone and flint tithe barn has elaborate roof timbers supported by thick oak posts. The manor house is mainly 19thC but incorporates part of a Tudor house which was owned by Francis Walsingham, Elizabeth I's spymaster. Remains of a medieval wayside cross can be seen near the Tudor vicarage which has notable mullioned windows. The yews in the garden are believed to be over 1,000 years old.

27. Tolpuddle   2 C8

Halfway between Puddletown and Bere Regis, A35. A name to conjure with in English history, where in 1831, under a sycamore tree in the centre of the tiny village, six poorly-paid farm labourers formed the Friendly Society of Agricultural Labourers to protest against the third wage reduction in four years. Three years later the local landowners and landlords, with the support of the government, had them arrested: they were tried at Dorchester, and sentenced to seven years transportation to Australia. A public outcry later resulted in a free pardon, but by this time they were in Australia. These were the Tolpuddle Martyrs, who suffered for the right of working men to combine.
The sycamore still stands, though propped up by wooded staves, and is cared for by the National Trust. Six cottages and a small museum were erected by the TUC in 1934 as a memorial, while the original cottage where the oaths were taken, bears a memorial plaque. A memorial service and trade union parade is held each year in July.

28. Wareham   2 D9

Once an important Saxon river port and a centre of conflict with the invading Danes, its harbour silted up during the Middle Ages and Wareham's chances of growing into a great town were ended. Now it's a quiet and friendly place, full of cheerful old inns, its ancient quays the haunt of fishermen and pleasure-trippers.
Like Blandford Forum it had a great fire in the 18thC and as a result is also largely Georgian red-brick, although less grandly and distinctively so, perhaps owing to the absence of fine architects. The strong walls, originally British earthworks and later reinforced by the Romans are best seen from the west of the town. St Martin's Church, mainly of the 11thC, is the oldest church in Dorset and contains Eric Kennington's effigy of Lawrence of Arabia. Largely Victorian, Lady St Mary's Church is distinguished-looking, with much rich medieval detail. Admirers of T. E. Lawrence will be interested in the small museum, including photographs, which could perhaps be combined with a visit to his home at Clouds Hill and to Bovington Camp where he was stationed. *Museum open most days.*

29. Weymouth   2 C9

One of the earliest, and still one of the most delightful of seaside resorts, here in 1763 the first bathing machine was used, and in 1789 George III came to try it out, dipping his toe in the water as the band played 'God Save the King'. Finding the experience agreeable, he was to return many times and under his generous patronage Weymouth grew into a fashionable and handsome resort. A fine equestrian statue cut into the chalk north east of the town commemorates the honoured royal guest, as does another statue at the south end of the Esplanade.

Weymouth is an ideal place for sands and bathing. Although much of it is modern sprawl, it does not entirely lack historical interest: it is mentioned in a Saxon charter of the 10thC and at Radipole Lake the Romans had a port. This is now the site of a swannery, a bird sanctuary and pretty gardens. The sea front is still remarkably handsome, with fine late Georgian terraces mixing in a dignified fashion with later Victorian building. The two 19thC churches are both fine: Holy Trinity is a spacious building of 1836, while St Mary's was constructed in 1816 on the site of a 17thC church. St Mary's contains the famous painting 'The Last Supper' by James Thornhill, born near here in 1675. His most famous works are those on the dome of St Paul's Cathedral in London.

30. Whitchurch Canonicorum   2 B8
4m NE of Lyme Regis, N of A35. Beautiful medieval church, standing rather apart from the modest village of the same name, reached by a delightful road from the A35 over the shoulder of Hardown Hill with fine views over Marshwood Vale. The church has work dating from the 12thC, its tower is c1400 and the Jacobean pulpit and the 17thC limestone monument to Sir John Jeffrey are both notable.

The name means 'White Church of the Canons' and is said to derive from St Wite, its patron saint, who is believed to have been a pious lady killed by the Danes. The church really is white all over, not with marble but with rich stone, and is the only church in England agreed to actually possess the bones of its patron saint.

31. Wimborne Minster   2 E8
Wimborne. One of the finest churches in all Dorset, rich in dark red and white stone, it embraces all periods from Norman to 15thC, but is largely Norman. It is twin-towered, and

its central tower bore a spire until 1600 when it fell.

The interior contains a wealth of treasures: a beautiful Norman font, a chained library in the vestry containing a 14thC manuscript and church accounts of 1403, Jacobean choir stalls and a 15thC Flemish window of rare beauty. Particularly not to be missed are two 16thC effigy tombs and an astronomical clock dating from 1320 in the west window which, according to medieval cosmology, shows the sun and moon rotating around the earth. The Minster's most eye-catching feature is the Quarter Jack on the west tower. This wooden figure, which strikes the quarter-hours with a hammer, is dressed as a grenadier but was originally a monk.

32. Worldwide Butterflies, Compton House   2 C7
Halfway between Sherborne and Yeovil, A30. Compton House is an ancient home with many fine rooms, but is now more interesting for having been turned into a unique

Compton House

showplace. Butterflies can be seen flying in exotic surroundings or hatching out before your very eyes while in the grounds the Lullingstone Silk Farm demonstrates the rearing of unique English silk. The children will love it, and it is certainly a treat for those interested in the fauna. *Open summer.*

❧ WILTSHIRE ❧

33. Alton Barnes Horse   2 E5
1m N of Alton Barnes. Poised to take off into the Vale of Pewsey at a quick canter, this is one of the numerous White Horses of this area of downland. Visitors are often deceived into thinking he is an ancient creature, but it is not so, for he was only cut in 1812: it is said a local farmer paid £20 to have a horse cut out of the chalk turf to esteem his village above others in the neighbourhood. Alton Barnes's little church was here 800 years before its sleek White Horse. At 162ft long he can be seen clearly as far as Old Sarum hill.

34. Avebury   2 E4
The largest and, in some ways, the most impressive of the great stone circles of the Bronze Age, it is not as well-known as Stonehenge, although Jane Austen thought it compared to Stonehenge as a cathedral does to a parish church. It is 29 acres in area, surrounded by a 15ft-high bank, and intersected by ancient causeways. Still an awe-inspiring sight, about 100 Sarsen stones remain, which, unlike those at Stonehenge, have not been worked into shape.

Avebury was probably built during the late neolithic period, some time before 1600BC, by the people called the Beaker Folk. Since that time it has been subject to desecration and robbery: one 14thC thief was killed by a stone falling on top of him.

Standing out from the flat plain like a huge pyramid is Silbury Hill, *1m SW of Avebury,* largely a prehistoric mound, with three quarters of it thought to be artificial. Made

Avebury

from the soft chalk it seems even more mysterious than Avebury, as we know even less of its date, purpose or builders. It is thought, however, to be late neolithic or Bronze Age, and it may have had some connection with the religious ceremonies that are thought to have been the purpose of Avebury.

35. Bradford-on-Avon   2 D5
One of Wiltshire's most pleasant market towns, it has an outstanding collection of historical buildings adorning its narrow, twisting streets, often connected by flights of steps as in the hill towns of Italy. Bradford was already an important place in the 10thC, and it has perhaps the finest complete Saxon church in England: St Lawrence's was only rediscovered in 1856, when the Vicar of Bradford, standing on a terrace, noticed what seemed to be a tiny church among the houses below. It turned out to be a gem – with its strong walls and the elegant simplicity of its

proportions, it is a potent memorial of Saxon England.

The Church of the Holy Trinity dates back to the 12thC, although it was restored in the 19thC. The windows are Norman and there are a number of rich tombs and figures. The old stone bridge of the town has two arches dating back to the 14thC; the rest is 17thC. The great tithe barn of the early 14thC is one of the biggest now existing in England, and houses a museum of Wiltshire agricultural implements.

Bradford has been prosperous throughout the centuries, and this is testified to by many fine houses from different periods, often in stone. Church House and the Old Priory are 15thC and there are Georgian houses. But the finest building is The Hall of the early 17thC. Quite original in its time it is a marvellous contrast to the quaint, gabled houses around it and an exquisite demonstration of the transition between Tudor and Palladian architecture. *View from outside only*.

36. Castle Combe   2 D4
Considered to be one of Britain's prettiest villages, its features have become better known to millions since it was used as the location for the film, 'Dr Doolittle'. Set in a pleasantly wooded valley, it has all the things an English village ought to have: charming stone cottages, an arched bridge over the brook, an ancient church which is Perpendicular and has fine 13thC fan vaulting, and a honey-coloured ancient market cross giving the village its centre. The most distinguished building is the Manor House of 1664, beautifully set and now a hotel, while the 17thC Dower House is also worth a look. A Roman villa and cemetery have been found near Castle Combe.

37. Chippenham   2 D4
Chippenham is an intriguing blend of ancient and modern, with industrial development and a brand-new bridge over the Avon masking its roots as an ancient market town. The Danes grievously ravaged Chippenham in AD878 and after their defeat, King Alfred used to relax by hunting in the nearby forests. Although much of the town is modern, it is not entirely short of buildings which testify to its long past: there is a 15thC town hall and St Andrew's Church retains some Norman work. Its 15thC Hungerford Chapel contains some interesting monuments. The secret of Chippenham is to look upwards – many attractive old houses have been converted to shops and offices, but the upper storeys retain their antiquity.

In the suburb of Hardenhuish (pronounced Harnish) is a charming Georgian church of 1779, designed by John Wood of Bath, with two especially beautiful Venetian windows.

38. Corsham Court   2 D4
Corsham, 4m SW of Chippenham, off A4. The history of a house on this site dates back to Anglo-Saxon times, and was originally part of the traditional dower of the queens of England. The present house, however, was built in the late 16thC by a wealthy customs collector and his pleasant structure of stone, gables and mullions substantially remains today. In 1777 Corsham Court came into the hands of the Methuen family, members of whom negotiated the famous 'port wine treaty' of 1703 with Portugal and founded the publishing house. Capability Brown, working as an architect, and later Nash, made many alterations, while in 1885 Thomas Bellamy rebuilt much of Nash's work.

The park with its elm avenue was laid out by Capability Brown and Humphrey Repton, adding great elegance to the original conception. But it is chiefly to see the magnificent collection of paintings built up by the Methuen family that people come to Corsham. Works by Coreggio, Van Dyck,

Corsham Court

Rubens and Reynolds to name but a few, are set off to advantage among the rich 18thC furniture and trappings. *Open certain days*.

39. Devizes   2 D5
Although an ancient market town, having largely grown around its Norman castle, Devizes is rich in 18thC building and even now retains an aura of the elegance and civilisation of that agreeable era. The unusual name is thought to derive from the Latin 'ad divisos' ('at the boundary'), because the castle was originally built at the meeting place of three parishes.

Devizes is still centred around the main street with its market place which culminates in the dignified 18thC town hall. The market cross of 1814 is inscribed: 'She instantly fell and expired': apparently a certain Ruth Pierce called upon God to strike her dead if she lied during a quarrel – and heaven obliged. Brownstone Hall and Greystone Hall are both good buildings of the 18thC, but there are some notable older buildings such as the 16thC Elm Tree Inn. Devizes has no less than three fine churches. St John's is the most interesting building in the town with a Norman tower, panelled ceilings and an impressive chancel. St Mary's is mainly 15thC, and St James's largely of the 19thC but with a fine Perpendicular tower. For a sunny afternoon's saunter, take one of the attractive walks by the Kennet and Avon Canal.

Devizes Museum, *Long St,* is a rich repository of the great archaeological heritage of Wiltshire, owned by the Wiltshire Archaeological and Natural History Society. Housed here are extremely important finds such as Bronze Age beakers, urns, grave goods and ornaments excavated from the barrows on Salisbury Plain and other prehistoric sites in the area. There are also good fossils, and a fine collection of water-colours of the county painted in the 19thC. *Open most days*.

40. Edington, Church of SS Mary, Katharine and All Saints   2 D5
1m E of Bratton. Soaring magnificently from the rather undistinguished village of Edington, this is one of the finest of Wiltshire country churches. As it was almost entirely built in the 1350s, it provides a superb demonstration of the transition between the Decorated and Perpendicular styles. Edington Church is beautiful both in its exterior and interior. Cruciform in plan, it is on a noble scale with a low embattled central tower and soaring battlements. The porch is hugely impressive and the sculpture-rich chancel is delicately patterned with pointed arches and has a white painted roof. Note also the magnificently carved 15thC screen leading into the chancel, the beautiful 14thC carving in the Lady chapel, and the great series of consecration crosses and fine tombs and monuments for which the church is particularly famous.

41. Fonthill
2 D6

Fonthill Gifford, 5m E of Mere. The site of many great houses, the most famous is Fonthill Abbey, a Gothic dream constructed by William Beckford. The brilliant but wayward son of an 18thC Lord Mayor of London, he inherited a large fortune and settled down to achieve some success as a writer of Gothic romances. To add to the image, he commissioned the architect Wyatt to build him a half-ruined and half-perfect abbey. Watched by a critical but fascinated public, the fantasy emerged, crowned with a huge Gothic tower. Hazlitt regarded it as 'a glittering waste of industrial idleness' and, indeed, less than 30 years after it was begun, the tower collapsed and the whole abbey fell into ruins. Significantly by this time Beckford had sold the estate and in 1859 a new owner built a house in Scottish baronial style.
Part of a wing of Beckford's fantastic abbey still remains, however, as do many hundreds of tall trees he planted in the grounds to enhance the atmosphere of sepulchral gloom. The whole area is attractively wooded, and both Fonthill Bishop and Fonthill Gifford are charming little places.

Icknield Way
One of the most ancient tracks of ancient Britain, the great trade route of the Iron Age, the Icknield Way once stretched all the way across southern England from the Wash to the Channel. It can now be traced from Thetford in Norfolk, to Cambridge, across Hertfordshire, over the Thames near Streatley, over the Berkshire Downs past Wantage to near the source of the River Kennet in the Marlborough Downs in Wiltshire.
However, the eastern section of the route was thoroughly Romanised and has in many places disappeared. The best walking country today is in Berkshire and Wiltshire: miles upon miles of public footpaths lead across hills and woods, passing archaeological barrows and sites, the soft but windswept downs evoking a strong sense of history and timelessness.

42. Lacock
2 D4

3m S of Chippenham. Owned by the National Trust, this delightful village of medieval character vies with Castle Combe as the prettiest in Wiltshire and one of the loveliest in England. The streets are narrow and twisting, and there are many fine half-timbered buildings dating from the 15thC onwards, often crowned with rich gables. None of the buildings are later than 1800 so the town gives a unique impression of English life before the advent of industry, suburbs and the motor car. The Church of St Cyriac is a real gem – a particularly fine example of 14thC Perpendicular with a remarkable Lady chapel. A 14thC barn with curved timbers opposite the Red Lion Hotel was once a part of the abbey estate.
Standing proudly in its broad meadow by the Avon is beautiful **Lacock Abbey**. It comes to us from the days when Magna Carta was still recent news, and was founded in 1229 by Ela, Countess of Salisbury who was its first abbess. Lacock Abbey was the very last religious house in England to be dissolved by Henry VIII, late in 1539, but its new owner, Sir William Sharrington, retained many of the original features in his new building.
Although the house was greatly altered in the popular Gothic mode in the 18thC, the spirit and some of the fabric of the original building still survive in a hotch-potch of styles, mysteriously blending into a deeply harmonious whole. The 13thC sacristy and chapter house, the 15thC cloisters and the grand late 18thC hall are all entrancing, and it was through one of the ancient oriel windows of the front that Fox Talbot, the pioneer of photography, made his first negative in 1835. The actual photograph can be seen here, as

can other curiosities, such as the Mechlin Vessel of 1500 which is said to have been the nuns' cooking pot. *Open most days, summer.*

43. Littlecote
2 F5

3m W of Hungerford, off A4. A little jewel of an early Tudor manor house, charmingly mixing stone, mellow brick and flint, set among water-meadows rich in flowers. It was almost all built between 1490 and 1520 and reflects both the provinciality but also the liveliness and lack of pretension typifying English architecture at that time.
There is a splendid long gallery and Great Hall with a unique collection of Cromwellian armour, and a most fine 17thC chapel. The house has several historical connections: Henry VIII is said to have courted Jane Seymour here and William III stopped here in his journey to conquer England in 1688.
If you feel a chill on the landing, don't be surprised. It's said to be haunted by a mother whose new-born child was murdered in 1575 by the owner of the house, 'Wild' Will Darrell. The story came to light when the midwife, who was bribed to keep silent, could bear it no longer and confessed all she knew to the local magistrate. No-one knows who the mother was, for she was masked. But speculation continues on why 'Wild' Will so desperately wanted to be rid of the child. Some say the lady was his secret mistress. Others claim she was his sister whose pregnancy brought shame on the family. Others agree that she was his sister – but the child a product of their incestuous relationship. *Open summer.*

44. Longleat
2 D6

One of the greatest of English stately homes and one of the first to be opened to the public, the safari park with its world-famous lions and other great beasts adds a touch of the exotic to what is essentially the epitome of an English Tudor mansion. An Augustinian priory stood here from the 13thC, and medieval fishponds remain, but the present house was first the creation of the Thynne family who came into the land at the Reformation and later became marquesses of Bath.
In the grand and slightly vulgar style of new wealth the present huge mansion was built complete with great mullioned windows, pillars, soaring turrets and balustrades. The house, however, was largely destroyed by fire in 1567 and most of what we see today dates from after that time. Much of the work was the responsibility of Robert Smythson, while the ubiquitous Capability Brown was hired to lay out magnificent formal gardens in the 18thC, and the 4th Marquess had the house decked out in Italian style in the 19thC with much marble and gilt.
A day out at Longleat is therefore a feast of varied splendours. Adorning the walls are some very beautiful French and Flemish tapestries and the house is renowned for its collection of paintings including works by Titian, Reynolds and Sutherland, family portraits by the 18thC English masters and Holbein's portrait of the Duke of Somerset. The magnificent panelling, velvet hangings and 18thC Chinese wallpaper are impressive features in the rooms and there are some priceless ancient manuscripts including a contemporary handwritten version of Wyclif's Bible.
In spite of all this grandeur the most impressive room is Bishop Ken's library, the retirement place of a bishop who refused to swear the oath of allegiance to William and Mary and also once refused to let Nell Gwynn stay in the Cathedral Close when Charles II visited. Hardly having changed at all since the 17thC it still conveys a unique impression of austere learning and holiness.

45. Malmesbury
2 D4

One of the very oldest boroughs in England, Malmesbury is the proud possessor of a charter of Athelstan given in AD930. There was an abbey here as early as the 7thC, while the earliest records of the town go back to before the Saxons came, when it was the stronghold of the 4thC British King Malmud, who gave it its name.

Many attractive stone buildings from across the centuries testify to a prosperity largely based on weaving. The Old Bell Inn has a window dating from the 13thC and may have been part of the Norman castle, while the White Lion may originally have been one of the abbey buildings. In the High Street is a marvellous battlemented market cross which is early 16thC. Attractive 18thC houses line the street and traces of the medieval walls can be detected near the Cirencester Road. High on its hill beside the Avon, Malmesbury remains a fine country town, proud of its past and quietly confident of its future.

Chief glory of Malmesbury, the Norman **Malmesbury Abbey** has survived wonderfully as the modern parish church, expressing with noble serenity the spirit of a long-dead age. The stone dragons in the great Norman nave have been looking down for 800 years, while here, too, is commemorate the first king who could claim authority over all England – Athelstan who reigned from AD925 and was Alfred's grandson. His magnificent tomb is in the north aisle.

The abbey was founded in the 7thC but is now substantially Norman with some 14thC additions. At the Reformation, a capitalist clothier of the time, Will Stumpe of Malmesbury, bought the abbey and set up his looms here. At least this spirit of desecration preserved the porch and nave of the abbey, enabling it to grow into the present parish church. The south porch has some of the best Romanesque sculpture in Britain, illustrating the Creation. Also of note are the superb 12thC arches, the later clerestory and the Porch Room which has a number of priceless ancient manuscripts.

Malmesbury Abbey

46. Marlborough 2 F4

Marlborough's long and wide High Street has been on the main road from London to the west of England for more than 1,000 years. Fringed with Georgian buildings and with two fine churches, the whole town has an air of serenity and beauty, modestly set in its hollow amid the high Marlborough Downs.

The town is famous for its public school founded in 1843 and contained in partly 17thC buildings. But the great mound in the college grounds connects Marlborough with much older history: it was the site of the Norman castle, and legend has it, too, that Merlin, the ancient British wizard, was buried beneath it. Stone Age and Roman remains have been found here, and some ruins of the castle can still be made out – but, sadly, evidence of Merlin is as elusive as ever. Marlborough was afflicted by a great fire in 1653 so there is little pre-17thC building, but the charming alleyways, colonnaded shops and fine buildings in the broad High Street make it one of the most impressive in England. Both Marlborough's churches, St Peter's and St Mary's, are largely Perpendicular but have been much restored. Marlborough makes an excellent centre for exploring not only the ancient Savernake Forest but also the many archaeological sites that abound in this part of Wiltshire. The White Horse near the town, however, is not an antiquity, but was cut by some schoolboys in 1804.

47. Old Sarum 2 F6

2m N of Salisbury. Britain's outstanding example of what was once a great town and which then shrunk away to nothing, 'Old Sarum' really means 'Old Salisbury' and may be regarded as the original model for that city. This great hill, covering 56 acres, was an Iron Age camp and a great Roman centre when the site of modern Salisbury was impassable marsh. William the Conqueror reviewed his victorious troops here in 1070 and there was a Norman castle and a cathedral for the episcopal See. But quarrels between the clergy and castle soldiers grew bitter, water was short, the land was cold and barren and in 1220 it was decided to build a new cathedral in New Sarum – or Salisbury.

This great centre gradually fell into ruins, and by the 16thC when Leland visited, it was virtually uninhabited. Later, Old Sarum was to become the most famous of the 'rotten boroughs' which provoked controversy before the 1832 Reform Act – places where a handful of voters continued to send members to Parliament because the town had once been important. Thus, Old Sarum has gone into every schoolchild's history book as the grassy hill that could influence politics more in the early 19thC than the great industrial cities of Manchester and Birmingham! The site can still be inspected and is cared for by the Ministry of the Environment. Salisbury Museum contains a model of what Old Sarum must have been like in its days of greatness.

48. Potterne, Church of St Mary 2 D5

2m SW of Devizes, A360. High on a hill and in the severe purity of Early English style, the magnificent cruciform church dominates the pleasant half-timbered village of Potterne. It dates mostly from the early 13thC but the great tower is 14thC and has a pierced parapet, a turret at each corner and fine lattice work. The large front porch is of the same date.

The interior is on a grand scale, and is relatively unadorned, although there are ancient paintings and beautiful carving around the organ that has been played since 1723. There is a 15thC pulpit, but perhaps of greatest interest is the older of the two fonts, unique in having round its rim a text from the Saxon baptism service: it may either be Saxon or Norman.

49. Salisbury 2 E7

One of the most beautiful, and also one of the most typical, of English cathedral towns, its narrow streets are busy and prosperous-looking, seeming to bear witness to the rather uneventful but nevertheless important record of the centuries here.

The history of Salisbury is not remarkably ancient, for it dates only from the early 13thC, when it was decided to transfer the episcopal See here from Old Sarum. It is said that the site for the new cathedral was chosen by the fall of an arrow from a randomly-chosen bow. The foundations were laid in 1220 and the building was substantially completed by about 1258. Ancient medieval bridges span the Avon, and from then begins the great succession of fine building in Salisbury which testifies to its prosperity and progress through the ages.

Salisbury is rich in late medieval gabled houses in narrow alleys, and has countless interesting buildings of later periods: the facade of the Joiners' Hall is 16thC; the Shoemakers' Guildhall is 17thC; the Banqueting Hall of John Halle, a 15thC mayor, was restored in 1834 by Pugin; the Council House is an attractive red-brick building of the 18thC; the Old George is an ancient inn begun in 1320 where Samuel Pepys stayed; St Martin's Church dates back to Norman times . . . indeed, the list of things to see here is almost endless.

Many of the most exquisite buildings are

concentrated in the Cathedral Close, a picturesque place of mellow peacefulness doing justice to its beautiful cathedral. The buildings here range from medieval to Georgian. The Tudor King's House, in which Richard III and James I both stayed, is a glorious, gabled building. The Old Deanery is partly 13thC and now forms part of a teacher training college and the medieval Bishop's Palace is notable. But the finest of the Georgian buildings is Mompesson House, built for a rich merchant of the time, and superb in its panelling, plasterwork and rich, gilded staircase. *Open certain days, summer. certain days, summer.*

The remains of the city's ancient ramparts can still be inspected, and of course Salisbury would be a marvellous centre for an archaeological trip centred on Salisbury Plain. The excellent town museum is very strong on prehistoric remains, including those from Stonehenge. *Open most days.*

49. Salisbury Cathedral 2 E6

St Ann's Gate. No cathedral rises so superbly from its setting as Salisbury Cathedral rises from the plain and marshes at the junction of five rivers. A landmark of the town, its soaring great spire, 404ft high, gives a unique impression of the austere spirituality which so inspired William Golding in his great novel, 'The Spire'. Salisbury is unique among English cathedrals in that it is all built in a single style: it rose almost entirely between 1220 and 1258, and is a pure example of Early English architecture. The spire, however, is later, dating from 1334.

Resting in deep harmony with its site and setting, the building is of a local Chilmark stone, while inside a simple and perfect beauty comes from the austere consistency with which dark Purbeck marble shafts are alternated with lancet windows. Especially beautiful are the nave, where the clustered columns support the ten great arches that support the triforium and clerestory, and the Lady chapel where the impression of logic and lucidity the whole building gives is at its height. An exquisite 13thC roof painting is the glory of the choir, there are many old manuscripts and, in the large cloisters, some beautiful medieval glass. In the north transept stands the oldest clock in working order in England, dating back to 1386.

Many of the cathedral's great treasures were lost, however, due to the late 18thC 'restorer', the architect Wyatt. Actually revelling in his nick-name 'destroyer', he swept away many fine tombs (although some remain), chantries, screens and ancient stained glass – he is even said to have thrown some of the latter down a drain! But enough certainly remains to make a visit to Salisbury Cathedral a rewarding and fascinating experience.

Savernake Forest 2 E6

One of the ancient forest lands of England, it is unique in England in that it has not traditionally been Crown property, but the hereditary property of its Wardens, the Esturmys. Granted the forest by William the Conqueror in 1083, they have held it in unbroken succession until the 20thC, the present warden being Marquess of Ailesbury. The forest covers some 2,300 acres, and some of its magnificent trees – oak, beech and elm – may date back to before the Conquest. In less popular glades rare birds and species of plants may be seen.

Savernake is by no means wild forest, because over the centuries the wardens have made themselves responsible for beautifying it. Many splendid beech avenues were laid out in the 18thC, including the Grand Avenue, a drive of nearly four miles which bisects the whole forest from north west to south east. Among famous monuments is the Ailesbury Column which the wardens erected to celebrate the recovery of George III from his

madness. You can take picnics into the forest, but there is a special picnic site just south of Marlborough on the Andover road which is also a good place to begin explorations.

50. Stonehenge 2 E6

Nr Amesbury. The most famous of the great prehistoric monuments of the British Isles, over the origin and use of which immense amounts of ink have been spilt. At a distance Stonehenge seems rather dwarfed by the immensity of Salisbury Plain and curiously small, but looked at close to, it assumes the full magnificence of a wonder of the world, and one marvels that primitive men equipped only with hand-tools could have constructed such a monument.

Strangely enough, in the eras after it was built, Stonehenge was forgotten for many centuries. Although it seems to have been familiar to ancient and medieval antiquaries abroad, its significance was first realised in England by the 17thC antiquary, John Aubrey, who excavated much of the site.

Stonehenge is now seen in the form of several circles of stones and a horseshoe, protected by an outer ditch. The stones seem to have been put into place in several phases during the Bronze Age, from about 1,900BC to 1,300BC, and by several different peoples. The massive blue-stones and sarsen stones, some from as far away as Dyfed in Wales, are now generally thought to have been transported here by glacial action rather than by the builders. It is not true that the Druids had anything to do with the building of Stonehenge, as they arrived in Britain much later.

No-one knows the exact combination of purposes for which Stonehenge was built, and there is certainly no evidence that it was ever used for human sacrifice. But we do know that its axis was carefully aligned with the sunrise on the longest day of the year, June 21st, and it is thought that its purpose was broadly religious, to do with the foretelling of the seasons and perhaps also with the worship of a sun-god. What remains very mysterious is the great sophistication which enabled the stones to be put in place – the labour force must have been both highly disciplined and immense. Some of the vertical and cross-stones we can still see today show the mortice and tenon shapings by which the stones were held in place.

Near Stonehenge are various other prehistoric barrows and monuments. The most notable is **Woodhenge**, *2m NE of Stonehenge,* a bank with a ditch inside with six concentric rings for holes: this may once have been a roofed building on wooden posts.

51. Stourhead House and Gardens 2 C6

Stourton, 3m NW of Mere. Stourhead is one of the truly great houses of Wiltshire, a magnificent Palladian mansion, and the nearby village of Stourton is also pretty. But the chief glory here is the gardens, acknowledged as among the most beautiful and elaborate in Europe, which were laid out from 1741–50 in the then fashionable romantic Italianate style by the owner of the house, Henry Hoare.

As you walk around the ornamental lake, you pass from one enchantment to the next: the grottoes, the Temple of Flora, the Pantheon, the Temple of the Sun, cottages, bridges and statues. A superb mingling of nature and artifice, these buildings blend most skilfully with the magnificent trees (note in particular the great conifers and the huge tulip tree), the plentiful rhododendrons and azaleas.

The manor was the property of the Stourton family from before the Conquest, and the ancient church and the 14thC stone cross just inside the gates to the park are their work. In the 18thC the estate passed to the Hoares, and they had the present mansion, which was completed in 1722. The house was badly destroyed by a fire in 1902, but much of the facade and some of the interior remains as it was. Today it is visited mostly for its wonderful paintings and an unusually good and comprehensive collection of Chippendale furniture. *House open most days, summer; gardens daily.*

52. Swindon 2 F4

The largest town in Wiltshire, this is thanks to the 19thC creation of the railway which converted Swindon from a quiet market town to a great industrial centre. Though some pleasant traces of the past remain, modern industry and commerce have completed the present townscape. The locomotive works were once among the largest in the world and the Great Western Railway has stamped its initials indelibly on the town's history: it was this company which was responsible for St Mark's Church in 1846 and many other buildings.

The Railway Museum has a permanent collection of historic locomotives and interesting railway relics. The Swindon Museum and Art Gallery, housed in one of the few really old buildings in Swindon, is exceptional, with many archaeological and geological exhibits, paintings, and an outstanding collection of seashells.

53. Wardour Castle 2 D4

15m W of Salisbury N of A30. A romantic ruin, standing on a lake and set against dark, wooded hills, Wardour Castle is one of the most impressive remaining medieval castles. It is unique among English castles because it is hexagonal, with two huge, soaring towers enclosing a hexagonal courtyard. Originally built in 1392 on the orders of Richard II, it has had an adventurous past, being besieged twice in the Civil War, once by Roundheads and once by Cavaliers. Severely damaged, it was never rebuilt, but the grounds were tastefully landscaped by Capability Brown in the 18thC to provide the present romantic scene. *Open certain days, summer.*

Near ancient Wardour Castle are two other historic buildings, 17thC Old Wardour House and 18thC New Wardour Castle, the three providing an interesting comparison of English building styles through the centuries. *Old Wardour House view from outside only; New Wardour Castle open certain days, summer.*

54. Wilton House 2 E7

Wilton. One of the greatest of the English country houses that were built on the wealth and land of the old abbeys. William Herbert, first Earl of Pembroke, described by the 17thC antiquary Aubrey as 'a mad, fighting young fellow' was given the nunnery and lands of Wilton by Henry VIII. Tradition maintains he built the house in the 1540s and 1550s on the designs of the painter Hans Holbein. The house was redesigned, however, after a fire in the mid 17thC by Inigo Jones, and only the delightful entrance porch remains from the 16thC. The east front is 17thC as are the seven magnificent state rooms, but further alterations by Wyatt in 1800 and others later, makes the present house a conglomerate of styles.

The Herbert family has always been noted for aristocratic style and taste, and never more so than in the late 16thC when Sir Philip Sidney's sister was second Countess, and Spenser, Jonson and Marlowe often visited. It is also claimed that Shakespeare may have played here in the first performance of 'As You Like It', and that a lady-in-waiting to the Countess, Mary Fitton, may have been the 'dark lady' whose tormenting attraction Shakespeare described in his sonnets.

The taste and artistic connections of the house are also expressed in the magnificent art collection built up by the Herberts, which includes examples of Rubens, Tintoretto, Van Dyck and Rembrandt. The state rooms are magnificently decorated, particularly the Double Cube Room, and there are some excellent examples of furniture by Kent and Chippendale. The lavish 18thC garden architecture, of which the Palladian Bridge is especially notable, is most impressive and a special attraction is the exhibit of 7,000 model soldiers. *Open most days, summer.*

Wilton House

🍂 HAMPSHIRE 🍂

1. Alresford Pond 2 G7

One of the oldest reservoirs in the world today, Alresford Pond was originally dammed up from the River Itchen in the 12thC by Godfrey de Lucy who wanted to construct a great trade waterway from Winchester to Southampton. Today part of the dam and pond still remains between Old and New Alresford, the pond lined with tall trees through whose trunks waters are reflected in the sun.

The pond remains an impressive monument to the engineering skill of men of a distant age, and it crowns the pleasant town of Alresford which has many ancient houses, a 14thC bridge and a partly Norman church.

2. Beaulieu 2 F8

One of the most intensively marketed of English country houses, Beaulieu certainly deserves its patronage for it holds more than enough interest for a splendid day's outing. Here is an example of where an ancient abbey was directly incorporated into the great house that was built on its ruin. A Cistercian abbey was founded by King John in the early 13thC, peacefully set among the woods and hills. Ruinous remains can still be seen today, with

well-preserved 15thC work in the outer gatehouse. The 14thC great gatehouse is now Palace House, although the outer walls and the four towers are an addition of the 18thC. Among ancient remains at Beaulieu is the 13thC conduit which supplied water to the abbey wine-press, and the old dormitory and graves of famous cricketers under the shadow within the modern house. Now the home of Lord and Lady Montagu, Beaulieu has been owned by the same family since 1538.

A modern attraction is the National Motor Museum, one of the finest museums of its

Beaulieu Abbey

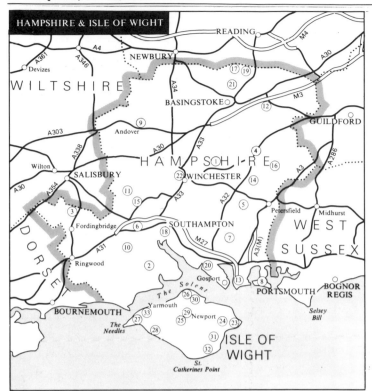

HAMPSHIRE & ISLE OF WIGHT

kind in the world, commemorating the
interest of a member of the family in old cars.
It opened in 1952, contains over 200 vintage
cars and bikes a World War Two Spitfire, and
presents the story of motoring from 1895 to
the present day.

3. Breamore   **2** E8
3m N of Fordingbridge. One of Britain's ancient
villages, Breamore has a particularly notable
Saxon church, with remarkable Saxon writing
on one of the arches. Some of the very oldest
words on any English wall, the translation
reads: 'Here the Covenant becomes manifest
to thee'. The writing helps to date the church
at cAD980. There is also a highly interesting
Saxon sculpture of the Crucifixion over the
doorway. All the walls and seven windows of
this church are Saxon, but there is also 14thC
and 15thC work.
Near the church is **Breamore House**, a
gabled Elizabethan building. To be seen
inside are fine paintings and furniture and in
the grounds is the Countryside and Carriage
Museum with agricultural tools and
machinery and a collection of steam engines.
Open certain days, summer.
In the dense little wood behind the house is a
mysterious maze, nearly 30 yards across.
No-one really knows the age, but it is believed

to be Anglo-Saxon. Many such mazes were
built for misbehaving monks who would be
forced to crawl through on their hands and
knees as an act of penance.

4. Chawton, Jane Austen's Cottage   **2** H6
1m S of Alton. Hampshire's greatest writer,
Jane Austen was a real local lass, for apart
from a few years at Bath she lived and died
entirely in the county, and it was the small
gentry of the area who formed the basis of the
characters in her novels. The unpretentious
red-brick house, respectable but cramped, is
where she lived from 1809–1817 following
her father's death.
Chawton Cottage provides a fascinating
insight into the environment of a great writer:
we can see the small sitting room where Jane
wrote alongside her sister and hypochondriac
mother, with its creaking swing door to warn
of any intruders, and we can marvel at the fact
that novels of the spiritual independence and
analytical power of 'Emma' or 'Persuasion'
were able to emerge from such a pressing
milieu. The final versions of her six completed
novels were all written here. The house is now
a museum with many personal relics of the
author. *Open summer; most days, winter.*

Jane Austen's Cottage

5. East Meon, Church of All Saints   **2** H7
East Meon is one of the attractive villages in
the delightful river valley of the Meon. Apart
from the charm of thatch and gables, it is
crowned by its magnificent church, one of
Hampshire's finest, a pure Norman piece of
parish devotion set among the flower-

Breamore House

meadows and the yews. The building is cruciform with a fine Norman tower topped by a lead spire. But the chief glory is the wonderful Norman font, from Tournai in Normandy itself, of pure black marble and enriched with fine carvings of grapes, doves and dragons as well as scenes from the life of Adam and Eve.

6. Eling Tide Mill   2 F8

Totton. Rare example of a 19thC tide mill, fully restored and in working order. Displays show how the mill used to work, from sacked grain to dressed stoneground flour and how the tide governed the miller's working life: about four hours' milling time was available each day from the tide, often at unsociable hours. Delicious stoneground flour is for sale. *Open most days.*

Pit Wheel, Eling Tide Mill

7. Hambledon   2 H7

7m NW of Havant. Hambledon is a pretty village, but it has earned its place in history for being the home of cricket. The game was, in fact, already long established when the Hambledon Club was formed in the 1760s by a group of wealthy landed gentry, but it was here that the first proper rules of the game were established. Between 1772 and 1787 the club was especially important in the history of the game, as with its help the MCC was founded.

The famous ground where the club played, at **Broadhalfpenny Down**, *2m NE of village*, is a place of pilgrimage to all cricketers. The church, which shows both Saxon and Norman work, has many ancient headstones and the graves of famous cricketers, under the shadow of its enormous yew. The Bat and Ball Inn, where cricket celebrations have been held over the centuries, still affords a good welcome, and opposite there is a granite monument to commemorate cricket played here in the 18thC.

8. Hayling Island   2 H8

Hayling Island was subject to intensive holiday development and today retains the atmosphere of a slightly old-fashioned resort area. But actually its history is as ancient as that of England itself, with an earthwork that pre-dates the Christian centuries and a living yew tree which has been here since the Saxons. The Early English church in North Hayling, has many ancient tombstones from the 18thC, a 13thC font and three old bells that have been ringing since 1350.

St Mary's of South Hayling is 13thC, has much fine carving, and has a beautiful stone bowl near the pulpit which may have been the Saxon font. South Hayling has the most modern holiday development, but also some fine 19thC building including part of a grand crescent. William the Conqueror gave Hayling Island to the Norman abbey of Jumièges, but the medieval priory does not remain.

9. Hurstbourne Tarrant   2 F5

5m S of Andover. Set in the fine valley of the River Test, one of England's most famous trout streams (together with its sister river, the Itchen), Hurstbourne Tarrant is one of the prettiest villages in Hampshire. William Cobbett, who could be very harsh in his views of villages and small rural towns, was a frequent visitor in the early 19thC and praised the village in his 'Rural Rides'. Hurstborne Tarrant belonged to a Dorset nunnery in the 13thC, which explains the second half of its name. Of great interest is the old flint church, partly Norman, with fascinating early 14thC paintings showing the Three Quick and Three Dead – standard symbolic figures at that time – and the Seven Deadly Sins.

10. Lyndhurst   2 F8

With woodlands lapping its boundaries, Lyndhurst is an attractive small town in its own right, proudly conscious of its historic role as the focus of this beautiful area. It has one main street, at the end of which is the Queen's House which was built in the 17thC for the Lord Warden of the Forest. The Verderers, who administer the forest, still meet here and their court-room is interesting to view, with a great axe-hewn dock where rough woodman's justice has been meted out through the centuries, and ancient panelled walls.

Lyndhurst has many other fine old houses, and a splendid Victorian Gothic church in fine red-brick with a commanding spire. Displayed over the altar is a magnificent painting of the Ten Virgins by Lord Leighton and there is some Burne-Jones and William Morris glass and a panel by Flaxman. The most famous person resting in the churchyard is Alice Hargreaves, who died in 1934, but who long before, in 1862, was the Alice Liddell to whom the story of 'Alice in Wonderland' was first told by her friend Lewis Carroll on the river at Oxford.

11. Mottisfont Abbey   2 F7

Mottisfont, 4½m NW of Romsey, off A3057. Posed charmingly on green lawns amid the trees, Mottisfont is an impressive Tudor and Georgian country house, which incorporates in its structure remains of an Augustinian Priory founded in the early 13thC. The builder of the Tudor house, Lord Sandys, who gave up the villages of Chelsea and Paddington to the King for this property, rather interestingly used the nave of the priory church for the main portion of his converted house.

The present north side is almost entirely Tudor and the south side is Georgian. Portions of the west side are underlain by a 13thC undercroft, with graceful circular stone columns remaining entirely unaltered. Other 12th and 13thC remains can be seen in the ground floor offices of the present house. The interior is notable for the drawing room designed by the fashionable 1930s artist, Rex Whistler, who created a charming painted Gothic fantasy here. *Open certain days, summer.*

The New Forest   2 F7

One of the greatest and most picturesque of the remaining forest areas of England, this royal forest was designated as hunting country for red deer by William the Conqueror in 1079. The forest was once much larger than it is today, stretching from the Wiltshire border to the coast, but it now covers almost 100,000 acres in south west Hampshire, which certainly seems extensive enough.

Nearly all this Crown land is available for the access and enjoyment of the public. Immensely varied within itself, areas of dense woodland alternate with heaths, glades and moors, ponds and rich valleys, with many different species of trees, animals and birds. For those seeking peace and solitude there are paths and trails to follow where deer browse and countless ponies roam free.

Interlaced with the forest are charming, small towns, such as Lyndhurst, and pretty villages like Cadnam and Minstead. Near the latter is the stone said to mark the spot where King William Rufus met his death by an arrow in 1100, probably fired by his trusted companion, William Tyrell.

The New Forest

12. Odiham Castle   2 H5

North Warnborough, Odiham. Only a ruin now, but once a great castle that played an important role in the history of England. It was from here that King John set out to sign Magna Carta in 1215, but his rebellious barons did not trust him and called in the French for support, who besieged the castle. Later, in the 14thC, King David of Scotland was held prisoner here. The ruin we see today is still impressive, picturesquely set by the towpath of the old Basingstoke Canal. One unusual aspect is the 13thC octagonal keep – the only remaining castle of this shape in the country.

Odiham itself is a pleasant market town where buildings of all ages from medieval to Georgian mingle in unpretentious harmony.

13. Portsmouth   2 H8

Of all English towns Portsmouth is the one that is most intimately connected with the history of the Royal Navy – the sight of 300 acres of docks and shipping installations, which you can see from Portsmouth Heights, remains a breathtaking sight. To the medieval kings, Portsmouth was 'the glory and the bulwark of these kingdoms': the first dock was built here in 1194, and the world's first dry dock in 1495.

Much of Portsmouth is not particularly picturesque: the town suffered greatly during the last war, so new building predominates. Miles of grimy 19thC terrace houses are rather depressing, but it was in one of these modest dwellings that Charles Dickens was born in 1812, the son of a Navy pay clerk. His house, now the **Charles Dickens Birthplace Museum**, *Commercial Rd*, is furnished in period style and contains personal relics plus many rare editions of his books in the library. Most of the interest in Portsmouth lies in old Portsmouth, with cobbled streets and narrow lanes. The Round Tower was built by Edward III in the 14thC, and the Square Tower was added by Henry VII. Many beautiful old buildings are found close to the dockyard, including some lovely Georgian houses (note especially the Navigation School). Gracious St Anne's Church dates from the early 18thC. In the smaller streets near this area more modest but still attractive old houses are to be found.

Portsmouth Cathedral was originally founded in the 12thC in honour of recently-martyred Thomas a Becket, but was partially destroyed during the Civil War and has suffered extensive 20thC alteration. The Garrison Church is mainly 13thC, but was bombed during the war. One of Portsmouth's most impressive buildings is the guildhall, with its great tower rising 210ft and the magnificent huge columns of its front. It was opened in 1890 by the Prince of Wales for Queen Victoria.

The **HMS Victory and Royal Navy Museum**, *Dockyard*, is a great monument to the most outstanding of England's naval commanders and one of her most lovable heroes – Horatio, Lord Nelson. The most remarkable example of ship restoration in the world, the Victory herself remains much as she was when she gave battle at Trafalgar in 1805. Nearby, the Royal Navy Museum houses relics of Nelson and the navy of his day which can't be conveniently displayed on board, as well as a large collection of model ships and figureheads. Its great centrepiece is the panorama of the battle of Trafalgar by W. L. Wyllie. *Open certain days.*

Portsmouth has now absorbed many settlements that were once independent, and among these the seaside resort of Southsea to the east, developed in Edwardian days, retains a dignified charm and still has paddle-steamers to the Isle of Wight. At the head of Portsmouth Harbour is the old town of Portchester, whose most notable possession is the fine, well-preserved medieval castle, built by Henry II, which stands on the site of a Roman fort.

14. Prior's Dean   2 H7

5m NE of West Meon. An isolated village set among the wild hills of Hampshire, Prior's Dean holds much for the traveller who is willing to venture off the beaten track. It has good thatch, and an ancient manor house, in the garden of which and in the fields nearby ancient Roman tiles have been found. Particularly attractive, if tiny, is the village church, mainly dating from the 13th and 14thC. As so often in this part of Hampshire, its churchyard is shaded by a majestic yew. It has a Norman doorway, and something else quite rare – the homely steeple is supported on four enormous baulks of timber, virtually tree-trunks roughly shaped with the adze, said to date from Saxon times or soon after. The church also has an ancient timber roof and good brass portraits on the chancel floor of people from the manor house.

15. Romsey Abbey   2 F7

Romsey was one of that species of English town that grew up in medieval times around its great abbey, and the church of the old convent buildings remains magnificent today. The abbey was founded at the start of the 10thC and Anglo-Saxon foundations in the church can still be seen by lifting a trapdoor, but the building we know today is almost entirely 12thC. The Norman nave, immensely long and high, is grand, the severe simplicity of the west front is an exquisite example of 13thC work, and the rich Norman doorway, standing next to a remarkable Saxon sculpture of the Crucifixion, is very beautiful.

Romsey Abbey is rich in treasures and antiquities: there is a small Anglo-Saxon rood behind the altar, in the south choir aisle an Anglo-Saxon Crucifixion scene hangs outside on the west wall of the south transept and there is a magnificent early 16thC painted reredos of the Resurrection. In the south transept lies Lord Louis, Earl Mountbatten of Burma, whose horrific assassination in August 1979 shocked the world.

The ancient market town of Romsey has much to see besides the abbey – it's full of houses of different ages, including the former home of Lord Palmerstone, Broadlands. **King John's House**, *nr Abbey*, a 13thC building fine Norman dog-tooth carving, is now a museum. *Open most days, summer.*

Romsey Abbey

15. Romsey, Broadlands 2 F7

A3057. One of the grandest Palladian mansions in the south of England. A house on this site was originally built in 1536 for the Abbey of Romsey, but after the property passed to the Palmerston family in the mid 18thC, new architecture and landscaping was completed by Capability Brown in 1767. The interior is very richly decorated, and the house has many fine works of art. Broadlands has had substantial connections with England's history, having been the home both of the 19thC Prime Minister, Lord Palmerston, and the late Earl Mountbatten. A special exhibition and audio-visual show gives a rich and detailed picture of Mountbatten's uniquely varied career of public service. *Open most days, summer.*

Broadlands

16. Selborne 2 H6

4m S of Alton. While retaining its charm, simplicity and modesty, Selborne has become one of the most famous villages in Hampshire, because here lived and died Gilbert White, the vicar of Selborne who will always be remembered for his classic work, 'The Natural History and Antiquities of Selborne'. For its intimate observation of the animate world this delightful minor classic, published in 1789, has never been bettered.

White's house, The Wakes, a 17thC building set in extensive grounds, is now a museum, and contains many relics of both Gilbert White and Captain Oates, the perfect gentleman who gave up his life for his friends on Captain Scott's Antarctic expedition of 1912. *Open most days, summer.*

The Church of St Mary was restored in the mid 19thC by a great-nephew of Gilbert White, but retains its Norman arcades and Perpendicular tower arch. White is buried in the churchyard and remembered by a stained-glass window depicting St Francis. The areas of common around Selborne Hill, with its adjoining woods, all of which was a favourite haunt of Gilbert White, is now in the possession of the National Trust.

17. Silchester Roman City 2 G5

Silchester is nothing today, hardly even a hamlet. But in ancient times it was an important place, because here there was a great Celtic earthwork and then a Roman city – under a waving cornfield lies what was once Calleva Atrebatum, which fell into decay after the Romans left and waited to be rediscovered until the 19thC.

Parts of the Roman flint wall can still be seen here, with the remains of three temples, houses, shops and a large basilica. But the most remarkable building that was excavated was a small Christian church of the 4thC, the only one known to have been built during the Roman occupation. There is a Calleva Museum on the site which houses some objects as well as models of what the city must have been like, but most of the important finds are now in Reading Museum.

18. Southampton 2 G7

Today, Southampton seems a very modern city, with industrial, commercial and educational functions added to the status it has enjoyed since the mid 19thC of a great passenger port – but Southampton has been a great port as long as Britain has been a seafaring nation. The Romans had a fortress nearby at Bitterne, the Danes often plundered the growing port in the 9th and 10thC, armies set off from here to fight England's medieval wars against France and it was from Southampton in 1620 that the Pilgrim Fathers left for their epic voyage to America in 'The Mayflower', an event now remembered by a column. As a great port Southampton suffered particularly heavy bombing during the last war, so much of the building is new, and sometimes, it must be confessed, rather unattractive. But much that is old also survives, and all but the undiscerning will find Southampton rich in interest.

Among the most interesting features are considerable survivals of the medieval city walls, and a historically interesting walk can be made around them. The finest surviving monument is Bargate, one of the outstanding medieval gateways in England. Built by the Normans it retains the original Norman arch as well as pointed arches from the 14thC. Nearby is a statue of George III, dressed in 18thC fashion as a Roman emperor. The south and west walls face the Rivert Test, and walks along the river here are particularly attractive.

Southampton retains some interesting old houses: Canute's House dates from the 12thC (so can in fact never have been used by that monarch who was offered the crown of England at Southampton in 1016) and The Wool House, now the maritime museum, is early 14thC. But the most beautiful house, with its exquisite Elizabethan garden, is The Tudor House, where Henry VIII and Anne Boleyn are said to have stayed in their courting days. *Museum and Tudor House open most days.*

St Michael's is Southampton's oldest church, with a Norman tower and tower arches now standing rather oddly isolated among the restorations of many periods. Its most outstanding feature is the black Tournai Norman font, rather similar to Winchester's but embellished with fantastic animals. Near Southampton are several prehistoric sites, including Woolbury Camp, an Iron Age hill fort with fine views.

19. Stratfield Saye 2 H6

Between Reading and Basingstoke, 1m W of A33. Stratfield Saye is a monument to one of England's greatest men, because in 1817 this rebuilt early 17thC house was presented by a grateful nation and Parliament to the Duke of Wellington. The Duke decided against building a new palace, and instead, thoroughly modernised the old house, installing a central heating and plumbing system still in use today.

Although not as full of relics as Apsley House in London, it is well-preserved and gives a good impression of this great soldier's character and tastes. *Open most days, summer.*

20. Titchfield 2 G8

One of Hampshire's most delightful small towns, Titchfield evokes a pleasant atmosphere of Stuart and Georgian days and has many individual buildings of great interest. Titchfield is rich in timbered and plastered houses, of which the early 17thC Market Hall may be singled out.

Part of St Peter's Church dates far back to the 9thC, although there is work of many periods here and the church as a whole does not give a great impression of antiquity. An attractive building, it has a particularly fine Norman doorway, and also a splendid south chapel, a magnificent 16thC monument paid for by the second Earl of Southampton.

The ruins of Titchfield Abbey and the Tudor House that was built on its site by the Wriothesleys, earls of Southampton, are magnificent: particularly imposing is the

Tudor gatehouse, with great turrets and gargoyles and particularly beautiful are the 13thC tiles to be seen in the ancient cloister of the abbey. It is possible that Shakespeare knew this house, because the third Earl of Southampton was his patron, and is thought by many to have been the young man who is addressed in Shakespeare's sonnets.

21. The Vyne 2 G5
4m N of Basingstoke, N of Sherborne St John.
Perhaps Hampshire's loveliest country house, The Vyne is of mellow Tudor red-brick, but has fine Georgian embellishments including a magnificent staircase. It was built between 1500 and 1520 and was the home first of the Sandys family and then of the Chutes.
Its glory is a most beautiful early 16thC chapel, once described by Horace Walpole as the 'most heavenly chapel in the world': it has a fine vaulted ceiling and particularly lovely tiered stalls with canopies, as well as exquisite stained glass from Flanders. Another distinguished room is the Oak Gallery, also dating from the early 16thC. The Vyne had the first classical portico to be added to an English country house, built on the north side in 1654 by John Webb. *Open most days, summer.*

22. Winchester 2 G6
Winchester was long one of England's greatest, as it is one of her most ancient, cities, and for many centuries it was a matter of dispute whether Winchester or London would be the eventual capital of England.
Winchester was a Celtic centre; it was already an important town in Roman times; it came to be the capital of the Anglo-Saxon kingdom of Wessex; and in Alfred's reign in the late 9thC it was a great centre of learning. William the Conqueror still considered Winchester his capital although London was already, as a great port, a town of equal importance. Naturally, then, Winchester is full of historic interest and is rich in ancient buildings.
The centre of Winchester is its ancient High Street, which has a restored 15thC cross and statue to King Alfred. Nearby is the fine 19thC guildhall. Some of the medieval city gates survive, including Westgate at the end of the High Street which is mainly 13thC: once a prison, it is now a museum of the history of Winchester. Winchester has a number of interesting museums, of which The Royal Green Jackets Museum, devoted to regimental history, is particularly interesting. *Museums open most days.*
There was a great Norman castle at Winchester, from which, in one of medieval history's most romantic episodes, Queen Matilda escaped concealed in a coffin. Little remains of the castle as it was destroyed after the Civil War but the 13thC Great Hall, a fine

example of the domestic architecture of this period, can still be visited. In this building Sir Walter Raleigh was condemned to death in 1603, after Queen Elizabeth had died and his enemy James ascended the throne. Here, too, Judge Jeffreys held part of the Bloody Assize in 1685.
The Bishop's Palace combines a fine 17thC building with medieval ruins and Winchester has many attractive old houses of all periods, often chanced upon down charming alleyways. Apart from the cathedral, the most interesting ecclesiastical building is the Church of St John the Baptist which is Norman and has a magnificent Decorated window and beautiful 13thC wall-paintings. Fine views of the city reward a climb up St Giles's Hill, a public park. Winchester's other hill, St Catherine's, has an Iron Age earthwork and a 'miz-maze', or labyrinth, cut into the turf, which may be of prehistoric origin. The story goes, however, that it was created by a Winchester College scholar who was kept behind during the holidays as a punishment for his misdeeds.

22. Winchester Cathedral 2 G6
Off High St. Although perhaps not as impressive in its exterior or approach as some, Winchester is one of England's grandest medieval cathedrals, as much the expression of earthly as of heavenly might. The first church at Winchester, the Old Minster, was begun in AD642 by King Cenwalh of Wessex, but after the Conquest the old building was pulled down, and a new one started by Bishop Walkelyn in 1079, which was consecrated in 1093.
During medieval times the See of Winchester was one of the most powerful bishoprics in England, and the cathedral was much embellished, especially by the great William of Wykeha, who in the late 14thC added a Perpendicular veneer to what had been basically a Norman building. The cathedral is therefore a mixture of medieval styles, and the best Norman work can be seen in the crypt, transepts and east cloister.
The cathedral is on a truly massive scale: it is the longest medieval church in the world with a nave of 560ft, and also has the largest Early English retro-choir to be found in England. One of its greatest treasures is the black 12thC marble font from Tournai, with magnificent carvings illustrating the life of St Nicholas, while other treasures include beautiful wall-paintings in the Lady chapel and the Winchester Bible and other ancient manuscripts housed in the Treasury. Many kings have been laid to rest here since Alfred, and their tombs are richly impressive. Izaak Walton and Jane Austen are two of the famous people who also lie here.

THE ISLE OF WIGHT

23. Bembridge 2 H9
Pleasant residential and yachting village, with large Victorian and modern villas. Bembridge has a wide, natural harbour, and nearby on a rock, joined to the mainland by a causeway built in 1878, is St Helen's Fort. One of a series of forts built on the suggestion of Lord Palmerston in the 1850s to guard against a French invasion, it never fired a shot in anger and became known as 'Palmerston's Follies'. Bembridge also has a much visited windmill of 1900. Nearby is Culver Cliff, scaled by many young Victorians as a test of courage, among them the poet Swinburne. He succeeded at a second attempt in 1854, only to pass out in a coma and be revived by a sheep poking its nose into his face!

24. Brading 2 H9
Modern holiday town, much modernised and motorised, but with some historic interest. It returned two members to Parliament in the Middle Ages, and has many old stone and thatched houses as well as Regency villas. St Mary's Church is much restored, but is the oldest on the island, being Norman and Early English, and has some notable tombs. The old town hall near the church is interesting for its lock-up, whipping-post, stocks and dolls' museum. On a lamp-post nearby is an ancient bull ring. A Roman villa, *1m SW of town,* has well-preserved mosaics and a hypocaust.

25. Carisbrooke Castle 2 G8
1½m SW of Newport. One of Britain's

best-known, this 20-acre castle standing proudly above its village is the historic focus of the Isle of Wight and conveys an immense sense of history and tradition.

A Roman fort first stood on this site and later the Normans built a keep here, set on an

Aerial View of Carisbrooke Castle

artificial mound above the plateau on which the castle stands. There is also much Elizabethan and Jacobean work: the Tudor buildings, consisting of outer walls at a lower level than the Norman keep, were built as an emergency measure against the Spanish Armada of 1588. Using local labour they were completed within 245 days. Carisbrooke achieved its greatest fame in 1647 when the defeated King Charles I took refuge with the governor, Colonel Hammond, hoping to be treated as a guest but only to find himself a prisoner.

There is an interesting museum recording the history of the Isle of Wight and the castle also possesses the oldest church organ in Britain. The well house is interesting; the 16thC water-wheel was once worked by prisoners, but today donkeys are considered more suitable.

26. Cowes 2 G8
Cowes is now internationally famous for its place at the August height of the yachting season, but it enters the marine history of the nation at many points, and is the entry port to the island from Southampton. Henry VIII built a castle here and there were also Tudor forts: very little remains of the castle now, although during the Second World War the site of the castle was the chief operations centre for the Normandy landings of 1904. The first English settlers for Maryland left from Cowes in 1633, and from the 18thC great ships for the Royal Navy were fitted here.

Sailing near Cowes

Cowes is a pretty sight when approached from the sea, with the houses hovering over the glimmering water's edge, but perhaps the greatest attraction now, apart from Cowes Week, is the proximity of Osborne House, Queen Victoria's much-loved home.

27. Freshwater and Farringford 2 F9
An area forever associated with the great poet Tennyson, who like so many of the Victorians, including his queen, was to find a seaside domestic idyll in the Isle of Wight. His monument, a great granite column on the summit of High Down at Freshwater, marks the height to which Tennyson would climb in all weathers, to drink in views of sea, woods and meadows.

Tennyson came here when he was a struggling young poet with a volume published and a little money invested in a railway. He lived for nearly 40 years at Farringford House to become a great sage and lyrical interpreter to the Victorian public. His house is now a hotel, but retains many relics of the poet, and the rustic bridge nearby, which he crossed so often on his walk to High Down, is named after him.

28. Mottistone 2 F9
2m W of Brighstone. Enchanting little place with fields, downs, sea, gorse and hay, which belonged to the Cheke family; the most famous member was a noted Tudor scholar and humanist, and tutor to Edward VI. There is a fine L-shaped Tudor manor house and a notable church dating originally from the 12thC, with a beautiful Tudor arcade on clustered columns, a charmingly-decorated Jacobean pulpit and an 18thC organ by John England. Behind the manor is Long Stone, the oldest man-made monument on the island, comprising two huge stones, one 13ft high. These are thought to be the remains of a burial mound used by Stone Age men. There are also several prehistoric barrows in the area, and the whole place has an air of antiquity and peace which once experienced will not easily be forgotten.

29. Newport 2 G9
The historic focus of the Isle of Wight and in many ways the island's most attractive and interesting town. It has been a port on the River Medina for many centuries, and the French sacked the town in 1377. Charles I held talks with the Cromwellian commissioners here to try and reach a political settlement, which led to the abortive Treaty of Newport (1648). Today it remains a pleasant hillside town, if also a busy business centre, and has many grand old houses, especially from the 17thC. Buildings to note include the old grammar school of 1619, where King Charles was lodged, and the 17thC Chantry House. There's an excavated Roman villa nearby. *Villa open most days, summer; or by arrangement.*

30. Osborne House 2 G8
Nr E Cowes. Queen Victoria's favourite home where she lived as often as she could, and also where she died; it remains still impregnated with the spirit of this remarkable if sometimes rather unpleasing lady. Overlooking the Solent near Cowes, Osborne House was designed by Thomas Cubitt in 1845–8, assisted by Prince Albert, and is in heavy Italianate style. The rooms, grand or domestic, remain much as they were when Victoria knew them: the miniature chairs still bear the initials of the little royal prince or princess who habitually sat there, the Billiard Room still breathes the pompous air of Victorian masculine leisure and the Antler Room retains its fusty gloom. In the Dining Room is a brass plate showing where the lying-in-state was held in 1901.

We can wander around all these rooms, and cherish the idea of the bagpipes being played at breakfast, or remember occasions such as the day in 1899 when, as Queen Victoria recorded in her diary, a young Mr Casals from Spain played to her most beautifully on the cello. On the terraces are tombstones to many favourite dogs, while the huge grounds, planted with every conceivable species of English tree, reward a leisurely stroll. *Open weekdays, summer.*

31. Shanklin   2 H9

One of the Isle's most elegant and welcoming seaside towns, crowned with many cliff-top hotels. A ravine with streams and pools, ferns and foliage. The Chine, where French raiders were defeated by Henry VIII's proud new navy in 1545, is a famous beauty spot. Later it had contact with the peaceful world of the imagination, as Keats was to write part of 'Endymion' looking out to sea in the shadow of the great trees. The Church of St Blasius was begun in the 14thC and is prettily set against the backdrop of Shanklin Down.

Shanklin

32. Ventnor   2 G9

Pleasant watering town with an almost sub-tropical climate and a touch of the Riviera, Ventnor is attractively Victorian as a whole but has few buildings of individual interest. The area was a centre for smugglers in days gone by, and the picturesque black crags of Blackgang Chine, a story-book adventureland all the young in heart will enjoy, was once the haunt of the notorious 'Black Gang'. In the town itself is an interesting smugglers' museum. Nearby **Appuldurcombe House**, *Wroxall*, comprises

the ruins of a Palladian building set in grounds laid out by 'Capability' Brown.

33. Yarmouth   2 F8

Cheerful small harbour, and one of the Isle of Wight's prettiest places, Yarmouth is a highly historic port. Here stand the ruins of one of the castles built by Henry VIII in the early 16thC on the south coast: this one is unique because it is square and has the first arrow-headed bastion in England.

Yarmouth

In St James's Church is a white marble statue of a colourful character, Sir Robert Holmes, the 17thC governor of the island who took New Amsterdam (later New York) from the Dutch in 1665. The head is of Sir Robert, but this was grafted onto what had originally been a statue of Louis XIV which had been captured from the French. There is a tiny 18thC town hall here, and many pleasant old houses which often seem more Continental than English in their ambience. Nearby is the pretty fishing village of Shalfleet, which has a Norman church.

THE HOME COUNTIES

The title 'The Home Counties' expresses this region's essential character very well: these are quiet, domestic counties at England's heart, nestling comfortably around the nation's capital, drawn to London by many links, and yet somehow resisting being dominated by it. Yet the pull of attraction between the metropolis and its surrounding rural counties is very strong, and movements between the two are a constant theme in history.

Great roads and rivers join the city and the countryside in unbreakable bonds. On the important roads, such as the Great North Road (M1) or Roman Watling Street (now the A5), there are a score of busy towns that have been staging posts through the centuries. The majestic silver line of the River Thames, with its many tributaries, links the capital of learning at Oxford, the smiling towns and villages of Berkshire, and the royal palace at Windsor to the great metropolis.

Being so close to London, the history of this area has been mainly quiet and peaceful. The region is long settled – there are plentiful records of every era from the Stone Age onwards – and the generations have led a relatively undisturbed life here. It was not the first landing-place for the invader, as the south east has been, nor has it seen constant battles, like the war-torn Midlands. No great medieval barons were able to set themselves up here as local rulers defying the king, and most of the Norman castles, once plentiful in the area, long ago became only mounds or ruins. The great medieval abbeys, too, were thoroughly destroyed at the Reformation. Instead, the region is dotted with a multitude of fine houses, both great and small, where people have devoted themselves to the art of living and pleasure, while solid 17thC market halls or 19thC municipal buildings complete dignified and prosperous townscapes.

The region, indeed, bursts at the seams with magnificent houses of all shapes and sizes, from great palaces to cosy manors. Some of them are the creations of great and powerful families. The Russells and the Greys were the two great families that divided Bedfordshire between them in amicable rivalry, and they have left their mark in the overpowering mansions that remain so impressive to the eye. Other families have left gorgeous palaces too – places as diverse but grand as Hatfield, Stowe, Moor Park and Windsor. In Buckinghamshire those outstanding 19thC immigrants, the Rothschilds, have left their imprint in a bevy of houses, of which Mentmore Towers is only the most spectacular. Smaller houses express the tastes and personalities of 19thC politicians such as Disraeli or Bulwer-Lytton, while a score of famous writers have chosen to retire from the hustle to the solitude of country retreats in this region: Milton, Cowper, Pope and Shaw are only some of the more notable.

This is a relatively small area, but because human development has been so intense, it is also a very diverse one. There is a world of difference between the green, winding lanes of Hertfordshire and the often inhospitable stone uplands of northern Bedfordshire. Parts of the Chilterns, hills which almost skirt London's border, seem immensely remote even today, although they are not far from rapidly expanding towns. Oxfordshire has towns and villages that seem to grow out of the local stone, while Berkshire sports a score of delightful Thames-side villages, wonderful places to stroll, punt, or just enjoy the lazy swirl of water.

From the courts and quadrangles of Oxford have gone forth countless men and women who have made a major contribution to the record of human achievement. Fighters for liberty, whether religious or political, like John Bunyan or John Hampden, have played a prominent role in the life of this region, as have some of those, like Cecil Rhodes, who have sought to impose tyranny on their fellow men.

In our own century no region, except perhaps London itself, has seen faster or more striking change than this one. A hundred years ago, the landscape was predominantly rural, the towns were market towns or county towns, and what industry there was tended to be local or traditional such as the straw-hat making or brewing of Hertfordshire and the duck-breeding of Buckinghamshire. But as the modern tide of development has swept relentlessly on, many quiet rural communities have been invaded by commuters and villages have been swallowed up by expanding or new towns to which many thousands of people have moved. Shocked by the London slums and determined to set up a settlement that would combine the best of town and country, in 1903 Ebenezer Howard planned the world's first garden city at Letchworth. Drawing on that experience, Welwyn Garden City was developed and remains the pride of English new towns. But though this is living proof that the 20thC planning dream need not always turn into a concrete nightmare, some places have been almost redeveloped or industrialised out of existence, while others are now in a precarious balance between ancient and modern. Recent developments have sometimes been imaginative, but the traditional character of the landscape is everywhere threatened. It will take constant vigilance and a strong conservation movement if the essence of this region is to be preserved, to delight future generations as it has done those of the past.

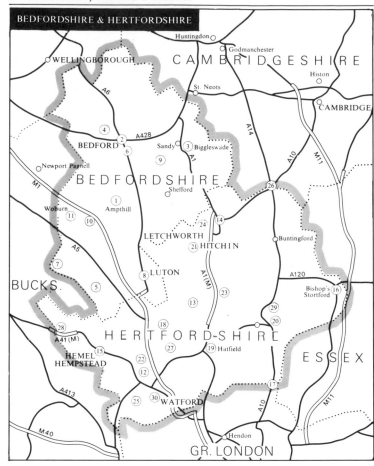

BEDFORDSHIRE & HERTFORDSHIRE

🏛 BEDFORDSHIRE 🏛

1. Ampthill
3 C2

Gracious, largely 18thC town where shops, houses and offices blend into a dignified and harmonious whole. The local great house was Ampthill Castle, first built in the 15thC by an uncle of Henry V and later in royal possession. Here Catherine of Aragon was sent to await divorce by her husband, Henry VIII, while on a more cheerful occasion, at a hunting party in the park, Henry's wife-to-be, Anne Boleyn, gave him a hunting-horn and a greyhound. The castle fell into ruin, but in the 18thC Lord Ossory built a splendid new house in its place. This is now a Cheshire Home, but the park, with its 300-year-old oaks and ancient crosses, is still a delightful place to stroll.

2. Bedford
3 C2

A modest but distinguished town. It was founded in the 10thC, and had an important Norman castle (now just a mound), but its history since then has been largely uneventful. There is a lack of historically interesting buildings, much of Bedford being 19thC. Bedford is forever associated with John Bunyan's two stays in its goal, when in the teeth of adversity and with the help of faith, he wrote much of his great works: 'Grace Abounding to the Chief of Sinners' and 'The Pilgrim's Progress'. Bedford did not make amends to its 'tinker oft in quod' until it unveiled a statue to Bunyan in 1874, 200 years after the second imprisonment! The Bunyan

Museum, *Mill St*, contains his surviving personal relics. *Open most days, summer.*

3. Biggleswade
3 D2

An unlovely town and with little that is old (mainly due to several disastrous 18thC fires), it is mentioned here because it was a coaching centre and has some fine old inns, of which the Sun Inn is the most interesting. Medieval St Andrew's Church is large, mainly Perpendicular, and contains some good carving and priests' seats.

4. Bromham Bridge
3 C2

Bromham. Good example of a surviving early medieval bridge: the narrow passage over the river with its 26 arches is a modern bottleneck for traffic, but the part over the river itself may well be 12thC. In 1281 a hard frost caused it to give way in parts, and a woman fell through and was carried to Bedford on an ice-floe! Until 1813, over the flood area, there was only a 6ft causeway, but in that year the bridge was widened. Nearby stands the old mill, and in the distance the 16thC Bromham Hall. Charles I once stayed here, and its Royalist owner, Sir Lewis Dyve, had a narrow escape during the Civil War when he swam across the river to escape.

5. Eaton Bray, Church of St Mary the Virgin
3 C3

A most splendid church, mainly of the 13thC, but with Perpendicular windows. There are exquisite arches with delicate carved capitals, and similar carving on the font. Note the ancient fire-hooks used to pull the thatch off roofs if they caught fire. Eaton Bray also has a Norman castle in a fair state of preservation, and an ancient mill-house on a stream.

6. Elstow 3 C2
Very close to Bedford, it was John Bunyan's home village, where he was born in 1628 and grew up to be a tinker like his father. In the Norman church he rang the bells as a young man and learnt the faith that was to sustain him through trouble and inspire his literary achievement. There are ruins of a medieval abbey near the church and many old cottages with overhanging upper floors. The ancient Moot Hall, standing a little secluded on its green, now houses a Bunyan museum.

Moot Hall, Elstow

7. Leighton Buzzard 3 C3
Sleepy but rather charming town with a traditional High Street, Leighton is ancient: two large Saxon cemeteries have been found here. In the early Middle Ages it was an important market town, and the present Market Cross dates from the 15thC and has fine sculptured figures of a king, a bishop, John the Baptist, Christ and the Virgin Mary. In the High Street are distinguished buildings from a number of periods, including grand Victorian houses now occupied by Barclays and National Westminster Banks. The church is medieval, largely Perpendicular and with a lofty spire. The town is now officially known as Leighton Linslade (although nobody calls it that) and in Linslade you can see the Grand Union Canal, which, with the railway, gave Leighton much of its 19thC prosperity.

8. Luton Hoo 3 D3
Luton. Great house of Luton, the present building is the composite creation of the 18th and 19thC. Robert Adam was commissioned to build a house by the Marquess of Bute in the mid 18thC on the site of an older house. Unfortunately there were several serious fires and his work is hard to find, although his magnificent library remains. The present house is largely the creation of Mewes and Davis, architects of the Ritz Hotel in London. There have always been architectural doubts about the house: an 18thC visitor commented pertly that 'the mixture of unfinished palace

and ruinous offices is odd', and many have found the house overdone. But the interior has a fabulous display of Edwardian wealth (vulgar as that may have been), and stunning trinkets by Fabergé. *Open most days, summer.*

9. Old Warden 3 D2
A good example of a 19thC estate village with honey-coloured thatched cottages built for his tenants by the Victorian Lord Ongley. But the main reason for coming here is quite different. The estate was bought from the Ongleys by the Shuttleworths, the last of whom was tragically killed in a flying accident. His mother set up the Shuttleworth Collection of Historic Aeroplanes and Cars here to honour his interest in flying. On flying days there are many fascinating old aeroplanes, and you may well see a genuine 1909 Blériot actually in the air.

10. Toddington 3 C3
Standing on a hill where five roads converge, it is a dignified town with fine houses from many eras. A market town from 1218, it always remained the peaceful centre of its rural district. Ancient St George's Church commands the hill: it is on a fine scale, the plan and some of the masonry dating from the early 13thC and the lofty nave is early 14thC. A Norman motte-and-bailey castle here has vanished, but traces remain of the Elizabethan manor house of those staunch Royalists, the Wentworths. Here the beautiful Henrietta Wentworth who was to attract the love of Charles II's ill-fated illegitimate son, the Duke of Monmouth, grew up. She herself was to die shortly after her lover was executed for attempting to win the throne. Only the kitchen-block, unfortunately, survives of this once fine house. However, the old forge and the village pump complete what is certainly a charming miniature townscape.

11. Woburn Abbey 3 C2
Woburn. Grandiose and famous stately home, it is a splendid monument to one of England's greatest families, the Russells, whose main home it has been since the mid 17thC. Much of the present house and gardens were created in the 18thC by the 4th Duke of Bedford, who added to a 17thC north wing. Despite the pulling down of part of the house in 1950 and the commercialisation (including a dolphinarium, an amusement park and a safari park), nothing can detract from the overwhelming view of the west front from the great park, or the magnificence of the treasures inside. One of the best private picture collections in the world includes examples of Van Dyck, Gainsborough and Reynolds. The state dining room is set out as if for a banquet and the tapestries and furniture are magnificent. Curious outbuildings include a lakeside dairy, an ice-house and stable blocks which contain a pottery, shops and an antiques centre. *Open most days.*

HERTFORDSHIRE

12. Abbots Langley 3 D4
It got its name from long ownership by the abbots of St Albans (Langley means 'long meadow'), and was once a pleasant rurally-orientated town, but has now been almost swallowed up by Watford. Here was born, 800 years ago, the only Englishman ever to become Pope – Nicholas Breakspear. Son of a poor farmer, he finally rose to the papal throne as Adrian IV in 1154, struggled against the Holy Roman Emperor and sanctioned the

English conquest of Ireland, which has caused so much trouble since. There is a memorial to him in the beautiful Church of St Lawrence which has a low Norman tower, arcades of carved Norman arches, and much graceful stonework and glass. Abbots Langley was also the home in the 17thC, of Elizabeth Greenhill, who holds the English record for childbirth. Pregnant every year from the age of 16 to 54, she died at 64 having had 39 children in 38 confinements. The town's large mental hospital was rather quaintly known in the 19thC as the 'Metropolitan Asylum for Imbeciles'.

13. Ayot St Lawrence 3 D3
Thrush-haunted hilltop village where, in Friar's Wood, was found a hoard of 230 Roman coins. There is also a 14thC ruined rose garden, a Georgian classical church, a Tudor house and many timbered cottages. In modern times the village has become a notable centre for retirement and for weekend cottages. The most famous dweller was George Bernard Shaw who lived here for 44 years until his death in 1950.

Ayot St Lawrence

14. Baldock 3 D3
Standing at the crossroads of the prehistoric Icknield Way and the Great North Road, Romans and Saxons were here. Its name, however, was given to it by the medieval religious and fighting order of the Knights Templar who settled here and named it after a city of their own, Baldach, near present-day Baghdad. Its main street has some fine old houses and has earned a respite from its career as a traffic bottleneck since the building of the new bypass. The many old inns include one where, we're told, Samuel Pepys, the 17thC diarist, fancied the landlady but 'durst not take notice of her, her husband being there'. For this, and many other fascinating details, we are indebted to an 18thC Baldock parson, John Smith; it was he who, over three years, patiently deciphered the six tiny books of the diary and thus gave it to the world. Baldock's church, where Smith preached, is spacious and almost entirely from the 14thC. The sad apology for a spire is a good example of the 'Hertfordshire spike'.

15. Berkhamsted 3 C4
Atmospheric town, especially on dark winter afternoons wandering down the old alleys or by the canal where its long history can be felt. The line of the prehistoric earthwork, Grim's Ditch, can be traced on the common, and great earthworks as well as some ragged walling remain from William the Conqueror's castle, once one of the most important in the country. Thomas a Becket lived here for a while in the 12thC, and this was where, in 1376, the Black Prince passed his last days. Berkhamsted Place is an Elizabethan mansion partly built with stones from the old castle and the large church is mainly 13thC. Ashridge Park is a great local haven. Built on the site of a 13thC monastery, it now contains an entertaining Gothic house designed by James Wyatt in 1809. Berkhamsted school is a famous public school founded in the 17thC, where Graham Greene was a pupil.

16. Bishop's Stortford 3 F3
Charming and historic town, not spoilt by being a traditional centre of the malting industry (the old red-brick and white weather-boarded maltings by the river are, in fact, worth a visit) but rather ruined by hideous modern developments. Ancient Waytemere Castle was the great stronghold of the bishops of London, who owned much of this area for 800 years, and was famous for its dark and terrible dungeons. Here Bishop Bonner is said to have kept Protestant prisoners during the reign of Catholic Queen Mary I, and there is a charred stump in the forecourt of the castle which is probably the remains of a stake where one Christian burned another to death. Very little remains of the castle now. There are two fine churches, one medieval and the other modern, both set on small hills.

17. Cheshunt 3 E4
A rose-laden little town, it is full of historic interest and has had many famous residents. The remains of Theobalds Palace, built by Elizabeth I's Burghley and later a home of James I, now only consist of a long wall. But in the park is London's original Temple Bar, which in the 17thC marked the western boundary of the City of London: it was later dismantled and bought by the 19thC owner of Theobalds. Cheshunt Great House, once a home of Cardinal Wolsey in the early 16thC, is a remnant too, but still has its panelled hall with a splendid 15thC timber roof. Another famous resident of Cheshunt was Richard Cromwell, son of Oliver Cromwell. Briefly ruler of England after his father's death, he lived here in retirement paying 10s a week rent to his friend Mrs Pengelly until his death in 1712. Outside the town is Waltham Cross, one of the series of crosses raised by Edward I in the 13thC to mark the resting-places of his dead wife's body on its way to London. Although now rebuilt in 19thC Gothic it remains very beautiful and still contains some 13thC stone.

18. Harpenden 3 D3
Exquisite little country town with a fresh gorse-clad common, charming walks through woods and fields, and wide avenue-like streets lined with gracious trees. The church was restored last century but the tower is 15thC and the font Norman. Turner's Hall is a 17thC house, and just outside Harpenden is Rothamsted agricultural research station. Founded in 1840, ever since then it's been spreading the gospel of agricultural improvement and experiment around the world.

19. Hatfield House 3 D4
Hatfield. One of the most important Jacobean houses, it was built by Robert Cecil, son of the great Lord Burghley and devoted servant of Elizabeth I and James I. The house has been home to generations of the Cecil family, and is simply magnificent. Built on a sweeping E-plan, it has a plain front and elaborate carving and stonework on the garden side. The traditional Great Hall with its sumptuous minstrel's gallery and beautiful carved staircase is one of the finest rooms. The house contains an abundance of treasures including fine tapestries and furniture. Of particular interest is a collection of Elizabeth I's personal belongings, including her silk stockings and gardening hat. *Open most days, summer.*

Hatfield House

20. Hertford 3 E4
Founded in the 10thC and already the county town by the 11thC, Hertford has long, however, been smaller than many other Hertfordshire towns. It remains relatively unspoilt, though much has been lost. The five medieval parish churches have either vanished or been restored out of existence, and it is the Friends' Meeting House, built in 1669, that is probably the most interesting religious building: it is the oldest Quaker meeting house in the world still in use. At Hertford Castle only a few walls and the rebuilt

gatehouse remain, although its site by the Lea is attractive. This Norman castle was built on the site of a Saxon stronghold, and was host to many a medieval monarch. Interesting old inns include the Salisbury Arms which was in business early in the 15thC.

21. Hitchin 3 D3

One of Hertfordshire's most attractive towns, it was a great coaching centre and therefore enjoys a wealth of old inns. The prosperous trade of the centuries has given rise to the fine houses, many of the older ones so low that you can almost touch the eaves from the pavements. Mercantile wealth also built Hertfordshire's largest parish church, rich in 14thC and 15thC craftsmanship. A charming Garden of Rest stands by its great tower, which is on Norman foundations and contains Roman bricks. Hitchin has grown considerably in recent years and has become a very fine shopping centre, but the town's basic character remains intact.

22. Kings Langley 3 D4

4m NW of Watford. Posh commuter village whose main street has some interesting ancient red-brick houses, many dating back to the 17thC, and a medieval cottage, all set against undistinguished shop-fronts. The place got its name because it was the seat of a royal palace: it was known as Chiltern Langley until the late 13thC when Edward I's wife, Eleanor, rebuilt a house here, and many future kings, especially the murdered pair of 14thC monarchs, Edward II and Richard II, were to spend much time here. Only fragments of the palace remain, and all that's left of the great medieval priory is now incorporated into a Rudolf Steiner school. The Church of All Saints is mainly 15thC, but the chancel walls are 700 years old. There is a fine 16thC chest and a canopied Jacobean oak pulpit stylishly decorated with carved dragons.

23. Knebworth House 3 D3

Knebworth. The 19thC novelist and politician, Bulwer-Lytton, rebuilt the originally Jacobean house in extravagant Gothic style, complete with battlements, turrets, and grotesque gargoyles which Lytton's gardener apparently always referred to as 'bloody monkeys'. The whole place has a slight atmosphere of vulgarity and 'Gothick' pretentiousness, perhaps reflecting Lytton's highly-coloured and rather overbearing character: Disraeli once described an acquaintance as 'the most conceited man I ever met, though I have read Cicero and known Bulwer-Lytton'. The carved screen and plasterwork of the ceiling in the Great Hall are both Jacobean and the rooms contain magnificent furniture and family relics, including some of Lytton's manuscripts. The huge gardens provide picnic areas and amusements. *Open most days, summer.*

Knebworth House

24. Letchworth 3 D3

The world's first garden city, built in 1903. This was the earliest dream-child of the great visionary of modern town-planners, Ebenezer Howard, a reporter and writer shocked by the London slums and determined to set up a settlement that would combine the best aspects of town and country. Business associates gave him the chance to experiment at Letchworth, and it is indeed a pleasant place, the many factories being hidden away behind rows of trees, quiet walks and wide avenues. The ancient Icknield Way runs through the town in a fine avenue of almond trees, and there are still many remains of old Letchworth: a 17thC hall, Stuart cottages, a dignified medieval church, and, nearby, the site of a British settlement inhabited before the Romans came.

25. Moor Park 3 C5

Nr Rickmansworth. One of the most magnificent houses ever built by a tradesman, the present 18thC palace was the result of the fortune Benjamin Styles made out of the South Sea Bubble, that riot of speculation that ruined so many people when it burst in 1720. The house is classical in style, fronted by a splendid portico with Corinthian columns, while the interior was lavishly painted by Italian artists with themes from Greek mythology. The house is now a golf club, and golfers drive off across the grounds landscaped by Capability Brown. *Open certain days.*

26. Royston 3 E2

A town of narrow streets and old inns, it is famous for a cave, a palace and a church. In 1742 some workmen in the market place discovered a cave beneath, cut in solid chalk, containing the skeleton of a woman and many colourful wall-paintings and carvings. The cave's history is mysterious – it may have been a Roman tomb, an early Christian oratory, a Saxon hiding place, or a medieval sorcerer's coven. The carvings, however, are definitely thought to be medieval. A fragment of James I's splendid palace (where he signed Sir Walter Raleigh's death warrant) remains. The King loved to hunt hares on Royston Heath which later became a haunt of highwaymen. The Church of SS John and Thomas is an amalgam of all periods from the 13th to the 20thC, and has many splendid brasses, ancient sculptures, a 14thC knight in alabaster and fine 14thC oak panelling.

27. St Albans 3 D4

Although not the county town of Hertfordshire, St Albans has exercised the greatest influence throughout history on the county, and it remains Hertfordshire's most interesting town. Despite some unattractive modern rebuilding, you don't have to look far for reminders of its long and proud past. Even before the Romans came, this was a great meeting-place of tribes – what Sir Mortimer Wheeler calls a 'prehistoric metropolis'. It was Roman Verulamium, and many magnificent remnants of the city – the mosaic floors, the semi-circular theatre, the walls – have been excavated. The whole complex is one of the finest examples remaining in England of the inventive town planning of the Romans. Bodicea sacked the city in AD61 in her revolt against the Romans, and it was then rebuilt more splendidly than before. In the Christian era the town grew up around the shrine of England's first martyr, St Alban, and in medieval times was independent of royal rule, being a 'Liberty' ruled by the abbot, one of the most powerful men in England. Two fierce battles in the Wars of the Roses were fought here in the 15thC and that great warrior-queen, Margaret of Anjou, held a council of war in 1455 in the Moot Hall, the building now occupied by W. H. Smith. In the same era printing was set up here, only four years after Caxton initiated the first press in London. It has long been one of the town's main industries. St Albans has much of interest apart from the abbey. The clock tower of 1402 is a rare surviving example of a town belfry, and among fine streets are French Row, so-called because French soldiers were quartered here in 1217, and the fashionable Fishpool Street. The Saxon Church of St Michael is worth a visit for its Anglo-Saxon nave and monument of Sir Francis Bacon.

27. St Albans Abbey   3 D4

The surviving abbey church of one of the greatest medieval abbeys in Europe, it is the oldest monastic church in use in Europe today, and has the second longest nave in England. The abbey first grew around the shrine of St Alban, the 4thC first English martyr, and the central tower used red Roman bricks taken from Roman sites nearby. The original church was 8thC, but little remains of it now, the present church being 11thC at its heart, and having grown irregularly and periodically since then (which accounts for the length of the nave). The church was disastrously restored in 19thC by Lord Grimthorpe in yellow-stone Gothic – the crown of his work was to erect an image of himself as St Matthew in the porch – and the result is an unhappy marriage of Victorian vulgarity with medieval austerity. Don't miss the medieval wall-paintings on the Norman nave-piers that were covered with whitewash for centuries.

28. Tring   3 C3

Ancient market town on Roman Akeman Street and near the even more ancient Icknield Way, it was known to King Alfred in the 9thC. The church is from many periods and stands now as a haphazard but striking patchwork of flint and stone walls and battlements. There are many pleasant chestnut-lined avenues of old houses and interesting canal-side walks.
Tring Park is a 19thC Rothschild home, and was rebuilt then, although there are still traces of the 17thC house which Wren designed and where Nell Gwynn stayed. It is set in 300 acres of magnificent parkland containing the wonderful zoo collected by the second Baron de Rothschild. He used to drive down the High Street in a carriage drawn by zebras! The Rothschilds did much for Tring, building a Geological Museum and much housing, and the name of this colourful and powerful family is remembered with affection.

29. Ware   3 E3

Famous for the trade of brewing and malting since the days of William the Conqueror, Ware is full of water-mills and malthouses. The High Street is a fine thoroughfare with many gabled houses, red roofs and a Regency town hall. That ill-fated monarch, Lady Jane Grey, was proclaimed Queen at Ware, and the town is also famous for 'The Great Bed of Ware', a huge Tudor bed built for one of England's kings (who, we don't know) and spoken of with reverence in the pages of Shakespeare, Jonson and Farquhar. It's now in the Victoria and Albert Museum, London. The spacious, cross-shaped Church of St Mary is mainly 14th and 15thC, and nearby Fanhams Hall is an interesting Queen Anne building.

30. Watford   3 D4

Hertfordshire's largest town but once described in the early 19thC by Charles Lamb as 'the pretty village of Watford'. It has now become ugly and noisy, but is worth visiting for certain historical buildings. The old church with its 13thC chancel is a haven of peace behind the busy High Street and beautiful Cassiobury Park is the old great house of the earls of Essex. Watford was originally a Saxon settlement, and although the 20thC has destroyed much, ancient and attractive old buildings are chanced upon round the most unexpected corners.

🏛 BERKSHIRE 🏛

1. Ashdown Park   2 F4

Nr Lambourn, 2¼m S of Ashbury. Odd-looking but interesting great house, very tall and narrow like a tower. It's made entirely out of creamy chalk blocks with brown-stone corner-dressings, and crowned with a little viewing room under a dome with a green cupola. The house is so tall that the great stairway, all there is to see inside, occupies a quarter of it. It is said that the first Earl of Craven put up this strange erection in 1665 when he was fleeing from the plague, and built the house when he felt he had hidden far away enough from London for there to be no risk of infection. Craven dedicated the house to Elizabeth of Bohemia, the 'Winter Queen' and daughter of James I who had been driven into exile from her throne during the Thirty Years War. Craven had been a cavalier at her court when young, and in later years contributed to her upkeep. *Open special days, summer*.

2. Basildon   2 H4

Home of the great agricultural pioneer, Jethro Tull, who first intended to be a politician but was forced to retire here through ill health. He used his intelligence to invent a seed-drill (1701) and later a horse-drawn hoe, laying the foundations for the great agricultural improvements of the 18thC. He is buried in the churchyard. The church itself, originally 13thC, was largely rebuilt in 1875 and is only of moderate interest. Basildon Park is a Georgian mansion, and there is a magnificent railway bridge of 1839 with four great Roman-style arches constructed by Brunel.

3. Binfield   2 J5

Charming village which seems to have been a sort of 18thC garden suburb, with many gentleman's seats of that period, such as Binfield Lodge, Park House and Manor House. The most famous resident was the poet, Alexander Pope, who spent his boyhood here in the early 18thC after his father grew rich on the trade of linen-drapery and decided to move out of London. Pope wrote many poems here which show the splendid promise of his early manhood, including 'Essay on Criticism' and 'The Rape of the Lock'. The church is mainly Victorian but partly medieval. Billingbear Park, once owned by the great Neville family, now remains only as its kitchen-block forming part of a modern farmhouse. Sandford Mill is a beautiful 17thC mill near where the Loddon often overflows its banks in winter.

4. Bray   2 J4

Famous above all for its 16thC turncoat vicar of the popular song, this trimmer of the age of religious dissent, Simon Aleyn, is buried in the churchyard he clung to so ably. Ockwells is a very fine example of a 15thC timber-framed manor house, and Jesus Hospital a distinguished charitable building of 1609. St Leonard's Hill, just outside the village, is thought to have been a Roman beacon and a Roman lamp of bronze was discovered here in the 18thC.

5. Buscot Park   2 F3

3m NW of Faringdon. Charming house and garden, both worth a visit. The garden lake was created by Capability Brown in the 18thC, while Harold Peto designed the rest of this water-garden, with a canal fringed with water lilies and decorated by statues dropping by stages to the lake. The house is equally charming, in 18thC Adam style and with 19thC interior decorations by Burne-Jones. *Open certain days, summer*.

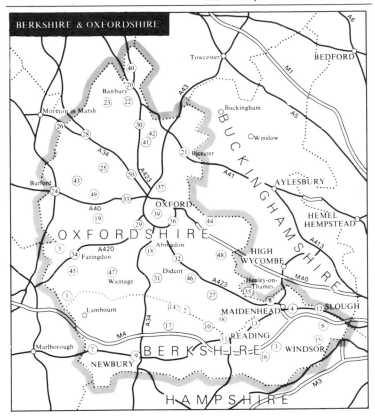

BERKSHIRE & OXFORDSHIRE

6. Eton College 2 J4

Nr Windsor. Premier public school of England, traditional provider of half the Cabinet (19 Prime Ministers have been Etonians), Eton College was founded in 1440 by Henry VI largely for the education of poor scholars. Its buildings are steeped in history and association. The oldest part is School Yard, and both this and Lower School are 15thC and still in daily use. Upper School dates from 1694: among names carved on school desks are Walpole, Fox, Shelley, Gladstone, Eden and Macmillan. Here, too, is the desk belonging to Dr Keate, the famous early 19thC headmaster who once flogged 80 boys in one morning. The old chapel, noted for its exquisite roof, has been much restored, but contains fascinating pre-Reformation wall-paintings as well as other treasures. The library is full of priceless manuscripts, including three printed by England's first printer, William Caxton, in the 15thC.

7. Hungerford 2 F5

Town of many picturesque ancient customs, including that of the tutti-men who snatch kisses from pretty girls at Hocktide, just after Easter. This is also when you can see used the horn which the 14thC great noble, John of Gaunt, presented to the town to celebrate an agreement concerning fishing rights that they had made. The Bear Inn has been visited by a record number of kings and queens, including Anne of Cleves, Catherine Howard, Elizabeth I, William III and Anne. The High Street is full of good-looking houses of all ages and is flanked by a canal bridge, built by John Rennie who constructed the whole of the 19thC Kennet and Avon canal. The local great family were the Hungerfords, a 17thC member of whom established a market in London: its site is marked by the northern end of what is still called Hungerford Bridge.

8. Hurley 2 J4

Riverside leisure and holiday village, ideal for punting idly along the Thames. The town also has much historic interest. William the Conqueror built a Benedictine monastery, later a priory, here: the nave of the largely Norman parish church, is part of the old monastery. Surviving medieval buildings include a barn and a dovecote. Lady Place is a great house built by Sir Richard Lovelace in the 16thC with money captured from the Spaniards on voyages with Sir Francis Drake. There are many half-timbered houses and the Bell Inn is one of the oldest in Berkshire.

9. Newbury 2 G5

Despite its interesting historical background, there's relatively little to show for it today: the Norman castle has vanished without a trace, as have the old guildhall and market cross. Many parts of Newbury are rather dreary, but there is a fine Jacobean cloth hall, now a museum, from the days in the 16th and 17thC when Newbury was one of the greatest centres of the cloth industry. There is also battlemented St Nicholas's Church, built at the expense of Jack Winchcombe of Newbury in the early 16thC. Jack was a great cloth

River Kennet, Newbury

master and one of the earliest of the really huge capitalists – he even entertained Henry VIII and Catherine of Aragon at his home.

His house is now gone, but the site is, rather fittingly, now occupied by Marks and Spencer. There are almshouses boasting a charter granted by King John in the early 13thC, and the sites of the two Civil War battles of Newbury can also be visited.

10. Pangbourne 2 H4
Where the jolly little River Pang joins the Thames, Pangbourne has a delightful river scene with boats, locks and weir, only slightly marred by the series of magnificently dreadful Victorian villas by Shooter's Hill. So redolent are they of the 'Belle Époque', they're known locally as 'The Seven Deadly Sins'. This stretch of water inspired Kenneth Grahame's 'Wind in the Willows', and Jerome's 'three men in a boat' stopped for a jar at the Swan Inn.

11. Reading 2 H4
A seemingly endless succession of industrial estates and housing developments strung out along the grim length of the 19thC railway that brought its prosperity. But Reading has a very ancient history, if well hidden. There are flint-tool records of human habitation on the site 400,000 years ago, and remnants of all historical eras since then, including Roman coins and pottery which indicate that Reading was an important Roman river port.
The seal of medieval success was given with the foundation of a great Cluniac abbey by Henry I in 1121: the remaining buildings – late 13thC gatehouse, part of the abbey church, the chapter house, a wall of the cloister – are scanty, but still impressive. But remains of medieval Reading are in general few, although the parish church of St Laurence is a notable one. Sadly, its beautiful stained glass was blown out by bombs during the last war. The town was substantially rebuilt during the 19thC, with buildings including a riotous, characteristically Gothic mid-Victorian town hall. The huge, grim outline of the jail where Oscar Wilde served out his martyrdom can be seen from the railway.

12. Slough 2 J4
Slough boasts an old centre, a famous astrologer, a famous murderer, and was the home of several men of letters, including that persistent 18thC correspondent and advice-giver, Lord Chesterfield. The astronomer was Sir William Herschel who discovered the planet Uranus in 1781 from the telescope in his garden. His house, Observatory House, has been demolished, but his grave is to be found in the ancient partly 13thC Church of St Lawrence, in Upton, nearby. The murderer was John Tawell, a Quaker who killed his former mistress by giving her prussic acid in a drink: the case caused a sensation because it was the first time a killer was caught by sending messages along the electric telegraph.
The old part of Slough is the ancient village of Upton, with beautiful 15thC Upton Court and the elegant Bayliss House of 1695, now sited rather incongruously next to the Horlicks factory.

13. Sonning 2 H4
Among the sunniest of Thames-side villages. The 11-arched bridge is one of the oldest crossing the Thames. Holme Park is the site of the palace of the medieval bishops of Salisbury, and fragments have been excavated, including the foundations of a 15thC hall and gatehouse. Among other finds have been innumerable flint axe-heads, showing that prehistoric as well as modern man appreciated this cheerful spot.

14. Streatley 2 H4
Pretty river-side village with a magnificent view of the river from Streatley Hill, the place is full of substantial-looking brick houses of the 17th and 18thC. Among the finest is Streatley House, late 18thC and with three large storeys, made charming by an attractive porch. Streatley has an interesting village hall which was converted in 1898 by the architect Ravenscroft from a row of disused old malthouses.

15. Windsor 2 J4
Its most famous possession is overwhelming Windsor Castle, but Windsor is also a place that combines present-day charm and dignity with a rich heritage. Edward IV developed the town in the late 15thC, and many houses remain from that time in plastered and timbered splendour. Wren's noble guildhall of the late 17thC is certainly well worth a visit, not least for its fine collection of paintings. *Open summer.*

15. Windsor Castle 2 J4
Windsor. The largest inhabited castle in the world, itself a small world of magnificent buildings the favourite home of the present Queen and of most monarchs since Victoria. The origins of the castle go back to William the Conqueror, and almost every monarch since has added his bit. Glorious St George's Chapel, where so many monarchs lie buried, was begun by Edward IV, and Henry VIII built the entrance gate in the early 16thC. The present grandiose silhouette that rises so nobly from Windsor Great Park on dark winter afternoons, is largely the creation of the 19thC. Windsor belongs to the history of the nation more totally than any other place in England, and there is an immense richness of things to do and see here: cloisters, barracks, great kitchens, animals, priceless paintings, armour, furniture, procelain – all the property both of their royal owners and of every Englishman. *Open most days.*

Windsor Castle

16. Wokingham 2 J5
Squeezed in by Reading and the unpleasant modern town of Bracknell, Wokingham precariously preserves the character of a country town, with many old buildings remaining. It was a traditional centre of the early silk industry, probably introduced by French Protestant refugees in Tudor times. In the 18thC it also became noted as a great centre for bull-baiting, badger-baiting and cock-fighting; the Red Lion Inn, still standing, was where spectators gathered to watch bull-baiting, while an alley called Cockpits Lane is where the cockpit is believed to have stood. The town hall is a splendidly monstrous Victorian building of 1860, combining Gothic, French chateau and Byzantine effects. Until recently, Wokingham was often colloquially known as 'Lousetown', because the aldermen were once unable to agree on who should be the next mayor – a louse was placed on the table which eventually bore down on one alderman, thus electing him mayor!

17. Yattendon 2 G4
Formerly an important market town, but now immensely peaceful amid its quiet trees. Yattendon Court is the great house standing high up in wooded grounds. Yattendon is notable for the famous 'Yattendon Hoard', one of the largest collections ever found of prehistoric bronze implements, discovered in front of the terrace of Yattendon Court. The Georgian rectory once belonged to lecherous Sir John Norreys, who entertained Henry VIII here and was later beheaded for being too intimate with Anne Boleyn.

OXFORDSHIRE

18. Abingdon   2 G3
Beautiful local market town and
administrative centre, still with the prosperous
atmosphere of the 18th and 19thC when it
was a great centre of the brewing and woollen
industries. There was a Bronze Age
settlement here and both neolithic and Roman
remains are plentiful around here. But the
town's rise to importance began with the
foundation of Abingdon Abbey in AD675,
one of the greatest of Saxon and medieval
abbeys: there is little left of it now, however,
except part of the great gatehouse and the
timbered 15thC long gallery. St Nicholas's
Church was built in the late 12thC and has a
surviving late Norman doorway. Perhaps of
greater interest is St Helen's, which is wider
than it's long and has a remarkable late 14thC
painted roof. The market place is dominated
by the town hall, a grandiose Baroque
building of 1678–82: the 18thC traveller,
Celia Fiennes, thought it the finest town hall
in England. There are many late medieval and
Tudor houses, surprisingly often in wood as
well as stone.
A real feast of local relics is housed in the
Abingdon Museum, *The County Hall*, itself a
historic building. Relics from the medieval
abbey, ornaments and tools from Saxon graves
found nearby, ancient toys and pewter, arms
and weapons from the 16th to the 19thC, all
add up to one of the finest provincial general
museums to be found in England.
Set in the nearby pretty little village of Milton,
but well-hidden by high walls from the road,
Milton Manor is a delightful 17thC house
with Georgian wings added later. In the
18thC, too, the chapel and the library were
refurbished in the elaborate Gothic taste
which was sweeping England at that time. A
walled garden is planted with vegetables and
flowers. *Open weekends, summer.*

19. Bampton   2 F3
Bampton is traditionally known as
'Bampton-in-the-Bush', because in the
18thC it was in the middle of an impassable
thicket by the Thames. Its isolation has given
us a rich heritage of local customs such as
morris-dancing, and the horse fair has been
held here from the 13thC. The town dates
from Saxon times and there was a medieval
castle here, the remains of which are now part
of Ham House. The medieval cross-shaped
church is lovely, there are many stone
thatched cottages, and dignified Georgian
houses stand by the market-place.

20. Banbury   2 G1
Famous above all for the cross of the nursery
rhyme (not to forget Banbury cakes), the
monument in fact was destroyed by the
Puritans in 1600, and the present cross, an
undistinguished piece of architecture, was
erected only in 1858. Much has been
destroyed in Banbury, largely by the citizens
themselves: in the 17thC they petitioned
Parliament to demolish their great 12thC
castle, in the 18thC they blew up the old
church with gunpowder because they did not
want to pay the cost of maintaining it, and in
1912 they sold the Globe Room of the
Reindeer Inn to America for a quick profit.
The people of Banbury, no sentimentalists,
have concentrated on industry and their town
is one of the chief stock distributing centres in
England. There are a number of ancient
houses, mainly 16thC, and a delightful
vicarage with gables, mullioned windows and
the date 1649 over the door. The new church
is like a concert hall: the chancel ablaze with
colour and with a blue, starry ceiling, the
whole concoction in rich red sandstone with
an apse, a portico, an extraordinary tower and
a small chocolate-box dome.

21. Bicester   2 H2
Sleepy market town in flat, damp countryside.
Bicester has a number of attractive, gabled
houses. But its chief interest is the medieval
church, which has a Saxon arch joined by
Norman arches and a fine roof with beams.
There are fragments of a 12thC priory and
also many old saddlers' shops as this is great
country for horse and hound.

22. Bloxham   2 G1
Between a town and a village, Bloxham is
distinguished by its pleasant narrow ways
between stone cottages, by a worthy old
building for its ancient grammar school, and
an outstanding church built by the Normans.
It has an ethereal 14thC tower and spire,
beautiful Norman doorways, great decorated
windows (one by Burne-Jones and Morris)
and a fine 14thC reredos.

23. Broughton Castle   2 G1
Broughton. One of only two castles in old
Oxfordshire still intact, it's a fascinating and
dignified building standing in a wide, watery
hollow. The ancient walls are substantially
14thC, there's a 15thC gatehouse and many
charming Tudor and Stuart additions such as
gables, tall chimneys, green lawns and oriel
windows, which soften the rather harsh
medieval effect. Inside are beautiful vaulted
passages and a great 14thC chapel up a 14thC
stairway, next to the fine dining room and
ancient priest's room. Nearby is a pleasing
church full of rich tombs of the families,
including the Broughtons, who have owned
the castle. *Open certain days, summer.*

24. Burford   2 F2
Beautiful, unspoilt Cotswold stone village set
in simple fields by the rushing Windrush
rippling among willows, and crossed by its
narrow, stone bridge. Burford is very ancient,
being first mentioned in AD683 when it was
the scene of a conference held by the King of
Mercia to fix the date of Easter – a thorny
question among Christians at the time. Here,
after the Civil War, the Levellers, men who
wanted to take reform more in the direction of
democratic revolution, were surprised by
Cromwell, 400 of them imprisoned in a
church, and three of their leaders shot against
a wall in the churchyard. Burford has an
ancient Tolsey, or customs house, now a
museum, a fine 17thC vicarage, an
Elizabethan mansion called The Priory and
many dramatic Tudor houses lining the
streets. But its chief pride is the magnificent
Norman church, the largest in the county after
Dorchester Abbey. Look for the fine carvings,
a rich 15thC south porch, many colourful
chapels and a stone Saxon coffin in the
churchyard, remnant of an obscure 8thC
battle.

25. Charlbury   2 G2
Unpretentious village in the pleasant valley of
the Evenlode, and close by the glory of
Wychwood Forest. It has enchanting stone
houses, a drinking fountain commemorating a
visit from Queen Victoria, a medieval church
surrounded by noble trees on its hill and a fine
17thC house in Lee Place. Cornbury House
with its magnificent 600-acre deer park was
the 'sweete park' of the 17thC diarist, John
Evelyn.

26. Chastleton House   2 F1
Chastleton. Beautiful house built between
1603 and 1618, and a shiningly pure example
of the Jacobean style. It has a dignified,
symmetrical facade of five soaring gables, but
with a great square tower at either end. Inside
is a splendid drawing room with elaborate
panelling and a glorious plaster ceiling, a
sumptuous state bedroom, and a high, oak

staircase. The kitchen-block is black with the smoke of centuries, and bright with a remarkable service of pewter. There is also a secret chamber where the Royalist captain, Arthur Jones, was hidden after the Battle of Worcester in 1651. He escaped in a hurry, after his resourceful wife gave his pursuers drugged wine. *Open most days.*

27. Checkendon 2 H4
5m W of Henley-on-Thames. Perfect little village smelling of cherry-blossom, in the heart of the Chilterns, with many charming brick and timbered cottages around its trim green. The church is largely Norman and only slightly restored, and contains fine brasses to the Reade family, once the owners of the great house, Checkendon Court. This house was built on the site of a medieval nunnery and ghostly grey nuns are said to walk at night among the yew-hedges.

28. Chipping Norton 2 F1
The highest town in the county, perched on a 700-ft-high hillside by the source of the Evenlode. Chipping Norton is rich in old Cotswold houses, mainly dating from the 18thC, when much of this gracious town was built. It has a long but rather uneventful history: already a market town in Saxon days, there was a Norman castle here and a Member of Parliament has been sent since Edward I's reign. But most of its days have been, and still are, passed in an atmosphere of immemorial peace. There are fine 17thC almshouses, hospitable old coaching inns such as the Crown and the White Hart, and a stately, largely Perpendicular church, mainly built during the 14th and 15thC.

29. Cumnor 2 G3
Pleasant stone-built village, very quiet and grave, where a late Norman church improved through the succeeding medieval centuries remembers one of the most puzzling events in the course of English history. Cumnor Place was the scene of the dramatic death of Amy Robsart, wife of Elizabeth I's favourite, the Earl of Leicester. She fell down a flight of stairs in 1560, breaking her neck. The household said it was an accident, but there were dark rumours that Leicester had murdered her so that he could marry the Queen. In any event, the scandal that ensued was enormous, and no such marriage ever did, or could have, taken place. Amy's letters and a statue of the Queen can be seen in the church.

30. Deddington 2 G1
Almost an overgrown village, Deddington is now a small and rather severe-looking town. Once of great importance as the Saxons settled on its steep hill, and later a great medieval castle was built. Only grass ramparts now mark the site, but there is a 13thC house, Castle House, where Charles I once slept, two ancient inns, and an eight-pinnacled 14thC church that dominates the market square. Sir Thomas Pope, 16thC founder of Trinity College, Oxford was born here. It was he who had the tragic task of breaking the news to Sir Thomas More, martyr to Henry VIII's religious policy, that he was to be executed the next day. More said to the tearful Pope: 'Be calm, Pope, my kind friend; I trust we shall meet in heaven, where we shall live eternally and enjoy each other's company in everlasting bliss'.

31. Didcot 2 G3
Modern Didcot owes its existence to being chosen by the Great Western Railway in the 19thC as their main junction depot, and it is very much a railway town, complete with modern industries and power-station. One interesting place to visit is Didcot Railway Centre, where many of the old steam trains can be seen in full working glory. Once a Saxon settlement, the old part still exists as a recognisable village round the church, and

even retains a cruck-cottage and an ancient unused footpath. *Railway Centre open certain days, summer.*

32. Dorchester-on-Thames 2 G3
Its history is immensely ancient, for there are two great Bronze and Iron Age ditches, and later it was the Roman town, Dorocina. Then, in the 7thC, it became a Saxon cathedral city, one of the earliest strongholds of the Christian faith in a pagan area. Of the Saxon cathedral nothing remains, and remnants of the medieval abbey, just a little timbered building, now house a museum. The large medieval abbey church is worth seeing for the 12thC walls in the nave, Norman arches, and the Jesse window behind the altar, where stonework and glass reach new heights of curvy splendour. With its proud history, Dorchester has, strangely, remained only a village, but with its old coaching inns and many stone cottages, a most attractive one.

33. Eynsham 2 G3
Ancient and beautiful village where a Saxon parliament once met in the 10thC days of Ethelred the Unready. There is an exceptionally tall cross in the market square, and the 14thC parish church has very handsome 15thC arches in the nave: a Saxon abbey stood on this site before.

34. Faringdon 2 F3
Old-world town with an air of dusty charm. All Saints Church, which lost its spire in the Civil War, has an Early English chancel and an almost entirely Norman nave. Faringdon House is a grand building built by Poet Laureate Henry Pye in 1870, and there are many good Georgian houses. The 18thC folly on the hill where the Norman castle once stood, was built to help relieve local unemployment.

35. Henley-on-Thames 2 H4
Smartest of Oxfordshire towns and world-famous for its July Regatta, Henley has an old-fashioned and slightly pompous air. It is, nevertheless, very pleasant, and its noble, 18thC arched bridge spanning the stately Thames, carries carved heads of Father Thames and the goddess Isis.
Henley is ignored by the Domesday Book and was only granted its charter as a market town by Elizabeth I in the 16thC: the earliest parts of the stone and flint church are 13thC but most is 15thC and the imposing tower is Tudor. In the churchyard lies a distinguished refugee, Charles Dumoriez. First a general of the 18thC French monarchy, then Foreign Minister during the Revolution and a soldier who won famous battles, he eventually fled to England to advise the British government in its war against Napoleon. Henley has many old inns and good Tudor houses, and the Regatta, which began in 1841 accompanied by boat-building and brewing, adds an air of timeless frivolity to the town.

36. Iffley, Church of St Mary 2 G3
Comfortably reached from the centre of Oxford by bus or car, this very famous church of the 12thC has much late Norman work, including two magnificent Norman arches, as well as an Early English sanctuary. The west front with its doorway is quite spectacular.

37. Islip 2 G2
Delightfully unspoilt village where many prosperous Oxfordians have settled. 'In this small village, by name Githslepe' Edward the Confessor was born in 1004, and he later gave it to the monks of Westminster as an act of piety. The thatched cottage which was the 13thC home of the monks can still be seen. The steep main street is medieval and there is a handsome 17thC hall. The mainly 15thC church has a great embattled tower, although the chancel was built in 1861 and there has been much restoration. Islip was the scene of three skirmishes in the Civil War. It's also

here that the first recorded flight in English history took place. In 1784 James Sadler, an Oxford pastrycook, took off on a balloon and travelled five miles to a height of 3,500ft, coming down at Islip.

38. Mapledurham House   2 H4

Mapledurham, 4m NW of Reading. All red-brick and roses, delightfully set in a valley by the Thames and complete with panelling, portraits and a priest's hole, Mapledurham is a dream of a Tudor mansion. It even has ghosts: it's reported that by moonlight the corpse of a manservant is dragged around by the master who killed him.

The mellow brick is finely arranged in diamond shapes with eight beautiful oriels and many delightful nooks and crannies. It incorporates parts of an earlier 15thC mansion. Great oak staircases and Elizabethan moulded ceilings in white plasterwork are of interest inside, and the late 18thC chapel is a most splendid example of 'Strawberry Hill Gothick'. Here lived the Blount family, among them the Martha Blount beloved by the poet Pope, a frequent visitor who advised much on the garden. Though she refused to see him when he was dying, he left her his books and one thousand pounds. *Open weekends, summer.*

39. Oxford   2 G3

Most renowned of university towns and also a beautiful city with its own history, Oxford cultivates a unique mixture of the pursuit of learning and of pleasure. Almost all the 30-odd colleges are worth a visit, and there is an immense amount else to see.

It was a city before it was a university. A king's daughter, Frideswide, refused to marry, and founded a nunnery here: she died cAD735 and it is said that Oxford grew up around her shrine. A royal mint was built in 912 and later a Norman castle, of which little remains but a mound. In 1258 Simon de Montfort and 23 barons signed the Provisions of Oxford, limiting royal power, and from this some historians have dated the birth of English democracy: seven years later the council met at Westminster as the first English Parliament. The meeting-place of four roads, among them the High Street, is called Carfax and this is the traditional centre of Oxford. It is dominated by Carfax tower, all that remains of the medieval church of St Martin. From this tower you can obtain a wonderful view of Oxford and of the green hills that surround it.

Oxford

Students were first attracted here in the 12thC. We first read of a Chancellor of the University in 1214, and although University College and Balliol dispute the title, the oldest college is thought to be Merton, founded in 1264. No-one will ever agree on which of the colleges is the most beautiful and all have their individuality.

Christchurch, founded in the 16thC by Cardinal Wolsey and favourite of Etonians, is the grandest, with vast Tom Quad superbly dominated by its great bell-tower. The College Art Gallery contains Old Masters, and portraits of former members hang in the dining hall. Largely built in the 15thC, **Magdalen College**, with its deer park, has a unique, ethereal beauty. **St John's** has its timeless garden. **Corpus Christi** has an almost Puritanical fineness and an ancient sundial in the main quad. **Merton College** boasts some of the most perfect buildings and quadrangles including largely 14thC Mob Quad, Oxford's oldest quad. A fine complex of Gothic buildings dating from 1380, **New College** has a famous chapel, and exquisite dreaming cloisters, like a timeslip into the medieval world. **Keble**'s red-brick and its magnificent chapel are in the height of 19thC Anglican revivalism, while Arne Jacobsen's **St Catherine's College** (1963) brings the austere but elitist spirit of the modern movement in architecture to the Oxford college.

Other great buildings abound. Wren's **Sheldonian Theatre** of 1669, based on a Roman theatre and roughly semicircular in plan, is surrounded by the much-weathered heads of Roman emperors. The University **Church of St Mary the Virgin**, Oxford's noblest church, is mentioned in the Domesday book and has an exquisite 13thC tower with a 14thC spire. This is where Archbishop Cranmer first denied his Protestant faith under fear of the stake and then recanted.

The **Bodleian Library**, greatest of university libraries, contains buildings which are masterpieces of late medieval and Stuart architecture. The jewel among them is the Divinity School, a perfect example of 15thC Perpendicular. All are set in what is arguably Oxford's finest quad, even if its modern buildings do rather resemble a 1930s municipal swimming baths. The library includes Radcliffe Camera, in beautiful Radcliffe Square. Built by James Gibbs, it's a great circular monument to 18thC Classicism. Glorious, too, are Oxford's open spaces: the semi-wildness of Port Meadow continues commons rights that have existed since William the Conqueror.

Oxford's place in history is incredibly multi-faceted: here penicillin was discovered at the Radcliffe Hospital, here William Morris started one of the great car businesses of modern times in the humble buildings where his father had been at school, and here the Royalists found their great Civil War stronghold. From these courts an endless stream of the young, bright and hopeful have gone forth to make names the world remembers.

39. Oxford, Ashmolean Museum   2 G3

Beaumont St. The Ashmolean is the oldest public museum in Britain, having been opened in 1683, and is devoted broadly to art and archaeology. Its collection of paintings and drawings is truly superb, including examples of Michelangelo and Raphael, while it is also very rich in Egyptian relics, especially mummies. Among interesting exhibits are much 16th and 17thC silver, an exceptional array of snuff-boxes, and the Hill collection of musical instruments.

39. Oxford Canal   2 G3

Opened in 1790, it completed the 18thC transport network between London and the Midlands, covering the stretch between Oxford and Coventry, passing through Banbury and Rugby on the way. It is a narrow canal that meanders and winds through pretty countryside and townscape in a way that only Brindley's canals do.

40. Rollright Stones   2 G1

Little Rollright. A noted prehistoric stone circle probably of the Bronze Age and older than Stonehenge although lacking its impressiveness. Gaunt and shrivelled, set among shabby fir and stunted elder, they stand on the windswept ridge which is the

border between Oxfordshire and
Warwickshire. The circle is known as the
King's Men, the King's Stone and
Whispering Knights – local legend maintains
they were members of an invading army who
were turned to stone.

Rollright Stones

41. Rousham House   2 G2
Rousham, ½m E of Oxford–Banbury rd. An
ancient house restored in the 18thC, with
substantial Jacobean remains. William Kent
redesigned the house for the
Coterell-Dormer family, adding two wings,
altering the facade and laying out the grounds
in the Italian manner. Horace Walpole
declared at the time: 'Never has Kent shown
so much taste', and certainly the house
epitomises the easy aristocratic grace of the
18thC. The Painted Parlour and Great
Parlour are particularly magnificent. Kent
took full advantage of the dramatic setting of
the house, on rising ground near the Thames,
and created a spectacular garden extending
over 30 acres. *Open certain days, summer;
gardens daily, all year.*

42. Steeple Aston   2 G2
A tangle of all sorts of buildings forming a
village, with many grey walls high above the
Cherwell valley. It is particularly notable for
its fine church set among firs and with a high
sycamore towering above the medieval tower.
Inside is much Early English work while the
font is older, being either Saxon or Norman.
The 17thC chancel contains much rich glass,
there are interesting brass portraits and the
carving is beautiful. The most striking feature
is a magnificent monument to the 18thC
hanging judge, Sir Francis Page, who
commissioned this work during his lifetime as
a personal tribute to his own greatness.

43. Swinbrook   2 G3
Delightful stone houses cluster by a brook
that tumbles through meadows to meet the
Windrush. It has a substantially 13thC church
containing a collection of monuments to the
Fettisplace family, who owned all the land
around here in Tudor and Stuart days and,
it's reputed, land in 14 other counties. The
walks near the river are very peaceful.

44. Thame   2 H3
Dignified and quiet market town with many
graceful 18thC houses in the broad High
Street. It was granted its charter to hold a
market as early as the 8thC. Among the finest
buildings is the gabled stone grammar school
with its deep mullioned windows, erected in
1569. Many famous people were educated
here: Dr Fell of the well-known rhyme, the
poet Milton, Antony Wood the 17thC Oxford
antiquarian, Edmund Waller the 17thC poet,
and John Hampden, staunch opponent of
Charles I and champion of liberty. Hampden
came here to die, too, after being fatally
wounded at the battle of Chalgrove Field in
1643. The 13thC Church of the Blessed
Virgin, almost a cathedral in miniature, has a
lovely 14thC south porch, a vaulted roof and a
turret stair leading to an upper chamber.
Thame Park is a beautiful open space of 300
acres with an 18thC great house.

45. Uffington White Horse   2 F3
2m S of Uffington. One of the most striking

hill-figures in England, most clearly etched
into the bare hillside, it is 360 ft long and may
date from about 100BC. Popular legend has it
that it played a role in the decisive victory won
by King Alfred over the Danes, although
no-one really knows where that battle was
fought. Controversy rages, too, about whether
it is really a horse or a dragon.

46. Wallingford   2 H3
In Saxon times a greater town on the Thames
than either Oxford or Reading, Wallingford
was also a prehistoric settlement and its
modern streets are still based on the Roman
plan. King Alfred and his successors fortified
it against the Danes, and their earthworks and
ditch can still be seen in the town park. There
was a medieval castle, of which only a few
ramparts remain (it was destroyed under
Cromwell), and most of the medieval
churches are also, unfortunately, gone. There
are, however, many medieval timbered and
brick Georgian houses, St Leonard's is
substantially a medieval church and the town
hall is 17thC. The present many-arched
Thames bridge is 700 years old, descendant
of one that was first built in AD600.

47. Wantage   2 G3
Famous as the birthplace in 849 of the only
English monarch to be called 'Great' – Alfred,
England's saviour against the Danes. The
town has erected a noble statue of him in the
market place. Once a great centre of the wool
trade, and in the 18thC famous for blood
sports and other nefarious activities, Wantage
now seems very quiet and respectable. The
13thC Church of St Peter and Paul contains
magnificent tombs of the Fitzwaryn family,
into which Dick Whittington married. Rather
than streets paved with gold, the passage
leading from Newbury Street to some old
almshouses has cobbles made from sheep's
knucklebones.

48. Watlington   2 H3
A mile from the Icknield Way and nestling at
the foot of the Chilterns, Watlington is a very
ancient place. Its name may derive from the
wattles which the early Saxons interlaced with
mud to build their houses. It was a manor at
Domesday, and a market town by the late
12thC. Though rather forgotten now, there's
a fine and spacious 17thC market hall, traces
of its medieval manor house, and a 14thC
church which has, unfortunately, been much
restored.

49. Witney   2 G2
Solid country town where nothing much has
ever happened, but whose weathered stone
buildings, wide main street, enormous green
and severe Early English church all testify to a
prosperity which has survived the centuries.
Witney was a prosperous market town as early
as the 11thC, and has been a blanket-making
centre from the 14thC to the present. Hardly
satanic buildings, the mills we see now,
dignified structures set among green fields by
the unpolluted Windrush, are mainly 19thC.
At one end of the High Street is the quaint
17thC Butter Cross, its gabled roof crowned
by a clock-turret and sundial.
To the west of the town is **Minster Lovell**,
most famous of the Windrush villages. Its
lovely stone houses and setting on the hillside
besides the river are so striking that it suffers
not a little from commercialism. The church
is cruciform, chiefly Perpendicular and
contains a magnificent 15thC tomb and
monument to William, Lord Lovell, one of the
local great family. Most famous of the tribe
was Francis Lovell known as 'Lovell the Dog',
who assisted the kitchen-boy, Lambert
Simnel, to revolt against Henry VII in the late
15thC. Legend states that after the Battle of
Stoke in 1487 he came to the now-ruined hall
and hid in a secret chamber only known to
himself and a trusted servant. The servant
died suddenly and Lovell starved to death. It

wasn't until 250 years later that workmen found 'the entire skeleton of a man, as having been at table . . . with a book, paper, pen . . . all much mouldered' while they were altering the house.

50. Woodstock 2 G2
Often viewed as a mere appurtenance to Blenheim Palace, Woodstock has a rich life and history of its own. It grew as a centre for royal hunts: in the early 12thC Henry I had a hunting lodge here and Henry II kept his mistress, 'Fair Rosamund' in state here. It is said (probably falsely) that she was poisoned by Henry's jealous wife, Eleanor of Aquitaine. King John established a market here, glove-making came in the reign of Elizabeth I, and in the Civil War Woodstock was staunchly

Blenheim Palace

Royalist but had to surrender to Parliament. Apart from Blenheim, Woodstock also has a magnificent medieval church with a classical 18thC tower and many splendid old houses.

50. Woodstock, Blenheim Palace 2 G2
Built by Queen Anne for her great victorious general, John, Duke of Marlborough, in gratitude for his victory at the Battle of Blenheim against the French in 1704. 'England's biggest home for England's biggest man', it certainly outdoes most kings' palaces in splendour. Even the gateway weighs 17 tons! The house covers three acres and is set in a park of 2,500 acres, laid out by Capability Brown in imitation of the battle. A masterpiece of English Baroque style, there are literally hundreds of chimneys and the buildings, designed by Vanbrugh, themselves form a huge block with wings joined by arcades forming courtyards. The roofline is crowned with trophies of war. The rooms are dazzling: that in which Sir Winston Churchill was born is one of the more insignificant. Blenheim is not to modern taste, which distrusts its military-style magnificence, but there is no denying that it is a staggering monument to one of Britain's most successful soldiers. *Open summer; park daily, all year.*

✥BUCKINGHAMSHIRE✥

1. Amersham 3 C4
Garages, traffic-lights, depots and factories are found here in conjunction with the medieval parish church, ancient inns, the 17thC town hall and the site of the original Chaloner's Grammar School, founded in 1624. The wide High Street is exceptionally fine, with much of its architecture ranging from Tudor to Georgian, while the alleyways leading off to the River Misbourne are also full of ancient houses. The 17thC market hall stands in the middle of the road, supported by arches above an open piazza, with a twin lock-up. The product of what has been called 'metroland', Amersham has a variety of buildings constituting a small history of suburbia, from Victorian villas and elegant Edwardian houses to the functional municipal housing of the 1950s.

2. Aylesbury 3 B3
An expanding town with many grim new office buildings, Aylesbury's town centre still retains its traditional charm. The market square is rich in ancient inns and courtyards and has an impressive clock tower, while in the streets around there are many curious winding passages and old houses. The Bull's Head has a 350-year-old barn for a garage. But the premier inn is the King's Head, which has a magnificent medieval leaded window as well as Cromwell's chair. Built in the 15thC, it still has the atmosphere of a medieval inn. The church was restored by Sir Giles Gilbert Scott in the 19thC, but retains its 13thC central tower and the 14thC Lady chapel. Near the church is the Bucks County Museum with many local Roman remains.
An interesting sight is the end of the Aylesbury arm of the Grand Union Canal, *W of town centre.* From this spot in 1832 departed Aylesbury's first emigrants to America: paupers on the verge of starvation, they travelled by narrow boat to Liverpool and thence to America, many of them dying on the way.

3. Beaconsfield 3 C5
The centre of Beaconsfield is an undistinguished modern shopping area that could be anywhere, but the original village is still pleasant. Here the wide, tree-lined High

Street supports many venerable coaching inns including the Royal White Hart, where Elizabeth I stayed. The striking landmark of St Mary and All Saints Church is less impressive inside due to a ruthless restoration of 1869, but the Old Rectory of 1500 is charming.

4. Buckingham 3 B2
Chosen by King Alfred as Buckinghamshire's county town in AD888 when he divided England into shires, Buckingham has never grown very great, but remains a pleasant country town set among green meadows and ringed on three sides by the river. The great market place in the centre of the town, embodying the ancient bull-ring, is a reminder of the rich wool trade of former days: the trade declined because of the town's inaccessibility. The red-brick town hall is crowned by the gilded swan of Buckingham. Close by is the little Norman chantry which became a classroom in the 16thC grammar school founded by Edward VI. Castle House on its hill

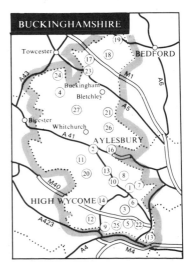

was where Catherine of Aragon, still then the happy wife of Henry VIII, was once entertained, and where Charles I presided over a council of war.

5. Burnham 3 C5

Famous throughout the world for Burnham Beeches, the noble 600-acre forest crowded with marvellously gnarled, weird-looking trees, some 1,000 years old. One of England's most acclaimed beauty spots, it was once part of the Chiltern forests. The remains of Burnham Abbey, founded in 1266, can be seen to the south of the village. Burnham is an ancient settlement where in Saxon times the kings of Mercia often lived. The church is 700 years old, with magnificent wood panels in the transept and on the altar rails. The town's many delightful old houses were haunts of poets and writers like Gray, Sheridan and John Evelyn.

6. Chalfont St Giles 3 C4

Lovely village in the pleasant valley of the River Misbourne. It was here that the 17thC poet John Milton, old, blind and in disgrace under Charles II for supporting Cromwell, escaped from the plague in 1665 and found peace in his last years. Here he wrote part of 'Paradise Lost' (for which he received the princely sum of £5), and 'Paradise Regained'. His tiny cottage, the only existing home in which he lived and worked, is now a Milton museum. *Open most days; closed mid-winter.*

Milton's Cottage

The church is charming, with 600-year-old ballflowers around the doorway, a display of 14thC paintings and 13thC angels looking down from the roofs. In the churchyard lies the circus man, Bertram Mills, remembered also for his widespread charity.

7. Chenies 3 C4

4m NW of Rickmansworth. Ancient home and resting place of one of Britain's greatest aristocratic families, the Russells, Dukes of Bedford. Chenies was laid out as a 'model village' for estate workers by the family in about 1850, and is a neat, simple place set in the lovely valley of the River Chess. Now only one wing of Chenies Manor House, once a vast Tudor mansion, remains, but with its warm red-brick and mullioned windows, it's still impressive. The church is mainly 15thC, and has specimens of styles from Norman font to Victorian hammer-beam roof. The chief glory is the Bedford Chapel, where through the glass grille you can glimpse the tombs of 400 years of Russells among the banners and marble, right from the founder, John Russell, who rose from a farmhouse to the position of royal adviser and earl in the early 16thC. Among later scions of this remarkable family have been the builder of much of Bloomsbury in London and chief drainer of the Fens, the introducer of the first Reform Bill into Parliament, a notorious pro-Hitler duke of the 1930s, and one of Britain's most notable philosophers. *House open certain days, summer.*

8. Chesham 3 C4

In the Middle Ages Chesham was regarded as part of Amersham and only won recognition as a separate town in 1454: the old rivalry can still sometimes be seen at football matches! Chesham has always been a more industrial and sober place than Amersham, with a long history of Puritanism – 15thC Lollards, 17thC Quakers, 18thC Baptists and 19thC Congregationalists were all strong here, and the town abounds in Victorian chapels – and on the whole Chesham is not as historical or

picturesque as its neighbour. But the old part of the town contains The Bury, a fine 18thC brick mansion, and Church Street has many old and architecturally distinguished buildings. The parish Church of St Mary was sensitively restored by Sir Giles Gilbert Scott in 1869, the best features of the old building being preserved.

9. Cliveden 3 C5

Nr Burnham Beeches. The most magnificent of the many mansions around Burnham Beeches, the present Victorian Cliveden is the third house to stand on this site. The first was built by the second Duke of Buckingham, a powerful Restoration nobleman and friend of Charles II. Cliveden has had a continuous reputation as a centre of political intrigue. In the 18thC it was the home of Frederick, Prince of Wales, and the centre of plots against his father, George II. It was under his patronage that 'Rule Britannia' was written by Thomas Arne, to be performed in the grounds in the 1730s. As the home of the powerful Astor family the house was the centre of the 'Cliveden set', who were said, with justice that may be disputed, to favour appeasement of Hitler. And in the early 1960s, it was the scene of the scandals involving John Profumo, Stephen Ward and Christine Keeler.

The house remains magnificent, and is now let to Stanford University. From its steep ascent there are magnificent views of the Thames. The huge grounds have many leafy arbours, and you may well round a corner to be confronted by a statue of Prince Albert wearing a kilt. *Open weekends, summer; gardens daily, all year.*

10. Great Missenden and Little Missenden 3 C4

Both medieval villages of much the same age, which have diverged over the course of history. Little Missenden is very quiet and small, extremely unspoilt, with ancient thatched cottages standing unselfconsciously by solid Georgian houses. Parts of the parish church go back to the 12thC, and it is famous for the magnificent series of 13thC wall-paintings, unearthed in 1931.

Great Missenden is very different. Almost a small market town, its smart High Street sports an amazing variety of architectural styles from Tudor to 19thC, managing somehow to create an impression of essential modernity. An ancient monument is Missenden Abbey, first established as an abbey in 1138, dissolved at the Reformation and rebuilt in 1814 in the then fashionable Gothic style.

11. Haddenham 3 B4

3m NE of Thames. There's a Mediterranean air to this large village of Georgian and Victorian houses interspersed with palatial modern residences. Many Haddenham houses have wichert walls (wichert, a chalk marl mixed with straw and water, is a traditional building material in this area). The parish church dates from about 1215 and has a 13thC tower and a 15thC chapel. By it is an old duck pond that was the traditional home of the Buckinghamshire industry of duck-breeding, once flourishing but now almost died out. Church Farm House is a well-preserved 15thC building, and Bone House has knuckle-bones of sheep on the outside walls.

12. Hambleden 3 C4

Beech-surrounded village like a scene transported out of old England: in its heart is the village pump under two large chestnut trees, by it, the big square with gabled houses and timbered cottages, and standing a little apart, the ancient church. By the Thames is one of the few remaining weather-boarded water-mills along the river. The Romans were here, and their tiles, mosaic floors and pottery can be found in a splendid little local museum. In Hambleden was born the Earl of Cardigan, the man who led the Charge of the Light

Brigade, and in the churchyard is a memorial to W. H. Smith, the man who founded the High Street chainstores.

13. Hampden House   3 C4
Great Hampden. Former home of John Hampden, defender of English liberties. A member of Parliament in 1636, he refused to pay Charles I's new tax, ship money, and was tried for it, only to be acquitted a popular hero and bring closer by his action the eventual Civil War. Much of the present exterior is 18thC, although the roof is medieval and Hampden would have known the gallery in the long hall. The house is now a girls' school, but with its tall chimneys, castellated roof and ivy-covered porches, is certainly worth a look.

14. High Wycombe   3 B5
Almost a new creation after modern wholesale replanning and expansion, some picturesque buildings remain in the new setting, mostly found in or close to the old High Street. There is a handsome guildhall of 1757 with an assembly hall, and a Robert Adam market hall. Many famous people have known Wycombe: Dr Johnson stayed here, Wesley preached here, Cobbett rode through on one of his rural rides (wondering in his customary querulous fashion why it was called 'High' Wycombe, it quite plainly being in a valley), while Disraeli and Churchill gave frequent speeches here. Just north of the town is **Hughendon Manor**, the home for over 30 years of one of Britain's most colourful politicians, Benjamin Disraeli, and his wife, Mary Anne. The house was originally Jacobean, but was extravagantly 'Gothicised' by Disraeli. In spite of the rather painful architecture involved, it remains charming, reflecting the curiously engaging private side of this rather slippery politician. Here Disraeli wrote his novels and entertained friends, while Mary Anne delighted in her peacocks. Here, too, Disraeli died. His library is still exactly as it was, and you can see his desk, writing paper and pens as well as letters from Queen Victoria. Across the valley is the red granite monument Disraeli built to his father, Isaac. *Open most days, summer.*

15. Iver Church   3 C5
Iver. A highly historic church with Roman bricks in its Saxon nave, and there are Norman arches, medieval art and Tudor monuments. Especially lovely are parts of the chancel, with its richly moulded pointed arch, and the graceful round columns of the double piscina and triple sedilia.

16. Mentmore Towers   3 B3
Nr Aston Clinton. Built in the mid 19thC by the great Victorian architect, Joseph Paxton, for the Baron Mayer Anschel de Rothschild, scion of the German Jewish family which had sprung to fame as the greatest of international bankers. Paxton used the Jacobean style, and the main ground floor rooms are richly decorated, if sparsely furnished. Once famous for its artistic treasures, most of these were sold in 1978 and the house is now the 'Seat of the World Government of the Age of Enlightenment' and the national centre of Transcendental Meditation. *Open certain days.*

Mentmore Towers

17. Milton Keynes   3 B2
Brand new city, created in 1967, it has as yet little history of its own and may be viewed, according to opinion, as an interesting urban experiment, or a planning disaster. The ancient villages of the area, pleasant little places like Simpson or Woughton, are being allowed to remain, and to become integrated into the urban structure. Also, the Grand Union Canal which flows through the town is being used, with canal-side walks, lakes and lagoons: a fascinating environmental idea. These features will certainly help to ensure that the legacy of the past is not entirely blotted out at Milton Keynes.

18. Newport Pagnell   3 B2
Built of brick of many colours but predominantly red, Newport Pagnell still retains the air of a 17th and 18thC market town. Many dignified houses from that time stand by the 14thC church with its pinnacled Tudor tower and ancient graveyard. It was first mentioned in Domesday Book as a town, and has been quietly flourishing ever since. There are two dignified old Nonconformist chapels, one Methodist and one Baptist. The Swan Inn, which has a lovely 17thC staircase, is first mentioned in 1543. Tickfield Abbey was the great medieval religious foundation nearby and fragments of it remain incorporated in a modern building, while Tickford Bridge is a sturdy iron construction of 1810, the oldest iron bridge in Britain still in daily use.

Tickford Bridge, Newport Pagnell

19. Olney   3 B1
Beloved home of the 18thC poet William Cowper in the last and happiest 19 years of his melancholy and madness-haunted life. His charming letters and pastoral poems give a wonderful picture of 18thC life in this remote country town. The house where he lived as a guest of his friend Mrs Unwin, is tall and ugly, although the garden where he often sat is lovely. The house is now a Cowper museum. Olney is a quiet place of grey stone through which the reed-fringed Ouse flows calmly. All has an air of peace: Cowper wrote in the 18thC: 'Occurrences here are as rare as cucumbers at Christmas', and you can still believe it to be true. *Museum open most days, or by arrangement.*

20. Princes Risborough   3 B4
Quiet but pleasant little town bursting with historic houses: some timbered, some thatched, some gabled, some 16thC timber-framed. Norman St Mary's Church was rebuilt in the 13thC and close to it lies the Mount, an earthworks thought to represent the site of a Saxon camp. The Manor House is early 18thC with a very beautiful 17thC oak staircase. In the centre of the town is the old brick market house with open arches where a weekly market was once held.

21. Stewkley, Church of St Michael and All Angels   3 C3
Stewkley. Built during the reign of Henry II, when Norman architecture was rising to its 12thC peak of majesty and richness of ornament, it is like a small cathedral, unbelievably imposing for this small village. Only the porch and vestry are modern: the pinnacles and gargoyles are mostly 14thC, but otherwise it is Norman. The central tower, on each side a beautiful arcade, is especially magnificent. The west front has a beautifully carved central doorway, and the whole interior is full of sculpted splendour.

22. Stoke Poges 3 C5

Prosperous commuter village famous for its golf-courses, but with a place in English history and culture. By the Church of St Giles is the country churchyard that Thomas Gray is said to have immortalised in his famous 'Elegy'. Indeed it is wonderfully peaceful, although only about two miles from the busy centre of Slough. There is a monument to the poet in the fields, and he and his mother and aunts rest under the south window of the 13thC church with its beautiful timber porch. Look for the kind of medieval bicycle featured in the stained glass window. Stoke Park, originally the Elizabethan manor house of the great lawyer, Sir Edward Coke, was rebuilt in the 18thC and is now a golf club.

23. Stony Stratford 3 B2

Old and prosperous market town but with a faint air of melancholy, it now forms one of the northern limits of the city of Milton Keynes. Nonetheless, it's an individual place, steeped in history. The body of Queen Eleanor, beloved wife of Edward I, rested here in the late 13thC on its mournful procession to London. The elder of the two Princes in the Tower stayed here on his way to London, expecting to be king, but only to be thrown into the Tower by Richard III when he reached his destination. Stony Stratford has always been a staging post: it is on Roman Watling Street (now Telford's great 19thC road to Holyhead), and the town has many memories of coaching days. The two splendid old inns, the Cock and the Bull, were great centres of gossip here, giving rise to the expression 'Cock and Bull Story'. In the peaceful market square there is a tree under which John Wesley preached in the 18thC. Only the tower of the graceful medieval Church of St Giles remains, as Stony was swept by two disastrous fires in the 18thC.

24. Stowe School 3 B2

Stowe, nr Buckingham. Stowe School was founded in 1922 by the notable public school educationalist, J. F. Roxburgh. The magnificent building in which it stands is, in fact, an 18thC palace, then home of the Temple family of Stowe, who became dukes of Buckingham. Especially notable are the huge grounds, designed by Bridgeman and Kent, full of sculptures and monuments such as the Temple of British Worthies, the Gothic Temple, the Palladian Arch, the sham castle and countless grottoes and follies – a true 18thC extravaganza. The exterior of the house, on which Vanbrugh, Soane and Robert Adam worked, is magnificent with its great sculptures and colonnades. Despite the fine, 18thC Marble Salon, inside it is now more school than palace, and the rooms that once knew 18thC gossip now resound to schoolboys. *School open by arrangement; grounds open certain days, summer.*

25. Taplow 3 C5

Stately, largely Georgian village, with Victorian railway development superadded in the middle of one of the Thames's most gorgeous stretches. The Saxon church has vanished and the present church is 20thC, while Taplow Court, with fake Tudor gables and tower, is in fact mid Victorian. Taplow belongs also to ancient history: a much older house stood on this site, and in the grounds of the house a Saxon tumulus marks where the 5thC Saxon king, Aella, clashed with the last Romano–British forces left in England, finally defeating them after a struggle lasting 12 years. Aella built a house in Taplow and was buried here. The treasures of his tomb, including a great iron sword and a silver drinking-horn, are now in the British Museum.

26. Wing, Ascott House 3 C3

Lovely timber-framed house built originally in 1606, but much altered when bought by Leopold Rothschild in 1874. It now belongs to the National Trust, but is still used as a family home and has a restful, pleasant air. The house is full of treasures, which include a fine collection of Dutch masters, an outstanding collection of Oriental pottery, Chippendale chairs and many Rothschild heirlooms. The charming grounds, with their French formal garden, are also well worth seeing. *Open certain days, summer.*

26. Wing Church 3 C3

Wing. The finest Saxon church in Buckinghamshire, a very impressive structure for its age, crowned with a 15thC tower. The nave is clerestoried, but with Saxon walls in the nave and chancel. Wonderfully mysterious is the Saxon crypt, 1,300 years old, but only opened up last century. The church is rich in monuments, which include 15thC brasses and 16thC tombs to the Dormer family.

27. Winslow 3 B3

Standing gracefully above its fertile valley, it was a home to the kings of Mercia in Saxon times, but carries its many years with ease and grace. It has many winding ways and 16thC thatched cottages, while the graceful hall, built in 1700 for a Secretary of the Treasury, keeps its beauty intact. The Church of St Lawrence has a fine 15thC porch leading into the clerestoried interior and the stump of a medieval cross pokes up its head in the yew-fringed churchyard. There is also a Baptist chapel of 1695, very interesting considering its age, built by the famous Baptist preacher Keach. It is typical of the severe outlook of those days that when Keach published a book saying Baptist children needed play as well as prayer he was sentenced to spend two hours in the pillory and his 'seditious and scandalous book' was publicly barred.

SOUTH EAST ENGLAND

The history of England's south east corner goes back a very, very long way. The remains of the first south easterner known to us were found in the gravel of Swanscombe, near Gravesend, and are more than a quarter of a million years old. Julius Caesar, landing in 'Cantium', found it to be culturally on a level with Roman Gaul and far ahead of the rest of Pagan Europe. And when St Augustine landed with 40 monks in AD597, he found an established kingdom under the Jutish Ethelbert. Being the nearest part of the British Isles to the mainland of Europe, the three south-eastern counties have borne the brunt of invasion and threatened invasion: three successful invasions, Roman, Saxon and Norman, and three unsuccessful ones, Spanish, French and German, have left their mark upon the land. Two thousand years of defence are summarised in earthwork and stone – first an arc of hill-forts facing the Continent, then an arc of castles: Pevensey, Hastings, Bramber, Lewes, Arundel and Chichester.

Subsequently, this region has been the first to feel the influence of important travellers – royalty, prelates and statesmen – who have passed through it on their way to London and other parts of the kingdom. Never cut off or isolated, Kent, Surrey and Sussex have always been lively, open to new ideas, fashions and customs, and yet (with the cynicism bred of long experience) never overwhelmed by them.

The south east really took off as a fashionable area from the 18thC. A time of peace and prosperity after the Civil War, the commercial development of the country hit this part in the most pleasurable ways. Two crazes in particular developed: taking the waters and bathing in the sea. Roads were considerably improved to carry the elite to health-giving spas such as Tunbridge Wells, or to lively resorts like Brighton, following the example of George IV. The exuberant and frivolous Royal Pavilion remains as a symbol of this new age. Later, Wellington's defeat of Napoleon paved a safe path to the Continent, and roads leading to the coast served a further purpose by taking young men of good standing for their obligatory tour. Many of the quaint inns we associate with this area were a result of this new, mobile society. Coaching inns prospered as weary, hungry travellers found comfort in a warm bed and a hearty meal along the way. Today, the tradition of welcome is upheld. On a Sunday lunchtime, whether small-talking with a gin-and-jag stockbroker from Surrey, or propping up the bar with a beer-and-bike farmer from Sussex, the warm atmosphere of 'the local' will be as strong in the 'cold, unfriendly' south east as anywhere in Britain.

Prosperity has made the south east the playground of England. Cultural pleasures are catered for thoroughly. Surrey has an abundance of concert halls and theatres, Kent has some of the most romantic castles in Britain, and in Sussex are magnificent stately homes. South easterners are spoiled further – parts of the coast here claim the highest average daily rate of sunshine in the country. This wealth of culture and activity draws a new breed of 'invaders' from the Continent – but this time brandishing weapons no more threatening than the latest Japanese camera.

The whole area is dominated by two ranges of chalk hills – the North and the South Downs – while Wealdon clay forms much of the low-lying region. Just south of the North Downs are the secondary ridges formed of greensand, including Leith Hill, crowned with a folly to make it the highest point in the area. South east England is very well watered and most of the rivers rise in the Wealdon Hills and cut their way through the North or South Downs to join the Thames or to flow into the sea.

The landscape has refused to be overwhelmed by the constant invasions of the past. Every step in the sequence can still be identified today: Stone Age cave, Bronze Age burial mound, Iron Age camp, Roman villa, Saxon church and parish, Norman castle and cathedral. There are hundreds of timber-framed buildings, some dating back to the 13thC, and the Roman roads, the pilgrims' ways, can still be followed. Visual history is spread all around.

Arriving by sea from Europe, you will see all the basic Englishness of this part of the world, from the white cliffs at Dover to the trim hedges, rolling downland and cosy cottages. Now Britain is a part of the European community this is, more than ever, England's doorstep to the Continent. But the distinctive landscape – the backcloth to all this human activity – though modified through the centuries, has not changed fundamentally. The vulnerable and lovely countryside needs to be taken care of to protect it from the advance of the metropolis, motorways and juggernauts, but miraculously the region essentially retains its rural nature.

Near the junction of the three counties is Ashdown Forest, which once formed part of the huge Wealden forest of Anderida. Iron Age man lived there, the Romans marched across it, the Norman lords hunted in it, the monasteries grazed their sheep on it – and the ancient rights persist to the present day. This unenclosed tract of primeval heathland and woodland is the very heart of the south eastern counties and the symbol of their continuity. Look across it, and you could be living now – or 2,000 years ago. The view is the same.

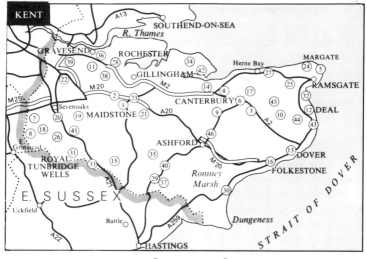

KENT

1. Allington Castle 3 G6
2m NE of Maidstone. Beautifully set in dense woodland, this is a late 13thC moated castle with a castellated curtain wall, a gatehouse and a fine Great Hall. Though much restored earlier this century, much of the original fabric has been retained. Named after Lord Conway of Allington, its former owner, the castle now belongs to the Order of Carmelites. To be seen inside are some valuable religious paintings, a collection of ikons, sculptures, and a priest's hole which was used during the reign of Elizabeth I.

Allington Castle

2. Aylesford, The Carmelite Friary 3 G6
3m NW of Maidstone. Well-restored 13th–14thC Carmelite house with cloisters. The original building was destroyed at the Dissolution, but much 13th–15thC work remains. See the monks' excellent pottery, the rose gardens and the sculpture and ceramic exhibition. Just to the north is Kit's Coty House, a neolithic burial chamber of c3,500BC comprising two standing stones and a third supporting a capstone at one end. 'Coty' derives from 'cot', meaning a little house.

3. Barham 3 J7
5m SE of Canterbury, off A2. There was a confrontation here between Romans and Britons, with barrows and ditches clearly visible today to prove it. Centuries later, Charles I picnicked with his wife-to-be on their way back from Dover to London. Nearby Broome Park is a fine mansion designed by Inigo Jones, and was later occupied by Lord Kitchener. *View from outside only.* Notice the church, with its distinctive copper spire.

4. Boughton, Monchelsea Place 3 G7
Once the home of Sir Thomas Wyatt, a leader of the revolt against Mary I, this is a battlemented Elizabethan house with Regency additions. There is a collection of historical dresses and vehicles.
Pause on the main staircase and look at the unusual pattern of the stained glass windows.

Originally in the church, they were smashed during the Civil War and reassembled here, only to be shattered again during the Second World War. The gardens contain deer and command magnificent views. *Open certain days, summer.*

5. Broadstairs 3 K6
Popular seaside town, dominated by the ghost of Charles Dickens with whom it has many associations. Bleak House, *Fort Rd*, was Dickens's summer retreat for many years, inspiring 'Bleak House' and 'David Copperfield'. Originally called Fort House, it's a castellated building standing above the harbour. Much of Dickens's own furniture remains plus some original letters, drawings and photographs. *Open summer.*
Across the bay the **Dickens House Museum**, *Victoria Parade*, the original of Betsy Trotwood's home. It contains Dickens's letters and possessions, Dickensian prints, costumes and Victoriana. The parlour is described in 'David Copperfield'. *Open summer.*

6. Canterbury 3 J6
If you sense antiquity in the air here – despite today's cars and crowds – you will be right. Canterbury is one of the oldest centres of habitation in Britain.
The site had already been occupied for 350 years when the Romans arrived in AD43. They landed on the south side of Pagwell Bay and advanced westwards, to find a settlement of the Belgae tribe at a key crossing point on the River Stour. This they turned into their encampment fortress of Durovernum. Long stretches of the town walls survive, built in the 13th and 14thC on Roman fortifications, and the picturesque 14thC West Gate, the only survivor of seven former gates to the city, has a Museum of Arms and Armour.
The poet Christopher Marlowe, who wrote 'Dr Faustus', was born here in 1564, and the King's School, where he was educated, still stands. One of the oldest schools in England, it has an unusual exterior Norman staircase.
Worth looking out for is Eastbridge (St Thomas's) Hospital, *High Street*. It is one of the oldest buildings in the city, dating from the 12thC, and has been used as almshouses since the 16thC. Inside, are a 13thC mural and many treasures, and there is also a vaulted crypt with two chapels.
The Poor Priests' Hospital, *Stour Street*, is an interesting 14thC building, now the

Regimental Museum of the Buffs. *View from outside only.*

Bombing in the Second World War uncovered a Roman town house, with a mosaic floor at Roman Pavement, *Butchery Lane.* There's a display of Roman pottery, coins and jewellery. *Open weekdays.* Not to be missed is the Royal Museum, *The Beaney, High St,* with the archaeology, geology and natural history of the area, including a hoard of Roman silver spoons, Roman coins, Anglo-Saxon glass and jewellery with the silver 'Canterbury Cross'.

The ruins of **St Augustine's Abbey** are one of the most important ecclesiastical sites in England. Layers of ruins include Saxon and Norman work and the medieval Benedictine abbey. Straddling the river in a series of arches, **Grayfriars**, *off Stour Street,* consists of the restored remains of the first Franciscan house in England, built in the 13thC. *View from outside only.*

6. Canterbury Cathedral 3 J6

This was the cradle of Christianity in Saxon England. The first cathedral was built in AD597 by St Augustine, when he arrived from Rome in the Saxon town of Cant-wara-byrig – 'the borough of the men of Kent'. Here he baptised King Ethelbert of Kent and so paved the way for the conversion of all England to Christianity. Soon after the Norman Conquest, work began on the present cathedral, on the site of the original. In response to Henry II's outburst 'who will deliver me from this turbulent priest?' Thomas a Becket was murdered before the high altar in 1170. Four years later the penitent Henry walked barefoot to the cathedral – the first of a steady stream of pilgrims to Becket's shrine. Pilgrimages continued until Henry VIII dissolved the monasteries in 1538, and the shrine was destroyed. The place of Becket's martyrdom is now marked by a plaque on the floor. The cathedral was damaged again both in the Civil War and the Second World War, but its surviving medieval stained glass is among the finest in the country. Don't leave without visiting the crypt, the oldest part of the building and the largest Norman crypt in Britain. Also look at the Trinity Chapel, which contains the site of the original shrine of Thomas a Becket, and the tombs of Henry IV and Edward, the Black Prince. Note, too, the lovely 12thC choir with its 14thC screen. Canterbury Cathedral is the Mother Church of Anglicans throughout the world.

7. Chartwell 3 E6

2m S of Westerham. The former home of Sir Winston Churchill (from 1924 until his death), with 79 acres of parkland, Chartwell was bought by a group of his friends and given to the National Trust in 1946. The rooms, furnished much as they were during the time that Sir Winston and Lady Churchill lived there, reflect his career and wide interests, and two have been arranged as a museum. In the garden is the famous wall Sir Winston built and also his studio, containing many of his paintings. The lovely terraced gardens descend towards a lake adorned with rare black swans. *Open most days, summer.*

8. Chiddingstone Castle 3 F7

5m E of Edenbridge. A 17th–18thC house in a park with lake and caves, adjoining the National Trust village of Chiddingstone. Much of the interior retains the original panelling and inside are pictures, furnishings, relics of the Royal House of Stuart, Japanese lacquer, metal-work, armour, and a collection of Buddhist images and paintings. There is a particularly outstanding collection of Japanese swords. *Open most days, summer.*

9. Chilham Castle 3 J6

5m SW of Canterbury. A hexagonal Jacobean castle, probably one of the earliest works of Inigo Jones. The 18thC landscaped gardens, designed by Capability Brown, contain the Battle of Britain Museum with Spitfire and Messerschmitt engines, propellors, airframes, photographs, uniforms, badges and swords. *View house from outside only; gardens open most days, summer.*

Chilham Castle

10. Chillenden Windmill 3 J6

½m N of Chillenden. Post mill originally erected in 1868, well restored in 1958. Post mills were built from the 12th to the 19thC with little change of design. The rectangular boarded body is turned around on a central post to face the wind. At the foot of the post are horizontal beams and diagonal bars to carry the weight of the uprights and masonry. In Chillenden Mill, these bars are left open, so this is an 'open post mill'. *Open by arrangement.*

11. Cobham Hall 3 G6

Cobham. Set in a park with fine trees, this is a 16thC mansion with later additions, including work by Inigo Jones and Wyatt. Elizabethan fireplaces and magnificent ceilings. The building is now a school. *Open certain days, summer.*

11. Cobham, Owletts 3 G6

A red-brick house of Charles II's reign, with five cottages and 25 acres of garden and orchard. There is a magnificent staircase and a plasterwork ceiling. Built by a farmer, its appeal lies in its modest character and attractive garden. *Open certain days, summer.*

12. Deal Castle 3 K7

A Tudor castle, with a dry Tudor rose-shaped moat, built by Henry VIII. It was one of five castles which were quickly built as a defence against possible invasion by the great Roman Catholic powers of Europe – the others were at Sandown, Walmer, Sandgate and Camber. Deal was one of the most powerful and is among the best preserved today. The massive central citadel houses exhibits of Iron Age weapons, early pottery and relics of Deal's history.

13. Dover 3 K7

Bustling, breezy front door to Europe, with the white cliffs on one side and the mighty castle dominating the other. Much of the town was rebuilt after the Second World War, but notice the 13thC Hall of Dieu, formerly a hostel where the Continental pilgrims used to stay before setting out on the road to Canterbury. The road still follows the route of the Roman Watling Street. The museum *Ladywell* contains exhibits of local history, early furniture, textiles, pictures, ceramics, coins, militaria, Victoriana and a collection of butterflies and moths. *Open most days.*
Crabble Mill, *Lower Rd*, is a six-storey water-mill built in 1812 to provide flour for the local garrison at the time of Napoleon's invasion scare. The mill was restored to working order in 1973. *Open certain days, summer.*

13. Dover Castle 3 K7

High up on the famous white cliffs, Dover Castle stands frowning like a clap of thunder, commanding this important harbour. Despite later invasions, Roman influence survives strongly here. The castle is 12thC Norman, but built on Roman foundations, and the

Normans left intact the stone Roman 'pharos', or lighthouse – the earliest in Britain – which stood outside the Roman walled city of Dubris. Peverell's Tower, constructed shortly after the Norman Conquest, is the oldest part of the castle. The keep and underground passages can be visited: you will see the ancient well, the splendid banqueting and main halls, and the huge kitchens.

14. Faversham, Chart Gunpowder Mills   3 H6
South Road. A late 18thC mill, believed to be the oldest of its kind in the world, is a reminder that this town was once the centre of the gunpowder industry. It supplied Nelson at Trafalgar and Wellington at Waterloo. Now well restored. *Open by arrangement.*

Chart Gunpowder Mills, Faversham

14. Faversham Society Heritage Centre   3 H6
Fleur de Lis, Preston Street. Local history and architecture going back over 1,000 years are vividly illustrated by unique displays, audio-visual programmes and antiques, in a former 18thC coaching inn.

15. Finchcocks   3 G7
1½m W of Goudhurst, off A262. Internationally known as a centre for early music, this fine Georgian house contains a magnificent collection of old musical instruments. Concerts are held in summer and informal music serenades you on your tour of the house. Set in lovely parkland, Finchcocks provides a rare opportunity to see and hear music performed on the instruments for which it was written. Entrance includes a conducted tour, demonstrations and a short recital. *Open certain days, summer, or by arrangement.*

Finchcocks, Goudhurst

16. Folkestone   3 J7
One of the most attractive of English seaside resorts, with narrow cobbled streets leading down to the original fishermen's quarters near the harbour. The Leas, a picturesque cliff walk, is ablaze with flowers for most of the year.
Famous men who have lived in Folkestone include William Harvey and H. G. Wells. Harvey, who discovered the circulation of the blood, was born here in 1578 and is commemorated by a window in the church of St Mary. H. G. Wells wrote some of his best

works at Spade House, Sandgate, now a restaurant.

17. Fordwich   3 J6
Worth visiting for its delightful old town hall, one of the smallest in Britain, timber-framed, overlooking the River Stour and complete with ducking stool!

18. Hever Castle   3 F7
3m SE of Edenbridge, off B2026. A miniature castle on the River Eden, scene of one of the most famous and influential romances in English history.
Originally a manor house, for prestige reasons Hever was converted by a nobleman in the 13thC into a residential castle with moat. In 1462 this castle was bought by the Boleyn family, and it was here that Henry VIII courted Anne Boleyn who became his second wife and the mother of Elizabeth I. The great dining hall is 40ft long, the courtyard on the scale of a country inn, but the interior contains magnificent panelling and carved screens. The spectacular gardens were laid out by the Astor family, who bought the castle in 1903 and still live there, surrounded by a lake and a magnificent Italian garden with Roman statues, fountains and topiary work. *Open most days, summer.*

Hever Castle

19. Ightham Mote   3 F6
Ightham, nr Sevenoaks. Delightfully romantic, this perfect 14th–15thC moated manor house is set among trees and meadows with peacocks in the grounds. The name derives not, as might be assumed, from the moat, but from the moot or council that met here in medieval times. There is a Tudor chapel with painted ceilings and the Great Hall, crypt and solar room remain much as they were. Ightham Mote was the source of inspiration for Anya Seton's romantic novel 'Green Darkness'. *Open certain days.*

20. Knole House   3 F7
S of Sevenoaks. Set in an undulating blanket of green, Knole House is surrounded by the deer, old oaks and beeches of its extensive park. The house is one of the largest and most famous country mansions in England. It was begun by Thomas Bourchier, Archbishop of Canterbury, in 1456. Queen Elizabeth bestowed it on Thomas Sackville, first Earl of Dorset, in about 1603 and it has remained in the family ever since.
The state rooms contain a large collection of pictures including notable works by Reynolds, Van Dyck and Gainsborough. Lavishly furnished and richly decorated, the rare rugs, tapestries and furniture of the 17th–18thC create a spectacle of ancient splendour. Of the 365 rooms, don't miss the Venetian and Ambassador's Room, the King's Room with silver furniture and a splendid state bed, the Reynolds Room, the Ball Room, the Cartoon Gallery and the richly furnished Brown Gallery. Note the magnificent Jacobean staircase. *Open most days, summer.*

21. Leeds Castle   3 H6
Leeds, Nr Maidstone, off A20. With a fairy-tale setting, standing romantically on three islands encircled by a lake, this gem of a castle has a long and dramatic history. Built originally of wood, it was named after Led, Chief Minister of Ethelbert IV, King of Kent, in AD857.

Among its many royal owners were Edward I who gave it to his beloved Eleanor of Castile and Henry V who presented it to Catherine of Valois – hence Leeds became known as the Lady's Castle. Henry VIII's first wife, Catherine of Aragon, lived here and Elizabeth I was a prisoner in the castle before she became queen. Passing through many hands, it housed French prisoners of war in the 17thC and finally was bought in 1926 by Lady Baillie, who made the castle's restoration her life's work.

It was Henry VIII who transformed the ancient medieval fortress to a splendid royal palace. His magnificent 75ft-long Banqueting Hall contains a remarkably fine 16thC oak folding table. Other treasures include a 15thC Flemish tapestry which is a rare example of medieval weaving, a 14thC Florentine altar piece, and a collection of Impressionist paintings.

Within the 400 acres of surrounding parkland are a wildwood garden and avaries. Rare swans, geese and ducks enjoy the lakes and browse beside sloping lawns and flower-carpeted woodlands. *Open most days, summer.*

Leeds Castle

22. Lullingstone Castle   3 F6
An 18thC castle in extensive grounds with a gateway dating from the reign of Henry VII and a dining room which was used by Queen Anne. It was the first large-scale building to be built of brick throughout with cut brick for detail. Inside is some fine panelling, the carved balustrade of the staircase incorporating the crests of the Hart family and the state drawing room with its Elizabethan ceiling. Look out for the ancient church of St Botolph in the grounds, which was restored in the reign of Edward III. *Open certain days, summer.*

22. Lullingstone Roman Villa   3 F6
Remains of a fine Roman villa with tessellated pavement and wall-paintings dating from the 1st–5thC, one of the most important archaeological finds in Britain. The excavations have given unique information on the life of a wealthy country family in Roman times. The mosaic floor is in excellent condition and the height of the walls is an unusual feature.

The villa is also notable for having been occupied by Christians as early as the 4thC, and has a specially adapted private chapel, one of the earliest known places of Christian worship in Britain. The villa is completely roofed. Additional exhibits are displayed in an illuminated gallery.

23. Maidstone   3 G6
A busy, prosperous town, Maidstone was probably a Roman settlement but didn't rise to prominence until the 14thC. The Archbishops of Canterbury lived here until 1538, and their gabled Elizabethan and medieval palace can still be seen by the River Medway. The gatehouse dates from the 13th–14thC and may originally have been a mill-house.
Chillington Manor, *St Faith's St*, originally a Tudor manor, is now an art gallery and museum. It contains Anglo-Saxon jewellery,

glass and exhibits relating to the history of Kent. There is also a Japanese Room. *Open weekdays*. In the medieval Archbishop's stables, *Mill Street*, is a museum of carriages. *Open weekdays, summer.*

24. Margate   3 K5
Popular with wealthy Victorians, this was where, in the mid 18thC, bathing machines were first used, invented by a local Quaker. But Margate was in existence long before bathing became fashionable. Salmestone Grange is a restored 12thC monastic building belonging to the Canonesses of St Augustine. And Tudor House, *King Street*, is Margate's oldest domestic building. It dates from the early 16thC and has fine beams and moulded plaster ceilings. Neighbouring Westgate, with two sandy bays, is best for bathing.

25. Minster-in-Thanet   3 K6
Traditional landing place of the Anglo-Saxons and once an important market town, Minster-in-Thanet has many historical associations. The abbey is one of the oldest inhabited houses in Kent, dating from the 11thC. Alongside are the ruins of a 7thC nunnery, one of the first in England. The Church of St Mary is an exceptionally fine parish church, incorporating Norman work with Roman tiles and 15thC choir stalls. *View abbey from outside only.*

26. Penshurst Place
Penshurst. Famous throughout the world as the birthplace of that perfect knight, Sir Philip Sidney. From medieval times, wealthy families who wanted to live outside London but within easy reach of court and Parliament were attracted to the Weald, where they built fine houses or converted older castles. The result is that splendid houses are thicker on the ground here than anywhere else in Britain. And the greatest of these is probably Penshurst, whose history goes back 600 years. Penshurst was given to William Sidney by Edward VI in 1552. The famous Elizabethan courtier, soldier, diplomat and poet, Sir Philip Sidney, was born two years later and his family have lived there ever since. The present descendant is the Viscount De L'Isle. The house still retains most of its original character. Its oldest feature is probably the 14thC Barons Hall, a fine example, with chestnut beams and a minstrels' gallery. In the state dining room a table is permanently laid to display a Rockingham dinner service, made for William IV. The great state rooms are splendidly furnished and contain pictures, tapestries, china and rare silver. Housed in the Gothic crypt is a historic collection of arms and armour.

The famous toy museum will delight the children and there's also a Venture Playground and nature trail to keep them out of mischief. The adults can take a genteel turn about the Tudor gardens, and regard the ancient yew hedges and typical Kentish orchards. *Open most days, summer.*

Penshurst village is notable for the original Leicester Square, named after the Earl of Leicester, Queen Elizabeth I's favourite.

Penshurst Place

27. Reculver Roman Fort 3 J6
3m NE of Herne Bay. On Kent's north shore, the site of the Saxon invasions, there are partial remains of a 3rdC Roman fort on older foundations. Reculver is part of a chain of mighty Roman forts, girdling the coast of south east Britain and guarding the natural gateways. Each could hold a substantial garrison and adjoined a harbour from which a Roman fleet could operate.
There are also remains of a Norman church – only the towers are left standing – which was built on the site of a Saxon church.

28. Rochester 3 G6
The ancient cathedral city of Rochester has been immortalised by Charles Dickens who spent his boyhood here. Under its own and other names, it appears in his books more often than any other place except London. Eastgate House, *High Street*, is an Elizabethan house described in both 'Pickwick Papers' and the unfinished 'Edwin Drood'. It is now a museum of local history, including Dickens' relics. His Swiss chalet from Gads Hill stands in the grounds.
Dickens also mentions Restoration House, *Maidstone Road*, built in 1587, which became 'Satis House' in 'Great Expectations'. It is so called because Charles II stayed there on May 28th, 1660 on his way from Dover to London to take possession of the throne. The house was refaced with decorative cut brickwork in the 17thC. *View from outside only.*
In the High Street are the 17thC red-brick guildhall with an interesting copper weathervane and the Corn Exchange, with its huge clock overhanging the street.
Rochester is not the most beautiful of towns, but rather endearing and with a long history. The Romans settled by a ford across the River Medway and Rochester really developed in importance when it was made a bishopric by St Augustine in AD604.
Realising the strategic importance of the town, **Rochester Castle** was built during the reign of Henry I, to defend the Medway crossing. It has a storeyed keep dating from 1126–1139 which is one of the best preserved in England and makes a prominent landmark. King John took the castle from the rebelling barons after a siege in 1215. Climb to the top past the banqueting hall, Norman chapel and mural galleries for an excellent view of the city and surrounding countryside. *Open most days.*
The Cathedral Church of Christ and the Blessed Virgin Mary was rebuilt in the 11th–12thC. Its full beauty has been revealed by cleaning. Notice in particular the 14thC chapter room doorway and the impressive 12thC west front and nave. The crypt is one of the finest in the country. The Cathedral library is outstanding and contains the Textus Roffensis (1115–24), Coverdale's Bible (1535), the Great Bible (1539) and numerous ancient documents. The Garth, with spacious lawns enclosed by ancient walls, makes a peaceful setting for the Cathedral.

29. Rolvenden, C. M. Booth Collection of Historic Vehicles 3 G8
Falstaff Antiques, High St. A unique collection including Morgan three-wheel cars dating

C. M. Booth Collection of Historic Vehicles

from 1913 and the only known Humber tri-car of 1904. *Open most days.*

30. Romney, Hythe and Dymchurch Railway 3 J8
New Romney. Claiming to be the smallest public railway in the world, this is a mecca for railway enthusiasts of all ages. This fascinating narrow-gauge railway runs for 13½ miles and is useful as well as decorative, since no other train goes to Dungeness. There is an engine shed where you can inspect the brightly-coloured miniature locos at close quarters, and a very large model railway exhibition. *Open summer.*

31. Royal Tunbridge Wells 3 F7
The Bath of the south east, this fashionable spa of Regency days still retains its elegance. From a rural hamlet its popularity as a spa grew so rapidly that accommodation could not keep up and Queen Henrietta Maria (wife of Charles I) and her court had to camp in tents on the common because so few houses had yet been built. West of the common is a sandstone outcrop among the trees called High Rocks, a picnic area since the 17thC.
The Pantiles – famous, elegant and unique – is a colonnade of 18th and 19thC houses and shops, with Italianate columns and a raised music gallery, shaded by lime trees. Its name is derived from the tiles laid in the early 18thC to lead as a paved walk to the medicinal springs. These have been worn out and replaced, but 15 of the original tiles still remain today. The springs, discovered by Lord North in 1606, are at the end of the parade, in Bath Square, where the waters can still be drunk.
The 17thC Church of King Charles the Martyr has an impressive wooden cupola, a fine plaster ceiling and a clock of 1759.

32. Sandwich 3 K6
An ancient Cinque Port forsaken by the sea – now two miles away – preserving much of its old charm. There are many superb timbered houses which were built by the Flemish weavers who poured into Kent towards the end of the 16thC.
An excellent town to explore on foot, start at the Barbican, a medieval conical-towered gate where a toll is collected for crossing the River Stour. The guildhall, built in 1578 and little altered, has a permanent exhibition devoted to the Cinque Ports, including original documents and interesting paintings. *Open certain days, summer.*
With much Norman work still in evidence including its fine tower, the Church of St Clements is worth a visit. Note the early 15thC intricately-carved stone font.
Just to the north of Sandwich is **Richborough Castle and Fort**. The legions of Emperor Claudius under Aulus Plautus landed in AD43, established themselves at Richborough building a castle and a fort as a base for operations in the south east, and thrust inland to Canterbury. Guarding the Wantsum Channel, this is the beginning of the Roman Watling Street. Richborough was the key fort in the Saxon shore defences and the remains of the 12ft-thick and 24ft-high walls are among the best examples in England. There is an interesting museum on the site.

33. Scotney Castle 3 G7
1m SE of Lamberhurst. Rust-stained ruins of a 14thC castle. Surrounded by a water-lilied moat, it is worth visiting for its magnificent setting in a romantic landscape garden, created by the Hussey family in the 1840s. Deer roam freely in the 1,000 acres of wooded country – perfect for a picnic.

34. Sheppey Island 3 H6
London's holiday island, the 'Isle of Sheep' is a flat, bleak wilderness of crumbling loam. Privately owned it has been a favourite haunt of pirates from Vikings to French and Dutch.

Along the north coast are the remains of Minster Abbey, perched on one of the highest points above the old village of Minster. The Abbey was founded by the Saxon Queen Sexburga in AD670. Shurland Hall, where Henry VIII and Anne Boleyn spent their honeymoon, was once a stately home on the scale of Knole, but is now sadly being allowed to crumble away.

Bright, brash and breezy, Sheppey has extensive sands and is a lively night spot.

35. Sissinghurst Castle 3 G7
1m E of Sissinghurst. In the Seven Years War, 3,000 French prisoners were put into this Tudor manor house: they called it a 'chateau' and the name stuck.

The badly-neglected manor house was rescued in 1930 by Sir Harold Nicolson the critic, and his wife, the writer Vita Sackville-West. They restored much of the building and created a series of gardens, some of the finest in the country. These include a herb garden, a 'white' garden and a delightful old-fashioned cottage garden. The gardens and also the long library and study where Vita worked, are National Trust property. *Open summer*.

36. Sittingbourne 3 H6
A rather unlovely small town, but worth visiting for the Sittingbourne and Kemsley Light Railway, *Milton Rd*, formerly the works railway of the Bowater Paper Co. A 2ft 6in gauge steam-hauled railway, it operates a tourist service between Sittingbourne and Kemsley Down where there is a display of narrow gauge locomotives. *Trains run summer weekends and BHs*.

There is also a Dolphin Sailing Barge Museum which includes exhibits relating to the Thames Spritsail Barge and the traditional sailing barges. *Open Sundays*.

37. Smallhythe Place 3 H7
2m S of Tenterden, B2082. An exquisite half-timbered house dating from 1480, which was the home of the actress Ellen Terry, who was a friend of Bernard Shaw. The house is now an actors' museum containing costumes worn by Miss Terry, with mementoes also of Mrs Siddons and David Garrick. Nearby is a priest's house, a cottage and a barn theatre. *Open most days, summer*.

38. Strood Temple Manor 3 G6
1m W of Rochester, A2. Overlooking the River Medway, the Manor was built in the 13thC by the Knights Templars. It became a nunnery which was destroyed at the Dissolution, and was then used as a farm house. Recently restored, the 13thC hall and 17thC brick extensions are of interest.

39. Sutton-at-Hone, St John's Jerusalem Garden 3 G6
Nr Sevenoaks, E of A225. The walls and chapel are all that remain of the 13thC Commandery of the Knights Hospitallers, where Henry III often stayed. A house was built on the site in the 16thC and altered in the 18thC. It was the home of Abraham Hall (1635–1721), Treasurer of the Royal Society, and of Edward Hasted, historian of Kent.

The River Darenth forms a moat round the lovely, large garden, which contains a weeping willow descended from the tree under which Napoleon was buried at St Helena. *Open certain days, summer*.

40. Tenterden 3 H7
Rows of weather-boarded shops line the wide, main street of this 'capital of the Weald', the reputed birthplace of William Caxton in 1472. A tiny Roman settlement, the town grew in importance as a wool-trading centre in the Middle Ages, affiliated to the Cinque Ports. There is an old town hall, now a museum, and a collection of old coaching inns around the great tower of the 15thC church.

To the west is the main station, and start of Britain's first Light Railway, the Kent and East Sussex Railway, constructed by Col H. F. Stephens at the turn of the century and re-opened with steam trains in 1974. There are now about 25 restored locomotives, the earliest built in 1872. *Trains run certain days*.

41. Tonbridge 3 F7
A mixture of a market town and a rail depot which grew up at the highest navigable point of the Medway. The castle, *off High St*, a key Norman bastion, dominates the town above the bridge, and has curtain walls of the late 12thC, a massive round-towered 14thC gatehouse, and a ruined shell keep. The huge mound inside the walls may have been the site of an Anglo-Saxon fort. After a dramatic history, the castle was eventually wrecked by Cromwell.

Tonbridge is the home of the famous boys' public school, founded in 1553 by Sir Andrew Judd, a Lord Mayor of London. The father of Jane Austen taught at the school and – in our own times – cricketer Colin Cowdrey learnt the game there.

42. Upnor Castle 3 G5
2m N of Rochester, at junction of A228, A226 and A2. Dating from 1561 and well-restored, Upnor Castle is more like a fortified manor house than a castle. It was probably built from stones taken from Rochester's medieval walls. Here, Queen Elizabeth I reviewed the fleet in 1581. There is a small but interesting museum.

43. Walmer Castle 3 K7
1½m S of Deal. Built in the 16thC on the coast to face France, the traditional enemy, this is now the official residence of the Lord Warden of the Cinque Ports. Today more of a stately home than a fort, the castle contains mementoes of its many famous residents such as Pitt and Wellington. The magnificent gardens were designed by Pitt's niece, Lady Hester.

44. Westerham 3 E6
1m S of Deal. A small town of half-timbered houses and narrow, steep roads, which has been the home of many famous men.

Sir Winston Churchill lived at Chartwell, on the outskirts, for 30 years. General Wolfe, who took Quebec, lived at the 16th–17thC Quebec House which is now a museum in his memory. *Open most days, summer*. Squerryes Court, built in 1681, was also once Wolfe's home and contains a collection of Dutch paintings and period furniture. *Open certain days, summer*. A timbered cottage which was the country retreat of Pitt the Younger is now a restaurant. Both Wolfe and Churchill have statues on the village green, close to two famous old coaching inns.

45. Wingham 3 K6
6m E of Canterbury. A large village where a market has been held since the days of Henry III. It has a wide, picturesque main street, timbered houses, a coaching inn which marks the halfway point of the road between Sandwich and Canterbury, a 13thC church and an 18thC vicarage. The size of the church, with its grand interior fittings, recalls the time when there was a college of priests here.

46. Wye 3 J7
1m NE of Ashford, off A28. The college (now agricultural) was founded in 1448 by Archbishop Kempe for priests. Original buildings, including the medieval hall, are still in use. There is an exhibition of old farm implements in a fine tithe barn dating from the 14thC. *Open certain days, summer*.

Of the many interesting old buildings in Wye, note in particular Olantigh House which, though rebuilt, still has many of its original features, and the 15thC Church of SS Martin and Gregory.

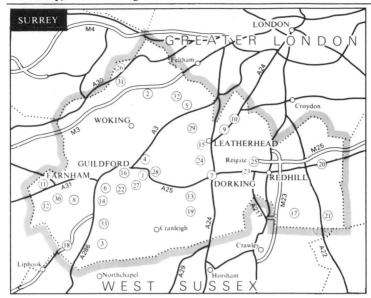

SURREY

1. Abinger and Abinger Hammer   **3 D7**
5m NW of Dorking. This site was inhabited by
mesolithic man, and it's possible to dig up his
pottery and flint tools today. The present
village, which lies in beautiful wooded land, is
very conscious of its more recent past. The
stocks and whipping post still stand on the
green.
Adjoining Abinger, the hamlet of Abinger
Hammer – which was the home of E. M.
Forster, the novelist – is so-called because of
the 'hammer pond' method of smelting iron
introduced in the 15thC by skilled craftsmen
from the Continent. The Surrey iron industry
was still flourishing in the 17thC. It is
commemorated here by the village clock,
which has a smith striking a bell – and there is
still a working smithy in the village.

2. Chertsey   **3 D6**
Ancient town which grew up round a
Benedictine abbey founded in AD666 – this is
one of the first certain dates in the chronology
of Surrey. The abbey was destroyed by
super-vandal Henry VIII, but traces of its
precinct can still be found in the land leading
to the river: fragments of walls, a section of
the floor of the nave, some pillars and arches
of decorated stone.
This riverside town has avoided the worst
features of 20thC commercialism. The
approach from the east crosses the Thames by
the graceful 18thC bridge designed by James
Paine, who was also responsible for
Richmond's fine bridge. The 18thC urbanity
of big trees and smooth brickwork abounds,
but Windsor Street, the extension of London
Road to the west, is especially handsome with
some fine 18thC town houses.
At the junction of London Road and
Guildford Street you'll find the library, the old
town hall of 1851 (now a museum) and the
church. A curfew bell in the church
commemorates the touching tale of one
Blanche Heriot who, at the time of the Wars
of the Roses, knowing that her lover was to be
executed at curfew, climbed the church tower
and hung onto the clapper of the bell until he
was reprieved!
Chertsey Museum, *Windsor St*, has an
exhibition of drinking glasses and decanters.
The museum includes local history relics, the

Matthews collection of costumes and
accessories and the Tulk Bequest of furniture
and porcelain. *Open most days.*

3. Chiddingfold   **3 C7**
An attractive village centred round a large
green and pond. It is in the middle of the
'fold' country, and is one of the 'fold' villages,
along with Dunsfold, Alfold and Durfold,
situated within a few miles of each other.
Chiddingfold was the best known
glass-making centre in England from the 13th
to the 16thC, and was subsequently famous
for its iron smelting trade. By making use of
the local ponds here, and in other villages, this
trade earned them the name of 'hammer
ponds' (hence the name of the village Abinger
Hammer).
Chiddingfold church has a fine lych gate built
in 1888, which contains a coffin rest for the
funeral bearers. A lancet window in the west
wall is the only example of Chiddingfold glass
in the church. The picturesque Crown Inn
was originally built as a rest house for monks
in 1285, and became an inn in 1383. The
interior has been well restored – and it's a
good place for a meal.

4. Clandon Park   **3 C7**
N of Guildford, A246. A house built about
1733 in the Palladian style by an Italian
architect, Giacomo Leoni, for the second
Lord Onslow. It has one of the finest 18thC
interiors in Britain, with a marble entrance
hall – a reception room of real grandeur with
resplendent plaster ceilings and other
decoration – furniture, pictures, porcelain
including the Gubbay Collection of Chinese
porcelain birds and a painting of the house
which shows the original setting. The 18thC
grotto is still in the garden, which was
re-designed by Capability Brown, but the
parkland is now farmed. *Open most days,
summer.*

5. Claremont   **3 D6**
Nr Esher, E of A307. Originally the house that
Vanbrugh built for himself in 1708, rebuilt in
1772 by Henry Holland and Capability Brown
for Clive of India. In 1816 Princess Charlotte,
daughter of George IV, and her husband
Prince Leopold lived there until the death of
the Princess following the birth of a stillborn

son. Had she lived, she would have succeeded to the throne instead of Victoria. Prince Leopold stayed on at the house, and Princess Victoria spent several holidays there as a child, and often returned after she became Queen. There's a columned portico and fine interior decoration by Holland, including good fireplaces and plaster ceilings. Claremont is now a school for girls.

The house is surrounded by the earliest surviving English landscape garden, which belongs to the National Trust, and has been restored. It was begun by Vanbrugh and Bridgeman before 1720, and extended and naturalised by William Kent in about 1760. It covers nearly 50 acres and includes a lake, an island with pavilion, a grotto, a turf amphitheatre, rare trees and magnificent rhododendrons. *House open certain weekends, summer; garden daily.*

6. Compton, Church of St Nicholas 3 B7

Here you'll find one of the most interesting and unusual parish churches in Surrey, a mixture of Saxon and Norman. The pillars of the nave, carved from startlingly white chalk rock, lead to the unique Norman double sanctuary, one built within the other. The Saxon chancel walls and the tower are some of the finest examples in the country.

Watts Picture Gallery is a memorial gallery with about 150 paintings by G. F. Watts, the Victorian painter, whose grave is nearby. *Open most days.*

7. Dorking 3 D7

Ancient market town with much literary association. Here you'll find one of Surrey's oldest inns, the 400-year-old White Horse. Dickens stayed there, and wrote part of 'The Pickwick Papers'. A neighbouring inn (now pulled down) which was called the King's Head became the Marquis of Granby in that novel. The novelist and poet George Meredith lived in a house at the foot of Box Hill and is buried nearby.

It was in Dorking also that the ailing Keats completed 'Endymion' in 1818 and the Burford Bridge Hotel, just north, was the scene of the final separation of Lord Nelson from his wife in 1800. The High Street is part of the Roman Stone Street but Dorking has recently boomed as a commuter town and is notable for its fine, modern houses.

8. Elstead 3 C7

A charming old village beside the River Wey with a wealth of interest: a 14thC church, a five-arched bridge and a Georgian water-mill. A riverside walk leads to the ruins of Waverley Abbey, the first Cistercian house in England, which inspired Sir Walter Scott's novel 'Waverley'.

9. Epsom 3 D6

Spa waters were discovered on the chalk downs here in 1618 – a decade after the establishment of Tunbridge Wells. The beneficial salts plus the bracing air and the short journey soon attracted health-seekers from London.

Epsom's heyday was in the 18thC. A large number of its houses blend with the landscape – almost by accident, for Barbara Villiers, having been given the Royal palace of Nonsuch by Charles II, promptly sold the building, stone by stone, to property speculators here. Epsom became one of the finest residential towns in England, the home of rich merchants and a fashionable spot for those wealthy enough to afford a second home. A new well and a new town were laid out in 1754. The well failed but the town, with diversions such as wrestling, athletics and horse racing on the common lands, flourished.

The Earl of Derby established two new classic races on the Epsom track in 1779 – the Oaks and the Derby – and these races have been run ever since.

10. Ewell, Bourne Hall 3 D6

Spring St. Cultural centre, museum, library and art centre containing all that remains of Henry VIII's Nonsuch Palace, and a large collection of maps and documents. *Open most days.*

11. Farnham 3 B7

An unspoilt town of Georgian houses, Farnham is extremely ancient, being reached by a route – still traceable – along the southern edge of the Hog's Back. This was used by Bronze Age traders long before the Canterbury Pilgrims, and, with its extensive views, is a favourite site for picnickers today.

Visually, Farnham is perhaps the most exciting town in Surrey. It is rich in good architecture that reflects the prosperity of many periods: the ecclesiastical Middle Ages, the woollen industry, corn and hops in the 18thC, and markets up to the present day. It is still one of England's most important corn markets.

Radical William Cobbett, author of 'Rural Rides', was born in 1763 at his father's inn, now called the William Cobbett, *Bridge Sq.* His memorial is in the parish churchyard. Another notable resident was the idiosyncratic John Henry Knight, whose inventive prowess embraced the first English motor car, a silent trench mortar and a brick laying machine!

With their combination of solidity and elegance, 18thC buildings stand in an almost unbroken line along the main streets. Notice in particular Wilmer House (1718) and Sandford House (1757), *West Street.* Wilmer House, a fine example of Georgian brickwork, is now the town museum. It contains archaeology, geology, local history, folk art and tiles and stonework from Waverley Abbey.

At nearby Moor Park, Jonathan Swift, the famous Irish satirist, met his 'Stella'. Her real name was Esther Johnson, and she was only eight when Swift, aged 22, became her tutor. Swift never married, as he had a dread that he might have inherited a tendency to insanity, but his intimate letters to her were collected as 'Journal to Stella'. *View from outside only.*

11. Farnham Castle 3 B7

Castle St. This, the finest fortified structure in Surrey, stands on high ground to the north of the town. It was built in the 12thC, with additions in the 15th–17thC. The castle has been occupied almost continuously until recent times. It belonged to the Bishops of Winchester until this century, when ownership passed to the Bishop of Guildford because the See of Guildford was created on the division of the diocese of Winchester. The Bishop of Guildford lived in the newer part of the castle, with its Great Hall and fine 16thC brick tower but moved out in 1956 and this part is now used as a training centre.

Royalty have been entertained at the castle through the centuries, from Edward I to Queen Victoria: Elizabeth I came frequently, James I used it as a centre for hunting, George III and Queen Charlotte visited it and Queen Victoria came with the Prince Consort to inspect the bible on which she had taken her oath at the Coronation.

The ruined shell keep, erected in 1129–71 by Bishop Henry de Blois is the most impressive part of the remains. *Castle open special days; keep open daily, all year.*

12. Frensham 3 B7

A lovely area, famous for its two ponds – Great and Little – but both sizeable. They were once used by the monks of Waverley Abbey for fish breeding but today are popular sailing and fishing spots and the vegetation on the shores is suffering from over-use by the human species. The Great Pond lies in open common land, an excellent area for walks, and the more secluded Little Pond is covered by water lilies in the season. Frensham Ponds

and 905 acres of heathland belong to the National Trust, who have established a Country Park on part of the property.
In Frensham church is what is claimed to be a true witch's cauldron, 3ft across, used by a Mother Ludlam who lived in a cave near Waverley Abbey in the Middle Ages.

13. Friday Street 3 D7

A perfect village not to be missed, reached by deep, narrow lanes. The inn, The Stephen Langton, is named after King John's Archbishop of Canterbury, born there in about 1150, who played a leading role in the signing of Magna Carta.
A street lined with old cottages leads to a tree-shaded lake with 59 acres of woodland stretching to Leith Hill, all belonging to the National Trust.

14. Godalming 3 C7

A sleepy, old, wool town with narrow streets, half-timbered houses and inns dating back to Tudor and Stuart times – but it has unexpected connections with Russia. Peter the Great stayed as a paying guest at the King's Arms in 1698, and Tsar Alexander I of Russia and King Frederick William of Prussia dined there in 1816. The Old Town Hall affectionately known as the 'Pepper Pot' due to its quaint design, dates from 1814 and is now the Borough Museum containing local antiquities. Godalming Church is mainly Early English and Perpendicular, with a fine spire. *Town hall open certain days.*
There is an interesting memorial in the public gardens nearby. It is to John George Phillips, chief wireless operator of the Titanic, who stayed at his post to the bitter end in a vain attempt to get help. In the cemetery just outside the town is the grave of Philip Heseltine, better known as Peter Warlock the composer, remembered especially for his 'Capriol' suite. A highly-strung man, he was parodied by D. H. Lawrence in 'Women in Love' as Julius Halliday. Godalming is particularly known for being the home of the famous public school, Charterhouse.

15. Great Bookham, Church of St Nicholas 3 D7

One of the finest Norman churches in Surrey, the nave was rebuilt in 1180 and the chancel added by the Abbot of Chertsey in 1341. Notice the 12thC font and the tombs of the Slyfields.

16. Guildford 3 C7

Guildford's records go back to the time of King Alfred in AD900, and the Domesday Book mentions it as one of the only two Surrey boroughs (the other being Southwark). Only the three-storeyed keep of **Guildford Castle**, *Quarry St*, survives. It grew up around Anglo-Saxon fortification and in medieval times was a popular royal residence. You can ascend the keep for excellent views of the town, and the castle grounds, with lawns and flower beds, are a favourite lunch-time haunt for local workers.
The attractive, steep, cobbled High Street contains a wealth of interesting, old buildings. Abbot's Hospital comprises fine brick-built almshouses founded by George Abbot in 1619 and is still inhabited. They have exquisite chapel windows, a dignified dining hall and unusual moulded chimneys. The Angel Hotel, an ancient coaching inn, has an old wooden gallery and a coaching yard. Guildford House, built 1660, is a timber-framed building with an intricately-carved staircase in oak and elm, and elaborate plaster ceilings. Art exhibitions are held here. In **Guildford Museum**, *Quarry Street*, is a collection of local history, geology, archaeology and needlework, plus items relating to Lewis Carroll who spent much of his time here. *Open weekdays.*
But the landmark of Guildford is the guildhall, with its fine, projecting clock. A

master clockmaker, John Aylward, had been refused permission to work in Guildford, so he made this clock in 1683, gave it to the guildhall – and was allowed to set up shop.

Guildhall, Guildford

17. Haxted, Watermill Museum 3 E7

The mill dates from the late 17th–early 18thC, and is weather-boarded, with a mansard roof. Adjoining it is the tile-hung mill house. There is a museum containing mill machinery, and two working water-wheels. *Open certain days, summer.*

18. Hindhead 3 B7

The highest village in Surrey, set among woodland and heath, built mainly in the health-conscious 19thC because of its clean air and spacious views.
Nearby, at 895ft, Gibbet Hill takes its name from the murder of a sailor in 1786 on the old Portsmouth Road. He was walking from London to Portsmouth and, as he passed through Esher, met three men. They followed him and at Hindhead, murdered and robbed him. They were soon caught, however, trying to sell his clothes near Petersfield, and were tried and hanged in chains here.
Gibbet Hill overlooks the spectacular plunging valley known as the Devil's Punchbowl, which is perfect for a hearty walk.

19. Leith Hill Tower 3 D7

1m SW of Coldharbour. A good climb through wooded country is rewarded by exhilarating views from the ridge of this beauty spot. It is crowned by a 64ft ragstone tower, and from here, on a clear day, you can see 13 counties. The tower was built in 1766 by Richard Hill, to make Leith Hill the highest point in the south east. He lived at nearby Leith Hill Place and is buried in the church.

20. Limpsfield, Detillans 3 E6

2m E of Godstone. A field day for military enthusiasts! A 15thC Wealden hall house with kingpost roof and inside, the largest collection of orders and decorations in the UK. Also collections of furniture, china, porcelain, militaria and guns. *Open certain days, summer, or by arrangement.*
Set in wooded countryside, Limpsfield is a quiet village with the composer Delius resting peacefully in the churchyard.

21. Lingfield 3 E7

An interesting village in the Weald with buildings dating back to the 15thC. The parish church was largely rebuilt in 1431 by Sir Reginald Cobham, who also founded the Carthusian college which used to be attached to the church and accommodated a provost, five chaplains, four clerks and 13 poor persons. The first Lord Cobham, who died in 1361, was a great soldier, and fought at the battle of Crecy. The brasses and monuments in the church commemorate the Cobhams, who lived at Staborough Castle (no longer standing).
In the centre of the village are St Peter's Cross and the village cage, by the pond. The cage was used as a temporary prison for those who had broken the local laws, and had its last inhabitant in 1882.

22. **Loseley House** 3 C7
2½m SW of Guildford. Set in a large park, this is an elegant, Tudor mansion, built in 1562 with stone from Waverley Abbey, which had been demolished at the Dissolution of the Monasteries. Its first occupant was Sir William More, kinsman of Sir Thomas, and the house has remained in the family ever since. Loseley House has received many royal visitors, including Elizabeth I and James I. Inside are fine ceilings, panelling from Henry VIII's Nonsuch Palace, old furniture and tapestries and a unique chimney-piece in the drawing room, carved from a single piece of local chalk. Today the name Loseley House is known throughout the country for its delicious dairy products. *Open most days, summer.*

Loseley House

23. **Outwood Mill** 3 E7
5m SE of Redhill. High up on Outwood Common is the oldest working mill in England: a post mill built in 1665. You can still buy bags of flour ground at the mill.
A post mill, built mainly of wood, has a rectangular boarded body which turns around on a central post to face the wind, as opposed to a tower mill, which just has the top half containing the sails revolving. *Open certain days, summer.*

24. **Polesden Lacey** 3 D7
3m NW of Dorking. Richard Brinsley Sheridan, the famous playwright, had his country home on this beautiful site, high on the North Downs, with magnificent views across the valley to Ranmore Woods.
Polesden Lacey has some of the loveliest gardens in Surrey, with herbaceous borders, terraces and miles of wooded walks. The gardens were begun in the 1760s, when the superlative Long Walk was planted, and developed by Sheridan who also made the terraced walk. Sheridan and the Master of Dramatists, Shakespeare, are honoured each year in the delightful open-air theatre situated in the grounds.
The elegant house that rests amid the fine trees today, was originally a Regency villa designed by Thomas Cubitt in the 1820s, and was restored by Mrs Ronald Greville, a well-known Edwardian hostess, in 1906. The leisured life of Edwardian society is faithfully preserved: the house contains a fine collection of important pictures, tapestries, furniture, porcelain and silver, plus many of Mrs Greville's personal photographs. We also have Sheridan to thank for the impressive library, which he stocked by levying contributions from his friends. King Edward VIII was entertained here, and the house was lent to King George VI and Queen Elizabeth the Queen Mother for their honeymoon. *House open most days, summer; gardens daily, all year.*

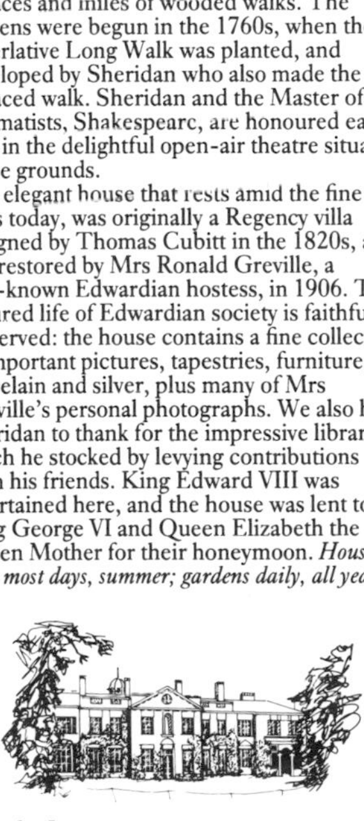

Polesden Lacey

25. **Reigate** 3 D7
Listed in the 'Railway Times' of 1850 among the 'salubrious sites' that were within half an hour of the city, Reigate, in fact, had been overtaken by the railway as early as 1841. Except for the early 18thC market house, there are few Georgian survivors, and even fewer Tudor. It is a Victorian expansion, with good open spaces, yet its lineage goes back to Saxon times, when it bore the name of Cherchefelle (Churchfield).
Reigate was first mentioned by its present name in 1170. The owners of the manor were the powerful Warennes, who were granted large areas of Surrey and Sussex after the Norman Conquest. The male line died out in 1148, but the name continued, since the heiress married the son of King Stephen, William of Blois, and their descendants took the name of Warenne. Today, Warenne's Castle is a mere mound situated within pleasant gardens called Castle Grounds. The enclosure is entered from a 'folly' – a mock castle gate built in 1777. Underneath is the Baron's Cave, from which run a number of medieval tunnels reaching for miles underground, some of which are open for investigation by the adventurous and non-claustrophobic. *Open by arrangement.*
The history of the **Priory Museum**, *Bell Street*, began in 1235 and went through many stages, including being converted into a Tudor mansion by Lord Howard of Effingham in 1541. The hall and fireplace of this period can still be seen. In 1710 a painted staircase by Verrio was added. The house is now partly used as a school, and part is a museum of local history, Victorian toys and costumes. *Open by arrangement.*
A 400-year-old smock mill, restored in 1964 and converted into a chapel, can be found just outside the town on Reigate Heath. A service is held there on certain Sundays in the summer. Although not in working order, it has been restored to its original appearance with the interior retaining much of its old form with a heavy, beamed ceiling. *Open by arrangement.*

26. **Runnymede** 3 C6
The fields of Runnymede are where King John reluctantly signed the Magna Carta on 15th June, 1215. The barons, led by Stephen Langton, made King John set his seal to the Great Charter of Liberties which has been of lasting significance to the Constitution. It contains 63 clauses, and it is clause 39 which states: 'No free man shall be taken or imprisoned save by the lawful judgement of his peers, or by the law of the land'. Marking the approximate spot of the signing is a memorial set up in 1957, inscribed: 'To commemorate Magna Carta, symbol of freedom under law'.
On a hill above Runnymede is a simple but moving memorial to President John F. Kennedy, assassinated in 1963.

27. **St Martha's** 3 C7
Nr Chilworth. Trundle up one of the wooded paths to the historic chapel of St Martha. Lonely and appealing, it stands high on a hill overlooking Chilworth village in the valley below. The chapel is on the Pilgrims' Way, and was one of their resting places en route to Canterbury. It was restored in 1848, but traces of the old Norman structure can still be seen. With fresh, country air and magnificent views of the Surrey countryside, this is a perfect spot for picnics.

28. **Shere** 3 D7
3m E of Guildford, off A25. Snuggled in the valley of the River Tillingbourne, with old cottages, and a 12thC church and the local pub on either side of the small village green, Shere is the perfect village. The south door of the church has some fine Norman decoration. The coffer dates from the 13thC and, as in other churches, was placed there to take gifts from the crusaders. There are four 12thC lancet windows, and some Chiddingford glass

in the south aisle. If you're in need of a thirst-quencher, you can't do better than the charming 16thC White Horse Inn, which has a frame of ancient ships' timbers.

29. Stoke d'Abernon, Church of St Mary   3 C6

St Mary's is in the grounds of Stoke d'Abernon Manor on the banks of the River Mole. The original church was built in the 7thC, and parts of the structure can still be seen on the south side.

St Mary's monuments and brasses are grander and more numerous than you'd usually find in a village church. Among them is the oldest known brass in the country, that of Sir John d'Abernon, dated 1277; that of his son, next to him, is dated 1327. The black marble slab nearby is the tombstone of Sir John Ackland, a Devon Royalist, who garrisoned his home, Columb St John, against the Roundheads. There is a fine 13thC chest, an Elizabethan pulpit made of English walnut, beautifully carved with an hour glass stand on the wall, and a 17thC lectern.

Old Kiln Agricultural Museum

30. Tilford Old Kiln Agricultural Museum   3 B7

Reeds Rd, 3m SE of Farnham. Well-displayed permanent exhibition of historic farm implements, machinery and crafts and trades allied to farming. The site covers some 10 acres and includes a smithy, a wheelwright's shop and old farm buildings, in a setting of gardens and woodlands. *Open most days, summer.*

31. Virginia Water   3 C6

An artificial lake in a lovely woodland setting, this is an excellent picnicking, rambling and boating spot. Virginia Water was designed in 1746 for the Duke of Cumberland by Thomas Sandby, the Deputy Ranger of Windsor Park, and is one and a half miles long and up to half a mile wide.

The original area was a marsh with a number of streams running from it, and the lake was formed by damming the streams, flooding the ground and building the cascade to take the overflow of water. It was laid out as a celebration of the victory at Culloden, and called 'Virginia' after the state in America, as the Duke had at one time been Governor there.

32. Walton-on-Thames   3 D6

Caesar crossed the river here, at Coway Stakes, in pursuit of the British Chieftain Cassivellanus. Today there is a wooden bridge to mark the spot. The restored church is Norman, and contains an interesting 'Scold's Bridle' – a steel cage shaped to fit the head. John Bradshaw, who put his signature to the death warrant of Charles I, lived in the 15thC manor house.

33. Witley   3 C7

4m SW of Godalming. Well worth visiting for the 600-year-old, tile-hung, steep-roofed White Hart – one of the oldest pubs in England, which was once part of a hunting lodge belonging to Richard II. George Eliot lived in neighbouring Wormley which inspired her to write 'Daniel Deronda'. Anglo-Saxon work can still be detected in the Church of All Saints, and the tower, chancel and transepts date from the 12thC. A window claimed to be over 1,000 years old is in the west gable.

SUSSEX

1. Alfriston   3 F9

2½m NE of Seaford, B2108. Once a busy harbour, now tucked away in the Cuckmere valley, this village was famous for smugglers, who met at the Star Inn. This inn is one of the oldest in the country and has beautifully-carved woodwork.

Alfriston has a particularly large share of historic houses, most notably the Clergy House. Dating from 1380, this was the first house to be purchased by the National Trust, in 1896. Half-timbered and thatched, the medieval living room has cambered tie-beams and moulded king-posts. Restoration has left the house much as it was when it was built in the 14thC. *Open summer.*

Have a look at the simple stone cross in the

Alfriston Clergy House

small triangular market place. It's the only surviving market cross in Sussex, apart from Chichester. The church, known as the Cathedral of the Downs because of its size, stands on an isolated knoll by the river.

2. Amberley   3 C9

3m NW of Arundel, B2139. This is as typical a Sussex village as you could find, with a ruined castle, an ancient manor house, thatched cottages with gardens full of flowers, and a Norman church. This has the 'catslide' method of roofing its walls, common in Sussex. The roof was brought down in one sweep from the ridge to within a few feet above the ground.

Looking down from the church, you'll see Amberley Wild Brooks ('wild' is derived from 'weald'), 30 square miles of grazing marshes watered by the River Arun – a paradise for walkers.

The Norman castle became the residence of the Bishops of Chichester and the ruined 14thC gatehouse and walls enclose an ancient manor house.

3. Arundel   3 C9

Arundel is dominated by its castle and two churches, the late 14thC parish church of St

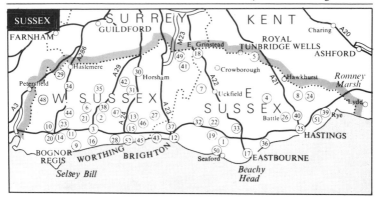

Nicholas (a good example of Early English architecture) and the 19thC Roman Catholic Church of St Philip Neri, designed by Joseph Hansom, of Hansom cab fame. Below, there is a pleasant collection of 18th and 19thC houses, the streets running down to the river bank. The Arun flows to the sea less than five miles away. In Norman times the town was a port. Arundel Museum and Heritage Centre, *High St*, is devoted to the town's history, and further along the road there is a splendid 18thC coaching inn, the Norfolk Arms.

3. Arundel Castle 3 C9

One of the most impressive in England, the seat of the dukes of Norfolk for over 700 years, Arundel Castle looms above the wooded cliffs of the River Arun. Its antiquity is, however, apparent rather than real. The original castle was built by the Normans just after the Conquest to defend the valley against sea raiders, almost ruined by Cromwell's cannon, rebuilt in the 18thC and extensively restored in 1890. Only the gatehouse and shell remain from the original fortification – the rest is rather the Victorian idea of a castle. Immortalised by Turner and Constable, this romantic and picturesque castle is well worth visiting for fine furniture dating from the 16thC, armour, state dresses, china, tapestries and the exquisite Fitzalan Chapel. The art collection is particularly good, with paintings by Gainsborough, Reynolds and Van Dyck. Each year at the end of August, the castle plays host to the famous Arundel Festival which attracts artists from all over the world. A Shakespeare play is presented in the castle's magnificent Tilting Yard. *Open most days, summer.*

Arundel Castle

4. Bateman's 3 F8

Burwash, 5m NE of Heathfield, A265. Lovely 17thC house which was Rudyard Kipling's home from 1902–36. He wrote 'Puck of Pook's Hill' here, and described the surroundings in it. Now a museum, the house contains many of Kipling's possessions and his study remains as he left it. Note the

magnificent Jacobean panelling and the noble staircase. The attractive gardens merit a stroll and there is a recently-restored water-mill. *Open most days, summer.*

5. Bayham Abbey 3 H8

Sussex/Kent border, A268. The most impressive group of monastic remains in Sussex, Bayham Abbey was founded in the 13thC by monks of the Premonstratensian order. Today you can see the walls of the nave and part of the cloisters still standing almost to their full height. A 14thC gatehouse of unusually delicate design stands by the River Teise. No wonder the earls of Camden used the ruins as the centrepiece of their romantic park in the 18thC!

6. Bignor Villa 3 C8

Nr Petworth. This is the site of one of the largest Roman villas in Britain, covering four and a half acres. There are fine mosaic floors with great delicacy of detail, made of fragments – less than one inch square – of chalk, sandstone, tile, limestone and glass. One depicts Venus and the Gladiator; another, Zeus as an eagle. Remains of workshops and a smithy are grouped around a courtyard. The size and quality of Bignor, with extensive quarters for farm animals and slaves, indicate that it was the seat of a wealthy man. *Open most days, summer.*

7. Bluebell Railway, Sheffield Park 3 E7

10m S of East Grinstead, off A275. This is the southern terminus of the Bluebell Railway. A 15 minute journey running through five miles of woodland (good bluebell country) takes you to Horsted Keynes. It is part of an abandoned Southern Region line, now operated most successfully by a private preservation company. The platform at Sheffield Park, its headquarters, is fine Victorian architecture, with slender cast-iron columns and marvellous old advertisements. *Open summer; certain days, winter.*

8. Bodiam Castle 3 G8

3m S of Hawkhurst, 1m E of A229. The original of every boy's model fort, rising complete and apparently solid from its moat and reached by a drawbridge across which feet have thundered for six centuries – those of medieval soldiers, Roundheads (who sacked it) and now tourists.

Bodiam Castle

It is in fact a shell, with 6ft 6in walls, the interior having been plundered and burnt out, not by French invaders, but by Cromwell's men. Enough remains, however, for the visitor to have an open-plan view of the various rooms – Great Hall, kitchen, servants' hall, steward's and household offices, chapel, lady's bower and bedchamber – and get a vivid idea of life as it was lived there. Floors have recently been relaid on some of the towers and visitors can now climb circular stairs and view some more of the interior.

Built in 1385 as part of a plan to protect Sussex from the French, Bodiam never, in fact, saw military service, and was used as a country house by various noblemen. The last owner was Lord Curzon, who excavated and repaired the ruins and bequeathed it to the National Trust in 1925.

9. Bognor Regis   3 C9
First a Saxon village, then a medieval fishing hamlet from the late 18thC, Bognor unselfconsciously developed for the fashionable wealthy. The 'Regis' was added in 1929, after George V convalesced there. Handsome Regency houses line the Steyne and Waterloo Square. But its finest mansion, the Georgian Hotham House, is unfortunately boarded up. Five miles of sand with safe bathing contribute to making this a popular holiday resort.

10. Bosham   3 B9
Cuddling round the water's edge, the softly-coloured flint, brick and tile-hung cottages make Bosham (pronounced 'Bozzam') a favourite haunt of artists and yachtsmen. It was here, on Chichester's harbour, that Canute tried to rule the waves. The church is immortalised in the Bayeux Tapestry, which shows Harold, with hawk on hand, going to hear mass there on the eve of sailing to Normandy in 1064. The chancel arch is one of the best Saxon arches in the country, and notice the unusual five-light lancet window in the east end.

11. Boxgrove Priory   3 C9
3m NE of Chichester. A one-street village which has a huge church with a magnificent nave, built between 1170 and 1220. An excellent example of Early English architecture, notice, too, the shafts and Purbeck marble. Lord de la Warr, Lord of the Manor, saved the church at the Dissolution in 1537 and converted it from a Catholic priory church into a parish church. The priory itself – once the centre of South Saxon Christianity – was destroyed, however, and a few Norman arches and walls are all that remain.

12. Brighton   3 E9
The pursuit of pleasure is responsible for this peer of resorts. First came the Duke of Gloucester, in the 1760s, but it was the Prince Regent's visit to his uncle, the Duke of Cumberland, in 1783, that gave Brighton its popularity and inimitable 'racy' reputation. The Royal Pavilion was its centrepiece. The Steyne, an elongated square planted with trees, still has an air of Regency promenade. Marlborough House is now an information centre and Mrs Fitzherbert's house, a YMCA hostel. The Dome, Royal Riding School and stables are now a concert hall, museum and art gallery, housing a collection of English and European paintings and drawings, pottery and Sussex folklore, as well as one of the best collections of old English musical instruments in the country. The town centre round Market Place is completed by the Corn Exchange and Old Town Hall of 1852.
Famous for antiques, tiny gourmet restaurants, cafes and pubs, the warren of small streets known as The Lanes follows the tracks of the old farming village. Consisting of elegant crescents and gardens, the 'New Town' to the east was built in the 1820s for wealthy residents. In recent years, however,

the face of the town has changed as Brighton has become a popular commuter base.

12. Brighton, The Royal Pavilion   3 E9
There is a picture by Rex Whistler in which a portly Prince Regent is shown awakening the sleeping maiden Brighthelmstone. She woke up, became Brighton – and has been very much awake ever since. The fishing village became a royal town, and its crown jewel is the Pavilion.
The Prince's ebullient taste bubbled up at its most exuberant in this extravaganza of Arabian Nights' domes. 'St Paul's went down to the sea and pupped,' quipped Shaw. 'A square box, a large Norfolk turnip and four onions,' jeered Cobbett. 'Chinese deformities,' laughed Cruikshank. Ever since it was completed by that normally restrained architect, John Nash, in 1820, the Pavilion has

Brighton Pavilion

roused strong passions – but it can never be ignored. A fantasy of lime-green and bamboo greets you in every room, with a predominance of Chinese lanterns and dragon and water-lily chandeliers. The kitchen, with excellent copperware, is a sober relief from the gaudiness.
Its history has been as dramatic as its appearance. The Pavilion took so long to finish that the Prince enjoyed his pleasure dome for a mere seven years. His brother, William IV, loved it, but he reigned for only seven years. Queen Victoria was definitely not amused by this 'strange, odd, Chinese-looking thing'. She had its whites and golds, pinks and blues painted over with chocolate and aspidistra green, and took its treasures away in 150 van loads to Windsor, Buckingham Palace and Kensington Palace. In the Royal Pavilion the Prince and Nash, knowing almost nothing of Eastern culture, were able to let their imagination run riot: the unique fantasy they created remains more magical than any copy could have been.

13. Chanctonbury Ring   3 D9
1m SE of Washington. One of the outstanding landmarks of the Downs, this is a superb defensive site – an Iron Age hill fort with a double rampart cut deeply into the chalk, forming a circular walk. Cross-dykes, which were the outer defences, are clear to the west. The whole encloses 12½ acres and includes an earlier neolithic causeway camp. An 18thC landlord planted a circular copse of beech trees on the summit. The climb is worthwhile for the unimpeded views inland and over the coast.

14. Chichester   3 C9
An unspoilt Georgian market town, Chichester lies between the South Downs and the coastal plain. There was already a settlement here when the Romans arrived in AD43 and set up a base camp: this is one of Britain's oldest towns. The Saxons gave it its name, Cissa's Ceaster (camp) cAD477 but it was the Normans who turned it into a cathedral city, replacing the See of Selsey, now under the waves. The city walls were built cAD200, and added to in medieval times.
The city has a magnificent simplicity of structure, shaped like a shield and quartered by four main streets – the fine market cross of 1501 at their junction. Each street leads to the site of a city gate, and within the walls it is the prosperous 18thC that dominates, its

apotheosis being the New Market House, built by Nash in 1807 and still in use. Also still lived in is St Mary's Hospital, built as an almshouse just before 1300, with a magnificent timbered roof.
In July every year the town is taken over by the famous Chichester Arts Festival.

14. Chichester Cathedral   3 C9
This is the only cathedral in Sussex, the only English cathedral whose spire can be seen from the sea, and the only medieval cathedral in the United Kingdom to have a detached bell-tower. This was to avoid putting the strain of bell-ringing on the spire, which is very exposed to winds off the sea.
Built mainly between 1091 and 1199, it is a Norman building with Early English additions. In the cathedral's chequered history it has been burnt down twice, damaged by Roundheads, and in 1861 its spire collapsed perpendicularly into the church. The present 277ft spire was designed by the Victorian architect Sir Giles Gilbert Scott.
By Norman standards Chichester Cathedral is by no means spectacular. It is relatively small, but does have two rare (and touchingly human) Romanesque reliefs of the raising of Lazarus, a fine retro-choir, beautiful windows and an interesting treasury. And it has something in addition – a welcoming atmosphere. It is not remote like some, more splendid, cathedrals, but very much a part of Chichester, and it is still being enriched by works of art: John Piper designed the reredos tapestry.

15. Cissbury Ring   3 D9
3½m N of Worthing, off A24. One of the largest hill forts in the country, Cissbury Ring dates from the Iron Age. A double rampart traces the outline of a chalk spur, some 80 acres. It was occupied in about 250BC when flint was mined in the area, and a number of shafts have been discovered.

16. Climping, Church of St Mary   3 C9
4m SW of Arundel, off A259. A bright spot in a rather dull corner of the Sussex plain, the church has such good proportions and purity of design that it gave rise to the Sussex saying: 'Climping for perfection'. It has a massive Norman fortress tower built of Caen stone, austere lancet windows, a window commemorating St Wilfrid, who evangelised Sussex, and a 15thC Crusaders' chest to provide funds for poor knights.

17. Eastbourne   3 F9
A fresh, sunshine resort, Eastbourne was developed by the 7th Duke of Devonshire when he inherited it, as a small village, in 1834. He intentionally made it quite different from Brighton – more elegant and less extrovert. Even today, there is not a single shop, let alone a kiosk, along the three-mile, flower-banked esplanade: instead it is backed by splendid hotels and gardens such as the Carpet Gardens.
During the Napoleonic Wars many fortifications were built along the coast. The Circular Redoubt was the most extensive and now houses an aquarium and a model village. The Wish Tower was named after the Wash, the 'bourne' that once flowed here. The Tower is now a Coastal Defence Museum where Napoleonic defence methods and equipment are displayed. *Open summer.*
The pre-Victorian nucleus of stone and flint houses still survives around the Norman Church of St Mary's. There's a medieval parsonage, timber-framed inns and a handsome 18thC manor house, now the Towner Art Gallery housing a good collection of 19th and 20thC British paintings, Georgian caricatures and sculptures by Henry Moore.

18. East Grinstead   3 E7
8m E of Crawley, A22. Described in the Domesday Book as 'una ferraria' (an iron-smelting place), this was a centre of the Sussex industry, which flourished from before Roman times to the 18thC. Here, iron grave slabs can be seen in St Swithun's churchyard. The town's charter dates back to 1221. It is dominated by one broad rising High Street and has an unbroken line of fine old houses on the south side – timbered as well as 18thC. Notice in particular the mid 14thC Amherst House, Cromwell House built in 1599, the 16thC Sackville House and Dorset House of 1705. Opposite is Sackville College, a beautifully preserved Jacobean building built of local sandstone. Founded by Robert Sackville, Earl of Dorset, in 1609 to house his old servants, it is still an old peoples' home.

19. Firle Place   3 E9
West Firle, 4m SE of Lewes, off A27. A Tudor house with Georgian additions, and a collection of European and British old masters, fine French and English furniture and porcelain. There are also paintings and documents relating to General Gage and the American War of Independence. *Open summer.*

20. Fishbourne Roman Palace   3 C9
Head of Fishbourne Creek, 1½m W of Chichester. Covering an area of 250,000 sq ft, this is probably the greatest of all the Roman villas in Britain. The northern wing of this Italianate-style Palace has been restored and is under cover of a modern building.
It began as a military establishment as, being on the shore, stone could easily be landed. Then a modest house with a colonnaded garden was added, which may have been occupied by Cogidubnus, the Briton made viceroy by the Romans. During the 2nd and 3rdC, the peak period of the Roman occupation, the house was developed into a palace, with four wings ranging round a formal Pompeii-like garden, now reconstructed and planted with appropriate shrubs. In the north wing 23 rooms have been converted into a museum devoted to an imaginative portrayal of life in Roman Britain. Sections of the walls, baths and underfloor heating systems can be seen, but the centre-piece is the superb mosaic floor, dating from the mid 2ndC, one panel depicting a winged boy astride a dolphin.
In about AD275 the palatial villa was destroyed by fire, to be buried in oblivion until 1960 when workmen laying a water pipe uncovered several walls and mosaic floors. Finds from the excavations are housed in the museum which contains pictures, plans and models. The story of the site is told by an audio-visual programme. *Open summer.*

21. Fittleworth   3 C9
3m SE of Petworth. A restful village of stone and timber-frame cottages, a favourite retreat of artists and anglers. Crossing the River Rother close by is Stopham Bridge, the best example of a medieval bridge in Sussex. The Swan Inn, *Lower St*, has accommodated many artists and its wood-panelled dining room is adorned with landscapes painted by George Constable, brother of John Constable.

22. Glynde Place   3 E9
4m SE of Lewes, off A27. Beautiful Early Elizabethan house of flint and brick, built round a courtyard. In the panelled Long Gallery are portraits by Hoppner, Lely and Zoffany, the original sketch by Rubens for the ceiling of the Banqueting House, Whitehall, 12thC documents, bronzes and fine needlework and pottery. *Open certain days, summer.*

23. Goodwood House   3 B9
3m NE of Chichester, off A285. This Jacobean three-sided mansion, rebuilt in Sussex flintwork in 1780, is the ancestral home of the Dukes of Richmond.
The 17thC Hunting Lodge has been enlarged

Goodwood House

to house the family collections. Paintings by Canaletto, Van Dyck and Lely together with sporting pictures by Stubbs and Wootton decorate the walls and the elegant Tapestry Room was built in the 18thC to accommodate tapestries purchased in France by the third Duke. There is also handsome French furniture and a collection of Sèvres porcelain. *Open certain days, summer.*

24. Great Dixter, Northiam   3 GH
4m SE of Hawkhurst, A268. Nestling cosily in the sleepy village of Northiam, Great Dixter is one of the finest timber-framed buildings in Sussex. Built around 1450 and recently restored, it has a notable Great Hall and oriel windows. The gardens, laid out by Sir Edwin Lutyens who restored the house, are known for their box and yew hedges. *Open most days, summer.*

Great Dixter

25. Hastings   3 G9
This original Cinque Port was once an isolated fishing village on the extremity of a ridge of sandstone hills. There is still a warren of narrow streets with a huddle of bent-backed timbered houses and red-tiled cottages leading down to the harbour area and the unique tall, dark, wooden huts once used for drying nets still stand on the beach. Otherwise, some Regency terraces remain, but most of the building took place after the opening of the railways in 1851 and is therefore Victorian.
A lift mounts the cliff face to the ruins of the 13thC castle. St Clement's Caves, three acres in extent and used for centuries by smugglers, are entered near the castle. Saxon Hastings is now lost to the sea; the pier roughly marks its position. The historical associations of the town are remembered by the Conqueror's Stone by the pier which is said to have been the 'table' at which William enjoyed his first meal, when he occupied the town on September 29th, 1066.
Hastings Museum and Art Gallery houses a good collection of Sussex ironwork. The Hastings Embroidery is on show in the town hall; it is a 243ft tapestry depicting scenes from British history from 1066 to the present day, created by modern embroiderers in the style of the ancient Bayeux tapestry. At the Fisherman's Museum in Old Town, you can see the last of the Hastings' sailing luggers. *Open most days, summer.*

26. Hastings Battlefield
Battle, 6m NW of Hastings. The one-day battle of October 18th, 1066, which shaped the face

of Britain, was fought not at Hastings but here, at the site now called Battle.
King Harold marched his army 240 miles from York and took up a good defensive position high on a hilltop. William, with his army of professional soldiers, was unable to break through. Several times Harold was very close to victory, but luck was against him – even the fickle English weather favoured William. After a number of unsuccessful uphill charges, however, William master-minded a brilliant plan. Pretending to flee, he led his army into retreat. Following in gleeful pursuit, the English army lost their dominant position. William rallied his army together to win the battle, Harold getting the proverbial arrow in his eye in the process.
Before the battle William made a vow to build an abbey, with the high altar on the spot where Harold fell. He honoured his oath, and St Martin's Abbey was consecrated in 1094 in the presence of William Rufus. The remains of the monastic buildings, a victim of the Dissolution, can still be seen on the hilltop. The abbot's lodgings were converted into a private house which is now a girls' school. The 14thC Decorated gatehouse, which dominates the town, is one of the finest in the country.
It is possible, without too much walking, to view the battlefield from both the Saxon and Norman positions. The local museum, in the centre of Battle, has an excellent relief plan of the battlefield and a reproduction of the Bayeux Tapestry, showing Harold's death.

27. Henfield   3 D9
6m N of Shoreham-by-Sea, junction of A281 and A2037. Worth a visit for Wood Mill, an 18thC water-mill in 12 acres of grounds. Inside there is a natural history display with small animals and insects, including a beehive – fascinating for the children who can also follow the nature trails. Traditionally these mills were the property of the Lord of the Manor, and anyone growing corn on his manor had to have it ground at the Lord's mill. The miller would then deduct a proportion of the grain as payment for his services. *Open most days, summer.*

28. Highdown Hill   3 D9
3m NW of Worthing, off A27. A conical hill, 266ft high, the site of an Iron Age hill fort beneath which a late Bronze Age settlement has been discovered. Saxons later used the site as a burial ground.

29. Hollycombe Working Steam Museum and Woodland Garden   3 B8
4m SW of Haslemere, off B2131. All the fun of an old-fashioned fair: 2ft gauge steam train, roundabout with steam organ, steam yacht, steam road loco, cake walk, steam swings and the only 'Razzle-Dazzle' still in existence. All working, they're set in a woodland of azaleas and rhododendrons with steam exhibits and demonstrations. *Open certain days, summer.*

30. Horsham   3 D8
This 'Capital of the Western Weald' was first recorded as a borough in 1236, returned two members to Parliament and held two fairs a year. The finest collection of houses in the town is in the Causeway, a tree-lined cul-de-sac. They are mainly 18th and 19thC, but some bulging-walled buildings date from the 15thC. There is one with a fine timber frame – Tudor Causeway House – which is the town museum concentrating on items of local and agricultural interest.
The Causeway leads down to the river and to St Mary's Parish Church, built by the Normans and enlarged over the centuries. The heavily-buttressed sandstone tower is 800 years old, and in the north wall a Norman doorway stands. The church contains a tablet to the memory of the poet Shelley, born at Field Place, Warnham a couple of miles away. *Gardens only open certain days, summer.*

31. Knepp Castle   3 D8
1m W of West Grinstead. High up on an earth
mound or 'motte', 30ft high, this ruined keep
is all that remains of a Norman castle dating
from the 11thC. Home of the de Braose
family, it is said that King John destroyed the
castle to prevent the French seizing it. Knepp
was finally demolished during the Civil War.

32. Lewes   3 E9
This – the county town of East Sussex – has
1,000 years of history behind it. The castle
which dominates it was built in about 1100 to
guard a gap in the South Downs, and the town
grew up on the hillside between the castle and
the river. Important already in Saxon times, it
was the site of the first Cluniac priory in
England. A few timber-framed houses remain
on the steep streets of the old town, but most
have been replaced by solid brick Georgian
houses, Cobbett's 'model of solidity and
neatness'. And Cobbett's favourite inn was
The White Hart.
Lewes claims more famous residents: the
Elizabethan Grange was the boyhood home of
the diarist John Evelyn (1620–1706) and
Thomas Paine lived in Bull House, *High St*,
from 1768 to 1774. The town was then a river
port and Thomas worked as an excise officer.
After writing a pamphlet demanding better
working conditions, he was firmly dismissed.
This incident spurred him to become the
famous pamphleteer.
Anne of Cleves's house in Southover, now a
folk museum with a collection of Sussex
ironwork, costumes and furniture, was one of
several houses given to her by Henry VIII
after their divorce in 1540. The 16thC
Barbican House is a fascinating museum of
local archaeology. *Museums open weekdays.*

32. Lewes Battlefield   3 E9
Mount Harry. This battlefield is best seen
today from the ramparts of Lewes Castle,
where there is an arrow pointing towards it. A
confined area, it is bounded by a town, a river,
and a steep slope: the perfect death trap, in
fact, where survival was more a matter of luck
than of skill.
Here, on May 14th 1264, Henry III
confronted Simon de Montfort. The battle
was particularly bitter as Simon, a former
favourite, was adviser to the King and
husband of his sister. Objecting to the King's
extravagance and the heavy taxes on his
people, Simon rallied the major barons,
supported by angry Londoners, to challenge
royal authority.
The battle, over by midday, was 'nasty, brutish
and short', and although Simon won a Pyrrhic
victory, this was reversed at the Battle of
Evesham in the following year. De Montfort's
soldiers, who wore the white cross of the
Crusaders, fought with inspired fervour. They
pursued the remnants of the King's army into
the marshes of the River Ouse to the south,
where they sank – to reappear next day when
the tide receded, making a macabre sight;
dead, yet still sitting erect on their horses, they
were held upright by their saddles and
armour. Bodies have been recovered at
intervals ever since, and a reasonable estimate
of the total would be 4,000 – one out of every
five engaged.
Apart from the battlefield and the castle (with
an adjoining museum) it is also possible to
visit the ruins of the Cluniac Priory of St
Pancras, *S of centre*. Here Henry III, having
had two horses killed under him and been
battered by sword and mace, eventually took
shelter. He was 56 years old, and although not
a soldier by inclination, had fought
magnificently. The Mise of Lewes, the
ensuing treaty, is considered the beginnings of
parliamentary government in England.

32. Lewes Castle   3 E9
One of the five Norman castles built to face
the enemies across the Channel (the others

were Pevensey, Hastings, Bramber and
Arundel), Lewes Castle has dominated both
the town and the surrounding countryside
since 1100. There are two mottes, one
overlooking the town and containing the keep,
and the other overlooking the river. This most
unusual feature indicates the military
importance of the castle. Remaining are a
Norman gatehouse, a 14thC barbican and
sections of the precinct walls. There is a
magnificent view from the top. *Open weekdays.*

33. Michelham Priory   3 F9
Nr Upper Dikter, B2108. Well restored by the
Sussex Archaeological Trust, Michelham
gives a vivid idea of priory-scattered,
pre-Henry VIII England. This was an
Augustinian priory founded in 1229. It is
surrounded by gardens and the moat, formed
by the diverted River Cuckmere, is 6½ acres
and one of the longest in England. There's a
14thC gatehouse and a 16thC Tudor house,
forming a splendid setting for the 17thC
furniture, stained glass, tapestries and Sussex
ironwork. Art exhibitions are held in the
Tudor great barn, and traditional Sussex
crafts are sold. A further attraction is the
working medieval water-mill. *Open summer.*

Michelham Priory

34. Midhurst   3 B8
A quaint old market town in one of the most
beautiful regions of Sussex. Local legend
states that a rider was led to Midhurst on a
dark night by following the sound of its
church bell. In gratitude he bought a piece of
land in the town (now called Curfew Garden)
and presented it to the town to pay for the
nightly ringing. The sound of the curfew
echoed the streets at eight o'clock every
evening up until only a few years ago when
frost-bitten bell-ringers voted to end the
tradition. Look out for the 16thC timbered
market house and the 15thC Spread Eagle.
Also here are the ruins of **Cowdray Park**,
built in 1520 by the Earl of Southampton and
burnt down in 1793. Queen Elizabeth I stayed
at Cowdray in 1591. The three-storeyed
gatehouse, hall and chapel are worth seeing
and Cowdray Museum contains paintings and
local exhibits. The famous polo grounds, a
favourite royal haunt, form part of the estate.
Museum open most days, summer.

35. Petworth House   3 C8
Nr Petworth, A272. Turner immortalised its
interior, and Petworth in return houses a
magnificent collection of his work as well as
paintings by Van Dyck, Holbein, Rembrandt,
Frans Hals, Gainsborough and Reynolds.
This is one of the finest private art collections
to be seen in England. Neo-classical sculpture
is found in the North Gallery and the house
also contains some fine furniture.
Facing the lake and 700 acre deer park
landscaped by Capability Brown, this
magnificent 17thC house was rebuilt from the
former Percy mansion by the 6th Duke of
Somerset. Of the former building, only the
14thC chapel remains. Most impressive of the
rooms inside is the superb Carved Room,
decorated by Grinling Gibbons. *House open
most days, summer; park daily, all year.*

36. Pevensey Castle   3 G9
Pevensey Bay. An immense castle, built right
on the sea within a fort constructed by the
Romans between AD250–300 as a defence
against the Saxons and other sea-going

peoples from Europe. Centuries after the departure of the Romans, the bastions were still strong enough for the Normans to use as the effective outer bailey of a compact stronghold.

The castle is shaped in a rough oval following the contours of the low promontory, and covers 10 acres. Many of the local stones were pressed into use in the 12ft-thick walls: sandstone, Eastbourne greensand, flint, ragstone, ironstone and brick.

The castle continued to be garrisoned until the 14thC, and was equipped for defence against the Spanish Armada, and then Napoleon. As late as 1940, blockhouses and gun emplacements were built among the ancient structures to meet threats from Hitler. The sea has now retreated, leaving the castle ruins two miles inland. Some parts, including the dungeons and the lower part of the keep, have been well preserved.

37. Preston Manor   3 E9
Nr Brighton, A23. Retaining the relaxed and comfortable atmosphere of the home of an English country gentleman, this Georgian house stands on the site of what was probably a Saxon settlement. Preston Manor was originally built c1250, assumed broadly its existing shape in 1738 and was remodelled in 1905.

Richly and elegantly furnished, the manor evokes the day-to-day life of a wealthy family before the First World War. Much of the original furniture of the Thomas-Stanford family remains and there is also an impressive collection of pictures, porcelain and silver. The house is set in beautiful grounds which contain a walled period garden and the family pets' graveyard. *Open most days.*

Preston Manor

38. Pulborough   3 C8
8m N of Arundel, A283. A large village on Stane Street, the road built by the Romans in AD70 from Chichester to London. The surrounding ground is rich in prehistoric remains – it's a good place to hunt for flint arrowheads. The church at Hardham, *1m S of village,* has fascinating 12thC wall-paintings.

39. Rye   3 H8
This ancient and most picturesque town, lying two miles inland, was once a coastal island with Mermaid Street as the main entrance from the sea. In Elizabethan times it was a fortified port and is still an important, busy place.

Rye is one of the two Antient (not misspelt!) Towns – the other being Winchelsea – of equal status with the Cinque Ports. Mermaid Street, hilly, cobbled and lined with timber-framed houses, must be one of the loveliest streets in England. It leads to the Mermaid Inn built in 1336 and destroyed a year later by the French. Rebuilt in 1420, it sheltered Roman Catholic priests fleeing to the Continent after the Reformation and later was the haunt of smugglers.

Across the street is The House Opposite; it was christened this by its irritated occupants who tired of the constant flow of people mistaking their home for the notorious Mermaid Inn. The Other House, *West St,* belonged to a carpenter. A family along the street bore the same name and found themselves constantly referring callers to 'the other house' – and so it was named. Further down is Lamb House, a Georgian building and the home of Henry James from 1898 until his death in 1916. National Trust Property, the three rooms that are open are kept as they were in his day.

The 12thC **Church of St Mary the Virgin** is so impressive it's known as 'The Cathedral of East Sussex.' It has a magnificently carved mahogany altar, dating from the early 18thC, and a remarkable clock with cherubic figures striking the quarter hours, claimed to be the oldest turret clock in England. An 18thC water-house built for public use stands in the churchyard. Don't miss the Augustinian Priory or the Ypres Tower, built c1250 when Normandy fell to the French crown, and part of the 15thC sea defences. It now houses the local museum.

40. Sedlescombe   3 G8
6m N of Hastings, A229. Charming village with brick and tile-hung cottages surrounding the green where, under a gable-roofed shelter, stands an old pump. Anglo-Saxon coins were found here in 1867, which are said to have been buried by Harold's paymaster after the Battle of Hastings.

At **Norton's Farm** is a small museum of rural life. Farming tools of the past are displayed in old farm buildings and 27 horse-drawn ploughs and hoes and 14 wagons can be seen in the farmyard. *Open summer.*

41. Sharpthorne, Tanyard   3 E8
6m SE of Crawley, off B2028. A fascinating medieval tannery and manor with 16th and 17thC additions, set in walled gardens. Inside, furniture and ornaments of the period are displayed in a setting of oak beams, timbering and large open fireplaces. *Open certain days, summer.*

42. Shipley, King's Mill   3 D8
12m N of Worthing, off A24. This fine smock mill is also called Belloc's Mill because it belonged to the poet and novelist Hilaire Belloc who lived nearby. It was built in 1879, restored in 1957, and is in full working order. Smock mills – so called because their shape resembles the smock worn by farm workers – are constructed from wood on a circular base. They are usually eight-sided and the sails rotate to work the grinding stones. The mill is now owned by Belloc's daughter. *Open special days, or by arrangement.*

King's Mill, Shipley

43. Shoreham-by-Sea   3 D9
At first sight, an untidy commercial port, but look closer and you'll find two superb Norman churches. St Mary de Haura (of the haven) at

New Shoreham and St Nicholas at Old Shoreham mark two distinct stages in the medieval growth of the old port. New Shoreham is a planned town of straight streets; Old Shoreham is the core of the original settlement established in the 5thC by the South Saxons at the mouth of the River Adur, the rest having been swallowed up by the sea. Marlipin's Museum is worth a visit – it's a 12thC chequered flint and Caen stone barn containing paintings, historic ship models and relics of local history, and belongs to the Sussex Archaeological Trust. *Open summer.*

44. Singleton, Weald and Downland Open Air Museum
4¹/₂m N of Chichester, off A286. A unique open air museum, where historic farm buildings from Sussex, Kent, Surrey and Hampshire have been preserved by moving them bodily to this wooded valley. Within the 37 acres of grounds you can see a 14thC house, a 15thC farmhouse, an 18thC granary, a 19thC forge and toll cottage, a market hall and a barn. There are displays of traditional crafts and rural industries. You can eat your lunch in one of the attractive picnic sites, then follow the nature trail. *Open most days, summer.*

45. Sompting, Church of St Mary 3 D9
The most famous Saxon church in Sussex and one of the oldest in the country, St Mary's has a unique roof, called a Rhenish helm. This is the nearest the Saxons ever came to building a spire and although this type of tower is common along the Rhine, it is unique in England. The chancel is mainly Norman and the chapel, 14thC.

St Mary's, Sompting

46. Steyning 3 E9
4¹/₂m NW of Shoreham-by-Sea, A283. A medieval town, Steyning has managed to withstand modern development. Church Street tells the story of Sussex building: timber frames, tile-hanging, Horsham slate roofs, knapped flints and river cobbles subtly intermingle with brick in the 15th to 17thC cottages. To the south of the town, *Mouse Lane*, is the 15thC poor house, and an old market house stands in the High Street. The 12thC Church of St Andrew is one of the noblest in West Sussex. Built of stone imported from Normandy, it has a lofty nave and a 12thC carved marble font.
Just to the south of Steyning is **Bramber**. This prettiest of villages was once William the Conqueror's provincial capital and a port on the River Adur. All that remains of its importance is a 76ft-high fragment of the Norman castle wall on a large natural mound. **St Mary's House** is the best example in Sussex of late 15thC timber-framing with marvellous panelling. Furnished in period style, it contains a large collection of handicrafts, costumes, tapestries and antique furniture. There is an exhibition of antiques in the restored music room. Finally, pop in to see the weird and wonderful **Potter's Museum** and **Exhibition of Humorous Taxidermy**. *Open summer; certain days, winter.*

47. Storrington 3 D9
8m NW of Worthing, A283. A market town since the 14thC, Storrington is still small, though superficially spoilt by some ugly modern concrete. Look closer, however, and you'll find: Edwardian shopfronts and houses of local stone in the High Street; a triangular space in the centre, once the site of the medieval cattle market, in Brewer's Yard; the 400-year-old brewery buildings imaginatively converted into cottages; a large town pond. The church is Norman and has a tower but no spire – this having been destroyed by lightning in 1731. Inside, two monuments commemorate Wellington's victories over Napoleon. The Old Pillery Gardens near the churchyard are called after a certain Mr Dixon's pink pills – a universal panacea for the local people.
Beyond the parish church stands Storrington Priory, where the Norbertine monks cared for the sick poet Francis Thompson so well that he was inspired to write some of his best verse, including 'The Hound of Heaven'. In the garden wall of the Abbey House there's an unexpected mahogany door carved with birds and fishes, copied by Indian craftsmen from a famous door in Lahore. *View from outside only.*
Nearby **Parham House** is a perfect Elizabethan mansion in a downland setting of large trees and bracken that has not altered since Tudor times. The Great Hall has unusually large mullioned windows and a plastered ceiling. The hall, long gallery and principal rooms contain superb period furniture, Elizabethan, Jacobean and Georgian portraits, china and fine needlework. Interesting grounds with a deer park, a walled garden – and a church on the lawn. *Open certain days, summer.*

48. Uppark 3 B8
Nr The Hartings, B2146. A copybook example of the Wren-type country house; this noble, red-brick mansion was built from around 1690, high up on the blowy West Sussex Downs. Its downland setting is beautiful, its views magnificent, and it was once the home of Emma, Lady Hamilton, Nelson's mistress. The interior has been virtually unaltered since 1790 and remains in a remarkable state of preservation, with the original flock wallpapers and damask curtains, as well as the furniture. *Open most days, summer.*

49. West Hoathly 3 E7
4¹/₂m SW of East Grinstead, off B2028. A Saxon village in the Weald, once a centre of the iron industry. Look out for the 15thC Priest's House, now an interesting folk museum, run by the Sussex Archaeological Trust. It has a 'bean' for a threshold – a large lump of unfused iron. The church door has '31st March 1629' spelt out in iron studs and monuments of 17thC ironmasters set in the south wall. The shingled tower of the church, which is 13thC, has weathered to a lovely silvery colour. Smugglers used to climb it to signal to their friends down the valley to come and meet at the Cat Inn. *Priest's House open most days, summer.*

50. Wilmington Long Man 3 F9
6m NE of Seaford, A27. One of the oldest, largest and most imposing hill figures in the country. The Long Man is 231ft tall, cut into the downland turf in a shady coombe of Windover Hill, overlooking Wilmington village. He holds a staff in each outstretched hand, and was first recorded in 1779, but may be the work of the Iron Age Celts.

50. Wilmington Priory 3 F9
6m NE of Seaford, A27. A 12thC ruined priory, which makes a delightful setting for a museum of old agricultural implements, ironwork and other artefacts of the past. *Open summer.*

51. Winchelsea 3 H8
10m NE of Hastings, A259. On the opposite hill to Rye is this skeleton of an ancient city. A unique exercise in medieval town planning by Edward I, this half-built town was laid out on a regular grid pattern – no narrow streets, but

wide avenues at right angles to each other. It was a port until the 14thC, when the harbour silted up. The population was then 6,000 – now it's a mere 600, so is a town by virtue of history rather than its size.

In the centre is the 14thC Decorated Church of St Thomas Becket, partly destroyed by French marauders. The 14thC Court Hall is a museum which traces the history of the Cinque Ports.

52. Worthing   3 D9

Princess Amelia, youngest daughter of George III, put Worthing on the map when she visited it in 1798. In the next 14 years the town developed from a fishing hamlet to a popular resort, with bathing machines and esplanade and a tree-lined promenading place, or Steyne. The first six streets laid out from 1802–1805 were 'occupied by persons of the first rate fashion and fortune in England'. In Worthing Museum are many early Victorian water-colours and local prehistoric finds. *Open weekdays*. There's a half-timbered 16thC house at West Tarring, *NW of centre*, with a collection of 19thC bygones and exhibits of local interest. *Open most days*.

LONDON

'The flower of cities all' as the 15thC Scottish poet Dunbar called it, London is Europe's largest city, a place of endless variety and fascination, packed with historical memories and associations even as it passes through the processes of constant change. Britain may not be any longer one of the world's great powers, and her economy may be shrunken, but in London she still possesses a great source of pride and importance. For almost 30 miles from east to west, London stretches along the shining line of the Thames, divided into its two unequal halves by the great stream that widens towards the sea.

London has 2,000 years of history. It was the Roman invaders who built the first city here, where two low gravel hills, now topped by St Paul's and Leadenhall Market, encouraged the building of a bridge and settlement. At this time the tide reached only as far as London Bridge, so the settlement was turned by the Romans into the centre of communications in England and also its greatest port. From this dual role all the greatness of the city sprang.

Through all the centuries London has grown and changed. We first hear of a Sheriff of London in the 7thC and the first Lord Mayor was elected in 1192. Soon afterwards a great stone bridge rose where London Bridge now stands, the wonder of medieval Europe as it was the first stone bridge that had been built since Roman times. As the years passed, the City of London, where the Roman city had been, developed into a great financial and business quarter, while the settlement the Saxon kings had developed upstream at Westminster, grew by extension into a series of palaces and parks and then into the fashionable 'West End' where, from the 17thC onwards, the town houses of the nobility were built. The 18thC added new streets to complete the modern central area, a second bridge at Westminster and a splendid new mansion house for the Lord Mayor. And with the 19thC began the great, sweeping process of suburban growth, swallowing up old villages and former proud towns, creating the sprawling metropolis we know today to which millions have flocked in search of fame and fortune.

A great story indeed, and yet the seeker of history may be a little disappointed in the first instance, as actual living fragments of the distant past are few. There have been two great episodes of immense destruction – the Great Fire of 1666 which decimated the medieval city, and the sustained bombardment of 1940–44 during the Second World War. Besides this, there have been countless individual acts of careless waste and catastrophe. You have to go elsewhere, in general, for medieval inns: even the historic pubs of London tend to be solidly 19thC. Only a handful of the 100 medieval churches in the City of London survived the Fire, and the Blitz put paid to large parts of some of them. Much of London's history is a form of palimpsest: under the modern surface, if you look carefully, you can trace the endless layers of the past, revealed in street names, foundations and archaeological fragments. The really ancient buildings that survive to delight us, Westminster Abbey or the Charterhouse, for instance, are the product of a sort of happy accident. The story of London is one of essentially unplanned growth, buildings going up to meet immediate needs. It does not try to stun us with great processional ways or broad vistas: much of its grandeur rises in a context of the unexpected and domestic, in the way that the massive facade of St Paul's greets us from narrow Ludgate Hill. Over large areas it is a higgledy-piggledy jumble of squares, mews, crescents and streets of the same name running into each other at odd angles; grand sights existing cheek-by-jowl with modern eyesores. This is why some visitors to London initially find it shabby, but long acquaintance will only teach how much it has to offer – how often the unexpected journey or the unpromising-looking corner will reveal a rich treasure. Going with this unplanned growth, too, is the intricate network of local character, which has given rise to the Londoner's traditional love of his own area, his familiar patch. Even in the centre this is evident: in spite of massive rebuilding, for instance, the City of London retains its own character, its strange little alleys, its churches in quiet spots of green. And what two areas, only separated by a quite narrow road, could be more different than Mayfair and Soho? As you go out into the suburbs, this sort of intricateness does not diminish. It is a cliché to say that London is a collection of 1,000 villages, but even so it is true, and these old village centres somehow survive, as do the old windmills, tollgates and commons.

London was not built in a day, nor can it be explored in one. Decades of living in this great city will still leave many unfamiliar streets, many delights waiting to be discovered. Start, by all means with the truly great sights – the Abbey and St Paul's, the Houses of Parliament and the Tower of London – but as your knowledge broadens you will find that your greatest joy in London comes from the less familiar – the exquisite parish churches at Battersea and Chelsea, for instance, or the statue of the soldier on Paddington Station lost in timeless contemplation of home.

CENTRAL LONDON

All Hallows by the Tower
4 F6

Byward St, EC3. One of London's most historic churches with fragments of all eras somehow surviving in a composite whole. It was bombed twice in 1940, leaving some walls and the tower standing, but very little else. In the course of the imaginative rebuilding by Lord Mottistone, some fascinating history was unearthed: the remains of a Roman tessellated pavement of the 2ndC and ashes from the sacking of London by Bodicea in AD61. Also discovered were a Saxon archway and parts of two Saxon crosses, built not long after the first Christian church on this site, founded in AD675. The modern rebuilding of All Hallows has produced clever concrete galleries and roof and a pleasant light interior. Some fragments of the old church, such as the pulpit of 1670, remain. *Crypt museum open weekends or by arrangement.*

All Saints Church
4 E6

Margaret St, W1. A true masterpiece of the Gothic revival, this church was built by Butterfield in 1859 with paintings by Ninian Comper. A highly original design, it still appears startling, with its gilding, mosaics and paintings a riot of colour.

Apsley House
4 E6

Piccadilly, W1. One of the few great mansions still remaining in the neighbourhood of Hyde Park Corner, the house was built in red-brick by Adam in the 1770s and later bought by the Duke of Wellington, when it became known, because of the Duke's greatness, as 'No 1, London'. It was opened to the public in 1952 as the Wellington Museum and contains some remaining Adam decoration, a magnificent picture collection and many personal mementoes including splendid dinner services presented to the Duke by the grateful crowned heads of Europe. You will avert your eyes, of course, from the huge nude statue of Napoleon, apparently an idea suggested to Wellington by the monarch. *Open most days.*

Bank of England
4 F6

Threadneedle St, EC2. Known as 'The Old Lady of Threadneedle Street', it stands magnificently on three acres on an island surrounded by five streets, and from Lothbury its sheer walls and towers make it look rather like an Oriental palace. The Bank started in 1694 but initially operated from the Grocers' Hall, and the first building on the present site was erected in the 1730s. Sir John Soane built the present, great windowless structure in the 1780s, but it was largely rebuilt by Sir Herbert Baker in 1921–37 who destroyed Soane's classic interior and made the exterior much larger. Of the interior, only the entrance hall, a powerful room with great Belgian columns, is open to the public, but this gives an adequate idea of the financial might within, embodied in the nation's gold reserves in the great vaults. The surrounding area, colloquially known as 'Bank', is the historic focus of the City, and the modern streets have evocative medieval names like Cornhill, Lombard Street and Poultry.

Bank of England

Banqueting House
4 E6

Whitehall. One of the very few parts of the ancient palace of Whitehall remaining, the Banqueting House was built by Inigo Jones in 1619. This is the first building in London to be carried out in the Italian Palladian style and is generally considered to be his masterpiece. Charles I, a great artistic and architectural patron, hoped to add many more splendid buildings, but it was from a window of the Banqueting House that he stepped to his execution in 1649. An unparalleled summit of 17thC art, the main hall has an allegorical ceiling by Rubens, describing the magnificence of absolute monarchy as personified by the Stuart dynasty. The other remaining part of the old palace is Henry VIII's wine cellar, part of ancient York House, which is substantially 16thC and may be viewed on written application to the Ministry of the Environment.

Bevis Marks Synagogue
4 F6

Heneage La. (off Bevis Marks), EC3. One of the earliest surviving places of Jewish worship in England, it dates from 1700, shortly after the Jews had regained the freedom to live in England. It is distinguished by fine windows and a brass chandelier from Amsterdam.

Billingsgate
4 F6

Lower Thames St, EC3. One of the oldest of London's great quays and markets, for in the laws of Ethelred, given out in AD979, we read of trade ships arriving at Billingsgate, and some have even claimed that a market on this site dates back to the ancient Britons! By Elizabethan times it was well established as London's fish market, and even then strong language seems to have been associated with the place, if contemporary reports are to be believed. The present market buildings were built by Horace Jones and are of brick with cast-iron pillars in arcades within. The market has now moved to East London.

British Museum
4 E6

Great Russell St, WC1. One of the world's greatest museums and libraries, it is an awe-inspiring creation, built by Robert and Sydney Smirke in 1823–47. Apart from the library, it is said to contain eight million permanent exhibits and it is also constantly holding special exhibitions. Many of the treasures, such as the Assyrian bulls and lions, the Egyptian mummies, the ancient Chinese relics, the Magna Carta and the Elgin Marbles, are quite literally priceless. The museum stems from when Sir Hans Sloane gave his collection of objects for a down-payment of £20,000 in 1753, and this was followed by many other gifts, including some royal ones.

The library, in the great, domed reading room designed by Sydney Smirke (quite simply one of the world's most beautiful rooms) was added as a sort of afterthought to fill the central open space: originally tickets were for gentlemen only, but over the years the place has become a home-from-home to all those who can demonstrate serious scholarly intent. Karl Marx and Metternich, the 19thC conservative statesman, were both readers and are said to have met once on the steps, and proceeded to blame each other for the ills of Europe! The fact that the library is a copyright library has caused a super-abundance of books.

Buckingham Palace
4 E6

St James's Park, SW1. The official residence of the Crown, it is in the tradition of English unpretentiousness by being more a house than a palace. The facade you see from the Mall is not the true front and dates only from 1913: the more magnificent facade faces onto the garden, but you won't see that unless you're invited to a palace tea party. The site of the palace was originally a mulberry garden set up by James I in the early 17thC to encourage the manufacture of silk in England, and the house was originally the property of the Duke of Buckingham, who built it in 1703. George III bought it in 1761, and after extensive redecoration by Nash, which created an interior of great magnificence, it became the official royal residence during the reign of Queen Victoria. She had the great gateway of the house removed to Tyburn, where it is now known as Marble Arch.

The interior is not open, although the Queen's Picture Gallery can be seen, but the approach to the palace along the Mall is splendid. The Changing of the Guard in the forecourt every morning is one of London's most publicised but, nevertheless, spectacular attractions.

Buckingham Palace

Bunhill Fields Cemetery   4 F6
Nr Finsbury Sq, EC2. 'The Campo Santo of the Dissenters' as the poet Southey called it, it was London's Nonconformist burial ground from 1685, and before that was a burial ground for victims of the Great Plague of 1665. Here lie those three great apostles of the English Nonconformist conscience: Daniel Defoe, John Bunyan and William Blake. Nearby, most fittingly, is the 18thC chapel of John Wesley, in the graveyard of which he, too, lies buried.

Charing Cross   4 E6
Long regarded as the historic focus of London and the place from where British distances are measured. The area developed in the early Middle Ages as the small village of Charing, exactly half-way between the growing twin cities of the City of London and Westminster. The original cross was erected here by Edward I in November 1290 in memory of his wife, Eleanor of Castile: it was the last of 13 crosses put up at each of the places her body rested on its way from Lincolnshire to London. The cross stood where the statue of Charles I stands today, but was destroyed by the Parliamentary government in 1647 as a godless image, and a fish shop was encouraged to open on the site. The Victorians erected a new cross, a fine piece designed by E. M. Barry. It stands in the forecourt of Charing Cross Station, that great monument to Victorian 'railway cathedral architecture', designed by Hawkshaw and opened in 1864.

Cheshire Cheese   4 E6
145 Fleet St, EC4. One of London's most historic hostelries, it was rebuilt after the Great Fire of 1666 and the interior, with its low ceiling and open fire in the hearth, has changed little since it was rebuilt in 1677. Many literary men have been associated with the pub such as Dr Johnson, whose favourite chair is marked, Thackeray and Dickens. Oak tables and sawdust floors provide atmospheric setting for stout English cookery such as the steak and kidney pud for which the pub is famed. The 14thC crypt of Whitefriars Monastery is still intact beneath the cellar bar.

City of London   4 F6
A part of London which tourists often never penetrate, it's a shame to ignore it because this was where London began. The Romans built the original Londonium on two low gravel hills now crowned by St Paul's and Leadenhall Market, between which a tiny stream, the Walbrook, ran to the Thames. Over this stream the Romans built the first bridge. This was Norman and medieval London too, as street names like Cornhill, Poultry, Lombard Street and Jewry testify and the area it covers is still known as 'the square mile'. It began to develop as a distinct business and financial quarter from the 17thC, and became famed for top-hatted businessmen, or young men wandering the streets carrying huge piles of scrolls.

In recent years the City, which was heavily bombed, has been redeveloped almost out of existence. But it is still a notable area for archaeology, with such sights as the Temple of Mithras and Cripplegate Roman Fort.

Cleopatra's Needle   4 E6
Victoria Embankment, WC2. Nothing to do with either Cleopatra or sewing, this is a great pink-granite monolith, 68½ft tall, presented to the British government by Egypt's ruler of 1819, Mohammed Ali, and finally erected in 1877. It dates from 1500BC and is one of the Embankment's most striking, if incongruous, sights.

Cleopatra's Needle

Covent Garden   4 E6
Old and interesting quarter of central London, in the 16thC it was the convent garden of St Peter's Church, Westminster. Here the monks sold their surplus vegetables, starting a tradition which was a long time dying. After the Reformation the area passed to aristocratic landowners, the dukes of Bedford, who developed it around London's very first square, the Piazza, laid out by Inigo Jones in 1631 in imitation of the Piazza d'Arme at Livorno. He also built St Paul's Church for the square, a rather squat structure not showing his genius at its finest, but notable for its many theatrical graves. In 1671 a small market was opened here which gradually filled the whole square. It was housed in grand 19thC market buildings by Barry and Fowler, and became the world's most famous fruit and vegetable market. Covent Garden has long associations with culture and entertainment. Punch's puppet show was performed in England for the first time in the Piazza in 1662 and many great theatres and one of the world's great opera houses gradually sprang up. Voltaire lodged in Maiden Lane where Turner was born, while Jane Austen stayed with her brother in Henrietta Street on her trips up from Hampshire. The area developed, too, as a great centre of the printing trade and other crafts, adding to a rich urban mix.

In 1974 the market moved to Nine Elms and the area lost its heart. Sweeping plans for redevelopment were thwarted at the last moment and conservation won the day, the old market buildings most skilfully preserved as a new shopping and entertainment centre with the London Transport Museum. The whole place retains a little of its traditional shabby charm, as in sad 19thC Monmouth Street, but it is now too full of expensive coffee bars and shops selling nothing in particular.

Cripplegate Roman Fort   4 F6
These remains of a 2ndC Roman fort were discovered during post-war excavations. It seems to have been a sort of ceremonial barracks, housing soldiers performing the guard duties connected with a capital city and the presence of an imperial governor, rather than a military installation. Sections of the stone wall of the fort can be seen in Noble Street and in St Alphage churchyard (in the latter corresponding with the Roman city wall), and the Noble Street section also has an internal corner wall and turret. Part of the west gate of the fort remains under London Wall.

Dickens' House   4 E6
48 Doughty St, WC1. This was Dickens's residence when he was a young writer in the first flush of success, from 1837 to 1839: he wrote 'Oliver Twist' and 'Nicholas Nickleby' here. He was later to live in larger and grander houses, but few of the others remain. The late 18thC terrace house has great charm, however, and is now a museum devoted to his life and work, with many personal mementoes. Doughty Street has many other fine 18th and 19thC buildings and is one of the most attractive and unspoilt streets in Bloomsbury. *Open most days.*

Downing Street   4 E6
Off Whitehall, SW1. The Prime Minister's official residence is found, with British domestic understatement, in a small, quiet street dating from the 17th and 18thC. It was laid out by Sir George Downing, a 17thC civil servant, in 1681. No. 10 has been the Prime Minister's residence since 1735, when Sir Robert Walpole moved in, and it is much bigger and grander than it looks from the front door. Next door, no. 11, is the official residence of the Chancellor of the Exchequer. The walk through Downing Street into St James's Park and then back to Whitehall by way of Horse Guards Parade is one good way of sampling the atmosphere of this historic quarter of London.

10, Downing Street

Drury Lane, Theatre Royal   4 E6
Drury La, WC2. Perhaps the most famous theatre in the world, even older than the Theatre Francais which was founded in 1680 by Louis XIV. The theatre has been burned down several times and the present building dates from 1812 though the splendid Doric portico and the colonnade on the north side were added later. Countless famous players have left their footprint on the stage – Nell Gwynn, David Garrick, Mrs Siddons, Peg Woffington, Kemble and Macready – and their statues and busts fill the auditorium. The theatre has played a great role in English life and has been the scene of several notable disasters: in 1668 the pit audience rioted when rain came through the roof; in 1780 the London mob attacked it as part of the Gorden

Riots; an attempt was made on George III's life there in 1800; and in 1809 it burned down again before the anguished eyes of the actor and manager, Sheridan. Interesting historical aspects are the two doors labelled King's Entrance and Prince's Entrance, dating from the time the Hanoverian kings quarrelled with their sons and preferred to proceed to their boxes by separate routes.

Fleet Street   4 E6
The 'street of ink' or the 'street of shame' as it is often known, is world-famous as the centre of the British newspaper industry, and almost all national newspapers have offices either in the street itself or in the surrounding area. The connection with printing and the written word is very old: from the early Middle Ages Fleet Street was one of the main thoroughfares between the City of London and Westminster, and Wynkyn de Worde, who had been an assistant to England's first printer, Caxton, set up his own press here in 1501. Fleet Street's first daily paper was the 'Daily Courant', founded in 1702. The most exciting time to visit Fleet Street is late at night before the morning papers go to press, when there is a discernible excitement in the air; most newspapers will admit visitors if application is made well in advance to the editor.
Notable landmarks of the area are St Bride's Church, the Cheshire Cheese, the fine 18thC house in which Dr Johnson lived, *Gough Square*, and the Printers' Devil Tavern, *Fetter Lane*, which has a fine exhibition of printing throughout the ages. The western end of Fleet Street is Temple Bar, the historic division between the Cities of London and Westminster. The site was marked until the 19thC by the Bar itself, but now has an obelisk surmounted with a griffin. The other end is Ludgate Circus where the road slopes down suddenly – this is because it is crossing the old valley of the River Fleet (followed by Farringdon Street), one of London's 'underground rivers'.

Gray's Inn   4 E6
Holborn. One of the four great inns of court, it was badly damaged during the last war but has been well restored. There was a gathering of lawyers at Gray's Inn as early as 1370, and among famous members have been the great 17thC philosopher, Francis Bacon, who was treasurer of the Inn, Thomas Cromwell and Lord Birkenhead. The public are allowed to stroll around the tranquil gardens. Nearby are many attractive Georgian streets of which Great James Street, Bedford Row and Doughty Street are perhaps the most notable. *Open by arrangement; gardens open weekends.*

Guildhall   4 E6
Gresham St, EC2. The centre of the civic life of the City of London, premier town hall of England. It was partially destroyed by fire in 1666 and by bombs in 1940, but parts of the medieval building have magnificently survived. The present facade leads into a 15thC vaulted porch and the Great Hall is a splendid 15thC room, with genuine medieval masonry, although the ancient figures of Gog and Magog, twin deities of London, did not survive the war, and the present figures are modern. The hall is used for ceremonial occasions. In the 16thC it was the setting for many famous and fatal trials: that of the unfortunate nine-days-queen, Lady Jane Grey, and her husband, of Anne Askew, the Protestant martyr burned under Henry VIII, and Henry Howard, Earl of Surrey, sent to the block for being suspected of plotting against the King. There is a magnificently vaulted crypt below the hall and a lovely library, begun in 1425, which has an outstanding collection of books about London.

Horse Guards Parade   4 E6
Whitehall, SW1. The magnificent sentries of
the Household Cavalry, immobile on their
mounts, decorate Horse Guards Parade, a
group of buildings around the open space of
the parade itself. It is usually surrounded by
an admiring crowd of tourists, who sometimes
attempt to stuff billets-doux into their boots!
The site was once the guard house of ancient
Whitehall Palace, but the buildings and
parade were redesigned by Kent in the mid
18thC. The site is used for trooping the
colour in June, a ceremony no visitor should
miss.

Houses of Parliament   4 E6
Parliament Sq, SW1. Seat of the modern
legislature but still officially known as the
Palace of Westminster, this was a royal
residence long before it housed Parliament.
Edward the Confessor, who also built
Westminster Abbey, started the medieval
palace in the 11thC, and during this period it
was enlarged to include Westminster Hall and
St Stephen's Chapel, which were the only
parts to survive the disastrous fire of 1834.
Henry VIII moved into Whitehall from
Westminster in the 16thC, and that was the
period Parliament began to meet here
regularly.
The new palace began to rise in the 1840s
(after a plan to use Buckingham Palace for the
new seat of Parliament had been turned
down) and was designed by Sir Charles Barry
together with his assistant, Pugin, in
neo-Gothic style. The building was badly
bombed in 1941, and the new Commons
Chamber is the work of Giles Gilbert Scott.
Lofty and beautiful, Westminster Hall is the
most historically interesting part of the palace.
First built by William II in 1097, in the late
14thC Richard II put in the superb oak
hammer-beam roof which is considered one
of the best in Europe. Until the 19thC, this
was also the seat of the Royal Courts of
Justice, and many famous trials were held
here through the ages: the Scottish patriot,
William Wallace, who had been betrayed to
the English, was hung, drawn and quartered
on the steps in 1305, in 1606 Guy Fawkes was
tried and here Charles I faced his accusers in
1649 before being executed. Outside is
Thorneycroft's dumpy, thigh-booted statue of
Oliver Cromwell, an over-awed-looking lion
at his feet, while Richard I waves his sword
outside the Lords. Much of the palace, which
has 1,100 rooms, is impressive, with many rich
hangings, staircases and pictures. Big Ben, the
striking bell of the great clock, finished in
1858, is one of Britain's most loved landmarks
– the bell weighs 13 tons! The long river
frontage of 300 yards shows the facade at its
most impressive, and while here, no visitor
should omit a visit to the lovely, largely 16thC
Church of St Margaret, just across the road.

River Thames

Leicester Square   4 E6
WC2. One of the great hubs of modern
London, Leicester Square began to develop
around the great house, Leicester House,
built by Robert Sidney, second Earl of
Leicester, in 1631. He laid out the old
Leicester Fields with pleasant walks and the
square began to become residential from the
later 17thC. The house was pulled down in

1791 and its site is now largely occupied by
the Empire Cinema. Many of the famous have
lived around Leicester Square: Hogarth
resided in the south east corner, Blake lodged
here when he and his wife were first married,
Sir Joshua Reynolds had his fashionable
18thC studio here and Sir Isaac Newton lived
in a house near the site of modern
Westminster Public Reference Library. From
the 19thC Leicester Square was a tatty area
and it still remains a garish complex of loud
entertainment and multifarious eating places,
with very little remaining from the past.

Lincoln's Inn   4 E6
Holborn. An ancient inn of Chancery and one
of the four modern inns of court, the
barristers' associations. No-one knows how
long lawyers have worked on the site: one
authority places the date at 1292 and believes
the contemporary Earl of Lincoln founded it.
The Inn consists of lovely and dignified
buildings set around courtyards and
quadrangles, and Old Buildings, the
courtyard just inside the gatehouse from the
Chancery Lane entrance, is genuinely
medieval. Old Hall was built in 1492 and has
sinister twisting stairways leading to the
chambers above. The other buildings span the
centuries: there are 17thC offices around
New Square, while the library is in attractive
19thC mock-Tudor red-brick. Most of the
buildings are open on application and the
public may walk in the gardens.
Lincoln's Inn Fields, separated from
Lincoln's Inn by just a wall, is a public space
laid out by Inigo Jones as a private park in
1618, and declared a public park by Oliver
Cromwell in 1656. This crowded park, where
thousands of office-workers eat their
lunchtime sandwiches, was once noted as a
duelling ground and as a great haunt for
pickpockets. The latter tradition is by no
means dead, so beware!

London Bridge   4 F6
In many ways the real historic focus of
London and the reason why it began; the
Romans built the city at the lowest bridging
point, which was also at that time the highest
place the tide reached and London therefore
developed as both the centre of
communications and great port of Roman
Britain. The Roman bridge was probably a
little downstream of the present one. No-one
knows how many bridges preceded this one,
but we first hear of a Saxon bridge in the 9thC
when a woman was found guilty of bewitching
a man to death, so 'they took that woman and
drowned her at London Bridge'. The rhyme
about London Bridge falling down derives
from the occasion in 1014 when King Olaf of
Norway attacked London: his Vikings lashed
ropes around the piles and rowed hard,
causing the bridge to collapse.
Since then there have been many
replacements, although all the bridges have
been in the same spot. The bridge was
wooden until the 13thC, but the great stone
construction that followed, carrying houses
and shops, was one of the wonders of
medieval Europe. The fortified gates at each
end had spikes which were often adorned with
heads of traitors. A granite bridge built in
1832 by Rennie was shipped off to Arizona in
1971, and the latest structure, distant heir to
the Roman bridge, went up in 1973.

London Stone and London Wall   4 F6
The great wall of Roman London began to be
built around AD200 and formed the main
boundary of the City. With episodes of
intermittent destruction the walls continued in
use until the late Middle Ages. Some
surviving portions of wall are Roman in date,
although most of the later-added bastions are
in fact medieval. Sections of the wall and
bastions can be seen at the Tower of London
behind the ruined Wardrobe Tower; at

Cripplegate Roman Fort, where the walls of the fort corresponded with the city walls; at Cooper Row; at Amen Court; and (with the permission of the GPO), at the Post Office in St Martin's-le-Grand. The modern street called London Wall, rebuilt after the bombing as a landscape of futuristic skyscrapers, follows the northern line of the Roman wall, and many surviving medieval street names – Aldgate, Bishopsgate, Cripplegate – recall that these roads were at the position of the wall gates.

London Stone, embedded in the wall of the Bank of China in Cannon Street, is said to have been the 'milliarium' of Roman London, the spot from which they measured distances. It has been moved about a few times in the thousands of years, but probably rests not too far from its original spot.

London Transport Museum   4 E6
Piazza, Covent Garden, WC2. Housed in the old flower market of Covent Garden, an attractive Victorian building in its own right, a piece of intelligent conservation has turned this into one of London's most fascinating museums. There are many interesting old trains, buses and trams, as well as photographs and posters in abundance, while the helpful commentaries give both a history of transport in the capital and a detailed explanation of the development of London Transport. For the children – and fun-loving adults – there are chances to stand at the controls of a tube train and to work the switches in the special tunnel exhibit.

Madame Tussaud's   4 E6
Marylebone Rd, NW1. Famous exhibition of waxworks and horrors. Madame Tussaud was a friend of Louis XVI's sister, who fled the French Revolution bringing with her a collection of the death masks of guillotined aristocrats which she had been forced to make, and her exhibition, embellished by English murderers, established itself here in the early 19thC. The collection has widened since to include all classes of celebrities, some very life-like, and almost all the other exhibits, including the guillotine, are genuine.

The Mall   4 E6
SW1. The processional way from Trafalgar Square to Buckingham Palace, the Mall is one of London's few attempts at conventional grandeur and is comparable in its dignity with the Champs Elysées. It was laid out originally during the reign of Charles II, but the Victoria Memorial and Admiralty Arch, which forms the grand entrance to the way, were put up in 1911. To the right as we enter from Trafalgar Square is Carlton House Terrace, magnificent stuccoed Nash mansions built in the 1820s. Among the great houses of the Mall are Marlborough House, built for the great duke by Wren in 1710 but long a royal palace, and 19thC Clarence House, home of the Queen Mother.

Mayfair   4 E6
W1. Long London's most fashionable quarter. Mayfair is the product of aristocratic development, and especially of those greatest of London landlords, the Grosvenors, since the 19thC, dukes of Westminster. In the late 17thC Mary Davies, the daughter of a city clerk, brought into the family as her dowry what was then marshy farmland, but which as modern Mayfair and Belgravia is now one of the world's greatest property assets. Until the 1920s the dukes would not allow a trade plate to appear in these dignified streets, but since then commerce has invaded the area and it is now full of travel agencies and fashionable shops. It has become less grandly residential, although most mornings you can observe dotty-looking old ladies walking their overfed poodles.
The name derives from a great fair which was held here for centuries when the area was

rough and raffish: it was closed down in 1730 when its goings-on became intolerable. Shepherds Market, where it was held, still remains a charming if rather dubious enclave of 18th and 19thC London. Mayfair is in general very well preserved, and some of the squares, particularly Berkeley Square, retain 18thC elegance. Among fine streets remaining are Mount Street, where the gentleman burglar Raffles resided and which is splendid in 19thC terracotta brick; Brook Street, where Handel composed the 'Messiah'; and Dover Street with that cosiest of grand Mayfair hotels, Brown's, where Agatha Christie always stayed on her trips to London.

Monument   4 F6
Fish Hill St, EC3. This 202ft-high fluted Doric column was designed by Wren to commemorate the Great Fire, and is only a stones'-throw away from where the fire started, in a baker's shop in Pudding Lane. Modern buildings have lessened the impact of the Monument, but from the public gallery at the top it is possible to get a splendid, detailed view of the City of London.

The Monument

Museum of London   4 F6
London Wall, EC2. One of London's most fabulous and comprehensive museums, in which it splendidly celebrates its own greatness. It comprises the collections of the former London Museum and Guildhall Museum, with extra material besides. Cast as a biography of the city, it has models, reconstructions and even the Lord Mayor's coach. The part of the museum illustrating the building of the Roman walls is cleverly arranged so that you can look at the model and at the same time look down onto the actual Roman wall, a fragment of which is below you. *Open most days*.

National Gallery and National Portrait Gallery   4 E6
Trafalgar Sq, WC2. The National Gallery occupies the north side of Trafalgar Square and was built from 1832–8 on the site of the old Royal Mews in order to dominate the new square: a William Wilkins design beat a Nash one in open competition. Parliament had accepted the idea of a national art collection in 1824, and since then the gallery has developed into one of the outstanding collections of the world. Rich in every artistic period from the 13thC onwards, it excels in early Italian, Dutch and Flemish, 15th to 18thC Spanish and, of course, English works.
The National Portrait Gallery is rather inconspicuous behind the National Gallery and it provides a magnificent biographical record of famous Englishmen and women. The earliest portrait from life is that of Henry VII: earlier kings are shown on coins.

Old Bailey   4 F6
Newgate, EC1. The Central Criminal Court and the associated buildings, it stands on the site of former Newgate Prison, established in the 13thC and for long one of Britain's most notorious places of incarceration. It was finally pulled down in 1903. From the 18thC to 1863

Newgate replaced Tyburn as the main site of public executions. Note the road widens outside the court – this was to allow room for spectators. The Central Criminal Court was set up in 1834, but the present building is 20thC. Though rather rugged from the outside, the Great Hall inside is of pleasing Edwardian elegance. Visitors are warned that there may be long queues to get into popular trials.

Old Curiosity Shop   4 E6
Portsmouth St, WC2. A little crooked and blackened house, an outstanding example of 17thC domestic architecture in an area that once contained some of London's most horrific 'rookeries' or slums. It is disputed whether this is the origin of Dickens's Old Curiosity Shop as some experts think he based it on a shop near the Charing Cross Road. Nearby is Clare Market, with Dick Turpin the highwayman associations.

The Old Curiosity Shop

Oxford Street   4 E6
W1. Oxford Street represents the main Roman road from London to the west and has long been one of its most important thoroughfares. From the Middle Ages onwards it was the road out to Tyburn, so-called because of the Tyburn Brook, where thousands flocked to watch public executions, near where Marble Arch now stands. The street became London's most important shopping street from the 19thC when it developed as the 'woman's mile', selling women's clothes and domestic goods, as it was conveniently situated close to a centre of the rag trade just a little to the north. The department stores began to appear towards 1900.

Pall Mall   4 E6
SW1. Highly historic street, which is said to take its name from 'pêle-mêle', a favourite game of Charles II and his courtiers. It was the historic home from the 17thC of many of the rich and fashionable, including Charles II's actress mistress, Nell Gwyn. John Evelyn, the diarist, writes of a morning in Pall Mall in March 1671: 'Mistress Nellie, as they call an impudent comedian, talking with the King, she looking out of her garden, on a terrace on top of the wall'. Pall Mall is now the site of several large London clubs, such as the Oxford and Cambridge founded in 1830 and the slightly later Reform, and they are housed mainly in palatial former mansions of the 19thC.

Piccadilly   4 E6
W1. The street that more than any other symbolises London, it was a country lane until the 17thC. Its name is thought to derive from one of the earliest shops in the area, that of an early 17thC tailor called Robert Baker who sold 'pickadils' (frillings on hems) and lived in a house called Pickadily Hall. Grand mansions began to be built here from the late 17thC and the area became a headquarters of fashion. It is now largely commercial but still undeniably grand, with the Royal Academy splendidly housed in 18thC Burlington House, other dignified premises of learned societies nearby, and massive 19thC facades everywhere. Piccadilly Circus, at the eastern end, was laid out as part of Nash's plan for

Regent Street in 1819, but has become very garish since. Its beloved statue, the Angel of Christian Charity (wrongly known as Eros), was erected in 1893 by public subscription as a tribute to the philanthropic Earl of Shaftesbury.

Piccadilly Circus

Queen Anne's Gate   4 E6
SW1. The best example in London of a totally 18thC street, it was built by William Paterson and was originally known as Queen Square (although it can never have been a proper square). The houses are now offices, but retain their character astonishingly with 18thC porches, torch extinguishers, railings and statues. Queen Anne's Gate runs into Petty France, once a fashionable street and in the 17thC the residence of John Milton.

Regent Street and Regent's Park   4 E6
W1. Part of the grandiose conception designed by Nash for the Prince Regent, later George IV, in the 1810s and 1820s, Regent Street was designed to link the administrative area of Whitehall and the King's residence at Carlton House to the great new Royal Park which had once been part of Henry VIII's hunting forest. Regent Street was a magnificent example of a 'grande route', but despite its great architectural merit it was largely rebuilt in 1925–6 in rather top-heavy monumental style.
Regent's Park was originally designed for private, royal pleasure, but was opened to the public in 1838. It contains the zoo, Bedford College, the delightful Queen Mary's Gardens and some of the most magnificent houses Nash designed – the Nash terraces of the Inner Circle, which remains magnificent despite suffering from the bombing of 1940.

Royal Exchange   4 F6
Cornhill, EC2. Dominating the great confluence of roads around the Bank is the Royal Exchange, one of the premier City institutions. The first Royal Exchange was built at the behest of the great Elizabethan banker, Sir Thomas Gresham, but was burned down in 1666, as was the second building in 1838. The present building is by Sir William Tite, and has a splendid range of classical columns in its facade, over which a tympanum shows City officials as well as both merchants of all races and commercial symbols. Inside it is a place of stone benches and echoing corridors, and the entrance hall shows a most interesting 18thC hand-operated fire-engine. *Open weekdays.*

Royal Mews   4 E6
Buckingham Palace Rd, SW1. One of the few adjuncts of Buckingham Palace open to the public, it contains many interesting examples of royal transport. There's the Balmoral sociable, Edward VII's 1903 Daimler, the current Rolls Royces and some of the carriage horses with their accoutrements, including a droshky harness given to Queen Victoria by the Tsar. But the prime exhibit must be the

gold state coach of 1762 made for George III, the epitome of ceremonial magnificence, much loved for its use on royal occasions. *Open certain days*.

Royal Opera House, Covent Garden 4 E6
Floral St, WC2. One of the great opera houses of the world, the present huge and magnificent building was built by E. M. Barry in 1838, who also designed Covent Garden Market. The interior is richly decorated and as well as opera it also houses the Royal Ballet and doubles as a concert hall.

The Royal Parks 4 E5
Great swathes of open land in the very centre of London, they have been preserved for use of the public by the generosity of the crown. The largest, **Hyde Park** which is joined to Kensington Gardens, was originally part of the Saxon manor of Eia which was bequeathed to Westminster Abbey soon after the Norman Conquest. Henry VIII took hold of it in 1536 and stocked its with deer to form a hunting park, and James I opened it to the public. Queen Elizabeth I held military reviews (still held on special occasions) and it was the site of the Great Exhibition of 1851. Until the 18thC it was a haunt of highwaymen, and even now is patrolled by the police at night. Sights to see include the wide Serpentine, created in 1730 by damming the Westbourne river which now runs underground, the mile of Rotten Row where the Edwardian crowds promenaded, the Tea House and the charming statue of Peter Pan. Hyde Park Corner originated as a toll-gate into London and was laid out in its present form by Nash in 1820.
St James's Park was also an acquisition of Henry VIII and was laid out in French style by Charles II, later being grandly redesigned by Nash in 1820 for George IV. Here you'll find the world's most pampered ducks. **Green Park** was once part of St James's Park, but has been considered a separate area since the 18thC. This was the scene of the celebrations at the Peace of Aix-la-Chapelle in 1749 when Handel's 'Music for the Royal Fireworks' was first performed in front of a vast crowd.

St James's Park

St Bride's
EC4. Fleet Street's beloved parish church, its history is pre-Christian, for the remains of a Roman mosaic pavement were discovered here and are displayed in the east end of the crypt. This is a remain of the only building known to have existed in Roman times between their city and Westminster. There was a Christian church here from the 6thC dedicated to Bride (Bridget), the Irish saint, but the present church is by Wren, built after the Great Fire and ready for use in 1675. It is one of his masterpieces, with a beautiful white and golden interior and stalls of honey-coloured wood, and also possesses one of his happiest steeples, which Henley called 'a madrigal in stone'. There are remains of a medieval crypt and walls, as well as some Roman walling which survived a new episode of destruction, the partial gutting of the church by fire bombs in 1941.

St George's 4 E6
Hanover Sq. One of the finest of London's 18thC classical churches, it was built by John James in 1721–4 and tastefully restored by Blomfield in 1894. Among its treasures is the original of the 'Last Supper' by Kent.

St James's 4 E6
SW1. A tight corner of aristocratic development around the royal palaces, it developed largely as the precincts of Charles II's court from the 1660s, and remains the part of London where the English gentleman still reigns supreme and finds his shops and his clubs. St James's Square, one of London's earlier squares laid out in 1660, is still largely 18thC and is the ultimate in aristocratic addresses: at one time six dukes and seven earls were living there. It also houses that unique institution, the **London Library**, founded by Thomas Carlyle in the 1840s, which has developed as a sort of socially-superior rival to the British Museum.

St James's Palace 4 E6
Pall Mall, SW1. Standing on the site of a 'hospital for maidens that were leprous' built before the Norman Conquest, Henry VIII took possession of it at the Reformation and built a palace to please Anne Boleyn. Only small parts of the remaining palace are Tudor – the Chapel Royal, with its magnificent ceilings by Holbein, the Presence Chamber and the Clock Tower – but most of it is of considerable antiquity and there is a 15thC gatehouse. Many kings and queens lived here, Charles II was born here in 1630, and although no monarch has resided here since William IV, it is still the official seat of the court. You can walk round the courtyards and look for the ancient lampholders. *View from outside only*.

St Magnus the Martyr 4 F6
Lower Thames St, EC3. One of Wren's finest churches, on the site of originally a Saxon church, it has a splendid steeple, 185ft high. The interior is in the height of Anglo-Catholic Baroque magnificence, immortalised by T. S. Eliot as 'inexplicable splendour of Ionian white and gold', and the 1712 organ is original. From 1176 to 1831 what is now its churchyard formed part of the roadway approach to London Bridge.

St Martin in the Fields 4 E6
Trafalgar Sq, WC2. One of London's most loved landmarks, this is a fine classical church of 1726 by Gibbs with a famous spire and portico. There is a Venetian east window, a white and gold moulded plaster ceiling and a cluttered but atmospheric crypt full of old monuments and abandoned furniture. St Martin's is famous for lunchtime music and has magnificent acoustics. When it was built, the area really was close to fields.

St-Mary-le-Bow 4 F6
Cheapside, EC2. One of London's symbolic churches, because it was Bow bells that recalled Dick Whittington to be thrice mayor of London, and a true Cockney must traditionally be born within sound of these bells. The original bells were lost in the Great Fire, as were their replacements in the Blitz of 1941, but the new bells were made from the remains. The Wren Church was built in 1670 on the site of what was originally a Saxon church. Although the exterior from Cheapside has been carefully restored, the interior was redesigned by Laurence King in a bold if not entirely successful design of white and gold with a turquoise ceiling and a black and white floor.

St Pancras Station 4 E6
Euston Rd, NW1. Truly magnificent Victorian Gothic building, more palace than station, designed by Sir George Gilbert Scott in 1868. Its dreaming spires and pinnacles are best seen on misty nights, when surrounded by the

attendant lights of London – it looks as if all the romance of the Middle Ages has united with the constructional skill of the Industrial Revolution to form a castle of enchantment.

St Paul's Cathedral 4 F6

Ludgate Hill, EC4. London's cathedral and perhaps the most potent symbol the great city has, St Paul's remains superbly moving even if its classic profile on the London skyline has been dwarfed by the skyscrapers of the industrial age. It is the crown of Christopher Wren's church-building in the City and the chief monument of 17thC English classicism. No-one knows how long the site has been the scene of Christian worship, but there is agreement that by at least AD604 a wooden church was built by Bishop Mellitus and that it was destroyed and rebuilt a number of times until a great medieval cathedral rose in 1220. But in the later Middle Ages it fell into decay and was even used to stable horses. In the 17thC plans were set afoot to rebuild it: Inigo Jones almost took on the job, and in the 1660s the young Christopher Wren advised replacing the tower by a great dome. Then came the Great Fire, and the cathedral became the cornerstone of Wren's plans for rebuilding London. After many difficulties it was finally finished in 1708, the final stone laid by Wren's son as the architect himself, now 78, was too old and infirm.

During the Second World War the area around the cathedral was subjected to continual bombardment. The building escaped narrowly many times including one occasion when an incendiary bomb lodged within the dome itself and all seemed lost, until as if by a miracle, it just fell into the Stone Gallery. But although there was damage to the High Altar and crypt, to the great joy of Londoners the great church did not fall. Much glass was blown out, but was replaced by the clear glass Wren originally wanted.

The massive interior, 513ft in length, is dominated by the presence of the great dome above. At 112ft in diameter, it's the largest in the world after St Peter's, Rome. You can ascend the stairs to the Whispering Gallery which surrounds the lower dome, but this requires stamina. The rich ornamentation everywhere conveys Wren's genius for detail, and he had the help of Grinling Gibbons in the carving. The dome frescoes are by James Thornhill, another close collaborator of Wren. The crypt is the biggest in Europe and contains many monuments and tombs, including those of Wellington, Nelson, and John Donne, poet and Dean of St Paul's. Wren himself lies there, covered by a simple slab, above which are his son's words, 'Si monumentum requiris, circumspice'.

St Paul's Cathedral

The Salisbury 4 E6

St Martin's La, WC2. In the heart of London's theatreland, the Salisbury preserves intact its atmosphere of late Victorian brilliance and artificiality. It was opened in the 1880s (having formerly been a venue for prize fights) and its decor is original: cut-glass mirrors, plush marble bar, statuettes, exquisite decorated lamp-stands. Oscar Wilde used to drink at the Salisbury, and it's now frequented by theatrical types, or people who look as though they ought to be theatrical types.

Smithfield 4 F6

EC1. Smithfield has a long history, associated with blood in various forms. This was the site for the burning of martyrs at the Reformation and of medieval tournaments. The longest-running fair in English history, the Bartholomew Fair which ran from 1123 to 1855, was sited here, and this was the scene of many a ruffianly deed, while the slaughter-house for cattle set up by James I has turned over the years into the largest meat market in Europe. The present market buildings were designed by Horace Jones from the 1860s and contain 15 miles of hanging rails for taking carcases.

Smithfield is a particularly interesting area to explore, as it has a large number of historic buildings. **St Bartholomew's Hospital** (Bart's) is London's oldest, founded by the monk Rahere in 1123 at the same time as the Priory **Church of St Bartholomew the Great**. The present hospital buildings were largely designed by James Gibbs in the 18thC. The church is the city's oldest, with a 13thC gateway leading in from west Smithfield. There are huge Norman columns and arches, the Lady chapel is of 1330, and there are medieval furnishings of great interest. It is one of those churches that initially seems dark and gloomy but which then broadens out before your eyes until you see it is the size of a small cathedral. The ancient **Charterhouse** is nearby, founded in 1349 as a site of the monastic order. When it was suppressed by Henry VIII, some brave monks were dragged on hurdles to Tyburn and disembowelled and hanged alive. In the 17thC it became a school which in 1872 moved to Godalming in Surrey.

Soho 4 E6

W1. A place of mystery and long London's foreign and raffish quarter. Its strange name is thought to derive from the old hunting call 'so ho' which was used as a rallying cry by the supporters of the Duke of Monmouth, Charles II's illegitimate son who lost his head in 1685 because of his attempt on the throne. The first, and predominant foreigners in Soho were the French who settled here in large numbers after Louis XIV's persecution of Protestants by the revocation of the Edict of Nantes (1685) drove them away. They were followed over the years by large numbers from Spain, Italy and Malta to form the cosmopolitan mix of an area where foreign languages are heard as often on the streets as English. The area has become a great centre for the media industry, good restaurants and London's vice quarter, the last progressively taking up more and more room. Visitors to London have often found room in Soho: Mozart stayed in Frith Street in his visit to London as a child prodigy and Karl Marx lived in scholarly poverty in Dean Street. William Blake, the greatest poet of his native city, was born in what is now Broadwick Street and lived here much of his life.

Soho's streets were largely built by private development in the late 17th and early 18thC and often bear the names of their developers – Panton, Frith, Whitcomb, Wardour. This haphazard tangle of streets and alleys has remained unchanged over time, so that Soho is full of strange passages and streets, like D'Arblay Street or Great Pulteney Street, which you think you know but which are always hard to find. Soho Square is one of the most interesting parts: it was grandly fashionable for a while when it was built in the 1680s and became a centre for foreign embassies. Although most of the modern buildings are undistinguished, there is still a delightful square garden, with Cibber's much weathered 18thC statue of Charles II.

Statues of London
London has over 1,700 outdoor statues and memorials, the subjects ranging from classical mythology to modern statesman, some of them famous works of art, even more, loved local landmarks. The oldest is the statue of Alfred the Great in Trinity Church Square, which was probably transported from Westminster Hall and is thought to date from 1395. Probably the finest of all is Charles I in Trafalgar Square looking down Whitehall: it was made by La Sueur in 1633 and ordered to be destroyed under Cromwell, but it was hidden and erected on its present site in 1677. Perhaps the most scenically impressive is the warlike Bodicea on Westminster Bridge, done by Thornycroft in 1902. Other very famous ones include Edith Cavell, Peter Pan, Lincoln, Florence Nightingale and Nelson on his column. But perhaps some of the most moving are equally familiar but less well-known, such as the soldier of the First World War on Platform 1 at Paddington Station, in trench warfare kit and reading a letter from home.

The Temple   4 E6
EC4. Containing two of the four inns of court, Inner and Middle Temple, it occupies a large area between the river and Fleet Street. It was originally the site of the headquarters of the Knights Templar, a medieval fighting religious order forcibly disbanded in 1312 and many of the buildings are 17thC or even earlier. You can enter from Middle Temple Lane through a gatehouse designed by Wren in the late 17thC, and inside are many courtyards, steps, trees and gardens, while the 17thC houses in King's Bench Walk may be by Wren. Middle Temple Hall dates from 1570 and saw the first performance, in 1601, of Shakespeare's 'Twelfth Night', in which he himself may have acted. Inner Temple has a 14thC crypt.
But the oldest part is **Temple Church**, consecrated in 1085 and only one of five round churches remaining in Britain. The earliest parts are Gothic in style, it has a beautiful oblong Early English chancel of 1240, and the reredos is by Wren. Extensive 19thC restoration and severe Blitz damage have not been able to destroy the unique historical interest of this church.

Temple of Mithras   4 F6
Queen Victoria St, EC2. One of the most spectacular of the finds made after bomb damage, this was the church of Roman soldiers who worshipped the Persian sun-god Mithras. Originally found 18ft underground in Walbrook it was moved here with other Roman relics. Some sculptures and a unique decorated silver canister which were found in the temple are now housed in the Museum of London.

Tower of London   4 F6
Tower Hill, EC3. One of the most impressive medieval fortresses remaining in Europe, the earliest part, the White Tower, was built by William the Conqueror in 1068 to overawe the people of his new capital city. The tower served throughout the years as a garrison, armoury, royal residence, zoo, prison, observatory, and Royal Mint. Although it was a prison as late as 1820, all these functions have now been moved and today it's an impressive showplace with grim memories. Many great names have languished here, including kings of England, France and Scotland, and from here unfortunates, such as Lady Jane Grey, Sir Thomas More and Anne Boleyn, went to execution blocks at Tower Green or Tower Hill.
There are many things of interest to see at the Tower, although it also has some aspects of tourist nightmare. Traitor's Gate, the main entrance from the river, is grimly impressive, and another water-gate, 13thC in date, has

recently been discovered. The Bloody Tower is where Sir Walter Raleigh was imprisoned for 13 years, and where the murder of the little princes is said to have taken place in 1483. The half-timbered Queen's House is the Governor's residence and looks out onto Tower Green with the much publicised Beefeaters and ravens: legend states that when the tame ravens depart, the Tower will fall. The ancient White Tower contains one of the finest collections of medieval armour in Europe and in the crypt of the Norman chapel of St John is the axe and block used to execute Lord Lovat. Dream of every burglar, the Crown Jewels are, of course, a must.

Tower Bridge   4 F6
EC3. Impressive Victorian Gothic structure with its familiar towers and hydraulic twin drawbridge. It was erected by Jones and Wolfe Barry in 1894.

Tower Bridge and Tower of London

Trafalgar Square   4 E6
WC2. Laid out between 1829 and 1841 in belated commemoration of Nelson's great victory on the site of the former Royal Mews. It's crowned with Nelson's Column, erected in 1847, on which he himself stands 17ft high, and at his feet are the Landseer lions which were added in 1867. A pleasing square with fine vistas and a great focus of the swirling crowds, it's famous for its pigeons, Christmas tree, New Year festivities and political demonstrations.

Westminster Abbey   4 E6
Broad Sanctuary, SW1. Premier of English abbeys, its long association with the Crown probably saved it from the general fate of abbeys at the Reformation, and it remains a pristine example of the glories of medieval architecture. The first abbey was built by Edward the Confessor in the 11thC, but it was magnificently rebuilt by the pious Henry III in the mid 13thC in the purity of the Early English style. This forms the basis of the building, but it was finally added to in the succeeding centuries by the great 14thC architect, Henry Yevele, and others. Its crowning glory, the Henry VII chapel, perfect example of the Perpendicular Gothic, was added in 1503. The towers were finished by Hawksmoor in 1734.
The association with English kingship is long and deep. Edward the Confessor's body was moved here when the new church was built in the 13thC, and until George III, monarchs were buried here. All English monarchs since Harold have been crowned here, except Edward V and Edward VIII who were never crowned. Many of the greatest Englishmen are buried here (with a special section for the literary at Poet's Corner) and at least one of the humblest – the grave of the Unknown Soldier, movingly edged with poppies, is in the foreground of the nave.
The wonders of the Abbey are many and full exploration of this great church will take time. But enter by the great West Door and savour the impressive length of the stone-flagged nave; do not miss the richness of the choir or the multiple memorials of the crowded east end; see the serene cloisters and the museum of funeral effigies carried in historic burials here; visit one of the sumptuous royal chapels, preferably the Henry VII chapel. To end, take a visit to ghostly Dean's Court outside, with its cobbles, gas lamps and secretive archway, seeming on misty evenings to call up all the mysteries of the Christian past.

SOUTH OF THE RIVER

Battersea
4 E7

In Roman times the area was composed of marshy islands, there was a ford near where Battersea Church stands, and many flints and bronzes that have been discovered testify to the importance of ancient British settlement. In Tudor and Stuart times Battersea was a flourishing village and manor, and traces of this settlement are still recognisable to the west of Battersea Bridge. The St John family were lords of the manor for generations and Old Battersea House, designed by Wren in 1700, is their monument. A gathering place for the wits of Queen Anne's day, it has a lovely row of dormers in the roof, rich rooms inside and one of the finest art collections in London.

Until the end of the 18thC, Battersea was only a market-gardening village – hence the name of the modern shopping street, Lavender Hill. In 1792 William Blake married the daughter of a Battersea market-gardener in St Mary's, Battersea's parish church.

St Mary's is one of the exquisite small churches of Battersea, with a commanding position above the Thames, a fine apse, a delightful copper spire, and a wonderful heraldic window, one of the few of the 17thC left in England. There has been a church here since William the Conqueror, but the present one is late 18thC.

In the 19thC Battersea began to change: at first it was fashionable, but then came industry and the endless rows of two-up two-down grimy artisans dwellings. Clapham Junction station was opened in 1845, and many Victorian industries are still open here today. The new society provided its landmarks: the great park, opened in 1858 on the site of old Battersea Marshes, and that magnificent monument, the Power Station.

Battersea Power Station
4 E7

Battersea Park Rd, SW8. This huge industrial building caused horrified protest from environmentalists when it was erected by Giles Gilbert Scott in the 1930s, but it is now recognised as a masterpiece of 1930s architecture, with its monumental red-brown facade and grand, symmetrical four towers.

Bermondsey, Rotherhithe and Deptford
4 G6

Three historic riverside boroughs between London Bridge and the Surrey Commercial Docks, they retain memories of a long past amid the process of urban renewal and change. Bermondsey has an old church, St Mary Magdelene, which was built in 1680, but is the direct descendant of one of the first Cluniac monasteries in England, built soon after the Conquest. Bermondsey's old industries are in decline, and it's quite spooky to walk along Shad Thames, just to the east of Tower Bridge, where the dark line of old warehouses sometimes breaks to give views of the river. Nearby is the site of Jacob's Island, that horrifying slum of rackety river-tenements which Dickens immortalised in 'Oliver Twist'. Rotherhithe, whose name derives from the Anglo-Saxon for 'mariner's haven' and which was a port for more than 1,000 years, seems haunted by the ghost of the Surrey Docks and by the sound of dead voices on the desolate quays. Deptford is livelier today. It was the site of Henry VIII's naval dockyard in the 16thC, but little trace of this remains. It was while drinking in a low tavern in Deptford that Christopher Marlowe, the playwright, was killed in a brawl in 1593: he is buried here in an unmarked grave.

Blackheath
4 G7

A high and windy common on a gravel hill on the southeastern outskirts of London, where medieval and Tudor rebels who wished to attack the capital used to gather. Wat Tyler's pathetic band converged here during the Peasants' Revolt of 1381, as did Jack Cade's followers in 1450. Henry VII fought a battle against Cornish rebels at Blackheath in 1497. As London became safer from attack, the common resorted to more peaceful uses (although it was still a haunt for highwaymen): early in the 17thC James I introduced golf to England here, and in the 18thC many fine Georgian residences were built, including a magnificent crescent, the Paragon, which now forms the nucleus of fashionable Blackheath. Morden College is an almshouse of 1700 built by Christopher Wren at the behest of a wealthy merchant in the Aleppo trade. It is a fine Queen Anne House and has some Lely portraits. Ranger's House is the 18thC home of the Earl of Chesterfield: it has wonderful rose gardens and is now a public tea-room.

Brixton Windmill
4 E8

Blenheim Gdns, SW2. An elegant windmill of the tower type, erected in 1816 in what were then open fields. It has recently been restored by the GLC. Other notable South London windmills are to be found on Wimbledon Common and Wandsworth Common.

Crystal Palace
4 F9

Crystal Palace, SE19. Named after Paxton's 1851 Great Exhibition building removed here from Hyde Park in 1854, and in turn, it gave its name to the late 19thC suburban area that grew around it. It was destroyed by fire in 1936, and a great modern recreation centre has arisen near the site. The superb foundations still remain.

Dulwich
4 F7

One of the most interesting and distinctive of the villages which have been swallowed up by the outward growth of London, Dulwich Village is basically a well-shaped street full of delightful Georgian houses. Dulwich profited much from the generosity of the Elizabethan actor, Edward Alleyn, who rivalled Shakespeare's top actor, Burbage. Having made a mint of money, he founded both the school, Dulwich College, and the most charming public park, notable for its splendid rhododendrons and beloved of the late Queen Mary.

Dulwich Village

Greenwich
4 G7

SE10. Heir to the great English traditions of royalty and naval enterprise, Greenwich is outstanding for the most magnificent assemblage of 17thC buildings in England, set at the foot of rising ground where Greenwich Park sweetly fronts the Thames. Greenwich has always been a lively riverside borough, because before the building of the docks in the 19thC the disembarking points for ships were on the South Bank, and at Greenwich the Great Howland Docks were built in 1696 to take the Greenland whalers. There was also a medieval palace by the river, a favourite residence of the Tudors: Henry VII and his three children, Edward, Mary and Elizabeth,

were all born here, Henry VIII courted Anne
Boleyn here, and Elizabeth spent many hours
walking in the woods in the great park.
The greatest glory of Greenwich began in the
17thC when the palace had collapsed into
ruin, and on its site Wren planned the great
Naval Hospital, now the Royal Naval College.
The building was largely executed by Wren's
two able assistants, Vanbrugh and
Hawksmoor, both to become great architects
in their own right, but the plan expresses
Wren's genius. The painted hall is one of
Britain's finest rooms, and the ceiling, painted
by James Thornhill, is perhaps the most
successful European example of provincial
copying of the glories of the Roman Baroque.
Open most days. Wren also designed the old
Royal Observatory on the hill, now part of the
National Maritime Museum. Marked on the
path in front of it is the Greenwich Meridian
from which Greenwich Mean Time is
calculated. The third great 17thC building at
Greenwich is the rather earlier work of Inigo
Jones, the Queen's House, completed for
Henrietta Maria, wife of Charles I.
As if all this were not enough, Greenwich has
more historic buildings and associations. St
Alphege's Church was built in 1718 by
Hawksmoor in massive Grecian style on the
site of an ancient church, but it suffered
terribly in the bombing of 1931, and many of
the medieval relics, including the organ of the
16thC musician Thomas Tallis who is buried
here, were destroyed. Vanbrugh's Castle, at
Maze Hill, is the early 19thC home of the
architect, its heavy solemnity reflecting its
owner's style. The Cutty Sark, most famous of
the 19thC tea-clippers, is moored on
Greenwich Reach. Gipsy Moth, the yacht in
which Sir Francis Chichester sailed
single-handed round the world, is nearby.

The Cutty Sark

Imperial War Museum   4 E6
Lambeth Rd, SE1. Museum of modern war
established in 1920 in what had formerly been
part of London's best-known lunatic asylum:
the Bethlehem Hospital for the sick or
'Bedlam' was where the fashionable crowds of
the 18thC went to mock at the imbeciles. The
modern museum is comprehensive in its
record of the two world wars, and of some
more recent ones, and contains models,
weapons, paintings and relics, as well as an
excellent collection of photographs and
posters and a most extensive archive.

Kew   4 C7
Kew grew up as a sort of royal appendage to
Richmond from the Tudor period and the
royal palace moved here in the 18thC. Kew
Green is the most picturesque part: the
elegant 18thC houses around the triangular
open space were mainly originally 'grace and
favour' residences for ladies of the court. The
elegantly classical 18thC Church of St Anne's
here has Gainsborough's grave in its
churchyard. Salubrious
Strand-on-the-Green, by Kew Bridge, is a
living picture of 18th and 19thC waterside
life, with charming cottages with decorated
verandas, trailing plants and wisterias over
their porches looking down onto a charming
towpath by the river.

The Royal Botanic Gardens, *Kew Rd*, are
one of the world's greatest, with 200 acres of
variety and colour. The scientific spirit of the
18thC founded it and the succeeding 200
years have constantly enriched the collection.
There are magnificent tropical orchid, palm
and Australasian houses as well as water and
Alpine gardens. The orangery and the
beautiful pagoda were designed by William
Chambers in 1760, and the glass palm-house
by Decimus Burton in the 1840s.

Kingston-upon-Thames   4 C8
Now one of London's most outlying suburbs
and famous for its noisy bypass, it is in fact an
ancient market town as can be discerned from
its narrow and picturesque main street and
Clattern Bridge, which dates from c1200. The
gaudy Victorian town hall is a landmark and
the street market which has continued for
centuries, is one of the most attractive in the
country.

Lambeth Palace   4 E6
Lambeth Palace Rd, SE1. On the side of
Lambeth Bridge is the London residence of
the Archbishops of Canterbury, in continuous
use for over 700 years. Much of the building
is 15thC, there is an extensive medieval crypt,
the Great Hall is largely 16thC, and there is a
magnificent collection of portraits
representing many styles from the 16th to the
19thC. *Open most days*.

Richmond   4 B7
More like a country town than a mere suburb,
Richmond is a prosperous and elegant world
of its own, with miles of wonderful riverside
walks. Richmond cherishes its long
associations with royalty: records of the royal
palace there go back to Edward III, and it
became a favourite residence of the Tudors,
especially Elizabeth. The palace was
demolished in the early 18thC and the
Georges grew up at Kew, but the royal
entourages created the delightful houses
around Richmond Green. The splendid view
from Richmond Hill was immortalised during
the same era by Gainsborough, Turner and
Reynolds. Huge **Richmond Park**, the
residue of the ancient palace, is magnificent
with its famous herd of deer: private shooting
of them only stopped in 1904. Richmond is
also an excellent centre for exploring the
numerous country houses of this area of West
London.

Richmond Park

Southwark and Bankside   4 F6
London's historic 'borough', Southwark grew
up from the early Middle Ages as an area
'without the city walls', therefore outside the
city's jurisdiction, and a centre for criminality,
pleasure and the theatre. Shakespeare's
Globe, as well as the other Elizabethan
theatres, were on Bankside. The site of the
Globe is now marked only with a plaque on a
brewery in an area full of derelict 19thC
warehouses. Here, too, was Chaucer's Tabard
Inn, from which his pilgrims set out to
Canterbury. Modern Borough High Street
may be noisy and undistinguished, but it is the
direct descendant of the medieval high street,
and the Old Kent Road is just what it says.
The George Inn, frequented by Dr Johnson,
is the last remaining example in London of a
17thC galleried inn, and you can look down

Southwark Cathedral

on a courtyard where Shakespeare may have acted in one of his own plays.
The cathedral of a great diocese, **Southwark Cathedral**, *Borough High St*, suffers from its surroundings of railway viaduct, swirling traffic, warehouses and cranes which belie its antiquity: first built in 1106, it is basically a 13thC church but was comprehensively rebuilt in 1890–6. A few arches of the original church remain and some fragments of wall, and there is also a most beautiful 16thC screen behind the altar, presented by Bishop Fox of Winchester. Shakespeare's brother is buried here, as well as the contemporary playwrights, Fletcher and Massinger.

The Roman Catholic Cathedral **St George's Cathedral**, *St George's Rd*, stands on the triangular site where in 1780 the mob gathered under the crazed Lord Gordon to riot against the English Catholics. But when, in the 1840s, Augustus Pugin designed the symbolically grand building, England was in the full flood of the Catholic revival. The cathedral was badly bombed in 1941, but was rebuilt by Romilly Croze from the original designs. It remains a severely unemotional but truly impressive structure, with a fine stone interior in a variety of styles.

Wimbledon   4 C8
An ancient place that even now retains its individuality. Julius Caesar had a camp here on his visit to Britain in 55BC, and it is marked on maps on the south western corner of the great, leafy common. More than 1,000 glorious acres of birch and heath, enlivened by the delightful windmill of 1817, provide countrified walks and Bronze Age remains have also been found on the common. Wimbledon itself is a suburban paradise with some fine old houses, such as Eagle House of 1613, at the top of Wimbledon Hill. The name of this area is, of course, synonymous with the world of international lawn tennis, and the Lawn Tennis Museum, *All England Tennis Club*, is the only one of its kind in the world. *Open most days*.

❧WEST LONDON❧

Albert Hall and Albert Memorial   4 E6
Kensington Gore, SW7. Epitome of the huge, popular Victorian concert hall, the Albert Hall is in the endearing chocolate-cake style of 19thC architecture. Particularly significant is that it was the first practical realisation of Albert's plan to build a great complex of learning and culture in this area, which has resulted in the many academic institutions and the South Kensington Museums. The Albert Memorial, just across the road in Kensington Park, is over-ornate but nevertheless touching as the tribute of a sorrowing queen and her people.

The Albert Hall

Belgravia   4 E6
Grand residential area of the early 19thC, with impressive but cold, white, stuccoed mansions in great squares like Eaton Square or Chester Square. It was designed by that inventive 19thC genius, Thomas Cubitt, from 1825 onwards, for the Grosvenor family who own much of the area. He also created more down-market Pimlico.

Brompton Oratory   4 E6
Brompton Rd, SW7. Inspired by that greatest of 19thC Catholic converts, Henry Newman, the Oratory is a wonderfully Italianate expression of the Roman church, built in 1884 by H. Gribble. It is a building on a massive scale with its great dome, large, sombre, richly-decorated interior, 51ft-wide nave and huge, marble apostles by Mazzuoli. It's best appreciated when a great concourse of richly-robed priests celebrate Benediction with much ceremony amid the smoke of incense.

Chelsea   4 D6
One of London's most elegant suburbs, with much delightful Georgian and typical

Victorian building. Chelsea first gained social cachet when Sir Thomas More, saint and politician, lived here in the early 16thC, and later the Tudors built a palace here. Under Charles II fashion made its renewed mark here: the Kings Road, now the mecca of the young, started life in the 1660s as a private road for Charles II to visit his mistress, while Wren's great Royal Hospital is an austerely impressive building of 1682. Some of the loveliest Georgian building is by the water-front and the Chelsea Embankment, and the beauty of the area tempted writers and artists to live here, including Addison, Swift, Steele, Whistler, Rossetti, George Eliot and Oscar Wilde. Chelsea Old Church, All Saints, dates from the 12thC, but was almost entirely destroyed during the last war. The More Chapel, rebuilt by Sir Thomas, survives, however, within the new fabric, and all the restoration has been tasteful. The church rejoices in a large number of memorials and is the only church in London still to have chained books. Chelsea Physic Garden nearby is a delightful haven of 18thC peace and quietness.

Chiswick   4 D6
Prosperous area full of fine Georgian houses and long a retreat for scholars and intellectuals from the bustle of nearby London: Pope lived in Chiswick in the beautiful but unpretentious red-brick house which is now the 'Fox and Hounds', Dr Johnson was a frequent visitor and Hogarth is buried in the churchyard. There were three great 18thC mansions by the river – Grove House, Sutton Court and Chiswick House – but only the latter remains. This, however, is a lovely Palladian villa of the 1720s which was built for the Earl of

Chiswick Mall

Burlington by his long-time partner, William Kent, who designed both the interior and the gardens. Chiswick still has a slightly aristocratic air as any visit to splendid Chiswick Mall by the river will confirm.

Ham House   **4 B7**
Petersham, Surrey. Superb Jacobean house built by the first Baronet Vavasour in 1606. It has a lavish Restoration interior and a most magnificent collection of Stuart furniture. *Open most days.*

Hammersmith   **4 C6**
Tatty but full of character and enterprise in art and entertainment, Hammersmith today is largely the creation of the 19thC. Before that, in 1720, Defoe described this as a well-to-do village with great houses and palaces and a noble square, the Broadway. In the 19thC, Hammersmith grew up as a basically lower-middle class suburb, with a large immigrant Irish community at Brook Green. But it never lost the trace of smartness, and Upper and Lower Mall by the river remain epitomes of 18thC elegance. Literary denizens of Hammersmith include Leigh Hunt, James Thompson (who wrote 'The Seasons' largely at that exquisite riverside pub, 'The Dove') and William Morris, while Holst wrote an orchestral suite to celebrate the area. St Paul's Church is very imposing Victorian Gothic, and St Peter's Square has exceptionally lovely stuccoed Victorian houses. Hammersmith also has one of the river's most beautiful bridges, Sir Joseph Bazalgette's light and airy conception of 1887.

Hampton Court Palace   **4 B8**
Hampton Court, Middlesex. Great Renaissance palace built in 1514 by Cardinal Wolsey, the great servant of Henry VIII who built a house so grand that he was forced to present it to his royal master. The Cardinal is commemorated in the sign of a nearby public house. Henry, who enlarged the palace, made it very much his own, and it was further beautified by Wren. From the gatehouse the red-brick facade looks immensely imposing and it is even more overwhelming inside with enormous amounts to see: sumptious state rooms painted by Laguerre, Verrio and Thornhill; the great gallery of Italian masterpieces; superb tapestries; gilded staircases; and cutlery, all of unbelievable ornateness. The extensive gardens are among the greatest in the world: you have an orangery, formal gardens in the French style, great vine, wilderness, knot garden, and of course, the maze of mazes.

Kensal Green Cemetery   **4 D5**
Harrow Rd, W10. Laid out in 1832 in imitation of the Père Lachaise in Paris, Kensal Green was the great mausoleum of the Victorians: among the graves are those of the writers Thackeray, Trollope and Wilkie Collins, the artists and architects Cruikshank and Smirke, the great actor Macready and the prince of engineers, Brunel. Not for nothing did Chesterton write in a poem about what he would do 'before we go to Paradise by way of Kensal Green'. The place is a rather odd but moving assemblage of obelisks, urns and ornate tombs, juxtaposed, in a flash of true urban poetry, with a gasworks and the railway line.

Kensington   **4 E6**
Chelsea's even grander neighbour, Kensington was laid out largely in the early 19thC in dignified squares and gardens, carrying on the classical tradition in 18thC London architecture, but with the added heaviness of Victorian stucco. It was more respectable and less Bohemian than Chelsea from the start, and John Stuart Mill, Macaulay and Gladstone were early residents here. Much of Kensington has now become unpleasantly hectic, but Kensington Palace Gardens remains a most impressive row of

19thC Italianate mansions and 18thC Kensington Square is lovely.

Olympia Exhibition Hall   **4 D6**
Hammersmith Rd, W6. The greatest of English exhibition halls until nearby Earl's Court was built, Olympia was opened in 1866 and extended to the edge of Hammersmith Road in 1929. It is an impressive landmark of this part of London, and earned perhaps its greatest notoriety when Sir Oswald Mosley used it for his monster-meetings of the British Union of Fascists (BUF) in the 1930s.

Osterley Park House   **4 B7**
½m S of M4 motorway, 1m N of Hounslow. One of the truly grand houses in Britain, its interior largely redesigned by the great decorator, Robert Adams. Starting work in 1760, he turned an Elizabethan manor house of 1576 into what Horace Walpole, the diarist, called 'the palace of palaces'. Adam worked on the house for over 20 years and you can still gaze astonished on his handiwork: walls of mirrors, rich carpets, delicate furniture and tapestries of unparalleled magnificence. Outside the house lies the great park with woods, ornamental lakes and huge cedar trees. The wealth that created this house came from banking: it was originally built by Thomas Gresham, the Elizabethan banker who entertained Elizabeth I here, and after being captured by the Roundheads during the Civil War, it fell into the hands of the Childs family of bankers who commissioned much of the redesigning. It is now owned by the National Trust and is close to the busy M4 motorway and the Great West Road – but a visit still evokes the magnificence of 18thC civilisation, when aristocratic splendour rested on the secure foundation of commercial strength. *Open most days.*

Osterley Park House

South Kensington Museums   **4 E6**
It was Prince Albert's idea in the 1850s to continue the work began by the Great Exhibition of 1851 by building a great complex of learning and culture in the South Kensington area. The **Victoria and Albert Museum** was the first to be built here in 1857, although the present overwhelming building is the 1907 work of Sir Aston Webb. It remains the largest, and surely the greatest museum of fine art in the world. Special exhibitions include Constable paintings and the Raphael Cartoons. *Open most days.* The Geological, Natural History and Science Museums came later. The extensive **Science Museum** includes collections of aero engines, transport, atomic and nuclear physics, telecommunications and astronomy. There are galleries on printing, paper-making and lighting and a children's gallery with working models. The **Geological Museum** contains the largest exhibition of basic earth science in the world and a piece of the moon, while the **Natural History Museum** contains national collections of zoology, entomology, botany and palaeontology and has superb dinosaur models. But perhaps because of the original conception, all of them, even the machine-minded Science Museum, have a rather fusty, old-fashioned air.

Sudbury Town Underground Station 4 B5
Bridgewater Rd, Wembley. The extension of the tube network in the 1930s was marked by the building of a number of fine new stations in the modern art deco style, of which this was the first. The architect of these stations was

Charles Holden and they were produced under the patronage of Frank Pick, the outstanding organiser of London Transport who also sponsored its poster-design tradition.

Syon House   4 B7
Park Rd, Brentford, Middlesex. One of the great houses of the London area, founded in 1415 as a monastery and remodelled in the 18thC. The exterior remains from the original date, but the interior was comprehensively redesigned by Robert Adam in the 1760s for the Duke of Northumberland, who also changed some of the architecture to get improved vistas onto the gardens that were being laid out by Capability Brown. In the 19thC another, less wise, duke encased the red-brick in Portland Stone which lessens the impact of the exterior. But the interior represents Adam at his peak, particularly in the superbly coloured ante-room and the gallery. *Open most days.*

NORTH AND EAST LONDON

Alexandra Palace and Park   4 E4
N22. One of North London's most loved open spaces, it was crowned by Alexandra Palace, a late Victorian building, named after the then Princess Alexandra. Concerts and exhibitions were held here and this was one of the earliest centres of BBC Radio and Television in Britain. In the summer of 1980 the Palace sadly was burnt down in the biggest London fire since the Blitz. The park has 200 acres, and from its hill there's a wonderful view over London, looking towards the City and the soaring new towers of the Barbican.

Archway Bridge   4 E5
N6. This impressive structure, which carries Hornsey Lane over the busy Archway Road, has historic interest as it was London's first flyover. It was originally built in 1813 but the present structure is of 1897.

Bethnal Green Museum   4 F6
Cambridge Heath Rd, E2. One of the outstanding tourist landmarks of the historic east end, the Bethnal Green Museum is part of the Victoria and Albert Museum, and is notable for collections of early toys, dolls and dolls' houses, ceramics and silver. Especially interesting is its history of costume, including examples of the delicate work of the Spitalfields silk weavers, introduced by the French Hugenot refugees who fled from religious persecution after 1685. This was the great precursor of the East End 'rag trade'.

Camden Town and Kentish Town   4 E5
The green fields of yesterday gave way to a surge of urban building here at the beginning of the 19thC, as London began to spread. We first hear of the manor of Cantlowes – Kentish Town – in the 13thC, but modern Camden Town started in 1791 when the first Earl of Camden, Charles Pratt, gave leases for the building of town houses, planning the area as a slightly down-market version of next-door Regent's Park. But in the 19thC Camden Town declined, and became an area of sad Victorian streets, populated by the sort of semi-genteel clerks and seedy semi-intellectuals who feature in the late 19thC novels of Grossmith and Gissing. This was also the haunt of Crippen who carried out his sordid little murder in one of its quiet little streets. Proverbially, because it was as far as you could walk from Euston Station carrying two heavy suitcases, in the late 19thC Camden Town became the centre of the Irish community. In the 20thC a Greek–Cypriot community added to the teeming social life of the area. Now Camden Town is newly fashionable again, and fine houses in Camden Road and Camden Square are being restored to their pristine glory.
A visit to Camden Town can show some excellent Georgian houses and some famous traditional Irish pubs. Picturesque Camden Lock on the Regent's Canal, where the locks start the 19ft drop to the river, is best seen on Sunday, the best day for the lively street market. Kentish Town is less picturesque, but retains more of the area's traditional character. It also has a curious and interesting Anglo-Norman parish church.

The Docks   4 F6
For 1,700 years London owed its greatness to the fact that it was Britain's greatest port, but before the 1800s, most ships docked in the river itself, in the Pool of London or downstream at Greenwich or Woolwich. The great, strange spaces of enclosed water that we know as the London Docks were created after 1802 and involved some of the country's finest engineers: it was Thomas Telford, for instance, who built St Katharine's Dock in 1825 by the Tower. Over the years the docks created a strong community pride and distinctive way of life. The area proved its mettle during the last war when the docks were a major target and endured first the Blitz of 1940 to 1941, then the flying bombs of 1944, then, as the final trial, the V2 rockets. From the 1960s the great London docks began to close as the port migrated downstream to Tilbury, and very little of them now remains, the area having been redeveloped for industry and housing. The few remaining old terrace dwellings seem increasingly forlorn. Some new life has now been brought to the dock area with the development of St Katharine's Dock with a yacht basin, a World Trade Centre, a luxury hotel and flats.

Ebonite Tower, Islington   4 F5
Tileyard Rd, York Way, N7. An interesting and distinctive example of early industrial architecture, it is an elegant, 150-ft-high brick tower of 1870 which once contained meter testing of water tanks.

Epping Forest   4 H2
Stretching between Chingford and Epping, this 6,000-acre area was once part of a royal hunting forest. Queen Elizabeth's Hunting Lodge from which sovereigns could watch 'the chase' may still be seen, and is now the Epping Forest Museum. Built in the 15thC, it came under the protection of the City of London in 1882. Get yourself lost in rolling miles of beech, oak and birch, enjoy the thousands of squirrels, and stumble across two ancient British camps, Loughton Camp and Ambersbery Banks, both more than 2,000 years old.

Hampstead   4 E5
Old Hampstead, high on the hilltop, is substantially 18thC and has some truly lovely Georgian houses. It first became a fashionable area because of the medicinal wells, hence Flask Walk and Well Walk. One of the loveliest streets is Church Row, a pot-pourri of building from the 18thC to the present, which still manages to convey true elegance. Much of the rest of Hampstead is solidly Victorian, and Hampstead Garden Suburb is one of the cluster of planned, experimental suburbs built around the turn of the century. Hampstead is notable for three famous and atmospheric public houses around the heath. The Old Bull and Bush and Jack Straw's Castle are early 19thC but largely rebuilt. The

Keats House

Spaniard's Inn is largely 18thC, retaining features from that date, and partly weather-boarded. A skirmish took place here during the Gordon Riots of 1780.
Fine historic houses include **Fenton House**, *Hampstead Grove*, built around 1693, with a charming garden and notable for its fine collection of furniture, porcelain and rare, historic musical instruments. *Open most days, summer; weekends, winter.* **Kenwood House**, *Hampstead Lane*, is an Adam house of 1767 built for the Earl of Mansfield: it was given to the nation by Lord Iveagh in 1927, together with its fine collection of paintings and furniture, a gift known as the Iveagh bequest. It has magnificent gardens with a lovely, wide lake. The poet Keats lived at Lawn Bank, now **Keats House**, *Keats Grove*, and wrote 'Ode to a Nightingale' in the garden. A charming example of the small-scale domestic buildings of the early 19thC, it contains many personal relics of the poet.

Highgate   4 E5
One of London's better-preserved villages, although very threatened by traffic, Highgate is an elegant clutter of Georgian and Victorian houses, perfectly set on its grassy hill. A haunt of poets, Highgate has been the home of Coleridge, Hopkins, Marvell and A. E. Housman who wrote 'A Shropshire Lad' here.
Designed by Stephen Geary, more famous for the construction of Victorian gin palaces, **Highgate Cemetery**, *Swains La*, is in highly romantic Tudor–Gothic style. Dark, winding paths, looming cedars and pillars and obelisks in Egyptian style all add to the atmosphere of strange gloom which is accentuated by the neglected appearance of much of the whole. Many of the famous and philosophic are buried here: George Eliot; Herbert Spencer, the 19thC positivist; Christina Rossetti; George Holyoake, organiser of workers' co-operatives; and, of course, Karl Marx. The older section has suffered from vandalism and is now usually closed to the public.

Islington   4 F5
This area has gone through many vicissitudes in its long role as neighbour to the historic City of London. The name appears first in an Anglo-Saxon charter as Gislandune or 'Gisla's Hill' and until the 18thC, Islington was largely open ground. Famous for its dairy produce, it was a noted pleasure ground for Londoners – here the Elizabethans loved to come to shoot wild-fowl, or 18thC Londoners to drink more than was good for them at Sadler's Wells. From the early 18thC Islington was famous for the great Caledonian market, then industry began to invade, and the area was built up for clerks and middle-income workers in the City. These were the days when Charles Lamb, East India clerk turned writer and burdened by the mad sister of whom he took such loving care, found peace as he relaxed with his book and tobacco by the canal.
In the 19thC the area took a social down-turn and Islington became a close-knit but rough working-class area. In recent years a remarkable social reversal has occurred – the professional middle class has moved in armed with Dulux Gloss, and such old Islingtonians

as remain often act as speech-models for television script-writers. But it all adds up to a lively urban mix in social and landscape terms, elegant Georgian houses close to the Regent's Canal often standing cheek-by-jowl with lowering council blocks, and the bright shops of elegant Camden Passage close to gaunt Victorian warehouses backing onto the wide railway lines.

Regent's Canal
London's premier canal, built for the busy trade route from the Thames via the link with the Grand Union Canal to Birmingham. Commercial traffic has almost stopped now, but pleasure boating and towpath walking are flourishing. The Grand Union Canal meets the Regent's Canal near elegant 'Little Venice', passes in a broad cutting through Regent's Park, starts its voyage through the series of locks at Camden and Islington and broadens out to the great City Road Basin. Below this the canal follows a secret path through the industrial towers and grimy warehouses of east London, finally reaching the Thames at Regent's Canal Dock, now sadly silent and empty of ships.

Spitalfields   4 F6
E1. Historic artisan quarter of the east end, it saw the beginnings of the rag trade and several historical waves of settlement, as immigrants have arrived here over the centuries. The area has always been poor and sometimes horrific – here, and in Whitechapel, Jack the Ripper carried out his gruesome attacks in the 1890s – but it is also full of interest, and even style. The first immigrants were the French Protestants or Huguenots who fled here from religious persecution in the later 17thC, bringing their silk-weaving skills with them. At the end of the 19thC more persecution brought a great wave of eastern European Jews to the crowded streets east and north east of Aldgate Tube Station, where they worked in the sweat-shops. More recently, many Bengalis have made their contribution to the rag trade in this area.
Spitalfields was built up in the 17th and 18thC as terrace dwellings, and Fournier Street is a good example of typical Dutch style houses of the time. Most of the Jews have now gone, but the shop-names of old tailors tell of the past in the Russian pale, and by Petticoat Lane Market you can see a low building of 1902 entitled 'Soup Kitchen for the Jewish Poor'. Monuments include the superb early 18thC Christchurch, *Commercial St*, built by Nicholas Hawksmoor, pupil of Wren: the exterior is monumental, although the interior is unfortunately closed. Nearby is Toynbee Hall, opened in 1884, a University Extension settlement where the idealistic young men of Oxford hoped to make contact with the poor of the East End, and to improve their lives. All in all, Spitalfields is a fascinating area, moving at times in urban dereliction, changing rapidly, but resounding with echoes of the past.

Wapping   4 F6
Once one of the most notorious areas of the East End – in the 18thC groups of thieves in Wapping High Street used to attack ships moored in the river in open daylight – it is now in the agonising process of dockland renewal. Wapping Old Stairs still exists, and nearby is the pub where in 1688 James II's hated 'hanging' judge, Jeffreys, was trapped dressed as a sailor and taken to the Tower. Near Tunnel Pier Warehouse is Execution Dock where the hanged bodies of pirates were once washed ritually three times by the rising tide. The most famous of its victims was Captain Kidd in 1701. Close by is the Prospect of Whitby, once frequented by so many thieves and smugglers that it came to be called 'The Devil's Tavern'.

WALES

Wales is the country of the 'Wealeas', a Saxon word meaning foreigner. The Welsh prefer to call themselves 'Cymry', which roughly translates as 'people like us'. The first word is that of a conqueror unable and unwilling to understand the people he has subjected to his rule: the second, that of the people themselves looking to find a national identity to sustain them. It is remarkable that, a mere 50 miles from the industrial heartland of England, Wales has retained a language and culture all its own.

To the Welsh their past is a vital element of their nation. Their roots can be traced back to the arrival of the Celts at the end of their great migration from the Mediterranean, in about 3,000BC. The civilisation they brought with them was capable of quarrying the huge stones of Stonehenge in Pembrokeshire and transporting them to their resting place on Salisbury Plain. In Wales they left behind them burial chambers or cromlechs, and standing stones, scattered about the desolate moors. Anglesey was the centre of learning for their priesthood, and became known as the 'Island of Druids'. The Arthurian legends, popular during the Welsh revolts of the Middle Ages, contain traces from the fertility cults of the Druids.

The Romans constructed a network of roads and camps by which to control their territory. Two legions were stationed for the duration of their stay, one at Chester, the other at Cearleon, to uphold a fragile Pax Romana.

After the Romans left, Wales split into a number of small, feuding kingdoms. Within this chaos the Celtic Church began to flourish in the 6th and 7thC. Monks and hermits carried on the Celtic tradition of learning in remote places, and in St David, Wales found a patron saint.

At the same time the boundary between England and Wales was demarcated with the construction of Offa's Dyke, while Wales suffered her fair share from Viking raids on the coast. Wild Wales was seen as a threat to the stability the Normans had created in England, and William the Conqueror created the marcher lords to control the border lands. They had absolute authority within their lands, which lasted until the 16thC. Motte and bailey castles were built in the south to consolidate their rule.

Welsh hopes for independence grew with the revolt of Llywelyn the Great and his grandson, Llywelyn the Last, who became recognised by Henry III in 1267 as the first native Prince of Wales. He was also the last. Twelve years later Edward I made sweeping inroads into Llywelyn's territory. Llywelyn was killed in battle and his brother captured and executed.

It was 100 years before nationalist hopes rose again, under the revolt led by Owain Glyndwr. The bitter struggle lasted 14 years, leaving Wales devastated. In the end Wales was as much under English rule as ever, but confidence was high. The old prophecy that Welsh blood should one day rule in Britain was revived.

With the ascendancy of the Tudors (or, more properly, the Tewdwrs) at the end of the Wars of the Roses, the prophecy was fulfilled. The Tewdwrs had a lineage that included a Prince of Gwynedd during the time of the Conquest. The Act of Union of 1536, passed by Henry VIII, removed the privileges of the marcher lords, gave Wales Parliamentary representation, and declared void all laws that discriminated against the Welsh. Wales kept loyal to the crown with the Stuarts and in the Civil War the Welsh castles declared for the King, and were subsequently slighted by Cromwell's forces.

The 18thC saw the spread of a specifically Welsh Methodism, determinist and theologically austere. The exploitation of iron and coal resources in the Industrial Revolution brought with it miserable conditions for the poor, and the chapels became the focus for social discontent. The Chartist and Rebecca Riots of the 1830s and 1840s indicate the strength of feelings at the time. The traditional alliance of chapel and socialism lasted well into this century, and brought men like Lloyd George and Nye Bevan into politics.

The past few years have seen a resurgence of Welsh nationalist sentiment, with the Welsh language coming back from virtual extinction and the devolution debate continuing. The long and often bitter relationship between England and Wales is still to be resolved. Wales remains a fiercely independent part of the United Kingdom and there can be no question of its difference. Sturdy from generations of mining and tough hill farming, the struggles of the past have produced a strong sense of community and warmth of character as the Welsh people strive to preserve their own language and traditions. Apart from the traditional friendly hospitality of the Welsh, one of their best-known characteristics is their love of music. The International Eisteddfod takes place every year in Llangollen and the National Eisteddfod is held every year in a different town. The Welsh are also proud of the beauty of their country. From the valleys and Black Mountains in the south, to the glories of Snowdonia in the north, it offers a feast of scenery. Not as barren and rugged as Scotland, Wales has a greener, more gentle beauty. A paradise for walkers, often the only figure to be seen for miles is the Welsh farmer, with his obligatory cloth cap, stick, wellington boots and ever-faithful sheepdog.

CLWYD

1. Bangor-is-y-Coed 5 J2
4m SE of Wrexham, A525. This was the site of
one of the first monasteries in Britain,
traditionally founded in AD180. By 596 there
were 2,400 monks established here. Disaster
struck, however, with the defeat of the Celtic
forces by the Saxons at the Battle of Chester
in 615: the victorious Aethelfrith sacked the
monastery, claiming that the monks had
prayed for the enemy. The few that survived
the massacre fled to Bardsey Island.
There are no traces remaining of this period,
but the village does boast a charming 17thC
stone bridge over the River Dee, said to be an
early work of the great Inigo Jones.

2. Bodrhyddan Hall 5 H1
2m NW of Dyserth, A5151. A mainly 17thC
manor house, the original 15thC building has
been lost in later additions. There is a 17thC
south front, a large 18thC dining room and a
19thC west front. The house contains a
collection of arms and armour from the 13thC
onward, and, in delicate contrast, a collection
of 18thC Chinese porcelain. There are also
portraits by Hogarth and Reynolds, mummy
cases, and gifts presented to the family by both
Charles I and Charles II.
The St Mary's Well Chapel in the
picturesque grounds, thought to have been
designed by Inigo Jones, is reputed to have
been used for clandestine marriages. *Open
certain days, summer.*

3. Caerwys 5 H1
10m NW of Mold, off A541. Famous for its
centuries-old tradition of eisteddfodau –
contests of music and poetry, the first of which
was held in 1568. At that time there were
many wandering vagabonds in the country,
products of the economic hardships after the
Wars of the Roses. As they were all claiming
the bardic right to food and hospitality, Queen
Elizabeth I granted permission for a
competition to be held at Caerwys to sort the
genuine poet and musician from the others.
Following this, the real artists were given
licences to practise their craft and
eisteddfodau were held regularly.
Caerwys retains its medieval street pattern: a
grid system popular during the reign of
Edward I. The parish church has traces of an
earlier Welsh foundation. Of the Roman
settlement indicated in the name of the town,
however, little has yet been discovered.

4. Chirk Castle 5 J2
1m W of Chirk, A5. No medieval ruin, but a
stately home of elegance and style cosseted by
pastures and parkland round its hilltop site.
Built to a traditional rectangular plan by
Roger Mortimer in 1310, with four corner
turrets and internal quadrangle, it is a unique
example of a marcher fortress and has been
inhabited ever since. Sir Thomas Myddelton
– a merchant adventurer who sailed the
Spanish Main with Walter Raleigh – bought it
in 1595 and his descendents still live there.
See his portrait at the foot of the stairs.
Interior delights are mainly 17th, 18th and
19thC, including armour and arms from the
Civil War, chandeliers, paintings, tapestries,
and a four-poster where Charles I snored.
Note the metal-framed beaver hat of the kind
he sometimes wore.
Beautiful 18thC wrought iron gates almost
rival the castle itself as a showpiece not to be
missed. Local lads Robert and Thomas
Davies made them, and they once stood on
the north side of the castle. A deep dungeon
to give you the collywobbles and a servants'
hall are two of the castle's more
out-of-the-way interests. Traces of Offa's
Dyke run through the grounds which include

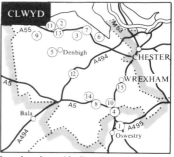

formal gardens with clipped yews. Chirk
Castle is managed on behalf of the Secretary
of State for Wales, by the National Trust.
Open most days, summer.

5. Denbigh Castle 5 H1
Denbigh. A large, straggling ruin overlooking
the town, Denbigh Castle was prominent in
the struggles of the Welsh revolts and in the
Civil War. Once the headquarters of the rebel
Henry Hotspur, the castle was built by
Edward I in 1282 to help secure his victory
over the Welsh, and completed in 1322. The
fortification included the garrison town within
its walls.
After his defeat at the Battle of Rowton Moor,
Charles I took refuge here. Denbigh was
besieged for 11 months before surrendering
to the Parliamentarians and its defeat marked
the end of the Royalist cause in Wales. The
remains of several towers and walls can be
seen, but the elaborate gatehouse is the most
impressive and complete building remaining.
The explorer Sir Henry Morton Stanley (of
'Dr Livingstone, I presume', fame), was born
in a cottage near the castle entrance, since
demolished. Mementoes of his life and local
archaeological finds are housed in the castle
museum.

6. Flint Castle 5 J1
Flint. Shakespeare's setting for the capture of
Richard II, Flint was the easternmost, and
first, of Edward I's Welsh defences. Brooding
on a low rock by the sea, it is now a sad ruin,
destroyed by the Parliamentarians when they
besieged it in the Civil War. The castle was
built on a simple square plan with drum
towers at each corner. The keep is outside the
square, isolated on a small island and
connected to the rest by a drawbridge.

7. Holywell 5 H1
18m NW of Wrexham, A55. Prince Caradoc
was a cad who tried to seduce Winefride,
young daughter of a 7thC prince. But she ran
away towards the church of her uncle, St
Beuno. Caradoc followed, and cut off her
head. Immediately, the earth opened and
swallowed him. Miraculously, Beuno replaced
the head and only a white scar round
Winefride's neck showed what had happened.
A spring gushed where the head had fallen,
and for 1,300 years pilgrims in sickness and
health have trekked here to worship its healing
powers. They still do.
Unfortunately, a local guidebook sniffily
rejects the story as 'commonplace in Celtic
hagiography and inherently unlikely'. But the
poet, Gerard Manley Hopkins, was more
receptive. Years later he wrote: 'even now the
stress and buoyancy and abundancy of the
water is before my eyes'. He also wrote a
poem about the well and an unfinished verse
drama about Winefride.
Modern visitors still feel the magic of the
place even though nearby mining diverted the
stream in 1917 and the well ran dry. Another

less powerful spring was connected to it. A chapel built in 1480, in itself a fine example of late 15thC Perpendicular architecture, now contains the well which fills a basin in the crypt. Bathers pray at a rough hewn block called St Beuno's Stone in a large pool outside the chapel. Rows of crutches left behind by the cured used to line the chapel, and graffiti carved by the pilgrims tell fascinating stories. *Open certain days, summer.*
Ruins of **Basingwerk Abbey**, *1m NE of Holywell, A548*, show evidence of how famous for its beauty and setting this 12thC monastery was. It was founded to house a community of Cistercian monks who had settled in the vicinity of St Winefride's Well and so many guests visited that they had to eat at two meal sittings. Wines from Spain, Aragon and Brittany flowed round the trestles. Features are: 12thC rubble walling on the west side; a bench in the chapter house where monks sat to hear the daily Rule; next to it a parlour where conversation was allowed; a hatch at the south where food was passed from the kitchen; a 13thC pulpit in the frater. Holywell's parish church is famous for its bell and knee pad. Built by mistake under a hill, no-one in town could hear its bells – so a man went about with a bell fixed to his leg!
While you're here, glance at Holywell Junction Station – Italianate brick and stucco and one of the few surviving examples of Francis Thompson's 19thC work. Also of interest are Holywell Textile Mills, built in 1777 for cotton spinning but later, in 1841, converted to flannel manufacturing.

St Winefride's Well, Holywell

8. Llangollen 5 H2
A hard-edged place built around the singing River Dee with high ridges of land closing in on both sides. It's a place of surprises, like a Welsh ballad. Of ancient note is **Elseg's Pillar**, more than 1,000 years old. Its long inscription tells us it was erected by Cyngen, prince of Powys, in memory of his great grandfather, Elseg. It stands on its original mound, where it was reset after being thrown down in the Civil War. Elseg himself may have been buried in the mound.
Striking a different chord is the **Canal Exhibition Centre**, *Canal Wharf*, a fascinating centre illustrating all the important aspects of the canal era. Films, slides, models and exhibits trace the history of the canals and the way of life of the people who built and worked on Britain's first major transport system. *Open summer; by arrangement, winter.*
Near the railway station is the eerie ruin of **Castell Dinas Brân**. Standing conspicuously at a height of almost 1,000ft, it has a history dating back to the Iron Age. The fort built at this time was replaced by a Welsh one, and this by a Norman castle about 1236.
The castle's Celtic origin is indicated by the typical circular construction, and by its name. Brân was a heroic figure in the Mabinogion, a 14thC compilation of early legends. There is evidence that this figure goes back to the Mediterranean fertility cults introduced in the Iron Age period of Celtic trading. These cults formed the basis of the Druidic religion.

Offa's Dyke 5 J2
Good view from grounds of Chirk Castle. For centuries Offa's Dyke marked the boundary between England and Wales. It begins on the north coast near Prestatyn and cuts down across hills and valleys to the Severn estuary. The rounded bank is in places 60ft across, and the ditch on the Welsh side 12ft deep. For 60 miles it coincides with the bank and ditch construction built in the late 8thC AD, by Offa, the powerful Mercian king.
Welshmen today still talk of 'crossing Offa's Dyke' – crossing the border – an adventure which in the past carried the penalty of imprisonment.

Offa's Dyke

9. Parc-y-Meirch 5 G1
2m SE of Abergele, off A55. An Iron Age hill fort with ditch and rampart defences incorporated in the natural steep scarp of the hill. Traces of a stone-built guard post, added during a reoccupation in the 6thC, can be seen.

10. Pontcysyllte Aqueduct 5 J2
4½m E of Llangollen, off A5. Sir Walter Scott thought it the finest work of art he'd ever seen. As you summon your courage to walk across this tremendous aqueduct, you won't think it an altogether excessive reaction. Hundreds of people gathered for its opening in 1805, and gasped as a procession of boats crossed it, heartily accompanied by the band of the Shropshire Volunteers.
Thomas Telford's wondrous feat of engineering was pioneer work in cast iron on the grandest scale imaginable and bore the Shropshire Union Canal 127ft above the River Dee. Nineteen graceful scts of airy arches – each with a span of 53ft – carried the iron trough of the canal and towpath 1,007ft. Industry began to flourish in this area while the aqueduct was being built, and today nearby you can see lime-kilns, an iron foundry site and tram-roads, plus canal-side pubs and workers' cottages. Learn all about canal life at the Canal Exhibition Centre, Llangollen. *Open summer; by arrangement, winter.*

11. Rhuddlan Castle 5 G1
Rhuddlan, 2½m SE of Rhyl. This noble castle was recorded at Rhuddlan in 1188, as belonging to the eldest son of Owain, Prince of Gwynedd. The present castle is Edward I's replacement, part of his massive Welsh defences, built in 1277. After deepening the river in order to bring ships up to Rhuddlan, Edward made the castle his headquarters. Rectangular in design, the castle had six turrets and two large gatehouses. Demolition and plundering for building materials have reduced it to a massive shell, its setting above the River Clwyd enhancing its majesty.

Rhuddlan Castle

12. Ruthin 5 H1
With many of its black-and-white half-timbered buildings huddled round the market square, Ruthin still has something of a medieval air. Here you will find the old court house and prison. Also in the square, in front

of Exmewe Hall, is the Maen Huail – the stone on which King Arthur is said to have executed Huail, a rival in a love affair. Nearby is St Peter's Church, which should be visited for its oak roof with 500 carved panels, a gift from Henry VII to the Welshmen who had helped him to the English throne. Ruthin castle was built by Edward I and constructed around the base of an earlier Norman building. It is now a luxury hotel.

13. St Asaph Cathedral   5 H1
St Asaph. The smallest cathedral in Britain at 182ft by 65ft, St Asaph has a quiet dignity of its own. It was founded in AD537 by St Kentigern, who was succeeded by St Asaph 13 years later. The original building was burnt by the English in 1282. Rebuilding began shortly after, and the earliest parts of the present structure, notably parts of the choir, are of this date. Much of the Norman building was destroyed by Glyndwr in 1402. Major restoration was undertaken by Gilbert Scott in 1875 and again early this century.
Note the curious Greyhound Stone in the north aisle and ask to visit the Chapter Museum. It has early bibles and prayer books, a copy of a Welsh–Greek–Hebrew dictionary written by the local tramp and celebrated genius, Dic Aberdaron, as well as autographs of Dickens, Darwin, Thackeray and others. Climb the tower for a wonderful view of the lower Vale of Clwyd.

St Asaph Cathedral

14. Valle Crucis Abbey   5 J2
1½m NW of Llangollen, A542. Romantically isolated, Valle Crucis is the most atmospheric religious ruin in North Wales. It was founded as a Cisterian Abbey in 1201 by Madog ap Gruffydd, Prince of Powys. A central tower collapsed in 1400 and it suffered under Henry VIII during the Dissolution.
The remains comprise the church and part of the domestic buildings, used for some time as a farm house. The noble and beautifully proportioned west front has three windows in a common frame, with a rose window above. There are six tombs in front of the choir, one of them of Iolo Goch, famous as Owain Glyndwr's bard.
Valle Crucis means 'vale of the cross' and derives from nearby Eliseg's Pillar. Now a weathered 8ft stump, it was erected to commemorate a battle fought between Eliseg, a Celtic prince of Powis, against the invading Saxons. Originally its Latin inscription was 31 lines, but weathering and vandalism have reduced this to 15.

15. Wrexham   5 J2
A no-nonsense town, centre of the North Wales coalfields. Its name, meaning 'hamlet of the king', suggests its origins were English rather than Welsh.
Wrexham's historical and architectural treasure is the Church of St Giles, traditionally counted as one of the 'Seven Wonders of Wales'. To begin with, the wrought iron churchyard gates are the work of the brothers Davies, masters of their craft. The church itself, with a richly ornamented tower of 136ft, was built in 1472 of a dark stone, appropriate to an industrial town.
In the churchyard is the grave of Elihn Yale, one of the founders of Yale University, Connecticut.
To the south of the town is **Erdigg House**, a late 17thC mansion, standing within grounds of 2,000 acres and with a complete range of outbuildings. It's now owned by the National Trust. Erdigg House was begun in 1684 by Joshua Edisbury, the High Sheriff of Denbighshire. Debt caused him to flee to London, where he died before the house was completed. It was then bought by a London lawyer who added two wings and filled the house with the furniture which is one of its principal attractions today.
The outbuildings with stables, bakehouse, laundry and kitchen are all in working order, and there are portraits of the staff who kept the whole place running. Varieties of fruit which would have grown in the 18thC are grown in the restored formal garden.
Nearby, is the **Erdigg Agricultural Museum**, *Felin Puleston*, which contains a collection of local farm machinery, some of it housed in a 17thC barn. *Open most days, summer.*
While you're in the area, delve a little further into Wrexham's history by following the Bersham and Clywedog Industrial Trail which starts by the village green. Eight miles long, it follows a route between the lead mining village of Minera and the Abenbury Forge, centring upon the iron-working village of Bersham.

✦ DYFED ✦

1. Aberystwyth   5 E5
A pleasant seaside resort and university town which began as a religious settlement in the 6thC. Prim Victorian and Edwardian buildings line the broad promenade at the end of which stands Constitution Hill, well-worth a climb for the view.
The castle was built by Edward I's brother in 1277, replacing an earlier wooden fortification. During the Glyndwr revolt it was besieged for three years, and on surrender it became a rebel headquarters. Sacked by Cromwell's forces, like virtually every other castle in Royalist Wales, all that remains are part of the curtain wall and the crumbling towers and gates. Some mysterious prehistoric stones stand in the castle grounds.
The National Library of Wales, *Penglais*, was founded in 1907 for the specific purpose of collecting ancient Welsh and Celtic texts. Included in its collection are the magnificent 12thC 'Black Book of Carmarthen', the oldest manuscript in the Welsh language, and the 'White Book of Roderick', the earliest version of the Mabinogion tales. *Open most days.*

Aberystwyth

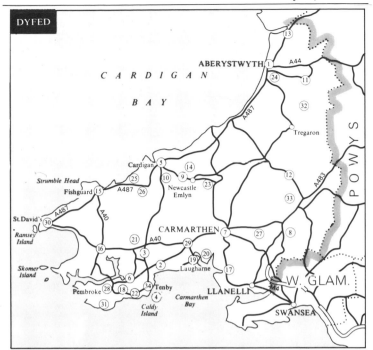

2. Amroth   5 C9
3m NE of Kilgetty, off A477. At very low tides a sunken, primeval forest is revealed on the beach of Amroth. On one of these occasions the skeleton of a small pig was found, containing an arrow-head estimated to have been about 10,000 years old. There was a medieval castle at Amroth, but no traces remain. The present 'castle' is a 19thC upstart, now used as a holiday centre.

3. Blackpool Mill   5 C9
Narberth, off A40 at Canaston Bridge. Built in 1813 for wheat grinding and flour making, this is one of the finest examples of a corn grinding mill in Britain. Within the mill there is an interesting display of old accounts, bills and wages, as well as a small restaurant. *Open summer.*

4. Caldy Island   5 C10
Boats from Tenby harbour in summer.
Lily-livered Norsemen re-named this island Caldy (cold) during a 10thC raid on the Celtic monastery there. Cold or not, people and animals have lived on Caldy for thousands of years. Mammoth, rhinoceros and elk bones found in Nanna's Cave show that prehistoric Caldy was no island, but a hill in the Forest of Coedrath.
Early Christian missionaries arrived in the Dark Ages, and Benedictines founded a monastery in the 12thC. Today, you can see their refectory, gatehouse and prior's lodging which is now the guest house. St Illtyd is thought to have taught here, and there's an Ogham stone in the church of his name on the island. Made of sandstone it has a cross and two inscriptions, one in Ogham, an early Irish alphabet, and the other a 9thC translation into Latin. It was this stone that helped scholars to decipher the Ogham script.
After the Dissolution the community disbanded and the abbey was used as a laundry and even a brewery. Various orders toyed with a permanent base here. Somehow, none ever stayed – until the Cistercians, who now farm and sell their produce and make perfume to sell in Tenby gift shops. Ironically, their creed doesn't allow women to visit the monastery! St Illtyd's church is 13th and

14thC and its sanctuary is paved with large, black pebbles from the beach. Paul Jones the pirate has a bay named after him which he's said to haunt.

5. Cardigan   5 C7
Cardigan originated as a port and fortification in the 11thC and remained prosperous until the 19thC when the river silted up and the advent of the railways took away its trade. Thanks to the destructive Roundheads, only two towers and the keep remain of the 12thC castle. It is now privately owned. The town's most interesting feature today is the bridge over the Teifi, built in 1726.
St Dogmael's Abbey, *1m W of town,* was founded as a Benedictine monastery in 1115 to replace a Welsh institution sacked by Vikings 150 years earlier. The original north and west walls of the nave survive, as well as fragments of the refectory. In the parish church is an interesting 6thC carved stone with both Latin and Ogham script.

6. Carew Castle   5 C9
Carew, 1m N of A477, off A4075. Gaunt and solid, the castle ruin stands above a tidal creek of Milford Haven. Replacing an earlier structure it was built from 1270 to 1320 by the Carew family. In 1408 it was sold to Sir Rhys ap Thomas, who added the Great Hall and entertained the future Henry VII. In the 16thC it was converted to a Tudor domestic manor but the fortifications were retained. The Carew family returned during the Civil War, and withstood two sieges on behalf of the King. Severely damaged, the castle was abandoned a few years later, but it is still owned by the Carew family today. Parts of the keep show the early 14thC work, and form an interesting comparison with the later Tudor additions.
Near the castle entrance is the 14ft-high Carew Cross, with elaborate geometric patterns, which was erected in 1035 to commemorate the death of Maredudd, King of Deheubarth.

6. Carew French Mill   5 C9
S bank of River Carew, 5m E of Pembroke, A4075. Fast-flowing streams and rivers were

often used to drive corn mills and this one was grinding back in Elizabethan days. It is the only tidal mill surviving in Wales, and the present three-storey building dates from the early 19thC when it produced flour. Rising water from the tidal River Carew fills a pond upstream of the mill and is stored there. On the ebb tide water is released from the pond to work the wheels. There's a picnic site on the north side of the mill pond.

Carew French Mill

7. Carmarthen 5 E8

An animated town of bent-backed houses and narrow winding streets, Carmarthen is built on the site of the Romans' westernmost fort, Caer Maridunum. The remains of the fort were excavated this century, and the Roman sites have since been built upon. Around the end of the 11thC the Normans established a castle and walled town, later reinforced by Edward I. In the following centuries Carmarthen became prosperous as a port and wool town. The castle, *Castle Hill*, like most others in Wales, was Royalist during the Civil War, surrendered, and was later demolished. Only parts of the curtain wall and a 14thC gatehouse survive.
Tradition has it that the magician Merlin was born at Carmarthen of a princess and a spirit. One of his prophecies ran:
'When Merlin's oak shall tumble down
Then shall fall Carmarthen town.'
Superstitious locals wrapped the oak in iron bands and embedded it in concrete, but it has recently been removed to Abergwili Museum to make way for roadworks.

8. Carreg Cennen Castle 5 F8

4¹/₂m SE of Llandeilo, off A483. Precariously poised at the very edge of a sheer 300ft limestone cliff, Carreg Cennen dominates both the sky and the valley. Its history is obscure. The date and name of the builder is unknown, but it is probably the work of a marcher lord in the late 13thC. It was destroyed in 1462, having degenerated into a haunt for brigands.
The castle is entered (after a steep climb) by a gatehouse with portcullis. It is rectangular in design, without a keep. The most remarkable feature is a passage cut into the limestone cliff leading from the south east corner to a well deep in the rock. The way is lit by arched openings in the cliff-face from which there are spectacular views over the river valley and Black Mountains.
A couple of miles to the north is **Carn Goch**, one of the largest Iron Age forts in Wales, with a drystone rampart walk on the western side some 20ft high. Excavations have shown the site to have occupied almost three acres during the 2nd and 3rdC BC.

9. Cenarth 5 D7

3m W of Newcastle Emlyn. A charming village on the River Teifi, and one of the few places where the ancient art of coracle fishing is still practised. The coracles are ribbed with ash of willow, and covered with a stretched tarred canvas. This craft dates back to the ancient Britons.

10. Cilgerran Castle 5 C7

2m S of Cardigan, 1m E of A478. Although not as striking as Carreg Cennen, Cilgerran's situation on a steep promontory above the River Teifi is romantic enough to have inspired many artists, including Turner. The castle was originally founded at the end of the 11thC, but was rebuilt many times. The present ruin is, in the main, mid 13thC. Two large round towers of the 13thC and a rectangular tower of a slightly later date are all that remain apart from traces of the curtain wall. The buildings contain original Norman doorways and windows.

11. Devil's Bridge 5 F5

11m E of Aberystwyth, A4120. Once upon a time an old lady lived near the river Mynach. One day her cow wandered across the river, and because of the steep gorge she did not know how to get it back. The Devil appeared and told her that he would build a bridge. Believing that she would be over first to fetch the cow, he made one condition – he would claim the first living thing which crossed it for himself. She agreed. But he hadn't reckoned for her quick wit. She threw a crust over the bridge, her dog ran after it, the furious Devil had the dog – and the old lady claimed her cow.
The legend of Devil's Bridge is mentioned in chronicles of 1188. This little stone bridge is now the lowest of three, one above the other, which span the River Mynach at the lip of a cataract that falls away at 300ft. An energetic descent into the depths of this spectacular gorge affords the best views of the five magnificent waterfalls which cascade into the river below. Various platforms en route offer unsurpassed glimpses of unspoilt Welsh countryside and there's an interesting nature trail to follow. A trip not to be missed, a real treat is to leave the car at Aberystwyth and take the Vale of Rheidol steam railway which chuggs through breath-taking scenery.

12. Dolaucothi Roman Gold Mines 5 F7

Dolaucothi, Nr Pumsaint, off A482. Gold is one of the keys to the development of culture in Wales. In the Iron Age it was traded among the peoples of the Mediterranean and it was of prime attraction to the Romans. Archaeological evidence has shown that it was the Romans who fully exploited this site, most probably to provide gold bullion for the Imperial Mints of Lyons, in France and Rome. They started up operations around AD75 and used both open cast and shaft methods – the information hut in the car park has literature explaining these complex workings. There are signposted walks past prominent features such as the aqueducts, sluices and reservoirs as well as the open casts and shafts.
To complete the day, visit the museum at Abergwili, near Carmarthen, where a mining display includes material found on the site during excavations. But before you go, take a look at the ancient five saints stone at the car park from which the nearby village of Pumpsaint took its name. *Open most days.*

13. Eglwys-fach, Dyfi Furnace 5 F4

6m N of Talybont, A487. A furnace for smelting silver in the early 17thC gave this small village its name. In 1755 a more ambitious blast furnace for iron ore was set up, using local wood for fuel. The iron ore was imported from the north of England by boat. The enterprise survived for 50 years or so, but the buildings have recently been restored – a fascinating piece of industrial archaeology.
For inveterate nature lovers, there is also a splendid waterfall on the River Einion to enjoy.

14. Felin Geri Flour Mill 5 D7

Cwm Cou, nr Newcastle Emlyn. This mill has been drawing its water from the River Ceri to grind corn since 1604. It is still grinding in the traditional fashion, using the original means of production, yet operating on a regular commercial basis. The mill, with its very old outbuildings, is set in the heart of the unspoilt Ceri Valley. You can see all the stages of production and the flour can be purchased at the shop. Alongside the mill is a rare example of a water-wheel-powered saw mill, now under restoration.

15. Fishguard 5 B7
Away from the Irish ferry terminal Fishguard remains an unspoilt fishing village with narrow streets and crooked old houses. Fishguard was the scene of the last foreign invasion of Britain. This was in February 1797 when a force of 1,200 mainly French convicts sent to seize Bristol were driven north by the wind. Having substantially partaken of some shipwrecked alcohol on landing, they were easily beaten by the local militia – helped by stout-hearted local women in traditional costume whom they took to be soldiers. The incident ended with a peace treaty being signed in the old Royal Oak pub in the centre of the town.

16. Haverfordwest 5 B9
A tight-packed market town of narrow streets, Haverfordwest grew up around the castle built by the Normans in about 1120. Flemish settlers arrived later in the reign of Henry I. The castle was strengthened with thick walls and when Cromwell's forces were ordered to destroy it, much was left intact. The remains are mainly those of the 13thC inner ward, with the addition of an 18thC county gaol. It now houses a museum and information centre.
The Church of St Mary is as English-looking as they come in Wales, with 15thC nave and clerestories and good 13thC work in the chancel.

17. Kidwelly Castle 5 D9
Kidwelly. Even in ruins, this noble castle standing above the River Gwendraeth dominates the little town of Kidwelly. Remaining, are a rectangular inner ward with a surrounding outer wall and associated buildings which date from the 13th to the 15thC. The first castle here was built by Roger, the Bishop of Salisbury, under Henry I but the present building dates from the time of Edward I. The intervening years were violent, the castle changing hands between Welsh and English many times, but it remains a splendid sight. Note the ruined 14thC gateway nearby.

17. Kidwelly Tinplate Works 5 D9
1m NW of Kidwelly. Next time you shop at a supermarket, spare a thought for the tin cans. Most of Britain's are made in Wales. John Hanbury started rolling tinned plates in Pontypool in 1728, and by 1750 the tinplate works at Kidwelly had opened. Out of 35 tinplate works in Britain during the 19thC, 22 were Welsh – hence the old rugby song 'Sospan Fach' (The Little Saucepan). Although the Kidwelly site can only be viewed from the road, you can see two great chimney stacks, flywheels, rollers, a large 'Foden' engine, and horizontal steam engines. Llanelli Borough Council have bought the site to open a museum of the tinplate industry there.

18. Lamphey Palace 5 B9
Lamphey, 2m E of Pembroke. One of the several estates of the Bishops of St David's Cathedral. The earliest building here is in the Early English style of the 13thC, seen in parts of the old hall. The gatehouse and new hall were added a century later, and in the 15thC a chapel and living quarters were built. The palace has welcomed many a royal visitor. The future Henry VII stayed here on his way to the Battle of Bosworth and it was the childhood home of Robert Deveraux, Earl of Essex and favourite courtier to Elizabeth I. Used only for a short time as a private house, Lamphey was soon abandoned – and later used as a stone quarry. *Open certain days.*

19. Laugharne 5 D9
One of Wales's most pleasing small towns, Laugharne (pronounced 'Larn') was the home of the poet Dylan Thomas for many years. He lived in the boathouse overlooking the 'heron priested shore'.
Locals at Brown's Hotel in the main street, his favourite pub, still love to recall their favourite tales of evenings spent in his company. His grave, marked with a simple wooden cross, is in the nearby churchyard.
Laugharne Castle was built on the site of an earlier Norman fortification. The ruin today is mainly of a mansion built in the reign of Henry VIII, the outer wall romantically clad with ivy.

Dylan's Cottage, Laugharne

20. Llanstephan Castle 5 D9
A friendly, crumbling ruin on a high ridge fronting the shore, and, naturally, a favourite with romantic artists. It dates from around 1280, and has a well-preserved gatehouse that seems to have been used as a keep, plus inner and outer walls. St Anthony's Well, *¼m SW of castle*, is a wishing well reputed to be particularly efficacious in matters of health.

21. Llawhaden 5 C8
An interesting ancient little town. The ruined castle on its small hill was the 14thC home of the bishops of St David's, providing them with a safe refuge in times of trouble. A solid-looking drum tower gatehouse and a section of the curtain wall remain: the latter has some fine windows and interesting five-sided towers. The early 16thC chapel, reached by a stair tower, was built by Bishop Vaughan, but soon afterwards the castle was abandoned. Llanwhaden church, with its two towers, was built in the 14thC on the base of a much earlier Celtic foundation and nearby stands an attractive 17thC water-mill.

22. Manorbier Castle 5 C9
6m W of Tenby, S of A4139. Built over the 50 years from 1275 to 1325, Manorbier is strikingly situated over the red sandstone Manorbier Bay. Still privately owned and occupied, perhaps the fact that it was never besieged accounts for the excellent state of preservation of many of the buildings. It has a series of towers linked by high curtain walls and the ruin is surrounded by all the features of a medieval community: castle, church, ponds, mill, dovecote and orchards. The castle has been peopled with model figures of knights and soldiers in an attempt to recreate the medieval scene. *Open summer.*

23. Museum of the Woollen Industry 5 D7
Dre-fach Felindre, 4m E of Newcastle Emlyn, off A484. Sheep, if they only knew it, could take over Wales since they outnumber the Welsh three to one! Instead, they surrender their fleeces to the ever-increasing number of tourists keen to buy good cloth or just curious to know how a traditional woollen mill really works – or worked.
Until the last century, wool was one of Wales's most important industries, and this complex is typical of the busy Yorkshire or Lancashire-style mills that once dominated every inch of the Teifi Valley. But Dre-fach Felindre isn't just a museum showing the usual machines and processes. Within a mile, every stage in the development of the industry from the Middle Ages to the present day can

be seen, from fulling mill to weaver's cottage, smithy to water-wheels. There is a working woollen mill actually on the premises. *Open most days, summer.*

24. Nanteos 5 E5
2½m SE of Aberystwyth, off A4120. Meaning 'brook of the nightingale', Nanteos is an apt name for this fine, Georgian manor, set in the shadow of a steeply-wooded ridge. It seems a shame, therefore, that rather than being a romantic gift from a handsome prince to his betrothed, it was built in 1739 for a certain Thomas Powell from the profits of the lead-mining industry.
But inside, the rooms with their rococo plasterwork are full of beautiful treasures: fine period furniture, porcelain and paintings. In the music room is a portrait of Richard Wagner who is said to have composed part of 'Parsifal' while staying here. *Open summer.*

25. Nevern 5 C7
7m SW of Cardigan, off B4582. Hidden away in a deep valley that drops some 300ft below the main road, Nevern is one of the most fascinating small villages in Wales. The Church of St Brynach contains a unique collection of carved stones, the earliest dating from the time of the Roman occupation, around AD400. Two others are inscribed in both Latin and Ogham script: the Maglocunus Stone and the Vitalianus Stone. The 10thC Great Cross, 13ft high, is one of the finest Celtic crosses in Wales, intricately and richly carved with Celtic patterning. Near the church is the so-called 'Bleeding Yew', which drips a blood-like sap.
On the slopes of Carn Ingli, which dominates the village, are the crumbling walls and towers of one of the best preserved Iron Age camps to be found in the country.

26. Pentre Ifan Burial Chamber 5 C7
3m S of Nevern, off A487. One of the most striking megalithic monuments in Britain, its capstone, 17ft long and weighing about 20 tons, is delicately balanced 7–8ft above the ground on four massive uprights. It is situated at the south end of a barrow of 135ft by 56ft, and was obviously one of the most important of its time – some 4,000 years ago. Its stones were hewed from the local Preseli Hills, which provided the famous 'blue stones' of Stonehenge.

Pentre Ifan Burial Chamber

27. Paxton's Tower 5 E8
6m E of Carmarthen, off B4300. A folly of 1805, looking rather like a cross between the Norman keep intended and a truncated rocket. It was built by local Member of Parliament and banker, William Paxton, to commemorate Lord Nelson's recent victories. There are fine views over the countryside from the top.

28. Pembroke 5 B9
Still watched over by the uncompromising ruin of its castle, Pembroke has a restrained, 19thC air, with dignified buildings and pleasant riverside walks. A typical town of Norman foundation, Pembroke retains its town walls, priory and streets laid out in the grid pattern. The town grew up around the castle, which was first founded in the late 11thC. In 1138 Pembrokeshire was given the status of County Palatine and the earls of Pembroke had supreme power over the area. Unlike many other towns, Pembroke suffered little in the Welsh rebellions.

Some attractive medieval cottages survive on Monkton Hill, where there are also remains of the town's west gate. The town wall dates from c1265 and further stretches overlook the town commons. Monkton Hill is named after Monkton Priory, founded as a Benedictine institution in 1098. Monkton Priory Church has a remarkably high chancel and an ancient holy-water stoup. Note the 'leper's squint', an opening through which ill monks could watch the service from outside.

28. Pembroke Castle 5 B9
Castle St. A superb castle, set on a high, rocky ridge and surrounded on three sides by the River Pembroke. Its great circular keep, nearly 70ft high, was built c1200 and is intact but for its floors. The towered curtain wall was added shortly after. Harri Tudor, later to be Henry VII and founder of the Tudor dynasty, was born in a first floor room of the Henry VII tower, in 1457.
Pembroke Castle was unique in Wales in declaring for Parliament at the start of the Civil War. After six years the town's mayor dramatically changed sides and Cromwell himself led the subsequent Parliamentary siege. Afterwards the castle was slighted and fell to ruin, although its excellent state of preservation belies the fact.
Beneath the northern hall is the 'Wogan' – a huge natural limestone cavern once used as a storehouse. Its walls are coloured a creepy blood-red and green by the damp.

29. St Clear's 5 D9
A small agricultural town founded, as its name suggests, by the Normans. Only the mound of the Norman castle remains, but the church is a remnant of a 12thC priory, one of only two established in Wales by the Cluniac order. The church has a pure Norman font, and a fine carved Norman chancel arch, quite rare in Wales. The priory was dissolved by Henry V and the property given to All Souls, Oxford.

30. St David's Cathedral 5 A8
St David's. With a population of around 2,000, St David's is the smallest city in Britain, thanks to its magnificent, medieval cathedral. Rather than dominating its surroundings, this purple-stoned building snuggles discreetly in a shallow, leafy vale. At the height of its importance, two pilgrimages to St David's were regarded as the spiritual equivalent of one to Rome.
St David founded the first church here in AD550. After being sacked it was rebuilt and is today basically 12thC, with 14thC alterations. The nave dates from 1180 and the central tower from 1250, although both were raised in height in the 14thC. Sir Gilbert Scott carried out an extensive renovation in the last century, adhering to the original design. The church is notable for its Irish oak nave and fascinating misericord carvings on the choir stalls, but perhaps the most beautiful feature is the intricate fan tracery of Bishop Vaughan's Chapel. The rood screen is also extremely fine.
In its time, St David's has had some notable bishops. Bishop Ferrar was burnt at the stake at Carmarthen by Queen Mary for refusing to accept the return to Roman Catholicism in the 16thC. Bishop Davies made the first Welsh translation of the Bible. Legend states that Bishop de Leia, in 1190, went to King Rhys of Wales to ask him to cease warring against England and bring peace to his realm. The King had him beaten for his pains, and the Bishop retaliated by excommunicating him and his sons. After the King's death, his sons came to the Bishop and begged him to pardon them. His answer to this was to have their father's corpse disinterred 'then sufficiently stinking' and flogged. He had the sons flogged too – and then pardoned them.
Lying in a tranquil valley beside the cathedral

are the romantic ruins of **Bishop's Palace**. St
David's was once the richest of the Welsh
dioceses, and this is reflected by the
magnificence of the palace. The ruins consist
mainly of a quadrangle with an open arcade
running round the top, and the associated
private chapel, kitchens and impressive Great
Hall, all built from 1280 to 1350. Note the
arcaded parapet, a unique feature of Bishop
Gower's work.

If, as tradition has it, the 16thC Bishop
Barlow had not stripped the roofs of their lead
to provide dowries for his five daughters,
these rooms would doubtless be in a better
state of preservation today.

St David's Cathedral

31. St Govan's Chapel   5 B9
1m S of Bosherton, 7m S of Pembroke, off B4519.
A fascinating, tiny chapel wedged in a narrow
cleft halfway down a cliff, rife with legend and
superstition. You can wander down the 52
steps that lead from the cliff to the tiny
sanctuary. The main fabric of the building is
11thC, but the altar, bench and other stone
fittings go back, in all probability, to the 5thC,
the time – we think – of St Govan. On the
plastered west wall is a circle with an as yet
undeciphered inscription.

Just who St Govan was, no-one is sure. He or
she could have been the Gawaine of King
Arthur's Round Table, St Gofen (wife of a
Celtic chief), or even Gobham (an Irish abbot
and contemporary of St David). The most
popular story states that St Govan was being
attacked by some pirates when a cleft
suddenly opened up beneath her. As she took
refuge, a well miraculously sprang up which
she took as a holy sign. This is why she built
the church – and where she is buried. But,
whatever, superstitions abound. It is claimed
that you can never count the steps to make the
same total twice; a human-shaped figure can
be seen in limestone behind the crude altar;
and that your wish will come true if you throw
a coin into the holy well, which is also said to
have great healing powers.

32. Strata Florida Abbey   5 F6
1m ESE of Pontrhydfendigaid. In the 12th and
13thC Strata Florida was the intellectual and
political centre of Wales, and this originally
Norman monastery was magnificent enough
to be called 'the Westminster Abbey of
Wales'. Welsh princes here swore their
allegiance to Dafydd, son of Llywelyn the
Great, in 1238, and Strata Florida was also
their burial ground. During the Owain
Glyndwr revolt the abbey was converted to a
military stables, but later returned to the
monks who added the cloister. When Henry

VIII dissolved the abbey, the monks took an
olive-wood cup with them which they believed
was the Holy Grail.

Meaning 'plain of flowers', from a Latin
translation of 'ystrad fflur', outlines of the
abbey's church, sacristy, chapter house and
cloisters can still be seen. The tile pavements
are finer than those of any other ruined abbey
in Britain and the decoration on the Norman
arch at the west entrance is unique.

The farmhouse nearby has an unusual
painting and some relics. Five miles south is a
great peat bog – the largest in Wales – known
as Gors Goch Glan Teifi, or Tregaron Bog.

33. Talley Abbey   5 F8
5½m N of Llandeilo, B4302. Established in the
monastic revival of the 12thC it stands in a
beautiful setting at the head of the Talley
Lakes. A curiosity is that while so much has
been swept away, part of the central tower of
the church survives almost to its full height. It
is evident from the design of the church that
an ambitious plan was left uncompleted.

34. Tenby   5 C9
With its town walls and narrow streets, Tenby
is a fascinating combination of the dusty
charm of a medieval town and the elegance of
a Georgian seaside resort. Its first claim to
fame is in a poem written in the 9thC,
remarking that the songs of the inebriated
bards at the fortress drowned even 'the beat of
the waves resounding below'.

The surviving gatehouse and tower of the
present castle are 12thC and now used as the
town museum. The town wall, *South Cliff*, is
of a slightly later date. Like the castle, it
suffered from constant Welsh attacks during
the 13thC but was substantially strengthened
in 1457. Tenby was held for the King at the
beginning of the Civil War, and was twice
bombarded from the sea before surrendering
in 1648.

Tenby

Tenby grew rich as a port during the 15th and
16thC, but then began to decline. Prosperity
boomed again in the early 1800s when
William Paxton, the local magnate and
Member of Parliament, developed it as a
fashionable holiday resort. The bustling little
harbour is a popular yachting centre.

St Mary's Church is largely 15thC with
considerable 19thC modifications. It is the
largest parish church in Wales and noted for
its finely carved nave roof. **The Tudor
Merchant's House**, *S of main street*, shows
the influence of the Flemish merchants who
came to Tenby in the 15thC. As well as some
beautiful furniture, it has Flemish pattern
murals and a fine Flemish chimney. It was
restored in 1938 and is owned by the National
Trust. *Open most days, summer.*

MID GLAMORGAN

1. Caerphilly Castle   5 H10
9m N of Cardiff, A469. The second largest
castle in Britain (the largest is Windsor) and
the strongest medieval fortress ever built,
Caerphilly shows Norman defensive ingenuity
at its most inventive. This muscle-bound
masterpiece must have daunted the heart of
any attacker. There are three lines of defence:
an outer moat, an inner one guarded by the

outer ward, and finally the inner ward,
protected by the four great drum towers at
each corner.

It was begun in 1268 by Gilbert de Clare, to
defend the Glamorgan lowlands against
Llywelyn the Last. Llywelyn destroyed the
foundations in 1270 and laid siege while it was
being rebuilt. Later, the castle was captured
during Glyndwr's revolt. The dramatic incline

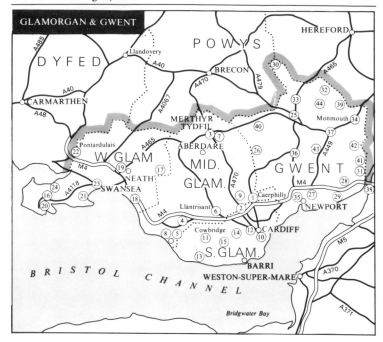

GLAMORGAN & GWENT

of the south east tower results from
Cromwell's attempts to blow it up during the
Civil War.
The castle has been splendidly restored and
the 14thC Great Hall is used for festivals and
concerts. Graced by swans, the moat and lakes
constructed by Clare provide the castle with a
beautiful setting.

2. Castell Coch   5 H10
3m NW of Cardiff, off A470. A glorious
medieval fantasy, beautifully situated on the
sides of a steep, wooded valley. It was built
from 1865–85 for the Third Marquess of
Bute as his country home on the site of a
13thC red sandstone castle, from which it
takes its name (Castell Coch is Welsh for Red
Castle). It was designed, as was the interior of
Cardiff Castle, the Marquess's town home, by
the famous Victorian eccentric, William
Burges.
The building is triangular in shape, with
round towers at each corner, each topped with
a fairy-tale conical roof. The interior is just as
fantastic, with murals of birds and animals
from Aesop's fables, and subjects from Greek
mythology.

Castell Coch

3. Cefn-Coed Viaduct   5 H9
Off A470 at Cefn Coed. At 725ft long, this is
the third largest viaduct in Wales and shows
the engineering skills and workmanship of the
Victorians at their best. It was built in 1866 to
carry the Merthyr–Brecon railway over the
Taf Fawr river. The viaduct has 15 arches, at
a maximum height of 115ft, built of stone –
with bricks underneath, because of a strike by
stonemasons during its construction!

4. Coity Castle   5 G10
2m NE of Bridgend, off A4119. Coity Castle has
the proud distinction of being one of the few

castles that Owain Glyndwr besieged
unsuccessfully. It's an extensive, rather
gloomy ruin, built at the end of the 12thC.
The walls of the keep and the curtain wall
date from this time but the remainder is
mainly 14thC, with minor Tudor additions.
The castle was later inherited by Sir Robert
Sidney, the poet Sir Philip Sidney's brother,
but shortly after his death it was abandoned.

5. Ewenny Priory   5 G10
2m S of Bridgend, B4524. The roadside offers
the best view of this 12thC monastery built
with military defences as a cell of the
Benedictine Priory at Gloucester. Much of
the remains are original Norman work and the
13thC circuit walls are virtually complete.
The crenellated precinct wall and portcullis in
the gatehouse indicate that the monks were
ready to defend their retreat at a moment's
notice.

6. Llantrisant   5 H10
10m W of Cardiff, A48. Llantrisant castle, of
which only a ruined drum tower remains, was
the scene of the ignominious capture of
Edward II, fleeing from his wife Isabella and
her baronial allies. The church, although
heavily and none too happily restored, is on a
scale which indicates the town's past
importance.
Llantrisant was the home of Dr Price, one of
the greatest of Victorian eccentrics. In 1884,
aged 83, he had a child whom he named Iesu
Grist, or Jesus Christ. The boy died in infancy
and Price, to the horror of the locals,
cremated him on the hillside above the town.
There was a riot and Price was arrested.
Later, he was acquitted on payment of a
farthing costs, establishing for the first time
the legality of cremation in Britain.

7. Merthyr Tydfil   5 H9
Of little beauty but great social interest,
Merthyr grew from village to boom town
during the iron and coal years of the 19thC.
Dynasties of ironmasters and colliery bosses
controlled it and Carlyle described it as one of
the 'sootiest, squalidest and ugliest' places he
knew.
Poor housing and food, bad drainage,
pollution and long working hours brought
high disease and death rates. Tradesmen

rarely lived beyond 32 years old, wroking men rarely beyond 17. People huddled in low rows of cottages – while William Crawshay, iron magnate, spent £30,000 on his mock-medieval Cyfarthfa Castle, *1m NW of Merthyr*. An impressive building, set in beautiful parkland, it overlooks a lake which supplied the Cyfarthfa Ironworks nearby, favouring the ironmaster with a vantage point from which to view his industrial empire. It now houses the town's museum and art gallery. Opposite the house is a church with a blue-faced clock. You will note that the clock has only three faces. It's said that the builders refused to put one on the side facing the house, saying they wouldn't give Sir William an hour of thcir time. Compare the castle with the ironworkers' cottages in Chapel Row, *nr bus garage*, and you'll understand their feelings. Next door to no. 1 is a ruined chapel built by the Crawshays in 1788 for their workers.

In February 1804, a historic journey was made – the first steam locomotive in the world, built by Trevithick, drew five rumbling wagons of freight and 70 men to the canal at Abercynon. From Penydarren Tramroad, *W of A470 at Quakers Yard*, you can still walk most of the route. A replica of Trevithick's engine is now on display at the Welsh Industrial and Maritime Museum in Cardiff.

8. Ogmore Castle   5   G10
3m SE of Bridgend. Once the 12thC stronghold of the hated William de Braose, it is now a romantic misfit more at home with some companionable cottages along the River Ewenny than with its bull-necked bully boys of old. The stepping stones across the river explain its siting: it guards a river crossing on the Ewenny and as such was of crucial importance to the Normans in the Vale of Glamorgan. With Coity and New Castle, Ogmore formed a defensive triangle which was strengthened when Ewenny priory was fortified about 1200. The earth banks and ditches of the early 12thC, the stone keep and the 13thC gatehouse remain.

9. Senghennydd   5   H10
4m NW of Caerphilly, B4263. Scene of the worst mining disaster in Britain. On October 4th, 1913, an explosion 2,000ft underground in the Universal mine claimed the lives of 439 men – a sharp reminder of the terrible dangers faced by the miners every day of their working lives.

🐚 SOUTH GLAMORGAN 🐚

10. Cardiff   5   H10
Attractive, lively, and with a cosmopolitan air, the capital of Wales is a city of contrasts. Its history goes back to the Romans – a 3rdC Roman fort and traces of a civilian settlement have been discovered to the south – but little is known of Cardiff's history between their departure and the coming of the Normans. The original primitive castle was strengthened after repeated attacks from Welsh rebels, and a prosperous town grew up within its protection.
Over the centuries Cardiff fell into slow decline, but the Industrial Revolution brought dramatic changes. In 1801 the population was about 1,000. By mid century this had increased 30-fold. Its proximity to the South Wales coalfields, its importance as a port and the arrival of the railways all contributed to this rapid growth.
Some excellent modern buildings have sprouted, notably the universally-acclaimed civic centre, *Cathays Park*. Look at the City Hall with its clock tower and magnificent Marble Hall. The imposing National Museum of Wales houses archaeological remains, industrial items and a world-famous collection of paintings which includes Welsh artists and French Impressionists. The Welsh Industrial and Maritime Museum, *nr Docks*, is a fascinating exhibition area occupying a four-acre site.

Cardiff Castle

10. Cardiff Castle   5   H10
Castle St. With its 1,900 years of history, Cardiff Castle stands in direct contrast to its modern city surroundings. The castle is a fascinating amalgam of a variety of styles from the Roman to the Victorian periods. You can see the remains of the 10ft-thick walls built by the Romans near the 13thC Black Tower entrance. The Normans used the Roman fort base to build their castle and it has been in constant occupation ever since.
Along the west wall are the apartments improved for domestic life during the Tudor and Stuart periods. In 1867–75 the Third Marquess of Bute employed the Victorian architect and genius, William Burges, on an extensive renovation project. He virtually rebuilt the entire south west part of the castle, transforming the interior with an extravaganza of elaborate and colourful Gothic decoration. It was also at the time that the ornate Clock Tower was erected.
Of interest are the drawing rooms with a rarc Louis XIII clock, the library, the Chaucer Room, the banqueting room and the collection of weapons and trophies of the Welch regiment, housed in the Black Tower.

11. Cowbridge   5   G10
Still a centre for the farming community and with historic inns and coaching houses scattered along its long main street, Cowbridge was once the market town for the area. Settlement here goes back to the Romans, but the town today is essentially a Norman creation. Parts of the 14thC town walls can be seen to the south west.
The surrounding area abounds in castles, and one was begun in the hamlet of **Llanblethian**, *1½m W of Cowbridge*. It was never completed, but the three-storey gatehouse still stands. To the east of the town is **Beaupré**, *by footpath, 1m SW of St Hilary*, the restored ruin of a grand Tudor mansion house, once the home of the Basset family. Their motto is on one of the two fine Renaissance style porches, and reads: 'Gwell angau na chywilydd'. It was later adopted by the Welch regiment, and is more familiar as 'Better death than dishonour'. *Open most days*.

12. Llandaff Cathedral   5   H10
2m NW of Cardiff. If not as glorious as some of the great English cathedrals, Llandaff can be proud of its determined survival. Cromwell's troops used the nave as their beer-hall and the font as a pig trough. In 1703 a storm blew down the south west tower. Twenty years later another claimed the nave roof. And that wasn't the end of its troubles. Disaster struck

again in 1941, in the form of a German landmine, which caused devastation second only to that suffered at Coventry.
Lying half-hidden in a hollow, it's hard to identify this turbulent past with Llandaff's tranquillity today. It was founded in 1120 by Bishop Urban on the site of an earlier church. The beautiful Lady chapel was added soon after its completion in 1266, and further refinements including the construction of Jasper Tudor's north west tower were made in the 14th and 15thC.
There followed 300 years of absentee bishops and appalling neglect but a sustained restoration began in 1835. Rebuilding after the war incorporated bravely modern elements, such as the parabolic arch that sweeps across the nave. Particularly interesting is the modern memorial chapel to the Welch Regiment, and the Processional Way. Look out for Epstein's remarkable sculpture 'Christ in Majesty'.

13. Llantwit Major   1 F2
B4265. A fascinating small town with a charming 15thC town hall and double church, divided into the Old Church and the New Church. The Old Church is built on the site of a monastery and clerical school founded by St Illtyd c500AD. It became one of the most important centres of learning in British Christendom and fostered some of the greatest minds of early Welsh history. Among its famous pupils were St Teilo and St David. Perversely, the New Church is about 100 years older than the main fabric of the Old Church, which was rebuilt in the 15thC around the core of the 11thC original. The Old Church contains a fine collection of Celtic stones, including an 8thC cross

dedicated to St Illtyd and a number of interesting medieval monuments.

14. St Fagan's Welsh Folk Museum 5 H10
4m W of Cardiff, off A48. You can almost smell the warm bread, leek pie and toasty cheese wafting from a traditional Welsh kitchen on show here at this beautiful folk museum. One glimpse of the iron range, hooks for curing hams, onion strings, blue-and-white china, copper lustre jugs, and the inevitable Welsh oak dresser is enough to send even liberated ladies straight back to domesticity!
Everyday life in rural Wales is what this museum is all about, and it's built in and around an Elizabethan mansion, itself standing within the walls of a medieval castle. Everything from crossbows and rapiers to flat irons and organs is here. Rather than the usual display in glass cases, everything here is animated (as far as any museum is able) by its setting. In the grounds Welsh buildings have been removed stone by stone, timber by timber, from various parts of Wales and re-erected here. See the tannery, cockpit, wool factory and tollgate house. Craftspeople demonstrate old techniques like weaving, basketry and wood turning. There is also a modern gallery complex housing exhibitions of costumes, agricultural and domestic implements and machinery.

15. Tinkinswood Burial Chamber 5 H10
St Nicholas, S of A48. A massive and well-preserved burial chamber, with a capstone of an estimated 35 tons. It was excavated in 1914 and found to contain the remains of about 50 people as well as fragments of pottery and worked flints. From these it was dated at about 4,500 years old.

✻ WEST GLAMORGAN ✻

16. Arthur's Stone   5 E10
1m E of Reynoldston. According to tradition, this irregular block of millstone grit split when King Arthur pierced it with his sword. There are other legends – one story identifies it as a pebble cast from Arthur's shoe, and yet another claims that on New Year's Eve, it miraculously shunted off down to the sea for a drink. What we do know is that it is the capstone of a burial chamber some 4,500 years old, and weighs a massive 25 tons.

Arthur's Stone

17. Cymer, Welsh Miners' Museum   5 G10
Afan Argoed Country Park, nr Cynonville, off A4107. Here, by entering the simulated coal faces, viewing pit gear and examining the miners' equipment, you can experience the harsh realities of coal-mining and understand its effects on the communities of the South Wales Valleys. *Open summer; weekends, winter*.

18. Margam Abbey Church   5 F10
Margam, N of M4. Built for the Cistercians in 1147 on the site of an earlier Celtic monastery, the abbey is now incorporated into the parish church. Much of the nave and west front are part of the original building, and the west end also has some fine glass by William Morris.
The ruined chapter house is about a mile away in Margam Park. It is a beautifully vaulted building, 12-sided without, but circular within. Adjacent to the church, the Margam Abbey Museum has a good collection of carved and inscribed stones, dating from Roman times onward. Beautiful Margam Park is renowned for its orangery and herd of fallow deer. *Museum open certain days*.

19. Neath Abbey   5 F9
S of A474 bridge. A fragmentary, smoke-blackened ruin of a 13thC Cistercian abbey. It was founded in 1130 by Richard de Granville who at the same time built Neath castle of which very little remains. After the Dissolution a large part of the abbey was made into a private mansion. With the coming of rapid industrial expansion at the end of the 18thC the abbey was converted to a forge, and the mansion used to house the workmen. The forge chimneys can be seen on the eastern side of the site.
The outer walls of the nave, and part of the west front are all that remain of the abbey church, but the mansion is in relatively good repair. The vaulted dormitory building houses a collection of carved stones from the abbey. While you're here, visit **Dulais Iron Works**, *2m NE of Neath*, an ancient industrial site where Turner painted a waterscape. In fact, you can see the remains of the iron works from the beer garden. There's a fine weir, a

waterfall, sluices, watercourses and a wheelpit. Downstream a single stone arch spans the river – all that survives of a twin-arched bridge that connected the site with a stretch of canal.

20. Oxwich   5 E10
Picture postcard village of quaint thatched cottages with an intriguing church and the ruin of a 16thC fortified manor. Sheltered by trees on a ledge above the sea is the 12thC church. The chancel is only 3 yds long, and thought to be based upon an early Celtic monastic cell. Equally ancient is the font, said to have been brought to the church by St Illtyd in the 6thC. Note the lovely 14thC de la Mere tomb.
Oxwich Castle, the manor house built by Sir Rice Mansel in about 1540, occupies the site of an earlier Norman castle. The ruins consist of a gateway with the family arms, a tower, and part of what must have been a huge columbarium where doves were kept to supplement the winter supplies of meat.

21. Oystermouth   5 F10
3m SW of Swansea, off A4067. A pleasant resort-cum-village that has been incorporated into Swansea since 1920, situated on that part of the coast known as the Mumbles. The name, which originated with the Normans, derives from the French 'mamelles' or breasts – a glance at the two islands at the tip of Swansea Bay provides the explanation! Oystermouth church is mainly 19thC, with a 12thC core and a font dated 1251. The church bells come from Santiago de Compostela, the Spanish pilgrimage centre. In the churchyard is the grave of the notable Dr Thomas Bowdler who, in his 1818 edition of Shakespeare, removed all passages 'calculated to deprave the youthful mind', and so added the verb 'to bowdlerise' to the language.
Oystermouth Castle is a squat, irregular ruin with a commanding hilltop siting to the north of the town. It was built in 1287 to replace an earlier version destroyed in a Welsh uprising two years before. The surviving keep, gatehouse and open courtyard are all connected by the high, towerless, curtain wall. *Open weekdays.*

22. Pontardulais   5 E9
8m NW of Swansea, A48. Rapid industrial expansion with the coming of a tin plate works in 1870 swept away whatever antiquities the town may have boasted. But in the early 1840s, Pontardulais was the centre of one of the strangest civil disturbances seen in Wales – the Rebecca Riots. They originated as a protest against the toll charges on the highways, but later came also to represent the plight of the poor. The name was taken from an appropriate verse in Genesis: 'And they blessed Rebecca and said unto her . . . let thy seed possess the gate of those which hate

them'. Rioters dressed as women and called their leaders 'Rebecca'. Only after considerable bloodshed was the movement quelled, but some time afterwards an act of Parliament put paid to the profusion of toll-gates once and for all.

23. Swansea   5 F10
The name Swansea is traditionally said to derive from Sweyn's Ea (Sweyn's island). Sweyn Forkbeard was a 9thC Viking marauder who chose this site as a base for plundering the coast. Another explanation is suggested by the name used by King John when giving the town its charter – Swinnzey. Sea swine was the common name for seals, abundant in this area. Whatever, Swansea has little to show of its past. Even Swansea Castle, *Castlewind St*, is a replacement: the original was built in about 1340 by Henry Gower, the Bishop of St David's. It was partially destroyed by Owain Glyndwr, and suffered further damage in the last war. An arcaded tower and turret are all that now remain. Swansea today shows the expansion of the previous century and post-war rebuilding. A bustling university town and commercial centre it is relieved by its 48 parks. Cwmdonkin Park was a favourite haunt of the poet Dylan Thomas and contains his monument. He used to refer to himself as 'the Rimbaud of Cwmdonkin Drive' – a street near where he was born.
The Maritime and Industrial Museum on the redeveloped seafront is a fine tribute to the city's seafaring past.
Near Parkmill are two interesting historic sites. Parc le Brear Burial Chamber is one of the best preserved passage tombs in Wales, in a 70ft long cairn. To the south are the impressive remains of Pennard Castle which dates from the 13thC.

24. Weobley Castle   5 E10
2½m W of Llanrhidian. From its lovely setting, this impressive 12th–14thC ruin overlooks the Gower marshland. It was mainly built at a time when Norman castles were giving way to more domestic fortified manor houses. The castle passed from the Beauforts to the influential Welsh knight, Sir Rhys ap Thomas, during Henry VII's reign, but in the 16thC was left to fall into decay. The remaining gatehouse, 13thC keep, kitchens and hall give a good impression of the conditions of domestic life in the late Middle Ages.

Weobley Castle

GWENT

25. Abergavenny   5 J9
The gateway to South Wales, Abergavenny is a pleasantly busy market town set in a mountain-ringed valley, whose settlement dates back to the Romans.
The modern town sprang from the founding of a castle by the Normans. It was inherited in 1177 by William de Braose, who became one of the most hated of the marcher lords. To avenge the murder of his uncle he invited the local Welsh rulers to Christmas dinner – and had them slaughtered as they dined. He then sent men to the chieftains' homes to kill their male heirs. William's just deserts came 30

years later when, after rebelling against the Crown, he was dispossessed of his lands and left to die a beggar. The castle fell to ruin in the 15thC, and all that is left are part of the curtain wall, gatehouse, and towers.
St Mary's Church, *Monk St*, is a more substantial reminder of the past: it's a 14thC building, replacing a Norman priory burnt during the Glyndwr revolt. The west front and parts of the nave date from a 19thC restoration. There are fine memorials in both the Lewis and Herbert Chapels, notably one in alabaster to Sir Richard Herbert who was executed in 1469.

26. Bedwellty House 5 H9
S of Tredegar, A4048. A massive block of coal
weighing 15 tons and hewn in 1851
symbolises the wealth that built this elegant
residence for iron boss Samuel Homfray, and
maintained it for the Tredegar Iron and Coal
Company until 1901. Certainly, it's the best
surviving example of an ironmaster's house,
set in beautiful grounds and with a history of
the town inside. Ironically, Tredegar was a
seething centre of political unrest during the
19thC, and mansions like this remind you of
the contrast between affluent industrialists
and their poverty-stricken workers. The
building is now used as council offices. *Open
weekdays.*

27. Caerleon, Roman Amphitheatre and Legionary Fortress 5 J10
3m N of Newport, B4236. 'Caerleon' comes
from 'castra legionis' or 'camp of the legion' –
and for three centuries from AD76, over
6,000 Roman soldiers lived in this massive
fortress. Civilians lived there, too, in a
bustling town outside the walls, and this is the
only known pairing of civil and military sites in
Roman Britain.
Modern houses have covered much of
Caerleon, but you can see the foundations of
the barracks, all laid out according to Roman
military textbooks with cookhouses and ovens,
dormitories and latrines. The fortress baths
with their long swimming pool, sunbathing
area, Purbeck marble steps and cold dip give
us an idea of how the average soldier spent his
off-duty hours. When he wasn't splashing
playfully in the baths he was probably
watching gory gladiatorial combat in the
marvellously-preserved amphitheatre at
Caerleon.

Caerleon Ampitheatre

The only completely excavated amphitheatre
in Britain, it is oval-shaped and with an earth
bank 26ft high that held tiers of wooden seats.
A stone wall 11ft high surrounded the arena –
mortar-smoothed so that no beast or person
could scramble to safety. Two main entrances,
one at each end, lead into the arena. Two
more went to private boxes. A small
half-domed recess in front of one probably
held a statue of Nemesis (Fate).
In the Middle Ages the ruins must have been
even more impressive, and Caerleon became
identified with the court of the legendary King
Arthur. An account by Geoffrey of
Monmouth in 1136 states: 'the royal palaces
with gilded roofs . . . made it rival even the
grandeurs of Rome'. Needless to say, there's
no historical evidence for the Arthurian
connection, but the atmosphere of the town
was sufficient to inspire Tennyson, who
stayed at the Priory Inn while writing 'Idylls of
the King'.

28. Caerwent 5 K10
8m E of Caerleon. A richly evocative Roman
town, known then as Venta Silurum. It was
founded in AD75 after the Romans had
defeated the local tribe, the Silures, who had a
hill fort a mile to the north. It was Roman
custom to remove local tribes to new Roman
settlements, both as an effective means of
control and to help 'civilise' the natives. At its
peak the population was probably about 2,000.

Today the greater part of the Roman wall still
surrounds the town. It reaches a height of 17ft
in places and is fortified by six octagonal
bastions which date from a re-fortification of
about AD340. The most impressive section is
on the south side of the town, where it is
unbroken for 500 yards. Material excavated
from Caerwent is on display at Newport
Museum.

29. Caldicot Castle 5 K10
5m E of Magor, B4245. A late 12thC
construction with typical round keep. The
rectangular gatehouse was added in the 14thC
by Thomas Woodstock, one of Edward III's
sons. Ruin came with neglect rather than any
military action, but the castle has since been
restored and is the setting for medieval
banquets and junketings.
An interesting museum of local history
exhibits rural crafts and the Woodstock
Tower now houses an art exhibition. *Open
summer.*

30. Capel Y Ffin 5 J8
4m N of Llanthony. A tiny village hidden in the
Black Mountains. Its little cottage-like church
was described in the diaries of the Reverend
Francis Kilvert in 1876 as 'short, stout and
boxy, with its little bell turret – the whole
building reminded me of an owl'. You can see
exactly what he meant.

31. Chepstow Castle 5 K10
Bridge St, Chepstow. Full of arrogant
detachment, this magnificently solid castle
was built along a high spur above the River
Wye shortly after the Norman Conquest.
Stone was used from the outset, making this
one of the oldest stone castles in Europe.
In 1189 the Marshall family substantially
strengthened both the castle and the town
walls. From them it passed to the Bigods and
finally, in the 15thC, to the Herbert family
who remained there for the following 400
years.
The ruined Great Tower dates in its lower
parts from the 11thC foundation. The
residential quarters are 13thC, and include
Marten's Tower with its chapel. Henry
Marten, one of the men who had signed King
Charles I's death warrant, was imprisoned
here for 20 years and his private rooms, on the
first floor, give the impression that he wasn't
too uncomfortable. There are fine views of
Chepstow's steep medieval streets from the
curtain walls and towers.
The graceful iron road bridge over the River
Wye next to the castle was built in 1816 by
John Rennie. It is one of the earliest iron
bridges in the country and had its first
extensive repairs in 1968.

Chepstow Castle

32. Grosmont 5 J8
16m N of Monmouth, B4347. Now a tiny,
cobwebbed village, Grosmont was a place of
national importance in the Middle Ages. Its
decline was officially marked when it lost its
borough status in 1860.
Grosmont was one of the three castle given to
Hugh de Burgh in 1201, erected to protect
the border between England and Wales: the
others were White Castle and Skenfrith.
Originally the most sophisticated of the three,
Grosmont has suffered over the course
of time, and only the Great Hall and parts of
the curtain wall and towers survive. In 1233
Henry III and his wife were forced to flee
from Grosmont in their nightclothes,
following a surprise night attack by Llywelyn
the Great. It is also known for marking the
end of the Glyndwr revolt: the Welsh rebel

was decisively beaten here in 1410 by the future Henry V. Glyndwr went into hiding and was never heard of again.

And thereby hangs an interesting tale. Grosmont church has, on the south east wall of the nave, a monument to a certain John Kent. Sent to Oxford by the local Scudamore family, he later earned a reputation as a bard and magician and died at the ripe old age of 120. The coincidence of Glyndwr's fall and Kent's rise proved too much for local imagination and a rumour persisted that they were one and the same man. True or not, the church is worth visiting for the rich Early English arcading in the choir and the Norman arches of the nave.

33. Llanthony Priory   5 J8
6m NW of Llanfihangel Crucorney, B4423.
People who come here seldom forget it. Asked why, they find it hard to put into words – peace, beauty, a place described by one 12thC writer as 'truly fitted for contemplation' – who knows?

Certainly, it affected the knight who founded it back in 1103. Renouncing worldly pleasures, William de Lacy took one look at the sun rising over the Black Mountains and decided to stay here as a hermit. A new church replaced the little rustic one William had stumbled upon, and an English monastery for Black Canons opened. Dissolved in the 16thC, the priory crumbled until an 18thC landowner bought it and turned the south tower into a shooting box. This has now been converted into a hotel.

Some of the 12thC buildings survive, astonishing in their grace and delicacy. Beguiled by its serenity, that eccentric 19thC man of letters, Walter Savage Landor, bought the Llanthony estate. He spent his honeymoon there and planned to found an ideal community on the spot. The visionary plans he had involving the planting of 10,000 Lebanon cedars, proved too much for his pocket and within a couple of years he was bankrupted, had quarrelled with everyone in sight – and departed.

Llanthony Priory

34. Monmouth   5 K9
A historic market town still with the important air of when it was a strategic stronghold of medieval Wales. The street plan has hardly changed since the mid 15thC, although much has been enhanced by fine Georgian buildings and coaching inns. Although there was a minor Roman settlement here, the town grew up around the Norman castle and priory founded at the beginning of the 12thC. Geoffrey of Monmouth was born in the town in about 1100. His great work, 'The History of the Kings of Britain', established the popularity of the Arthurian legends in the Middle Ages. In 1387 the future Henry V was born in the castle keep, a 12thC structure which is the only surviving part of the castle. His statue can be seen in the 18thC Shire Hall. Note the 13thC Monnow Bridge: with its fortified gateway through which the road passes, it is unique in Britain.

35. Newport   5 J10
A fiercely thriving commercial centre, it was given its name by the Normans: it was their new port, replacing the old port of Caerleon upstream. A true product of the Industrial Revolution, its importance grew dramatically

when it became the natural outlet for the iron and coal industries of the Monmouthshire valleys.

On a site guarding the river stand the ruins of the castle. Rebuilt in the 14th and 15thC it was left to fall into decline and was eventually restored in 1930. The ruins consist of a square central tower with chapel on top and watergate beneath, plus two adjoining octagonal towers.

St Woolos Cathedral, *Stow Rd,* takes its name from a corruption of Gwynllwy, a 6thC lord who founded the first church here on his conversion to Christianity. The present building is 15thC, replacing the Norman one destroyed by Glyndwr. With the creation of the Church of Wales in 1921, St Woolos became a pro-cathedral, attaining full cathedral status in 1949. The Lady chapel occupies the site of the Celtic church, and parts of it are 12thC. The columns at the entrance to the fine Norman nave with clerestory were taken from Caerleon and are thought to be Roman in origin.

Ingenious and odd, **Newport Transporter Bridge,** *end of Brunel St,* is one of only two in Britain (the other is in Middlesborough) and four in the world. Two steel towers, 242ft high, support a platform spanning the river from which a transporter car – rather like a large Alpine cable car – is suspended. It runs along the platform powered by an electric motor and drum mechanism located in the engine house on the car. There's a good view of Newport – urban and industrial landscape – from the catwalk of the bridge, and the cab itself holds six cars. It opened in 1906 when Newport was heaving with new factories and needed quick transport.

Just to the west of the town is **Tredegar Park.** The house is set in grounds which are now a country park, run by the local council, but they once belonged to the Morgan family before passing out of their ownership in the 1950s. By far the best spectacle of the architecture is the design and execution of the Gilt Room, a symphony in wood panelling bordered in gold leaf with paintings let into the upper panels. The Brown Drawing Room is no less remarkable with exquisitely carved wood panelling setting off a fine ceiling and candelabra. One of the finest 17thC brick houses in Wales, the facade is particularly striking. *Open most days, summer; grounds daily, all year.*

36. Pontypool   5 J9
Among the first places in Wales to experience industrialisation, and fortunately there are still many industrial relics to be seen in and around the town. A 2½ mile waymarked walk in Pontypool Park has been designed around several points of interest. Not to be missed is the Valley's Inheritance Centre in the restored Pontypool Park Stables, which tells the story of the Torfaen area through exhibits and audio visual displays.

37. Raglan Castle   5 K9
7m SW of Monmouth, off A40. Veteran of Agincourt, Sir William ap Thomas, built this handsome castle in about 1430, more for social grandeur than military need. He was a gentleman of aggressive tactics. To ensure the appointment of a new prior, for instance, he simply carried off the rival candidate and threw him in chains at Usk Castle!

His 'Yellow Tower of Gwent' is a gruesome moated keep, hexagonal and built outside the main castle walls. Watch out for signs of the two drawbridges – one wide for VIPs, one narrow for everyday use. A prominent Yorkist during the Wars of the Roses, William's son continued building at Raglan until he was beheaded in 1469. A string of aristocrats spent the next two centuries glamorising it with long galleries, niches for statues, gazebos, and a Pitched Stone Court so-called for its cobblestones, most of which were found intact when the grass was uprooted there in 1947.

The siege of Raglan in 1646 was one of the most important in the Civil War. A garrison of 800, under the 84-year-old 5th Earl of Raglan, held out against a force double that number. Reinforcements arrived, and attackers numbered 3,500. Still Raglan held. Then Cromwell's Commander-in-Chief, Sir Thomas Fairfax, came in person to direct the siege. And Raglan fell, bringing to an end the first phase of the war.

Severely battered by 'slighting' – the usual policy after any defeat – Raglan crumbled until 19thC travellers, hooked on the cult of romantic ruins, partly restored it. In 1938 the government took over. See the buttery, pantry, kitchen tower, office wing, closet tower and chapel. The magnificent Grand Staircase at the north west corner of the Great Hall leads to the apartments in which Charles I stayed after his defeat at Naseby.

38. Severn Bridge 5 K10

Regarded as the gateway to Wales (as opposed to the way out to England), the Severn Bridge is an extraordinary light and elegant structure, with a main span of 3,400ft, the seventh longest in the world. Opened in 1966, it's one of the most successful of modern engineering projects.

![Severn Bridge photograph]

Severn Bridge

39. Skenfrith Castle 5 K8

7m NW of Monmouth, B4521. Skenfrith Castle was, along with Grosmont and White Castle, one of the three castles granted to Hugh de Burgh by King John in the early 12thC. The smallest of the three, it has a circular, three storey keep surrounded by an irregular outer wall. Skenfrith saw little action during its lifetime, and was abandoned by the mid 16thC.

The last governor of the three castles, John Morgan, lies buried in Skenfrith church. There's a fine monument to him and his family, remarkable for the detail of contemporary clothes carved upon it. The church, with its thick-walled tower, is a good example of the semi-defensive type found in the Marches.

40. The Round Houses 5 H9

Nantyglo, nr Brynmawr, off A467. Iron bosses Joseph and Crawshay Bailey were so hated by their workers that they built themselves a tower as a refuge from rioters. Ruthless working conditions, abject poverty and lack of representation bred violence. Nantyglo was also a centre for the 'Scotch Cattle' – a secret society of men dressed in skins and horns who held midnight meetings on the hillsides and intimidated blacklegs. *View from outside only.*

41. Tintern Abbey 5 K9

Tintern, 4m N of Chepstow, nr A466. Thanks to Wordsworth, Tintern is one of Britain's best-known monasteries. With its beautiful setting on the Welsh side of the River Wye, among green pastureland and wooded hills, and still with an aura of sanctity, it seems to nurture the poet in people. Many 18th and 19thC tourists waxed lyrical over it: 'this venerable relic', 'beauty in decay' and 'indescribably fine' were phrases flashed around ad nauseam by those enthusiastic travellers – and the magic remains.

Chosen for its wild remoteness, Tintern's founding Cistercians arrived in 1131 well-pleased with the martyring austerity of the site – and its fortunate abundance of nearby fish (the monks ate no meat). All prospered, and by 1220 plans were afoot for rebuilding Tintern on a grander scale. Money came from estates, and donors who expected a spiritual return on their cash. One demanded a holy lamp kept alight permanently beside his mother's tomb!

After the Dissolution, Tintern's monks dispersed and the Earl of Worcester (the abbey's patron) rather irreverently melted down lead from its roof and bells to use at his castles in Raglan and Chepstow. Much of the nearby Anchor Inn is built from abbey stones. Yet Tintern has survived assorted cannibalisings. The church itself is graceful and delicate, with majestic arches and a beautiful traceried rose window in the east end. Some carved bosses lie on the ground. Drainage problems meant that the cloisters were built to the north instead of the more usual sun-facing aspect. Here you can see book shelves, a fine 14thC doorway, the dining hall and alcoves for washing hands and holding towels. Stairs led to a pulpit where a brother read aloud during meals. A small museum adds facts and exhibits of abbey life to the very special atmosphere of the place.

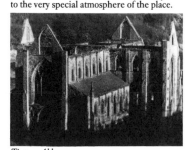

Tintern Abbey

42. Trellech 5 K9

6m S of Monmouth, B4293. Nothing remains to show that Trellech once rivalled Monmouth in prominence during the Early Middle Ages, but the village does have monuments of an earlier time.

The Harold Stones, three standing stones near the village crossroads, have nothing to do with that Harold of Hereford who died at the Battle of Hastings. They date from the earlier Celtic civilisation, before the arrival of the Romans. The preaching cross in the churchyard is 7thC, the contemporary of the first church built on the site.

The Virtuous Well, *SE of village on rd to Tintern,* is of the same age, and its healing qualities were advocated as late as the 18thC. It contains some interesting medieval stonework.

43. Usk 5 J9

Gentle town situated on the east bank of the river of the same name, Usk probably occupies the site of the Roman town, Burrium, although no extensive remains have been discovered. Looking wistfully over broad meadowlands are the remains of a small Norman castle. These include the keep, gatehouse and a tower from the curtain wall, mostly dating from the 12th and 13thC, when the castle was owned by the powerful de Clare family. *Open by arrangement.*

The Church of St Mary occupies the site of a Benedictine priory founded by the de Clares in 1236. The choir and tower show some remarkable 12thC work and the rest of the building is 13thC with extensive 15thC renovations. The glory of the church is its Tudor screen which extends the whole width of the building, and the 17thC pulpit and organ are from Llanduff Cathedral.

44. White Castle   5 J8
5m E of Abergavenny, B4521. A magnificent isolated ruin, the finest of the three castles given to Hugh de Burgh, it owes its name to the white plaster which once coated it. The present remain dates from both de Burgh's time and from a re-fortification in 1263. The castle began to decline after Edward I's successful subjugation of Wales.

Outwardly, at least, the castle shows little of the effects of time. Its six-sided curtain wall with drum towers at each angle seems as rock-steady as ever. This solidity, plus its isolated setting high on a hill, make the White Castle one of the most memorable in South Wales.

GWYNEDD

1. Aberffraw   5 A2
From shortly after the departure of the Romans until the early Middle Ages, Aberffraw enjoyed the status of capital of the kingdom of Gwynedd. Rhoderic the Great had a palace here in the 9thC with an attendant court of poets, priests, princes and warriors. The last Prince of Aberffraw was Llywelyn the Great in the 13thC.

But of all this glory, nothing remains and today Aberffraw is a grey village of spick-and-span cottages with little but an ancient hump-backed bridge to show of its historic past.

2. Bardsey Island   5 C3
Regular summer boat service from Aberdaron. Bardsey is also known as the 'Island of 20,000 Saints' – that is the number of the blessed buried here. It was first used as a sanctuary for the monks from Bangor Is Coed, near Chester, after forces sympathetic to them had been defeated at the Battle of Chester in AD615. During the 6th and 7thC it became a major place of pilgrimage. There are no great monuments, but the church is built on the foundation of the 6thC Abbey of St Mary.

Bardsey Island is an excellent bird watching centre, particularly for spring and autumn migrants.

3. Barmouth White House   5 E3
Barmouth, nr harbour. The White House (or Ty Gwyn) is said to have been originally built for Henry Tudor, later to be King Henry VII of England and used when he was plotting against Richard III in the Wars of the Roses. Although substantially rebuilt it retains its original 15thC door.

4. Beaumaris Castle   5 C1
3m NE of Bangor, off A545. Edward I ordered his architect, Master James of St George, to build Beaumaris as the last link in a chain of fortresses across North Wales. Work began in 1295 and three years later Beaumaris was more or less defensible. Notice the arrow slits in the curtain walls. Round holes mark where scaffolding was fixed on a slope to allow loads of stone to be wheeled up during building work.

The castle was taken by Owain Glyndwr in 1403, but retaken two years later. The last military action seen here was during the Civil

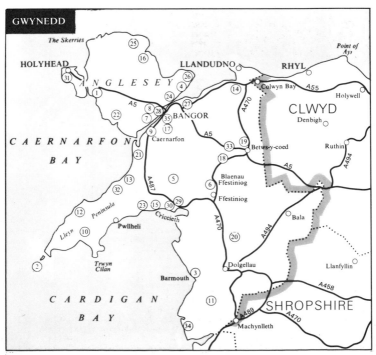

War when it was originally Royalist, but capitulated to the Parliamentary forces in 1646.
'Beaumaris' means 'beautiful marsh' and the castle was built to control the rich corn lands of Anglesey. Sea once lapped the southern edge of the castle and 40-ton vessels could sail right up to the main gate. You can still see the mooring rings. At the end of Gunner's Walk is a platform used for hurling stones or painful liquids on enemies.
Don't miss the limewashed chapel: for many people it's the highlight of their visit. Ironically, work on the castle was never completed, and that's why the towers look so truncated – they were stunted by lack of cash and interest. But Beaumaris remains a magnificent ruin, with particularly fine views from the outer ramparts and towers.

Beaumaris Castle

5. Beddgelert   5 E2
Crisp, compact, mountain village, the meeting place of three valleys. 'Beddgelert' means 'The Grave of Gelert', referring to a popular legend surrounding Llywelyn the Great. One day he returned home from hunting to discover his baby son savaged to death in his cradle, and his faithful hound, Gelert, covered in blood. In fury he slew the beast, only to discover that it had killed the wolf who attacked his child. The grief-stricken Llywelyn buried Gelert with full regal honours.
The story was popularised in an 18thC poem and Gelert's grave 'discovered'. Recently spoil-sports discovered that an 18thC inn-keeper invented the tale and passed it on to a writer of ballads. But if this imaginative man had the interests of his town at heart, he was certainly successful, for thousands of visitors are still drawn to pay tribute to the noble beast.

6. Blaenau Ffestiniog Railway   5 E2
Between Porthmadog and Ffestiniog. The Ffestiniog Railway Preservation Society has re-opened the derelict line, offering tourists a scenic eyeful in fine weather, through the Vale of Ffestiniog. The 13-mile-long narrow gauge railway was built to carry the slate from the mountain quarries to the coast. It opened in 1836, but the first steam engines were not introduced until 1863 – before that, horses had done the pulling.
Passengers are not a new thing – the novelty value of the charming little coaches was realised as early as the 1870s and it claims to be the oldest narrow gauge passenger line in the world. For the record, the gauge is 1ft 11ins. *Open summer; certain days, winter.*

Blaenau Ffestiniog Slate Quarrys   5 F2
1m N of Blaenau Ffestiniog, A470. Slate everywhere: quarries of it, heaps of it, tombstones of it, garden walls of it; the town seems engulfed by it, especially on rainy days when it glistens bluely. It seems incredible that people live close to such towering desolation – at 900ft above sea level with 100ins of rain a year. But despite dire unemployment, many do, and many have even chosen the town above all others: the novelist John Cowper Powys (1872–1963) spent his last eight years here.
Blaenau ('blaen' meaning 'head of the valley') grew up during the slate boom of the 1800s. Worldwide demand for it led to tramways and railways which linked the quarries with ports like Porthmadog. Slate quarrying ended in the 1960s after years of decline, but the skills of

the quarrymen and how they and their families lived haven't been forgotten. At Lechwedd Slate Caverns, an exciting train ride through tunnels and caverns jolts you to the 200ft-high Cathedral Cave formed by slate extraction. Victorian mining conditions are recreated in another cave showing how quarrymen worked by candlelight. Try splitting the slate at the mill museum. Quarrymen's cottages at Gloddfa Ganol Mountain Centre are furnished to reflect three eras of slatework, and there's a museum-cum-works which tells the story of the struggles and aspirations of the workers. Keen explorers might enjoy a landrover tour of some of the 42 miles of tunnels and caverns (helmets provided). Wear warm clothes for any of these activities. Don't worry about the children – the fairy grotto and play area will keep them amused. *Open summer.*

7. Bodowyr Burial Chamber   5 B2
1³/₄m WNW of Llanian Church, Bryn-Siencyn. How did neolithic people lift this 8ft by 6ft capstone onto these three upright standing stones without rupturing themselves? The probable answer is that they positioned the uprights and then built an earth mound around them until only their tops were visible. Then they dragged the capstone up the slope with ropes and wooden rollers. Finally, capstone in place and burial completed, the tomb was entirely covered with earth. Bodowyr's communal tomb is only a framework: it, too, was once covered with a mound of earth.

8. Bryn-Celli-Ddu Burial Chamber 5 B2
4m SW of Menai Bridge, off A5. Many people were buried in this temple-like tomb which is reckoned to be the finest Bronze Age cairn in Wales. The original mound, 160ft in diameter, was surrounded by a stone circle and ditch. Archaeologists excavated the mound, and then replaced it. A long entrance passage leads to a 10ft inner chamber near the centre of the mound. A carefully rounded upright stone still stands within it – not as a support, but presumably for some religious purpose. Passage graves are more common to Scotland and Ireland than England and Wales, but they are usually found near the Atlantic.

9. Caernarvon Castle   5 E1
Castle St. A baby was once presented to the Welsh people at this magnificent castle – he was Edward II, son of Edward I, who subdued the Welsh during the 13thC and built a series of castles to keep them in their place. Caernarvon was one of them. By calling his son Prince of (all) Wales, he hoped to appease and reconcile the hostile Welsh princes. In the end Edward failed: Owain Glyndwr angrily besieged Caernarvon in the early 15thC. During the Civil War both sides took possession of the castle in turn, and eventually abandoned it. Many offices and walls within were dismantled and, though from the outside the castle appears complete, inside you see it's little more than a shell.
Ironically, since it was built to suppress the natives, this great medieval fortress with its varying bands of stone that some folk liken to the ancient walls of Constantinople, is today one of the showpieces of Welsh tourism. Curtain walls, galleries and drum towers are kept repaired by the Department of the Environment, and architecturally it still displays much of its original uniqueness. Of particular interest are the seven polygonal towers, an innovation at the time, the largest of which is the western-most Eagle Tower. From the top there are marvellous views, while in the dungeon you can appreciate the thickness of the walls – 18ft in places. The shouldered arch of the castle is copied elsewhere and widely known as the 'Caernarvon arch'.

Prince of Wales is a title given to the heir to the British crown (the Queen was once Prince of Wales!) since baby Edward's time. The reigning monarch 'invests' it on the heir – it isn't automatic – which is why Prince Charles had his investiture at Caernarvon in 1969.

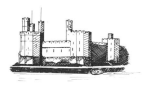

Caernarvon Castle

9. Caernarvon Roman Town   5 E1
1/2m SE of Castle Sq, A4085. Originally called Segontium, it was founded by the Romans in AD78, and they remained in occupation until c AD400. Tradition states that this was the birthplace of Constantine the Great, but there's little supporting evidence. Only the outlined foundations remain to be seen, but the museum dealing with Roman life is worth a visit.

10. Capel Newydd   5 D3
3m W of Llanbedrog. A lonely little chapel on the Lleyn peninsula, it was granted its licence in 1769, making it the earliest surviving Nonconformist chapel in North Wales. The earth floor and general barn-like atmosphere convey the humble intentions of the first worshippers here and their break from the established church. Recently the building almost collapsed but was saved by rapid restoration. Note the doors – they were originally windows!

11. Castell-y-Bere
Abergynolwyn. Dramatically situated in the shadow of the Cadair Idris, now a lofty ruin. If battlefields are haunted, Castell-y-Bere must be full of ghosts. There were scenes of epic struggle in this lonely mountain stronghold as the tides of war ebbed and flowed in the Middle Ages. Edward I captured it but failed to hold it, and after its fall in the uprising of 1294, it was abandoned. This Welsh castle lacked sophisticated devices like portcullis and drawbridge, but occupied a strong position with a precipitous descent to the north. It was here that the castle building stood, backed by a long and narrow courtyard extending to the more vulnerable southern side, where a curtain wall – now traceable only with difficulty – provided protection. The castle was entered by way of a timber bridge crossing a moat cut out of the rock.

12. Cefnamwlch   5 C2
Tudweiliog, off B4417. One of the largest and most impressive of the Bronze Age burial chambers, or cromlechs, to be found in the area. Its capstone, resting on three uprights, is 11ft long, 8ft wide and 3ft thick.

13. Clynnog-Fawr   5 D2
Here is one of the finest Perpendicular churches in Wales. It has a splendid, simple west tower and, inside, a notable 16thC screen and pulpit of c1700. Also of interest is the Bachwen megalithic burial chamber, *W of village, by sea.* It has standing stones and a capstone which is carved with cup-shaped markings.

14. Conwy Castle   5 F1
One of the most picturesque of Edward I's Welsh defences. Sited on a broad, precipitous rock, the castle, built in 1283, has been the scene of many a dramatic historical event. During a Welsh uprising of 1294, Edward was besieged here, and driven close to surrender through famine. The chapel was the scene of the betrayal of Richard II to Henry of Lancaster. The outer walls are 15ft thick and

have eight cylindrical towers, from which there are fine views over the Conwy estuary. Conwy town walls, with 21 towers, were built by Edward at the same time as the castle, and are one of the finest remaining examples of this kind of work in Britain. They extend for 1,400 yards with an average height of 30ft.
Telford's Suspension Bridge, over the Conwy estuary, was finished in 1826. It was built in the same style as the Menai Bridge, except that its towers were built to match those of Conwy Castle.
Aberconwy House, a three-storeyed building with a picturesquely asymmetrical front, is one of Conwy's last remaining 14thC timber-framed houses. The intricate leaded casement windows are of a later period. Housed here is the Conwy Exhibition, depicting the life of the borough from Roman to present times. *Open summer.*

15. Criccieth Castle   5 E2
Criccieth. Dramatic in its setting, with its gatehouse silhouetted against the skyline, the crumbling ruins of Criccieth Castle perch on a rocky hill above the town. A native Welsh fortification, the castle was built c1230. It was prominent in the fighting between Llywelyn the Great and the princes of Powys and Merioneth and after Edward I conquered the land, he strengthened the defences and formed a chain of coastal strongholds. Criccieth remained occupied until Elizabethan times. Still in good repair are the outer walls, the gatehouse flanked with towers and the small rectangular inner ward which dates from the original building.

Criccieth Castle

16. Din Lligwy   5 B1
11/2m W of Moelfre, off A5025. A walled village dating from the end of the Roman occupation, it was probably built on the site of an earlier, Iron Age, settlement. Traces of the irregular defence wall can be seen as well as the stonework of two circular buildings and some rectangular ones, covering about half an acre in all.
Nearby are two other archaeological sites: Capel Lligwy, a roofless 12thC church, and Din Lligwy Tomb. This was found to contain the remains of 30 bodies when excavated in 1908. Its huge, 28-ton capstone is supported on short uprights above a natural fissure which formed the burial chamber. *Open certain days.*

17. Dolbadarn Castle   5 B2
Llanberis. Its ancient stones blending with the grandeur of the Llanberis Pass, Dolbadarn is notable for both its precipitous location and imposing tower. The castle is a relic of the time when the Llanberis Pass was invaded not by pleasure-seeking tourists but by armies hot for conquest. See how it commands the entrance to the pass from its platform of rock. It dates from the late 12th or early 13thC and was built by the princes of Gwynedd. The tower, 40ft high, is the dominating feature. It is of mortared masonry and was probably the idea of Llywelyn the Great. There were two other towers guarding the western and southern approaches to the castle and the curtain wall was 4ft thick.

18. Dolwyddelan Castle   5 F2
1m W of Dolwyddelan. Traditionally the birthplace of Llywelyn the Great, the castle

was originally built for his father around 1170. Though there's not much evidence to support this, it's certain, anyway, that Llywelyn used the castle as a major residence. Dolwyddelan was occupied continuously until the early 16thC, but was then left to fall into ruin.

19. Gwydir Castle 5 F1
1m S of Llanrwst. Beautiful, romantic, Tudor manor house, whose importance merits the title of castle. It was begun about 1500 and added to throughout the 16thC using stones from the dissolved abbey at Maenan. In 1944 Gwydr was bought by Arthur Clegg who took upon himself the mammoth task of restoring the building. Many relics of the past were brought to light including a carved stone bearing the date 1171 and a secret priest's hole. Nearby is the Gwydir Uchaf Chapel, the private chapel for the Wynn family who lived at the castle. It was built at the end of the 17thC and has a finely painted ceiling depicting the Holy Trinity.

20. Gwynfynydd Gold Mine 5 F3
Coed-y-Brenin Forest, 3m N of Ganllwyd, nr Dolgellau. Wedding rings of Welsh gold glint on many a royal finger, and The Princess of Wales's is no exception. Modern gold mining began here in the 1840s, but Romans had discovered the 'California of Wales' in the 4thC and supplied bullion from it to their imperial mints in Lyons and Rome. Rich yields were struck in the 1860s, 1880s and 1890s, but by the 1930s the mines had closed. Gwynfynydd is scenically sited in the heart of the forest near the famous falls of Rhaeadr Mawddach where two waterfalls merge into one river. You can still see remains of the dressing mill, and the cast iron pipe that brought water from the river to work the turbine. There's an old strong room for storing gold with a steel door brought from the old county gaol at Dolgellau. Near it is an adit level leading to a chamber. Tramway remains follow the path of the river. Prospectors still poke about in these mines, and many people believe they still have much gold to offer.

21. Harlech Castle 5 E3
Harlech, off B4573. Standing splendidly on its rock platform 200ft above the surrounding grass-covered dunes, this majestic castle is remarkable for its excellent state of preservation. Originally the rock was a promontory overlooking the sea which has since retreated about two miles to the north, mainly as a result of 19thC reclamation work. Completed in 1289, after six years work, Harlech has offered fierce resistance to invaders over the years. It was besieged by Madog from 1294–5, but the garrison of 37 men withstood the ordeal. A similar feat of heroism is recalled when the castle was in Lancastrian hands and attacked by Edward IV. Famine eventually required the defending forces to surrender. The future Henry VII, then aged 12, was one of the survivors. It was this steadfast resistance that is said to have inspired the song 'Men of Harlech'. Harlech Castle stood up to its reputation by being the

last Welsh castle to hold out for Charles I during the Civil War.
The principal feature of the building now is the gatehouse, three storeys high, and with four towers. Needless to say, there are fine views to be had from the towers and walls.

22. Llangadwaladr 5 A2
1½m W of Aberffraw, A4080. An inscribed stone on the north wall of the nave of the rugged 13thC church marks the final resting place of 'Cadfan the King, wisest and most renowned of kings'. He was king of Gwynedd and died cAD625. The church has some beautiful stained glass of the 14th and 15thC.

23. Llanystumdwy 5 E2
1m W of Criccieth, A497. David Lloyd George came to Llanystumdwy as a child to live with his uncle, and their cottage, Ty Newydd, is marked with a plaque. He was educated at the village school and successfully stood as local Member of Parliament in 1890, to go on to hold the seat for the next 54 years. His body was brought back to Llanystumdwy after his death in 1945.
There's a simple, dignified memorial to him on the banks of the River Dwyfor. Opposite this is the Lloyd George Museum which houses many mementoes and relics of his often turbulent and controversial political career. *Open weekdays, summer.*

24. Menai Straits Bridge 5 B2
Menai Straits, 2¼m W of Bangor. Thomas Telford, the engineer, had already constructed what is now the A5 road when he began work on the Menai Bridge in 1819. It was opened in 1826 and at that time had the longest span in the world. The original graceful design was adhered to as far as possible in a rebuilding of 1938–41, when the road was widened and the number of supporting chains reduced to four from Telford's 16. The bridge is nearly half a mile in length and has a central span of 579ft.

25. Mynydd Parys Copper Mine 5 B1
2m S of Amlwch, off B5111. Spectacular but dangerous, this shaft-bored mountain once had the biggest copper mine in Europe with 1,500 men, women and children on its payroll. Women were known as 'ledis copor' – copper ladies. Mined on and off since Roman times, in 1768 a super-rich seam was struck. Amlwch boomed, the mountain became a feature of The Welsh Tour – and artists arrived by the cartload to paint miners swinging over the cliff face.
During the 19thC, Amlwch (pronounced 'Amlooch') harbour exported thousands of tons of copper and it is said that the mine made copper sheathing and bolts for every ship in Europe. Welsh people also claim that copper's power to clean marine growth off ships was first discovered here, when copper solution pouring from Parys streams into Amlwch harbour left all the ships anchored there spotless.
Today, a vast, arid crater gouges the summit of this lunar landscape and you can spot the sheen of copper green in many of the rock screes and terraces. Circular cakes of Roman copper – 1ft across and 3ins thick – have been found all over Anglesey, often stamped with Latin. A disused windmill, once used to assist a steam engine in draining the workings, can be seen from the road. The Wales Tourist Board do not recommend this site for families with young children because of its mine shafts.

26. Penmon Priory 5 C1
Penmon. Originally a Celtic foundation of the 6thC, the Priory Church of St Seriol now displays some of the best 12thC stonework in North Wales. To the north is a well and monastic cell that is thought to be 10thC, and there is an early cross in the surrounding deer park.

Harlech Castle

27. Penrhyn Castle   5 E1
2m E of Bangor. The first impression is that
this is another of Edward I's great
fortifications. Wrong. It's a marvellous
example of Victorian 'Norman', a joke so
absurd that it works. Built in the early 19thC
to designs by Thomas Hopper, it was
commissioned by George Pennant whose
riches came from the nearby Bethseda slate
quarry. His successor was made Baron
Penrhyn by Queen Victoria. She visited the
house in 1859 and you can see a Californian
Sequoia she planted which has now reached
considerable proportions.
The Norman theme is successfully carried
through in the Great Hall, and the library and
Ebony Room, though more subdued, are
equally impressive. There are some
interesting examples of slate craftsmanship,
notably the extraordinary and beautifully-
made slate bed, weighing over a ton. A
collection of dolls includes examples from
Victorian times to the present day, and there is
an interesting industrial Railway Museum in
the stable yard. There are lovely grounds to
explore, including a walled garden. *Open
summer.*

28. Plas Newydd   5 H2
Llangollen, A4080. The heavily-timbered
home of the 'Ladies of Llangollen' – two
ladies, Eleanor Butler and Sarah Ponsonby,
who eloped together to lead a life devoted to
'friendship, chastity and the knitting of blue
stockings'. After settling in Llangollen their
wit, hospitality and mannish clothes attracted
many celebrated visitors: Wellington, Scott,
de Quincey and Wordsworth among others.
Each visitor was required to present a gift of a
curio, particularly of carved oak, which the
ladies liked to collect. Wordsworth wrote a
sonnet for the occasion, tactlessly calling the
house 'a low roofed cot'. He was not invited
again.
Notable rooms in the house include the music
room with its exquisite woodwork and the
amusing Gothick Hall with gallery. There are
mementoes of the ladies and their visitors,
splendid period furniture and paintings and
interesting murals by the 1930s society artist,
Rex Whistler. Take a turn about the
splendidly-constructed garden.

29. Porthmadog Maritime Museum 5 E2
Garlandstone, Harbour Station. Porthmadog
became a slate-exporting harbour once a light
railway was completed in 1836 to carry slate
from the busy quarries at Blaenau Ffestiniog
nine miles away. As the slate industry
declined, so did the railway. But enthusiasts
re-opened it for passengers and today it is so
successful that the amateurs have handed it
over to professionals to run. Painfully
engineered through difficult terrain, this track
claims to be the oldest narrow gauge railway in
the world.
Porthmadog is now a pleasure port full of
small craft and yachty visitors. Garlandstone
worked the west Wales ports during the
heyday of the slate boom, and it's a fitting end
for her cargo hold to tell the story of the
harbour's life 100 years ago in a series of
displays and exhibitions. An authentic slate
quay has been re-created at No 3 wharf. *Open
summer; certain weekends, winter.*

30. Portmeirion   5 E2
2m W of Penrhyndeudraeth. With carefully
planned viewpoints, gardens and flights of
steps, Portmeirion is undoubtedly an
attractive village – but about as Welsh as
spaghetti bolognaise. This exotic Italianate
village fantasy was created by the Welsh
architect Sir Clough Williams-Ellis. It was
begun in the 1930s, and a second period of
construction followed in the 1950s.
The Campanile building with columns and
cornices at the top of a small hill could have
come straight from Sorrento. Also of note is

Portmeirion

the 18thC Bath House Colonnade, rescued
from demolition in Bristol in 1957.
Acres of woodland surround this harbour
village and it has often been used as a film set.
Here, in the space of one week, Noel Coward
wrote his popular comedy 'Blithe Spirit'.

31. South Stack   5 A1
3m W of Holyhead. An early 19thC lighthouse
perched on a small rocky island on a turbulent
headland of Holy Island. It's reached by a
dramatic cliff descent of some 400 steps,
leading to an early suspension bridge which
connects the lighthouse to the mainland.
Little altered since it was first built, the
lighthouse is still in service.

South Stack

32. Tre'r Ceiri   5 D2
1m SW of Llanaelhaearn, N of B4417. The
'ong, uphill walk is worth it for, at 1,591ft,
Tre'r Ceiri is one of Britain's most
spectacular Iron Age forts. The site occupies
about five acres in all and is enclosed by a
rampart with drystone walls 12ft high and 15ft
thick in places. Inside are the remains of about
50 huts of varying shapes and sizes. The stone
remains have been dated c2ndC AD, but
settlement goes back much further.
Looking out across the desolate hills you see
much the same view Tre'r Ceiri's inhabitants
enjoyed 2,000 years ago.

33. Ty Hyll   5 F1
4m W of Betws-y-Coed, A4086. Named 'Ugly
House' this small cottage was built out of huge
boulders hurriedly heaped together, almost in
a parody of traditional stone building. It dates
from the 15thC and has been said to have
been used as a hideout for highway robbers
and as an overnight shelter for drovers.

34. Tywyn, Church of St Cadfan 5 E4
St Cadfan's Stone in the parish church is one
of the earliest examples of written Welsh. It
dates from the 7thC, but no satisfactory
translation has yet been made.

35. Vaynol Old Hall   5 B2
1½m NE of Port Dinorwic, off A487. One of the
best preserved Elizabethan manors in Wales.
It was replaced by the larger Vaynol Hall in
the 18thC and so escaped additions and
improvements. Look at the fine mullioned
windows and stout doors, and there is a
notable 17thC oak staircase. Adjoining the
house is a private chapel of c1580. The
gardens are beautiful and incorporate a large
Elizabethan barn. *Open certain days, summer.*

POWYS

1. Abbeycwmhir   5 G6
4¹/2m NE of Rhayader. Abbeycwmhir means
'Abbey of the Long Valley', and,
extraordinarily enough, this tiny, isolated
hamlet once possessed the largest abbey in
Wales. Its nave of 242ft was exceeded only by
the abbeys at Winchester, York and Durham.
A Cisterian foundation and never fully
completed, it was sacked during Owain
Glyndwr's rebellion and the Dissolution
completed its destruction. All that can be seen
now, in a wooded meadow by the small River
Clywedog, are the traces of walls and
columns.

2. Aberedw   5 H7
3m SE of Builth Wells, off A479. One of the
most secluded villages in Wales, worth visiting
for its typical primitive, rugged, Welsh
mountain church. Dating from the late 13thC,
it has Tudor restoration work. Worth noting
are the fine hammer-beam roof and a late
14thC rood screen.
Deep in the limestone crags of Aberedw rocks
is a tiny cave where the last of the original
princes of Wales, Llywelyn ap Gruffydd, is
said to have hidden in 1282. The story goes
that it was bleak mid-winter, and Llywelyn
had his horse's shoes reversed so the English
couldn't follow his tracks. But the local
blacksmith spilled the beans and Llywelyn was
found and killed shortly afterwards.

3. Brecon   5 H8
An attractive, peaceful market and cathedral
town, one of the oldest in Wales, which grew
up around a Norman castle built at the end of
the 11thC. Traces of this remain in the
grounds of the Castle Hotel. It was destroyed
during the Civil War when the citizens of
Brecon demonstrated their neutrality by
demolishing the castle and the town walls.
The main attraction now is the cathedral,
formerly the Priory Church of St John
Evangelist. It was founded about the same
time as the castle as an outpost of the
monastery at Battle in Sussex. The 13th and
14thC saw extensive rebuilding, much of
which survives, although its character is
influenced by Gilbert Scott's restoration of
1865. Note the side chapels, dedicated to
various local trades such as shoe-making and

tailoring. The priory church was made
cathedral of the diocese of Swansea and
Brecon in 1923, and the domestic buildings
were restored for chapter use.
Local history and folklore is the theme of the
Brecknock Museum, *Glamorgan St.* Here you
can see a collection of charming love-spoons,
traditional gifts carved by young men for their
sweethearts.

3. Brecon Y Gaer   5 H8
3m W of Brecon, N of A40. An impressive
remain of a Roman fort covering five acres. It
was excavated by Sir Mortimer Wheeler from
1924–5, and much of the defence wall and
gates are visible, including one section 11ft
high. It is thought to have been built around
AD75 and occupied for just over 200 years by
a garrison of about 500 men.

4. Bronllys   5 H8
1¹/2m N of Talgarth, A470. A motte and bailey
castle was constructed here in 1088 when the
Normans, under Bernard of Newmarch,
made their first advance into Wales. An
excellent example of the smaller type of castle
in Wales, all that remains is the 80ft-high
tower which has two passages inside the wall.
Bronllys church has a detached 14thC tower,
probably built for semi-defensive purposes by
the villagers after the castle had fallen to ruin.

5. Builth Wells   5 H7
The fine six-arched 18thC bridge over the
River Wye introduces the visitor to a town of
mid 19thC prosperity. The local wells are no
longer in use, but the Victorians poured in to
sample the healing qualities of the two springs
here. Now a sober market town, there is little
of historic interest due to a disastrous fire in
1691, but Builth Wells makes an excellent
centre for exploring the lovely Wye valley.

6. Crickhowell   5 J8
An attractive small market town on the banks
of the River Usk. The fragmentary remains of
a castle by the post office date from the early
12thC. It was destroyed during the Glyndwr
revolt and never rebuilt. Porth Mawr, a 15thC
castellated gatehouse, is all that remains of a
Tudor mansion that belonged to the Herbert
family.
The most attractive feature of the medieval
town is undoubtedly the 13-arched stone
bridge over the river. Beneath it anglers can
be seen fishing for Usk salmon.

7. Hay-on-Wye   5 J7
Truly a border town, with the parts east of the
river traditionally thought to be English, the
rest Welsh. As a result, Hay-on-Wye has
suffered both from the Welsh and the English
whenever the borders were disputed.
Attached to a Jacobean manor house in the
town centre are the remains of the castle, built
by the ruthless marcher lord, William de
Braose, to replace one burned down by King
John.
A haven for scholars, the town has more than
its fair share of book stores, including the
world's largest second-hand bookshop, whose
stocks occupy another seven buildings in the
town.

8. Knighton   5 J6
With an attractive hillside position in the
Teme Valley, this is a charming little market
town. There are a number of fine 17thC
houses and pubs, and the church has some
notable Norman architecture.
Offa's Dyke can be seen to the west of the
town: it was constructed cAD784 by Offa,
King of Mercia, to defend his lands against
the Welsh. An excellent centre for hill
walking, the long-distance footpath which
partly follows the line of the dyke, was opened
in 1971.

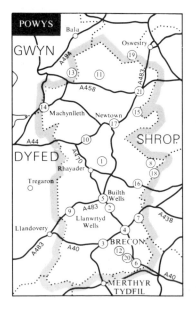

Looking like the stump of a decayed tooth planted high on a hill top, **Knucklas Castle**, *2m NW of town*, is the legendary home of the giant Cogfran, and it was here that King Arthur married Cogfran's daughter, Guinevere. In fact the castle dates from the early 12thC. Vavasor Powell, one of the earliest Welsh Nonconformists, was born here in 1617. He spent the greater part of his life in prison, having attacked Cromwell in numerous sermons, and his castle decayed along with its master.

9. Llandrindod Wells   5 H6
Victorian health-seekers flocked to Llandrindod Wells in their thousands to take the waters, for this was once the largest and most popular of Welsh spas. The town has a number of solid red-brick buildings of the period to show for it.
The history of the spa waters is far older than that, however. The town was known to the Romans as 'Balnae Silurum' – the Baths of the Silures, who were the Celtic tribe of the area. Artefacts from the Roman period are on display in the museum, while, at Llanyre, *1¹⁄₂m W of town*, remains of the Roman fort, comprising the earthworks and traces of the stone buildings, can be seen. There is also a museum of veteran cycles in Llandrindod Wells.

10. Llanidloes   5 G5
In the centre of the town there's an excellent and rare example of a type of half-timbered market house once common all over the country. Standing on wooden posts, its ground floor is open to the street to become a cobbled market place. It was built in 1609 and believed to be the only surviving example of its kind in Wales. In front of it is a stone on which John Wesley is said to have stood while delivering a sermon.
The market hall was also undoubtedly the meeting place for those involved in the Chartist riots of 1839. Although there was more talk than rioting, the militia were sent in and many of those arrested were transported to Australia.

Llanidloes

11. Lake Vyrnwy   5 G3
1m W of Llanwyddyn. Snuggled between the trees in the heart of the Welsh countryside, Vyrnwy is the largest man-made lake in Wales, and one of the most beautiful in Britain. It was constructed for the Corporation of Liverpool between 1880 and 1890 and the 1,200ft-long, 160ft-high dam holds back 12 million gallons of water. On the north shore is a fairy-tale Gothic tower which marks the beginning of the 75-mile aqueduct and canal to Liverpool.
The deeply-wooded valley, has an ancient history – it was cut by a glacier during the Ice Age. The village of Llanwyddyn is an interesting example of a Victorian model, built to replace the original village which now rests under the waters of the lake.

12. Llansantffraed   5 H8
6m SE of Brecon, A40. The birthplace and home for many years of Henry Vaughan, the 17thC poet, and his twin brother, Thomas, an alchemist and mystic. Thomas held the living of Llansantffraed all of his life, while Henry,

after studying in Oxford and London, returned to be the local doctor. They both spent much time in their family home, nearby Tretower Court. Henry is buried outside the east wall of the church and his tombstone bears a Latin epitaph composed by himself. The brothers were born in a house called Newton, since demolished, but Newton Farm was probably built on the site.

13. Llowes Church   5 H7
2m W of Clyro, A438. The church is notable for its Celtic cross with two faces, known as the Great Cross of St Meilig. The simpler side dates from the 7thC, while the other is 11thC. It was probably brought into the churchyard from some local prominence during the 12thC and was moved into the church itself a few years ago.

14. Machynlleth   5 F4
An attractive market town on the banks of the Dyfi, serving the sheep-farming community of the surrounding hills. Settlement has been shown to go back beyond the Romans to the Celtic Iron Age.
Its great moment in history came in 1404 when Owain Glyndwr held a parliament here and was proclaimed King of Wales, after his recent victories over Henry IV. His Parliament House, *Maen Gwyn St*, more or less completely rebuilt in the 16thC, now serves as the local library and has murals representing Glyndwr's military achievements. The giant 19thC clock tower marks the centre of the town.

15. Montgomery   5 H4
Half village, half town, Montgomery is a place of cobble-stoned, bow-windowed charm, with a host of fine 17th and 18thC houses.
The town gets its name from Roger de Montgomery, a Norman who built the first castle here in about 1072. This was replaced by a second during Henry I's reign, and a third, built about 1224 by Henry III. The brothers George Herbert and Lord Herbert of Cherbury, the first a poet and priest, the second a poet, philosopher and diplomat, were both born at the castle. This was pulled down in 1649, five years after it was besieged by Sir Thomas Myddleton, and finally collapsed in the 19thC. The fine view over the town makes the castle ruins well worth visiting.
The 14thC church is one of the grandest in Wales, with fine monuments and a glorious rood screen. In the churchyard is the grave of John Davies, a convicted murderer. Swearing his innocence at the gallows, he proclaimed that to prove it, grass would never grow on his grave. And, apparently, it is only in recent years that any greenery has begun to sprout.

16. New Radnor   5 J6
3m W of Walton, A44. Beautifully situated at the foot of the Radnor Forest, this town was, in fact, 'new' at the time of Edward the Confessor. Old Radnor was destroyed by Haraold, Earl of Hereford, later to become King Harold, and Edward established New Radnor a few miles away as his defensive base in the area. This castle was destroyed by King John, rebuilt by Henry III and destroyed again by Owain Glyndwr in 1401. Today only a grassy mound remains, but from here you can see the typical Norman grid-iron pattern of the original town. The scenery around here is spectacular – the perfect base for walks, picnics and rambles.
Old Radnor, *2¹⁄₂m E of New Radnor*, has one of the finest churches in Wales. Its imposing west tower shows late 14thC work at its best. Inside are noteworthy stalls and panelling, and what is believed to be the oldest, and possibly the largest font in Britain. Its crude circular shape was hewn from a glacial boulder, and it may be a relic from pre-historic rituals. The organ of c1500 is claimed to be the oldest in Britain.

17. Newtown   5 H5

A variety of different styles of local architecture over the years jumble happily together, showing little sign of Newton's 13thC origin.
Robert Owen, factory reformer and founder of the co-operative movement, was born here in 1771. After successfully going into business as master spinner, he devoted himself to social reform and the spread of education. Anticipating Marx, he saw the origin of all the injustices of society in the capitalist economic system, and urged for the creation of co-operative communities both in Britain and America. He died here in 1858 and a statue in Shortbridge Street pays him tribute. The Robert Owen Museum, *Broad St*, houses items relating to his life and has a recreation of the room in which he was born. The Royal Welsh Warehouse, *nr railway station*, was used by Pryce Jones, a leading figure in the textile industry, who started the world's first mail order business based entirely on Welsh flannel, in 1859. *Open most days, summer.*

18. Presteigne   5 G6

Languishing among the gentle slopes and wide vales, Presteigne was until 1971 the county town of Radnorshire, then the most sparsely populated county in England and Wales. There are some crisp half-timbered cottages, typical of the border country, as well as fine Georgian houses. The beautiful Perpendicular Church of St Andrew has a Renaissance Flemish tapestry, one of a set originally woven for Canterbury Cathedral. The medieval castle associated with the town now lies over the border – and in ruins.
Pilleth Hill, *3m SW of town*, was where Owain Glyndwr achieved a significant victory over the English forces of the Earl of Mortimer.

19. Sycharth Castle   5 J3

N of Welsh border, B4396. Once the main residence of Owain Glyndwr; if his court bard, Iolo Goch, is not to be accused of sycophancy it must have been a splendid place. He writes of it as including nine halls, many guest rooms and a church. The 16-year-old future Henry V laid the castle to waste in 1403 – one of the first English victories over Glyndwr.

20. Tretower Court and Castle   5 H8

Tretower, 2m N of junction with A40. This is the 14thC mansion of the influential Vaughan family, and much frequented by the 17thC mystic poet, Henry Vaughan, who was born at nearby Llansantffraed. In a splendid state of preservation, entrance is through the gatehouse of 1480. Although parts of the north wall are original, the main fabric of the building dates from Sir Roger Vaughan's 15thC restorations, but these are in keeping with the original style. The oak craftsmanship of the spacious rooms is very impressive.

The castle, within the Court grounds, was originally built in the early 12thC to guard the valley pass. It was raided by both Llywelyn the Last, and Owain Glyndwr, after which it was abandoned. The design is interesting in that the ruin of a circular tower lies within an earlier square keep.

21. Welshpool   5 J4

A distinctive Georgian market town whose Monday market dates back to 1263, the time the town first received its charter, and holds the largest livestock sales in Wales. At one time Welshpool had both town walls and a castle, but both have now vanished. One of the half-timbered houses on the road to Powis Castle has the motto 'God Damn Old Oliver' spelled out in nail studs, hammered home, no doubt with relish, by its Royalist occupant. With all the whims and fancies of an elaborate wedding cake, **Powis Castle**, *1m S of town*, is a massive red sandstone building rising from tiers of gardens. Early castles on this site had been built and destroyed in the turbulent 13thC. The present castle, dating from the reign of Edward I, has an Italianate rather than a medieval look. It was substantially renovated over the following centuries, particularly in the Elizabethan and Jacobean periods. The last re-modelling was by Capability Brown in the late 18thC. The most famous connection with Powis Castle is with Clive of India, whose son inherited it in 1784. As well as a collection of Clive memorabilia, the house contains beautiful furniture and porcelain, many fine portraits, and murals by Lanscroon. Of the many grand rooms the 18thC ballroom and the long gallery with its 16thC plasterwork are probably the most impressive. The terraced gardens, laid out at the end of the 17thC in the formal style the exiled Stuarts brought back with them from France, are exceptionally impressive, with superb topiary, ornamental trees, hedges and statues. A Douglas fir claims to be the tallest tree in Britain. *Open most days, summer.*

Powis Castle

SHAKESPEARE AND THE HEART OF ENGLAND

There is a solid core of truth in the oft-quoted saying that this is the true centre of England and its real heart. The region gave England its greatest poet and its second city. It throbs with the industry of towns and factories, but the traditional rural landscape brings the life of the past into the present as through a kaleidoscope, and you can still wander in Shakespeare's forest of Arden and see his hawthorn and his holly tree. Nature has constructed a meeting place here for the lowland plain of southern and eastern England, and the harder upland country of the north and west. The Midlands plain was dubbed the 'cockpit of England' because it was a battleground for so long. Here invaders were repelled and civil war raged, while great barons, like Simon de Montfort or Warwick the Kingmaker, made the Midlands the focus of their power. At Edgehill, Warwickshire, the first battle of the English Civil War was fought on October 23rd, 1642, when Charles I confronted the Parliamentarian Lord Essex and his army.

The exact geographical centre of England is said to lie at Meriden, and the region is England's natural communications centre. Many Roman roads – Watling Street, the Fosse Way, Ermine Street – cross-crossed each other here. Later the region was to be the centre of the 'silver cross' of canals that James Brindley and others built during the Industrial Revolution, just as today the nation's motorway system comes to a shuddering climax at Birmingham's Spaghetti Junction.

As the centuries progressed, much of the wealth of England was gradually and painstakingly created here. The Middle Ages saw the build-up of a rich network of villages, and of large towns, proudly centred around their great cathedrals and parish churches, practising many trades. Despite this flowering, a toll of decaying towns and deserted villages was also the legacy of the Middle Ages; the Black Country, to the north west of Birmingham, remained a largely undeveloped and unwelcoming moorland until in the 18th and 19thC local coal and iron turned it into the grimy industrial wasteland that Dickens painted with such horror.

The Midlands area was at the centre of progress: here, at Birmingham, James Watt perfected the steam engine, and at Coalbrookdale, iron was first successfully smelted with coke. The city of Birmingham, first a Domesday manor and then a small town, grew into an enormous red-brick city, manufacturing a thousand and one articles. But what strikes the visitor most about the landscape is its very varied nature, and this everywhere expresses the impact of local character, history and resources. In the Cotswolds the local woollen cloth trade gave rise to Tudor and Stuart prosperity. This gentle, rolling countryside, covered with fine beeches, is the setting for the rich Cotswold village, with the traditional house, built in the local limestone and with slates, mullions and dormers.

In the central sandstone plain, trim Georgian farmhouses and cottages stand among the red sandstone churches, shaded by the oak and hawthorn, although sadly not often now with the elm, once known as the 'Warwickshire weed'. Further east in Shropshire there is lonely moorland, rough hills and towns with grim castles. The Vale of Evesham is different again: long centuries of prosperous farming have given it an air of bucolic cheerfulness.

Different human traditions have also written themselves into the landscape. Leicestershire is fox-hunting country, and here horses as well as traditional forges and smithies are common. And Warwickshire's strong tradition of Roman Catholicism has given many of its fine country houses a legacy of priest's holes and hiding places, a reminder of past persecutions.

Warwickshire also provided the inspiration and background for many of Shakespeare's plays. Shakespeare was born in the attractive, old market town of Stratford-upon-Avon, probably on April 23rd, 1564, and never lost touch with his birthplace. This is one of the world's most famous tourist centres and, though the town may be over-commercialised with Shakespeare's face smiling down from every shop-front and restaurant, the sights associated with the great bard remain unspoilt. In Stratford itself are his birthplace and Holy Trinity Church where he is buried. Places in the surrounding countryside with Shakespeare connections include Charlecote Park, Wilmcote, Quinton and Shottery where Anne Hathaway's Cottage keeps coach-loads of history-hungry Americans happy for hours.

In the 20thC the Midlands is struggling to adapt itself to a rapidly changing world and technology. Coventry is a city that has risen from the ashes of wartime destruction and which has been rebuilding furiously ever since, while the old heart of Birmingham has been torn out to make way for the reinforced concrete hub a modern city needs – or is thought to need. Everywhere, the new shows signs of overwhelming the old with redevelopment, but threads of continuity with the past are preserved in the rural seclusion of many villages.

GLOUCESTERSHIRE

1. Berkeley Castle   2 C3
Between Bristol and Gloucester, off A38.
Magnificent if grim medieval castle, with
great, grey-buttressed walls, 14ft-thick in
places, a Norman keep, and a splendid 14thC
Great Hall. Home to the ancient Berkeley
family for 700 years, the castle has seen a
bloody past, for it was here that the deposed
king, Edward II, was brought in the 14thC,
starved and tormented by the knights who
were his keepers, and finally murdered with a
red-hot poker. You can still see the ancient
bowling alley where the murderers may well
have played. Of particular interest: the
medieval kitchen; the state apartments with
their magnificent furniture, tapestries and
silver; the terraced gardens and the deer park.
The tranquil town of Berkeley has a fine
Norman church where many of the Berkeleys
lie.

Berkeley Castle

2. Bibury   2 E3
Exquisitely pretty Cotswold village which
shows local architecture at its most beautiful
and typical. Once occupied by weavers,
Arlington Row is a group of stone cottages
which William Morris first hailed as
architectural classics in the 19thC. Arlington
Mill is a fine 17thC example which stands on
the site of the earlier Domesday mill and is
now a folk museum. Bibury Court is an
interesting 17thC country house and St
Mary's Church has Saxon work.

3. Bourton-on-the-Water   2 E2
With the little River Windrush running right
through it parallel to the main street and
spanned by several delicate stone bridges, this
picturesque town has not surprisingly suffered
much tourism. But the remains of its past are
still evident: a primitive pit-dwelling from
Saxon times was discovered, Roman relics
have been found and there are many fine 17th
and 18thC Cotswold houses, complete with
mullions and dormers. The church has been
much modernised, but has retained the 14thC
chancel. Another tourist attraction is the
famous model village.

4. Cheltenham   2 D2
Doyenne of English spa towns, nestling snugly
in the shadow of the Cotswolds, it is the
epitome of Georgian elegance with miles of
fine 18thC houses in wide, tree-lined
avenues.
Cheltenham was only a small settlement at the
time of the Domesday Book (although even
then it had five windmills), and in the 18thC it
was still a straggling village. But a saline
spring was discovered in a field and in 1738 a
local man built a simple pump-room and
gardens. From there the spa mushroomed, a
visit from George III in 1788 adding the final
seal of respectability. These developments led
to the creation of a perfect Georgian town.
Cheltenham also has the fine medieval church
of St Mary, with a 14thC rose window and
transepts as well as some Norman work. The
town is famous for fashionable schools,
including Cheltenham College and
Cheltenham Ladies College, run for 50 years
by the great pioneer of women's education,
Dorothea Beale.

5. Chedworth Roman Villa and
Museum   2 E2
Chedworth. One of the best preserved and
most interesting of the several Roman villa
remains in Gloucestershire, discovered
accidentally in 1864 while a lost ferret was
being dug out. Almost the entire outline of the
original building is clearly visible. There are

two sets of Roman baths, several mosaic floors and a lovely ornamental fountain over a spring. The small museum on site contains many finds from the villa. *Open certain days; closed mid-winter.*

6. Chipping Camden   2 E1
Perfect example of a Cotswold wool town. The local limestone is beautifully laid out with canopied doorways, rich gables and oriel windows in streets many of which have changed little since Tudor times. There are gracious 17thC almshouses, a wool hall that dates from 1380 and a town hall, parts of which are 14thC. But the finest building is the 17thC Market Hall, standing noble and erect on an island in the traffic. It was built by the wealthy merchant, Sir Baptist Hicks, who laid the foundations of the town's prosperity. He also built the manor house, Campden House, which now lies in ruins as it was burned by loyal Royalists after the Civil War to prevent it from falling into the hands of Parliament. The town also has a stately church which mostly dates from the 14thC and is rich in 13thC glass, 15thC embroidery, marble tombs and magnificent brasses: a veritable treasure house!

7. Cirencester   2 E3
Known in Roman times as Corinium, this was once the second largest town in England. Cirencester has fallen much in eminence since then, but still has a wealth of Roman remains to remind us of its past glories. Remnants of large houses, public buildings and an elaborate drainage system have been discovered, while tools and implements indicate that Corinium was a centre for cloth-making. The Roman walls were so strong that they stood until the 14thC, but have now made way for new buildings. Cirencester has much that is interesting from other eras too: a magnificent 15thC parish church, fine Georgian houses and Earl Bathurst's vast 18thC landscaped park which gives directly onto the town.

Cirencester Parish Church

8 .Gloucester   2 D2
Solid provincial city, perhaps a little dull on the surface, but where the remains of the past are everywhere if you look. The settlement was already well established when the Romans built 'Glevum' here as the great fortress of the west. In later centuries Gloucester was the scene of many incidents in the lives of kings: in 1085 William the Conqueror ordered the Domesday Book to be compiled here; Stephen came here as a prisoner during his war with Matilda in the 12thC; the murdered Edward II was carried here from Berkeley Castle to be buried; and Elizabeth I visited the town to award it the status of a port.
The city still stands on its Roman plan, centred around the town cross and on a cruciform pattern, with four 'gate' streets. Roman remains have been found under all the main streets and the guildhall in Eastgate Street is believed to be where the Forum stood. The city museum contains relics including many Roman votive tables, sculptures, pavements and querns. Besides its wonderful cathedral Gloucester has many lovely churches and fascinating historical buildings. Don't miss the New Inn, a 15thC

hostelry where pilgrims often stayed, or the many quaint houses in the byways around the cathedral precincts, such as the Fleece Inn, with its 14thC timbers.
Robert Raikes, the 18thC founder of the Sunday School movement, lived in Gloucester and the site of his first school can be seen in Catherine Street. The beautiful city park was laid out in the early 19thC, when it was hoped the town might become a spa. Industry and docks (due to the 1827 ship canal), a nearby railway line and pollution of the spring soon put paid to this idea, but the park still has many shady trees and magnificent lawns.

8. Gloucester Cathedral   2 D2
Off Westgate St. Gloucester's chief monument, the constant feature of its industrial skyline, the cathedral with its great Perpendicular tower, is an unmistakable sight. The 15thC work, however, masks a long history, for there was once a Saxon abbey here. The great Norman nave, built around 1100, remains, as does the 14thC transept and cloisters. The 15thC Lady chapel is as enchanting as summer flowers in bloom, with its mullions, delicate tracery and lovely glass. Another glory is the great East Window – 72ft high and the largest painted window in the country – which fills the east end of the choir with a riot of colour. Gloucester Cathedral is full of historic monuments: the tomb of murdered Edward II, figures of Osric and Serlo, founders of the Saxon and Norman abbeys, and of Edward Jenner, 18thC discoverer of vaccination, who lived and died in the county.

8. Gloucester and Sharpness Canal   2 D2
Gloucester to Sharpness. A 16-mile ship canal, it was constructed in 1827 to ensure Gloucester's future as a port: the Severn was tidal, shifting and in places dangerously shallow. The engineer was the great Thomas Telford, responsible for so much superb engineering in the west of England. It is still very much a working canal – ocean tankers are a common sight – and although there are only two locks, one at each end, there are plenty of swingbridges for the canal enthusiast.

9. Moreton-in-Marsh   2 F1
The main street is part of the Roman Fosse Way, and 6ft-thick remains of the Roman road have been found. Moreton is a cosy little town, which was once a centre of the wool-weaving trade. Historic buildings and monuments abound: there is a medieval tower with a 17thC clock, the beautiful 17thC Creswyke House with oriel windows and a mulberry tree, and the Four Shires Stone which until 1931 marked the boundaries of the old counties of Gloucestershire, Warwickshire, Oxfordshire and Worcestershire.

10. Paradise   2 D2
N of Painswick. Charles I gave this tiny hamlet its name when he visited it briefly during the Civil War. Enchanted by its beauty, on hearing that it had no name, he is said to have declared: 'Call it Paradise'. The 19thC Adam and Eve Inn is delightful and there are lovely wooded slopes by the River Slad. Nearby is peaceful Prinknash Abbey, a Benedictine house which is the descendant of the medieval abbey.

Ridgeway Path
Nr Avebury, Wiltshire to Ivinghoe Beacon, Buckinghamshire. Prehistoric routeway across the Cotswolds, and now one of the long-distance paths designated by the Countryside Commission. The Ridgeway was a trade and drovers' route of Celtic Britons, and on the way there are many burial mounds, barrows and hill forts worth investigating. In Gloucestershire there is a well-excavated ancient camp, Norbury Camp, as well as many long-barrows and prehistoric sites.

11. Stow-in-the-Wold   2 F2

Now a quiet, dreamy country town but once one of the most important wool towns of the Cotswolds, where in the days of the great sheep fairs 20,000 sheep might be sold in one session. The town has a quaintly irregular market square with an ancient cross and is lined with Cotswolds merchants' houses. The Church of St Edward is a graceful amalgam of all styles from Norman to Tudor. Lovers of antique shops will find that the town richly rewards a visit.

Sudeley Castle

12. Sudeley Castle   2 E1

½m S of Winchcombe, off A46. Delightfully graceful castle which was the home of Catherine Parr, the sixth wife of Henry VIII, after his death and her marriage to the ambitious Sir Thomas Seymour. She died here giving birth to her first child, and there is a picturesque 16thC window in the lovely old room which is still called 'Queen Catherine's nursery'. Also of interest are pictures, furniture and stained glass. *Open summer.*

13. Tewkesbury   2 D1

Laid out in a great Y-shape where the Rivers Severn and Avon meet, Tewkesbury is a medieval town which has retained its charm despite roaring traffic (now much reduced owing to the motorway). High Street and Barton Street are full of fascinating 15th and 16thC half-timbered houses, while behind them are warrens of alleys, once slums, but whose ancient houses and blue-brick pavements are delightful. The two rivers are crossed by the 13thC King John's Bridge, and one built by Thomas Telford in the 19thC. The Swan Inn is a dignified Queen Anne red-brick house while the Bear Inn dates from 1308 and is the oldest inn in the county. Tudor House, built in 1540 and now a hotel, has a fine Jacobean staircase and beautiful panelled rooms: it was a centre for 17thC Baptists and the room where they held their meetings can still be seen.

Just outside the town is the field, still called 'Bloody Meadow', where one of the most ferocious battles of the Wars of the Roses was fought in 1471 and the Lancastrian cause was finally lost.

Near Tewkesbury is **Bredon Hill,** a notable hill site where there was a great Iron Age hill fort equipped with multiple bank and ditch defences. This must have been one of the outstanding defensive points of the area and the remains of an Iron Age cemetery can be seen. Interesting finds are housed in a private museum at the nearby great house, Overbury Court.

13. Tewkesbury Abbey   2 D1

Church St. Dominating Tewkesbury's skyline is one of the finest examples of Norman church architecture in England: the Norman tower standing 132ft high on interlocking arches is of unparalleled magnificence. A monastery has stood on this site since the 8thC but nothing remains from Saxon times. Much of the finest work is Norman, including the majestic nave with its seven high columns on each side. The exquisite choir with its traceried windows and lovely parapet is 14thC.

Tewkesbury Abbey escaped the destruction that befell many abbeys at the Dissolution because the townspeople, who loved their great church, purchased it for £483. Inside the church stand the tombs of a veritable gallery of medieval nobility associated with the town: de Clares, Despensers, Beauchamps and Nevilles, their richly marbled tombs bearing witness to the pride and splendour with which they lived and died.

HEREFORD AND WORCESTER

14. Abbots Morton   6 E8

Charming black-and-white village, lying sleepily along a quiet, country lane beautiful enough in itself to make a visit worthwhile. On a hill at the end of the main street is the simple but attractive village church. The nave is barn-like with some Norman masonry and solid roof-timbers, and the quiet churchyard is pleasantly fringed with trees and flowers. But the serenity of this place belies a particularly violent past: in medieval times nearby Feckenham Forest was the home of outlaws who would attack the village in bands 100-strong. Terrorised by these robbers and murderers the residents flocked to the church for refuge – difficult to imagine today in this peaceful place.

15. Bewdley   6 D7

Once very important for its trade along the Severn, this fine town perches on a steep hillside by a graceful three-arched bridge designed in the 19thC by Thomas Telford. There are many medieval merchants' houses as well as 17th and 18thC buildings, houses, shops, chapels and almshouses. The 18thC parish church is of no particular interest, but the nearby great house, Tickenhill, standing on a hill which was inhabited in prehistoric times, is fascinating. Tickenhill was first home to the medieval baronial family, the Mortimers. It later became a royal residence, housing successive princes of Wales, and was besieged during the Civil War. The present house is largely Georgian, but there are 13thC beams and Tudor work in the hall. In the garden Roman coins and Celtic flint tools have been found.

16. Bredwardine   6 A9

Peaceful village on the wooded banks of the Wye, Bredwardine has much of interest. The church is curiously shaped and mainly Norman. Its best-known priest was Robert Francis Kilvert, whose diary kept in the 1870s gives a riveting picture of Victorian rural life. Old Court is a stone farmhouse dating from the 14thC, and the early 18thC Red Lion Inn is a pleasant brick-fronted house with rubble sides and back. There is also a fine 18thC brick bridge.

17. Croft Castle   6 B8

5m NW of Leominster, N of B4362. Fine 15thC manor house, standing neighbour-like beside its simple church, and surrounded by handsome chestnut trees. The castle was the residence of the Croft family who headed the plot to put Lady Jane Grey on the throne. Members of the family still live here although the house now belongs to the National Trust. Refurbished in the fashionable 'Gothic' style with a particularly fine staircase and ceilings, it is now a rather pleasing mixture of medieval and 19thC characteristic architecture. *Open certain days, summer.*

18. Evesham   6 E9

Cheerful town at the centre of the prosperous fruit-farming region. Evesham is set on a grassy hill and affords many shady walks by the wide Avon. The town was founded around an abbey at AD714, which is said to have been built after a shepherd, Eoves, saw a vision of the Virgin Mary in a field. The ruins of the abbey, which was largely destroyed at the Dissolution, are still impressive, especially the great 14thC entrance arch and the bell tower. Among very fine buildings in the town are the 15thC Booth Hall, the 17thC Dresden House and the two medieval parish churches which strangely stand in the same churchyard. All Saints Church has a glorious Lady chapel and St Lawrence's, rebuilt in the 16thC, has good Perpendicular panelling and fan vaulting.

18. Evesham, Battlefield   6 E9

1m N of town. Culminating act in the life of Simon de Montfort, great medieval baron and popular hero, who, in pursuit of baronial power, used the English people and Parliament as a weapon against Henry III. In 1265 he had been virtual ruler of England for a year, having defeated the King. But Henry's son, the Lord Edward, was thirsting for revenge.

After defeating another Montfortian army at Kenilworth, Edward caught Montfort off-guard with his tired forces resting. Montfort was outnumbered seven to one and hemmed in by the river. There was no hope for him. In the midst of a terrible storm, on August 4th, 1265, he and his son were slain with most of their followers. The place where Montfort is thought to have fallen is marked by an obelisk. The Abbey Manor House nearby, built in the 19thC, houses relics of the battle.

19. Goodrich Castle   6 C10

Goodrich. Very well preserved ruined castle standing in a magnificent spot overlooking the Wye. First built in the 12thC and enlarged in the 13thC it was the last Herefordshire defence to hold out for Charles I during the Civil War. It is a place of fascinating glimpses: the graceful arches in the Great Hall, the curious fire-place hoods preserved intact across the centuries, the views of the river below, and the ruined 14thC priory half a mile away.

20. Great Malvern   6 D9

The centre of six settlements on the Malvern hills with Malvern in their name, Great Malvern is a mid-Victorian spa town. Reflecting the austerity but also the comfort of that era, grey ragstone and red-brick villas mix with a few Georgian houses. The chief glory of Malvern is the lovely 14thC priory church with its fine setting amid cedar, pine and yew. The impressive Norman nave has massive piers, and there is much beautiful glass, most of which was laboriously pieced together again after being smashed at the Dissolution.

21. Hagley Hall   6 D7

Hagley. Grand 18thC house, lying snug in a hollow of the Clent Hills, which has long been the seat of the ancient Lyttleton family. This notorious family is remembered for its record both of eccentricity and fine public service. Early Lyttletons were a squire to Henry V and a Gunpowder plotter. The first baron, who built the hall, apart from being a friend to poets and wits, was Chancellor of the Exchequer. His son, however, was known as 'the bad lord Lyttleton' and lived a life of vice until he had a dream that a bird flew into his room, turned into a woman and told him he had only three days to live: three days later he did, in fact, drop dead. The third Baron was a strong advocate of parliamentary reform and was once smuggled onto a ship to meet Napoleon, while the fourth, apart from being a famous cricketer, collaborated with

Gladstone on classical translations. As befits such a family, Hagley Hall is an individual and rumbustious house, and although the exterior is not beautiful, the rooms are decorated in the height of 18thC lavish taste. The gallery has a rococo ceiling, there is a fine collection of Chippendale furniture and the landscaped park is of interest. *Open summer.*

22. Hereford   6 B9

Ancient market and county town which still enjoys a rumbustious life of pleasure. It is famous for sport (you can still see the 16thC bowling green), drama (Garrick was born here and Kemble and Siddons played here), and music. The three choirs festival, which is hosted here triennially, was founded in 1720 and is the oldest music festival in Europe. A bishopric was founded in Hereford as early as AD676, and the first cathedral is said to have been built by Offa of Mercia in the 8thC. The present cathedral is 11thC and is very fine with a massive Norman nave, a beautiful chantry chapel with fan vaulting, and a great central tower of red sandstone, built in 1300. In medieval times Hereford was a border town against the Welsh, and parts of the impressive medieval walls still remain. The motte of the Norman castle survives as a municipal park. Hereford has many attractive timber-framed houses and some street-names, such as Bakehouse Lane, the Butchery and Cooken Lane, stem from medieval times.

Hereford

23. Kilpeck Church   6 B9

Kilpeck, 7½m SW of Hereford. Interesting as one of the best-preserved and most attractive Norman churches in Britain, certainly worth a special trip. There is a huge, Norman font, a spacious nave and on the south doorway, some magnificent carving.

24. Leominster   6 B8

A black-and-white timber-framed town where Georgian avenues mingle happily with huddled medieval streets. It has a fine 17thC town hall with elaborate carvings and a 12thC priory church built of rich red stone and with a Norman west door. A curiosity in the priory's possession is the old town ducking stool, which was used to punish scolds and sellers of shoddy goods. The last recorded ducking was in 1809: one villain was condemned to it in 1813 but there was not enough water in the River Lugg to carry out the punishment!

25. Pershore   6 E9

Perfectly preserved Georgian town, with solid red-brick 18thC houses in the High Street and the town square. Many of them still retain their canopied balconies and are graced by Venetian windows and pillared porches. Pershore was founded around a 7thC abbey. The present abbey is Norman, with a beautiful 600-year-old lantern tower, but it is now only half its original length. The part used by the monks was destroyed at the Dissolution, leaving only the area where the townsfolk worshipped. Over the River Avon is a graceful 14thC footbridge. The middle arch was wrecked by Royalist soldiers fleeing from the battle of Worcester, to hamper Cromwell's men who were in hot pursuit.

26. Redditch 6 E8

Redditch is a child of the Industrial Revolution. It developed in the early 19thC from the many mills which sprang up on the banks of the little River Arrow to manufacture needles, nails and fish-hooks. There are traces of a small settlement here, however, in the 14thC. Bordesley Abbey, lying nearby, is now in ruins but was once a great medieval abbey. The ancient burial ground stands next to the church.

27. Ross-on-Wye 6 C10

A gentle, pretty town on a cliff beside the Wye. Ross-on-Wye was largely developed in the late 17thC by the 'man of Ross', John Kyrle, who donated land generously for building. A market was held here as early as 1120. In the early 19thC the citizens hoped that Ross would become a fashionable resort, and many of the medieval-looking buildings, such as the defensive tower, the lock-up and the town hall, were in fact erected in the 1830s to give a suitable 'Gothic' atmosphere for tourists! But the 14thC church, rich in monuments and tombs and the dumpy but engaging 17thC market hall are genuine products of their respective periods.

28. Wigmore 6 B8

Only a small village now, but a cluster of half-timbered houses in the main street, the mound of a Norman castle and the remains of 12thC Wigmore Abbey testify to a grand past. Both the Romans and the Saxons had forts here and in the medieval period Wigmore was a great centre of the powerful Mortimer family. Although Wigmore has been classified as a borough for 800 years, it never grew into an important town.

29. Worcester 6 D8

'The city faithful in peace and war': Worcester's motto declares its loyalty to the King during the Civil War, and also bears witness to the repeated sackings and gallant defences against invaders throughout the ages. Originally a Celtic fording point on the Severn, Worcester was later, because of its strategic importance, to be the scene of battles fought by Romans, Saxons, Danes, Welsh and Civil War forces. At the same time it grew prosperous on trade and industry. Ancient and beautiful, it also seems a rather melancholy place, redolent of forgotten, troubled summers.

Built on both sides of the Severn, but mainly on the steeper eastern bank to avoid flooding, Worcester retains some delightful old buildings despite having suffered much from modern redevelopment. The 18thC guildhall is an exceptionally gracious Queen Anne

Worcester

building, and among fine old houses are the Queen Elizabeth House, where she is said to have slept, King Charles's House and the 15thC guest house of the Franciscan Friary in Friar Street.

The greatest historical event of the town was the Battle of Worcester in 1651 when Charles II attempted to recover his father's throne from Cromwell. He failed, but his dramatic escape has stirred the imagination of the romantic ever since. For six weeks he wandered the country in disguise, always hotly pursued by the Roundheads, and was helped on his way by many loyal subjects who risked their lives for him. Among his amazing adventures were to hide in an oak tree and to have his ears boxed by a cook who took him for a kitchen boy! The city walls and many houses were destroyed in the battle, and little remains of the battlefield today.

29. Worcester Cathedral 6 D8

Between College St and River Severn.
Dominating the city from its superb setting poised above the Severn, Worcester Cathedral is a superb amalgam of all styles from Norman to Tudor, which have fused to create a deeply satisfying whole. The original cathedral was 7thC, but the earliest surviving parts are the Norman crypt, transepts and a Norman circular chapter house. The medieval nave was built gradually over two centuries. In the centre of the choir stands the magnificent tomb of King John, who so loved Worcester that he wished to be buried here. The 14thC choir stalls have magnificent misericords, and the cloisters leading out to College Green still carry an air of immemorial peace.

30. Worcestershire County Museum 6 D7

Hartlebury Castle, Hartlebury, nr Kidderminster.
A fascinating museum housed in the old bishop's palace which is especially rich in exhibits of traditional Worcestershire rural life. Among bucolic items on show are gypsy caravans, horse-drawn carriages and an impressive cider mill.

🏰LEICESTERSHIRE🏰

1. Ashby-de-la-Zouch 6 G5

Lying in the centre of the Leicestershire coalfield, but itself with no coal, this pleasant 15thC market town was the romantic setting for Scott's 'Ivanhoe'. Austerely beautiful, 15thC St Helen's Church contains the only known surviving finger pillory which was used until the 19thC to fasten the hands of those who misbehaved in church. But the chief monument is **Castle Ashby**, a ruin since the Civil War with only one majestic tower standing. Smouldering memories linger of Mary Queen of Scots who was imprisoned here and Charles I who stayed here on his way to Naseby. *Open certain days only.*

2. Belton 6 J6

Pretty hilltop village with a broad main street which, for its small size, is richly endowed with historic buildings. Here lie the pathetic

ruins of Grace Dieu Priory, its fragments of towers and walls covered with ivy; founded in the 13thC it was ruthlessly suppressed at the Reformation. The money from the priory was used to build Grace Dieu, a magnificent Tudor house, and Westbourne House is of the Queen Anne period. A lofty spire tops the finely-proportioned 14thC church.

3. Belvoir Castle 6 J4

7m WSW of Grantham, off A607. Peeping over the hilltop to overlook the Leicestershire Wolds, Belvoir Castle more than merits its name, which originally meant 'beautiful view'. The first castle was built by Robert de Todeni, who carried William the Conqueror's standard at the Battle of Hastings. Undergoing a history of destruction and rebuilding, the present, romantic, medieval-style building is deceptively only

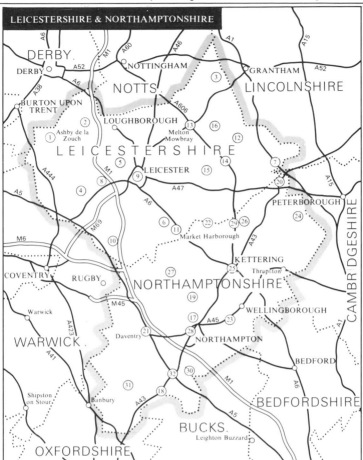

170 years old. It was remodelled by James Wyatt on instructions from the 8th Duke of Rutland, whose family still own the castle. Elegant rooms are veritable glory houses of treasure. The magnificent ceiling in the Grand Dining Room is worth stretching your neck for. Hand-painted wallpaper is the main attraction of the King Rooms which were used by George IV when he visited the castle as Prince Regent. Don't miss the chapel with its lovely Murillo painting and the interesting old kitchen. The Elizabeth Saloon, decorated in French rococo style, with superb painted ceilings, is the most beautiful room in the castle. But, above all, Belvoir is known for the Goblin tapestries and its collection of paintings: offerings by Van Dyck, Reynolds and Poussin, plus one of the best portraits of Henry VIII by Holbein.

For those more inclined towards tipples than treasures, there is the Beer Cellar; beer was brewed in the village and stored here until the 19thC and the beer barrels are between 150

Belvoir Castle

and 200 years old. Finally, go for a stroll around the splendid gardens. *Open most days, summer.*

4. Bosworth Battlefield　　　　**6 G6**
3m S of Market Bosworth. Culminating battle of the medieval period, it took place on 22nd August, 1485. In an hour of fierce, clumsy, hand-to-hand combat Plantagenet Richard III lost both throne and life to Henry VII, the first Tudor monarch, ending the Wars of the Roses. Although the battle may not have inaugurated the modern world, as old history books used to state, the passing of the throne to the great Tudor dynasty was by any standards a most significant event.

The battlefield is in pleasant, hilly country and no road passes through it. King Dick's Well, in a field, is where Richard is said to have taken his last drink, and from there is a good view of the hill above a marsh over which the battle was fought. In Bosworth Park is a spinney called King Dick's Clump where Richard is said to have raised his standard. Richard was not the monster that is usually supposed: he was a good administrator and certainly a brave man. He fought like a lion at Bosworth, declaring: 'I live a king: if I die, I die a king'. After he had been killed, his battered crown was said to have been found in a bush and placed on Henry's head while Richard's army was still being slaughtered. The town of Market Bosworth nearby is picturesque with charming buildings. Originally a Bronze Age and Roman settlement it became a prosperous medieval town.

5. Bradgate Park   6 G6
3m NW of Leicester, off M1. Childhood home of Lady Jane Grey, nine-days Queen of England, in the 16thC the park was part of the country house. Roger Ascham, the Tudor scholar, visited Bradgate and records that all the family were hunting in the park, except Jane who was reading Plato in Greek. Torn from her learning and solitude to a plot and crown she never wanted, she was finally sent to the block under Queen Mary I.
The house was set fire to in 1694 (some say, deliberately by the Greys themselves, who disliked living there) and now there are only ruins. But the park is really lovely, set amid gentle hills, with turf that has not been ploughed since the Conquest. *Open most days, summer; park daily, all year.*

6. Foxton Canal Junction   6 H7
Nr Market Harborough. In the 18thC the Midlands became covered with an intricate network of canals, which James Brindley, greatest of the builders, called a 'silver cross'. At Foxton is a particularly intricate junction, with a fine flight of 10 staircase locks and the remains of the ingenious 'inclined plane' that once replaced them.

7. Great Casterton   6 K6
A place half as old as time, it was a Stone Age settlement, and the skeleton of a Stone Age man has been found, still with his weapons and grinding stone. Roman Ermine Street ran here, and pieces of the road as well as part of the defensive ditch of the Roman camp are still visible. Great Casterton has a stately 13thC church with fine arches in the nave. John Clare, the peasant poet of neighbouring Northamptonshire, worked in Great Casterton as a labourer in the early 19thC. It was here that he met his wife, 'sweet Patty of the Vale', who bore him seven children before hardship and ill-health drove him to an asylum.

8. Kirby Muxloe Castle   6 G6
Kirby Muxloe. The main sight of this village, Kirby Muxloe Castle was built by Lord Hastings, a powerful baron of the late 15thC. He constructed it of strong brick and with a wide moat so it could be easily defended during the Wars of the Roses. It never achieved its purpose, however, because it was left incomplete when Hastings, denounced at a royal council meeting, was executed by Richard III. But the great stone gatehouse and the tower are still fiercely impressive.

Kirby Muxloe Castle

9. Leicester   6 H6
Modern as the city may be, behind the endless rows of red-brick terraces lie the remains of a past that is as old as England itself. There is so much history to Leicester that sometimes the town ignores it; for years a Roman milestone acted as the foundation for a lamp-post! Many medieval streets have been demolished to make way for new development, but there is enough history left to make a visit worthwhile.
Leicester was a Bronze Age settlement, and later became the Roman town of Ratae. Magnificent Roman remains have been discovered, including a great forum on the site of which no other building is now allowed. At its centre are the relics of one of the largest Roman public baths found in England. The Jewry Wall has been visible since medieval days; then it formed the boundary of the

Jewish ghetto but in Roman times it was part of the fortifications. Its brick-and-stone length of 75ft still seems very solid. Parts of Roman mosaic pavements form the cellar floors of many Leicester houses.
Throughout the centuries Leicester has remained an important centre. After the Romans departed, Saxons and Danes poured in, and Shakespeare's King Lear is said to have ruled here. The Church of St Mary de Castro was built by the Norman earl of Leicester, and the motte of the Norman castle remains behind the 17thC facade. In the 13thC, Simon de Montfort ruled England for a time from Leicester. Cardinal Wolsey, fallen from Henry VIII's favour and on his way to face trial, died at the abbey of St Mary, and is buried in the Lady chapel. A moving inscription from Shakespeare marks the stone: 'Give him a little earth for charity'.
Since the 19thC Leicester has had a prominent place in industrial history, too, as the centre of the hosiery and boots trades. The guildhall, begun in 1390, is one of the most dignified civic buildings in England, and the grammar school dates from 1573. The city hall, the county assembly halls and the Corn Exchange are fine symbols of 19thC prosperity. Leicestershire's moving Arch of Remembrance – Lutyens' tribute to the tragic history of our own age – is in Victoria Park. The Jewry Wall Museum is a fascinating museum devoted largely to Leicester's Roman remains. There is a magnificent mosaic pavement, together with ornaments, columns and a coffin. There are also remains from other ages, including a well-preserved Saxon skeleton.

Lost Villages of Leicestershire
Deserted medieval villages are scattered all over the Midlands, mainly a result of plague, famine and natural disaster. Leicestershire is especially rich in them because in the 15th and 16thC landlords here carried out a large-scale conversion from crop to dairy farming, forcing many villagers to leave. One of the best-marked sites is Elmsthorpe with its church nave lying open to the sky. It was already deserted when Richard III stopped here on his way to the Battle of Bosworth in 1485. Forton, abandoned in the 16thC, is now marked only by earthworks and Noseby is today just a hall and private chapel.

10. Lutterworth   6 G7
Home of the most famous of medieval English religious reformers, John Wycliffe, Lutterworth is a pleasant steep town, dominated by the parish church where he preached in the late 14thC. The church has changed little since his day (it was 200 years old even then), and the chancel, clerestory and roof are all more than 500 years old. The spire caused havoc in 1780 when it crashed down in a great storm. We know the spire was handsomely restored, but there are no reports as to the long-term effects on the passing vicar whom it narrowly missed.
Under the protection of the powerful baron, John of Gaunt, Wycliffe fearlessly preached doctrines here that were forerunners of later Protestantism. He was laid to rest in his church – but not for long. Forty three years later the Catholic church ordered his remains to be dug up and unceremoniously burnt. Wycliffe is now honoured in Lutterworth Church with a fine mural.

11. Market Harborough   6 H7
Ordinary but pleasant agricultural town, perfect for a relaxed stroll. The delightful market place has many fine houses and is dominated by a 14thC parish church, magnificent for the great spire rising above its tower. The old grammar school, founded by a rich citizen in 1613, is a delightful timbered and gabled building.
A market town since Henry III, Market Harborough saw great excitement during the

Civil War. Charles I held a council of war here on the way to Naseby and Cromwell's men massacred its citizens after their victory in the battle. Charles I later passed through on his way to trial and execution.

12. Market Overton
6 J5

A village rich in remains of many centuries. There are traces of Roman earthworks, some important Anglo-Saxon finds, including a remarkable Saxon clock, and the old stocks and whipping-post are still displayed on the village green. The 14thC church has a 13thC font, said to stand on a Roman base.

13. Melton Mowbray
6 J5

Resounding to the sound of horses' hooves, this pleasant market town has been the centre of the fox-hunting of the shires since the early 19thC. It is a very old town: Bronze Age hunters gathered here, it was a Roman and a Saxon settlement, and the Mowbrays were lords here in the Middle Ages. Many interesting old houses, some in the ancient market place, testify to this past, but the glory of Melton is its church, among the most beautiful of parish churches in England. Begun in the 13thC in the shape of a cross, it has a superb 14thC galilee porch and chancel, noble 16thC ornamented battlements and pinnacles in the lower part of the tower. Don't forget to try one of those famous pork pies and a piece of Stilton.

14. Oakham
6 J6

This elegant, small but spacious town was once the county town of Rutland. Its magnificent church dates partly from the 13thC and has particularly fine sculptures, and the old market square really seems to evoke the Tudor and Stuart world. Remains of Oakham Castle, a manor house of the late 12thC, can be seen, with curiously carved gables and richly decorated doorways. Oakham was the birthplace of one of the most unpleasant men in English history, Titus Oates, who concocted the Popish Plot.

15. Quenby Hall
6 H6

8m E of Leicester. Fine example of Jacobean architecture, built in rich red brick and with an interior that has changed little since that time. The story goes that Stilton cheese was invented by an 18thC housekeeper at Quenby Hall, who later moved to the village of Stilton, taking the cheese with her.

16. Stapleford Park
6 J6

7m SE of Melton Mowbray. Magnificent 17thC stone house with high gables and long rows of mullioned windows, the home of the Sherards until the 19thC. The north wing is Tudor, while the exquisitely decorated dining room is the epitome of 18thC splendour. The house contains some fine furniture, paintings and tapestries and houses a unique collection of Victorian Staffordshire pottery figures. *Open certain days, summer*.

Stapleford Park

🐾 NORTHAMPTONSHIRE 🐾

17. Boughton House
6 J7

4m N of Kettering, off A43. Northamptonshire seat of the dukes of Buccleuch, the house was modelled on the palace of Versailles in the late 17thC by its owner, Lord Montagu, the ambassador to France. Fine French furniture and china remain, and there is also a good collection of paintings and tapestries.
Laid out complete with formal gardens, Boughton was graced with magnificent statues and the avenues surrounding the house were enriched by elms in the 18thC, planted by the second Dukes of Montagu. Much of the gardens and many of the elms have now vanished, but it remains a magnificent place. Receiver of many royal guests, Queen Mary, wife of George V, particularly loved Boughton and visited it often. *Open most days, summer*.

Boughton House

18. Brackley
6 H9

Tiny but handsome town of shady trees and cool lawns, Brackley has a long history. It was a centre of the medieval wool trade, and was also well known for medieval jousting. Bayard's Green, where the jousts were held and which later became a 16th and 17thC racecourse, can still be seen. Brackley was the first headquarters of the rebellious barons of King John, whose revolt led to the signing of the Magna Carta in 1215. In the 16thC it was a refuge from the plague for the scholars of Magdalen College, Oxford. The place they occupied, the 12thC hospital of St John and James, was later to become famous as the site for Magdelen College School.

19. Brixworth, All Saints Church
6 J7

Dark, and even rather sinister, this church is very interesting as it was built largely during the 7thC – in the middle of the Dark Ages when Roman Britain was dead and the Anglo-Saxon world not fully emerged. It is surprisingly sophisticated for its date, and used bricks and tiles from nearby deserted Roman villas. Although the church was extensively added to in the medieval period, its ancient feeling predominates.

All Saints Church, Brixworth

20. Collyweston
6 K6

Fine village of solid stone houses roofed with the famous Collyweston tiles. The present manor house is late 17thC, but remains of an Elizabethan dovecote and an older house can be seen to the west of the church.

21. Daventry
6 G8

Quiet and pleasant hilltop town. The site of its Stone Age fort was chosen as the site for the BBC radio station in 1925: quite a juxtaposition of ancient and modern! The town was famous for coaching – 80 coaches a day changed horses here during the 18thC. It is not surprising that the principal industry of the town then, was making whips.

Many pleasant old coaching inns remain; try the Wheatsheaf Inn, where Charles I stopped on his way to Naseby. Daventry has fine Georgian houses, often following the line of medieval streets.

22. Drayton House 6 K7
Drayton, 2m W of Rockingham. Fairy-tale castle with turrets and battlements reflected in its shimmering lake. Originally built in the 12thC and much beautified since, it hasn't been let or sold since 1361. James I was entertained here by the owner, Lord Mordaunt, only weeks before the Gunpowder Plot. This did not prevent Mordaunt being arrested for supposed complicity in the plot: he finally died in the tower before coming to trial. *Open by arrangement, summer.*

23. Earls Barton, All Saints Church 6 J8
The church is contained in a wonderful Saxon building, with a magnificently commanding Saxon tower. The building has stood almost unchanged for 1,000 years. It is probable that it was built as a fortress or a place of refuge from attack. The interior work in the church is largely Norman.

24. Fotheringay 6 K6
Green, tranquil village of melancholy beauty, enriched by historical memories. A 12thC castle, now just a mound, was the scene both of Richard III's birth, and the execution of Mary, Queen of Scots in 1587. The old house called Garden Farm is said to be where the executioner slept. The church is magnificent, even in spite of destruction of the choir at the Dissolution. As well as a superb lantern tower, there is a great lofty nave with flying buttresses.

25. Kettering 6 J7
Largely a modern town, but with ancient roots; our records of Kettering go back to AD956. At the time of the Domesday Book it was only a manor, but it has grown tremendously, particularly since the 19thC, on the manufacture of boots and shoes.
The old manor house is one of the oldest and most interesting buildings remaining in Kettering. The Baptist Missionary Society was founded here in 1792 – the town coat of arms includes a negro with a broken chain – and the town was the home of William Knibb, an outstanding 19thC missionary who campaigned against the slave trade. He established 61 mission stations in Jamaica, one of them called Kettering.

26. Kirby Hall 6 J6
2m SE of Gretton. Stately palace lavishly designed in the 16th and 17thC but which has fallen into ruin over the centuries. It was begun in 1570 and later superbly embellished, probably by Inigo Jones. Now open to the sky, in its setting of rich grass and tall trees, it is still a place of sombre magnificence.

27. Naseby Battlefield 6 H7
6m SW of Market Harborough. Culminating battle of the English Civil War, fought on 14th June, 1645.
After many skirmishes, Charles I's army was tired and spies reported to Parliament's commander, Fairfax (later joined by Cromwell), that the horses were out at grass and the men in bad shape. When battle commenced Prince Rupert, the King's nephew, led a brilliant cavalry charge. But, as so often, he pursued the enemy too far. Eventually the disciplined charge of the New Model Army – the crack troops who had been raised to fight under Cromwell – took the day for Parliament, leaving a horrific trail behind them; dead bodies of Royalist soldiers stretched towards Market Harborough for four miles. Later, the Puritan soldiers murdered all the women of the Royalist baggage train, most of whom were prostitutes or soldiers' wives.
Naseby Field now rests peaceful and undisturbed. There is little evidence of its bloody past but you can still see the parallel ridges across the valley on which the rival armies faced each other, and Prince Rupert's Farm, which is said to have been his headquarters.

28. Northampton 6 J8
Rather gloomy modern Midlands town, with few old buildings, and yet of some historical interest. It was a Saxon town sacked by the Danes, and the Normans made it a centre of their communications, building a great castle here where the railway station now stands. Thomas a Becket was tried here before being exiled to France in the 12thC. Since King John bought a pair of boots here for ninepence in the early 13thC, the boot and shoe trade has flourished mightily. It has been said that every English army since the Civil War has been shod in Northampton. The Central Museum has a collection of shoes including Queen Victoria's wedding shoes and a pair made for an elephant!
Northampton's chief interest is in its churches. The Church of the Holy Sepulchre, built by a returned crusader in 1100, is one of only four round churches in England. Although on a Saxon site, St Peter's is also Norman and has fine sculptures. St Giles is Norman, too, while All Saints is the newcomer, dating only from the 14thC. The medieval market square is thought to be the largest in England. There was a great fire in 1675, which destroyed almost all of medieval Northampton. Among the more recent buildings, of interest are the two 19thC prisons, the Borough and County—rather grim reminders of what the Victorians considered a philanthropic gaol.

29. Rockingham 6 J6
A long line of stone cottages mounts the steep hill from the River Welland. In medieval times it was an important market town and jousting centre and you can still see the meadow, known as the Tilting Ground, where the jousts were held.
The church has a fine Jacobean pulpit, but the village's chief glory is **Rockingham Castle**, built by William the Conqueror. The present building is a superb collection of gables and bastions dating from many centuries, and it is very rich in historic associations: among kings who have stayed here are William II, Henry I, Henry II, Richard I, Edward I, Edward III and Henry V. The original site of the Norman keep is now a rose garden. *Open certain days, summer.*

30. Stoke Bruerne, Waterways Museum 6 J9
Stoke Bruerne, 3¹/2m E of Towcester. This village was created by the canal network, and its waterways museum is a must for lovers of canals and rivers. As well as machinery used on the canals, the museum contains many fascinating photographs, signs and paintings.

31. Sulgrave 6 H9
8m NE of Banbury. Owing to its connections with the Washington family, this village is of great interest to Americans. In 1539 Laurence Washington bought Sulgrave Manor from Henry VIII and rebuilt it: he was twice mayor of Northampton and an ancestor of George. The Manor contains a collection of George Washington's personal possessions, including his black velvet coat, and the Washingtons have a pew in the village church.

32. Towcester 6 H9
On Roman Watling Street and known to the Romans as Lactodorum, Towcester is a traffic-laden town, linking London to the Midlands and the North. In the 18th and early 19thC Towcester was a great coaching centre and was beloved of Charles Dickens: Sam Weller and Mr Pickwick enjoyed a 'werry good dinner' at the Saracen's Head.

SHROPSHIRE

1. Acton Burnell   **6 B6**
Sleepy black and white village, with many
echoes of the past. The splendid 13thC
Church of St Mary was largely built by Bishop
Burrell, devoted adviser of Edward I. The
chancel is magnificent with very fine lancet
windows and many carvings. Burrell's ruined
house, with two embattled towers still
standing, is one of the oldest fortified houses
in England. It is claimed that, in 1283, this
small village was the scene of the first properly
constituted parliament.
Remains of the Roman Watling Street and a
Roman bridge lie nearby. Just outside the
village at Langley is a deserted 17thC chapel,
its simple benches and dignified reading-desk
a reminder of the simple style of Puritan
worship in those days.

2. Boscobel   **6 C6**
5¹/2m ENE of Shifnal. Small village
surrounded by many fine oaks, forever
associated with the most romantic story told of
Charles II's escape after the Battle of
Worcester. The King hid in a great oak in
Spring Coppice to avoid Cromwell's men. A
stately veteran tree, said to be the one, is
marked, but in fact the actual tree seems to
have been cut down by souvenir hunters. We
could presume, however, that this oak has
grown from the other's acorn!
Boscobel House, where Charles hid, aided by
his faithful Royalist friends, is still standing, as
is Hobbal Grange where he also stayed.
Soldiers were often hot on the King's trail as
he went from house to house in this pleasant
countryside and it was the loyalty with which
he was received by many as their rightful king
which was to ensure his final escape.

3. Bridgnorth   **6 C6**
Romantic town perched dizzily across a great
sandstone ridge by the River Severn.
Bridgnorth is really two towns, High Town
and Low Town, 200ft apart, and joined by
countless sets of steps often cut into sheer
rock. Linking the towns is a cliff railway, the
shortest and steepest in England.
With its steps and arches and its steep
medieval streets, Bridgnorth is rather like an
Italian hilltop town. It even has a leaning
tower, which is part of the keep of the ruined
12thC castle and is even more precariously
inclined than Pisa's. Bridgnorth was an
important town in the Middle Ages, but has
never grown much since; its ancient houses
are therefore well-preserved, and fragments
of the medieval walls remain. There are also
some interesting more recent monuments,
such as the 19thC Church of St Mary
Magdalene. Its curious tower incorporates a
dome and the church was built not by an
architect, but by one of Britain's greatest
engineers, Thomas Telford.

4. Church Stretton   **6 B7**
Quiet and pleasant town, famed for its golf
course and set among some of Britain's most
ancient hills, such as the Long Mynd and
Caer Caradoc. Many ancient camps and
tumuli lie in the surrounding area. There are
few old houses in the town, but the
cross-shaped church goes back 800 years. Its
oldest occupant is a stone fertility figure, with
arms akimbo, over the Norman north door,
who may have been around before the
Normans came. On the inside arches of the
tower are beautiful rafters, the oldest in
Shropshire, covered with statues of
cheerful-looking people of the 13thC.

5. Cleobury Mortimer   **6 C7**
Exquisite 18thC town where timbered
cottages blend discreetly with fine Georgian
houses. The Vicarage and the Manor House
are both fine early 18thC buildings and the

Talbot Hotel, once a coaching inn, dates from
the 1860s. The grand church tower has stood
for 800 years and has a crazily-angled spire of
oak, while the church porch, with beautiful
carved doorways, is 700 years old. Cleobury
was probably the birthplace of William
Langland, one of the greatest medieval poets:
we can easily picture his Piers Plowman in the
eternal fields of the lovely surrounding
countryside.

6. Clun   **6 A7**
Remote, mysterious border town,
immortalised as one of Housman's 'quietest
places under the sun' in 'A Shropshire Lad'.
It lies near the wild moorland of Offa's Dyke
which was built in the 8thC as a fortification
against the Welsh. There are five ancient
camps here, one said to be the camp of
Caractacus, the chief who held out against the
Romans. Gaunt remnants of the Norman
castle, veteran of many medieval border
skirmishes, can be seen and the Norman
church has a great flight of steps up to a lovely
18thC lych-gate. The Town Hall museum
contains prehistoric relics including the
remains of a Bronze Age inhabitant.

7. Ironbridge   **6 C6**
The town, perching precariously on its
limestone cliff, holds an immortal place in
industrial history. It was a great centre of the
iron industry in the 18thC, and the iron bridge
over the Severn, constructed in 1777, was the
first in England. Spanning the Severn's great
gorge, the bridge is magnificent. The suburb
of Coalbrookdale was the site of the great
ironworks of the Abraham Darby dynasty in
the 18thC, a strange mingle with the ancient
timbered houses. It was at Coalbrookdale in
1709 that the first successful smelting of iron
with coke is thought to have been achieved.

8. Llanyblodwel   **6 A5**
With a Welsh name (meaning hamlet of
flowers) and on the Welsh border,
Llanyblodwel is, in fact, an English town in
character. There is a stone bridge and a
16thC black-and-white inn which was
managed by the same family for 300 years.
The Church of St Michael the Archangel is
one of the strangest in the country, an odd
amalgam of the centuries. Its curious almost
detached 19thC tower has a spire growing out
without any parapet, there is a fantastically
elaborate south porch, a fine 12thC doorway
and much unusual carving.

9. Longden-upon-Tern Aqueduct   **6 B6**
Longden-upon-Tern, 5m SW of Shrewsbury.
Long iron duct on four graceful arches, it
carries the Shropshire Union Canal over the
River Tern. This spectacular piece of

engineering, constructed in 1794 by Thomas Telford, was the first cast-iron aqueduct in England.

10. Ludlow   6 B7
Classic hilltop Shropshire town which John Betjeman has called 'the loveliest town in England'. You can still wander through the ancient, cobbled streets on a warm summer's day, look down from the steep hill to the ring of three rivers and the answering hills on the skyline, and imagine yourself in an unchanging England.
The great tower of the Norman castle is darkly impressive: from this great hill fort successive medieval princes of Wales attempted to govern their troubled principality. The castle, though partly a ruin, remains magnificent; the great stone steps of the massive Norman keep have been echoing to feet for 800 years, and you can still see the state apartment from which the unfortunate princes in the Tower began their fateful journey to London in 1483, never to return. Prince Arthur, elder son of Henry VII, brought his young bride Catherine of Aragon (later wife to his brother, Henry VIII) here, and the flowery walk through which they strolled is still known as the Queen's Walk. There is a magnificent Tudor gateway, and the Great Hall is where Milton's Jacobean masque, 'Comus', received its first performance. Most touching of all is the little round chapel of Mary Magdalen, 800 years old, its great chancel arch and walls open to the sky.

Feathers Hotel, Ludlow

Ludlow's other monument is the parish Church of St Laurence which stands on the site of a Saxon graveyard. It is one of the finest churches in England and at 203ft from east to west, is as big as a cathedral. It is mainly 15thC and has a stately nave, richly decorated medieval roofs and great stained-glass windows.
Besides these great buildings, the tortuous streets of Ludlow are a delight. There are lovely Tudor houses with gables and oriels, and the old grammar school has a 14thC room. The 17thC Feathers Hotel, especially the interior, is very fine and many dignified Georgian dwellings observe the cobbled ways.

11. Market Drayton   6 C4
Bustling but dignified market town, with a fair that has been held annually for centuries, Georgian houses, and many 19thC cobblers' and sadlers' shops. The grammar school was founded in 1558 and here Robert Clive, founder of the 18thC Indian empire, was educated. His desk, engraved with his initials, is still there. The centre of the town is the High Street, which is more like a market place. From here, the main streets fan out with the church appearing only in odd glimpses. The church has a 14thC tower of great height with a Norman doorway at its base.

12. Much Wenlock   6 C6
Intimate market town sleeping in the shadow of ancient Wenlock Edge. The charming guildhall, all in oak, is 15thC, and there are many ancient houses: a timbered Elizabethan manor house, a 14thC leper hospital with a 16thC chimney-stack, and by St Owen's Well, a 15thC house with an archway made of three

Much Wenlock Priory

pairs of great oak boughs. But the greatest attraction of the town is the ruined priory. Originally founded as a nunnery c680 AD, in the 12thC it was the greatest centre of Cluniac worship in England. Although it was destroyed during the Reformation, there is still much of interest: great masses of masonry, beautiful decorated arches and rich Norman carving and arcading which miraculously have survived the centuries of neglect.

13. Oswestry   6 A5
Ancient border town in remote north Shropshire country. It was named after St Oswald, 7thC king of Northumbria whose body was nailed to a tree after he was slain in battle with the Mercians. The Norman fortified castle is where Richard II held Parliament in 1398, but as the town was repeatedly burnt by the Welsh during the Middle Ages, the buildings are generally modern and the castle is a ruin. The Lloyd Mansion, however, is a fine Tudor building.

14. Shrewsbury   6 B5
Lying within a great loop of the Severn, this is one of the few medieval towns still beautiful after recent rebuilding; it's crammed with dignified streets, graceful church spires, extremely narrow alleys and old houses, known locally as 'shuts'. The Norman castle has been much restored but the gateway is the original. Round St Mary's church, also Norman, is especially notable for fine medieval and Tudor glass, much of it imported from Flanders, and for its stone spire. There are remnants of three medieval friaries as well as the medieval Abbey Church and many modern churches. Fine 16th and 17thC houses are in abundance, and the old buildings of Shrewsbury School are 16thC. Shrewsbury has figured much in history. It was originally a Roman town, and during the Middle Ages was often the scene of skirmishes against the Welsh. Here, in 1282, where the High Cross stood, David, the rebel Welsh prince, was hung, drawn and quartered. Henry V won his spurs in battle here against the rebel Hotspur in the early 15thC and the town held out gallantly for the King during the Civil War after a traitor let in the Cromwellians.

Shrewsbury

15. Stokesay Castle   6 B7
3m S of Craven Arms, A49. Fine, medieval survival, this 13thC castle has a moat which in summer is strewn with flowers, a splendid gatehouse with a gabled stone roof and overhanging storey, and two great towers at either end of the banqueting hall. The rooms are most handsome and in one of them is a 700-year-old fireplace – almost as old as the

house itself. The accompanying Norman church, largely rebuilt in the 17thC, is simple but dignified. *Open certain days.*

16. The Wrekin 6 C6
2½m SW of Wellington, S of A5. Great hill, from which on clear days there are magnificent views over the centre of England, and which has a large Iron Age hill fort crowning its top. It was probably the great gathering-place of the Cornovii tribe.

17. Wroxeter 6 B6
Sleepy, provincial town, chiefly interesting for its Roman remains: it was once the great Roman city of Uriconium covering an area of 180 acres, the fourth largest in Roman Britain. The city was destroyed during the Dark Ages, but the Roman thumb-print remains. The Saxons built the church by the Severn with great stones from the old city – the font, for instance, grows from the base of a Roman pillar – while nearby are the remains

of a Roman bridge. Countless generations have embellished the church: there are fascinating Saxon carvings of dogs and birds, the chancel is Norman, there are Elizabethan arches on the choir-stalls and the altar table is Jacobean.
But the chief interests in Wroxeter are the excavations of the Roman city. On the open plain is a brick tower, pierced with an arch – it was once a great building and you can still see a hall which was probably once a law court, a smithy and bronze-working furnace, and the remains of the public baths. Even the coal and charcoal used to heat them has been found in a storehouse. Many remains have been found in a field nearby: a tablet with writing, and other more touchingly human relics, such as a beautiful silver mirror with a twisted handle and a diploma giving an old soldier his discharge and Roman citizenship. There is a good site museum where many of these finds can be seen.

WARWICKSHIRE

1. Alcester 6 E8
Old town, set amid cool woods, laden with delightful byways and Tudor timbered cottages with overhanging storeys. Once a Roman market centre (the name means 'camp on the Alne'), present-day Alcester is a perfect example of a medieval town. The church has a magnificent 14thC tower, and there are also many old needle-mills, as Alcester was once the centre of this industry.

2. Arley 6 F7
Nr Anstey. Fascinating example of a 19thC colliery village, with a pit-shaft actually in the village, and many 19thC miners' cottages. The church, set amid Elizabethan yews, is 600 years old.

3. Astley 6 F7
Ancient village lying amid green fields, with a sundial in the church tower that dates from Saxon times. The great house, **Astley Park**, *1½m S of village*, now a hotel, is largely the work of the past few centuries, but in the former house Lady Jane Grey, nine-days Queen of England, grew up. Here, too, her father, the Duke of Suffolk, fled during the Catholic Mary I's reign. He hid for three days in a great oak until he was betrayed by his gamekeeper, later to be executed. The withered stump of the tree is marked with a small monument.

4. Atherstone and Mancetter 6 F6
Two ancient settlements, now merged together, both founded by the Romans on Watling Street. At Atherstone, Roman paving stones have been found with the marks of chariot wheels clearly visible, and Mancetter may have been the site of Bodicea's defeat by the Romans. Mancetter has a 13thC church around the green, and was the home of two martyrs burnt by the Catholic Mary I in the 16thC: Robert Glover, a sick man, was arrested in his bed, and Joyce Lewis (who actually came from a strict Catholic family, but was so revolted by Mary's cruel policy that she became a Protestant) was finally brought to trial and execution by her Catholic husband.

5. Barcheston 6 F9
Tranquil village that was the birthplace of tapestry-weaving in England: here in the 16thC William Sheldon set up his looms to compete with those of France and Flanders. Manor House Farm, where the industry began, is still there. When paper-hanging grew in popularity, however, the industry died. The church has stood since 1200 and has a Norman doorway and a charming 13thC leaning tower.

6. Bidford-on-Avon 6 E8
Typical but outstandingly beautiful village of the Shakespeare country. The bard himself must have been familiar with Bidford as he is reported to have been involved in drinking bouts at the Falcon Inn. The 15th and 16thC stone and timber houses and the quiet byways are a delight.

7. Charlecote Park 6 F8
5m NE of Stratford. Gracious Elizabethan house, site of one of the most famous Shakespeare stories. It is said that Sir Thomas Lucy, Elizabethan founder of the house, caught young Shakespeare poaching deer in the park and his flogging and prosecution caused Shakespeare to fly to London to win fame as a playwright. Later he satirized Lucy in the figure of Justice Swallow. Lucy, who built the house with its cascading copper domes in the shape of an 'E' to flatter Queen Elizabeth I, was rewarded by a visit from her in 1572. Whether or not the legend regarding Shakespeare is true, the house is worth a visit for its museum collection of carriages and deer park. *Open most days, summer.*

Chesterton Windmill

8. Chesterton 6 F8
4½m SW of Southam. Remote and lonely village with only a handful of buildings, but a long past. Particularly attractive is Chesterton windmill, built in 1632 and restored recently. Looking down the west slope from there, you can see clearly Roman earthworks on the Fosse Way: 2,000 years ago this quiet place was a Roman staging post.

9. Coleshill 6 F7
Delightful and varied town, a royal manor in Norman times. It has a gracefully-arching medieval bridge, many Georgian houses and a magnificent and huge Norman font in the parish church. On the old market place, by the church, you can still see the town stocks, pillory and whipping-post – harsh reminders of the style of punishment suffered by our ancestors.

10. Compton Wynyates 6 G9
10m W of Banbury, off B4035. Perhaps the most magnificent of all English country

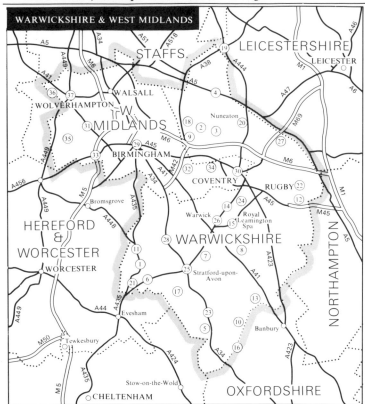

WARWICKSHIRE & WEST MIDLANDS

houses, now sadly closed to the public, but still worth seeing for its magnificent setting. Reached by winding country lanes, you come across it in a grassy hollow between low hills and protected by great yew trees. The house is a serenely grand blend of wood, stone and brick, of every hue from pale pink through rich red to sombre black. It is complete with battlements, turrets, oriel windows and a flower-decorated moat.

The house is home to one of England's greatest families, the Comptons, who have been lords of the manor here since the 12thC and are Marquesses of Northampton. The house was made into a grand home in the early 15thC by William Compton, boyhood friend of Henry VIII, who cleared out the local villagers to create the park! Later generations of Comptons have entertained British monarchs here.

Compton Wynyates

11. Coughton Court   6 E8
3m N of Alcester, off A48. Seat for five centuries of one of England's staunchest Catholic families, the Throckmortons. The house, at the end of a great elm avenue (now sadly depleted by disease), has a magnificent 16thC gatehouse and is filled with Throckmorton heirlooms including many family portraits. There is a priest's hole in the turret, and secret passages and hidden stairways. The Throckmortons often suffered for their faith:

one was executed under Elizabeth I, during the Civil War the house was sacked, and it was ransacked once again after the deposition of James II in 1688. It was here, too, that the wives of the Gunpowder plotters gathered to wait for the results of the plot. *Open certain days, summer.*

12. Dunchurch   6 G8
2m SW of Rugby. Placid old town where the town stocks stand together with the medieval cross on the pleasant green. The most interesting place is Guy Fawkes House, formerly the Lion Inn, where the gunpowder plotters met to arrange their final plans. It was here, too, that the news burst in on them that the plot had failed.

13. Edgehill Battlefield   6 G9
5m N of Banbury, off A4. A steep ridge crowned with monumental beeches is the site of one of the most famous battles in the English Civil War. The Parliamentary commander was the Earl of Essex – he pessimistically insisted on carrying his coffin and winding-sheet in his baggage! Charles I commanded the Royalist forces assisted by his gallant nephew Prince Rupert. Fought on 23rd October 1642, the battle raged for control of the road to London which was blocked by Parliamentiers. Although Rupert's charges, attacking from the slopes, were brilliantly successful, the battle was finally inconclusive: Charles was unable to march on to London.

Hundreds of the slain lie in Graveyard Coppice and the battlefield is now mainly part of a large army camp. Edge Hill Tower, an 18thC building which is now an inn containing relics of the battle, marks the place where the king raised his standard.

On the slopes of the hill lies another piece of history: a red horse carved in the hillside is said to have been cut by Warwick the

Kingmaker in memory of his red charger slain in battle.

14. Kenilworth Castle 6 F7
Kenilworth. Darkly impressive with its ruined stark red walls open to the sky, this castle is 800 years old. A great fortified place, it saw wars between Henry II and his sons in the 12thC and the imprisonment of Edward II in the 14thC after he had been deposed. Robert Dudley, Earl of Leicester, entertained Elizabeth I here with great magnificence in 1575, perhaps still hoping to marry her. The great Lancastrian, John of Gaunt, lived here in the 14thC, after Simon de Montfort, greatest of medieval rebel barons: he was defending the road to Kenilworth when he was killed at the Battle of Evesham in 1265. Cromwell ordered the castle destroyed after the Civil War and now it is a shell. But there is much to see, in particular the 12thC keep, the 14thC Great Hall and the Tudor barn.

15. Leamington Spa 6 F8
Elegant 19thC spa town with magnificent stuccoed houses, lovely gardens and delightful lanes leading down to the fragrant River Leam. The healing properties of the waters was known in the 16thC, but in the 17thC they were used mainly for curing meat. Fostered by local pioneers, the development of the spa town began in the 1780s. The gracious pump-room, much beloved by Queen Victoria, still recalls the 19thC upper-class taking the waters. So do the 19thC gardens, especially the magnificent Jephson gardens named after the doctor who administered the waters. Explore the broad walks by the river, passing multi-coloured flower displays, rockeries, roseries and fountains.

16. Little and Long Compton 6 F10
The southernmost villages of Warwickshire, in the lush fields by grassy Barton Hill. At the manor house in Little Compton lived Bishop Juxon, friend and comforter to Charles I on his scaffold. The church has a touching memorial to the King. Long Compton is a place of mysterious beauty, with a Bronze Age monolith called the King Stone. The Rollright Stones, a similar group, lie just across the border in Oxfordshire. The town holds a long tradition of witchcraft: as late as 1875 a local farmer killed a 79-year-old woman with a pitchfork because he thought she was a witch.

17. Long Marston 6 F9
5¹/₂m SW of Stratford. Charming, leafy village with a 12thC church which is forever associated with one of the most famous stories told about Charles II after his escape from the Battle of Worcester. He came here disguised as a servant of Mistress Jane Lane, the Warwickshire lady who had befriended him, and was sent to work in the kitchen of a local house (today called King's Lodge). A cook, enraged by his clumsiness with a meat-jack, boxed his ears just as Roundhead soldiers were coming in. Naturally they did not penetrate the disguise!

18. Maxstoke Castle 6 F7
3m SE of Coleshill, 4m NE of Bickenhill. Magnificent medieval fortress with massive turreted gatehouse and octagonal towers, built in the 1340s. Richard III stayed here before Bosworth (haunted by the ghosts of those he murdered, if Shakespeare is to be believed). He was followed shortly afterwards by Henry VII who stayed here after he had defeated and slain his rival. *Open by arrangement, summer.*

19. No Man's Heath 6 F6
6m NE of Tamworth. A fireplace at an inn was once the meeting place of this extreme northern part of Warwickshire with three other counties: Derbyshire, Leicestershire and Staffordshire. The picturesque heath became a haunt for the lawless: 18thC squatters and cockfighters, highwaymen and bare-fisted prizefighters who could escape police forces by popping into a neighbouring county. The ancient weathercock, still to be seen today, often had to be repaired, having been riddled with holes by guns!

20. Nuneaton 6 F7
A town that grew prosperous and ugly on 19thC industry and suffered from war damage, but still retains traces of the long past that dates back to Saxon times. The abbey church was begun in the 1150s and St Nicholas's Church dates partly from the 15thC. Nuneaton is George Eliot country: she was born at Chilvers Coton (now a suburb), and most of her novels celebrate this sedate corner of north Warwickshire where she saw the traditional rural Midlands of her childhood give way to industrial hum.

21. Ragley Hall 6 E8
2m SW of Alcester, A435. Designed in 1680 by Robert Hooke, this is one of the grandest Palladian mansions in England, well-fitted to play its traditional role of country seat of the Marquesses of Hertford. The house is enriched by very fine paintings and furniture, as well as an outstanding collection of traditional china. The grounds are well laid out for enjoyment, for in addition to the gardens, park and lake there are also an adventure wood, a country trail and a picnic area. *Open certain days, summer.*

Ragley Hall

22. Rugby 6 G8
Modern industrial town, but with an impressive past: ancient British tribes fought each other here before the arrival of the Romans. The town's most famous monument is Rugby School, endowed in the 16thC, and immortalised by the figures of Dr Arnold and Tom Brown. The heart of Rugby is the chapel, and the attached war memorial chapel with its touching epitaph to its Old Boys who died in the First World War (nearly one in four of those who served). Beneath the chancel Dr Arnold lies surrounded by figures of famous Rugbeians: Matthew Arnold, Rupert Brooke, and two archbishops of Canterbury. The Close is where Rugby Football was invented.
Also of interest in the town are the 12thC Church of St Andrew and the house in Hillmorton Road where Rupert Brooke, lost soldier-poet of the First World War, was born.

23. Shipston-on-Stour 6 F9
Once a great centre of the traditional wool trade of England, Shipston now seems to lie dreamily untouched by the modern world. Stately Georgian houses in profusion testify to the one-time prosperity of the 'sheep's town' and there is still a Sheep Street. Shipston was founded by Offa of Mercia in the 8thC.

24. Stoneleigh 6 F8
One of the loveliest villages in Warwickshire with medieval bridges, Tudor almshouses, and a smithy dating from 1851: not for nothing is this great riding country. The largely Norman church has one of the most ancient fonts in England.
Stoneleigh Abbey, the most magnificent Georgian mansion in Warwickshire, has been home for 500 years to the Leighs, staunchest of Royalist families. Charles I stayed here on his way to raise the Royalist standard in the

Civil War, Bonnie Prince Charlie may have been entertained here secretly (the Leighs would not go to church where they would have to pray for the Hanoverians), and Queen Victoria dined here in magnificent state in June, 1857. *View from outside only.*

25. Stratford-upon-Avon 6 F8

Proudest of English provincial towns, one of whose 2,000 inhabitants in the 16thC happened to be William Shakespeare. From shop windows, pub fronts and cafe signs, we see gazing down at us the wise, austere, kindly features that we recognise as the authentic face of England's greatest writer.

But there is much of historical interest in Stratford besides Shakespeare. It was a Bronze Age settlement, a Roman village and a manor at the time of the Domesday Book. A weekly town market has been held from 1196. The bridge over the Avon was built in the 15thC as was the old grammar school where Shakespeare studied, its timber-framed roofs and red walls a living monument to late medieval and Tudor England. The streets of Stratford are full of beautiful old houses and fascinating inn signs, many connected with Shakespeare. By the Avon bridge is the Alveston Manor Hotel where a Saxon cemetery has been discovered and more than 50 skeletons unearthed.

Anne Hathaway's Cottage

The Shakespeare relics themselves are sometimes ambiguous. The birthplace in Henley Street, although looking very Tudor, has been much restored and, although it is likely, we are not absolutely certain that Shakespeare was born there. Shakespeare's house in retirement, New Place, was knocked down by its owner in the 18thC to avoid paying the rates (this was before David Garrick started the first modern Shakespeare festival in 1769). The present estate is, however, charming. Just outside Stratford are the hamlets associated with Shakespeare's family: Snitterfield, from where his father came, and Shottery, where Anne Hathaway's charming cottage, owned by her family until 1911, stands. But perhaps the most potent associations are to be found in Holy Trinity Church, set in its avenue of tall limes, with rose windows, beautiful choir-stalls, and a font by the door which has been in use for 500 years.

26. Warwick 6 F8

Warwick is perhaps more full of historic interest than any town of comparable size in Britain. To stand on its steep heights with the distant view of shimmering fields overlooking the gabled medieval houses in the huddled streets is to understand instinctively the medieval world.

Chief glory, apart from the castle, is the parish Church of St Mary. Though it was partly destroyed by the great fire of 1694, its 12thC crypt and 14thC chancel remain. The most beautiful part is the 15thC Beauchamp Chapel, built in accordance with the will of Richard Beauchamp, Earl of Warwick, the Englishman who presided at the trial and burning of Joan of Arc. A magnificent central monument to him comprises a gilded statue on a Purbeck marble tomb. There are tombs of other earls of Warwick, a splendid Gothic reredos and stained glass and sculpture of rich beauty.

Historic buildings abound in Warwick: the grammar school was founded in the 11thC, there is a dolls' museum in an Elizabethan house and Leicester's Hospital, named after its founder, favourite of Queen Elizabeth I, is now a home for retired servicemen. Mill Street is a steep street by the castle, with Tudor houses, and Northgate Street has some of the finest Georgian houses in the Midlands.

26. Warwick Castle 6 F8

Castle Rock, Warwick. The view towards the massive grey wall of the castle from the tree-fringed Avon bridge is truly unforgettable. Warwick is among the most magnificent castles in Britain and incomparably rich in historic association. It is one of the few remaining medieval fortresses in England that are still inhabited.

The castle was founded in AD914 by Ethelfleda, daughter of King Alfred, as a bulwark against the Danes. The mound that was the centre of her fortress can still be seen. William the Conqueror had a motte-and-bailey castle here, but the present Caesar's Tower and Guy's Tower, inhumanely impressive, are largely the creation of the 14th and 15thC. The rooms, many of them with splendid views of the Avon, are filled with treasures of the ages: sumptuous tapestries, carved cedar and priceless furniture.

For centuries the most powerful families in England – Beauchamps, Nevilles and Dudleys – were earls of Warwick, and great events here were almost commonplace: here Piers Gaveston, friend of Edward II, was tried by the King's barons before being executed; here Richard Beauchamp entertained Henry V; here Warwick the Kingmaker plotted his successive changes of allegiance during the Wars of the Roses.

Warwick Castle

26. Warwick, Guy's Cliffe 6 F8

Henry V, Elizabeth I and Ruskin all stopped at this delightful, romantic spot by the River Avon. Guy, a Saxon earl, is said to have retired to this cave in order to die a hermit, having killed dragons and slain a giant. He is commemorated in a 600-year-old statue. Sarah Siddons lived here as a 17-year-old servant at the great house before she became a famous actress.

Nearby is Blacklow Hill which has a bloodstained niche in history – it was here that the rebellious barons of Edward II took his young lover and adviser, Piers Gaveston, to cut off his head.

27. Wolvey 6 G7

Quiet hilltop village which was a thriving millers' town in the Middle Ages. Many of the windmills still remain in the neighbourhood. It was at Wolvey Heath that Edward IV, encamped and asleep after a disastrous battle in the Wars of the Roses, was surprised and captured by Warwick the Kingmaker, his one-time friend.

28. Wootten Wawen Church 6 F8

Wootten Wawen. The best-preserved Saxon architecture in Warwickshire in its oldest church. The church is well worth a visit for its fine carvings and screens, richly decorated statues and perfect early 11thC tower. Outside is a Tudor sundial.

WEST MIDLANDS

29. Birmingham   6 E7

Second city of Britain and home to 1,000 trades, Birmingham has its share of soulless ugliness, but makes up for it with liveliness and abundant interest. Time and time again the city has made industrial and social history, and long acquaintance with these hilly, red-brick streets gives them a charm that they lack at first sight. Birmingham started life as a small line of stations on Roman Icknield Street. At the time of the Domesday Book it was a manor, and by the 17thC, a fairly substantial town. Though it tempered 10,000 swords for Cromwell's men, it was the Industrial Revolution of the 18thC that made Birmingham the great centre of the canal and road network that confirmed its rise to greatness. Old buildings are few, although there is some fine Victorian architecture. Even that has gone, however, in the re-designed central square, the Bull Ring, which dates back to medieval times.

Birmingham has, among its many fine buildings, some interesting churches. Most of St Martin's is modern, but it has a 600-year-old spire with a weathercock standing triumphantly at 200ft. The 18thC cathedral church of St Philip has magnificent windows contributed by Burne-Jones, while the 19thC Roman Catholic cathedral, designed by Pugin in 14thC Gothic style, seems to express the ebullience of the Catholic revival in England. The town hall is a monument to 19thC civic pride, as are the remains of Birmingham's old railway stations. The City Art Gallery houses a fine collection of the artistic treasures of the ages.

Matthew Boulton's Soho Works at Handsworth is both where gas lighting was invented and where James Watt perfected the steam engine. Nothing remains of the 18thC factory now, but Boulton's home, Soho House, can still be seen. Among the interesting monuments of Birmingham's industrial and social history is Gas Street Basin, the meeting place of two canals. Here, in the heart of the city, a traditional and colourful houseboat community thrives. As it grew and prospered, Birmingham became a pioneer city giving Britain its first children's court, its first municipal bank and its first municipal orchestra. Much of this lively, go-ahead atmosphere is still evident in the bustling streets today.

Birmingham has many areas and suburbs of distinctive interest. The old jewellery quarter, near the city centre, is full of 18thC narrow twisted alleys. **Bournville**, *4m SW of city centre*, built as a model industrial settlement by the Cadbury family in the 19thC, expresses a more modern ideal of industrialism and has a striking swimming baths, built from 1902–4. **Edgbaston**, *3m W of city centre*, is different again with its crumbling 19thC villas set among leafy roads. The civic university is situated here.

Birmingham University

30. Coventry   6 F7

A phoenix risen from the ashes of war, Coventry is a city of endless town plans and rebuilding, its past seemingly forgotten. Not surprisingly, considering the scale of the air-raid on the night of November 14th-15th 1940, old buildings are few. But Coventry has a fascinating past, because in the Middle Ages it was one of the most important towns in England.

Coventry originally developed around a 7thC convent (hence the name) and later around a large 11thC Benedictine abbey, founded by Leofric and Godiva who were Earl and Countess here. It is not certain if Lady Godiva's famous ride ever took place, or whether she was naked merely of her expensive ornaments and jewels, but she and Leofric are buried in the ruins of the abbey. Coventry has three great medieval churches whose delicate network of spires dominates the skyline: St Michael's, Christchurch and Holy Trinity. The 14thC St Mary's Hall, complete with medieval kitchen and with a splendid 15thC tapestry, is also worth a visit. Ford's Hospital, founded in the early 16thC is a beautiful example of a Tudor timber-framed building. But, overall, modern Coventry is a city of car-works, shopping precincts and housing estates – the past certainly has to be dug for here.

30. Coventry Cathedral   6 F7

Off Priory St. Moving symbol of the devastation of the Second World War and of the efforts to build anew, Coventry Cathedral is the newest of Britain's great historical monuments. The old cathedral of St Michael was totally gutted during the appalling raid of November 1940, and only the great spire, the outer walls and the crypt remain to remind us of Coventry's medieval glory. By 1962 a new cathedral had arisen to the north of the old, after what its architect Basil Spence described as 'eleven years of toil, frustration, hope and ecstasy'. The exterior is not very beautiful, although the outline of the circular Chapel of Unity is impressive. But the inside is filled with a wealth of modern artistic jewels: impressive stained glass, the huge tapestry by Graham Sutherland showing Christ in majesty, Elizabeth Frink's lectern eagle and Ralph Beyer's incised lettering. It may all be very modern and a little brash, but as a symbol of so much senseless destruction and noble endeavour, the whole experience is deeply affecting.

31. Dudley   6 D7

Historic centre of the grimy Black Country, Dudley was important long before the Industrial Revolution. Its castle, standing proudly on a high ridge, is said to date back to the time of Dud the Saxon. The medieval market square is still very fine, set round its fountain, but industry has set its heavy hand on Dudley and there are many smoky industrial estates and drab housing developments. It is said that here, in the late 17thC, coke instead of charcoal was first used to smelt iron, the process being discovered by Dud Dudley, illegitimate son of Lord Dudley and a miner's daughter. True or not, the great ironworks have belched out smoke in a towering demonstration of industrial power ever since.

31. Dudley Castle   6 D7

Fumes, factories, railways and canals form the view from this superciliously-sited medieval castle which still has its 14thC gatehouse, barbican, and keep. Most surprising of all, though, is the zoo here that opened in the 1930s. Sea-lions romp in the one-time moat, but the concrete buildings of the zoo are below the castle ruins and don't impinge too much. Beyond the north gate a strange enclosure houses dinosaurs and headless and extinct animals.

32. Hampton-in-Arden   6 F7

Smelling of the hawthorn, this leafy village in the middle of the ancient forest of Arden, is said to have been the setting for Shakespeare's

'As You Like It'. The sunlit rural world of the play is certainly perfectly mirrored in these steep streets and 16thC timbered houses with overhanging storeys decorated walls, and pretty, enclosed gardens. The packhorse bridge is 500 years old and the church has a late Norman nave, a medieval font in the shape of an hour-glass, blue and white tiles behind the altar dating from the 15thC, and an exquisite finely-crafted Jacobean clock.

33. Halesowen   6 E7
Standing between the industrial grime of the Black Country and the cool Clent Hills, Halesowen has managed to retain the air of a country town despite many metal factories. Its past goes back long before the Industrial Revolution: the church is Norman and thought to be on the site of an earlier Saxon church. With its fine 15thC tower and spire, and superb Norman arches and doorways in the chancel, it is like a small cathedral. Near the town stand the ruins of Hales Abbey. Founded in 1215 by King John, it is one of the most important monasteries of the Middle Ages.

34. Meriden   6 F8
5¹/₂m NW of Coventry. Ancient village with a 500-year-old headless cross said to mark the central point of England. The church, with its Norman chancel and mainly 14thC interior, has views from its steep hill both of the ancient wooded Midlands and Birmingham lying hazily below. The 18thC Forest Hall is where the Woodmen of Arden, the oldest archery society in England, hold their meetings. The many ancient farmhouses and inns are interspersed with great factories, such as the Triumph Works just a stone's throw from the M6 motorway: Meriden is a strange juxtaposition of ancient England and the industrial world of today.

35. Stourbridge   6 D7
Lying at the centre of the Black Country, this is the great centre for glass-making, a trade founded in the 16thC by Continental refugees fleeing religious persecution. The Stourbridge air has been blackened by coal-mining, clay-mining and industry, but there are still many fine features: colourful churches, one dating back to the 13thC; the Bluecoat School, founded by the local industrial magnates, the Foleys; and King Edward's School where Dr Johnson was once a pupil.

36. Wightwick Manor   6 D6
3m W of Wolverhampton. Built in 1887 for Theodore Mander, prosperous industrialist and mayor of Wolverhampton, this is a delightfully characteristic Victorian house, in the medieval style, with many gables and mullions. The house is given distinction by its great collection of Victorian art from the hands of William Morris, Burne-Jones, Holman Hunt, Millais and Rossetti. *Open most days*.

37. Wolverhampton   6 D6
The capital of the Black Country with, in Auden's words, a landscape of 'tramlines and slagheaps, pieces of machinery'. Although Wolverhampton may be an industrial jungle, it is not without historical reminders. There was a Saxon settlement here and an 8thC cross remains by St Peter's Church which has a 1,000-year-old Christian burial ground. The interior of St Peter's is very striking with its blend of medieval and Jacobean and its elaborately-panelled tower, while the Church of St John is almost a replica of St Martin-in-the-Fields in London and houses one of the most famous organs in England. Wolverhampton has some fine Tudor houses which survived a great fire of 1696, but in the 17thC the great ironworks (there had been iron furnaces as early as Roman times), came to dominate the town. Eventually the industries – buckles, jewellery, heavy iron goods and motor-cars – created in Wolverhampton suburbs the Black Country landscape in all its smoky power and ugliness.

PEAK AND PENNINES

Far from the sea and densely forested, this was not one of the first areas to be inhabited. Impenetrable undergrowth deterred early wanderers and, as few of the rivers were navigable, it was impossible to sail in. When settlers finally arrived, it was to hunt for caves and leave possessions for us to fathom 11,000 years later. In their quest for land, subsequent settlers cleared patches of forest for primitive crops. They beat trade routes to north Wales, the Lakes, even Devon and Cornwall, leaving behind a trail of stone circles, cairns, urns and cists.

In the porous limestone country of Peakland, water was often hard to find and communities grew up around wells. Names they gave to their settlements reflected the wooded surroundings, and still today 'birch' and 'ash' crop up frequently. In Norman times the forests were still large enough to hide an outlaw like Robin Hood, or swallow up kings and nobles for a weekend's hunting. Then local lead and iron smelters began to fell them for their foundries. By the 17thC, great forests of the High Peak, Cannock Chase and Sherwood had dwindled to scrubby woodland. Coal mining reprieved them for a while, by offering alternative fuel, but subsequently other demands, such as those of naval ship builders, left the landscape decimated.

Rich resources underground directly affected what happened overground. Deposits of clay found close to timber and coal led to the development of the Potteries, which was further encouraged by the importation of tea in the 17thC, creating a demand for a multitude of articles from which fashionable people might administer the new beverage. Teapots and sugar bowls, tea-caddies, cups and saucers poured out of the Potteries, and as the Industrial Revolution advanced, overworked, underfed pottery producers strove to meet the growing demand for wares.

Lead mining brought prosperity to many towns and villages. Their lavish churches and civic buildings reflect that boom, just as, later, commercial wealth born of the Industrial Revolution was given expression in stately homes and mansions. In the 19thC, expansion of towns overflowed into a battle of architectural styles, in which Gothic fought for ascendancy over Classical. The adherents of the Gothic style sought resurrection of what was seen as the inspired and fervid expression of the medieval age, while those who stuck to the Classical style continued to express the measured reasonableness of the 18thC. Pugin explored his passion for medieval purity in constructing Alton Towers in Staffordshire, while town halls everywhere tended to present a front of classical virtues, befitting the sober task to be performed within.

Coal and iron concentrated industry in these three counties. They became a centre of innovation and invention, developing water and steam power from vast catchments in Derbyshire, and refining industrial techniques in the cauldron of intense competition. England's first successful silk mill was built in Derby, and Hargreaves and Arkwright set up a mill to spin cotton in Nottingham. The resources that brought prosperity to the area brought much ugliness to the landscape, and generated jobs that were often dark, dirty and dangerous: Luddites broke machines to defend their status as artisans and resist factory slavery. But out of these conditions also grew a ripe, cynical humour.

The years of industrial development have contributed, as well, to our cultural inheritance, inspiring some of the greatest works in the English language. Eastwood, a mining town in Nottinghamshire, was the home of D. H. Lawrence, fourth son of a miner. Stoke-on-Trent was the home of Arnold Bennett, whose novels are set in the towns of the Potteries, which he immortalised as the 'Five Towns'.

Today the contrasts between a landscape gobbled up by industry and mining and a landscape protected from their ravages, are vivid, with sometimes no more than a handful of miles separating a curlew's cry and a factory chimney. This is far more than a region of coal-field slagheaps and identical rows of identical houses stained by the grime of the Industrial Revolution, for each of these counties has its own expanse of unspoilt countryside.

In Staffordshire, between the Black Country of the south and the Potteries of the North, is Cannock Chase. An amazingly wild spot for central England, you can get quite lost in the 16 square miles of forest and heather. Towards the east is lush farmland and the best dairy-producing area of the region. The deep, rich soil of south Derbyshire grows wheat and barley for breweries in Staffordshire. The pastoral scenery here provides good walking country, but the favourite among hikers is the rugged beauty of the Peak District to the north, with its rough stone crags and wooded dales. The tough-footed and hardy might like to trudge some way along Britain's first and longest national footpath, for from Edale you can start along the Pennine Way – even if you don't make the 250-mile stretch to the Scottish border.

Neighbouring Nottingham is as proud of her pastureland as she's ashamed of her collieries. Her beauty lies in the green woodlands of Sherwood Forest. Few of the oaks and beeches associated with the merry adventures of Robin Hood remain, but the firs and pines planted by the Forestry Commission provide enough leafy coverage to let your imagination relive the days of the chivalrous hero who robbed from the rich to give to the poor.

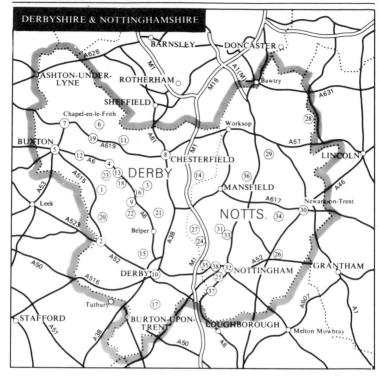

DERBYSHIRE & NOTTINGHAMSHIRE

🏵DERBYSHIRE🏵

1. Arbor Low   6 F3
8m SE of Buxton, off A515. Coach parties
rarely visit this mysterious grassy plateau, so
you can sit on it quietly, pondering what
happened here 4,000 years ago. Although it is
one of the most important henge monuments
in Britain, don't expect another Stonehenge
or Avebury. This circle, 230ft in diameter, is
much smaller, with some 50 stones or
fragments which once formed an outer circle
and an inner horse-shoe. Surrounding the
henge is a bank still more than 6ft high. Views
are headspinning. But they are not necessarily
what the builders of Arbor Low saw, as pollen
analysis shows that this area was probably
thickly forested.
Nearby is **Gib Hill**, an early Bronze Age
barrow where archaeologists found cremated
bones and pottery in stone cists. They believe
that this whole summit was a cultural and
religious centre, and that monuments on Gib
Hill were prototypes of Arbor Low. Many
questions are unanswered. The skeleton of a
man lying flat out and without the usual
grave-goods to ease his passage into the next
world was found at Arbor Low in 1902. It's
possible he was a human sacrifice. 'Low'
crops up in many local names. It comes from
Old English 'hlaw' meaning 'a burial mound'.

2. Ashbourne   6 F4
Attractive market town with a cobbled market
place and fine buildings of the 16th to 20thC.
Wander down Church Street and St John's
Street and note the original grammar school
building of 1585 and the 18thC Mansion
House opposite. Dr Samuel Johnson was a
frequent visitor here. Almshouses from the
17th and 18thC can be seen, plus what is left
of Ashbourne Hall (now the library and
offices), where Bonnie Prince Charlie slept on
his advance to and retreat from Derby.
Called the 'Cathedral of the Peak', the
Church of St Oswald with its 212ft spire is,

George Eliot claimed, 'the finest mere parish
church in the kingdom'. Unusually decorated
wrought-iron gates lead to the church where
you can spend an interesting time examining
the many monuments. The most famous is the
18thC white marble sculpture of five-year-old
Penelope Boothby. A child genius, it is
claimed that she could speak four languages
and died from the strain her ambitious parents
put upon her.

3. Ashover   6 G3
4m NE of Matlock, off A632. Unspoilt valley
village whose church with its 128ft spire is a
landmark for miles around. Inside is one of
the few remaining Norman lead fonts in
England and some lovely carved memorial
tablets. Note the closeness of the church and
the inn. Organists have been known to nip out
for a jar during the sermon. If you need an
excuse there are two interesting inscriptions
on the walls of nearby Crispin Inn. Ashover
means 'ash tree slope' and part of it is now a
conservation area.

4. Bakewell   6 F3
Famed for puds (not tarts, please) and spa
waters, this Anglo-Saxon settlement is
well-mannered and sprightly enough to
warrant a longish visit.
The bath house is 17thC, but no good for
chalybeate dips – the water was found to be
too cold. Fragments of Anglo-Saxon work in
the fabric of the Church of All Saints suggests
that it was originally 10thC. There are some
splendid alabaster tombs and in the
churchyard stands a 9thC sculptured cross.
Jane Austen stayed at the Rutland Arms
Hotel, *town centre*, while writing 'Pride and
Prejudice'. You can still see her room and it is
believed that the town of Lambton in the
novel is, in fact, Bakewell. The first tart, sorry,
pud, was made accidentally by a cook at this
hotel, who put jam at the bottom of a pud

mixture and filling at the top instead of the other way round. Guests gobbled it enthusiastically and it became such a regular feature of the menu that the cook bequeathed the recipe to a friend of the family which still use it. Ingredients are no secret. But the actual mixture is.

Visit the **Old House Museum**, *off Church Lane*. Local enthusiasts have unearthed a lot of fascinating new information about this 16thC house which was occupied in turn as a parsonage, 18thC 'flats' and a private house. The last tenant left in 1967, four centuries after the first one moved in. Work is well on the way to restoring it to its original 16thC condition as a typical yeoman's house and there are exhibitions of costumes, local bygones and kitchen and household utensils. *Open summer.*

4. Bakewell, Chatsworth House　6 F2
Half a million visitors assail this peakland palace every year to savour its classical grandeur and root round priceless art treasures within it. Described as 'a town' by the lady who lives there – the Duchess of Devonshire – Chatsworth employs a labour force of anything from mole-catchers to masons.

A Tudor house once stood on the site of the present one built between 1687 and 1707 by the 4th Earl of Devonshire. Devonshire was originally meant to be Derbyshire, but a 17thC secretary seems to have mis-read his shorthand. Chatsworth is very 'Derbyshire'. Its materials are local: gritstone from nearby quarries, grey marble from Calver and Blackstone from Sheldon Moor. The magnificent state rooms contain wood carvings by Samuel Watson, painted ceilings by Verrio and Laguerre, paintings by Rembrandt and Reynolds and a fine collection of books and furniture.

Many people like the park and gardens best – and with good reason. They're so huge there are milestones. See the orangery, rose garden with its busts, Dolphin House, grand cascade (a staircase with water running down), fountains, waterfalls and rocks. The arboretum includes trees from all over the world, and in 1830 a full-grown weeping ash was brought from Derby which was so unwieldy the turnpike gates were demolished to get it through. The Emperor Fountain, built for Tsar Nicholas I's visit, can throw a water jet 296ft high. *Open most days, summer.*

Chatsworth House

5. Buxton　6 E2
Heady yet sedentary, Buxton is a graceful, elegant town which has drawn health seekers rich and poor to take the waters, for four centuries. As a prisoner, Mary, Queen of Scots, who was being treated for rheumatism, even scratched a poignant ditty on a local window (since removed) with her ring:
'Buxton, whose fame thy milkwarm waters tell, Whom I perhaps shall see no more, farewell.'
The 5th Duke of Devonshire's 18thC development of the Crescent (modelled on Bath) really set Buxton on the map. It's been called one of the finest buildings in England, and contained three hotels all with rooms having private access to adjoining baths, assembly rooms, and shops. Getting to Buxton was awkward until the arrival of the railways. Then tourists swarmed in. Today, Buxton's baths are closed, but you can swim in the healing waters in the new swimming pool and drink them from a public well in the Crescent.

6. Castleton　6 E2
Magnificently-sited village of huddled stone cottages, renowned for its natural beauty spots. The settlement grew up round **Peveril Castle**, now a well-restored ruin glowering over Castleton. William the Conqueror built the castle unassailable on three sides, to control the wild High Peak, and its officers guarded the royal forest, too. Henry II added the 60ft-high keep, but from the 14thC onwards Peveril slumped. Look for the Norman herring-bone masonry on its curtain wall. Used as a gaol, Peveril fell empty and by the 17thC cottagers in Castleton were snaffling stone from it to build their homes. The area of Castleton contains four spectacular caverns which draw countless visitors every year. Nearest the village is the largest, **Peak Cavern**. The entrance lies deep in a recess between two great limestone cliffs with the River Styx spurting between. Victorians of the sort who clothed piano legs in knickerbockers to prevent indecency just couldn't stand the original name for this awesome cavern. So they dropped Devil's Hole in favour of Peak Cavern. Victorian visitors who swarmed through its 42ft-high, 120ft-wide entrance could ask the local church choir to sing from a ledge in the great hall and show off the cave's acoustics. Modern symphony orchestras have since taken up the idea elsewhere. *Open summer.*

Speedwell Cavern, *off A625*, is part artificial, part natural. Lead miners blasted a passage through 2,000ft of solid rock and used its subterranean waterways to transport waste rock and ore in the 18thC. This 'bottomless pit' described by one Victorian guide book as 'so huge as to make roof and bottom invisible to the eye' is reached by a half mile boat trip along dark underground canals. Unlike them, today's visitors don't have to push their boat using pegs driven into the walls at 6ft intervals. They descend 104 concrete steps, climb aboard, and arrive at a platform looking down on a black lake which is really only 35ft deep, but appears more.

The **Blue John Cavern**, *Treak Cliff*, is named after the beautiful amethyst-like, semi-precious stone found nowhere else in the world. Ornaments and jewellery made from Blue John were popular in the 18thC and 19thC and several local manor houses have fireplaces inlaid with it. At Chatsworth, nearby, is a huge Blue John vase shot with a variety of magical colours. Blue John is basically fluorspar, a common enough rock, but Castleton is the only place where it occurs in such a spectrum of colours ranging from purples and blues to creams and greys. Romans are believed to have worked Blue John in this area and vases made from the stone were found at Pompeii. The hill originally had 14 Blue John veins, and all are nearly exhausted. But local shops still sell superb collections of jewellery made from it. The only place where all 14 combinations of colour can be seen is at Vernon Park Museum, Stockport where 150 pieces of polished spar are displayed in a 7ft by 3ft window.

Treak Cavern, also rich in Blue John, glistens with fine-as-straws stalactites in eerie colours. Remembering that this area is composed of crushed animals and plants from a shallow sea that once covered it 280 million years ago, it's not surprising to find lots of fossils here too. Over 70 different species of brachiopod (shellfish) have been identified at Treak Cliff alone.

6. Castleton, Mam Tor　6 E2
1m NW of town, A625. This 'shivering mountain' is so-called because the shale on its eastern side is continually slithering away – and taking chunks of road with it. Centuries

ago it was regarded as one of the Seven Wonders of the Peak because it never seemed to get any smaller despite constantly wasting away. 'Mam' meant 'breast' in Irish and 'mother' in Welsh.

On Mam Tor summit is the most impressive Iron Age hill fort in the southern Pennines – and probably the most rewarding to visit because of superb views from its 1,696ft over the Hope and Edale valleys. Archaeologists think that a large community once lived on Mam Tor and grazed surrounding hillsides. Pottery found there has been dated cAD50. Lead mining relics pock the limestone uplands of the Peak – often dangerously. At the foot of Mam Tor are a crushing wheel and its circular iron track, remains of Odin Mine. Mine buildings and mine shafts – 70,000 of them – are uncovered or only partly protected. Lead mining vocabulary explains some of the odd place-names in this area: rake (a vein of minerals), scrin (a mini rake), flats (horizontal deposits), pipes (long, thin veins) and T'Owd Man. He is confusing because he can mean the mine itself (rather like Ole Man River), the ore, the hummock of waste, or even the spirit of long dead miners. Notice the name on many Peak pubs.

7. Chapel-en-le-Frith   6 E2
Foresters built a chapel here in 1225 which was replaced by a church in the 14thC. Hence the name: chapel in the forest (frith – forest). Today's remains are from the 14thC, but with 18thC alterations and box pews from the early 19thC. The little town retains its old stocks and a 17thC market cross.

8. Chesterfield   6 G3
A twisted church spire – 228ft high and made of lead-covered wood which has warped through the centuries – gives character to this rather dull town. The oldest inn is the Royal Oak, a timber-framed Tudor building. Revolution House is where conspirators met in 1688 to plot the overthrow of James II in favour of William of Orange. It was then the Cock and Pynot (magpie) Inn and is now a museum. *Open summer.*

9. Cromford   6 F3
One man's brainwave launched an industrial revolution in this quiet nook of the Derwent valley which triggered a movement that swept the country. Richard Arkwright found a way of using water instead of horses to power machines in his cotton mills, and established the first mechanised textile factory in the world here in 1771. He built it beside Bonsall Brook where water gushes especially fast through a narrow gorge. Part of that mill is still standing and used as a laundry. Arkwright found water so successful that within 10 years he had built mills all over the area, ending with Masson Mill where he tamed the rapid River Derwent. Though rebuilt and extended, it still dominates the river and is a landmark for travellers approaching nearby Matlock Bath along the A6. Upstream is the weir he designed. It still carries water to turbines which replaced the mill wheels in 1920.

But Arkwright was more than a businessman. He built an industrial community for his workers, and his houses and school are still standing beside the Wirksworth road.

Arkwright's Mill, Cromford

Arkwright lived in Willersley Castle and also built the church in which he is buried. Cromford today is much the same as he left it. See the 15thC bridge-chapel – one of six surviving in England – and an 18thC fishing house with a pyramid roof.

10. Derby   6 F4
Fought over by Romans, Saxons and Danes, by the 12thC Derby was already a busy trading centre with a population of over 2,000. But after this impressive start, it grew little over the next 600 years.

Crippled by plague during the 16th and 17thC, this now bustling town recovered during the Industrial Revolution and started making silk, stockings, porcelain and china. Railways turned it into an engineering centre. Wrought-iron work is remarkable here – the old silk mill gates by Robert Bakewell are a masterpiece.

Rooms in the museum and art gallery remember Bonnie Prince Charlie's arrival at Derby in 1745, and there's a working railway model and a collection of Derby porcelain. The cathedral has a splendid 178ft-high pinnacled tower, built during the reign of Henry VIII, which contains a remarkable wrought-iron screen by Bakewell.

Drystone Walls
You can't miss them – they're everywhere: coiling over moors, disappearing over horizons, fluffed here and there with snags of wool, tumbled by arrogant walkers. Rugged and fascinating, these walls date mostly from the enclosures around 1760 to 1830. Some are much older – 13th and 14thC. They do three things: use up stones and rocks strewn naturally over the land, divide one man's land from another's and separate field from field.

11. Eyam   6 F2
Heroism is part of village history here. In 1665 the local tailor received some cloth from London. With it came the plague. It spread rapidly and many terrified villagers prepared to leave. But the rector, Mompesson, persuaded them to stay rather than take the virus to other districts. Within a year 259 of Eyam's 350 inhabitants were dead. Each year on the last Sunday in August a memorial service is held with a procession to Cucklet Dell where the villagers worshipped during the plague. A row of six 17thC plague cottages can still be seen.

Mompesson's Well, ¾m E of village, is where neighbouring villages left supplies. The plague-ridden inhabitants washed the coins they left in payment in vinegar and water which they believed to act as a disinfectant. Eyam's 7thC preaching cross, found on a nearby hillside, is one of the most famous in Peakland. Unusual in that it retains its cross-head, it has vine scroll designs from Northumbria.

12. Five Wells   6 E2
5m E of Buxton, 1m W of Taddington, off A6. Labourers and clumsy archaeologists smashed up much of this remarkable neolithic tomb standing at a height of 1,400ft – but its features are still fairly clear. Two stone chambers inside a giant bell-shaped mound (70ft diameter) were approached along passages lined by upright stones. Many bones were found in the vaults, but most of its stones, including the capstones, were taken 100 years ago by workmen building field walls nearby.

13. Haddon Hall   6 F3
2m SE of Bakewell, A6. 'A good old house' is how one lady traveller described this fine medieval mansion in the 17thC. Others were more imaginative – the redoubtable Pevsner captured it perfectly: 'A large, safe, grey, lovable house of knights and their ladies.' Beautifully set in a vale by the River Wye, Haddon is exceptionally well-preserved and

dates in parts (Peverel Tower and chapel) from the 12thC. It was built by William Peverel, a bastard son of William the Conqueror, and eventually acquired by Richard Vernon whose family then held the house for four centuries. Richard Vernon built a 12ft wall round the house in 1195 which is still standing, but the battlements are 14thC additions.

The Great Hall, long gallery and Dorothy Vernon's Steps are full of atmosphere. Note the panelling and ceiling in the dining room and the tapestries on the staircase landing. A series of grey stone terraces forms the backbone of the garden which contains an abundance of flowers including the enchanting roses for which Haddon Hall is justly famous. *Open most days, summer.*

14. Hardwick Hall 6 G3

6m SE of Chesterfield, off M1. Elizabethan property developer, Bess of Hardwick, built this magnificent house between 1591 and 1594 – at record speed considering its size. By 1597 it was decorated, furnished and ready to live in. Much-married Bess did most things at top speed. Intolerable but irresistible, Bess was one of the most powerful personalities of Elizabeth I's reign. She married a Peakland lad-next-door when she was 12 and was widowed within months. Three husbands later – each wealthier than the last – she died at a great age, immensely rich and, it's said, without a friend.

Hardwick Hall has four great towers at each corner and huge windows that increase in size the higher they are. Parapets displaying her initials ES (Elizabeth Shrewsbury) stand out against the sky. Fine furniture, needlework, tapestries, portraits, huge chimney-pieces and a rambling staircase can all be seen indoors. Gardens are extensive. The ruins of Bess's birthplace (the Old Hall) stand beside the new house she built for herself. *Open most days, summer; gardens daily, all year.*

15. Kedleston Hall 6 F4

4m NW of Derby, off A6. Curzons have lived here for 800 years, but this glamorous house is 18thC and designed by the most fashionable architect of the day, James Paine. 'Kedleston' comes from 'ketill' meaning 'a round pot' which was an ancient nickname for a man with a round head who presumably had some connection with this spot.

Robert Adam worked amiably with Paine for several years here, bequeathing huge classical flourishes like the unique marble hall with pink columns, statues and scenes from Homer round the walls – one of the most magnificent rooms in Europe. The dining room, music room, library and drawing room are also Adam's work. Look out for a gilded mirror of palm design and a gilded sofa with the torso of a naked man growing out of one of its legs. Paintings include works by Reynolds, Van Dyck and Veronese and the Indian Museum has ivories, poisoned arrows, ancient weapons and works of art collected by Lord Curzon when he was Viceroy of India. *Open certain days, summer.*

16. Matlock 6 F3

Thermal springs brought fame to this dramatic town lying deep in a gorge of the Derwent during the 17thC and, bar a hiccough or two, it has never looked back. Architecturally, you can trace its 18th and 19thC growth in hotel and assembly rooms where young, pining Byron endured gnawing jealousy watching Mary Chaworth dance with other men. Railways turned Matlock into a resort with day-trippers from Derby and Nottingham. You can see petrified wells here and old lead mines, and the enormous, indigestible block of John Smedley's Victorian health hydro – now county council offices. To the south of Matlock is the **Cromford Canal**. Overgrown basins and wharfs show

Kedleston Hall

how important this 'water road' once was to the mills and quarries of this area. It runs 15 miles south from Cromford to link up with the Erewash canal at Langley Bridge. Cromford Canal Society has restored the engine in Leawood pumphouse which is itself a handsome gritstone building with a tall chimney. Fine scenery along much of this canal.

17. Melbourne Hall 6 G5

8m S of Derby, off A514. A fragile tracery of beautiful wrought iron is the showpiece at this 18thC home of Lord Melbourne, the statesman. Worked by a local craftsman, Robert Bakewell, the exquisite birdcage pergola stands at the far end of a pond in the gardens. Little is known about Bakewell except that he remained very poor and was certainly underrated. Other examples of his work are at Derby Cathedral, Okeover Hall (Derbyshire) and in Oxford.

Homely Melbourne Hall's charming rooms contain an important collection of portraits and furniture. But people come to see the gardens as much as the house, which were laid out in Versailles style by a royal gardener with long avenues, yew tunnels, fountains and a shell grotto. *Open most days, summer.*

18. Nine Ladies 6 F3

Stanton Moor, Stanton, 4m SE of Bakewell. A Lilliputian Stonehenge, this lonely circle (99ft diameter) stands only 3ft high and has a small cairn in its centre. Stanton Moor is covered with barrows and cairns which contained bones, charcoal, stone hammers, jet objects and a small red star-shaped bead of porcelain that originated in Egypt c1400BC.

Near the Nine Ladies is a prehistoric field. Bones found there show that its people were slender, squatted a lot, and suffered from rheumatism. Women not only outnumbered men, but also had the best tools. Nearby is a single standing stone called The King's Stone.

19. Snake Inn 6 E1

8m ESE of Glossop, A57. A turnpike inn built by the 6th Duke of Devonshire rather along the lines of a 19thC motorway service. It catered for travellers riding and walking along the newly-built Manchester–Sheffield route which replaced the old, windy one through Whaley Bridge, Chapel-en-le-Frith, Sparrowpit and Hathersage. It continues to provide good facilities for hikers and drivers today.

The Snake road and inn is named after the snake on the Cavendish armourial bearings, not the road's sinuous coiling. The Snake was the last important turnpike road built in the Peak. Give or take a by-pass or two, today's road system here looks much as it did then.

20. Tissington 6 F3

Picture-book village clustered round a hall, church, mere and greens with not a leaf out of place – except during the well-dressing season when visitors squeeze in for a view of this ancient folk-art which belongs almost exclusively to Derbyshire. Villagers 'dress' the wells in spring with elaborate designs worked in flower petals. People think the custom may have started in 1348 when the water's purity is said to have given the village immunity from the Black Death, but it is more likely an older pagan ritual.

Walkers wanting a break from high moorland rigours can amble the Tissington Trail. This grassy track is the old, now rail-less line from Buxton to Ashbourne and it has splendid high scenery.

21. Tramway Museum 6 G3
Matlock Rd, Crich, off B5035. Ride on tram cars from places as remote as Sheffield and Johannesburg, Glasgow and Vienna at this Edwardian-decorated museum set in the countryside that first thought of trams – though not the city sort. Trams grew out of 'tram roads' that linked quarries and mills with canals. Four miles away at Matlock was the steepest passenger-carrying tramway in the world – up a 1 in 5½ gradient. Its gritstone house and tram shed still stand on top of the hill. *Open most days, summer.*

22. Wirksworth 6 F3
Ancient lead mining centre which may have been the 'Lutudarum' that Romans stamped on each pig of lead they mined. People ordered Wirksworth lead from far and wide – Canterbury, for instance, sought lead for its cathedral roof. Inside the Moot Hall, built in 1814, is an oblong brass dish holding 14 pints;

this was a standard measure for lead ore. A stone slab in the wall of the north aisle at Wirksworth church is 7thC and covered the tomb of a Celtic missionary. Experts agree that the swirly carvings have strong Eastern links.

23. Youlgreave, Church of All Saints 6 F3
3m S of Bakewell, off A6. Edward Burne-Jones designed stained glass for this church built during a lead mining boom. There are several monuments and alabaster effigies worth seeing. Youlgreave means 'yellow grove'.

All Saints Church, Youlgreave

NOTTINGHAMSHIRE

24. Beauvale Priory 6 G4
7m NNW of Nottingham, off M1. Stone remains of the prior's lodging and church wall take on an extra dimension with the story of two men who stayed here during Henry VIII's reign. Both priors, they refused to accept Henry as supreme head of the church and tried to explain their reasons to Thomas Cromwell. He refused to see them, and gaoled them in the Tower, hoping to break their spirit. He failed, and ordered a trial. The jury found them innocent – until Cromwell intimidated them enough to get the verdict switched. A week later the priors were brutally tortured and executed, having refused a conditional pardon. Sir Thomas More watching them leave the Tower said: 'They went as cheerfully to their deaths as bridegrooms to their marriage.'
Beauvale (meaning 'beautiful valley') was founded in 1343 as a stern Carthusian order. It became a prosperous monastic centre – the monks even mined coal – and you can still see the handsome fireplace on the first floor, and the spiral staircase.

25. Beeston 6 H4
Hardly a tourist honey-pot of sweet buildings and history, but with enough industrial archaeology to occupy an enthusiast's afternoon. Villa Street has one of the oldest surviving lace factories – a four-storey building in which machines rolled 20 hours a day. Workers trained to handle small, metal parts for hosiery and lace making easily adapted themselves to the similar skills of bicycle building. And part of Humber's original factory with the adjoining company houses where the workers lived, remains at the junction of Queen's Road and Humber Road. Nottingham bicycles first appeared in the 1860s and by 1880 over 1,000 people in Beeston were making them.
Jesse Boot opened his first shop in Nottingham in 1877 and won success by popularising medicines and packaging attractively. Boots giant chemical and pharmaceutical works came to Beeston in the 1930s and now employs over 5,000 people here. Each year 15,000 visitors trundle round the 300 acres of factory to see the 'wets' (liquids, pastes, creams) and 'drys' (powders, tablets, lozenges).

26. Car Colston 6 H4
10m ENE of Nottingham, off A46. Reckoned by some to be the shire's prettiest village, Car Colston guards its seclusion with gates at either end of lanes leading to it. Cottages, pub and stocks cluster round the biggest village green in the county. Parts of the church belong to the 13th and 14thC. A poor-box there is 400 years old but the oldest relic is the Norman font.

27. Eastwood 6 G4
At the top of the list for lovers of D. H. Lawrence, Eastwood, lying in the heart of the colliery area, still retains its quiet, rural air. Townspeople here often dismiss Lawrence as 'that mucky man' – as much because of his love–hate descriptions of Eastwood in his novels as the embarrassment of 'Lady Chatterley'. A reluctant plaque marks his birthplace, *8a Victoria Street*, and if you stand outside it and look downhill you can see why Lawrence called this 'the country of my heart'. Wander on to the third house in Walker Street where he lived from 1881 to 1902 and look across to Crich on the left and Underwood in front, and you'll see the view Lawrence lived with from the age of six to 18. The corner house in Garden Road (formerly The Breach in 'Sons and Lovers') was bought in 1969 by the Association of Young Writers to save it from demolition. Funds from American fans and the British Lawrence Society have recently restored the house and it is now a museum. The Lawrences' last home was 97 Lynn Croft Road – a semi they moved to in 1902.
Despite recent activity to 'promote' Eastwood as a place of literary pilgrimage, a feeling of 'he were nowt but a big soft gel' lingers locally. Maybe Lawrence described Eastwood's ugliness too accurately.

Fosse Way 6 H4
Leicester to Lincoln, A46. Straightest road in England cleaving across the south east wolds of Nottinghamshire on its way to Lincoln, it marked the effective northern limit of Roman conquest. A chain of forts ran along it and four have been identified.
Archaeologists have studied **Margidunum**, *nr East Bridgford*, carefully and found that it covered seven or eight acres – large enough to

garrison 1,000 men and some cavalry. They unearthed Roman coins from AD100 to AD400, a little sepulchral stone carved with two figures, great jars and cooking pots, vessels moulded with human faces, fragments of glass, ladles, bucket handles, bone and bronze pins and horse trappings. Although Margidunum was a Roman camp, it was inhabited prehistorically, too, and some of the finds date from then. It was probably sacked and burnt in AD61 by the Coritani, Celtic people who lived in Nottinghamshire. By the end of the first century it was de-militarised and became a village settlement along the great road. Nottingham University holds the remains discovered on this site.

28. Littleborough 6 J2
Romans settled here and spoke dramatically down the centuries one day in 1860 when a sexton digging a grave in the Norman churchyard found a stone coffin. Raising the lid he saw the perfect body of a young woman, her garment fastened by a Roman brooch. The spectacle of a moment, she immediately crumbled to dust.
Altars, urns, pottery and coins have been found on the church site of this tiny village which was once called Segelocum. A Roman link road, now called Till Bridge Lane, crossed the River Trent by a stone-paved ford discovered in 1933 when severe drought lowered the water level. Built in Hadrian's time, it is said to be the oldest in England. Harold and his Saxons crossed here on their way to Hastings. The aisleless church itself is one of the smallest in Nottinghamshire. See the herring-bone masonry of the walls and the Roman tiles built into them.

29. Lound Hall Mining Museum 6 H2
Bothamsall, 5¹/₂m S of East Retford, B6387.
Nearby Bevercotes colliery was the world's first push-button pit. Ultra-modern, its training centre at Lound Hall houses a mining museum officially opened in 1972. Among its interesting exhibits is the pitch pine tandem headgear from Brinsley which featured in the film of 'Sons and Lovers'. Other exhibits include locomotives, coal face machinery, hand tools and electrical equipment. *Open certain weekends, or by arrangement.*

30. Newark-on-Trent 6 J3
Voted one of the best 50 towns in the country by the Council for British Archaeology, Newark is only just beginning to think of itself as a tourist lure. Until recently, it seemed to take its medieval self for granted. But a scheme to conserve and restore the town's many beautiful buildings is well on the way to completion.
See in particular the attractive, half-timbered late 16thC Governor's House, the 18thC town hall and the former White Hart Inn that stands in the fine market place. Twenty four painted figures peer out from canopies on this 15thC building which has a pantiled roof. Experts agree it's one of the finest inn fronts in England. The handsome Saracen's Head, a former coaching inn, and the Clinton Arms were both once frequented by Walter Scott and Gladstone. Jovial Victoriana beams over the rooftops in the Ossington Coffee House, built by Lady Ossington to promote temperance. Kirkgate has good Tudor buildings, too.
One of the finest churches in the county, St Mary Magdalene's, *nr market place*, has a remarkably tall spire – 30ft greater than the length of the ground-plan. Take some time to look at the walls – they're knobbly with sculpture: gargoyles, foliage, figures and shields. Humour coils round philosophy in this medieval medley – owls carry off rats, lions and lizards scramble over the stalls, two men in a boat are pushed off by a third, two men quarrel and pull each other's hair. A colossal Flemish brass shows Alan Fleming

who founded a chantry here in 1349. A sort of pay-and-pray service where a priest prayed daily for his household, was established – which presumably saved Alan from having to bother himself. Note, too, the rood screen and choir stalls of c1500 and the tremendous east window in the chancel.

30. Newark Castle 6 J3
Elizabeth I, sad Cardinal Wolsey, wretched King John – they all came to Newark castle, and some of the views they saw from it are still the same today. Although ruined in the Civil War for its steadfast Royalist support, Newark's walls and towers remain. The huge, elaborate north gateway and its chapel date from the 12thC. A fine, vaulted crypt contains a collection of ancient stones carved with zigzag and key patterns which once adorned the castle walls. They were rescued from the canal. You can see a passage where the sentry kept watch on the Great North Road, and a groove for the portcullis. Down below is a dungeon, beehive-shaped and shivery. Newark withstood three sieges during the Civil War and south of the town are the Scone Hills – surviving fortifications of the Royalists and one of the most perfect examples of military engineering of that time. *Castle closed for repairs; gardens open daily, all year.*

Newark Castle

31. Newstead Abbey 6 H3
8m N of Nottingham, off A60. Lord Byron dragged his lame foot round the crumbling estate he inherited from his wild old uncle and wondered how he could sell enough poems to pay for it. With oddly modern turn of phrase, he admitted considering 'marrying a golden dolly or blowing my brains out'. Though he spent little time there, Newstead Abbey is full of Byron – and his belligerent ancestors. Henry II founded it in 1170 as a priory to atone for the murder of Thomas à Becket. After the Dissolution, Henry VIII handed it over to Sir John Byron, known as 'little Sir John of the great beard'. Newstead stayed in the family until the poet sold it to a schoolfriend in 1817 to pay his debts. Three owners later it was acquired by the city council.
Byron lived passionately at Newstead. Boozy bachelor parties and a violent love affair, a disastrous marriage and the death of his beloved dog Boatswain compounded his feeling for the place. Today you can see his bedroom and personal belongings, Boatswain's huge brass collar, letters, miniatures, locks of hair and the helmet he designed for the Greek campaign against the Turks in which he died. The house was reconstructed in the 19thC but you can still see the great drawing room where monks once munched, the cloisters and chapter house, and there's a crypt with memorials to Byron antecedents. Locals will tell you of the black friar who haunts the building.
The gardens include waterfalls, a Japanese water-garden and a teahouse, Monk's Stew Pond, and rare shrubs and trees. Boatswain's memorial must be one of the most beautiful epitaphs a dog ever had: '. . . one who possessed beauty without vanity, strength without insolence, courage without ferocity, and all the virtues of man without his vices'. *House open summer; gardens daily, all year.*

32. Nottingham 6 H4
A vast old market place – six acres of it – marks the heart of ancient and modern

Nottingham which has triumphed over the centuries to become 'Queen of the Midlands'. First settlers there were the Snotingas, followers of Snot, an Anglian leader, and they established themselves on the sandstone hill behind the modern council house around AD500. Hence, Snotingham. The city's colourful market moved to Huntingdon Street in 1928 and a year later the great domed council house opened – to a mixed reception – with its great clock with booming bell called Little John.

Prosperous Nottingham is very much a product of the Industrial Revolution. Lace made Nottingham in the 19thC and it soon became a boom industry rivalling Guipure and Torchon. Traditional hosiery and knitting know-how gave it a start. Then a Nottingham businessman patented his bobbin-net machine and the plain net it wove was instantly successful. Other machines refined techniques to pattern the mesh, and immigrants swarmed into Nottingham – mostly German Jews – prising European markets away from the French lace monopoly. Today the working conditions in Nottingham factories are not bettered anywhere in the country – a sharp contrast to the early days when cotton workers had a life expectancy of 20 years.

The Lace Market was never a market with stalls and jostling customers, but a commercial enclave in the heart of the city where many Victorian lace manufacturers built their offices and warehouses. Walk round during the weekend when it's quiet. Notice the continuous row of windows on top floors which gave maximum light for mending and finishing.

Beer drinkers world-wide know the famous pubs of Nottingham. Cuddling into the castle rock Ye Olde Trip to Jerusalem Inne calls itself the oldest in England. It was built in 1189 and has a floor so porous that spilled beer dries before the barman can mop it up. 'Tryppe' is Old English for 'halt', and this was the stopping place of Crusaders from the Holy Land. Earthy-smelling and well worth a visit, it has rooms and cellars cut back deep into the castle rock.

Tales of Dick Turpin, 13thC oak beams and rock cellars believed to have been part of a Saxon cave dwelling are just some of the lures of The Salutation Inn, *Houndsgate*. This genuine medieval pub has a 70ft well sunk in solid rock.

Nottingham Brewhouse Yard Museum, *Castle Boulevard*, is spread throughout ramshackle houses, inns, brothels and caves which once seethed with vagabonds, cutpurses and whores. Later it held the water-mills, dovecote, maltings and brewhouse for Nottingham castle. Today it tells a tale of ordinary Nottingham folk in five brick town houses built around 1670. Rooms, shops, and models give glimpses of the city's past. Rock-cut caves used for storage, cooking and air-raid shelters are part of the project. Historic, local plants are preserved in the grounds – Nottingham and Trent Crocus, Broadmarsh, and Nottingham Catchfly.

An elegant row of Georgian terraced houses contains the **Museum of Costume and Textiles**, *Castlegate*, with the history of lace – and 200 years of underwear.

32. Nottingham Castle   6 H4

City centre. Local people carted away Nottingham's medieval castle by the barrowful after its demolition in the Civil War. That's why the present 'castle' is hardly the sort Robin Hood might have leapt death-defyingly from in the gutsy 12thC. William Cavendish bought the site in 1674, but died when the walls were only a yard high. His son completed it four years later and fortunately never saw it gutted by fire during a Reform Bill riot in the 1830s.

Caves honeycomb the castle's underparts and the best known is Mortimer's Hole, through which murdering conspirators crept towards their aristocratic prey. Wine cellars and dungeons are part of the subterranean guided tour.

The Corporation rescued the castle from dereliction in 1875 and opened it with much pomp and circumstance as the first municipal museum outside London. Exhibits span Bronze Age dug-out canoes found nearby, to Picasso paintings; 18thC English glassware to souvenirs of a World War Two flying ace. Note the lovely alabaster statuette, Virgin and Child. Buried to escape destruction at the Dissolution, it was unearthed in the 18thC.

33. Papplewick   6 H3

7m N of Nottingham, B6011. At the end of a twisty lane in Sherwood Forest is the intriguing Church of St James. It has a squire's pew with a fireplace near it. Squire Walker, one-time proprietor of 'The Times' who lived at neighbouring Papplewick Hall, used to poke the fire noisily when he'd had enough of the sermon. Coffin slabs here dating from the 13thC show the occupations of the men beneath them: bow and arrow of a forester, knife of a woodward and bellows of an iron-worker from the forest smithy. The figures of Faith and Hope in the east window are copied from Sir Joshua Reynold's picture in New College Chapel, Oxford. An old yew in the churchyard has a trunk circumference of 14ft, with a seat round it.

On the outskirts of Papplewick is a cave known as Robin Hood's Stable where he's supposed to have kept his horses. Papplewick Pumping Station is a fine, landscaped example of a late Victorian waterworks with two beam engines by James Watt and Co, a working forge and other exhibits.

Sherwood Forest   6 H4

Believing in Robin Hood definitely adds zest to any trips round his county. In popular imagination, he and his merry green men represented democracy against tyranny, the struggle of poor people against vicious forest laws and national pride in England's bowmen. Fleecing unworthy rich to give to the worthy poor is how Robin spent his outlaw days, and as you wander round the ancient woodland remains of that once-mighty forest, it's easy to imagine a chivalrous ambush.

Although Sherwood Forest once covered some 200 sq miles stretching from Nottingham to Worksop, only patches survive, mainly round the Dukeries of Clumber, Welbeck and Thoresby. Just past Edwinstowe you enter Sherwood Country Park where there's a forest information centre. This area is called Birklands and is famous for old oaks and birches. Major Oak here is 1,000 years old, hollow, 30ft in girth and is said to have been Robin's hideout. Many people believe that Robin was the rightful Earl of Huntingdon born about 1160 at Locksley. Man or myth, he's leapt from bough to bough through woods and literature for 700 years. And, hopefully, many more.

34. Southwell   6 H3

Byron had girlfriends here and belonged to the local amateur dramatic society. He drank at the still-welcoming Saracen's Head and even wrote a ditty for one of its customers who died of over-indulgence. It was here, too, that Charles I gave himself up to the Scots in 1646.

Apart from Byron, Southwell (pronounced 'Southwell' by locals and 'South'll' by 'furreners'), boasts one of the most beautiful churches in England. James I is said to have exclaimed: 'By my blude, this kirk shall jostle with York or Durham or any other kirk in Christendom'. The present building was begun in 1108 and the choir was rebuilt in

Southwell Minster

1234. It was a collegiate church under York and since 1884 has been a cathedral in its own right.

People come here to see the remarkable carvings. The pulpitum or screen of 1330 is the work of men trying to describe ordinary life: there's a master mason, a man with toothache, another pulling at his beard and one scratching his leg. The chapter house contains the finest examples of 13thC stone carvings in Britain. A triumph of detail and delicacy, figures and foliage cluster all over it and no two leaves are alike. Bold and glowing stained glass in the chapter house is 13th, 14th and 15thC. The east window in the choir contains Flemish glass from a church destroyed in Paris during the French Revolution. It came to Southwell in 1818 via a pawn shop. Sit quietly on a bench in the south transept, lift a trap door, and you'll find a tessellated Roman pavement 1,700 years old – it was the floor of the Saxon church that preceded the present one.

35. Stapleford 6 G4

Greatest historic treasure of this stockings-and-pencils town is its fine, famous Saxon cross now standing in the churchyard. It was here 1,000 years ago when Saxons worshipped in a little church of timber and wattle. The top and base were renewed in 1820, but the 10ft-tall shaft is covered with complex carving and on one side shows what is believed to be the symbol of St Luke – a horned figure with wings treading on a serpent.

Stapleford also has an odd natural phenomenon called The Hemlock Stone – a 70ft-high and 30ft-round mass of red sandstone rearing from a green mound, capped by a layer of granite. It is remarkably unweathered and can be seen best from Coventry Lane. A row of stockingers' cottages still fronts the old Derby–Nottingham road showing their long line of top floor windows designed to give maximum light to the homeworkers at their framework knitting machines.

36. Thoresby Hall 6 H3

7m SSE of Worksop, off A616. Largest Victorian house in England, this neo-Tudor exuberance has housed at least two rather striking women. Lady Mary Wortley Montagu, traveller, blue stocking, and pioneer of smallpox innoculation, lived there during the 1800s. Later that century, socialite and wit Elizabeth Chudleigh moved in. She married several men and was eventually charged with bigamy. Before dying, she's said to have downed two glasses of Madeira to ease her passage heavenwards.

However, both ladies lived in the old Thoresby. The present house dates from 1864 and has some splendid features: Great Hall with lavish hammer-beam roof, blue drawing room, state apartments and a clock collection. No-one seems to know exactly how many rooms there are, but it's around 200. Standing in 12,000 acres of parkland, there's much to explore: river-side walks, adventure woodland, avenues of chestnut trees and ornamental waters. *Open certain days, summer.*

37. Thrumpton Hall 6 H5

7m S of Nottingham, off A648. Hiding a wanted man cost the Putrell family their home. They'd lived at Thrumpton for 600 years. But they were Catholic, and concealed one of the Gunpowder Plot conspirators in a priest's hole built at the foot of a secret staircase behind a chimney-breast. You can still see it today.

Thrumpton was given to the Pigot family by James I in 1607. Mr Pigot junior hooked a wealthy wife, rebuilt the house and created a splendid interior. The carved grand staircase and panelled saloon are ample evidence of his enthusiasm for interior decor. When he died, his widow was so poor she had to pawn the whole estate. It went to the Emertons, then the Westcombs, who tarted it up in 1820 with Dutch gables. Lucy Westcomb married the 8th Lord Byron which is why the house contains relics of the poet.

A ha-ha divides the gardens, and there's a 200 acre estate. One of the first larches in England grows here, and Thrumpton has a custom of planting cedar trees to commemorate historic occasions, including the Queen's Coronation in 1953 and her Silver Jubilee. *Open by arrangement.*

38. Wollaton Hall 6 H4

2m W of Nottingham, off A609. Flamboyant tycoon Sir Francis Willoughby built this Elizabethan setpiece in 1588 from the industrial profits of coal and glass. It now houses Nottingham Corporation's Natural History Museum. Where Francis, his wife, 12 daughters and 32 servants once ate and argued, cuddled and connived, are stuffed gorillas, pickled jellyfish and Brazilian butterflies.

Poor Francis seemed determined to impress. Wollaton is a giddy mixture of towers, pinnacles and statues. The Great Hall soars 50ft to its hammer-beam roof, and the park is surrounded by a seven mile wall that took seven men with seven apprentices seven years to build. But Wollaton ran Francis badly into debt. Finally, he quarrelled with his family and died unhappily alone in London. Later Willoughbys were an odd lot too. One of them was so angry to see a stranger looking over the park wall that he ordered an extra course of bricks to be laid along its whole length of seven miles. Later he learned that the man was a giant from Nottingham's Goose Fair.

☙ STAFFORDSHIRE ☙

1. Alton Castle 6 E4

Nr Alton Towers, Alton. Colditz or fairy-tale, depending on the weather, this odd 19thC fortress was built as an occasional residence by the earl who completed Alton Towers. Now a Catholic boys' school. Remains of a medieval castle stand in the garden. *View from outside only.*

1. Alton Towers 6 E4

Alton, 4½m E of Cheadle, off B5032. Nightmare contraptions like The Corkscrew whirl you round at breakneck speeds here – then give you a certificate for surviving without fainting. But that's just the pleasure park. We've got Charles Talbot, the 15th Earl of Shrewsbury, to thank for this marvellously

STAFFORDSHIRE

[Map of Staffordshire showing Leek, Stoke-on-Trent, Derby, Stafford, Telford, Bridgnorth, Lichfield, Birmingham, with numbered locations 1-12 and road markers A6, A523, A50, A53, M6, A518, A51, A442, M5, M6]

awful, horribly delightful complex. Between 1814 and 1827 he hired huge numbers of labourers and craftsmen to convert 600 acres of wild countryside into a massive, fanciful, ornamental park. Playing Kubla Khan he wound up master of terraces and gardens, with lakes, colonnades, Chinese temples, a Swiss cottage and a model railway. An island pagoda throws its fountain so high you can see it for miles around.

The Earl, we're told, was a shy nobleman who obviously expressed his extrovert side in outrageous schemes like this. While creating his pleasure dome, Charles lived in the house on the site which he named Alton Abbey. His nephew enlarged it in Gothic style and renamed it Alton Towers. Only the shell remains, but parts are in use and you can see its original design. The grounds are immaculately maintained and it's certainly an extravaganza – but crowded. *Open summer.*

Cannock Chase   6 E5
Kings and nobles once hunted in this wild, oak forest now dwindled to 26 sq miles of moorland, scrub, streams, bracken and conifer plantations. Six thousand Germans who died in Britain during both World Wars are buried here in a vast cemetery. And close by is the graveyard of young New Zealanders who travelled half-way round the world to fight with Britain in 1918 only to die in the Spanish flu epidemic that ravaged the country during the month of the armistice. Freda, dog mascot of the New Zealand Rifle Brigade, is buried with them.

Cannock Chase was used as a huge military camp during the First World War and is now listed as an area of outstanding natural beauty. Gravel workings have exposed rock composed of round pebbles solidly embedded in sand. These are known as Bunter pebblebeds and are 100 million years old. Coal and charcoal industries scarred Cannock's natural beauty so that only a few of the original great oaks remain – mainly at Brocton Coppice in the north where deer roam. Bracken is prolific and was once gathered, burned, and its ash used for bleaching cloth. Three estates dominate the Chase – Hatherton, Lichfield and Anglesey.

2. Chartley Castle   6 E4
Nr Hixon, 8m NE of Stafford. Disaster-prone Mary, Queen of Scots, was imprisoned here in the Earl of Essex's castle following the discovery of letters connected with plots to kill Elizabeth I. A 'double agent' brewer smuggled them for her in the false bottoms of his beer casks only to tip off one of Elizabeth's ministers. All that remains of the scene today are a couple of crumbly round stone towers on a hilltop.

Chartley cattle – white beasts with black ears and branching horns descended from the primitive English aurochs – roamed the park for 700 years until tuberculosis almost wiped them out. The survivors were moved to Woburn Abbey where you can see them today.

3. Chatterley Whitfield Mining Museum   6 E3
3m SSE of Kidsgrove, off A527.
Claustrophobics are not advised to take full advantage of this rather alarming museum's facilities – unless they want to confront their terror eyeball to eyeball. Because its speciality is trips 700ft below ground wearing helmets, cap-lamps and belts – supervised by experienced miners. Warm clothes and stout shoes are recommended, and for anyone who has never been down a mine and seen conditions there for themselves, this is a marvellous opportunity to do so. For faint-hearted above-grounders, there are shows of coal-mining past and present, a lamp room, a colliery canteen, and a museum shop. *Open most days.*

4. Ilam   6 E4
14m E of Stoke-on-Trent, off A52. Someone once spitefully said that the best parts of Derbyshire are in Staffordshire. By that, they meant this area round Dovedale which is usually associated with the Peak District. Ilam is a Swiss-like model village rebuilt by 19thC tycoon Jesse Watts-Russell. An unusual Gothic cross in memory of his wife, Eleanor, graces the village centre. Ilam church has a carved Norman font and a strange relic known as a maiden's garland – white gloves and artificial flowers from the coffin of an unmarried girl. Its oldest relics are Anglo-Saxon crosses which stand in the churchyard. Part of stately Ilam Hall is now a youth hostel. Built in 1821, it was partly pulled down in the 1930s.

5. Ingestre   6 E5
4m NE of Stafford, off A518. Christopher Wren probably designed the 17thC Church of St Mary – but documents proving it were destroyed in a fire at nearby Ingestre Hall. It's highly likely he did because he was friendly with the builder of the Hall, and the fine quality of the church suggests someone with more experience than a provincial builder of that period. Ingestre is one of only two churches outside London with claim to Wren (the other is at Farley in Wiltshire). Notice the plasterwork, woodwork, monuments to the occupants of Ingestre Hall (Chetwynds and Talbots) – and electric lighting on delicate wrought iron fittings. This was installed in 1886 and was the first of its kind in any parish church.

Rebuilt in the 19thC after a fire, the impressive 17thC Ingestre Hall is now used as a centre for residential arts courses. *View from outside only.*

6. Lichfield   6 E6
'Lichfield' probably comes from 'lych' field meaning 'field of corpses' – Christians slain by decree of the Roman Emperor Diocletian. Lichfield's seal, which you can see on the railway bridge across St John Street, shows three British kings who defied the Romans, lying dead with their swords beside them. They are said to lie beneath a tumulus on

Litchfield Cathedral

Borrowcop Hill south of the city.
Samuel Johnson was born here in 1709. His birthplace is now a Johnsonian Museum and his statue stands in the cobbled market square. St John's 15thC hospital with its eight chimney-breasts facing the street has a peaceful little chapel inside where the public are allowed to attend services. Other notable buildings include Georgian houses, especially the George Hotel with its magnificent ballroom on the first floor; the Swan Hotel opposite, West Gate House, the Angel Croft Hotel and St Chad's medieval church.
Museum open summer; most days, winter.

6. Lichfield Cathedral   6 E6

Pilgrims paid for this sumptuous cathedral. Thousands of them journeyed each year to Lichfield to honour St Chad, Bishop of Mercia from AD669, and their cash raised this intricate, treasure-stuffed monument that is now dedicated to him. Built between 1195 and 1235, Lichfield is the only cathedral in England with three spires. They are called Ladies of the Vale, and you can see them from miles away. 'Ladies' emphasises the cathedral's fine-boned, delicate splendour. The west front is encrusted and pitted with over 100 statues, trefoils, quatrefoils and cinquefoils so that from a distance it looks like a piece of rich embroidery.
Listing Lichfield's items of interest would fill 10 pages, but Sir Francis Chantrey's 'Sleeping Children' is one of the most famous. Chantrey came back every year and sat in front of it hoping for similar inspiration with his current work. The Lady chapel contains some of the best 16thC stained glass in England and the St Chad Gospels, illuminated 7thC manuscripts, are the cathedral's most treasured possession.

7. Shugborough Hall   6 E5

5m SE of Stafford, off A513. Dilettante gentlemen created this complex of Classical and Oriental splendour which is now owned by the National Trust and houses Staffordshire's county museum. From the square entrance lodges and iron gates, you know you're in for an afternoon of architectural refinement. The astonishing portico of 10 Ionic columns – each an oak trunk covered with painted and sanded slate – confirms that, and after the oval entrance hall, saloon, bust gallery, ante room, red drawing room, blue drawing room, swallow passage, staircase hall and library, you wonder how anyone managed to find his or her way down to breakfast before lunchtime. They probably didn't.
Thomas Anson, descendant of the William Anson who built Shugborough in 1694, was a romantic bachelor and member of the Society of Dilettanti. His younger brother, George, was a celebrated admiral who revived the Royal Navy in the mid 18thC. The admiral left his brother a fortune and Thomas used this to renovate Shugborough in Classical style with the help of 'Athenian' Stuart, a fellow dilettante and Greek enthusiast.
The stable block and kitchen wing house the Museum of Staffordshire Life, with horse-drawn vehicles and an 18thC brew-house. Magnificently furnished, the house itself contains notable paintings. Remarkable monuments feature in the gardens. There's the Cat's Monument, James Stuart's temples and follies, and the Chinese House – pink outside with red lacquer, gilded monkeys and rococo scrolls – influenced by drawings made in Canton by one of Admiral Lord Anson's officers. *Open most days, summer.*

8. Stafford   6 D5

Knowing that Stafford was once an island in the middle of marshes on an ancient trackway, its name 'staithford' meaning 'landing place' makes more sense. You can still see these marshes and the site of medieval fish ponds beyond Eastgate. Green Bridge is the site of the original ford.
A trip round historical Stafford takes you past the ruined town walls and then to William Salt's library of books, deeds, drawings and engravings, which was given to Stafford by his nephew 100 years ago. Pitcher Bank refers to a crockery street market held here until 1881. St Mary's and St Chad's churches are both worth visiting. Izaak Walton, renowned angler, was born in Eastgate Street in 1593 and baptised in the Norman font at St Mary's. En route you'll see Staffordshire's oldest building, the High House. Built in 1595 from local oak, it's the largest timber-framed house in England and lives up to its name by standing four storeys high. Charles I stopped here in 1642 and Royalists were gaoled here during the Civil War. The Swan Hotel, converted from a 17thC town house and now an important coaching inn, has quenched the thirst of both George Borrow and Charles Dickens. Tenterbanks is where medieval weavers stretched their cloth dry on tenterhooks – and it gives an insight into the familiar expression 'on tenterhooks'. Broad Eye Windmill on the edge of town was built in 1796 and worked until 1880.

8. Stafford Castle   6 D5

1½ms SW of Stafford. Motte-and-bailey. Motte-and-bailey was the name for early castle-forts built of earth and timber – and Stafford castle was one of them. Workmen humped clay to shape an artificial hill, then dug complicated ditch defences topped with wooden stockades. All that happened around 1070, but the original contours remain.
Two centuries later, a stone keep appeared on top of the existing motte and the castle grew to accommodate the Stafford family and their 40 yeomen and grooms. Documents record a mill-house, a brew-house, a forge, barns and stables there, too. Parliamentarians demolished the castle in 1643 during the Civil War and it stayed a ruin until the 19thC when it was rebuilt in Gothic style on the surviving medieval walls. Unfortunately, the scheme was dropped half-way through, and the poor old castle rotted until the borough council took it over in 1961. Apart from work on the castle, excavations have revealed a medieval village with roadways and house sites. It was probably Monetvile – mentioned in the Domesday Book of 1086 and meaning 'vill', or village near a mountain.

9. Stoke-on-Trent   6 D4

Otherwise known as The Potteries, six towns make up this 14th largest city in England. Tunstall, Burslem, Hanley, Stoke, Fenton and Longton form a straggling group of haphazard communities stretching eight miles along the north Staffordshire moorland. Clay deposits found close to coal deposits meant that pottery was inevitable in this region. It was made in towns and villages as early as the Bronze Age and the Roman occupation, but expanded dramatically from the Middle Ages. Many great potters came from Stoke: Wedgwood, Davenport, Minton, Copeland and Spode. Bottle ovens, most of which have ceased operating, once made its skyline distinctive. Thick haze used to hang over Stoke, but this has been greatly reduced. Firing is done by gas or electricity now in smokeless tunnel ovens.
The best way of exploring this spread-out city is on foot, and three town trails make the going easier. Six Towns Road Trail and the Potteries Walkway Trail link the main points of interest in the six towns, and another covers canals and footpaths through the heart of the city. The Arnold Bennett Museum houses a collection associated with Stoke's most famous author, who lived here seven years. The City Museum and Art Gallery possesses

one of the finest and largest international pottery collections in the world.
Ford Green Hall Folk Museum, *Ford Green Rd, Smallthorne*, is a 16thC furnished manor house which has been beautifully restored as a folk museum. The timber-framed house has an 18thC east wing and dovecote in the garden. *Open most days.*
Reginald Mitchell, designer of the Spitfire, was a local lad – born at 115 Congleton Road, Butt Lane, Talke, for those bent on pilgrimage. The **Spitfire Museum**, *Bethesda St*, houses a Spitfire, and various pubs in the area have aerodynamic names like The Tiger Moth at Meir and Man in Space at Trentham. *Open most days.*
Bone china (actually made from bone) was Josiah Spode's greatest contribution to the history of ceramics and you can see extraordinarily beautiful examples of his work at the **Spode Factory**, *Church St*, on the site of the original Spode works. During the 18thC, Josiah perfected a process of underglaze blue printing and developed engraving techniques. He created over 40 dinner-ware patterns in as many years. His son, Josiah II, promoted his father's discovery of pure white sparkling bone china that rivalled European porcelain in its translucence. Craftsmen could use brilliant colours on this new china and embellish it with burnished gold. Josiah junior also introduced Stone China which copied Oriental designs. It is still highly prized today. Spode's itinerary includes mould-making, cup and plate making, a biscuit tunnel oven, a biscuit warehouse, printing, and transferring and painting. *Factory and museum open by arrangement; shop open most days.*

Bottle-shaped brick kilns, Longton

Spectacular bottle ovens still dominate the cobbled yard of the **Gladstone Museum**, *Longton*. Named after Mr Gladstone's visit north to open the Wedgwood Institute in 1863, this working museum tells the story of British ceramics. You can visit the engine house, slip house, clay preparation rooms, casting shop, and one of the bottle kilns.

10. Tutbury Castle   6 F5
Tutbury, 4m NNW of Burton-on-Trent, off A50.
Mary, Queen of Scots, anguished here during one of her many spells of imprisonment. At first she was allowed the courtesy of 60 attendants. Then security tightened as plots against Elizabeth multiplied. She lived rheumatically in an old hunting lodge, sparsely furnished and overlooking the castle lavatories which were used by over 130 people living at the castle during that period. Sir Ralph Sadler, her gaoler, tried to make life bearable for her and took her riding and hawking in Needwood Forest. But her next warder worsened conditions. He opened her letters. By 1587 she was dead, and the old castle was 'slighted' by Cromwellians in the Civil War. Little remains today but John of Gaunt's 14thC gateway, the south tower with its winding staircase, and the high tower.
The Church of St Mary, founded as a priory in the 11thC, is one of the most beautiful Norman churches in the Midlands. Especially impressive is the decorated west front with its magnificent doorway. Inside are some good arcades, an ancient parish chest and the old village stocks.
By 1831, Tutbury made history again. Workmen building an embankment nearby found some silver coins. Upstream next day they found more – and eventually uncovered a hoard of Scottish, Bohemian, Polish, Flemish and English episcopal coins. A 'silver rush' ensued and crowds descended on Tutbury waving spades and shovels. Records show that the Earl of Lancaster probably buried his army's pay chest at Tutbury as he fled from Edward II in 1321 after the Battle of Burton Bridge.

11. Wedgwood Museum and Visitor Centre   6 D4
Barlaston, 5m S of Stoke-on-Trent, off A34.
Fans of this distinctive and historic pottery can ogle to their heart's content in this award-winning complex of museum/cinema/demonstration hall/shop/refreshment lounge that opened in 1975. An 18 minute film describes the making of Wedgwood's fine bone china, Queen's Ware, oven-to-tableware, and the fine-grained stoneware of Jasper and Black Basalt. The museum houses early and modern Wedgwood from its 18thC founding in the pioneering days of Josiah, 'father of English potters'. Traditional hand processes, throwing, figure-making and ornamenting are all in action in the demo hall. *Open weekdays.*

12. Weston Park   6 D5
Weston-under-Lizard, 6m W of J12, M6.
Disraeli often visited this country house at the invitation of the Countess of Bradford and many of his letters can be seen here. Today it is still owned by an earl of Bradford – the 6th – and his special interest is forestry. George Michael Orlando Bridgeman took over Weston in 1957 and although he has 30 tenant farmers, he farms much of the 15,000 acres himself. Weston was designed by a gifted lady without the aid of an architect, in the 1660s. It is square, blockish and brick built, but elegant inside with its tapestry room, dining room, marble staircase, and superb collection of paintings by Holbein, Gainsborough and Reynolds. Especially charming are the small portraits in the breakfast room. Outside, the impeccably tailored grounds with terraced lawns and lakes were laid out by Capability Brown. See in particular the Temple of Diana and the Roman Bridge. *Open most days, summer.*

Weston Park

Attached to Weston Park and built in 1700, the little parish church has some touching memorials. One is to Lucy and Charlotte, daughters of the second Earl, who died in 1858 when Lucy accidentally set fire to her nightdress and Charlotte tried to beat out the flames. There's also an unusual window showing St Andrew crucified on his diagonal cross. Note the early 18thC wrought iron altar rails.

EAST ANGLIA

The area of East Anglia, though it has no definite boundaries, is as complete and easily recognisable a piece of country as it was in Saxon times. The name comes from the district of the 'East Angles', which was divided in its turn into 'North Folk' and 'South Folk', Norfolk and Suffolk. The area adjoining belonged to the 'East Saxons', which became known as Essex but also included the kingdom belonging to the 'Middle Angles', stretching to what is now Cambridge and the Isle of Ely. So, by long association these areas were thought of as a region called 'East Anglia', though strictly speaking it is bounded just by Norfolk and Suffolk.

In pre-Roman times East Anglia was comprised largely of one great forest, of which Epping Forest is the only survival. To the north lay the equally impenetrable swamps of the Fens. In the depths of the forest the Iceni people built settlements in cleared forest land, at the fording points of rivers and on what high ground there was. This great Celtic tribe penetrates the 20thC in the names of villages such as Ickworth, Ickleton and Icklingham, and in the Icknield Way, an Iceni trackway. Evidence of their highly organised culture exists in the flint mines at Grimes Graves in Norfolk, which are on an almost industrial scale.

The most famous of the Iceni was Queen Bodicea, who led them in revolt against Roman rule. They routed the Ninth Legion and reinforcements had to be called in. At her eventual defeat, Bodicea committed suicide, the gesture expected of a fiercely proud warrior race. The Romans subsequently asserted supremacy over East Anglia by building garrisons in Colchester, Caister, Cambridge, Lincoln, Brancaster and Horncastle.

The vacuum the Romans left behind them in the 4thC was soon filled. A kingdom of East Anglia was established, bordered by the Stour to the south and the Ouse to the West. Fortifications such as Devil's Dyke at Newmarket suggest that relations with neighbouring Mercia were none too cordial.

From the 9thC to the 10thC there followed a period of recurrent Danish invasion, rasing villages and sacking religious institutions – at Ely, North Elmham, Crowland, and many others. But the Norman conquerors put a stop to all that, and planted physical evidence of their dominance by raising great castles all over the area, considerable remains of which are still visible. They also re-endowed the Saxon religious institutions, building on a scale and to a quality never seen before or since. Ely, Lincoln and Norwich cathedrals displays some of England's most sublime medieval architecture. The Fens remained the last outpost of revolts against the Normans, led by Hereward the Wake, who had a little help from the Danes in the beginning. Norman culture expressed itself through the activities of the great baronial families – the Bigods, the de Burghs, the de Warennes, the d'Albinis – and in their castles at Norwich, Framlingham, Castle Rising and Orford.

On a less grandiose scale the East Anglian cloth trade began to grow. Resulting prosperity was poured in part into the construction of magnificent churches, large out of all proportion to the towns and villages they tower over. In north Norfolk, in the Fens and in the Suffolk cloth towns of Long Melford, Lavenham, and others, there are churches which would be wonders anywhere else, that are quite taken for granted by the locals. Fine domestic building, too, was produced by this wealth, and East Anglia has many 14th and 15thC wooden framed houses surviving as well as good building from later periods. Holkham Hall, Ickworth Hall, Blickling, Oxborough and Sawston all lie within the area, and are among the finest of their kind.

On the agricultural front, the gradual clearing of the forest and the enclosures of common land were catalysts for profound change. Over the years repeated attempts were made to drain the Fenlands which, even as late as the mid 18thC, were a virtual wilderness. Eventually the Fens were drained and the resulting rich soil made a great contribution to prosperity.

Cambridge grew up on the periphery of the Fens at the junction of a network of Roman roads with canals and rivers, but began to develop its collegiate character in the 13thC, with the building of Peterhouse College. Successive centuries brought the establishment of numerous other colleges, from many of which peaceful, green lawns, the Backs, run down to the river.

Cambridgeshire and Lincolnshire had their share of the mainstream of English history, particularly during the Civil War. But the rest seems to have been bypassed and to have had a history unique to the region itself. And, as East Anglia is not on the road to anywhere, and has no mineral or industrial resources, it has not suffered some of the worst advances of the century. Major roads here would be minor elsewhere, and some of the unclassified roads that lead to the treasures of the past have high, overgrown hedges, grass growing in the middle, and room for no more than one car at a time. In Suffolk is Constable Country, a land of streams and woods, of hills and tiny valleys, of villages and hamlets that have little changed over the centuries. You can look up at the sky and see if the racing, swirling clouds of his paintings are reflected there. Or, in Norfolk, stop in surprise at the sight of a ship seeming to sail through the fields, as it glides through the peaceful Broads.

🐚CAMBRIDGESHIRE🐚

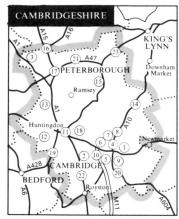

man admitted having started the fire in pursuance of a grudge.

To the west of the churchyard are the remains of Burwell castle moat. The castle was begun in 1143 but never completed.

5. Cambridge 7 E9

Situated between the Fens to the north and swamp to the south, the site of Cambridge was established as a ford over the River Cam. Soon it became a busy and important commercial centre. The Romans used Cambridge as an inland port and built a bridge over the river, giving the town its name. For them it provided a useful base for incursions into the wild Fenlands, and for the Normans, a useful base from which to fight the Fenland rebels under Hereward the Wake. In 1068 William the Conqueror built a castle and lived there for a while but no remains of the building survive.

No-one is very sure how or why the university started at Cambridge. It is thought that a school run by the monks of Ely was established in the 11thC, and that others followed to cater for a growing demand. By the 13thC several religious orders had come into being, with schools attached and in 1284 the first college proper was founded – Peterhouse. The academic community in Cambridge was quickly established and more colleges sprang up to house the growing number of students.

Cambridge has a wealth of historic buildings and much of its charm lies in the winding back streets and passages, such as Botolph Lane and St Edward's Passage. Medieval houses and cottages line Northampton and Magdalene Streets. The willow-strewn 'Backs', sloping to the peaceful riverside, make a perfect picnicking spot for a lazy summer's day. You can envy the nonchalance with which the well-practised students manipulate the poles – or rise to the challenge and take a punt out yourself.

Visitors are welcome to wander around the colleges and grounds, but during term time there may be restrictions. **Christ's College**, *St Andrew's St*, accommodated Milton from 1625 to 1632 and he wrote 'Lycidas' while sitting under the mulberry tree in the gardens. The hall has been much altered, but the gatehouse survives and has good heraldic carving.

The third oldest college, **Clare College**, *Trinity Lane*, was founded by Elizabeth de Clare in 1339. Fire destroyed the hall in 1521 and the earliest part is the east range of the old court, dated 1638. For the best view of this beautifully-unified building, look over from the lawns of King's College. **King's College Chapel**, *King's Parade*, is considered one of the world's most famous buildings. A glorious Gothic wonder of delicate fan vaulting and stone carving, it was begun in 1446 by Henry VI. The windows, which flood the building with an array of beautiful light, date from 1517 to the 1530s. Behind the altar sits Ruben's magnificent 'The Adoration of the Magi', painted c1634 and presented to the college in 1962.

1. Anglesey Abbey 7 E8

6m NE of Carbidge, off B1101. The house, given to the National Trust by the first Baron Fairhaven, was built in 1600 on the site of a 13thC Augustinian abbey. It contains a fine collection of books, furniture and paintings accumulated by the Baron, and its 100 acres of garden are outstanding. Created in 1926 to rival the masterpieces of Georgian times, they certainly succeed. *House open most days summer; gardens daily, summer.*

2. Bourn 3 E1

The 16thC but much restored, red-brick Bourn Hall is built on the site of an earlier, Norman, castle. No traces of the castle remain. While in the village visit the church which has a 13thC maze on the floor of the tower, symbolising the journey through life to salvation. Bourn also has the oldest windmill in England – a post mill on wooden legs built in 1636. *Open summer, or by arrangement.*

3. Burghley House 7 C6

1m S of Stamford, off B1081. Completed in 1598 for William Cecil, Lord High Treasurer of Elizabeth I. Royalist during the Civil War, it was taken by Cromwell who, to his discredit, destroyed some of its treasures. The original Great Hall with its glorious ceiling survived. The lovely state apartments contain pictures, furniture, tapestries and silver fireplaces. In 1694 the artist Verrio was called in to paint the Heaven Room, and his work justifies the title. The gardens in the walled park were laid out by Capability Brown. *Open most days, summer.*

Burghley House

4. Burwell, Church of St Mary 7 F8

1½m N of Newmarket, W of A142. Burwell church is in the 15thC Perpendicular style with large, light-giving windows. The upper part of its tower is octagonal, a design copied from Ely Cathedral. Note the beautiful, carved tracery over the chancel arch.

A monument in the churchyard recalls a terrible tragedy in the village which took place on 8th September, 1727. A travelling puppet show was giving a performance in a local barn. The show was so popular that the barn doors were nailed shut to keep others out. There was a fire and 82 members of the audience were burnt alive. Years later a dying Fordham

'The Backs', Cambridge

Corpus Christi College, *Trumpington St*, was founded by the townspeople in 1352. It was formerly called Bene't College from the partly Saxon church of St Bene't (St Benedict), which was used as the college chapel. Two of the college's most famous students were Christopher Marlowe and John Fletcher, the Elizabethan dramatists. Marlowe had first floor rooms and Fletcher came to the college in 1593, the year Marlowe was killed in a tavern. Both are commemorated on a plaque on the wall of the Old Court.

Emmanuel College, *St Andrew's St*, was founded in 1584 by Sir Walter Mildmay, Chancellor of the Exchequer to Elizabeth I, on the site of the Dominican or Black Friars house. The chapel was designed in 1666 by Sir Christopher Wren, in the new Classical style.

Jesus College, *Jesus La*, accommodated Thomas Cranmer who was made a Fellow in 1515. The poet Coleridge was also here and writes of the college in his 'Biographia Literaria'.

King's College, Cambridge

Attractive **Magdalene College**, *Magdalene St*, with its two charming courtyards, is particularly known for the **Pepysian Library** which contains 3,000 books which the diarist left the college. Among the collection his diary, written in cypher, was found and decyphered for publication in 1825. The books are housed in his own bookcases and his own desk is still there, too.

Edmund Spenser, Thomas Gray, and the younger Pitt were all sons of **Pembroke College**, *Trumpington St*. The New Chapel was the first building that Christopher Wren ever designed, commissioned by his uncle, the Bishop of Ely. The west end, quietly classical, remains his work: the rest has considerable Victorian additions.

Just along the road is the first of the colleges, **Peterhouse College**, founded in 1281 by the Bishop of Ely as a secular institution. Little remains of the original hall due to 19thC restoration but it has retained a Tudor fireplace. The William Morris windows are an addition.

One famous fellow of this college, if short-lived, was the poet Thomas Gray. With a phobia for fire, the ladder which he left permanently attached to his window proved too tempting for his mischievous fellow students. One dark night in 1742 they raised the alarm outside his window. Thomas belted down the ladder clad only in his nightshirt – and landed straight in a tub of icy water. Predictably not amused, he left for Pembroke College.

Queens' College, *Queens' Lane*, was founded by two Queens: Margaret of Anjou, wife of Henry VI, and Elizabeth Woodfield, wife of Edward IV. Begun by Margaret in 1448, it was taken over by Elizabeth in 1465. It remains, essentially, the same great Tudor mansion constructed then.

Arching quaintly over the river is the famous wooden Mathematical Bridge, so called because it was based upon geometric principles and constructed in 1749 without the use of any nails or bolts. A curious Victorian took it to pieces to see how it worked, didn't succeed, and couldn't put it

back together again. So now it has bolts and nails just like any ordinary bridge.

The largest and richest, **Trinity College**, *Trinity St*, was founded by Henry VIII who added new buildings and joined together the existing colleges of King's Hall and Michaelhouse. There are many grand buildings: the Great Gate of the chapel with a statue of Newton, a marvellous hall and the Great Court, the most impressive in Cambridge and said to be the largest university court in the world. Trinity men include a half-dozen Prime Ministers, the poets George Herbert, Dryden, Byron (who kept a tame bear and was sent down for bathing naked in the fountain), Tennyson and Housman, and, in the field of science, Isaac Newton and Rutherford who, for better or for worse, split the atom.

Second largest of the Cambridge colleges, **St John's College**, *St John's St*, was founded by Lady Margaret Tudor after Christ's, but not built until after her death. Notable buildings include the splendid turreted gatehouse, the Tudor hall with its hammer-beam roof and the handsome Combination Room. Crossing the Cam is the famous Bridge of Sighs based on the one at Venice, and built in 1831. St John's men include Wordsworth, Palmerston, Wilberforce and Herchel the astronomer.

If you've any energy left, there's plenty more in the way of churches and museums. **The Round Church**, *Round Church St*, was built in 1130 on the model of the Holy Sepulchre and is the largest of the four remaining round churches in England. The tower of **St Benet's Church**, *Benet St* is one of the few Saxon survivals in England, and is thought to date from the reign of Canute or even earlier. Note the long-and-short work (alternate vertical and horizontal stones) in the tower and the tower arch inside which is decorated with many strange mythical beasts.

The Fitzwilliam Museum, *Trumpington St*, is one of the world's great museums, housing paintings by Turner, Breughel, Canaletto and Constable. There is also a large Egyptian section, and collections of illuminated manuscripts, sculpture, furniture and clocks. *Open most days*. Also of interest are the **Cambridge and County Folk Museum**, *Castle St*, containing interesting articles of daily use from medieval times until the 20thC, *open most days*, and the **Scott Polar Research Institute**, *Lensfield Rd*, a memorial museum to Scott and his companions containing relics of their expeditions, *open weekdays*.

6. Carr Dyke   7 E8
4m N of Cambridge, ½m S of Waterbeach, off A10. The remains of a Roman canal that connected with Lincoln, and so, from there, to York. Much of the canal has been lost in later Fenland drainings. About a mile to the north are the fragmentary remains of Denny Priory, founded by the Countess of Pembroke, who also founded Pembroke College, Cambridge.

7. Devil's Dyke   7 F8
Reaches to Ditton Green across Newmarket Heath. A huge ditch and bank earthwork, the dyke runs for seven miles, cutting across the Icknield Way. Archaeologists have differed about its date and purpose – it has been said to be Roman, pre-Roman or Saxon. The consensus seems to be that it was built in the 7thC to defend East Anglia from the neighbouring kingdom of Mercia.

8. Ely   7 E8
A charming, predominantly Georgian market town watched over by its magnificent cathedral. The name is a contradiction of 'eel-eye' – eel island – which is exactly what it was before the draining of the Fens. Old folklore insists that the eels in the surrounding marsh were 'uncelibate' priests miraculously transformed by St Dunstan.

Ely was the last stronghold of revolt against

William the Conqueror, led by Hereward the Wake who was eventually betrayed by the abbot of the monastery. Another famous, and more successful rebel lived at Ely: Oliver Cromwell occupied the vicarage adjoining St Mary's church, and was responsible for collecting the tithes.

Ely has many attractive old buildings. Strolling along the Riverside Walk, you'll see 18thC cottages and a maltings which has been converted into a public hall.

Ely Cathedral

8. Ely Cathedral   7 E8
Off High St. A religious settlement was first founded at Ely in AD 673 by St Etheldreda. Her relics were placed in the cathedral choir in 1252. After the Conquest William laid the foundation of the present cathedral. It took a mere 286 years to reach completion. A magnificent Gothic palace, it has two glories for which it is universally acclaimed. When the Norman tower collapsed in 1322, the magnificent Octagon was constructed. An engineering masterpiece, its crowning wooden lantern is a fine example of medieval carpentry. The lovely, light, Lady chapel has some marvellously intricate carving in white stone. Note the ceiling and the detail of each of the many bosses.
Associated with the cathedral is the beautiful chapel of Kings' School, which recently celebrated its millenium. While you're there, take a look at the Headmaster's House, which retains its splendid Norman doorway. Also of interest is Ely Porta, the great gate of the old monastery.

9. Gog Magog Hills   7 E9
4m SE of Cambridge, A604. Gently rising to 234ft, these chalk slopes are named after two Celtic giants – although no-one knows quite why. One theory is that the Romans quartered Vandal auxiliaries there, who were, to the shorter Celts, giants. This would also explain why the great earthwork on top of these hills came to be called Wandlebury. This area provides popular walks with good views for the otherwise hill-deprived East Anglians.

10. Grantchester   7 E9
3m S of Cambridge, A603. A leisurely punt ride from Cambridge along the Cam, Grantchester was beloved, and mentioned by both Byron and Tennyson. But it is in Rupert Brooke's nostalgic and comic poem that this tranquil little village has gained immortality. Brooke lived at Grantchester before being killed in the First World War and becoming one of the most famous War Poets. There are thatched cottages, and a fine church with Roman bricks and a Saxon window. Look to see if the clock still stands at ten to three.

11. Huntingdon   7 D8
A plaque on a house in the High Street marks the place where Oliver Cromwell was born in 1599. During the Civil War Huntingdon was in turn Cromwell's and Charles I's headquarters. The Cromwell Museum, *Market Sq*, a small Norman building, was once the grammar school which Cromwell, and later Samuel Pepys, attended. It has a good collection of Cromwellian memorabilia, including the Lord Protector's death mask. The remains of a motte of a Norman castle can be seen behind Castle Hill.

12. Kimbolton Castle   7 C8
Kimbolton. A fortified Tudor mansion, much restored in the 18thC. Catherine of Aragon, first and ill-fated wife of Henry VIII, spent her last four years here, hastened to her end by fear of poisoning and the execution of so many of her supporters.
Part of the house collapsed in 1707 and Vanbrugh was commissioned for the rebuilding. The Queen's Room, where Catherine died, remains the same, and her ghost has been spotted a number of times. The splendid square gatehouse was added by Robert Adam in 1776. Inside, there are fine ceilings and Pellegrini mural paintings. Kimbolton Castle is now a school. *Open certain days, summer.*

13. Little Gidding   7 C8
Little Gidding – a humble church and a huddle of houses – is a place with a cultural significance much greater than what is physically present would suggest. In 1625 Nicholas Ferrar, son of a prosperous merchant, gave it all up and founded a small religious community here. It was visited by Charles I and at one point during the Civil War he took refuge here from Cromwell's forces. T. S. Eliot found inspiration in Ferrar's life and principles for the last of his 'Four Quartets', entitled 'Little Gidding'. Since then it has become a place of literary as well as spiritual pilgrimage.

14. Littleport   7 E7
A typical Fenland village, and scene of the Littleport Riots of 1816. Famine in the area drove men from Littleport to riot. They marched on Ely behind a home-made tank of four punt guns mounted on a wagon. Although concessions were granted them, the next day the military rounded up 80 men. In his last exercise of temporal power the Bishop of Ely elected judges for their trial. Five were publically hanged and another five were transported to Botany Bay.

15. March   7 D7
No traces remain of the Roman settlement at March, but the town should be visited for the medieval church of St Wendreda. Its lovely interior is famed for the double hammer-beam roof with about 200 angels, carved in oak with outspread wings – a breathtaking sight.

16. Northborough   7 C6
6m N of Peterborough, A15. John Clare, the 'peasant poet', lived here from 1832 to 1837 when he was admitted to Northampton General Lunatic Asylum. Although his years here were not happy, he succeeded in producing some of his best work. His stone cottage, with two acres of land, *opposite Pringle Lane*, was built for him by his patrons. Clare had the door put at the back as an easy escape from sightseers.
Elizabeth Claypole, Oliver Cromwell's daughter, lived at Northborough manor house. Now a restaurant, this 14thC building retains much of the original work. Elizabeth died just three weeks before her father, and Cromwell's widow, who came to live with her bereaved son-in-law, is buried in the village churchyard.

17. Peterborough   7 D7
Excavations and aerial photography have revealed that settlement here, on what was the edge of the Fen swamps, goes back to prehistory. From Norman times it has enjoyed the prosperity associated with an important religious site and country market town.
This century has seen much development, but the old market place dominated by the 17thC guildhall, remains the focus of the town. Priestgate contains the museum and art gallery and has some fine Georgian houses. Remains of Civil War fortifications can be seen outside Old Fletton.

17. Peterborough Cathedral 7 D7

A monastery was first founded on this site in
the 7thC and this eventually became the
Abbey of St Peter. The present Barnack stone
building dates from the early 12thC and is one
of the most impressive Romanesque buildings
in England. Henry VIII gave the abbey church
cathedral status in 1541 and his first wife,
Catherine of Aragon, lies buried in the north
choir aisle. A memorial marks where Mary,
Queen of Scots, was buried after her
execution at Fotheringhay: she was later
removed to Westminster Abbey.
The most striking feature of the exterior is the
13thC west front. The spacious nave has a
unique painted roof, dated c1220 which is
magnificently decorated with figures. There is
some early Norman work in the sanctuary, the
oldest part of the building. Look out for the
Hedda Stone, an interesting piece of
Anglo-Saxon sculpture dated cAD800.

Peterborough Cathedral

18. St Ives 7 D8

Picturesque town with refreshing, riverside
views and fine Georgian and Victorian houses.
In the market place, is a bronze statue of
Oliver Cromwell who had a farm nearby. A
six-arched stone bridge built in 1425 spans
the River Ouse. There's a small chapel in the
middle, one of only three of its kind in
England.

St Ives

19. St Neots 7 C9

St Neots came into existence with a 10thC
Benedictine monastery, of which nothing
remains. The beautiful, late medieval Church
of St Mary is one of the largest in the country,
and has intricate roof carvings of angels,
animals and birds.

20. Sawston Hall 7 E9

5m S of Cambridge, off A130. Occupied by the
Catholic Huddleston family for over 400
years, Sawston Hall, a four-square house built
around a central courtyard, has hardly
changed in that time and remains one of the
most complete examples of an Elizabethan
manor.
On the 7th June 1553 Mary Tudor stayed
here while on her way to Norfolk. Early next
day the troops of the Duke of

Northumberland, a supporter of Lady Jane
Grey's claim to the throne, attacked the
house. Mary fled, disguised as a dairy-maid,
accompanied by her host, John Huddleston.
From the Gog Magog hills they looked back
to see the house in flames. Mary is reported to
have declared: 'Let it blaze. When I am
Queen I will build Huddleston a better
house.' The present hall was built between
1557 and 1584 and used the bricks of
Cambridge Castle.
It was a Huddleston who helped another
monarch: Father John Huddleston was the
priest who hid Charles II in the oak tree after
the Battle of Worcester and absolved him at
his death.
Inside are some interesting rooms, notably the
Great Hall with oak panelling and a bedroom
with marvellous Flemish tapestries dating
from c1500. This is the room that Mary slept
in – and, it is reported, occasionally revisits.
Open by arrangement.

21. Thorney Abbey 7 D6

1/2m N of village, off B1040. A great Norman
abbey was built on the site of a monastery
originally founded in the 7thC. After the
Reformation it was left derelict for 100 years
until in 1638 part of the great abbey church
was incorporated in the parish church. The
surviving remains are impressive, although
only about a fifth of the size of the original
building. There is a fine west front with two
12thC turrets with octagonal tops, separated
by a screen containing medieval statues. The
nave is also from the original building, but the
chancel and transept were added in the
19thC.

22. Wimpole Hall 7 D9

Wimpole. Standing gracefully in an enormous
park, Wimpole Hall is Cambridgeshire's most
spectacular mansion. Basically 18thC, it's a
red-brick building with elegant rooms
containing appropriate period furniture with
work by Gibbs, Flitcroft and Soane.
In the chapel are outstanding painted
decorations by Sir James Thornhill. Note also
the pulpit and wrought iron altar rails. The
formal gardens were landscaped by Capability
Brown then later by Humphrey Repton.
Wimpole Hall was recently bequeathed to the
National Trust by Rudyard Kipling's
daughter. *Open most days, summer.*

23. Wisbech 7 E6

Glorious in blossom time and active in the
fruit-picking season, Wisbech began as a
coastal port at the mouth of the River Nene.
The sea has since retreated, but coasters still
come up the river to discharge their cargoes.
In Norman times there was a castle, the
mound of which can be seen to the south of
the town. King John probably stayed there in
1216, shortly before his death.
The elegant houses of rich merchants on the
North and South Brinks overlooking the River
Nene, are a reminder that the Georgian era
was the time of Wisbech's great prosperity.
Peckover House, *North Brink,* built in 1722,
is owned by the National Trust. John
Peckover, a Quaker banker, bought the
property at the end of the 18thC and the
family stayed there for 150 years. The interior
testifies to a prosperous yet restrained way of
life. *Open certain days, summer.*

🐚 ESSEX 🐚

1. Audley End 7 E10

1m W of Saffron Walden, off A130. Immense
though this magnificent Jacobean mansion is,
Audley End is but a shadow of its former self.
A Benedictine monastery here was handed
over by Henry VIII after the Dissolution to Sir

Thomas Audley, who built himself a house on
the site. The estate passed to Lord Howard de
Walden, the first Earl of Suffolk, who began
to build one of the largest Jacobean houses in
the kingdom. Sir John Vanbrugh was
commissioned to make extensive alterations in

1721, and further changes were made throughout the 18thC. The result is that Audley is now about half its original size. The house contains a fine collection of paintings and 18thC furniture and in the Great Hall the original Jacobean woodwork remains. The entrance hall and staircase are splendid and there is much work by Adam. The grounds, on the banks of the River Cam, owe their attractive design to Capability Brown. A miniature railway with steam trains runs through the woodland and over the river. **Ring Hill**, an Iron Age camp across the A11 from Audley, has a Doric 'Temple to Peace', built by Robert Adam in 1763 to commemorate the end of the Seven Years War. *Audley End open summer; railway runs most days, summer.*

2. Bradwell-on-Sea, Church of St Peter's on the Wall   3 H4
1½m NE of village. This church is one of the oldest in the country, in all probability the very one built by the priest St Cedd cAD654. As its name suggests, it was built on the walls of a Roman fort, and it is evident that Roman bricks were used in its construction. Up until the end of the 18thC its tower was still standing. Used as a barn by local farmers until its significance was realised in the 1920s, the restored church is now the focus of an annual pilgrimage.
Bradwell's other claim to fame is in direct contrast – the massive, brooding, atomic power station which dominates the coastal marsh.

3. Bures, St Stephen's Chapel   7 G10
½m E of Bures, off B1508. This restored, almost reconstructed, thatched chapel is where, according to tradition, the 15-year-old St Edmund was crowned King of East Anglia, on Christmas Day AD855. There is no hard historical evidence for this, but the chapel looks the part perfectly.

4. Coggeshall   3 G3
Coggeshall was an affluent wool and lace-making town in the late Middle Ages. One of the most prominent of merchants then was Thomas Paycocke, whose house, named after him, still stands and is considered one of the finest examples of Tudor domestic architecture. A half-timbered, two storey building, it is richly carved (notice the repeated motif of an ermine tail, the family trade mark) and has fine oriel windows. Other attractive buildings in the town are notably the Woolpack Hotel and the Lamb and Flag pub. There's a memorial to Thomas Paycocke in the church. Another monument, to Mary Honywood, records the remarkable fact that she left no fewer than 367 descendants.

5. Colchester   3 H3
The oldest recorded town in England, Colchester was the first colony the Romans established cAD50. Less well-known is that before this Colchester was the capital of the Belgic kingdom, and named Camulos after the Belgic war god. King Cunobelin (better known as Shakespeare's Cymbeline) was in power when the Romans arrived, and they adapted the name to Camulodunum.
It was here that the Romans met their fiercest resistance, the revolt led by Queen Bodicea. After her father's death the Romans claimed the whole of the Iceni Kingdom. Bodicea protested and the Romans had her publically flogged. This outrage united the Iceni against the Romans and the Iceni stormed Camulodunum in their thousands. The town was burnt, its people mercilessly slaughtered and every trace of Roman art and custom destroyed. Eventually Bodicea was defeated near London, and she committed suicide. The Romans retook Camulodunum and remained there until well into the 4thC.
After the Romans came the Saxons, traces of whose pottery and wooden fortifications have been found. The Normans, who followed, left here their largest castle and remains of religious institutions. From this time onwards, Colchester flourished as a local market, port and textile town. Balkerne Gate, *Balkerne Lane*, is the ruin of the west gate of the Roman town. Topping the gate is the Hole in the Wall pub, which obstructs what would have been the original thoroughfare. Just opposite, the foundations of Colchester's eighth Roman temple can be seen.
Only parts of the west front and nave remain of the 12thC **St Botolph's Priory**, *S of castle*, which was the first English Augustinian house. The ruins, however, are impressive, with massive columns supporting tiers of Norman arches. St John's Abbey was founded in 1096 by Eudo Dapifer who built the castle. Only the 15thC gateway, with pinnacled towers on either side, remains. Housing a collection of 18th and 19thC household objects and costumes, **The Hollytrees**, *High St*, is a beautiful Georgian red-brick building. *Open certain days.*

5. Colchester Castle   3 H3
High St. Built on the site of the Roman Temple of Claudius, the building incorporated many of the Roman bricks from local ruins. It was begun c1080 by Eudo Dapifer, Steward to William the Conqueror. Only the keep which, at nearly 100ft high and 150ft long are the largest in Europe, remains. At half its original height it is still a mighty building. From the end of the 13thC to 1835 the castle was used as the county gaol, and one of the nastier aspects of English history is recorded in a monument to James Parnell. He died here in 1656, aged 19, the first of the Quaker Martyrs. The castle is now the Colchester and Essex Museum and has a fascinating collection of local archaeological finds.
Another monument in Castle Park records the spot where the defeated Royalist leaders were executed by Cromwell's men, after a protracted siege of the city.

6. Dedham   7 H10
1m S of A12, B1029. Possibly the most attractive of all Essex villages, situated in the Constable country of the Stour valley. Constable was born across the river in Suffolk, but used to come each day to Dedham to school. Dedham water-mill was one of the many in the area owned by his father, Golding Constable.
The other artist associated with Dedham is Sir Alfred Munnings. The Sir Alfred Munnings Art Museum at Castle House, where he lived and had his studio, now houses a number of his paintings, drawings and sketches. *Open certain days, summer.*

Essex Flats
South Essex. Once closely forested with oaks in the Middle Ages, now a large tract of low-lying land sliding muddily into the North Sea beyond marshes and creeks.

7. Greensted-Juxta-Ongar, Church of St Andrew
7m SE of Harlow, off A128. Greensted church is England's only surviving Saxon log-built church. It used to be thought to date from 1013 when the body of St Edmund was carried through the village on its way to Bury St Edmunds. Recent scientific tests, however, suggest something close to AD850. The nave is built of oak logs split vertically in two and set in an oak sill. The date of the wood tower is uncertain, but the flint chancel is Norman, rebuilt in the 16thC, while the six dormer windows are Tudor additions. Note how well the exposed timbers have weathered during the course of 1,000 years.

8. Hadleigh Castle   3 G5
1m S of Raleigh, off A129. Immortalised by Constable, the ruins of Hadleigh castle stand on a cliff overlooking the Leigh marshes. Hugh de Burgh began the work in 1231, but before he had completed it he fell from royal favour and the castle was seized by Henry III. It remained a royal property and was rebuilt by Edward IV as a defence against a threatened French invasion. It was afterwards sold and demolished, the stones used for other local building projects. The most impressive remains are the two 14thC towers at the east end of the curtain wall.

Hatfield Forest   3 E3
Nr Bishop's Stortford, Essex. Forest and lakes rich in wildlife. Fallow deer, badgers, tufted duck and teal. The trail starts at the Shell House by the lake.

9. Hedingham Castle   7 G10
Castle Hedingham, 5m NW of Halstead, off A604. The towering, grim, 100ft keep of Hedingham Castle is one of the best preserved Norman remains in the country. It was built around 1140 by Aubrey de Vere, the first Earl of Oxford, and the de Veres remained in possession until the 20th Earl died in 1763. Throughout that time they were one of the most powerful families in the realm, with much royal influence.
The 7th Earl led the English to victory at Poitiers, and the 9th Earl rode with the young King Richard II to meet the rebels of the Peasants' Revolt of 1381. Henry VIII was a regular guest at Hedingham, and gave the 13th Earl the ostentatious title: 'Lord High Admiral of England, Ireland and Aquitaine'. The four storey keep is decorated with the typical Norman zig-zag pattern on the arches inside. On the second floor is the 30ft-high Great Hall which has original plastering and a circular gallery halfway up the wall. Over the moat a 15thC bridge leads to the Norman interior. *Open certain days, summer.*

10. Hempstead   3 F2
6m E of Saffron Walden, B1054. The church register here records the birth, in 1705 on 21st September, of: 'Richardus, filius Johannis et Maria Turpin' – in other words, Dick Turpin. His father was the landlord of the Bell Inn. Dick later moved to Whitechapel as a butcher's apprentice before becoming a sheep stealer and later a highwayman. Romanticised today, this unpleasant fellow met his end at York, aged 34.

11. Laver Marney   3 H3
5m SW of Colchester, off B1022. The Marney family who rose to prominence during the reign of Henry II, intended to build themselves the grandest mansion in the kingdom. The eight storey (higher than anywhere else at the time) four-towered gatehouse was as far as they got. In 1523 the first Lord died, to be followed by his only son two years later. Work on the house stopped and work on their tombs began. A black marble effigy of the second Lord lies beside the alabaster one of his ancestor. The gatehouse, with lovely, 16thC Italianate decoration, still stands in fine repair, overshadowing the church and surrounding buildings. *Open certain days, summer.*

Layer Marney

12. Maldon   3 G4
8m E of Chelmsford, A414. Maldon's long history begins with a small Roman settlement, later taken over by the Saxons. An Anglo-Saxon poem, 'The Battle of Maldon', celebrates the heroic English defeat in an important battle against the Danes, AD991. Under the Normans, Maldon was the first Essex town to be granted a charter, in 1171. Built originally for lepers, the ruined Hospital of St Giles is a relic from this time. Moot Hall, *High St*, a brick tower built c1440 by Sir Robert d'Arcy, has been used as a council meeting place since the late 15thC. Just along the road, The Blue Boar is a Tudor timber-framed building with an added 18thC front.
The unique, triangular 13thC tower of All Saints Church, built on a small hill overlooking the Blackwater estuary, is a landmark for sailors. The church also has fine 14thC windows, the buttresses between them holding statues to St Cedd, and others of local connection.
Maldon's other church, St Peter's, has only the tower remaining. It houses a 6,000 volume library donated to the town in 1704 by Dr Thomas Plume. Access to the collection is by a small spiral stone staircase, which leads to the charming library furnished with early 18thC fittings. *Open certain days.*

13. Manningtree, St Michael's Church   3 J2
Much restored in the last century, this church is the burial place of 17thC witch hunter Matthew Hopkins. Commissioned by Parliament, he bestowed upon himself the title 'Witchfinder General' and for three years combed the East Anglian countryside torturing confessions from those bewildered and terrified women unfortunate enough to fall into his hands. At the height of this frenzy, 68 were hanged in one day. In 1636 public outrage insisted upon an investigation into his methods, which were subsequently roundly condemned. Hopkins published a pamphlet to defend himself, but later in the same year, 1637, he conveniently died.

14. Pleshey Castle   3 F3
5m N of Chelmsford, 3m W of A130. Pleshey village lies entirely within the one-and-a-half-mile circumference of a pre-Roman ditch and rampart earthwork. During Saxon times a 50ft-high earth mound was constructed inside the rampart walls and the Normans saw this to be the natural place to build a stone castle. Pleshey Castle has seen violent days. It was besieged by King John during the baronial revolt and had turbulent times during the Wars of the Roses, too. In 1397 it belonged to the Duke of Gloucester, Richard II's uncle, who was killed upon the King's orders, in Calais. His body was brought back for burial. Later, the Duke of Exeter, who was involved in Richard's

downfall, was beheaded outside the castle walls.

The only remaining building is the beautiful 15thC brick bridge which spans the Saxon moat to the castle mound. The earthworks are very impressive, and from the top of the mound there are splendid views of the Essex countryside.

15. Saffron Walden   3 F2

Almost a museum of late medieval and Tudor architecture, few towns have retained their medieval street pattern as well as Saffron Walden. Prosperous since the Middle Ages, today it remains a bustling market town and lies attractively surrounded by lovely old villages and scattered hamlets.

The town got its expressive prefix in the Middle Ages when it was a centre for the production of saffron. This delicate spice is made from the dried stigmas of the saffron crocus – it takes about 30,000 flowers to make one pound.

At the top of the hill on the common are the crumbling remains of a great Norman castle built by Geoffrey de Mandeville c1100. It was destroyed by Cromwell's army during the Civil War. The Lord Protector himself had headquarters at the former Sun Inn, a many-gabled 15thC building. There are some fine medieval houses in Castle Street, Bridge Street and Church Street with good timber and plasterwork, and late Georgian houses in the High Street.

The Church of St Mary is the largest in Essex, and a fine example of the Perpendicular style with a glorious clerestory. The spire, at 193ft, is a 19thC addition which blends surprisingly well. Note the magnificent roofs and carvings inside the church.

Finally, it is worth considering an earlier, pre-historic culture. On the east end of the common is a maze cut into the ground, thought to be around 2,000 years old. One supposes it had some religious significance, possibly connected with a fertility cult.

16. St Osyth's Priory   3 J3

7m SE of Colchester, B1027. First, the legend of St Osyth. She had been devoted to the contemplative life from an early age. On the day of her wedding to Sighere, King of East Anglia, she slipped away while he was hunting, and took the veil. The King was sympathetic to her calling and handed her land to found a priory. Beheaded by marauding Danes in AD653 – as she prayed,

it's said – she picked up her head and carried it over to her chapel, and died there. Her tomb gained the reputation of being able to cure afflictions and St Osyth's became an important religious centre.

Come the Reformation, the 12thC abbey was swept away all but for the marvellous flint-patterned gatehouse. The house built on the priory site has a fine collection of jade and ceramics, and a beautiful garden. The parish church, across the street from the gatehouse is worth a visit for its hammer-beam roof and red-brick arches. *Priory open summer; grounds all year.*

17. Thaxted   3 G2

Often, and wrongly, thought to be another Essex cloth town, Thaxted's wealth, evident in its church and medieval buildings, in fact originally derived from a cutlery industry. A document of 1381 recorded 78 cutlers and 11 smiths at work in the town. The guildhall, *Town St,* a splendid half-timbered building with an open ground floor which was used as a trading area, was built by the Cutlers' Guild c1390. The industry declined by the 16thC and the guildhall was taken over by the town council. It has recently been fully restored. Stoney Lane, running from the church to the guildhall, has some of the finest of the many 15thC houses in the town.

The glory of the Church of St John the Baptist is the magnificent slender, soaring spire, originally built in 1475, but replaced in 1814 after lightning damage. A host of grotesque gargoyles glares down from the nave roof.

18. Waltham Abbey   3 E4

One of the best surviving examples of Norman architecture in the country. Waltham Abbey was actually founded as a collegiate church before the Norman Conquest, and was consecrated in 1060. King Harold's body was brought here after he was slain at the Battle of Hastings and a black marble slab recently excavated is thought to be part of his sarcophagus.

Until the Dissolution, the Abbey was one of the richest and most important monastic sites in Britain. What survives, however, is magnificent. The great 12thC nave, with its majestic circular piers and fine clerestory, is comparable to Durham Cathedral. Remains of a 14thC painting can be seen in the Lady chapel. An interesting later addition is the east window, with stained glass by Burne-Jones.

LINCOLNSHIRE

1. Alford Mill   7 E3

10m NW of Skegness, A1104. One of the three working windmills in the county. Known as Myer's Mill, it was built in 1837 and has six storeys and five sails.

2. Ancaster   7 B4

5m N of Grantham, off A153. A pleasant village, spread out along part of the Roman road, Ermine Street. The Roman town was known as Causennae, and it must have been a prosperous place as thousands of coins have been discovered as well as pottery artefacts and part of a mosaic pavement. These are housed in Grantham Museum. Earth ramparts and ditches, probably dating from the 4thC and originally enclosing all nine acres of the camp, are near the church. In the churchyard are two coffins reputed to be Roman.

3. Belton House   7 B5

2½m NE of Grantham, A607. This attractive, if somewhat forbidding, yellow-grey stone manor house was built from designs by Christopher Wren in 1689. The copula high

above the roof is the dominant exterior feature.

Inside there are elegant and beautifully-proportioned rooms with fine furniture (note the 'blue bed' of William III) and collections of porcelain and silver. Marvellous paintings adorn the walls, including works by Titian, Rembrandt, Reynolds and Van Dyck.

The pleasantly wooded park is home to deer and black sheep – and to the Bellmont tower, built in 1750. There's a sundial, formal gardens and scented rose gardens, too. *Open summer.*

Belton House

4. Boston 7 D4

Landmark for miles around, the Boston 'Stump' is the misnomer applied to the 272ft tower of St Botolph's church. A climb up the 365 steps to the top is rewarded with splendid views over sea and land, and on a clear day Lincoln Cathedral can be seen. The octagonal lantern on top of the tower allows sunlight to flood into the spacious interior. Note the handsome pulpit, the embossed roof and the magnificent carved stalls.

Boston's fame as a port was second only to London's by 1204 when King John granted it a charter. But the Black Death, floods and the development of American trade, ensured its decline by the 16thC. John Cotton, vicar of St Botolph's in 1612, was instrumental in encouraging the Lincolnshire Puritans to emigrate to America, where they founded Boston, Massachusetts.

Shodfriars Hall, *South St*, is a beautifully restored 16thC half-timbered building, once part of a Dominican Friary, from which it takes its name. It is now a local theatre and arts centre. Along the road is the 15thC guildhall which now houses a museum with items of local interest. These include the iron-gated cells in which the first Lincolnshire Pilgrim Fathers were held after their abortive attempt to leave for America in 1607.

Boston Stump

5. Bourne 7 C6

Reputedly the birthplace of Hereward the Wake but the evidence connecting Hereward with the de Wake family, who held a Norman castle here, is slight. The de Wakes founded Bourne Abbey in 1138, but this was destroyed at the Dissolution, with only the nave of the Abbey church remaining, incorporated into the parish church.

Red Hall, *South St*, is a restored Tudor house that once belonged to the Catholic Digby family, who were involved in the Gunpowder Plot. It was subsequently used as the local station master's house (surely the grandest in England!) and is furnished with period pieces.

6. Crowland Abbey 7 D6

Crowland Abbey was founded in the early 8thC in what must have then been an almost inaccessible mosquito-ridden swamp. The first of many Viking raids came in 870, when all but three of the monks were slain. Abbot Theodore died while praying at the altar for his assailants' souls. His skull is preserved in a glass case on the north wall, and you can see where the sword went in. More sacking followed, and it wasn't until the 12thC that the monks enjoyed peace and prosperity, entertaining kings and nobles.

At the Dissolution most of the buildings were demolished, and it was further damaged by Cromwell in the Civil War. The north aisle of the Abbey church survives, and there is the great west front, adorned with statues of saints and abbots, apostles and kings. Perhaps the most evocative remain of all, however, is the great isolated Norman arch spanning the empty Fenland sky.

7. Grantham 7 B5

Mentioned in the Domesday Book, Grantham is a very ancient town. The Angel and Royal Hotel, *High St*, is one of England's finest medieval inns. The front is 15thC, but parts

of the building date back to the 12thC when it is believed to have been a manorial hall. Tradition has it that King John held a court here in 1213, and Richard III was staying here when he signed the Duke of Buckingham's death warrant. Almost directly opposite is the George Hotel, the north wing of which lodged Isaac Newton when he was a pupil at the grammar school.

St Wulfram's Church is one of the finest in Lincolnshire. Its beautiful 28ft spire is 14thC, as are the splendid windows that enlighten the interior. There is a library of chained books above the south porch, and a crypt which was once the simple shrine of St Wulfram.

8. Grimsthorpe Castle 7 C5

4m W of Bourne, A151. The grandest house in Lincolnshire, the oldest part of which dates from the 13thC – a turret from an earlier abbey. The castle was substantially (and hastily) rebuilt in 1541 when the owner, the Duke of Suffolk, wished to entertain Henry VIII. Grimsthorpe was where Henry accused his wife Catherine Howard of having committed adultery, when he wished to dispose of her.

In 1724 Vanbrugh was commissioned to rebuild the house on a grand scale. He died before the work was finished, but the north front was completed according to his plans before the money ran out. Work began again in 1840 when the west front was built in Gothic style. Inside are sumptuous state rooms with numerous treasures including a Van Dyck of Charles I and the costume he wore for the sitting, and the House of Lords clock which stopped at exactly the moment George III died. Vanbrugh's Great Hall rises on a double tier of arches to the roof. *Open summer.*

9. Gunby Hall 7 E3

7m W of Skegness, off A158. A rectangular red-brick building with stone dressings, built in 1700 for Sir William Massingberd. The oak staircase and wainscotting of the interior were added 35 years later. It is often thought that Gunby is Tennyson's 'haunt of ancient peace', for he was a regular visitor. Superbly panelled rooms contain fine furniture and portraits by Reynolds. There are formal gardens and herbaceous borders within the 1,400 acre grounds. *Open certain days or by arrangement, summer.*

10. Harlaxton Manor 7 B5

2m S of Grantham, off A607. A strange, fevered place, Harlaxton was built over a 20-year time span from 1827 by Anthony Salvin for Gregory Williams who, for reasons best known to himself, preferred to be known as Gregory Gregory.

A long drive leads to the house, a jumble of Jacobean, Gothic and Tudor styles, with turrets, towers, great banks of windows, cupolas, bays and arches – in short, Victorian imagination gone mad. The interior is in a similar vein, with a number of trompe-l'oeil effects.

Harlaxton was used, highly appropriately, as the setting for the film 'The Ruling Class'. It's now a part of the American University of Evansville. *Open by arrangement.*

11. Harrington Hall 7 D3
3m W of Partney, 1½m N of A158. A beautiful, red-brick mansion situated at 300ft, one of the highest points in Lincolnshire. It was the home of Vincent Amcotts, a good friend of Tennyson and it is often thought that the lovely garden here is the famed one into which Maud was invited. *Open certain days, summer.*

12. Heckington, Church of St Andrew 7 C4
4m E of Sleaford, A17. One of the most outstanding Decorated churches in Britain, the exterior is a monument to British architecture. It has a fine tower and spire, beautiful windows and tracery. Built in the 14thC, the possible founder was Richard de Potesgrave, Edward III's chaplain. The Easter Sepulchre, three sets of panels depicting the Easter story, is an exquisite work with fascinating detail. The tracery work in the east window has been hailed as a masterpiece. Nearby is an eight-sail windmill, one of the few still operating in England.

13. Horncastle 7 D3
An important market town whose origins can be seen in the 13ft-thick wall which remains from the Roman town of Banovallum. Roman coins have also been discovered nearby.
St Mary's Church has a collection of early chained books. There's also a collection of scythe blades and pikes said to have been used at the Battle of Winceby and a painted memorial to Sir Ingram Hopton who died for the Royalist cause on that field. His adversary, Oliver Cromwell, made the arrangements for his burial in the church.
Horncastle's huge 10-day August horse fairs, held until the last century, were famed throughout Europe. Of the many attractive pubs, note the Fighting Cocks Inn which still has a cockpit in the yard.

14. Lincoln 7 B3
Built on a steep hill rising from the surrounding plain, the silhouette of the cathedral, one of the major glories of European religious architecture, dominates the town. Also in evidence are the remains of William the Conqueror's impregnable castle and a wealth of medieval buildings.
Lincoln's prominent position made the site a natural one for settlement, and Iron and Bronze Age artefacts have been found. The Romans arrived in AD47 and established a military settlement called Lindum, a corruption of the British 'Lindon' which meant the association of a pool and hill fort. Later, the settlement became a 'colonia' – a civilian town with amenities. The Danes followed, bringing prosperity by using Lincoln as a port, and after them, the Normans, establishing the wool and cloth trade to produce the famous Lincoln Green and Scarlet cloth.
Dating from the early 12thC, Jew's House, *The Straight,* is one of the oldest surviving examples of domestic architecture in England. Note the chimney and the marvellous decorated doorway. Lincoln had, like many a cathedral city, a large Jewish population. In 1255 serious anti-Semitic riots broke out in Lincoln, connected with the usual medieval accusations of ritual murder. Many Jews were murdered, both by rioters and the judiciary. In 1290 Edward I expelled all Jews from England. It should be remembered that without their help many of the greatest medieval monuments in England would never

have been built. It is said that half of Henry II's income was in the form of loans from Aaron the Jew. Certainly Lincoln Cathedral would never have been completed without Aaron's money. His 12thC house, *Steep Hill,* is well-preserved and is claimed to be the oldest inhabited house in England.
Also of interest is the guildhall which occupies the upper storey of the Stonebow, a 15thC town gate with four arches. Before each council meeting at the guildhall the 14thC Mote Bell is rung.

14. Lincoln Castle
Castle Hill. Even today an awesome spectacle, this once invulnerable stronghold was built by William the Conqueror c1076. Entrance is through the massive 14thC eastern gateway, opening onto lawns fronted by the 19thC Gothic Assizes. Next door to these are the prison buildings, in use for about a 100 years, from 1787.
In the south east corner of the grounds is the Observatory Tower, built on a Norman base by a Victorian prison governor with a taste for astronomy. Beyond this is the 12thC keep, or Lucy Tower, named after Countess Lucy Thorold who fortified it. King Stephen was held prisoner here in 1141. The prison chapel has a depressing atmosphere and the grisly prisoner's stalls are ingeniously designed to allow minimum movement for the prisoner and no view of his fellows. The iron rings which bound them to the walls, can still be seen.

Lincoln

14. Lincoln Cathedral
Off Bailgate. The third largest and perhaps the finest of the English cathedrals, both in its position and architecture. Sitting above the River Witham its triple-towered stone exterior shimmers various shades of honey and peach in the changing light.
The first cathedral was consecrated in 1092, built by the first Bishop of Lincoln, Remigius, and the west front, between the recesses on either side of the doorway, incorporates his work. Hugh of Avalon became bishop in 1186, and began a complete rebuilding, for in the previous year the cathedral had been cracked down the middle by an earthquake. The work went on long after Hugh's death in 1200: it wasn't completed until 1280. The result became a model of English Gothic architecture, a commanding, beautifully proportioned building, alive with intricate detail. The west front is unsurpassed, and behind it soars the 271ft central tower, a miracle of richly-ornate carving.
Inside is a host of treasures. The elaborately carved choir stalls, the alternating black and white marble of the nave piers, the 13thC glass in the north transept, Remigius's black marble memorial, and many excellent brasses, are all deeply impressive. Undoubtably the finest of all, however, is the Angel Choir, an elegant delicate, and detailed Geometrical Decorated work: one of the loveliest pieces of architecture in the world.

15. Louth 7 D2
In the Middle Ages second only to Lincoln in prominence, today Louth is a pleasant, mainly Georgian market town, with a relaxed lived-in feel about it. Profits from the wool trade and loans from Jews funded the building of a

Cistercian abbey here at the end of the 12thC, on a scale slightly smaller than Lincoln Cathedral.

Louth was severely affected by the Dissolution. The local priests had raised a protest against this royal act of vandalism, and were publicly executed in Louth market place for their pains. Revenge was also taken on the buildings, and nothing survives of the great abbey.

But consolation can be found in the Church of St James, built by the townsfolk for their own use, and one of the loveliest churches in England. It has a graceful pinnacled tower of 140ft, which is topped harmoniously by a slender spire of equal height supported by flying buttresses. The main part of the church is mid 15thC, and the tower and spire were added in 1500–1515.

16. Somersby Rectory　　　7 D3
Somersby, 5m E of Horncastle, 2m N of A158. Alfred Lord Tennyson's father, Dr George Tennyson, moved into Somersby Rectory in 1808, and it was here that his son was born. Tennyson's early life here was not happy due to his father's moods of depression. Having had a short spell at Louth Grammar School, he was educated by his father at home and did much of his writing in an attic reached by a separate stair. He continued his studies at Trinity College, Cambridge. *View rectory from outside only.*

Next door is a fine moated grange said to have been designed by Vanbrugh. There is a small collection of Tennyson relics and photographs in a glass case in the 15thC Church of St Margaret, including a valentine he sent.

17. Spalding　　　7 D5
There are over 10,000 acres of bulb fields in Lincolnshire, and in order that the bulbs are at their best, the flower heads must be cut in early spring. In their millions they are used to decorate the floats of Spalding Tulip Festival. This is a recent custom, but for the historically-minded there's Ayscoughfree House, built in the 15thC but with extensive later additions and repairs. In 1710 it was the meeting place of Spalding Gentlemen's Society, whose members included Alexander Pope, Joseph Addison and Sir Isaac Newton. Beautiful walks in the grounds and around the area often surpass the glory of the Dutch fields.

18. Stamford　　　7 C6
A fascinating, ancient town, with over 300 important medieval and many 16th–18thC buildings. The best streets for seeing Stamford's Queen Anne, Georgian and Regency houses are Barn Hill, Broad Street and St Martin's High Street.

Although there was a Roman settlement here, it wasn't until medieval times that the town reached the height of its importance as a wool centre. In the 13thC it had a castle, mint, priory and 17 churches. The Bastion is the only remaining part of the 13thC town wall which once encircled Stamford. St Paul's St has the remaining 14thC gatehouse of Brazenose College, occupied by rebellious Oxford students as an alternative to their university. Opposite is the grammar school,

founded in 1532, and with a 13thC chapel. The ruins of the Benedictine Priory of St Leonard, *Priory Road,* include a fine west front of c1149. Stamford also has a number of medieval almshouses. The most interesting are the late 15thC Browne's Hospital and Burghley Hospital, originally an 11thC Benedictine foundation which was much enlarged by Lord Burghley in the 16thC. Of Stamford's 17 churches, only six remain. Of these St Mary's and All Saints are the finest, both 13thC, and both with elegant spires. St Mary's is particularly notable for the chapel of the golden choir.

The George Hotel, *St Martin's High Street,* is one of the original coaching inns on the Great North Road. It's built upon the 12thC crypt of the Hospital of the Knights of St John of Jerusalem. One of its more hidden attractions is a 14thC wooden screen incorporated in one of the lavatories. The hotel has a portrait of England's heaviest ever man, Daniel Lambert, who died while passing through the town (exhausted by its architectural treasures, no doubt). Not even 6ft tall, he measured 9½ft round, and weighed in excess of 52 stone.

19. Tattershall Castle　　　7 C4
1½m N of Dogdyke, off A153. The 100ft-high keep of Tattershall Castle is perhaps the finest example of medieval brickwork in Britain. Built on the base of an earlier, 13thC, castle, the design seems to be aimed more at ostentation than defence, and the interior rooms were planned on a palatial scale. The third Baron Cromwell, who built the castle, died without an heir and, passing through many hands, by the early 18thC it had become derelict. But when interest was shown by an enthusiastic American group who wanted to dismantle the castle and take it to the States, Lord Curzon came to the rescue. Having restored it, he presented Tattershall Castle to the National Trust.

A set of the original fireplaces has survived, decorated with heraldic devices, but other fittings perished during the castle's long neglect. There are good views of the countryside from the keep.

Tattershall Castle

20. Woolsthorpe Manor　　　7 B6
7m S of Grantham, off A1. Sir Isaac Newton was born in this attractive 17thC manor house on Christmas Day, 1642. In the orchard in front of the house is a descendant of the apple tree which caused the young man to formulate the laws of gravitation. This event (probably apocryphal anyway) happened while Newton had returned home from Trinity College, Cambridge in 1665, when the college closed because of the plague. *Open certain days, summer.*

✺ NORFOLK ✺

1. Binham Priory　　　7 G5
1m N of Binham. Founded in 1091 by William the Conqueror's nephew, Binham Priory is one of the finest surviving examples of Early English architecture. The west window, with its great window now unfortunately bricked up, dates from 1226–44 (even earlier than Westminster Abbey).

2. Blickling Hall　　　7 H5
2m N of Aylsham, B1354. The manor of Blickling was first the property of King Harold. It passed through many hands down to Sir John Fastolf, who sold it to Geoffrey Boleyn, grandfather of Anne, second queen of Henry VIII and mother of Elizabeth I. The present building, one of the finest in the

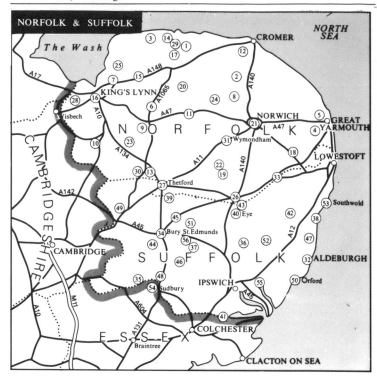

NORFOLK & SUFFOLK

Jacobean style in the country, was built from 1616–27 by Sir Henry Hobart, Lord Chief Justice under James I.
The pinnacled and gabled facade in red brick gives a deceptive impression of Blickling's size, for the house is deeper than it's wide. The State Rooms, largely in elegant 18thC style, are truly magnificent. The Long Gallery is unquestionably the finest of the rooms, extending 127ft along the east front. The plasterwork ceiling here is a delight, as are the slightly bizarre decorated allegorical panels. There's more good plasterwork in the south drawing room, and an excellent chimney-piece. The State Bedroom is particularly handsome and the Peter the Great room has a splendid tapestry, showing the Tzar surveying the Battle of Poltowa. It was given to the second Earl of Buckinghamshire by Catherine the Great while he was ambassador to Moscow.
The second Earl's pyramidical tomb is secluded in the park woods to the north west of the house. Have a picnic in the famous gardens and take a walk alongside the mile-long lake or through the wooded Pleasure Gardens. *Open most days, summer.*

3. Burnham Thorpe   7 G5
1½m SE of Burnham Market. Most famous of the seven villages in the area with the prefix Burnham. Lord Nelson was born at the vicarage here, which has since been demolished. But a local legend has the old flint barn next to the village pub as his birthplace: Nelson's mother is said to have been out riding when the moment came upon her and she was unable to reach home. The church and the Nelson Hall next door contain Nelson memorabilia: his medicine chest, some letters and a ragged white ensign, amongst other personal items. The church lectern is made from timber from HMS Victory. *Nelson Hall open certain days.*

4. Burgh Castle   7 K7
3m W of Great Yarmouth, off A143. Called Garianoum by the Romans, it was built

around AD290 to guard what was then an estuary. Three massive walls of flint and brick remain. Records give evidence of a Christian mission here in the 7thC, and there are traces of a Norman castle.

5. Caister Castle   7 K6
1½m W of Caister, off A1064. Sir John Fastolf for whom this castle was built c1430, was probably the model for Shakespeare's Falstaff. His claim to fame was leading the English archers at Agincourt, and besieging Caen and Rouen during the French Wars. After his death the castle passed to the Paston family, who wrote many of their famous letters here. They sold it in the 17thC, and it was demolished for building materials.
The ruined keep built of an attractive pinkish yellow brick, remains, and there are traces of the surrounding wall, the whole surrounded by a moat. A museum of old cars has been sited recently in the castle grounds. *Open most days summer.*

5. Caister Roman Town   7 K6
Off A149. A Roman port, surrounded by a stone wall, was built here cAD125. The site occupies about 30 acres, and apart from the wall, about 10ft high in places, the foundations of the houses can be seen.

6. Castle Acre   7 G6
5m N of Swaffham, off A1065. One of the largest castle earthworks in England, with a charming village situated in the outer bailey. It was built by William de Warenne, son-in-law of William the Conqueror, shortly after the Conquest, and it's probable that he chose a pre-existing Saxon site. Settlement here is thought to go back even further. The effort involved in raising the 100ft mound can be imagined. Of the original building only traces of the ruined walls and the recently exposed foundations remain, although there is a 13thC gatehouse, picturesquely straddling one of the village streets.

6. Castle Acre Priory   7 G6
Off A1065. This grand ruin is beautifully

situated in lush green meadows by the River Nar. The Priory, built in 1090 by the son of William de Warenne, enjoyed wealthy endowment until the Dissolution. The entrance is through an early 16thC gatehouse, leading to the magnificent west front of the priory church, a beautiful example of elaborate Norman blind arcading. Behind are the crumbling walls, columns and exposed foundations. There's also a charming Tudor prior's house in perfect repair.

During the last century, while a bridge was being built over the Nar, workmen discovered two massive stone coffins, possibly those of William de Warenne and his wife. The vicar ordered the men to drag the coffins up to the village, but it seems there was an argument about payment, and the coffins were thrown back in the river, and where, somewhere, they remain. *Open most days.*

7. Castle Rising   7 F6
An attractive village containing one of the best preserved Norman keeps in the area, and an interesting 17thC hospital. Rising was a port from Roman times, and only declined in the 14thC with the silting up of the River Babingley.

The castle was built c1150 by William d'Albini, whose father had been William the Conqueror's butler. In Edward II's reign it became royal property, and Edward's widow, Queen Isabella, was imprisoned here on the suspicion that she was involved in his death. Richard II sold Rising in 1397. The castle fell into decay and the village subsequently declined.

The 50ft keep is in surprisingly good condition. Access is by steps leading to the Norman vestibule of the impressive, but now roofless Great Hall. A massive stone staircase leads to a fascinating sequence of rooms, galleries and minor staircases.

Bede House, or Howard Hospital, was built in 1614 by Henry Howard, to provide for 12 women 'single, 56 at least, no common beggar, harlot scold or drunkard' as the provisions state. Twelve such upright ladies can still be found living there today, and they may occasionally be seen on their way to church, dressed in their distinctive red cloaks with the Howard arms, and wearing tall steeple hats. *Hospital open most days.*

8. Cawston Church   7 H6
4m W of Aylsham, B1145. One of Norfolk's finest churches, begun by Sir Michael de la Pole in 1414, and completed by his widow after his death a year later. It has an impressively austere grey stone tower, contrasting with the magnificent hammer-beam roof inside, richly carved with cherubim and angels. A mile away, on the Norwich road, is the site of the duelling ground where Sir Henry Hobart of Blickling was killed by his adversary, Oliver le Neve. A small urn on a pedestal commemorates the event.

9. Cockley Cley   7 G6
4m SW of Swaffham. An atmospheric reconstruction of an Iceni village of about AD160. All in wood, it contains the fortified stockade and drawbridge with watchtower, a round house for the village chief, a long hut that would have been the communal quarters for the warriors, and smaller huts for the

everyday occupants.

The interiors are complete with domestic detail, and with its low-lying setting in a marshy field, it is easy to imagine the daily life of pre-Saxon times. The 15thC forge house, a remarkable building, is used as a museum of local archaeological finds.

10. Denver Sluices   7 E6
1m S of Downham Market, A10. The first attempt to control the tidal waters of the River Ouse and to drain the fens was made in 1652. The purpose was to bring agricultural prosperity to the area and the scheme was master-minded by Vermuyden, Charles I's Dutch engineer. The present Denver Old Sluice was built in 1832 by Sir John Rennie who also built the old Waterloo Bridge. The steel gates have been added since Rennie's time, and the load has been lessened by the opening of the Cut-off Channel. This is good fishing and sailing territory.

11. East Dereham   7 G6
Still 'the pattern of an English market town' that the novelist George Borrow observed. He was born at Dumpling Green, about a mile away.

East Dereham today is a bustling town with a number of Georgian houses. St Nicholas's church is impressive, with two towers and a mixture of styles from Norman to Perpendicular. The seven-sacrament font is particularly lovely. In the churchyard a small sunken chamber is known as the well of St Withburga, who founded a church and convent here in the 7thC. Her grave became an important shrine and influenced the growth of the town. Jealous of Withburga's posthumous popularity, monks from Ely stole her remains and reburied them in their cathedral. The story goes that as a sign of her disapproval she caused a spring to issue from her desecrated grave, which still feeds the well in the churchyard today.

William Cowper, the poet, lived and died at Dereham, and the monument to him in the church is by John Flaxman.

12. Felbrigg Hall   7 J5
3½m N of Matlask, B1436. A stately Jacobean hall, built for Sir Thomas Windham in 1620, and subsequently enlarged, the last time in 1750. The motto 'Gloria In Excelsis Deo' is spelt out in giant stone lettering on the front balustrade. The interior rooms are principally 18thC, and contain period furniture and pictures.

Felbrigg church, isolated in the Hall's extensive parkland, is famous for its monuments by Grinling Gibbons and Nollekens, and its excellent brasses, notably that of Sir Simon de Felbrigg and his wife. Save time for a walk around the grounds which contain an orangery with remarkable camellias and a walled garden. The park and lake can be seen from the lakeside walk. *House open most days, summer; park daily.*

13. Grime's Graves   7 G7
7m NW of Thetford, off A134. Named after the Anglo-Saxon god Grim, this is one of the most interesting and extensive neolithic sites in Europe, in the appropriately desolate setting of heathland. The Graves are flintmines dating back 4,000 years. There are over 360, which descend to a depth of about 40ft. These are the only ancient flint mines accessible to the public and you can climb down a straight iron ladder to explore the inter-connected tunnels below. The pick marks (the pick was made from a deer's antler) made by the men who worked here, are still plainly visible. At the site office is a display of some of the items that have been found, including antler picks and carved flints. Skilled men at the town of Brandon, a few miles away, still practise the craft of 'flint-knapping' – shaping the flints.

Cockley Cley

14. Holkham Hall 7 G5

1½m W of Wells-next-the-Sea, A149. A massive place, Holkham Hall was built in the Palladian style for Thomas Coke, first Earl of Leicester, by William Kent. It took from 1733 to 1761 to complete.

The interior is breathtaking. The Grand Hall, of pink Derbyshire alabaster and gold, rises 60ft to the ornate plaster ceiling, and leads into a gallery of Ionic columns and the grand staircase. The whole place is packed with treasures that many a national museum might envy, picked up on Coke's Grand Tour of Europe. Paintings by Van Dyck, Titian, Lorrain and Poussin compete for attention with delicate Sèvres porcelain, tapestries and Roman statuary.

The great park, designed by Capability Brown, extends for miles, with flocks of geese on the lake and deer grazing in the woods.

The third Thomas Coke to occupy Holkham, known as 'Coke of Norfolk', became famous for his agricultural innovations. He introduced crop rotation and experimented with new breeds of livestock, increasing his revenue tenfold, and ushering in a period of agricultural prosperity for the county. *House open certain days, summer; park daily.*

15. Houghton Hall 7 G5

4m SE of Great Bircham. Standing in a beautifully-landscaped park, Houghton Hall was built for Sir Robert Walpole in 1721–35. Comparison with Holkham is inevitable, and from the outside Houghton is a mellower, more attractive building.

The interior is less ostentatious than Holkham and displays equally beautiful craftsmanship. Much of the original furnishings by William Kent remain in the superb State Rooms, and the house is noted for the brilliance of its ceilings and carvings. Debt forced Walpole's descendants to sell many of their treasures, including a magnificent collection of paintings, and in the mid 19thC Houghton was described as a 'picture only of magnificent desolation'. This century has seen a turn for the better, and the house has been restored by the present Lord Cholmondeley. *Open certain days, summer.*

Houghton Hall

16. King's Lynn 7 F6

Lynn, as it is known to the locals, was established long before the Conquest, but it was under the Normans that it began to flourish as one of the most important ports in the country. A wealth of fine buildings from the 15th to the 19thC testifies to its enduring prosperity.

In 1100 Herbert de Losinga, first Bishop of Norwich, founded St Margaret's Church, and the town was then known as Bishop's Lynn. King John granted the town its first royal charter in 1204, but it wasn't until Henry VIII confiscated the bishop's lands in 1537 that Bishop's Lynn became King's Lynn.

Two buildings of special note are the guildhall and St George's Guildhall. The first, built of flint and chequered patterned stone in 1421, overlooks the Saturday market. The civic regalia housed inside gives an idea of Lynn's wealth. The gold and enamel King John's cup (dated 1340, so not really his) is one of the finest treasures of its date anywhere. There are also charters dating from the reign of King John, and one from the days of King Knut, better known as Canute. St George's Guildhall, is the largest surviving medieval guildhall in England. In its time it has been a corn exchange, a theatre (Shakespeare's company is known to have played here), a warehouse and a painter's workshop. It's now a theatre again, focus for the town's annual festival. *Guildhall and St George's Guildhall open most days.*

17. Little Walsingham 7 G5

The famous pilgrimage centre of the Shrine of Our Lady, attracting thousands of visitors every year. It all began in the early Middle Ages, when the Virgin Mary appeared in a dream to Lady Richeld, wife of the lord of the manor. Lady Richeld was commanded to build a replica of the House of Annunciation where the Angel Gabriel appeared to the Virgin Mary, at a site indicated by a spring of water. This she did, and Walsingham became second only to Canterbury as a place of pilgrimage. Among its visitors were Edward I, Henry III, Henry VIII and Cardinal Wolsey who hoped the change of air would cure 'the weakness of his stomach'.

Because the pilgrims were as numerous as the stars in the sky, and because one of the shrine's most precious relics was a phial of milk supposedly from the Virgin's breast, the Milky Way became known also as Walsingham Way.

A great church and priory were built to cater for the many pilgrims, but only scattered relics remain – a reminder of the chilling efficiency of Henry VIII's Dissolution of the Monasteries. The pilgrimages began again in the 1930s, when a replica of the shrine was established by Anglo-Catholics. Built of brick, it is not distinguished architecturally, but it exudes an atmosphere of tranquillity. In the tradition of the shrine it has the relics of two saints, and two pieces of the True Cross.

18. Loddon 7 J7

Once a Broadland port serviced by the now sadly disappeared Norfolk Wherries. It remains a delightful, compact town with many 17th and 18thC houses and a fine old water-mill on the River Chet. The Church of the Holy Trinity is a prepossessing building of 1480. The poor box, on a pillar facing the door, is carved from a solid piece of oak. A relic from an earlier Saxon church, it is one of the oldest in the country. Also of note is the medieval painted screen depicting the martyrdom of St William of Norwich.

19. New Buckenham 7 H7

New Buckenham became 'new' in 1146 when a Norman baron, William d'Albini, gave his castle at Old Buckenham to the Augustinians, and built a replacement here. It was demolished in the 1640s and only the overgrown moated mound is left. Remains can be seen of what is thought to be the first round keep in England. The village which grew up round the castle was planned on a grid-iron pattern: this is a rare medieval example. In the middle of the market square is the 17thC market house, its first storey supported on wooden columns, one of which was used as a whipping post.

Norfolk Broads 7 K6

A number of shallow lakes within the triangle of Norwich, Lowestoft and Sea Palling, interconnected by the Rivers Bure, Yare and Waveney. Now a crowded resort of amateur summer sailors and motor-boat cruisers, their origin was long puzzled over. In fact they are the result of Saxon peat diggings which carried on into early Norman times. Considering their extent, over 200 miles, an immense amount of peat must have been obtained.

20. North Elmham 7 H6

5m N of East Dereham B1110. The ancient seat of the Saxon Bishops of East Anglia from AD800 until AD866 when it was pillaged by the Danes. The See was briefly restored in

955, but removed to Thetford in 1075. The cathedral has been excavated so that the foundations may be seen, and there are also traces of a Saxon fortification.

21. Norwich   7 J6

The county town of Norfolk, and truly the 'fine city' it proclaims itself. Its irregular street plan indicates its Saxon origins, while a wealth of surviving buildings testifies to its continued importance from the early Middle Ages onward. In addition to its magnificent cathedral, Norwich could once boast a church for every Sunday and a pub for every other day of the year.

Norwich Market

Modern development has been judiciously restrained (with one or two exceptions) and many of the city's old buildings have been saved and restored. With its twisting streets and alleys, the great castle keep or the cathedral spire rising up from around every other corner, Norwich is the ideal place to explore on foot.

Begun in 1450, St Peter Mancroft, *off Haymarket*, is a glorious Perpendicular church, with an added Victorian Gothic tower. The nave columns and clerestory give a spacious, lofty feel to the interior, and the hammer-beam roof is particularly notable. There are some fine monuments, including one to Sir Thomas Browne, author of 'Religio Medici'.

Stranger's Hall, *Charing Cross*, is a 15thC merchant's house built upon an early 13thC undercroft. Its name derives from immigrant cloth workers who lived here in the 17thC. Furnished rooms show a variety of fashions between the 16th and 19thC and it now houses a museum of costume and period furniture. *Open weekdays*. Flint-faced **Bridewell Museum**, *Bridewell Alley*, was built upon a 14thC vaulted undercroft. The museum has exhibits relating to local crafts and industries from the Middle Ages to the present day. *Open weekdays*.

The 13thC vaults of a Dominican Priory have been converted to an arts centre at Blackfriars Hall, *Elm Hill*. The adjoining St Andrew's Hall, a venue for concerts, is the 15thC priory church. Elm Hill is one of Norwich's most picturesque streets.

21. Norwich Castle   7 J6

Castle Plain. From its high mound the castle dominates the city centre. The magnificent keep was built in the 12thC, but owes its pristine condition to a refacing in the 19thC. It had a turbulent early history and was made into the city gaol in 1220, a function it maintained until 1887 when it was converted to become the county museum.

Although the museum has recently been modernised, the Great Hall on the first floor remains much as it must have been 600 years ago. Of major interest are a fine natural history section and a comprehensive collection of paintings of the Norwich school, as well as archaeological exhibits, Lowestoft porcelain and Norwich silver.

There are regular conducted tours of the castle battlements and dungeons.

21. Norwich Cathedral   7 J6

Tombland. This beautiful example of Norman architecture was begun in 1096 by Herbert de Losinga on the Pope's orders, as a punishment for the sin of simony. Herbert certainly paid his penance well.

The splendid vaulted roof of the nave has over 300 carved bosses, and there are more in the cloisters (the largest in England), totalling 1,200 in all. The Bishop's Throne, behind the altar, may be 1,000 years old. This would make it the oldest in any English cathedral. The graceful, slender spire is second in height only to that at Salisbury, and equally as lovely. It's a 15thC replacement of an earlier spire that collapsed in 1362.

The cathedral close stretches down to the River Wensum, and the 15thC river gate, Pull's Ferry. There are a number of excellent Georgian buildings in the close.

The two cathedral gates face the cobbled square of Tombland. The Erpingham Gate is regarded as one of the finest in the Perpendicular style in the country. St Ethelbert's is slightly earlier, built jointly by the townspeople and monks as a penance after one of their periodic riots in the Middle Ages.

Norwich Cathedral

22. Old Buckenham   7 H7

3m SE of Attleborough, B1077. Scattered around a 40-acre village green with duck ponds and playing fields, Old Buckenham is composed of a number of hamlets with such names as Chattergate, Hog's Snout, Loss Wroo, Hungry Hill and Puddledock. The old castle, which William d'Albini gave to the Augustinians to use to build a priory, has disappeared but for the mound; there is also only scant trace of the priory itself. The church is a small gem with a thatched roof and roses in the churchyard.

23. Oxburgh Hall   7 F7

Oxborough. A magnificent, early Tudor semi-fortified dwelling, with embattled walls, slender, decorated chimneys and a magnificent gatehouse. All of softest yellow-red brick it stands romantically, surrounded by a fine, wide moat.

Licence for the fortifications was received by Edmund Bedingfeld from Edward IV, and work must have begun soon after. Although there was considerable restoration this last century, it is in all but detail the original house we see today. The Bedingfeld family, who still live here, arrived with William the Conqueror and have a staunch Catholic and Royalist background.

Adjacent to the King's Chamber, which once welcomed Henry VII, are the Marian Hangings, with over a 100 needlework panels showing animals, birds and fishes, worked by Mary, Queen of Scots and Elizabeth Hardwick during Mary's long imprisonment at Tutbury Castle. In better days, Queen Mary I is known to have stayed at Oxburgh, and Sir Henry Bedingfeld led a force to Framlingham in support of Mary against Lady Jane Grey. Later, Elizabeth I visited the house during her royal visit to East Anglia in 1578.

The bridge over the moat is 18thC, replacing the original drawbridge. There's an exceptional staircase in the west gate house and, inside the house, a priest's hole – essential for a Catholic family during the Reformation. Bedingfeld Chantry Chapel forms part of the church and fortunately escaped damage when that building collapsed in 1948. It was built in 1513 and contains two beautiful terracotta monuments, fine examples of early English Renaissance. *Oxburgh Hall open most days, summer.*

24. Reepham   7 H6
A quiet market town-cum-village, which has two large churches in the one churchyard. There used to be three, one for each of the parishes of Hackford, Whitwell and Reepham that make up the town. Why they were built so close to one another (the two surviving ones are connected by a vestry) is a mystery – a healthy medieval rivalry between the three communities seems the likely answer.
Whitwell church, the one facing the attractive Georgian market square, is noted for its taller tower and its fine Jacobean pulpit. Reepham church proper, behind the other, has the finer interior, with a grand 14thC monument to Roger de Kerdiston, clad in his armour and reclined on a bed of cobbles. The third church, Hackford's, burnt down in the 18thC, and only a fragment of wall remains.
Just to the north of the town is **Salle**, the original home of the Boleyn family, but now visited for its church, one of the grandest in Norfolk, with a 111ft tower. The interior is spacious and inspiring, with some fine oak bosses on the beams and a beautiful pinnacled font cover.

25. Sandringham   7 F5
Country home of four generations of monarchs, Sandringham was traditionally the Christmas, but is now the New Year venue of the Royal Family.
Purchased by Queen Victoria, it was greatly rebuilt by Edward, Prince of Wales, in 1870. You can wander through the main rooms used by the Royals: among the many treasures to be seen are paintings of both British and European members of the Royal Family. In the ballroom is an exhibition which changes every year. Vintage cars are on show in the museum, as well as a variety of gifts received by the Queen. There are also local archaeological exhibits.
The original 7,000 acre estate has been extended to 20,000, most of which is farmed by tenant farmers. About 2,000 acres remain pine woodland, and the area provides scenic drives and healthy walks. *Open most days, summer.*

26. Scole Inn   7 H8
2m E of Diss, A140. Scole Inn, formerly the White Hart, was the finest posting house on the Norwich–London road. It was built in 1655 by John Peck, a Norwich merchant who spent the remarkable sum of £1,057 for a richly-carved sign which stretched across the road, advertising his establishment in a riot of allegory, mythology and heraldry. This

Scole Inn, Diss

wonder proved too costly to maintain, and was taken down in the 18thC, but there are pictures of it in the pub.

27. Thetford   7 G8
Now a centre for the light industry of the area, in the Middle Ages Thetford was one of the most important towns in the country. After repeated Danish attacks in 1011 it became the court of the Danish King Sweyne, who was succeeded by King Canute. The mound of their castle remains, 80ft high and 1,000ft in circumference, to the west of the town.
After the Saxon bishop of North Elmham had been deposed, Thetford became the See of East Anglia. Three bishops held office before the See finally settled at Norwich in 1095.
Religious life flourished with the founding of the cluniac Priory of Our Lady by Henry I in 1107, which remained an important institution until the Dissolution. The ruinous remains can be seen near the railway station.
Thomas Paine, author of 'The Rights of Man', was born in White Hart Street, in 1737. There's an excellent statue of him in front of the King's House. An earlier building on this site was once used as a hunting lodge by James I. Cage Lane has an old building that Paine, as a libertarian, would not have approved of – the two-storey 16thC lock-up gaol and stocks.

28. Walpole St Peter   7 E6
3m W of Terrington St Clement. Known as the 'Queen of the Marshes', Walpole St Peter is arguably the loveliest of the many fine churches in the Norfolk Marshlands, which are themselves among the best in England. The tower was built in 1300 and the nave, a beautifully-proportioned example of early Perpendicular style, shortly afterwards. The interior has a calm, spacious feel, lit by the large Perpendicular windows. On the south porch there are some fascinating bosses depicting scenes of sinners at the Last Judgement and allegorical images of natural life. Also of note are an unusual rood screen, c1610, the chandelier of 1701, the Jacobean pulpit and the 16thC octagonal font.

Walpole St Peter

29. Warham Camp   7 H5
3m E of Wells-next-the-Sea. A double-banked circular earthwork rising to 30ft, situated by the River Stiffkey. Iceni in origin, it probably dates from between 50BC and AD50. The great banks, fragrant with wild thyme in summer, make excellent deserted picknicking spots.

30. Weeting Castle   7 G7
1m N of Brandon, B1106. A lovely, seldom visited place, it comprises the romantic, ruined tower of William de Warenne's Norman castle, surrounded by a dry, square moat. Like many other Norman sites it was built at a pre-existing Saxon settlement, and there are burial mounds in the area. The settlement was probably connected earlier with nearby Grime's Graves.

31. Wymondham   7 H7
An old market town with a charming market cross, dated 1616, and one of the grandest churches in Norfolk.
The Abbey Church of SS Mary and Thomas was once part of Wymondham Abbey. The ruins, which were destroyed at the Dissolution, can be seen in the churchyard.

Two huge towers dominate the church, and were a result of differences of opinion between the monks and the townspeople in the 14thC. The church was divided down the middle, the monks building a wall to separate themselves and the high altar from the parishioners. They also built the beautiful octagonal tower. In retaliation, the parish built the square west tower larger than the monks'

tower. The church interior is distinguished by its hammer-beam roof and a number of fine monuments.

Robert Ket, who led a peasants' rebellion in 1549, was a Wymondham tanner. He was captured and hanged from the walls of Norwich castle until his body rotted away. His brother met a similar fate, suspended from one of the church towers.

SUFFOLK

32. Aldeburgh   7 K9
A sedate seaside town, full of character, and the birthplace of the poet, George Crabbe. He wrote a series of stories about the town, entitled 'The Borough'. One of the tales related was 'Peter Grimes', which the composer, Benjamin Britten, made into his first, and often considered his finest, opera. Britten came to live at Aldeburgh shortly after World War II, and, in 1948, initiated the world-famous Aldeburgh Festival of Music and the Arts. Small and intimate, the festival concentrates on performances of new works. The Martello Tower was one of those built along the East Anglian coast as a defence against a Napoleonic invasion that never materialised. Built of flint, timber and brick, the 16thC Moot Hall was once the centre of commercial activity in the town. It now stands alone by the edge of the sea.

33. Bungay   7 J7
Interesting town whose antiquity is indicated in the Saxon titles of Town Reeve and Feoffees (antedating Mayor and Councillors) which are still used. In the town centre is a domed, octagonal butter cross, built to replace an earlier one in 1688. Close by is a light standard surmounted by a weather vane depicting a huge black dog and lightning spear. This commemorates Black Shuck, the Devil Dog of East Anglia whose fearsome appearance is eternalised in the rhyme:
'All down the church in midst of fire
The hellish monster flew,
And passing onwards to the Quire,
He many people slew'.

33. Bungay Castle   7 J7
Off High St. The stumps of two gatehouse towers plus the exposed foundations and earthworks are all that remain of a castle which once had a 90ft-high keep and a surrounding curtain wall. At the south west corner of the site is a mine gallery: a tunnel running diagonally across, with two cross cuts into the masonry. Henry II's engineers made this after the King had ordered the castle to be dismantled. The practice was to dig such a tunnel and then set fire to the wooden props, hoping the fire would spread to the rest of the building.

34. Bury St Edmunds   7 G8
The historical importance of Bury St Edmunds is summed up neatly in the town's motto: 'Shrine of a King, Cradle of the Law'. The king was Edmund who, tortured and beheaded by the Danes in AD869, was brought to a monastery here about 30 years after his death. For many years he was patron saint of England. The monastery was given abbey status by King Canute in 1020, and throughout the early Middle Ages it remained one of the most important centres of pilgrimage in Britain.
The second event of historical significance which gave the town its motto, took place on St Edmund's Bay, 1214. It was here that English nobles gathered to draw up the 'Petition of the Barons' which formed the basis for Magna Carta.
The Abbey, *off Angel Hill*, was virtually

destroyed by rioting townspeople in 1327, and a fire of 1465 gutted what was left. After rebuilding was completed in 1538, the abbey church rivalled the great cathedrals in architectural glory. But sadly the effects of the Dissolution and subsequent neglect have left relatively little to admire. The most complete surviving buildings are the two gatehouses, one Norman and the other 14thC. The west front of the abbey church stands, but brutally stripped of its facing stone. The rest is but a few lonely columns and the exposed foundation.
This is an appealing market town which retains the original medieval grid pattern of the streets. Look out for **Bury Moyses Hall**, *Corn Hill*, a rare 12thC building, probably once a Jewish merchant's house. It now houses a museum with items from prehistoric to medieval times. The 13thC Monk's Chronicle, written at the Abbey, is one of its finest treasures. *Open weekdays.*
The town's finest remaining church is St Mary's, *Angel Hill*, built in the 15thC. The nave roof is beautifully carved with a host of angels, and the church contains the tomb of Mary Tudor, Henry VIII's daughter. Later prosperity left the town with many fine 17th and 18thC buildings.

35. Clare   7 F9
5m W of Long Melford, A1092. Set in the heart of Constable country, Clare is an ancient and beautiful little town, with the remains of a 13thC castle and priory. Its domestic houses cover all periods from the 13th to the 18thC, many of which display some fine pargetting (intricately moulded plasterwork). This art was at its most popular during the reign of Charles II.
The mound and fragmentary keep are all that remain of **Clare Castle**, *½m E of village*, built by Gilbert de Clare. The de Clares were one of the most influential families in the Middle Ages, but their power declined with the ascendancy of the Tudors. The castle declined with them. Edward III was often a visitor here, and excavations in the 19thC unearthed a beautiful gold cross set with pearls, thought to have belonged to him.
Originally a 13thC Augustinian foundation, all that remains of **Clare Priory**, *½m SW of village*, is a 17thC dwelling house incorporating 14th and 15thC features. The grounds, surrounded almost entirely by the River Stour, are most beautiful.

36. Debenham   7 H8
A picturesque village of overhanging timbered houses and many interesting, old buildings. The former guildhall is a timber-framed building dating from around 1500, and the Red Lion, dated 1600, still has its original plaster ceiling. The tree-lined main street rises to St Mary's Church which has a superb Galilee porch. The lower parts of the church tower are thought marginally to pre-date the Norman Conquest, and the alternating hammer-beam roof inside is a fine example.

37. Drinkston Mill   7 G8
Nr Beyton, 6m E of Bury St Edmunds, off A45. One of only three 17thC post mills left in

Suffolk, and this one still in working order. With four large, white sails, white weather-boarding, black cap, and the smaller sails behind (used to turn the whole structure with the wind) it really is a glorious sight. *Open by arrangement.*

38. Dunwich   7 K8
For the melancholic contemplation of the ravages of time and the sea's implacability, there is no better place than this desolate, evocative little spot. For Dunwich was once a thriving town and port, and in AD632 the See of East Anglia where the Anglian King Sigebert was crowned. The Domesday Book gives Dunwich's population at 508 and mentions three churches: a Benedictine monastery and both Dominican and Franciscan friaries. By the mid 13thC, at the height of the town's prosperity, the number of churches had risen to nine, plus another for the Knights Templar.
Erosion by the sea began early – in 1239 the Franciscan friary had to be moved away for safety. In 1904 the last of the churches fell, the tower finally collapsing in 1919. All that remains of old Dunwich are traces of the removed Franciscan friary. Today there is little to see but a few recently-built cottages and the town museum which tells the tragic tale.

39. Euston Hall   7 G8
4m S of Thetford, A1088. A huge place, built in the 1660s for Lord Arlington, and much added to in the Palladian style about 100 years later. The house contains period furniture and fittings, and has a collection of paintings which includes Van Dyke, Lely and Stubbs. Lovely gardens by John Evelyn and Capability Brown – and the 17thC Wren-style parish church.
The French writer de la Rochefoucald stayed here in 1784 and observed: 'The sideboard is furnished with a number of chamber pots and it is common practice to relieve oneself while the rest are drinking, one has no kind of concealment and the practice strikes me as indecent'.

40. Eye   7 H8
A lovely, small town, tucked into the countryside, with ruins of the castle, founded shortly after the Norman Conquest. There are also remains of a priory in a farmyard near the church, and a guildhall dating from the early 16thC. It is the noble church, however, that attracts visitors to the town today. Its 101ft, late 15thC tower, panelled in Suffolk flushwork, is beautifully built, and inside there's a marvellous medieval rood screen depicting saints and kings.

41. Flatford Mill   7 H10
1m SE of East Bergholt. One of the mills owned by John Constable's father: the family lived in attractive East Bergholt nearby. He later wrote of the Stour Valley: 'those scenes made me a painter'.
Constable painted the mill and the adjoining buildings as well as local scenes. 'The Cornfield' can be placed midway along the little lane to East Bergholt. But it should be remembered while trying to place a certain painting that Constable was not averse to shifting a church tower a few hundred yards to better suit his composition.

Flatford Mill

The mill has remained unaltered from his day, the rural harmony expressed in his famous canvases broken only by a crowded cafe. Owned by the National Trust, the mill is still used as a field study centre.

42. Heveningham Hall   7 J8
2m E of Heveningham, off B1117. Beautiful Georgian mansion in grand Palladian style, designed by Sir Robert Taylor, architect to George III. The young James Wyatt, who took over from Taylor, was responsible for the interior decoration. His original furniture remains. The house has continuously belonged to the Vanneck family.
The great entrance hall is one of the finest rooms in England, with a skilfully decorated barrel vault ceiling, marble floor and open screens supported by elegant, yellow-brown marble columns. The Etruscan room, library and dining room are also very impressive.
The gardens, laid out by Capability Brown, contain Wyatt's beautifully-proportioned orangery and the walled garden is an excellent example of a 'crinkle crankle' wall. There's an exhibition of their plans and designs in the house.

43. Hoxne   7 H8
4m E of Diss. Pronounced 'hoxen', this is where, according to legend, King Edmund was captured and killed by the Danes in AD870. There is no real evidence that this is so, but neither is there for any other place, and at least the villagers have gone to the trouble of erecting a small plaque to commemorate the event.

44. Ickworth Hall   7 G9
3m SW of Bury St Edmunds, off A143. Vast and portentous, Ickworth Hall was built between 1794 and 1836 for Frederick Hervey, 4th Earl of Bristol, to house the works of art he'd collected on his Grand Tours of Europe. The central feature of the house, the domed rotunda, was to contain the domestic apartments, and the two wings were to serve as gallery space. Unfortunately, Hervey was in Rome when Napoleon invaded Italy, and his collection was confiscated and he himself imprisoned. He died four years later, having never laid eyes on his magnificent house.
The interior rooms are lavish, with much elegant marble and plasterwork complemented by fine furniture, some of it Louis XV. Paintings by Gainsborough, Reynolds, Titian and Velasquez adorn the walls, and there is a fine collection of silver. *Open most days, summer; park daily, all year.*

Ickworth Hall

45. Ixworth Abbey   7 G8
½m N of Ixworth. Founded in 1170 for a community of Augustinian monks, a measure of the abbey's wealth is seen in the fact that the Norman church built for the community was 220ft long. Henry VIII exchanged Ixworth for the site on which he built Nonsuch for his second wife, Anne Boleyn. After this the abbey passed through many hands and many changes, reflected in the present building which contains portions from all ages. The house incorporates the recently restored 15thC Priors' lodging. *Open certain days, summer.*

46. Lavenham   7 G9
Picturesque Lavenham, with 15thC half-timbered houses quaintly lining the irregular streets, was one of the most

important Middle Age wool towns. But for the traffic, it is easy to imagine the scene hundreds of years ago.

Lavenham church was built in the 15thC at the height of the town's prosperity. There are some interesting memorials inside, but the 141ft-high flint and stone tower is its glory. The story goes that it would have been higher if the master mason hadn't fallen from the top during the building. Climb to the summit for a magnificent view over the town.

Among many fine old buildings are the Corpus Christi Guildhall in the market place and the 15thC Woolstaplers, *Prentice St.* There are also some lovely Tudor shops with original windows.

Lavenham Church

47. Leiston Abbey   7 K9
1/2m N of Leiston. Standing romantically in the open fields, Leiston Abbey is Suffolk's principal monastic ruin. The earliest part dates from 1388, built to replace an earlier building destroyed by fire. The Lady chapel survives complete, having been used as a granary after the Reformation. It was restored in 1920, and again during World War II, when it was used as a furniture store. The dwelling house near the abbey incorporates some of the materials of the destroyed church, and is now used as a Church of England retreat.

New contrasts with old in the village of Leiston – for this is the site of Summerhill, A. S. Neill's famous progressive school.

48. Long Melford   7 G9
Lavenham's rival as a preserved wool-town, Long Melford has been called the Rolls-Royce of Suffolk towns. It is known for its beautiful straggling main street which leads past dignified 18th and 19thC houses and charming shops to the magnificent church set behind the loveliest of village greens.

A miracle of grace and lightness, the 15thC Church of the Holy Trinity built in Perpendicular style, is considered the finest church in Suffolk. The 'greenhouse' effect of its 97 windows is heightened inside by the slender columns that support the nave roof. The well-proportioned tower is a replacement, built early this century around the 18thC brick tower.

Flanking the green is Melford Hall, one of our best surviving early Elizabethan houses. A red-brick manor, it has Georgian additions and four distinctive pepperpot towers. Before the Reformation, the Hall was a hunting lodge used by the abbots of Bury St Edmunds. Henry VIII gave it to one William Cordell, a lawyer, who, in 1578, entertained Elizabeth I here. There are some fine rooms, decorated

Long Melford

in the 18thC style, with good Regency furniture, and also a number of portraits and memorabilia of the Parker family, who have lived in the house since 1786. The gardens are worth a visit. *Open most days, summer.*

49. Mildenhall, Church of St Mary   7 F8
Notable for its roof and wood carvings, Mildenhall church is one of the finest in Suffolk. In the aisle are carvings of birds, beasts and saints. The wonderful elaborately-carved roof is peppered with shots from 17thC iconoclast Puritans. Note, too, the attractive north porch and exceptional east window.

Mildenhall's greatest treasure, however, will be found in the British Museum. It's a perfectly preserved collection of Roman silver, ploughed up in a local field during the last war.

50. Orford Castle   7 K9
Orford. Orford Castle has seen military service for almost 800 years: it was built in 1165 for Henry II, and was used as an observation post in the last war. Only the unique polygonal keep with its three towers remains, but this is in wonderful condition. Climb to the top and you'll be amazed at how much of the countryside and coast it commands. Inside the keep are a chapel and the Great Hall with a cellar below.

Attached to the castle is a curious legend that a wild man, half man and half fish, was captured and held in the dungeon. No amount of torture could get him to speak English, and, mercifully, he escaped back into the sea.

Orford was a major port from Elizabethan times until the mid 17thC, and many of the town's buildings indicate this former prosperity. *Open most days.*

51. Pakenham Mills   7 H8
5m NW of Bury St Edmunds, off A143. Pakenham is notable for its two working mills, one water and one wind. The windmill is of the tower variety, the latest development in windmills before their demise. It is worked by the Bryant family who follow the old miller's processes, and, incidentally, own a fine collection of old traction engines.

Aerial photography has shown Pakenham to have been an important pre-Roman settlement. *Open certain days, summer.*

52. Saxtead Green Windmill   7 J8
Saxtead Green, nr Framlingham. A beautifully preserved 18thC post mill, with three-storey roundhouse, four patent sails and a fantail. You can climb up inside and see the machinery, still in perfect order. There's also a set of stocks on the green and, if those didn't deter the offender, a whipping post in the church porch.

Saxstead Green Windmill

53. Southwold   7 K8
A distinguished seaside resort, with fine flint and brick cottages, still with an aura of Edwardian elegance. The wide greens were incorporated into the town when it was rebuilt following a catastrophic fire of 1659.

Southwold was the scene of another disaster 13 years later: The Battle of Sole Bay. British and Allied French ships fought a bloody battle against the Dutch navy, watched by the people of Southwold who lined the cliffs. It was estimated that over 6,000 men lost their lives. The battle is remembered with a strong beer brewed by local brewers, named Broadside Ale.

The Church of St Edmund, one of the finest Perpendicular churches in England, has a fine panelled roof. A 15thC oak Jack O'the Clock strikes the bell of the church clock. Both the Sailor's Reading Room on the cliff top and the town museum contain a number of interesting exhibits.

St Edmund's, Southwold

54. Sudbury   7 G10
An ancient market town with fine houses of the 18thC and earlier, Sudbury's best medieval and 18thC buildings can be seen in the streets leading from Market Hill.

Thomas Gainsborough, the painter, was born at 46, Sepulchre Street, now called Gainsborough Street. Gainsborough House contains a good collection of his work as well as period furniture, silk, and paintings by Constable. The 14thC St Gregory's Church, has a fine font canopy, and the skull of Sudbury's other famous son, Simon of Sudbury. Under Richard II he was, at the same time, Archbishop of Canterbury and Chancellor of England. Sudbury was killed by rioters in the Peasant's Revolt of 1381.

55. Woodbridge   7 J9
A sailing centre, this is one of Suffolk's most attractive towns. Stately buildings of the 15th to 18thC abound, the finest of which is the Shire Hall, built c1575, originally with an open lower part which formed a covered market.

Edward FitzGerald, the Victorian poet and translater, lived in a house near Market Hill, now marked with a plaque. Opposite is the Bull Hotel where FitzGerald's many famous friends, including Lord Tennyson, stayed. The Crown Hotel was the birthplace of the extraordinary John Fox, in 1528. Captured and held in slavery for 14 years by the Turks, after his escape he became something of a celebrity. The last years of his life were spent quietly in his home town.

Nearby **Sutton Hoo** was the burial site of the Saxon kings of East Anglia. They were placed in long ships and surrounded with their treasures to prepare them for the journey into the afterlife. There are 11 barrows on the site, and excavations yielded trinkets of gold, silver and enamel, and a super gilded helmet. This wonderful treasure is now in the British Museum, with replicas in Ipswich Museum. The site, now filled in, is not accessible.

56. Woolpit   7 H9
9m E of Bury St Edmunds, A45. Originally 'Wolf-pit' so this town does not, as might be expected in Suffolk, have anything to do with wool. The last wolves in England were said to be trapped here. There are still pits, but these are the result of brick quarrying. Woolpit bricks built much of 19thC Suffolk, and, it's said, the White House in Washington, too. Presumably the bricks found their way across the Atlantic as ships' ballast.

Woolpit is also the stage for one of Suffolk's most haunting legends, that of the Green Children. A boy and a girl are said to have sprung from the ground one harvest time. Both were totally green, and ate only green food. When they had been taught to speak English they said that they came from St Martin's Land, a country of perpetual twilight beyond a great river. The boy is said to have died shortly after baptism, but the girl grew up to marry and live at King's Lynn. The legend probably derives from ancient fertility rites practised by the Celts.

LAND OF THE RED ROSE AND ENVIRONS

The north western area of England is one of aggressive contrasts in landscape, architecture and people. The fascinating amalgam of the green countryside of lush farmlands, remote villages and attractive old market towns, the famous holiday resorts and the sprawling urban industry provides a visual record of the inexorable march of progress which changed a largely agrarian community into an industrial and commercial one. But it is this very diversity that gives the area its unique charm. Volcanoes threw up the Lake District 450 million years ago and made a natural playground of peaks and fells. Melting glaciers filled eight major lakes, and Stone Age settlers inched northward leaving behind their flints and cairns like historic visiting cards 8,000 years old. As if to puzzle and confuse us, Bronze Age people chose panoramic Cumbrian hilltops for their mighty stone circles, leaving us with a chuckle to work out their meaning 4,000 years later. Several Roman roads traverse the district, Hard Knott Castle is an excellent example of a Roman fort, and at Ravenglass stand the remains of an old Roman bath-house, one of the best preserved in the country.

Cumbria takes in the last northern thrust of the Pennines that leads to the fells and pikes of the Lakes. The coast on the west alternates between the wild and the industrial, from coal-mining under the sea to the cool power of Britain's first atomic plant at Calder Hall. Farmed and grazed for many centuries, green and mellow Lakeland was discovered like a starlet by Romantic poets in the 18thC. One of the most beautiful parts of Great Britain, it has become a symbol of spiritual as well as geographical grandeur. Today, however, the weekend invasion of campers, small boats and water-skiers means you will have to wander further off the beaten track to find the peace that inspired the poets.

Nearby Northumbria is no placid sister. But lacerating border and coastal warfare created a bloodier history for her so that today you could spend a lifetime of holidays visiting castles built to attack or defend as politics demanded. A green balm of forest now covers thousands of acres of remote Northumbria – recreating the ancient forests of the county and establishing the largest man-made forest in Europe. Romans built part of Hadrian's Wall here to mark the northerly limits of their empire, and centuries later, valiant market towns grew up, some still surrounded by their protective outer walls.

Further south, border wars were a problem for Cheshire, too. Once covered by a great lake, Cheshire acquired a treasure of salt beneath her soil when the waters retreated. Plundering bands from Wales or Yorkshire and pirates from the coast itched to get their hands on those salt mines – and frequently did. Salt is now the basis of a chemical industry, and it's no accident that ICI started here. Notice the brine baths, and sailing lakes sunk into old salt workings.

Chester was built by Romans as defence against the Welsh and contains enough antiquity to keep history-hungry American tourists happy for a year. In later years, rich farmland brought wealth, and Cheshire is renowned for her 'magpie' buildings – the half-timbered black-and-white manor houses characteristic of Tudor England. Here, too, are the deep meadows, slow-winding rivers, secluded meres and picture-postcard villages which draw visitors from all over the world to see 'old England'.

Nudging ever nearer came the great connurbations of Merseyside, Manchester and Lancashire. Liverpool was, and is, a major port and today you can read her maritime history in the buildings, wharves and pubs. The proximity of a great port like Liverpool and a humming commercial centre like Manchester, helped Lancashire to develop into the queen of the cotton industry. The first cotton mills were built near tumbling streams with folk working contentedly in their own homes. When the cottage industry came to an end, new sources of power worked the great looms in factories and the soot-caked stacks of their chimneys came to dominate the countryside. Today, the grimmer aspects of the Industrial Revolution are being treated with a sort of nostalgia as the first factories and neglected mills are lovingly painted, photographed and even restored in the interests of history. Meanwhile, modern development has opened fine vistas of green spaces between the new housing estates.

Out of this region came the Industrial Revolution, grinding poverty, soaring affluence, the first passenger railway, the Beatles, Rolls-Royce, atom-splitting Rutherford, the first free lending library – and Gracie Fields. The people of this area of contrasts are friendly and warm-hearted, with a rich sense of humour. Join them in the 'local' for a pint, or pop along to the corner shop for a loaf of bread, and you'll find yourself drawn into conversation. When you come 'up north', you will find you are welcome.

🦚CHESHIRE🦚

1. Adlington Hall
8 D9

5m N of Macclesfield, off A523. Two great oak trees support one end of the Grand Hall in this zebra-patterned, black-and-white Elizabethan mansion which is still occupied by the Legh family who built it. The oaks are said to have come from an 11thC hunting lodge which stood where the house stands now: that would make them at least 800 years old. Handel once was a guest at the house and the organ he tinkered on is still here.

Many people think Adlington has the finest hammer-beam roof in Cheshire: it dates from 1450, and angels cavort all over it. Roundheads attacked the house during the Civil War because the Leghs were loyal Royalists. Being made of wood, considerable damage was done and Adlington needed extensive patching up. By the mid 18thC the Leghs had partly recovered from the huge fines imposed on them by the Parliamentarians, and Thomas Legh began rebuilding with bricks baked in his own kiln. Judging by his portrait, Uryan Legh was a lively character. Knighted for services in Cadiz in 1596, this smiley, lace-collared wag wooed a senorita so successfully that she insisted on following him to England. How he dealt with the situation isn't known, but the gold chain she gave him is in the picture. *Open certain days, summer.*

Adlington Hall

2. Arley Hall Gardens
8 C9

6m W of Knutsford, 5m from M6. Nibble home-made buns under the trusses of a 16thC cruck barn here at the home of merry Squire Rowland Warburton. Squire Rowland was a lovely fellow given to leaving rhyming couplets about the place. Above a handsome doorway is: 'This gate is free to all good men and true/Right welcome thou if worthy to pass through.' Assuming that you are, you will find huge yew hedges high as castle walls, the very first herbaceous border in Britain, rhyming epitaphs for the squire's beloved horses, and even signposts in verse. Incidentally, herbaceous borders were one of the results of an interest in botany during the 19thC. Viscount and Viscountess Ashbrook seldom open the century-old hall to visitors, but they like to point out that the estate has been in the same family for 500 years. Generations of care have made the gardens very beautiful and they even won a top British Tourist Authority award in 1975. Squire Rowland liked people as well as plants and he laid out Arley village as a model estate complete with a maypole and dancing on appropriate days. Grandad oaks survey the scene, including one that the Squire experimentally squeezed 11 boys into, paying them a shilling each for their discomfort. *Open most days, summer.*

3. Beeston Castle
8 B10

3m S of Tarporley, off A49. Ranulf de Blunderville chose his site thoughtfully when he plonked this eerie fortified castle on top of the steepest hill in Cheshire in 1220. It was built as a bulwark against Llywelyn of Gwynedd, other Norman earls, and dodgy pals of Henry III. As politics changed, it fell empty and Tudor tourists spent days off throwing stones down its wells to guess how deep they were. Picnickers have always loved Beeston. After a challenging climb via the old gatehouse, outer walls (30ft high in some places), moat and round towers, you're rewarded with lungfuls of crystal air and dazzling views that set your appetite for sandwiches zinging. You can still trace the foundations of the banqueting hall, and see the 366ft-deep well.

A guerilla force of eight Parliamentarians finally finished off Beeston during the Civil War. Royalist officers used it mainly as a store-house for arms and provisions, and they left a cheese broker in charge thinking they could rely on his 'godliness' if not his military know-how not to betray the cause. Unfortunately, the gentlemen defended his soul more successfully than the castle, and ordered his 60 soldiers to surrender Beeston at the first hint of attack. He died shortly afterwards confessing an illicit love affair with a maid at one of his favourite inns.

4. Bunbury
8 B10

2m S of Tarporley, off A49 or A51. Commuters are seeping into this Cheshire heartland village, but its thatched cottages and medieval church manage to preserve their quietness despite development. See the huge painted tomb of Hugh Calverley, a 7ft, 14thC giant in jewelled armour, gauntlets and spurs. Hugh ate like two men and fought like 10, lived fast and furiously, and came home to found this church. Many ancient personalities are remembered here, including Sir George Beeston who was knighted at the age of 89 for helping to defeat the Armada. He died at 103. A busty wooden lady, dated 1741, was unearthed in the 19thC from the churchyard where a vicar, scandalised by her 'bulging udders', had buried her a century earlier. He claimed that young men of his congregation were 'disturbed' by her, but later, people have taken her to be a rare effigy of the Virgin Mary. Bunbury's water-mill has been restored and you can buy stone-ground flour there.

5. Capesthorne Hall
8 C9

Nr Chelford, A34. Bulging with arty treasures brought back from Grand Tours, this Victorian home of the Bromley Davenports looks romantic from a distance but rather stodgy close up. Capesthorne has a sturdy 'back bencher' tradition. The present owner and his two predecessors sat in the Commons for a combined Conservative total of 58 years, but never became ministers. Their political allegiance is satirised in a crest on one of the main staircase roundels — the felon's head is that of Gladstone. Capesthorne is the work of two famous Victorian architects, Blore and Salvin. Very little of the house they replaced remains, but next door is a beautiful Georgian chapel where services are still held. Walks round the gardens and nearby pools are enjoyable. *Open certain days, summer.*

6. Chester
8 A9

No city in Britain is richer in archaeological and architectural treasures than Chester, and one of its specialities is the Rows – a double row of shops one on top of the other. They first appeared around 1485, but the oldest surviving ones are Tudor and Stuart. Best and least altered examples are Leche House and Bishop Lloyd's House, in Watergate St, and they still line Eastgate and Bridge Street. Even contemporary writers remarked on them and their usefulness for 'keeping a man dry in foul weather', but no-one really knows how or why they came about.

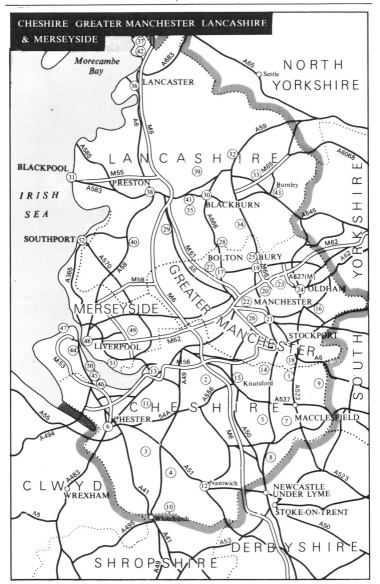

CHESHIRE GREATER MANCHESTER LANCASHIRE & MERSEYSIDE

Romans set up camp at Chester around AD70 and built a fortress for their 20th Legion. They called it Deva – or city on the Dee. Archaeologists have spent many years digging up what they left behind, and Chester is riddled with Roman building, foundations, inscriptions and artefacts. Many of them are packed into the remarkable **Grosvenor Museum**, *Grosvenor St.* Tour the city first, and see its Roman past in Watergate and Eastgate Street, parts of the north and eastern walls and an angle tower north of Newgate. South east, outside the walls, half the amphitheatre lies exposed. Then, seeing the coins and altars, gravestones and weapons that were part of everyday life to a Roman soldier, brings archaeology alive.

The 19thC colonnaded buildings generally known as **Chester Castle**, were probably once the site of a Saxon fortress. Strengthened by successive kings, the oldest bit still surviving is a square tower with thick walls of red sandstone, variously known as Caesar's Tower, Agricola's Tower, or the

Magazine Tower. Though mainly medieval, its foundations are Norman and inside it has three 'compartments', one above the other. On the ground floor is a crypt, the first floor has a beautiful little 13thC chapel and the second floor houses the Regimental Museum. Here you can see many interesting things collected by the Cheshire Regiment during different campaigns: the Amir of Scinde's marble armchair, caps with bullet holes, flags, maps, medals and even part of the framework of a Zeppelin.

6. **Chester Cathedral**   8 A9
Fabric woven from a spider's web and preserved between glass is just one of the fascinations of this 11thC cathedral which began as a shrine for the bones of a Mercian princess called Werburgh. In 1092, Hugh Lupus, one-time lecher and rascal, repented enough to found a Benedictine abbey on the site of the old church. Cloisters, chapter house and refectory where the monks read, wrote and meditated, survive today in a mass

of detail. Rare illuminated manuscripts, classic folios, and a book printed by the suitably-named Wynken de Worde are all on show. Inside, the cathedral tells its own story from Norman days to the present. Look out for superb 14thC carving and a grotesque figure known as the Chester Imp in the northern clerestory of the nave. Chester's nave is one of the smallest in England, and its chancel is one of the biggest! During the Middle Ages the monks here became known for the mystery plays they wrote. These dramatised Bible stories were performed in the street and became an important part of the city's life and tradition.

Chester Cathedral

7. Gawsworth 8 D9
3m S of Macclesfield, A536. Shakespeare's 'dark lady' may well have been Mary Fitton, maid of honour at Elizabeth's court, whose family owned Gawsworth's 16thC timbered hall. It's easy to romanticise here when you see the great windows overlooking lawns and beautiful gardens. Close by is probably the finest jousting ground in England – 200 yds long and 60 yds wide. An avenue of elms leads to the lovely 15thC rectory and yews round the churchyard were probably growing in the days of Magna Carta. St James's Church, full of Fitton family monuments and gargoyles, is also 15thC.
Set apart from the main churchyard is the grave of Maggotty Johnson, dancing master and jester, who wrote an 18thC box office hit called Hurlothrumbo which ran at the Haymarket for 30 days. Its unexpected success inspired him to write more plays, all of which flopped, and today he is remembered more for his eccentric personality than his literary prowess. Flamboyant even in death, Maggotty's ghost roams neighbouring lanes on a white charger. Gawsworth is one of Cheshire's prettiest villages, and descendents of the Fittons still live there. Evidence of far older inhabitants can be seen at a tumulus to the east of the village, where early Bronze Agers cremated their dead 3,500 years ago in ceremonial urns. *Gawsworth Hall open summer.*

8. Little Moreton Hall 8 C10
4m SW of Congleton, A34. Endlessly reproduced on cards and calendars, this prime example of the olde worlde English timbered mansion stands today almost as it stood when it was built in 1580. It's never been reconstructed, and despite odd tilts and sags the structure is still very sound. In 1977 a painted wall of the late 16thC was discovered which had been hidden behind 17thC panelling. Little is known about who lived there, or what happened behind its black-and-white walls: the Moreton family

Little Moreton Hall

left just after the Civil War and put in tenants until their descendents handed it over to the National Trust in 1937. Furnishings are few, so interest centres on the jumbled skeleton of the house itself – Great Hall, kitchen, buttery (now the shop), pantry (now the tea room), parlour, withdrawing room, various chambers, chapel and long gallery. *Open most days, summer.*

9. Lyme Hall and Park 8 D9
6½m S of Stockport, A6. One family can't live in a house for 600 years without giving it a feeling of continuity – so although Lyme Hall is a potch of different styles, somehow it hangs together as a home, albeit a stately one. Piers Legh started the ball rolling in the 14thC when he married Margaret Danyers, and inherited Lyme Hall from her father. Leghs lived there until 1946 when one of them gave it to the National Trust.
The present hall is a mixture of Elizabethan and 17thC Italian. Giacomo Leoni, a famous Italian architect, designed its astonishing columned portico which experts agree is one of the great examples of English Palladianism. Inside takes you through dark Tudor panelling and long galleries to elegant salons and grand staircases. Watch out for Grinling Gibbons carving and Chippendale chairs upholstered with material from Charles I's cloak. Deer roam the 1,300 acre park which is 800ft above sea level and straddles the borders of Derbyshire and Cheshire, offering stunning views of the Pennines. *Open most days, summer; park daily, all year.*

10. Marbury-cum-Quoisley 8 B9
3m N of Northwich, off A533 or A559. Imagine a picture-book village and you'd probably come up with something like Marbury. This gentle spot is tucked away in a green corner of Cheshire and boasts no more than a few houses, a church, a pub, and some farms. The village, snoozing peacefully beside two meres, is 700 years old and funny faces have squinted from the church walls for five centuries – a carved Punch, a monkey and jolly twins. The walls list with age. Many generations of local families have sat or dozed through sermons booming from the 15thC pulpit which is still in use.
Marbury country park was based on the former parkland of Marbury Hall (now demolished). It overlooks one of the county's most attractive stretches of water, Budworth Mere, where rich and varied bird life can be watched from a hide.

11. Mouldsworth Motor Museum 8 A10
Mouldsworth, 6m from Chester, E off B5393. Fifty vintage and post vintage cars, motor cycles, a 1920 replica garage, old signs, mascots, models, pumps, classic cars from the 1950s, pedal cars and toys for children – all on show at this museum near Delamere Forest. So after you've trundled nostalgically through a history of motor vehicles, reflect upon England's peacefulness before they were invented in this one-time hunting ground of the Earls of Chester. There are 4,000 acres of pines with museum and nature trails. *Open certain days.*

12. Nantwich, Churche's Mansion 8 B10
Fire burned down most of Nantwich in 1583 in a 20-day scorching that destroyed 600 buildings. Elizabeth I gave money to rebuild the town and a dedication to her hangs in Churche's Mansion. This old Elizabethan tanner's house escaped the fire because it was outside the original old town. Although it was built by Thomas Cleese, it is called Churche after its owners, and in particular Mr Randol Church, said to be 'a gentleman of singular integrity'. *Open summer.*

13. Norton Priory 8 B9
Warrington Road, nr Astmoor, Runcorn. Foundations so complete they look like a

life-size diagram laid out on the ground are all that remain of this 12thC Augustinian priory. Amazingly, they have survived two or three houses being built on top of them. When the monastery was dissolved, up went a Tudor hall, then a Georgian mansion, then Victorian extensions. When the Victorian house was finally pulled down, Runcorn Corporation wisely employed an archaeologist to excavate the site, which they planned to convert into a public park. He carried out one of the most thorough excavations of any monastic site in Britain, and uncovered foundations that clearly show church, chapter house and cloisters. There's a small museum displaying a large collection of mosaics and inlaid tiles found on the site. *Open most days, summer; certain days, winter.*

14. Quarry Bank Mill   8 C9
Styal, 1¹/2m NW of Wilmslow, off B5166.
People worked from 5.30am to 8pm at this cotton mill. Their boss was Samuel Greg, a successful businessman who built Quarry Bank and the nearby village of Styal into one of the finest examples of a complete 18thC industrial community. Greg chose the site because of the River Bollin which tumbles and rushes passionately through this woody valley. More practically, it falls 14ft and powered the original water-wheel.
Greg believed in thrift, hard work and paternal benevolence. Despite the hours – long even for those days – he was a good employer. He fed his apprentices well and built a chapel, a shop, cottages, and a school for families of the estate. The World Health Organisation recognises the records Greg kept of his workers' health as one of the first schemes of its kind ever. Some years ago the National Trust took over this 250 acre estate

and they have restored the mill, cottages and church and created an exciting museum in the beautiful mill buildings. *Open most days.*

15. Tatton Park and Hall   8 C9
Ashley Rd, 3¹/2m N of Knutsford. Tatton Hall and Park top the National Trust's tourist popularity poll, though neither are any grander or more luxuriant than many other stately settings. Perhaps the secret of Tatton's success is that even if you arrive hot and bothered from a suburban semi, the house itself is small enough to identify with and gives the impression of being designed more for elegant comfort than to impress the Georgian Joneses. Peacefulness seems to blow in off the deer-grazed parkland and mile-long mere. The Egerton family have bequeathed their personalities as well as their possessions which gives the estate a particular atmosphere.
All the predictable treasures are there: Canalettos, Van Dycks, silk-covered walls, silver and china. But it's the personal mementoes that grasp the attention: early cars, wireless sets, a spade Lord Egerton used to cut the first sod of the Manchester Ship Canal, and – if you like that sort of thing – a grisly collection of animal heads nailed on the wall, called sporting trophies. There's an old fire engine, family stage coaches, a 400-year-old hall and 16thC cruck barn on the site of a deserted medieval village. *Open most days, summer; certain days, winter.*

Tatton Hall

🏛GREATER MANCHESTER🏛

16. Astley Cheetham Art Gallery   6 E1
Stalybridge, 7m S of Oldham, B6175. Medieval and Renaissance Italian paintings at this just-out-of-the-city gallery which also has a collection of British 18th and 19thC work. *Open most days.*

17. Bolton   6 C1
The distant moors and outlying stone cottages serve to redeem the otherwise industrial features of this town. Bolton's prosperity came about from the growth of the cotton industry. Crompton's spinning mule could spin a pound of cotton to a length of many miles and you can see one at Tonge Moor Textile Museum, *Tonge Moor Road,* along with Arkwright's water-frame and Hargreaves's Spinning Jenny. Crompton is buried in the parish churchyard and there's a Saxon cross in the north aisle. The town's museum and art gallery, *Civic Centre, Le Mans Crescent,* houses important collections of British birds, Egyptology, English water-colours and porcelain, and Bolton's local history museum, Little Bolton Town Hall, *St George's St,* opened in 1978 to tell the story of Bolton from prehistoric times to the present.
The public library has one of the most splendid editions of the Bible in the world – 45 folio volumes published in 1800. It is a superb specimen of typography and full of engravings collected by an enthusiast and inserted into the volumes in the fashion of the day popularised by James Granger, who added the word 'grangerising' – illustrating a book – to the English language.

17. Bolton, Hall i' th' Wood   8 C7
1¹/2m N of Bolton, off Crompton Way, A58.
Photogenically Tudor, this lovely

black-and-white house now peeps through roads and houses rather than the woods of its name. Several important Bolton families lived here, but by the 18thC it had fallen from high estate and was let as tenements to poor people for a few shillings a week. Lord Leverhulme, a soap millionaire, found the hall derelict in 1899 and lovingly restored it. A graceful and interesting building, it's now furnished as a 17thC yeoman's dwelling.
Gifted Samuel Crompton, the gentle and brilliant inventor who designed a spinning mule that revolutionised the cotton industry, lived and worked here with his parents until 1780. He built the mule originally for cottage spinners, but the fineness and strength of his yarn soon brought tricksy and ambitious businessmen to the hall to discover how he managed to produce such high quality cotton. Trying to keep his secret so harassed Crompton that he agreed to make his mule public in exchange for voluntary gifts from

Hall i' th' Wood, Bolton

those set to gain from it. Many made fortunes. Crompton received £60. *Open most days.*

18. Bramall Hall   8 D8
1m N of Bramall, 3m S of Stockport, off A5102.
Perhaps the finest example of half-timbering in England. Wooded parkland holds off suburbia that once threatened to slink right up to Bramall's door and swallow it in a gulp of redevelopment. So effective is the parkland screen that you feel in real countryside here. Most of the hall dates from 1590 and has been held by the Davenport family for 500 years. The ballroom has medieval wall-paintings and the banqueting hall has an ancient roof of great arched timbers. Fragments of old glass wink among thousands of leaded panes, and there's a spiral staircase of solid oak up to an Elizabethan drawing room. Watch out for the grand four-poster and a great tapestry patiently worked by a lady of the house, Dame Dorothy Davenport. It was started in 1600 and took 36 years to complete. *Open most days.*

19. Bury Museum and Art Gallery   8 C7
Moss St, Bury. Best known for the Thomas Wrigley collection which includes Turner's 'Calais Sands' and Landseer's 'Random Shot'. Wrigley was a 19thC liberator keen on compulsory education. Paper-making, not chewing gum, made his money for him, much of which he gave to Bury. There's a museum in the basement telling the story of Bury's social and industrial history. This town is also where the fiercesome recipe for Black Pudding was born and bred. Try it.

19. Bury, The Lancashire Fusiliers Regimental Museum   8 C7
Wellington Barracks, Bolton Rd. Relics from 1688 to 1979 tell the story of this regiment and the British Army, in an outstanding collection of medals, silver and period uniforms. Bury was depot town of the Lancashire Fusiliers and in the First World War, more members of this regiment won the Victoria Cross than any other. There's a special Victoria Cross section in the museum. *Open most days.*

20. Heaton Hall   8 C8
Heaton Park, 4 1/2m N of Manchester, A665. Set in suburbia and surrounded by a large but rather bleak park, this 18thC masterpiece is reckoned to be one of the finest neo-classical buildings in the country. James Wyatt altered a plain building of 1750 for the first Earl of Wilton and it contains one of the few surviving 'Etruscan' rooms, with painted walls and ceiling, by Biagio Rebecca. The organ in the music room was built by Samuel Green in 1792. Furniture from the 18th and 19thC adds to the atmosphere of the house, though it still seems in conflict with its dreary city setting. *Open summer.*

21. Manchester   8 C8
An important weaving centre in the Middle Ages, the arrival of canals in the late 18thC brought raw cotton right into the centre and the city boomed – the Industrial Revolution had arrived. Manchester's prosperity is reflected in its great Victorian buildings, such as the Gothic town hall. Much of the central area, Piccadilly, has been rebuilt since the 1950s, but without distinction. Acres of slum housing have been cleared, but replaced by ugly tower blocks.
But in this huge city, there is much of historic interest. **The Town Hall**, *Albert Square*, is a Gothic extravaganza like all your fantasies of fairy-castles mortared into a single building. Alfred Waterhouse designed it for Manchester Corporation in 1866, and 11 years later it was finished – at a cost of £1 million. The outside, with its turrets and carvings, is magnificent, but the inside is truly spectacular. Ford Maddox Brown painted 12 splendid murals for the hall and their pre-Raphaelite atmosphere seems ideally

suited to this concerto of sandstone and glass. **The Free Trade Hall**, *Peter St*, is the home of the world-famous Halle orchestra. Called after the 'freetraders' who held meetings in the original hall, much of Manchester's emotional history took place inside it. It was built in 1840 as the headquarters of the Anti-Corn Law League. During the American Civil War, cotton workers met here to pledge support for the Unionists, whose blockade of Confederate ports caused much hardship – Abraham Lincoln called it 'sublime Christian heroism'. Dickens, Gladstone, Disraeli, Lloyd George and young Churchill often spoke here. Suffragettes drew attention to their campaign when they were carried from the hall after noisy dissatisfaction with Churchill's answers to their questions. Only the facade of Edward Walter's original design remains. Bombs destroyed the interior in 1940 and it was re-opened in 1951.
Two minutes from Victoria station is **Chetham's Hospital and Library**, the first public library in England and a school of music, built in the 15thC. Humphrey Chetham, bachelor and benefactor, made pots of money from textiles and banking and decided to spend it on educating poor boys. A school was founded in 1654, which has recently specialised in music. Although the school can only be visited with prior consent of the bursar, the library, containing many priceless books, has always been freely open to the public.
Researchers from all over the world come to **John Rylands Library**, *Deansgate*, an intellectual temple housed in some late flowering Victoria Gothic of 1890. A 'wicked Bible' condoning adultery, a manuscript by Petrarch, writings on skin, silk and stone are just a minute part of the priceless collection given to Manchester by the widow of John Rylands, a self-made textile merchant who loved books. In 1972, the Rylands library merged with the university library to become one of the greatest research libraries in Europe counting early Bible fragments among its 3,000,000 volumes.
There's plenty for art lovers as well as book-worms in Manchester. Sir Charles Barry, architect of the Houses of Parliament, designed the **City Art Gallery**, *Mosley St*, in the 1820s and it now roofs an outstanding collection of paintings by Gainsborough, Stubbs, Turner and Constable, plus pre-Raphaelites, and modern work by Nash, Ben Nicholson and Henry Moore. Beautiful silver, pottery, jade, enamels and glass, too. **Whitworth Art Gallery**, *Whitworth Park*, was founded in 1889 by Royal Charter. Its principal collections are British water-colours including work by Blake, Turner and the pre-Raphaelites. There are also Continental water-colours, a collection of Japanese prints, textiles, and special exhibitions.
It's not surprising to find a museum of science and technology in a city that has its roots in the Industrial Revolution. The **North Western Museum of Science and Industry**, *Grosvenor St*, contains optics, steam engines, electrics, hand papermaking, internal combustion engines, railway photographs, a Royce engine, dyes and textiles. Equally loved by studious adults and inquisitive kids, there's more than enough to occupy a whole day at **Manchester Museum**, *Oxford Rd*. Over 1/4 million visitors annually browse through exciting exhibits from dinosaurs to Egyptian tombs, aquaria to coins.
Though hardly historic – though they may be one day – don't miss the Royal Exchange Theatre suspended UFO-like inside the great hall of the city's magnificent Cotton Exchange, and the Barton Swing Aqueduct, Stretford, like something a child might build from Lego. While you're here, see the Great Stone entrance to Gorse Hill Park. People in plague areas who wanted to buy goods or food

had to leave the money in 'plague stones' so as not to spread the disease. This stone has two hollows on top which were filled with vinegar or other 'disinfectant'.

21. Manchester Cathedral 8 C8
Unflustered by all the big-city bustle around it, this 15thC church-turned-cathedral stands imponderably near Victoria station. Jarred incessantly by railways and traffic in one of Manchester's grottier spots, it seems to symbolise closer contact with reality than lovelier churches more picturesquely protected from urban sprawl. Henry V gave Thomas La Warr permission to turn the church into a college for clergy in 1421. Bits of it remain, but its striking tower was added in 1868. Look closely at the delightful 16thC choir stalls showing a husband in trouble with his wife for dropping his beer mug, rabbits roasting a huntsman and backgammon players. Notice especially the beautiful modern embroidery – altar cloths and vestments. There's a brass rubbing centre here, too.

21. Manchester, Wythenshawe Hall 8 C8
Wythenshawe Park. A socialist mayor and his wife gave this 16thC manor house and estate to Manchester Corporation in 1926 as part of a massive redevelopment programme in southern Manchester. Post war idealism envisaged a garden-city suburb there. Today, it is a problem area of council flats, high crime and suicide rate. You can still see parts of the original dwelling, and paintings, arms, armour, Oriental prints, ceramics, jade and beautiful 17thC furniture are all on show.

22. Monks Hall Museum 8 C8
Wellington Road, Eccles. Tudor farmhouse with later additions converted into a small museum and art gallery in 1961. Steam-hammers, longcase clocks, an observation beehive and an underground canal boat are just some of its interesting exhibits. There's a toy museum of dolls and games, too. *Open most days.*

23. Old Boar's Head 8 C8
Long St, Middleton. Crooked and bent with age after centuries of booze, this inn is unusual in that the local authority own it as a scheduled building of historic and architectural interest. Bang in the middle of Middleton, its perpendiculars now lean at drunken angles due to the antiquity of its timbers. It was first licensed as an inn in 1753, but many tankards of ale were brewed and consumed on the premises long before that date – the sign on the outside claims it's 12thC, but there's no conclusive evidence for this date.

24. Oldham 8 D7
Windy mill town that succoured such unlikely talents as William Walton and early English water-colourists. Oldham's central art gallery, *Union St,* has long been notable among provincial galleries for the excellence of its collection – a gift from Charles Lee at the end of the 19thC.

25. Peel Tower 8 C7
4m N of Bury at Holcombe village. Fans of Sir Robert Peel, Prime Minister and founder of the police force, erected this 128ft tower in 1851 to celebrate his repeal of the Corn Laws. Working at 1,162ft above sea level must have given the poor masons chilblains, but perhaps the breathless views made it all worth while. The top of the tower was sealed off many years ago for safety reasons.

26. Salford Art Gallery and Museum 8 C8
The Crescent, Peel Park, 3m SW of Manchester. Lowry covers the walls of this splendid gallery which contains the largest public collection of this Salford-born artist. Downstairs is Lark Hill Place, a full-scale walk-round replica of a period street with shops and houses typifying a scene in the north at the turn of the century. Everything from chemists to cobblers, beer to bonnets.

26. Salford, Ordsall Hall 8 C8
Taylorson St. Guy Fawkes may have hatched the Gunpowder Plot in the Star Chamber of this stately home in Salford dockland. Built in the 14th and 16thC, this once-moated home of the great Radclyffe family opened in 1972 as a period house and social history museum. The Radclyffes probably brought the first Flemish weavers to England and settled them in Salford. Outstanding features are: the half-timbered Great Hall built in the 1520s, with its seven-sided oriel and massive timbers, the great chamber, and the kitchen which shows how Ordsall must have looked when it was a Victorian farmhouse.

Ordsall Hall

27. Smithill's Hall 8 C7
Off Smithill's Dean Road, 2m NW of Bolton. Bang in the middle of a Bolton suburb, this 14thC manor house tugs your imagination back to trestle-tables and rushlights with its timbered Great Hall and medieval quarters. More refined day-dreamers might prefer the Tudor withdrawing room with its large square bay window overlooking the gardens. Andrew Barton, who built it, divided the ceiling into squares – each richly carved – and oak-panelled the walls. Make sure you see the 16thC linenfold panelling and carved medallion portraits – a test of skill for any student of heraldry.
The impression of a foot on a flagstone at Smithill's tells the story of a Catholic martyr, George Marsh, who was interrogated in the Green Chamber and ordered to recant. He wouldn't, and stamped his foot to make his refusal clear. People say that sometimes the print has a red glow. Marsh was burned as a heretic one year after his appearance at Smithill's. *Open most days.*

28. Turton Tower 8 C7
Turton, 4m N of Bolton, off A4666. This 15thC peel tower with its half-timbered Tudor wings stands 600ft up on the edge of Turton Moor and when gales seeth round the eaves you can almost believe in its claim to a resident ghost. The Timberbottom Skulls, reburied here after a local farm murder, should keep you shivering, too. It's said that if they're moved, or treated with disrespect, untold troubles will occur. Orrells lived here from 1420 to 1628 when financial problems forced John Orrell to sell the tower to Humphrey Chetham. Greater Manchester is full of Humphrey's thoughtfulness for the poor, and one of his gestures was to give Turton church a library of 52 chained books – still prized by the village. The tower was probably begun in the 12thC as a defensive structure, and traces of its original spiral staircase can still be found, despite considerable 16th and 19thC alterations. See the splendid 17thC arms and furniture brought from nearby Bradshaw Hall before it was demolished, and the large oak bedstead where Oliver Cromwell is said to have slept. *Open most days.*

⚜LANCASHIRE⚜

29. Astley Hall
8 B7

Park Road, Chorley. Guests visiting Astley's new wing for the first time must have toppled out of their 17thC carriages in sheer disbelief at the all-glass-and-no-wall effect of its windows. Soaring octagonally in two great bays from ground to roof with little more than a band of stone to keep them anchored, they have more in common structurally with a New York skyscraper than a Lancashire stately home. And despite doomy forecasts by friends and neighbours, they have survived magnificently alongside the rest of this Elizabethan hall.

Cherubs squint down from the ceiling at panelled walls hung with a curious collection of worthies and unworthies. A huge oak bed is known locally as The Cromwell Bed because Cromwell is supposed to have slept in it the night after the Battle of Preston – it's certainly big enough for several Cromwells to have done so simultaneously. He may also have supped off the famous 24ft-long shovel board table in the long gallery. The drawing room features early 18thC English walnut furniture, and Astley's pottery and painting collections are well worth seeing.

Astley Hall

30. Blackburn
8 B6

The town grew up in a clearing of the royal forest of the Ribble, round a church founded in Saxon times. Packhorses bringing wool from the fells, Flemish weavers and Irish flax all helped Blackburn to become one of the most famous textile towns in England. Wool and linen gave way to cotton, and handloom weavers were sucked into a factory system by the tide of the Industrial Revolution. The story of the textile industry in this area is told in the Lewis Textile Museum, *Exchange St*, which has full working models of Hargreaves's Spinning Jenny, Arkwright's frame and Kay's flying shuttle. *Open most days.*

31. Blackpool
8 A6

Playground of the North and Britain's largest holiday resort, at the beginning of the 19thC Blackpool was but a little-known fishing village. The 19thC passion for sea bathing first drew small groups of visitors here and they stayed in hostels along the seafront. Improving public transport fed its popularity, and by 1863 the North Pier was standing. It was followed by two more in 1868 and 1893. Blackpool Tower took three years to build – between 1891 and 1894 – and it stands 518ft high with views of the Lakeland, Welsh mountains and the Isle of Man from the top. Traders opened shops and stalls in forecourts of sea-front houses, and this was the start of the Golden Mile. Blackpool may have lost a lot of seediness, but you can still peer through beady curtains at black-haired ladies with crystal balls, lurch home sticky-fingered with dentures of rock, or ride in a tramcar.

Apart from its jolly Victoriana (Opera House, theatre, and hotels), Blackpool's 'history' resides in All Hallows Church which has a Norman porch carved with signs of the zodiac and epitaphs. The Grundy Art Gallery, *Queen St*, exhibits a fine collection of paintings by 19th and 20thC artists. *Open weekdays.*

32. Clitheroe
8 C6

Thugs and soldiers, nobles and henchmen have clattered through the streets of Clitheroe up to the castle on the hill built by an 11thC Norman family. Today, its 9ft-thick ruined walls peer through slit eyes at municipal flower-beds and afternoon strollers. Although the smallest Norman keep in England, it commanded a full view of the Ribble valley and was extremely difficult to attack. Medieval barons farmed many miles of land from this castle and gained a reputation for the horses and cattle they reared. Scattered in nearby Pendle and Rossendale forests were cattle booths or vaccaries; each booth held about 80 cattle, and Pendle area names like Barley Booth and Goldshaw Booth show where some of them were.

Clitheroe church, much changed through the centuries, has some interesting historical nuggets: a rough hewn church-warden's bench with built-in poor box; an old font; a 15thC altar tomb of Sir Richard Radclyffe in full armour; a brass engraved with the horoscope of an astrologer called John Webster; and a mural tablet about Captain Cook who was accompanied on his third voyage by a parson's son from Clitheroe.

33. Gawthorpe Hall
8 C6

Padiham, nr Burnley. Laces, shawls, tapestries, embroideries, costumes, textiles – Rachael Kay-Shuttleworth left such a beauteous collection here at her home that any visit to Gawthorpe is more than a shuffle round another lovely building. It is an experience of history through thread. Although much is displayed, much more is available on prior request and experts come from all over the world to study this superb collection. The house, built in the 17thC, is unusual in that the servants' quarters are in the basement and the Great Hall is at the back, not the front. *Open most days, summer.*

34. Helmshore Textile Museum
8 C7

Holcombe Rd, Helmshore, Rossendale. Clinging to much of its original character, this 18thC mill was built for wool textile finishing processes and is one of the oldest in Lancashire. The mill-owner's house and workers' cottages have scarcely changed in 200 years. At the museum you can see demonstrations of fulling and other operations. Textile machinery, including some of Arkwright's, is on show and there's a 20ft water-wheel. *Open most days.*

35. Hoghton Tower
8 B6

5m W of Blackburn, off A675. A crimson carpet woven especially for the occasion was just one of the crippling expenses that landed Sir Richard Hoghton in debt after a royal visit to his home in 1617 by James I and a gaggle of court cronies. For three days the company ate, drank and caroused in this now-restored Tudor hall and James grew so merry it's said he even knighted a joint of beef Sir Loin, creating the word sirloin. The long table where he probably did it is still there today. Richard's uncle built Hoghton in 1565 and a century later it had lost its tower in a gunpowder forray with attacking Parliamentarians. Later Hoghtons allowed the hall to decline and in the early 19thC it was used as a workshop by local hand-loom weavers. Charles Dickens describes its dilapidation in one of his short stories. But by 1860, a 9th baronet decided to repair it and today you can see the state rooms, a Tudor well-house with its horse-drawn pump, and stone cells used for cattle thieves. *Open weekends, summer.*

36. Lancaster   8 A5
The Romans took root here and the town
became a flourishing port, only to lose trade as
the silt moved up the river. Now with all the
attractions of a busy county town, Lancaster
retains a sense of its past importance in its
many old buildings, from the Norman castle
to the Georgian merchant houses.
Roman basilica, Saxon shrine and Norman
church have all stood on the site of the **Priory
Church of St Mary**, *Castle Hill*, and left their
traces in the present building. Although most
of the church is late 15thC, the belfry was
added in 1754 and there's a Jacobean pulpit.
A small museum on the south aisle shows bits
of Roman pottery and glass found in the walls,
a fragment of Roman millstone and an array of
ancient broken crosses, one carved by a Viking
1,000 years ago. The 14thC west door opens
onto an assembly of old gravestones. But most
famous of all are the 14thC stalls, minutely
carved with faces and figures, foliage and
flowers.
Judges Lodgings, a fine mid-17thC town
house, was home to visiting assize judges from
1826 to 1975. Recently converted to a
museum, the house has a furnished judge's
bedroom of 1840 and the Barry Elder Doll
Collection of 1,000 dolls, dolls' houses and
toys. *Open most days, summer.*
Overlooking the town is the folly to end all
follies – the **Ashton Memorial**. In 1909,
Lord Ashton built it as a fantastic memorial to
his first wife, Alice, for the headreeling sum of
£87,000. After remarrying – twice – the
monument was tactfully rededicated to
'deceased members of his family'! Its green
dome is a cross between the Taj Mahal and St
Paul's Cathedral and locals often call it 'the
jelly mould'. Views from the summit are
superb.

Lancaster Castle

36. Lancaster Castle   8 A5
Cobbled paths caterpillar up Castle Hill to
where Lancaster's 800-year-old castle
contemplates the centuries of bloodshed and
torture, battle and beauty it has witnessed.
Norman barons built it to fend off Scottish
marauders, then John of Gaunt repaired it,
and Elizabeth I fortified it to resist the
Armada. Royalists and Roundheads fought
for it and countless prisoners have wept within
its dungeons. The gatehouse, massive and
strong, is one of the greatest in England, and
still shows where the drawbridge chain and
portcullis grooved the stonework.
Lunatics, criminals and those gone mad with
torture were incarcerated behind these
terrifying studded doors. Grisly exhibits like
strait jackets, chains, irons, cat-o'-nine-tails
and scold's bridle are on show. Probably the
only one left in England, there's even a
branding iron and clamp which held the
person's hand as 'M' for malefactor was
scorched on it. Near the gallows there's a
chapel where prisoners attended services –
men partitioned from women, and a special
enclosure for those about to die. The library
houses a complete collection of the laws of
England since 1225, and in the Shire Hall are
600 painted shields and javelins. *Open summer.*

37. Leighton Hall   8 B4
3m NW of Carnforth, off A6. Brilliant white
limestone mansion built originally by the
Middleton family in the 15thC and restored in
the Gothic style by the Gillows in 1800.
Richard Gillow, the cabinet-maker, became
famous and the house contains unique
examples of early Gillow furniture, plus
paintings and the third largest dolls' house in
the world. Eagles and other birds of prey are
flown most days in the superb grounds of this
hall which is arguably one of the most
beautifully sited in the north. *Open summer.*

38. Preston   8 B6
A spiky skyline of steeples, towers, chimneys,
factories and flats is one of the most
memorable things about Preston. Reckoned to
have a church on every corner, none is
conspicuously old, nor has Preston generally
clung visibly to much of its past. St
Walburghe's 300ft white spire is reminiscent
of Salisbury cathedral in its startling
proportions, and was designed by Joseph
Hansom of cab fame.
Preston was the scene of one of the most
decisive battles of the Civil War. In 1648,
encouraged by Charles I, the Scots rose in
revolt and were defeated here in three hours.
Battles of a different nature took place in the
18thC, when the Industrial Revolution took
hold of the town. Workers fearing their jobs
were threatened by the new machines, rioted,
demanding their destruction, and Arkwright,
who invented the Spinning Jenny to cheapen
cotton production, had to flee to Nottingham
to escape their attacks. But when John
Horrocks set up the first cotton mill in
Preston, the town thrived. Before the
Industrial Revolution the gentry lived
decorously in places like Winckley Square
which still has some fine town houses: at no 7
the poet Francis Thompson was born. The
handsome Harris Museum and Art Gallery
houses ceramics, 2,000 glass and porcelain
scent bottles, and paintings.

39. Ribchester Museum and Fort   8 B6
Ribchester. A thousand Romans lived on this
six acre fort of Bremetennacum. One of the
biggest in Britain and of great archaeological
importance, it is sited in the attractive village
of Ribchester. Today you can see remains of
two great granaries, barracks, armoury,
houses for the governor and his captains and a
temple. The churchyard was their
headquarters and the church their shrine to
Minerva.
Finds here have been breathtaking, and many
are now in the British Museum. A perfect
bronze ceremonial helmet, one of the most
beautiful in existence, was unearthed in 1796,
9ft down in the gravel. The original is in
London, but Ribchester has a copy. Hundreds
of delicately-decorated urns were found,
along with shoals of Caesar-stamped coins.
An altar to the dastardly brothers, Caracalla
and Geta, was dug up in the churchyard.
Caracalla murdered Geta in front of their
mother and ordered his name to be erased
from all monuments – you can see it almost
obliterated on this stone. *Open most days.*

40. Rufford Old Hall   8 A7
7m N of Ormskirk, off A59. Exciting 15thC
house considered one of the National Trust's
most precious possessions – which is certainly
saying something. Rufford seeps craft and
curiosity from every corner and crack and has
one of the most impressive medieval halls in
England. Carved angels support a spectacular
hammer-beam roof and there's a weighty
screen that 10 men can shift with a lot of
puffing. It possibly assisted in the theatricals
Sir Thomas Hesketh enjoyed staging at
Rufford. Researchers have found convincing
evidence that Shakespeare spent some
unaccounted-for years of his youth here as a
member of Sir Thomas's company. A certain

William Shakeshaft sang and acted in this area and a sequence of coincidental contacts seems to suggest that he was the bard. Rufford also has Victorian dresses, four-posters, Georgian dolls' houses, a collection of children's games, a folk museum, arms and armour, coins, tapestries and antique porcelain – to mention just some. *Open most days; closed mid-winter.*

Rufford Old Hall

41. Samlesbury Hall   8 B6
4m E of Preston, off A677. Motorists and overnight guests claim a ghostly white lady prowls round this 14thC estate remembering how her brothers murdered her lover because he was an Anglican and she a Catholic. Whether she's fact or fantasy, no-one of course can prove, but the skeletons of two young men were found in the moat during road excavations in 1826. Speculation said they were lover and brother, slain in the feud.

Samlesbury Hall

Samlesbury's Great Hall and mullioned windows give instant olde worlde appeal, but its pedigree is varied to say the least. Begun in 1325, the Southworth family lived in it until 1678 when Edward Southworth sold it to pay off penalties and fines incurred as a Royalist. During the 19thC it became a beer shop, a

boarding school and back to a private house again. Each owner changed it a little, which is why the present house, though beautiful, is rather a mongrel. See secret rooms, massive open fireplaces and the family chapel. The beautifully-kept informal gardens include an archery field. While Samlesbury Hall is owned and administered by Samlesbury Hall Trust, it has for tenants a local branch of the Council for the Preservation of Rural England. *Open most days.*

42. Steamtown Railway Museum   8 A4
Warton Road, Carnforth. Climb aboard the footplate of the Flying Scotsman, ogle Sir Nigel Gresley, film Lord Nelson, or take a brake-van ride. Steam fanatics know precisely what all this means and should be tooting with delight at the mere mention of Jane Darbyshire, a Midland Railway signal box, and vintage coaches. All of them are on display here at this gigantic locomotive shed built in 1945 where 80 engines could 'stable' at once in the good old days of steam and smuts. Much of the English, French and German collection is in working order and is in steam on Sundays in summer and in July and August. You can even arrange trips to Ravenglass and York. For long-sufferers who don't know steam from diesel, there's a gift shop of non-railway souvenirs, carvings and pottery.

43. Towneley Hall Gallery and Museums   8 C6
½m SE of Burnley. Direst dungeons, blowy battlements, sweaty kitchens, secret hidey holes – this hunting lodge turned Tudor mansion turned Georgian showpiece has all of these and more. Burnley now uses it as an art gallery and museum, too. This was the home of the Royalist, Catholic Towneleys who sheltered fugitives and were themselves persecuted. Note their sparrow-hawk crest on walls and rain-pipes, a magnificent Jacobean table, the sweet family chapel with Tudor panelling and old Sir John's praying stool and chair. A secret room sound-proofed with daub and rushes leads off the long gallery from behind a family portrait. The baroque entrance hall of this mainly 14thC house is a particularly fine 18thC room and a large glass case contains some lustrous embroidery. *Open most days.*

⚜MERSEYSIDE⚜

44. Birkenhead Priory   6 A1
Priory St, Birkenhead. Benedictine monks arrived at this 'headland of birches' and built themselves a priory. They earned a modest living ferrying travellers across the Mersey and in 1330 Edward III recognised this route as part of the King's Highway. Like so many other places then, Birkenhead began as a religious settlement. Most of the buildings were neglected after the Dissolution. Only ruins remain but the original chapter house of 1150 still stands. All the priory ruins at Monks' Ferry are open to view and there's a museum on the site, too. *Open most days.*

45. Bromborough   6 A2
5m S of Birkenhead, off A41. Price's Patent Candle Company built this industrial village – one of the oldest examples in Britain – in 1854 for its workers. Marshes cut it off from surrounding areas which increased its isolation and until a causeway was built, the only way out was by footpath to New Ferry. Self-sufficient for many years, it had a community school, hospital, church and recreational facilities. The factory is now part of Unilever.

46. Eastham, Church of St Mary   6 A1
3m S of Port Sunlight, off A41. A 2,000-year-old yew tree in the churchyard here makes this 12thC church a mere historical beginner. When the abbot and monks of St Werburgh received the Manor of Eastham in 1152, local villagers begged them 'to have a care of ye olde yew'. They did, and today it still flourishes. The church itself has one of only two old spires in the Wirral, built in 1754. The oldest bits of the church are the Norman foundations of the north wall, and the 10thC font.

47. Fort Perch Rock   8 A8
New Brighton, off A554, Wirral. Enthusiasts from the Aircraft Wreck Recovery Group have assembled a wide range of World War II relics in this historic fort on the River Mersey. Occasional high tides may prevent access. Look out for the Union Jack which flies when the fort is open. *Open most days, summer.*

48. Liverpool   8 A8
Psychologist and philosopher C. G. Jung described Liverpool as 'the pool of life'. And floating round its old and new docks, you

begin to understand what he means.
Settlement dates back to the 1stC and by 1200
there was a busy fishing village. The real
boom came in the 17th and 18thC with the
growth of Atlantic trade, and the coming of
the steam ships in the 1840s made for further
expansion. Here emigrants to Australia and
America departed, and thousands of
potato-famined Irish arrived. Nowadays,
London and Southampton nab most of the
passenger traffic, but Liverpool is still
Britain's biggest export port, and a city with a
history created by water.
The best way to see the docklands is to take
that famous 'ferry cross the Mersey'. In one
sweep, you take in the Cunard building, the
green-domed Port of Liverpool building and
the monumental mass of the Albert Dock
warehouses. Get off at Pier Head and walk
the canyon between the Royal Liver and
Cunard buildings into Water Street,
Liverpool's main shopping street. Desolate
and lonely though many of the old docks are,
it's easy to understand why conservationists
want to protect their grace and special
atmosphere. Contrasts between old and new
are stunning – the Royal Seaforth dock,
opened in 1973, covers 500 acres of land
reclaimed from the Mersey: a port within a
port, it's the biggest docks project carried out
in Europe since the war.
Dockside pubs tell Liverpool's history as a
port, and you can find them near Chinatown:
The Baltic Fleet, rounded like a ship's stern;
The Flying Dutchman where slave trader
crews drank their pay; and the tiny Old Red
Lion sandwiched between tall warehouses, a
good example of an 18thC water-front ale
house. Beyond Pier Head are the emigrant
pubs where many pioneers bound for America
and Canada supped their last British beer.
The pubs are where you'll find the essence of
Liverpool. You could well be propping up the
bar alongside a budding comedian practising
his gags or be elbow-to-elbow with a musician
in the Beatles' old haunt, Ye Cracke, *Rice St.*
Rigby's Hotel, *Dale St*, has a Nelson room full
of his relics, and bow-windowed Denbigh
Castle, *Hackins Hey*, is still sniffily Victorian –
men only at lunchtime, women admitted
5.30pm, pub shuts 7pm! Thackeray and
Prince Louis Napoleon used to booze at the
Poste House, *Cumberland Street.*
Bombed in 1941 and rebuilt 25 years later,
The County Museum, *William Brown St*,
specialises in recalling the city's maritime
history. Superb models of Liverpool's
development as a port are on show, plus an
exciting transport section featuring the
Titfield Thunderbolt locomotive of 1838,
from the Liverpool and Manchester Railway.
Aquarium and vivarium are both favourites
with children and the planetarium was the
first in Britain outside London. A
3,000-year-old mummy and archaeological,
ceramic and applied art collections are here
too, and there's a beautiful historic musical
instruments gallery. Don't miss the Chinese
water-clock.
More marine exhibits can be seen at the
Merseyside Maritime Museum. Shanty
singing, net and sail making, and boat
repairing are some of the activities and you
can follow a quayside history trail, discover
how a great port works, and see full size craft
in the boat hall.
Liverpool is renowned for its enlightened
patronage of the arts. The **Walker Art
Gallery**, *William Brown St*, contains paintings
and sculptures from all periods, including
work by Stubbs, Lowry, Rubens, Rembrandt,
Hogarth and Degas. British painting of the
18th and 19thC is the speciality of the **Sudley
Art Gallery**, *Mossley Hill Rd*, a 19thC
merchant's house set in its own breezy
parkland. The **Hornby Library**, *William
Brown St*, contains letters from Nelson, Byron,
Gladstone and Verdi, signatures – legible and

otherwise – of many British monarchs, and
poems by Johnson and Cowper. Over 1,000
rare books, first editions, illustrations and
displays of binding and printing make this a
feast for book-worms.
St George's Hall has been described as the
finest Greco-Roman building in Europe. This
imposing eyeful is the first of the city you see
as you step out of Lime Street station.
Completed mid 19thC, the complex – with its
16 Corinthian columns towering 60ft high – is
used for regular organ recitals, law courts and
civic occasions.
Another interesting building is **Croxteth
Hall**, *Croxteth Hall Lane*, a sporting estate
pickled and preserved from the days of
Victorian and Edwardian indulgence. It's
retained even now by the Earls of Sefton, one
of Liverpool's oldest families. Formal
gardens, a rare Victorian walled garden,
farmland, woodland and fine rural buildings
belie the city's presence only five miles away.
*Open summer; certain weekends, winter; park
open daily.*

Roman Catholic Cathedral, Liverpool

48. Liverpool, Cathedrals   8   A8
Hope St. Largest Anglican cathedral in the
world, the Gothic giant built of dark pink
sandstone was finally consecrated in 1978
after 74 years of building. It was the lifetime's
work of one man – Sir Giles Gilbert Scott –
who won a competition to design it in 1901
when he was only 22. Every corner of this
silencing building seems to house a
record-breaker. The organ has 10,000 stops
and is the biggest in the world; the bells have
the highest (219ft) and heaviest (31 tons) peal
in the world; one of the stained glass windows
alone took 18,000 sq ft of glass. Children from
Liverpool gave the Lady chapel porch, so it is
generally known as the 'children's porch'.
'Paddy's wigwam' was how angry critics
described the Roman Catholic Metropolitan
Cathedral when it was consecrated in 1967.
Others find Sir Frederick Gibberd's conical
design of glass and concrete with its use of
colour, light and space, very effective.
Circular, and seating 2,250 people, the centre
focus of the cathedral is its altar. A cylinder of
coloured glass – the Lantern Tower – rises
centrally over the altar and bathes the whole
interior in a spectrum of different colours
depending on the time of day.

49. Pilkington Glass Museum   8   B8
Prescot Rd, St Helens, off A58. Phoenician glass
to plate glass – see it all at this handsome
industrial museum that skilfully describes the
evolution of glass-making and the many ways
glass can be used. Letting light into dark
corners began here with Jean de la Bruyère, a
Frenchman who settled in St Helens in the
mid 18thC because of its plentiful coal and
sand with grains of almost uniform size – ideal
for glass-making. In 1783, the British Plate
Glass Company built a factory here and part
of the original glass house (known as the
'cathedral') is still used today in the famous

Ravenhead works of United Glass Ltd. Pilkingtons built their ultra-modern complex in 1964 and it's reckoned to be one of the finest industrial buildings in Europe.

50. Port Sunlight   8 A9
Wirral. Famous 'garden village' which was built originally to house employees making soap at Unilever's nearby factory. It has become a model for town planners and all 900 buildings – some Tudor-style – in the village are now listed. One of the most interesting collections in the world, the Lady Lever Art Gallery is the place to come for an ogle at the pre-Raphaelites, English furniture, Wedgwood, Chinese ceramics, enamels, tapestries and antique needlework.

51. Speke Hall   8 A9
Nr Speke Airport, 8m SE of Liverpool, off A561. Dominating the cobbled courtyard of this timbery 16thC Tudor mansion are two great yews, older than the hall itself. If trees could talk, they'd have some tales to tell – about soldiers hiding in the attic during the Civil War, who passed the time cock fighting, and priests arriving at the dead of night and bundled into secret passages till danger passed.
Speke has four wings surrounding the

courtyard and its timbering uses the distinctive herring-bone and four-leaf clover designs characteristic of buildings in south Lancashire and Cheshire. Luckily, it escaped 18thC modernisation, and when in 1796 the Watts took over from the Norrises who built the mansion, Sir Walter Scott soon started such a fad for the Middle Ages and Tudor times with his Waverley Novels that Speke was left untouched – except to be furnished in the way the 19thC thought the 16thC ought to have looked like. Early vacuum cleaners and irons are on show in the impressive Victorian kitchen and servants' hall. The Great Hall is the oldest part of the house, and of note are the blue drawing room, the Victorian morning room, and the great parlour with its magnificent stucco ceiling and carved oak overmantel describing three generations of Norrises. Tapestries and William Morris wallpapers hang throughout the house.

52. Steamport Transport Museum   8 A7
Derby Rd, Southport. See steam and diesel locos, buses, trams, rolling stock, traction engines and all the rest beloved by railway enthusiasts. 'Steam-ups' and brake van rides on Sundays and Bank Holidays in summer. *Open summer; weekends, winter.*

CUMBRIA

1. Belle Isle   9 C9
Lake Windermere. John Curwen gave Isabella Curwen this round Georgian house on its 38 acre island as a wedding present – hence the name 'Belle'. He bought it from a Mr English who, according to Wordsworth, was the first man to settle in Lakeland for the sake of the scenery. Mr English built this completely circular house, the first in England, in 1774. The locals were furious – Mr English felled many of the island's trees and they hated the odd shape of the house. Fed up with all the fuss, he sold the estate at a loss and left in a huff.
Isabella placated the locals by replanting most of the trees, and today the house is almost as it was built. The 20-bedroomed mansion has no corridors and all the rooms connect. Staircases are hidden, and the furniture was carpentered by Gillow especially for the curved walls. Paintings by Reynolds and Romney, a round-the-island path, and the garden make this a gently enjoyable afternoon's visit. The Romans are thought to have used Belle Isle (originally Long Holme) and from 1250 it was the seat of the Lord of the Manor of Windermere. *Open most days, summer.*

2. Brantwood   9 B9
2½m SE of Coniston, off B5285 to Hawkshead. John Ruskin, philosopher and art critic, built this rambly house in 1871 and lived his last 28 years in it. Far from London society scandalised by the annulment of his marriage on grounds of impotence, Ruskin collected paintings by Turner and promoted pre-Raphaelites like Rossetti, Burne-Jones and Millais. He bought Brantwood as a cottage and added 12 rooms and a fancy bedroom tower to it. His hair, handkerchief, tie, baby chair and other personal belongings are on show along with pictures and furniture. Some people think it has a morbid atmosphere – certainly Ruskin suffered from depression and melancholia during his final years – but daffodils, azaleas and rhododendrons are beautiful enough in season to banish dark forebodings. *Open most days, summer.*

3. Carlisle   9 C5
King-pin in the line of defence against Scotland, Carlisle Castle has been fought over for centuries. William Rufus started building the great keep in 1092 with walls 8–15ft thick. Mary, Queen of Scots, stayed here for 2 months in 1568 – as so often, she arrived as a guest and ended up a prisoner. See the

Carlisle Cathedral

famous 'licking stones' in the dungeons and the erotic pictures on the walls of one of the cells, drawn by Major Macdonald after the '45 Jacobite rebellion. The portcullis, ramparts and a museum of the Border Regiment are also worth seeing.

Carlisle Cathedral is one of the most battle-scarred in the country. Chunks of it were pulled down during the Civil War and the stone was used to repair the city's defences. Built between 1092 and 1419, it was neglected in the 18thC and restored in the 19thC. Treasures are the huge east window with much 14thC original glass, and the merrily-carved choir stalls with cartoon figures, monsters and allegories. Tullie House is a stylish Jacobean mansion housing the city's art gallery, library and museum – including Roman finds from Hadrian's Wall, which ran through Carlisle.

4. Cartmel Priory 9 C9
Cartmel, 5m SE of Newby Bridge, off B5271. Augustinian monks settled here in 1188 and funded their priory by fishing and wild-fowling in the salty marshes. Although Norman bits survive from this period, so many styles have been grafted on that the church has a 'box of bricks' look to it. This squat assembly was dissolved as a priory in 1536 and the roof torn off, leaving the chancel to rot in rain and snow. It weathered remarkably well and the wittily pictorial woodwork makes it worth a visit.

5. Castlerigg Stone Circle 9 B7
1m E of Keswick, off A66. Draw a line from Skiddaw summit to Helvellyn summit and you'll find it passes straight through the two highest stones of this 1,400BC circle. Draw another line from the outer stone, through the centre of the circle and you'll find it ends on the horizon at Fiends' Fell in the Pennines, marking the line of sunrise on May 1st. This 'sunrise line' also passes through Long Meg stone circle which suggests a relationship between the two ancient sites. The circle itself is 100ft wide with 38 stones.

Castlerigg Stone Circle

6. Dove Cottage 9 B8
Town End, Grasmere. William and Dorothy Wordsworth lived frugally in this tiny, cramped cottage for nine years. William dictated much of his best poetry to Dorothy in one of its chilly upstairs rooms which Dorothy papered with newspapers to try and keep warm. William brought his new wife, Mary Hutchinson, there and the three of them shared a passionate and intense relationship. Coleridge, Mary's sister and William's brother sometimes joined them for day or night hikes over the fells discussing poetry, nature and life. The locals never quite came to terms with these strange goings-on, and continued to view their neighbours with the utmost suspicion. Today, the humble cottage is more or less how they left it – two rooms downstairs, and four little rooms upstairs. Opposite the cottage is the Wordsworth Museum, which contains his straw hat and walking boots as well as photographs, portraits and manuscripts.

Although Dove Cottage is famous all over the world, the Wordsworths never knew it by that name. Their address was simply Town End – a collective name for a group of cottages at one end of the village. Dorothy and William nurtured the little garden, grew peas and beans, and built a hut in one corner which is still there. When the Wordsworths moved out

of Dove Cottage, De Quincey and his thousands of books moved in. It is said he could lend them to Coleridge 500 at a time and not notice that any were missing. *Open most days, summer.*

Dove Cottage

7. Furness Abbey 9 B10
Barrow-in-Furness, off A590. Monks ran a big business round Furness during the 13th and 14thC based at this huge abbey founded in 1127. Wool, hunting, fishing, mills, salt-pans, iron mines, export, and even a spot of smuggling were all on the clerical agenda for these Cistercians, and it became one of the richest abbeys in England. Sheer size makes this settlement impressive. The dormitory was over 200ft long, the infirmary 126ft and the rectory 150ft – compared with the 100ft rectory and 110ft dormitory of Fountains Abbey, this is enormous. Everything is laid out in a functional manner: church, chapter house, cloisters, infirmary, kitchen, abbot's bedsit, even the drainage and sewerage system. You can also see the recess for a towel beside a basin and the rings in the walls where farmers tethered their cattle. Although much of the abbey remains, and rivals other great monastic ruins like Tintern, Melrose and Fountains, it is enclosed within the suburbs of a large industrial town and depends on its tree shield for peace and quiet.

8. Hill Top 9 C8
Nr Sawrey, Ambleside, B5285. Beatrix Potter beats Wordsworth into first place in the Lake District tourist league – perhaps because Peter Rabbit, Mrs Tiggy Winkle and Squirrel Nutkin are more widely known today than 'The Prelude'. She bought Hill Top in 1905 as a bolt-hole to get away now and again from dominating parents, and it was here that she wrote most of her books. Royalties from them bought more land and stock, including Castle Cottage which is across the road from Hill Top.

At 47 Beatrix married a local solicitor and moved into Castle Cottage where she lived for the next 36 years as wife and farmer. She wore a tweedy ragbag of clothes and was often mistaken for a tramp as she trailed over the fells with a sack round her shoulders, inspecting sheep. She became a passionate conservationist and gave generously to the National Trust. Her prize-winning flock of Herdwick sheep and 4,000 acres went to them on her death in 1943. Hill Top became a sort of personal museum where she deposited old plates, oak furniture and other random possessions. Today, the 17thC farmhouse contains her china, pictures, the longcase clock she drew in 'The Tailor of Gloucester', and originals of her books. *Open most days, summer.*

9. Holker Hall 9 C10
Cark-in-Cartmel, Grange-over-Sands. A popular 17thC mansion restored in 1873 after a fire with all the 'props' of a stately home: fine furniture, paintings, carving, gardens and a deer park. Keep the children quiet at the model railway, baby animal farm, or museum of curios and inventions.

The real treat here is the Lakeland Motor Museum, where a sumptuous feast of motoring history awaits anyone with a taste for old vehicles. On show are veteran, vintage, classic post war and unusual cars, plus bicycles, tricycles, model cars, motor cycles, and even the replica of a 1920 garage. *Open most days, summer.*

10. Kendal   **9 C9**
In the 14thC Flemish weavers settled in 'The Auld Grey Town' – so-called because of its many limestone buildings – and established a woollen-weaving industry. The town grew famous for its dyes, especially 'Kendal Green', mentioned by Shakespeare in 'Henry IV'. When fashion lost interest, Kendal started exporting to American cotton growers who weren't particular what colour their workers wore. They in turn sent tobacco and snuff to Kendal, and the town is still one of the main centres of snuff manufacturing. See the negro snuff-taker on a wall in Lowther Street.
For rummaging and rambling down old alleys and yards, pubs and shops, Kendal is a must. Catherine Parr once lived at the crumbly 12thC castle in the public park, which has a tower, dungeons and exhilarating views. Kendal church is a great square building dating from the 13thC and boasting four aisles with pillars which create curious optical effects. Find the jaunty little autobiographical poem inside the altar rails, composed by a local 17thC clergyman. Kendal is justly proud of the Abbot Hall Art Gallery, a Georgian house filled with 18thC furniture, porcelain, silver, objets d'art, paintings and a historical display of Lakeland life in the stable block.

Kendal

11. King Arthur's Round Table   **9 C7**
1m S of Penrith, off A6. Named after King Arthur and his knights who are said to have roamed this area, this is in fact a prehistoric earthwork, 300ft across with an inner ditch. There were once two entrances, but the one on the north side has disappeared. Two monoliths once stood by it and another stone structure stood near the centre of the circle. Mayburgh lies a few hundred yards to the west. It's circular like the Table, but with a single entrance on the east. Near the centre is a single standing stone, the sole survivor of the original four.

12. Levens Hall   **9 C9**
5m S of Kendal, A6. Bright Cordova leather

Levens Hall

covers the dining room walls of this house which grew out of a Norman pele tower. From 1170 when it was built, Levens has been added to, mainly in the 16thC: plaster ceilings, staircases, wainscots, carved fireplaces, overmantels, and a topiary garden of yews which is as well known as the house itself. Fine pictures and Charles II furniture make this an elegant afternoon's sojourn. Levens has the only deer park of 15 that once surrounded Kendal. Its fallow deer are particularly dark and local lore says that the birth of a white fawn forecasts either great good or great evil to the house. A unique steam collection includes small engines and traction engines which are in steam some weekends, and there's a collection of harpsichords. *House open most days, summer; park, daily summer, weekdays, winter.*

13. Long Meg Stone Circle   **9 D7**
6½, NNE of Penrith, off A686. Long Meg and her Daughters is the largest of three major stone circles in Cumbria but not as bleak as Castlerigg: a farm track runs across it and stray trees soften the savagery of the primitive skyline. Although Long Meg herself is a sandstone menhir and the oval of 27 stones stands on sandstone, all the other stones are volcanic rocks from the fells. One explanation is that it was easier for neolithic builders to carry boulders from the fells than hew rocks from the sandstone, even though they were nearer to hand. Cumbria had at least five other stone circles, now destroyed. The Grey Yards near Carlisle was the second largest one in England, but along with the others it has vanished under plough, tractor, and stone hunter.

14. Muncaster Castle   **9 A9**
Ravenglass, A595. Arson, rape, murder and robbery were all part of the guerilla warfare waged by Scots on the Border counties during the 14thC. The old line of defence gradually gave way and landowners realised they needed more local defences where each family could hold out for a few days against the raiders. Pele towers were the answer – and Muncaster was one of them. Design was defensive with little consideration for comfort or elegance. A basement with two or three storeys above meant that even if raiders broke into the basement, they still had to fight up a narrow spiral staircase to reach people on the upper floors.
Muncaster is one of many fortified manor houses in this area, and it has 15th and 19thC additions plus shimmering views over the Esk valley. Furnishings are 16th and 17thC, there's an excellent collection of portraits and the magnificent gardens have one of the finest rhododendron collections in Europe. One treasure understandably not open to the public is the engraved glass bowl given to the Pennington family by Henry VI after they sheltered him during the Wars of the Roses. It's said that as long as the bowl remains intact, a Pennington will hold the castle. *Open most days, summer.*

15. Rydal Mount   **9 C8**
Rydal, Ambleside, off A591. Wordsworth and his household of ladies moved here in 1813 after a couple of miserable years in Grasmere's leaky rectory, where two of Wordsworth's children died. They all welcomed the move to a bigger and better house which William's literary success made possible. In readiness for visitors the Wordsworths decided to splash out on some expensive carpets and new furniture. Apart from the windows, Rydal Mount hasn't changed since then, and you can still see the garden as the poet himself dug and designed it. Today, the house contains many personal mementoes, the very furniture they used, and several family portraits. Wordsworth died here in 1830 – 16 days after his 80th birthday.

Rydal Mount

Gordon Wordsworth, the poet's grandson, gave the house to the National Trust in 1935 and it is now famous for its spring show of daffodils – flowers most popularly associated with Wordsworth.

16. Sizergh Castle 9 C9
4m S of Kendal, off A591. Border castle of the 14thC which has been home to the Strickland family for 700 years. Like other manor houses fortified to repel the Scots, Sizergh has Tudor 'extras' – a Great Hall, and wings decorated with very fine early Elizabethan woodwork. Many people feel that the house has a great presence, and certainly that it is one of the most interesting in Cumbria. Some of the best Early English woodwork in England is found on the first floor and apart from locks of hair, old coronation tickets and family photographs, the grand furnishings are English and French, and there're silver, china and Jacobean things to intrigue. Gardens are 18thC. *Open certain days, summer.*

17. Swarthmoor Hall 9 B9
Ulverston. Quaker pilgrims still travel to this handsome Elizabethan house with mullioned windows, oak staircase and panelled rooms – because George Fox, founder of the Society of Friends, lived here. Not a particularly remarkable building from the exterior, it's worth a visit for the unusual staircase which has a heavily timbered open well in the centre. Nearby is **Conishead Priory**, *Priory Rd*, a Victorian Gothic house where Buddhists meditate. There are decorative plaster ceilings, marble fireplaces, famous wood panelling, plus gardens and woods. *Hall and Priory open most days, summer.*

18. Travellers' Rest Inn 9 C8
Kirkstone Pass, 4m N of Troutbeck, off A592. Highest Lakeland inn where you can sup a well-earned pint at 1,476ft. Its licence was granted in 1840.

19. Troutbeck 9 C8
3m N of Windermere, off A592. Pre-Raphaelite glass by Burne-Jones tints the light in Troutbeck's church. It has three lych gates and leads to one of Lakeland's prettiest villages, with cluster after cluster of low-roofed cottages lining its long main street. Townend is a typical 17thC yeoman's house which the National Trust has polished and restored. George Browne built it in 1623 and generations of Brownes lived there until 1944, adorning it with fine carving. Their books, papers and furniture are still there to be seen. *Open most days, summer.*

NORTHUMBERLAND

1. Alnwick 9 G2
Scholars have studied the layout of this greystone market town more closely than almost any other urban area in Britain because of the detectable way it grew from Saxon village to castle settlement and trade centre. Street names speak for themselves: Bondgate, Narrowgate, Pottergate, Bailiffgate ('gate' often means 'street' rather than 'gateway'). Only one of the old gates remains – the Hotspur Tower with its massive stonework. Cottages and little shops all popped up round the four and a half acre market triangle and the 18thC turnpikes prompted rebuilding. Built in the 15thC, St Michael's Church with its battlemented tower and interesting tombs, is well worth a visit.

1. Alnwick Castle 9 G2
A yawning young Percy used to sit down here to a breakfast of beer, wine, salt fish, red and white herrings, and a dish of sprats. On 'flesh days' he had half a shin of mutton or boiled beef. But breakfasts weren't the only excesses of this 16thC earl. Known as 'The Magnificent', he wore a golden coat garnished with pearls and precious stones for his wedding, and rigged out at least 400 horsemen in complementary colours. A powerful family, the Percys virtually ruled north east England for 600 years, and lived at Alnwick from 1309. The first one restored and strengthened the original 12thC castle and successive generations added wings here and towers there, usually to make the draughty old medieval building more comfortable – or more secure.
Although the present, dramatic castle is mainly 14thC, it was greatly restored in the 18th and 19thC. Robert Adam blundered badly in his overall redesign, but this is usually blamed on the then Duchess of Northumberland's poor taste. A century later, 300 workmen arrived to convert the interior into Italian Renaissance and this is how it stands today. See the keep, armoury, guard

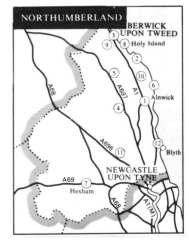

chamber, library and other apartments with works by Titian, Tintoretto and Canaletto adorning the walls. There's a family coach on view, a museum of Roman and British antiquities, and the Regimental Museum of the Royal Northumberland Fusiliers. *Open most days, summer.*

Alnwick Castle

2. Bamburgh Castle   9 G1

Bamburgh. Dazzling views, possibly the best in
Northumberland, await those with energy to
climb the keep of this stunning cliff-top castle.
If you're lucky with the weather, you'll see
Berwick, Holy Island, the Farne Islands,
Dunstanburgh castle and the Cheviots. As a
natural and almost unchallengable fortress,
the site was occupied by Romans and then
seized in 547 by an English chieftain, Ida, who
ruled one of the two Anglo-Saxon kingdoms
later to become Northumbria. He gave the
wooden fortification he built here, to his
grandson, Ethelfrith, who bestowed it on his
wife, Bebba. It became known as
Bebbanburgh, from which the modern name
derives. Bamburgh was often attacked or
besieged and on one occasion the ascetic
Aidan, in retreat on the Farne Islands, is said
to have changed the wind direction to prevent
the wooden walls from burning down.
When the Normans invaded Britain,
Bamburgh became a private stronghold. It was
frequently rebuilt and maintained as a border
fortress, but fell into decay as its usefulness
declined. Between 1894 and 1905 it was
heavily restored much to the annoyance of
antiquarians, historians and architects who
felt the job was carried out inaccurately.
Ordinary visitors, on the other hand, are
generally impressed by the stature and scale of
the castle with large airy rooms, such as the
King's Hall, dressed in the style of the Middle
Ages. See the 150ft well, 11ft-thick walls,
armoury, and windmill where grain was
ground for the poor of the manor. *Open
summer.*

Bamburgh Castle

3. Berwick-upon-Tweed   9 F1

Historic border town on the River Tweed, still
hugged by its ancient walls. Parkland and
fields lap against its northern bulwarks and
from the top you can see the busy market,
coils of the great river, and out to the North
Sea. Berwick's 16thC fortifications are a
unique example of European styles of
defence, comparable with Antwerp and
Verona.
A highly picturesque town, legend states that
during the temptation when the Devil was
showing the kingdoms of the earth to Jesus, he
kept Berwick hidden beneath his thumb
wishing to reserve it as his own little nook!
Twisty lanes and market, three beautiful
bridges and a 17thC church of classic purity
are four good reasons why. Military
enthusiasts will enjoy the Museum of the
King's Own Scottish Borderers, *The Barracks*.
Designed by Vanbrugh, they're said to be the
oldest barracks in Britain. If you like salmon,
Berwick's the place. Medieval monks started
the fishy business and it grew to become one
of the area's leading industries from 1787.

4. Callaly Castle   9 F3

Whittingham. Snuggled in the shadow of the
Cheviots, this smart 17thC mansion was once
the subject of a marital barney. According to
legend, the Lord of Callaly wanted to build a
castle on the nearby hilltop where earlier forts
had been. His wife preferred the sheltered
vale. All womanly persuasions failed and
building went ahead. So she dressed a servant
in boar's costume and secretly sent him each
night to pull down the previous day's work,
instructing him to hum ditties and dance

around wildly as he worked. Alarmed, the lord
sent his servants up at night to investigate.
Terrified, they returned to report a boar
demolishing the half-finished building.
Fearing divine disapproval, he relented and
sited the castle where you see it today.
Callaly is built round a 13thC tower which still
has a spiral staircase. Fireplaces, facades and
a magnificent entrance hall were added in
Georgian and Victorian times, but the
showpiece is the huge drawing room of 1750
with rich plasterwork and fine furniture. The
ballroom has tapestries and some interesting
paintings. The seclusion of its formal gardens
give the castle an almost perfect setting. *Open
weekends and B. hols, summer.*

5. Chillingham Cattle   9 F2

Chillingham, 2m SE of Wooler, off A697. Wild
white cattle have somehow survived here from
the days when a great forest stretched over the
Tweed into Northumberland. They were
'emparked' at Chillingham and are
descedents of the prehistoric wild oxen which
used to roam this rough parkland. A unique
herd – now numbering about 36 cattle – it has
miraculously escaped border raids,
trigger-happy sportsmen, savage winters and
recent foot-and-mouth outbreaks. The cattle,
found on the Earl of Tankerville's estate, are
now protected and maintained by the
Chillingham Wild Cattle Association,
founded in 1939. Although anyone can view
the animals, they are dangerous to approach
and you need patience to tramp far enough to
spot them.

6. Dunstanburgh Castle   9 G2

1m N of Craster. Writers topple about under a
heap of superlatives when it comes to
describing this wild-eyed 14thC castle. Sea
sucks and surges into the joints of rock under
Dunstanburgh's mighty walls and great cliffs,
and columns stand like sentries on centuries
of duty. Weather has bitten the stonework into
curious patterns. Turner fell for this castle,
too, and painted it at least three times.
Although it's the largest castle in
Northumberland, Dunstanburgh figured little
in the county's history because it was neither a
border fort nor the seat of a local lord. Why
Thomas, Earl of Lancaster, started it in 1313
is evaded in all the history books. He was
executed for treason nine years later, and the
castle passed to John of Gaunt, who added the
gateway. It changed hands five times during
the Wars of the Roses, and by 1538, was in
ruins. Many writers tell the story of Sir Guy,
the castle's ghost, whose cries of anguish are
often heard at midnight, as he searches vainly
for a lovely lady once seen in the Great Hall.

Hadrian's Wall   9 E5

*Bowness-on-Solway, Cumbria, to
Wallsend-on-Tyne.* This great Roman frontier
work was built during the AD120s, after a visit
by the Emperor Hadrian to Britain. It marked
the northern-most boundary of their empire
and was a show of strength to surrounding
hostile tribes. Altogether the wall was 72 miles
long, generally 10ft wide, 15ft high, and lined
with deep ditches, but the system was
composed of several types of defensive works,
of which the wall itself was only a part. Forts
and garrisons guarded it at intervals and
between them were milecastles, small forts
built every mile along its length, and between
them, smaller turrets. Soldiers policed it and
views from most points are still superb.
Archaeologists have thoroughly excavated
most of the great garrison forts like Chesters,
Housesteads and Corbridge. The finds reveal
a very 'Roman' precision. Chesters is the best
example of a cavalry fort in the whole of the
uncovered Roman empire. You can see two
parallel streets cutting the interior into three
sections – two for barracks and stables, and
the central bit for headquarters, granaries and

Hadrian's Wall

workshops. The commander's house had heated rooms and a bath suite. Four gateways are still visible and there's a museum. Housesteads, like other forts, guards one of the wall's vulnerable gaps, and at 750ft the wind must have whistled up a toga or two. Based on a similar plan to Chesters, it's the most interesting of the Roman forts and you can learn more about it at the information centre in Twice Brewed, or at Housesteads Museum. Corbridge also has a good show of relics, especially sculptures. Halfway between Chesters and Housesteads, the foundations of a little Mithraic temple with weather-worn deities huddle out of the wind at Brocolitia. Look out for Roman stones in buildings throughout this area.

7. Hexham   9 E5
Travellers interested in history find much to absorb them in this ancient market town. There's the Moot Hall (a 14thC tower house now used as library and exhibition centre), a 14thC prison, a grammar school founded in 1599, an Elizabethan house and a market square with a colonnaded shelter of the 18thC.
But of major interest here are the 7thC remains of **St Wilfred's Abbey**, built of Roman stones from nearby camps and known in its day as the finest of its kind north of the Alps. Danes destroyed it 200 years later, but the crypt survived, and you can see inscriptions on some of the Roman stones. This is the finest Anglo-Saxon crypt in England and steps and passages lead to a display of relics. The Frith Stool (peace chair), was probably used for coronations and also gave sanctuary to anyone who sat in it. The chair, as you can see today, was carved from a single chunk of stone. Another abbey was built on top of the Saxon one in 1113. See the huge staircase in the south transept which lead up to the canons' dormitory, and imagine them stumbling sleepily down it to sing the night offices.
Hexham's church is rich in interest with medieval misericords, a Roman monument to Flavinus and the Anglo-Saxon Acca cross.

8. Holy Island   9 F1
The island was named 'Holy' when Benedictine monks re-colonised the abandoned Lindisfarne Priory during the 11thC. It hardly warranted its title during the centuries after the Dissolution of the Monasteries, when monks had once again left Lindisfarne – infested with smugglers and wreckers, the old priory was used as a military stonehouse and stones from it were carted off to build Holy Island Castle.
Ruins of this 16thC fortress, perched high on its seaside rock, witness the fear of border raids throughout this area of England. After the Act of Union between Scotland and England, the castle lost much of its usefulness, though a garrison remained there until 1820. Although decaying, it was converted into a coastguard station and then the headquarters of an island detachment of the Northumberland Artillery Volunteers. Edwin Lutyens, the famous architect, restored the castle as a private dwelling in 1903, and today you can view its fine furniture, pictures and ornaments. Don't forget to check your tide times before crossing to Holy Island.
Castle open most days, summer.

8. Lindisfarne Priory   9 F1
Holy Island. The cradle of Christianity, missionaries from Iona settled here in the 7thC and succeeded in evangelising the whole of Northumbria – and beyond. They were led by Aidan, a bishop from Iona with fire in his heart and a message of love for the pagan tribes of northern England. When Aidan died, a shepherd boy from the Lammermuir Hills put on a habit and decided to tend a different kind of flock. St Cuthbert, 'wonder worker of Britain', ran the monastery at Lindisfarne for many years after Aidan. When he needed to be alone, Cuthbert retreated to a flat, grass-topped rock called the Hobthrush which you will find below the ruins of Fort Osborne, on the Heugh. Traces survive on the Farne Islands, of a little chapel, St Cuthbert in the Sea. He finally chose solitude in a stony cell among the rocks and seals and seabirds of the nearby Farne Islands. Little remains of that great Celtic centre except a museum and collection of inscribed stones. After Cuthbert's death, Lindisfarne contemplated God and the sea for over a century. But in 793, in a dawn raid, Danes murdered many of the monks, plundered silver and gold, and spent the next 1,000 years living down the atrocity. Threatened by further invasion, the monks fled and the community that had produced superb illuminated Lindisfarne Gospels (now in the British Museum) whispered a last Benedictine.

Holy Island

In 1093, a bishop in Durham decided to open a 'branch office' at Lindisfarne, and the priory you see today is the result. Until the 16thC Dissolution of the Monasteries, a handful of monks from Durham lived and worked here under a prior. Judging by their bills and shopping lists – ginger, sugar, olive oil, herrings, boots, robes, spices, geese – home comforts and running the estates were as important to them as art and study had been to their gifted predecessors. And enough of their quarters remain to imagine life as a monk during the Middle Ages. See the church with its 'rainbow' arch of carving, bits of the cloisters, dormitory, parlour, common room, prior's bedsit, guest room, dining hall, kitchen, brewhouse, pantry and buttery. Ledgers show that the monks bought weapons to defend themselves against possible Scottish attack, and during the 14thC the monastery was fortified. Taste monkish mead at the Lindisfarne winery, opposite, before you go.
Open summer; most days, winter.

9. Norham Castle   9 E1
6m WSW of Berwick-upon-Tweed, off A698. 'Most dangerous place in England' is how people once described this 12thC fortress strategically positioned in the border country. Built to guard an important ford across the Tweed, Norham was attacked and taken, battered and reclaimed, for over four centuries during battles between Scots and English. Every century until the 16th can be seen in its stonework. It was so strategically important that James IV and his Scottish armies dragged Mons Meg, the greatest cannon in the country, all the way from Edinburgh to grind its garrison into submission before continuing south. The keep was reckoned to be one of the finest in

the country and from its summit – 90ft high –
you can see the Cheviot. Parts of the gateway
and curtain walls are still standing, too, and
the picturesque grey-pink ruins were a
favourite subject of Turner.

10. Preston Tower 9 F2
1m SE of Ellingham, ½m E off A1. Look across
the fields from Ellingham and you'll see this
fine 14thC fortified pele tower. Originally it
was a long building with towers at four
corners. Two of the towers and their
connecting wall remain to carry a lovely clock
which chimes the hours.

11. Wallington Hall 9 F4
Cambo, 12m W of Morpeth, B6342. Beautiful

Wallington Hall

17thC courtyard mansion, outside it remains
almost exactly as it was built, but inside, it was
entirely remodelled in 1727 and is now famed
for its rococo plaster and work by Ruskin.
There's elegant furniture, Dutch blue and
white porcelain, pictures, exquisite grounds,
and a clock-tower where you can eat. On
certain days, the Northumbrian pipes are
played there. *Open most days, summer; gardens
daily, all year.*

12. Warkworth Castle 9 G3
Warkworth. Shakespeare set three scenes of
'Henry IV Part 1' here at the lofty part-12thC
home of Northumbria's champion, Harry
Hotspur. Rather rudely, he described it as
'this worm eaten hold of ragged stone'.
Today, he'd be more polite as Warkworth
boasts some proud ruins including Grey
Mare's Tail tower which shows the finest
loopholes for crossbow shooting in Europe. A
large and mysterious blue stone lies near the
Lion tower. Legend says that a guard
dreamed he'd find treasure under it, but was
pipped to it by a neighbour to whom he had
recounted the dream three days earlier. The
best-preserved part is the keep which shows
how a fortress gradually became a house as
danger diminished over the centuries, and still
conveys an impression of medieval living
conditions. A 19thC 'lantern' lights most of
the rooms and provided water for the most
advanced sanitary arrangements of the day.
Past guardroom, wine cellar, pages' room,
Great Hall, buttery, pantry and kitchen you'll
come to the chapel which has a vivid view of
the sea.

LAND OF THE WHITE ROSE AND ENVIRONS

A region of contrasts and variety, both geographically and historically, industrial Tyneside and South Yorkshire are an hour or two, at most, from the glorious countryside of the North York Moors or the Pennines. Historical remains exist from all periods: prehistoric standing stones, stretches of Roman road, Saxon churches, Norman castles and cathedrals, great stately houses, and factories and workshops from the beginning of the Industrial Revolution.

The fertile Vale of York is the key to the area's prosperity and was the supply line for the Romans in their conquest of the north. Roman York was known as Eborcum and was one of the leading cities of the Roman Empire. It had a population in excess of 10,000 and the Roman remains there are some of the most extensive in Britain. In medieval times it became a major religious centre and also prospered as a port and centre of trade. Stone city walls and gates were built in the 13thC and a great abbey and priory, friaries, nunneries and over 40 churches appeared. York remains a beautifully preserved city at the heart of a region full of great houses and warm villages. It still looks almost totally medieval, encircled by giant, grey, stone walls and dominated by the majestic Minster. The medieval tradition is upheld today in the world-famous York Mystery Plays. A series of medieval plays originally written and performed by the ancient craft guilds of the city, they are performed now every three years, still largely by York citizens.

In the Dark Ages, when the area was split between the kingdoms of Mercia and Northumbria, Anglo-Saxons from the North Sea settled here, bringing with them names ending in -ton (enclosure), -ing (place of) and -worth (homestead). The Danes in the 9th and 10thC used names ending in -by (settlement) and -thorpe (farm). From Norway came distinctive words such as dale (valley).

Jarrow had European importance in the scholarship of the Venerable Bede and his followers. This religious tradition was built upon after the Norman Conquest. Great monasteries were founded in the early 12thC, and magnificent abbey churches were built from the profits of the wool trade. Splendid even now in ruins, Fountains Abbey and Rievaulx were two of the richest in England. Durham and York cathedrals were begun at about the same time and both are pre-eminent in England – York for its medieval glass, Durham for its architectural unity.

Durham, secure behind the defenses of the north, has long been a settled and peaceful area. This quiet and security brought early religious scholars from Holy Island and Durham became a great religious centre. The combination of affairs of church and state established the prince-bishops in Durham. The title carried unique status and with their own parliament, coinage and ability to levy taxes, they ruled like kings. Though their powers gradually declined over the centuries, they were not finally abolished until 1836.

Many of the region's castles were strengthened and re-fortified during the period of the Wars of the Roses, which flared up from the end of the 14th to the late 15thC. The great baronial families switched allegiance frequently, as the fortunes of the opposing Yorkist and Lancastrian houses varied. Richard Neville, Earl of Warwick, of Middleham Castle, was influential in the rise and downfall of both Henry VI and Edward IV, hence his designation 'Kingmaker'. These dynastic struggles came to an end with the accession of Henry VII, of Tudor and Lancastrian descent, who took Elizabeth of York as his wife. A period of stability ensued until the Civil Wars of the mid 17thC. The great families and towns of the region were staunchly Royalist, with the exception of Hull, which refused the king entry to the city. The ensuing battle at Marston Moor in 1644 resulted in a victory for Cromwell's forces which in effect put paid to the Royalist cause.

Wool had always been the basis of the area's prosperity, but the introduction of factory techniques in the late 18th and early 19thC created vast new fortunes. The great textile towns of the West Riding, along with those of Lancashire, commanded the bulk of world trade. Textile wealth financed the Industrial Revolution, and the coalfields of Durham and Yorkshire powered it. Ship-building, glass making and chemical and iron works sprang up along the banks of the River Tyne.

Middlesborough grew into a prosperous industrial iron town and Sheffield became the great city of steel. The final requirement of an industrial society – transportation – was met in the birth of the railways at Stockton and Darlington.

This century has seen the decline of some of the traditional industries of the area. Grimy towns such as Sheffield have been cleaned up and we remember this region for the magnificent cities of Durham and York, and tough scenery such as the rare, remote beauty of the York Moors. Life in the Moors and Dales has changed little, the monuments from the past remain, and the friendly, warm-hearted people in this land of the White Rose are justly proud of them.

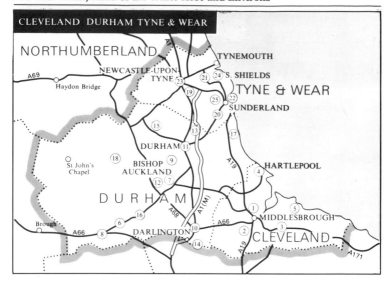

CLEVELAND

1. Billingham, Church of St Cuthbert 9 H7
2m N of Middlesborough, A19. A gem of a church, hidden in the urban sprawl of Teeside. Its west tower is 9thC Saxon, and the nave is a 12thC Norman alteration. The chancel was added this century, but blends with the older parts of the building with surprising harmony.

2. Egglescliffe 9 H8
9m E of Darlington, A67. Situated on the high left bank of the River Tees, Egglescliffe is a seductive village, with the almost Italianate 15thC tower of the church rising from the top of the crest. The medieval stone bridge was an important crossing point over the river, leading into Yorkshire. It was built originally in 1400 by the Bishop of Durham, but has since been extensively repaired and enlarged. Behind it is the beautifully graceful, 43-arched railway viaduct of 1849, 2,250ft long in all.

3. Guisborough 9 J7
The fragmentary ruins of a 12thC priory, once the third richest in Yorkshire, are next to the much restored 15thC parish church. The most important remains are the 12thC gatehouse and dovecote, and the late 13thC east end has a delicately carved window.

4. Hartlepool 9 H7
A monastery was founded here in AD640, authorised by St Hilda of Lindisfarne. It was sacked by Danes in 800, and it wasn't until 1833 that the site was rediscovered, during building work. The place is marked by a bronze plate on Marine Drive. After the arrival of the Normans, Hartlepool began to flourish as a port. A substantial part of the medieval town wall, built in 1330 with 10 towers, can be seen by the harbour. After the Civil War destroyed the town's defences, Hartlepool declined, only to boom again with the development of the coalfields and the coming of the railways.
Despite a number of renovations, the Church of St Hilda has retained a unity of Early English style. The large, buttressed (and slightly sinking) west tower, and the fine clerestory windows are dominant in the exterior. The interior is spacious and noble, and contains some fine monuments.

5. Kirkleatham 9 J7
2m S of Redcar, A174. Kirkleatham Hospital is a charitable foundation begun in 1676 by Sir William Turner, a wealthy local draper. Sir William was a friend of Pepys and Christopher Wren, and Wren's pupil, James Gibbs designed the splendidly classical Gibbs Chapel at the hospital, which can be viewed on prior arrangement. Inside the chapel is a beautiful Venetian window and a figure of Sir William dressed in the mayoral robes of London, an honour he held in 1668. Across the road from the hospital is the Free School, a quietly dignified building founded by Sir William's son in 1709.
A model of Georgian grace, the Church of St Cuthbert was built in 1763. Inside is an interesting child's stone coffin of the 9thC, and a large 14thC chest. An octagonal mausoleum topped with a pyramid, built to Gibbs designs in 1740, is a distinguishing feature.

DURHAM

6. Barnard Castle
A prosperous, dignified town on the River Tees with a grand church, fine 17th and 18thC buildings, a medieval bridge and an excellent museum. The town is overseen by the gaunt ruin of the medieval castle from which it takes its name. Settlement began with the building of this castle in around 1100 by Guy de Baliol. His nephew, Barnard, rebuilt in stone 50 years later, and gave his name to the town. The Baliol family were one of the most powerful in Britain. Barnard's successor, John Baliol, founded the Oxford college and his son, also called John, was crowned King of Scotland in 1292, to rule for four difficult years. The castle passed to the throne of England when it was inherited in marriage by

Richard III, who substantially strengthened it. Perched 100ft above the river, the massive circular keep, built in 1300, rises another 50ft. The whole imperious structure is said to have inspired Sir Walter Scott's 'Rokeby'.
The double-arched brown stone bridge, almost directly below the castle, dates from the end of the 15thC.
St Mary's Church, *Marketplace*, is of Norman foundation, heavily restored in the 19thC. The nave roof, and parts of the chancel are 15thC. A monument in the churchyard recalls the '143 inhabitants of Barnard Castle who died of Asiatic Cholera from August 18th to October 18th 1849'.

7. Bishop Auckland   9 G7
From the market square, an 18thC gatehouse leads to Auckland Park and Castle. The bishops of Durham have had a residence here since the 12thC and the town grew up around the market at its gates. The castle has been altered by successive bishops, and contains work of all periods, the earliest dating from the 14thC. The result is a rather austere building that seems neither one thing nor the other. Inside is some fine oak panelling, and the King Charles Room, where Charles I stayed as a prisoner in 1647. The adjoining chapel, a Norman hall converted after the Restoration, has undoubtedly the finest architecture of the castle. The clerestory and 17thC roof, added by Bishop Cosin, are among the finest examples of their period in the country. *Open by arrangement; park daily.*

8. Bowes   9 F8
3m W of Barnard Castle, A67. Dickens used the school at Bowes, then run by a William Shaw, as the model for the infamous Dotheboys Hall in 'Nicholas Nickleby'. Shaw became Squeers and Smike, the pathetic bullied cripple of the novel, was modelled on a pupil of the time, 19-year-old George Taylor. The school was closed following the scandal after publication of the book, but the building remains. Dickens stayed at the King's Head, Barnard Castle, while investigating the conditions at the school. The ruin of the late 12thC castle keep is only a shell, but contains stones from an old Roman fort.

9. Brancepeth   5 G6
5m S of Durham, W of A690. Standing in the grounds of a Norman castle is the 12thC Church of St Brandon. People come here to see woodwork at its finest – the carving of the pulpit, screen, choir stalls, pews, font cover and roof is magnificent. The castle passed through several hands including the powerful Neville family, and was heavily restored in the 19thC. There are surviving sections of the curtain wall, but the 'Norman' gatehouse is a reproduction. *View from outside only.*

10. Darlington   9 G7
On September 27, 1825, George Stephenson drove the world's first passenger train, Locomotion No I, from Darlington to Stockport-on-Tees. It was probably the most important event of the century, ushering in a new mobility that totally transformed western societies. Locomotion No I served the Stockton and Darlington Railway until 1841. It now rests, on its original rails, at North Road Station Railway Museum, housed in what is probably the oldest railway station in Britain (1841). Alongside is the locomotive Derwent, built in 1845. A portion of the re-laid track, using original sleepers, can be seen at the London end of the station.
Of less historical importance, but of greater beauty, is the Norman Church of St Cuthbert, founded in the late 12thC by Bishop Pudsey of Durham. An outstanding example of the Early English style, its slender, ribbed 14thC spire soars 180ft to dominate the city centre. Inside: beautiful 14thC sedilia, fine carved bench-ends and misericords, and a huge Restoration font canopy.

11. Durham   9 G6
The monks of Lindisfarne had long been looking for a site secure from marauding Danes and Scots, where they could have their shrine to St Cuthbert. At Durham, on a 70ft rock in a hairpin bend of the River Wear, they found it. A small cathedral and fortification was completed by 1020, to which King Canute made a bare-footed pilgrimage. Steeped in history and with magnificent views from every vantage point, Durham is one of the most picturesque cities in England. Elegant bridges span the river which is dotted with punts in the summer, and the trees almost completely hide the civic centre. Thanks to its semi-island position, the old town of Durham hasn't been encroached upon by modern development, which has mostly taken place on the opposite banks. With its impressive cathedral soaring above the wooded cliffs, it remains a monument to the two great powers of Church and State.

11. Durham Castle   9 G6
Off Palace Green. William the Conqueror had rightly seen that the commanding position of the castle would help it act as a buffer between England and the unruly Scots, and Durham is unique among England's northern strongholds as it never fell to the Scots. Durham castle was, from 1072 to 1831, the main residence of the prince-bishops, titles held by the bishops of Durham. The title carried unique status, giving the bishops powers to be lay rulers as well as religious leaders. It was the last of the prince-bishops, Van Mildert, who founded Durham University College in 1832, part of which is now housed in the castle. The octagonal keep, on its steep mound, was rebuilt in the 19thC from the ruins of the 14thC keep. It now provides rooms for students.
The 13thC Great Hall, hung inside with portraits of bishops, banners and armour, has entertained Edward II, Sir Walter Scott and the Duke of Wellington to dinner. The kitchen dates from the 15thC and is still used today. The Senate Room, once the bishop's drawing room, is hung with a glorious 16thC Flemish tapestry depicting the life of Moses. An intricately carved oak mantel commemorates James I's stay here while on the way to London to be crowned. Below this is the Norman chapel, the oldest part of the castle, dating from the late 11thC, and possibly incorporating an older building. The nave and aisle are beautifully vaulted, and the stones are carved with birds and animals and geometric designs. *Open certain days.*

Durham Cathedral

11. Durham Cathedral   9 G6
Palace Green. One of the finest examples of Romanesque architecture in Europe, outstandingly situated on a high, wooded rock above the River Wear. The Norman work, including the breathtakingly magnificent high, vaulted nave, was begun in 1093 and completed by 1133. Soaring marble columns support the delicately ribbed, vaulted roof, and with slender columns of sandstone and Purbeck marble, the Galilee Chapel was added at the end of the 12thC. The Chapel of

the Nine Altars, at the east end, was added in the middle of the 13thC. The great central tower rises to 200ft and was rebuilt in 1470–1490, following lightning damage. Climb to the top for unsurpassed views of the town and countryside.

Entrance is through the north door which has a grotesque 12thC bronze sanctuary knocker. In medieval times, anyone who grasped the knocker was granted freedom from arrest. The Sanctuary Book tells us that 331 criminals sought refuge between 1464 and 1525, most of them murderers. Because of blatant abuse, the Rights of Sanctuary were abolished in 1540. Don't pass by the cathedral museum. It contains the remains of the original oak coffin of St Cuthbert, lovingly carved by the monks of Lindisfarne. In the 14thC Monks' Dormitory you can see one of the oldest surviving embroidered stoles in Western Europe, still in remarkably good condition.

12. Escomb, Church of St John the Evangelist 9 G6
7m N of Durham, off A1(M). Probably as a result of its obscurity, this little church has survived, almost without alteration, from the 7thC. Much of the stone used came from a Roman fort at Binchester, about two miles away, and the quality of the beautifully-squared ashlar blocks is remarkable. One of the stones in the chancel doorway has inscribed, set upside down, the legend 'LEG VI', referring to the Sixth Roman Legion. Look at the raised rosette on the north wall – it may have been a sacrificial stone. Of particular interest are the five small Saxon windows, set high up in the nave wall. On the south wall is a Saxon sundial, carved with a serpent, and believed to be the oldest in England in its original position. The slim chancel arch, with traces of a 12thC painting on its underside, was taken complete from the Roman camp.

13. Finchale Priory 9 G6
3m N of Durham, 1m W of A1. Nestling in the crook of a bend on the River Wear, Finchale Priory ruins are the most romantic the county has to offer. The priory was founded by St Godric in about 1110, after he had given up an adventurous life as a tinker and seaman. After his death in 1170, aged 105, a stone chapel was built on the site of the hut where he lived as a hermit, and later was extensively enlarged to accommodate about 20 monks. Ruin began with the Dissolution, and continued with neglect. What remains is the nave of the priory church, and parts of the cloisters and domestic buildings.

14. Hurworth-on-Tees 9 G8
2½m S of Darlington, 1m E of A167. A village-cum-suburb, stretched along the north bank of the River Tees, with a good number of attractive Georgian houses. The Croft Bridge over the river traditionally marked the Durham–Yorkshire boundary. It was built in 1400, but has been much restored and enlarged since.

William Emerson, the mathematician, was born in 1701 in what is now the Emerson Arms pub, and is buried in the local churchyard. An eccentric and a genius, he dressed like a tramp and liked to show off his encyclopedic knowledge over a few pints. Convinced he must be some sort of a magician, the villagers infuriated him by expecting him to solve their problems with a wave of his wand. But despite his wizardry, he never became a member of the Royal Society – he refused to pay the subscription, saying it was too dear.

15. Lanchester 9 G6
8m NW of Durham, A691. Little remains of the Roman encampment of Longovicium, which guarded the route from York to Hadrian's Wall. The stones of the old walls have been incorporated into farm buildings, and some were used in building the church. At its peak, though, the camp occupied about nine acres, and some of the impressive archaeological finds are now housed at Durham. Lanchester church contains a Roman altar dated AD244, dedicated to the British goddess Garmangabis. Incorporating local deities was one of the Roman methods of establishing the Pax Romana. The church, a fine example of Norman and Early English styles, also has some good 13thC glass in the south window.

16. Raby Castle 9 F7
N of Staindrop, off A688. Set in a splendid 250-acre deer park, Raby Castle is one of the largest in the north of England, displaying, with its nine great towers, a rugged, enduring strength. A minor fortification at Raby is mentioned during the reign of Canute, but it was the arrival of the Nevilles in the 12thC that set the beginning of its important role in the Middle Ages. They were a powerful family: Ralph Neville led the English to victory over the Scots at the Battle of Neville's Cross in 1346, and included amongst his grandchildren, Edward IV and Richard III. The family's downfall came with the failure of the Northern Rising of 1569. This attempt to put Mary, Queen of Scots, on the throne instead of Elizabeth I, was planned in the great Baron's Hall, built by Ralph Neville's son to accommodate 700 barons. When the movements failed, Raby was fortified to the crown, and sold to Sir Henry Vane in 1626. It remains in the family to the present day. Raby, although much restored by the Vanes in the 18th and 19thC, contains a good deal of 13thC work. Most impressive are the Neville Gateway, commanding entrance to the inner courtyard, and the nine distinctive towers. To see inside: portraits, furniture, ceramics and a superb Victorian drawing room. The gardens are famous for their majestic trees, clipped yews, and sweet peas. *Open most days, summer.*

Raby Castle

17. Seaham 9 H6
5m S of Sunderland, off A19. The ancient Church of St Mary, with Saxon work visible in the nave and a 13thC tower, was the scene, in January 1815, of the marriage of Lord Byron to Ann Isabella Milbanke. Ann lived at Seaham Hall, now used as a hospital. The marriage, seldom happy, lasted a little over a year. Byron wrote of the ceremony: 'I trembled like a leaf, made the wrong responses, and after the ceremony, called her Miss Milbanke'.

18. Stanhope 9 F6
12m W of Crook, A689. The Heathery Burn Cave Treasure, turned up in quarrying in the last century about a mile from the village, was one of the most important Bronze Age discoveries ever made in Britain. It comprised of a complete collection of the implements of a Bronze Age family who probably took refuge in the cave and drowned when the waters rose rapidly. The finds are now on display in the British Museum.

A relic of an even earlier past is to be found in the village churchyard – the fossilised trunk of a tree estimated to be 250 million years old. It was discovered in a nearby quarry in 1964. The church itself contains some fine medieval Flemish carvings, and a Roman altar dedicated to the woodland god, Silvanus.

TYNE AND WEAR

19. Gateshead 9 G5

A severely practical businessman's place, devoid of pleasantries. Linked to Newcastle by five bridges, it's been a natural bridging point over the Tyne from Roman days. The Roman bridge was replaced by a fortified stone one in 1250. This was swept away in floods of 1771, and its replacement in turn made way for the present swing bridge. The two churches, St Mary's and Holy Trinity, are lonely reminders of Gateshead's past. St Mary's, near the Tyne Bridge, was the scene of the murder, in 1080, of Bishop Walcher, attacked by a mob for refusing to punish the killers of a local Saxon noble. Norman in origin, the church was substantially rebuilt following a fire in 1854 when a nearby factory exploded, showering the church with burning timber and red-hot metal. Holy Trinity Church is another Norman establishment, originally a monastery. It too was rebuilt, damaged by fire in the 18thC after a mob had set alight a neighbouring house. Famous residents of Gateshead include the great engraver, Thomas Bewick, and Daniel Defoe, who probably wrote 'Robinson Crusoe' here. A famous visitor was Dr Johnson, who dismissed the town as 'a dirty lane leading to Newcastle'.

20. Houghton-le-Spring, Church of St Michael 9 G6

4m S of Sunderland, A690. A well-proportioned 13th–15thC building, at one time this was one of the largest parishes in the country, and one of the richest livings went with it. The most famous rector was Bernard Gilpin, whose huge altar tomb is in the church. Here from 1556 until his death in 1584, his generosity to poor and rich alike, was legendary. He held open house on Sundays, fed whoever turned up, and earned the sobriquet 'Apostle of the North' by his many trips into the wilds of Teesdale. His death came as a result of being knocked over by an ox at Durham market.

21. Jarrow 9 H5

A sprawling, industrial town on the mouth of the Tyne, Jarrow grew with the founding of Palmer's shipbuilding yard in 1852. At its height, it employed a force of 10,000. When it closed in the slump of 1933 it was the last nail in the coffin of the ailing town. On October 5th, 1936, 200 of the town's unemployed marched to London to demonstrate their plight to a smug and apathetic Westminster. The Jarrow march was for many in the more affluent south, the first glimpse at the dire, poverty-stricken condition of their northern neighbours.

The most interesting building in the town is **St Paul's Church**, part of the monastery where the Venerable Bede spent most of his life from the age of seven, first as a novitiate and later as a world-famous teacher and scholar. He wrote 79 books in all, ranging from medicine and mathematics to philosophy and music. His greatest work is undoubtably 'Ecclesiastical History of the English People', a model work for centuries to come. The monastery was sacked by Danes twice in the centuries following his death in AD735. Parts of the Saxon building survive in the fabric of the present church. The slender central tower dates from a rebuilding of 1069, but in the western arch is the dedication stone of the original Saxon church, inscribed in Latin and recording the date: 'the 9th of the kalends of May in the 15th year of King Ecgfrid' – in other words, April 23rd, AD685. The chancel is pure Saxon, with crude stone walls. Bede's Chair, by the north wall, probably dates from the 14thC.

22. Monkwearmouth 9 H5

Sunderland, N of River Wear, A183. Monkwearmouth monastery was Jarrow's elder sister, founded 10 years earlier, in 674. They both shared Benedict Biscop as founder. The monastery suffered from Danes and Normans, but was rebuilt in 1076 and served until the Dissolution as a cell of Durham. An extensive restoration was begun in 1866, and this uncovered considerable portions of the original Saxon church. Most impressive is the barrel-vaulted porch roof, the only example of Saxon vaulting in England. The doorway contains two pairs of Saxon pillars, and there is Saxon work in the lower west wall of the nave and the tower. Over a window, traces can be seen of a large sculptured figure, the earliest major sculpture in England.

23. Newcastle 9 G5

Dreary streets and drab houses break out into a flourishing hotch-potch of culture at the centre of this important city. It began as a minor fort and bridge on Hadrian's Wall, and was known to the Romans as Pons Aelius. The modern town, and its name, derives from a castle founded in 1080 by Robert, William the Conqueror's eldest son. The town suffered from Scots incursions in 1342 and 1348, and was besieged in 1644. It was here that, two years later, Charles I was handed over to the English Parliament. Industrialisation and prosperity came with the development of Newcastle as a coal-carrying port, and as a centre of the railway industry. There are a number of dignified early 19thC buildings in the centre of the town. Of particular interest is the High Level Bridge, *St Nicholas St*, built by Robert Stephenson in 1849 to carry road and rail traffic on separate levels.

Newcastle Castle is bisected by the railway. On one side is the keep, built in 1172–77 by Henry II. The hall occupies the whole of the interior, and is reached by an external staircase. A fore-building contains a beautiful Norman chapel of c1175. There are more stairs to the battlements. On the other side of the railway lies the Black Gate of 1247, with an upper part added in the early 17thC, housing the library of the local Antiquarian Society. Towering above the quayside is the 18thC Church of All Saints, with some extravagant woodwork inside. Museums include the Science Museum, *Exhibition Park*, and the Hancock Museum, *Barras Bridge*, one of the finest natural history museums in England.

Tyne Bridge

23. Newcastle Cathedral

Mosley St. St Nicholas gained cathedral status in 1882, but its construction in the mid 14thC was on a near cathedral scale. Externally, the most important feature is the rare 194ft spire and crown, supported by flying buttresses. Inside are a number of fine monuments, including one by Flaxman, and a superbly ornate early 16thC font cover. The magnificent Thorton Brass in the south aisle is one of the earliest Flemish brasses in the country.

24. South Shields   9 H5
The Roman fort and supply base, Arbeia, has been excavated and the foundations of the barracks and other buildings can be seen next to the Roman Museum, *Baring St.* The museum has an excellent collection of inscribed Roman stones and other items, such as the inlaid sword with a figure of Mars on one side, boxes, coins and pottery. The world's first lifeboat service, the Tyne Lifeboat Society, was founded here in 1790.

25. Washington Old Hall   9 G5
5m W of Sunderland, off A182. A fine Jacobean stone mansion, built in 1610 by Bishop James of Durham, but incorporating parts of an earlier mansion that was the seat of George Washington's ancestors.
The Washingtons arrived here in 1183, when William de Hertburn obtained the manor and took its name. The family remained here until 1376, when they sold up and scattered to various parts of Britain while George Washington's grandfather, John, emigrated. The house contains fine 17thC furniture and a collection of Washington relics. *Open most days, summer; weekends, winter.*

HUMBERSIDE

1. Beverley   8 J6
Set in the greenery of Beverley Pastures, common land granted the townsfolk in medieval times, Beverley is one of the most attractive and interesting market towns in the area. The town began with the founding of a monastery by John of Beverley around AD700. He was canonised in 1037 and his shrine became a popular centre of pilgrimage. Henry V came to give thanksgiving after his victory at Agincourt.
Beverley flourished during the Middle Ages as the centre of the wool trade, and in 1377 was the 10th town in the kingdom on the basis of taxes paid. The wool trade declined, but the town remained quietly prosperous, indicated in the fine Georgian and early 19thC buildings. Plans for making Beverley a walled town during the Middle Ages advanced no further than the construction of five gateways. North Bar is the only survival, the north face displaying the red brickwork of 1409.
One of England's most beautiful churches, St Mary's is often overlooked in favour of the Minster. It was built, of white limestone, mainly in the 14th and 15thC, as a chapel-of-ease for the Minster, but soon became the church of the town's merchants. The Perpendicular west front and the south porch are particularly attractive, while the tower is crowned with 16 pinnacles. The panelled ceiling of the chancel has mid 15thC paintings of the kings of England. Carved misericords in the choir depict a bewildering array of foxes, monks, monkeys, kings and pelicans. There is fine statuary throughout the church. Look for the stone rabbit – it's said to have inspired Lewis Carroll's White Rabbit in 'Alice in Wonderland'.

1. Beverley Minster   8 J6
A splendid church, equal to the finest of cathedrals in the purity of its Early English architecture and the majesty of the Perpendicular work. Standing in proud isolation slightly apart from the town, the slender twin towers, 200ft of soaring white stone, are a triumph. The great west door is the work of the 18thC architect, Hawksmoor, whose restoration saved the Minster from falling into decay. The transepts date from 1220–1260, and express the purity and grace of Early English style. The Percy Tomb, dated about 1350, is to the wife of the second Lord Percy, and is the Minster's most outstanding feature.

2. Bridlington   8 K4
A popular seaside resort, once famed for its great Priory. It was founded c1114 by William de Gant, but the main buildings were constructed during the 13th and 14thC. John of Bridlington, a 14thC prior, was canonised in 1401, and subsequently the Priory attracted kings and knights to a pilgrimage. The remains form the body of the Church of St Mary, restored in the mid 19thC by George Gilbert Scott. Note the lovely west doorway,

the rich decoration of the north porch and the black grave slab in the south west tower. Intricately carved, it may belong to William de Gant and has been used as a table for distributing food to the poor. The Bayle Gate is a stone and brick building of 1388, and served as the gatehouse to the Priory. It is now a museum housing local relics, weapons, jewellery and paintings.

3. Burton Agnes Hall   8 K4
5m W of Bridlington, off A166. Comfortable red-brick mansion, built from 1590–1610, and typically Elizabethan but for the bay windows rising three floors. It is thought to have been designed by Robert Smithson, who was also responsible for Longleat. After falling into decline early this century the Hall has been restored and furnished to its original condition. The long gallery, running the whole 100ft of the south front, is the most impressive of the rooms. The house contains an excellent, still-growing collection of French Impressionist paintings, with works by Cézanne, Manet, Corot and Renoir. There's also a collection of beautiful Oriental china. In the inner hall is a portrait of a young girl who is said to haunt the Hall. *Open most days, summer.*

4. Burton Constable Hall   8 K6
1½m N of Sproatley. A castellated Elizabethan mansion with fine oriel windows, built around 1570 and altered in the mid 18thC by Adams and Wyatt. Another storey was added to the east front, and a central pediment with coat of arms gave a fashionable symmetry. There's a Tudor gallery, a Georgian dining room, and an excellent collection of pictures. The grounds, laid out to designs by Capability Brown, now contain a model railway, a playground, a zoo and a caravan site. There is also a museum of old carriages and cars. *Open most days, summer.*

Burton Constable Hall

5. Dane's Dyke   8 K4
Bempton. An immense Bronze Age earthwork stretching from Bempton Cliffs in the north to Sewerby Rocks in the south, cutting Flamborough Head from the mainland. Built by the Brigantes, a local Celtic tribe, it is still 60ft wide and 20ft deep in places.

6. Epworth, Old Rectory   8 H8
Home of Methodism, for John Wesley was born here in 1703, and his hymn-writing brother, Charles, in 1707. Two years later the building was set on fire by a mob who objected to Wesley's father's political views. The house was immediately rebuilt and parts of the old building are retained in the attractive bayed

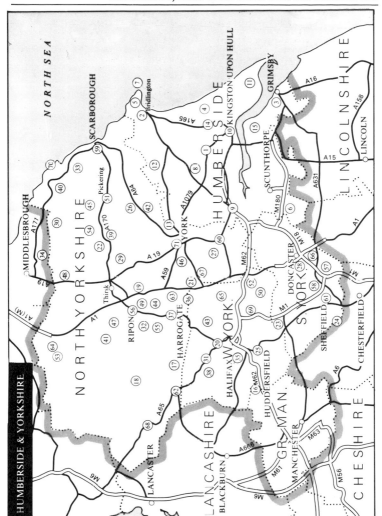

front. The house contains a number of relics of the Wesleys. *Open summer, or by arrangement.*

7. Flamborough Head   8 K4

A startling and dramatic chalk headland, rising some 300ft above the sea. The old Flamborough lighthouse, an octagonal building of local chalk was built in 1674. The 'new' lighthouse, built in 1806 to replace it, took just nine months to complete, and no scaffolding was used at any stage of its construction. Flamborough church is partly Norman and partly Early English, but was extensively renovated in the 19thC. The father of poet and parliamentarian, Andrew Marvell, was once the rector. A monument to

Flamborough Head

look out for is to Sir Marmaduke Constable – his bared heart reflects the grisly story that it was eaten by a toad he swallowed.

8. Goodmanham, Church of All Saints   8 J5

3m NE of Market Weighton. The 12thC church is thought to occupy the site of an ancient pagan temple. It was destroyed by the Saxon King Edwin after he and his high priest, Coifi, were converted to Christianity by the missionary Paulinus, early in the 6thC. The church has two fonts: one, once used as a horse trough, is possibly Saxon and the other, ornately carved, dates from the 15thC.

9. Howden, Church of St Peter   8 H6

Magnificent church, built on a scale fitting for a prosperous market town. It's tall tower is one of the area's finest, and the 14thC west front is very beautiful. The woodwork inside the church is modern, by Robert Thompson's workshops in Kilburn, and bears his charming signature of a small carved mouse. A copy of the *Quarterly Review* of 1859 on display has Dickens's description of Howden Horse Fair.

10. Hull   8 K6

The city's full name, Kingston-upon-Hull, records its unique origins when, in 1293, Edward I purchased the land from the French Abbots of Meaux and set about developing it as a seaport. But for Holy Trinity Church,

little remains from this period although part of the town wall has been excavated. A castle built by Henry VIII survives only in archaeological traces. Hull is known for the first overt act of rebellion in the country at the beginning of the Civil War when, in 1642, Charles I was refused entrance by the town governor, Sir John Hotham.
Hull today is Britain's third port, a bustling commercial centre and university town. Despite modern development, parts of the town retain an individual character.
At 272ft, the **Church of the Holy Trinity**, *Market Place*, is the longest parish church in England. It was begun in 1291 and finished just over a hundred years later, the influence of the Low Countries showing in the early use of brick. The tomb of Sir William de la Pole, the first mayor of Hull, is in the south aisle, and there is an interesting 14thC font.
Housed in the old Corn Exchange, the **Transport and Archaeological Museum** contains interesting Roman and Saxon material found in the Humberside district, as well as old carriages and cars.
Along the road is **Wilberforce House**, an Elizabethan building visited by Charles I in 1639. In the 18thC it was remodelled and bought by the Wilberforce family, and William Wilberforce was born here in 1759. At the age of 21 he became Member of Parliament for Hull, initiating a parliamentary career that lasted 45 years, devoted to the abolition of slavery and the slave trade. His fifth bill in 1807 succeeded in banning the slave trade in Britain, and a further bill, in 1833, shortly before his death in the same year, outlawed slavery in the British Empire. The Slave Room has relics of his campaign, and a life-size figure of the emancipator himself sits in a Chippendale chair in a corner of the room. There's a statue of him in Queen's Gardens.

11. Patrington, Church of St Patrick 8 K7
Called 'The Queen of Holderness', it's a beautiful Decorated church with a central spire soaring 189ft. It was built in the 50 or so years before the Black Death of 1348, and has an impressive unity of design inside and out. A magnificent wedding-cake of a font and a beautiful Easter Sepulchre are the highlights.

12. Sledmere House 8 J4
Sledmere. A Georgian mansion owned by the Sykes family, who first came to Sledmere in 1748. They replaced the Elizabethan manor house with a Queen Anne brick building, and in 1783 Sir Christopher Sykes faced this building with stone and added two wings, to give it its present Classical appearance. The house contains some exquisite French and English period furniture, and fine collections of porcelain and paintings. Unquestionably the finest room is the library, 100ft long and occupying the whole of the first

Sledmere House

floor. In 1777 Capability Brown was commissioned to set out the 2,000 acres of park. He also transformed the surrounding, uncultivated countryside into some of the most productive farming land in the area. *Open most days, summer.*

13. Stamford Bridge, Battlefield 8 G5
8m E of York, A166. Scene of a great English victory, led by King Harold, over the Norse forces led by Harold's banished younger brother, Tostig, and Harald Hardradra, a Norse warrior of 6ft 6ins. Harold's army, levied in the course of an incredible four-day march covering the 180 miles from London, caught the Norsemen completely by surprise as they rested by the River Derwent. The battle, fought on 25th September, 1066, lasted from midday to dusk, and both Tostig and Hardradra fell. Of the original 200 longships of the Norse invasion, a mere 24 were needed to carry the survivors home. But this was a victory that cost the English dear. Severely weakened, the army was unable to fend off the Norman assault at Hastings, a mere two and a half weeks later.

14. Swine 8 K6
6m S of Long Riston. A dead-end village – the road literally ends here – its name is straightforward enough as this was where an important pig market was once held. The Church of St Mary, with its 12thC nave, is all that remains of a Cistercian nunnery founded in 1150. Throughout the 13th and 14thC it had a suspect reputation, then monks were discovered living on the premises! It was dissolved in 1539, and the priory church retained for parish use. The church has a number of fine effigies, including three of the 14thC in alabaster. Also of note is the 16thC screen and a beautiful east window of 1531.

15. Thornton Abbey 8 K7
2m E of Thornton Curtis. At the Dissolution, Thornton Abbey was described as 'one of the goodliest houses of England'. Now, apart from traces of the abbey church and chapter house, all that remains to give an idea of its 'goodliness' is the splendid gatehouse. It was built in the late 14thC, partly in brick and partly in stone. The facade is decorated with five of the original statues, while inside there is a Great Hall, and rooms for the accommodation of guests. A small museum has some of the surviving treasures and stonework. The abbey was originally surrounded by a defensive wall and moat.

YORKSHIRE

16. Blackstone Edge Roman Road 8 D7
7m W of Ripponden, off A58. Running across the border between West Yorkshire and Greater Manchester is one of the most remarkable stretches of paved Roman road to have survived in Britain. It connected Manchester with the fort at Ilkley. Between the 16ft-wide kerbs it has a central channel which was probably planted with turf to give a good foothold for the horses.

17. Bolton Abbey 8 D5
6m E of Skipton, N of A59. A priory founded for the Augustinians in 1151 by Lady Alice de Romilly. Legend states that she built it in memory of her son who was drowned in the

River Wharfe: trying to leap across the Strid, a narrow gorge two miles away, his hunting hound held back on its leash, causing him to miss his footing. The tale is told by Wordsworth in 'The Force of Prayer', but there's probably little truth in it. The priory church has an alluring location by the River Wharfe. The Early English nave has been used as the parish church since the Priory's foundation. The west front was added in the 15thC, as a base for a tower which was never completed, while the choir and transepts are in romantic ruin.
The ruins are said to be haunted by the White Doe of Rylstone, written of by Wordsworth in

the poem of that name. The doe apparently still seeks its mistress, Emily Norton, who died of a broken heart after her brother's death in the Rising of the North in 1569.

18. Bolton Castle · 8 D3
Castle Bolton. A grim castle, overseeing Wensleydale from its hill-side position. It was built by Richard Scrope, Lord Chancellor under Richard II. Mary, Queen of Scots, was brought a prisoner here in 1568 and remained six months. The rooms she occupied are among the best-preserved in the castle. In the Civil War it was besieged by the Parliamentarians and the garrison was reduced to eating horseflesh before they surrendered! Subsequent slighting by Cromwell's men made the castle uninhabitable.
The interior is as forbidding as the exterior appears. A maze of stairways and corridors with smaller corridors leading off, connects the large, bare rooms. The Great Hall now houses a Dales Folk Museum, with the reconstruction of a traditional Dales farmhouse kitchen. *Open most days.*

19. Boroughbridge · 8 F4
Established in Norman times, this town became an important road centre. Of the 22 inns it once boasted, a good many remain. To the west are the **Devil's Arrows**, three great standing stones of the Bronze Age, each about 20ft high, all in a line with each other: at one time there were seven. The story goes that they were bolts fired by the Devil to destroy the town.
To the east of the town is the pretty village of **Aldborough**, site of the Roman town Isurium Brigantum, the headquarters of the Ninth Legion. Before the Romans' arrival it had been called Iseur, and was the capital town of the largest Celtic tribe in Britain, the Brigantes. A signposted path from the village green leads to two huts which contain two splendid, excavated tessellated pavements. One has the image of a panther beneath palm trees, the other, an eight-pointed star. Further Roman remains can be seen in the small museum by the village green, which has coins, jewellery, fragments of pottery, and the dice the legionnaires used to pass the time. The 14thC church is built on the site of the Temple of Mercury, and a battered statue of the god has found its home at the west end.

20. Bradford · 8 E6
Prosperous Victorian cloth town of the old West Riding, developed by local builders and architects in a fairly undisciplined mixture of styles. Its Italianate City Hall and the Gothic Wool Exchange are among the finest Victorian buildings in the country. In 1920 Bradford was made a cathedral city, and in 1966 its technical college, founded in 1880, was raised to university status.
Bolling Hall, *1m S of city centre*, is a 15thC manor converted in the Adam style in 1780. It now houses a museum of local history and folk culture, with a particularly fine collection of English furniture from the 16th to the 19thC.
Cartwright Hall, *Lister Park*, is a late Victorian building in the classical vein, donated to the city early this century by Lord Masham, to serve as a memorial to Edmund Cartwright, inventor of the power loom on which the city's wealth was founded. It houses a fine collection of paintings and sculpture. Formerly the 14thC parish church, **St Peter's Cathedral**, *off Forster Sq*, was given cathedral status in 1920, and was greatly enlarged from 1951–63. The modern Lady chapel has excellent glass by William Morris, and there is a beautiful 15thC font cover, as well as notable monuments.

21. Bramham Park · 8 F6
Bramham, W of A1. A grey stone country house built by the first Lord Bingley in 1698. He was Lord Chamberlain to Queen Anne, who gave him the portrait of herself which hangs in the hall. The grounds are laid out in the French style, with long avenues of beech leading to an eye-catching pedestal or temple. *Open most days, summer.*

22. Byland Abbey · 8 G4
8m E of Thirsk. Founded by the Benedictines in 1134, and transferred to the Cistercians 13 years later, Byland is overshadowed somewhat by the more famous Rievaulx to the north. Only the splendid Early English west front and south transept of the church remain, but the latter has some rare green and yellow patterned medieval tiling. The foundations of the rest of the abbey have been exposed and a small museum houses interesting finds excavated from the site. Nearby is the famous Roman Catholic public school for boys, Ampleforth.

23. Cannon Hall · 8 F7
6m W of Barnsley, off A635. A small 18thC mansion, built by John Carr of York on the base of an earlier building. It is now owned by Barnsley Council. Now a country house museum, it has some superb furniture, and a collection of glassware and paintings, including a portrait by Constable. The house is set in beautiful parkland with a lake.

24. Carl Walk · 8 E9
4½m SW of Sheffield, N of A625. An impressive ancient fort, isolated on a moorland scarp with three steep sides. On the south and west side the earth rampart is faced with stones. Some authorities have placed it in the Iron Age, while others, considering the remarkable preservation of the stonework, have thought it to date from shortly after the departure of the Romans.

25. Castle Hill · 8 E7
3m S of Huddersfield, nr Almondbury. An Iron Age hill fort of the Brigante tribe, with bank and ditch defences. The hill is now topped with a Victorian tower. The Romans had a fort, Camulodunum, about five miles away to the west, named after Camulos, a Celtic war god. It's not an unreasonable guess that this commemorated the resistance the Romans met from the Brigantes of Castle Hill.

26. Castle Howard · 8 H4
6m W of Malton. But for a quarrel over money that Charles Howard, third Earl of Carlisle, had with the architect he originally commissioned, Vanbrugh would never have had the chance to build his magnificent Castle Howard. Vanbrugh, until then famed as a soldier and poet, met Carlisle in the notorious Kit Kat Club, and on the strength of a few sketches was given the job. In collaboration with Hawksmoor, Christopher Wren's assistant, Vanbrugh produced one of the most original and spectacular buildings in Britain. Considering he had never designed a building in his life before, it is little short of miraculous.
Work was begun in 1700 and was not completed until 1737. By then, Vanbrugh, Hawksmoor and the Earl had all died. A domed central block, containing the magnificent Great Hall, is symmetrically flanked by two smaller wings. The building faces a classical parterre of lawns with a central fountain and pond. The grounds are a credit to the designers, too, and no-one should miss the delightful Temple of the Four Winds by Vanbrugh, and Hawksmoor's elegant circular colonnaded mausoleum.
The Great Hall is one of the grandest rooms in England, rising 70ft to its domed ceiling. The splendid frescoes are by Pellegrini. The two other great rooms are the long gallery in the west wing, and the Norman style antique passage, packed with classical statues and busts. Castle Howard's treasures equal many a museum: statues by Bernini, paintings by Reynolds and Gainsborough, a glorious painted relief by Sansovino, a portrait of

Henry VIII by Holbein, and enough period furniture to fill a fleet of removal vans. The stables house a massive costume collection. *Open summer.*

27. Cawood   8 G6
4m NW of Selby. A 14thC gatehouse, rather out of place between a barn and a farmhouse, is the only reminder of the days when Cawood was the resort of bishops and kings. It belonged to the palace of the bishops of York, the land originally donated by King Athelstan in 930. The palace was built in about 1273. Edward I's wife, Marguerite of France, stayed at Cawood for five years while her husband was busy in his Scottish campaign, and their son, Edward II, came here to recover from his defeat at Bannockburn. Another historical visitor was Cardinal Wolsey, who retired here after his fall from favour following his failure to obtain a Papal annulment of Henry VIII's marriage to Catherine of Aragon. The day before he was to be enthroned Bishop of York, he was arrested by the Earl of Northumberland on a charge of high treason. His death at Leicester, while on the way to London, saved him from the executioner's axe.

28. Conisburgh Castle   8 G8
5m SW of Doncaster, off A18. A 90ft-high, circular, white, limestone keep looking sternly over the town. It was probably built by Hamelin Plantagenet, Henry II's half-brother, in the latter part of the 12thC. The circular construction of the keep, an innovation at the time, is one of the best-surviving examples of 12thC architecture. Sir Walter Scott wrote 'Ivanhoe' while staying locally, and on the third floor, built into the buttress, is a tiny chapel which was the setting for one of the scenes.

29. Coxwold   8 G4
8m SE of Thirsk. The novelist Laurence Sterne came to the living of Coxwold after his instant success with the publication of 'Tristram Shandy'. There was no vicarage so he moved into a homely cottage which he named 'Shandy Hall', both to commemorate his novel and amuse the locals, for shandy is a Yorkshire word for daft or eccentric. He lived there eight years, dying of the tuberculosis which accounted for his appearance: 'tall, thin and hectic-looking' according to a contemporary. He was buried in London, but his body was removed to Coxwold churchyard in 1969. Shandy Hall has a collection of his papers and mementoes, in the care of the Sterne Trust. *Open certain days, summer.*

30. Danby Rigg   8 H2
1m N of Lealholm Sleights. The archaeological remains of what must have been a large and important Bronze Age settlement. There are hundreds of small burial mounds on the steep side of the hill at about 700–1,000ft. These are protected by a double earth dyke. Nearby are some standing stones, known as Old Wife Stones, possibly a reference to the earth goddess worshipped by the Celtic tribes.

31. East Riddleston Hall   8 D6
1m E of Keighley, A657. A typical Yorkshire manor house of 1648, built for the Murgatroyds, notorious rakes who were excommunicated for their various sins. Notable features include the rose window and battlements of one wing. The Hall is now National Trust property and has fine panelling, period furnishing, paintings and armour. A medieval tithe barn in the grounds is one of the best preserved in the north of England. *Open most days, summer.*

32. Fountains Abbey   8 E4
3m SW of Ripon, off B6265. The hauntingly lovely ruins of what was once the richest Cistercian monastery in Britain. The buildings date from the mid 12thC, with the exception of the church tower, which was completed shortly before the Dissolution.

Unlike many other monastic sites, the domestic buildings have survived alongside the religious ones. Kitchens, guest houses, the fine vaulted dormitories, the infirmary, cellars and workshops amount to almost a small town, and give a good idea of the day to day business of monastic life. The nave of the church is grandly austere, a strong contrast to the slightly later Chapel of Nine Altars, with its exquisitely delicate Early English design. During the 18thC the ruins were landscaped with pools, waterfalls and lakes. On a summer's evening, with the sound of plainsong echoing around the lofty walls, there is no more atmospheric place in Yorkshire.

Fountains Abbey

32. Fountains Hall   8 E4
3m SW of Ripon, off B6265. A fine Jacobean hall, built around 1610 with stones from the Abbey ruin. It is furnished in the period and contains some of the Abbey treasures.

33. Fylingdales Early Warning Station   8 J3
9m N of Cloughton, off A171. Three giant golfballs on concrete tees, with the broad, desolate sweep of Fylingdales Moor for a fairway. Fylingdales is part of NATO's missile defence system, and will give us four minutes' warning should the worst happen. Just time enough to make a nice pot of tea.

34. Great Ayton   8 G2
Captain James Cook, the great navigator and discoverer of Australia, was born at Marton, now a suburb of Middlesborough, but the family moved to Great Ayton while he was still a child. He went to the village school and an upper room contains mementoes. A small obelisk marks the place where the family's cottage stood. The cottage itself was bought in 1934 by the State of Victoria, Australia: it was dismantled to be shipped (along with a piece of the creeper which grew on the walls) and re-erected in Melbourne. There is also a larger monument on nearby Easby Moor. Cook's mother and some of his brothers and sisters are buried in All Saints churchyard.

35. Halifax   8 E7
One of the great textile towns of the north of England, still retaining a good number of buildings from its heyday in the 19thC. The finest of these are undoubtably the town hall and All Souls Church, which Sir George Gilbert Scott thought to be the best of all he'd designed. St John's, dating from the 12thC, has excellent woodwork. The Piece Hall provides a contrast from a different period, the late 18thC. Its name derives from the merchants taking their pieces, or lengths of material, to be sold here. The old cloth market was held in its colonnaded courtyard. In Gibbet Rd is the base of the infamous Halifax Gibbet, a precursor of the guillotine. Until 1650 anyone caught stealing more than 13½d worth of cloth was summarily executed, hence the famous saying: 'From Hell, Hull and Halifax, good Lord deliver us!'. There's a model of the gibbet in Bankfield Museum,

Ackroyd Park, the town's museum housed in the 19thC home of Edward Ackroyd, a local mill owner and philanthropist. Finally, everyone is familiar with Halifax's greatest invention – the reflecting 'cat's eyes', dreamt up in 1934 by Percy Shaw.

36. Harewood House   8 F5
Harewood village, junction of A61 and A659, 8m N of Leeds. A magnificent 18thC mansion, set in an equally magnificent tree-studded park. The house was built from 1759–71 by John Carr of York, with Robert Adam responsible for the interior decorations. Alterations made in the 19thC have changed the strictly Classical style of the building, but Harewood lost nothing in sumptuousness and is still one of the best places to see 'Adam style'.
The rooms are glorious, with intricately plastered ceilings, painted panels, rich complementary carpeting and fittings. Most of the furniture was designed by Adam specifically for the house, and made by Chippendale. There are also fine collections of silver and Sèvres porcelain, including Marie Antoinette's tea service, and important Italian paintings, including two Bellinis. The Earl of Harewood has created an exotic bird garden with brilliantly plumaged birds from all over the world, in an enclosure by the lake. There's also an adventure playground. *Open summer; certain days, winter.*

Harewood House

37. Harrogate   8 F5
The stately hotels of Harrogate were built to cater for the fashionable and hypochondriac Victorians who came to take the famous spa waters. The first spring was discovered in 1576, but it wasn't until the 18thC that the spas became popular resorts. Harrogate could offer both chalybeate and sulphurous waters, and its most celebrated spring was known as 'The Stinking Spaw'. At the height of its popularity, 1,000 glasses of water were stomached per morning.
The Tewit Well is preserved in the Stray, the town's main park, and the Royal Pump Room of 1842 now houses a museum. The English passion for municipal gardening reaches its apogee in Harrogate, and the happily haphazard scattering of spa and bath buildings among the buxom blooms, still gives the town a restful, recuperative air.

38. Haworth, Bronte Parsonage   8 D6
2m S of Keighley, A6033. Home of the famous and tragic Bronte sisters, and now one of England's most popular literary pilgrimages. It's in a sombre village, caught between the industrial outskirts of Keighley and the moors. The Bronte family moved into the parsonage in 1820. The children grew up close to one another, and the three surviving sisters, Charlotte, Anne and Emily, collaborated in their writing. Charlotte's 'Jane Eyre' and Emily's 'Wuthering Heights' were written here, but they had only just begun to be successful when a series of tragedies struck. Branwell, their unhappy brother, died aged 31, his end hastened by opium addiction and

alcoholic binges at the Black Bull. A year later he was followed by Emily and Anne, aged 30 and 29 respectively. Terrible as these deaths were, they were nothing strange in Haworth at the time. An investigation in 1850 found the average age of death in the village to be 28 years 5 months, the legacy of poor sanitation, polluted water and overcrowded housing. The parsonage was acquired as a public memorial to the sisters in 1928. It contains the family's furniture and many of their possessions, some of them very touching. There are the miniature books the sisters made as children, with stories about the adventures of Branwell's toy soldiers, and the sofa on which Emily died, and the tiny slippers that were Charlotte's, as well as manuscripts and drawings. The Bronte family tomb is marked by a brass plaque in the church. Haworth is on the Worth Valley Railway line, which uses old steam engines in summer.

39. Helmsley Castle   8 G3
Helmsley. A 12thC keep enclosed by a dry moat and earthworks. The site also has the ruin of a 12thC chapel, and a 16thC hall with fine oak panelling. This was the home of the Duke of Buckingham, a notorious rake during Charles I's reign, and a favourite at court.

Helmsley Castle

40. High Bridestones   8 H2
2m S of Sleights, W of A169. The remains of two prehistoric stone circles. A few of the stones stand upright, others have fallen, and some have been removed. There are also a few stones standing outside the circles. Dating from the same time as Stonehenge, their purpose is just as obscure.

41. Jervaulx Abbey   8 E3
2m S of East Witton, A6108. Founded in 1155 by monks from Byland Abbey, Jervaulx prospered to become one of the great Yorkshire abbeys. The destruction following the Dissolution was particularly severe, with much of the church virtually levelled. Some columns and tombs remain in the chapter house, and the altar and south west door of the church are intact.

42. Kirkham Priory   8 H4
8m S of Malton, off A64. The ruins of Kirkham Priory contain a magnificent late 13thC gatehouse, carved with images of David and Goliath and St George fighting the dragon. Apart from this the ruins are scanty and overgrown, but see the lavatorium where the monks washed in leaded troughs before eating. The Priory was founded in the early 12thC by William l'Espec, to commemorate his son who died in a hunting accident in the surrounding woods.

43. Kirkstall Abbey   8 E4
Nr Horsforth, 4m W of Leeds. Another of Yorkshire's ruined Cistercian abbeys, and one which has survived the passage of time remarkably well. It was founded in the mid 12thC, and the chapter house and church display some fine late Norman work. The two sides remaining of the collapsed tower have been in their seemingly precarious state since the mid 18thC. Look out for details such as the beautifully carved door leading into the cloisters. In the restored abbey gatehouse is a museum of local archaeology and folk studies, with an interesting collection of toys and games.

44. Knaresborough   8 F5
2½m E of Harrogate, A59. An attractive, mainly 18thC town, situated in the steep limestone valley of the River Nid. Near High Bridge are Mother Shipton's Cave and the

Dropping Well. Mother Shipton was a celebrated witch of the 16thC, as much famed for her ugliness as her prophecies. There's a grotesque model of her in the cave that's supposed to be her birthplace. The prophecies, which included the foretelling of the submarine and the end of the world in 1881, were the confessed invention of one Charles Hindley of Brighton in 1862. The Dropping Well is so rich in calcium that it 'petrifies' anything left in it for a few months. A number of hats and various other objects that have undergone the process can be seen. On the other side of the river, *below Low Bridge*, is the remarkable Crag Chapel, carved out of the limestone cliff in 1409. About a mile downstream, *nr Grimbold Bridge*, is St Robert's Cave, the retreat of a monk from Fountains Abbey, who died here in 1218. The cave was made a roughly hewn shrine, unique in England. The crudely carved figure of a Knight Templar on the outside by the door is an 18thC embellishment.

44. Knaresborough Castle   8 F5
Castle Hill. Standing high above both town and river, this is where the murderers of Thomas à Becket resorted after committing their crime, in 1170. Later the castle became the property of John of Gaunt, and Richard II was imprisoned here in 1399, during the Wars of the Roses. In the Civil War the castle withstood a siege by Fairfax, the great Parliamentary commander, until the threat of starvation brought surrender. The castle was then slighted and the 14thC keep is the most complete building remaining. The king's chamber and the dungeon also survive.

45. Lastingham, Church of St Mary 8 H3
2m N of Hutton-le-Hole. The church is built on site of a monastery founded by St Cedd in the mid 7thC. In 1078 monks came from Whitby Abbey to build a church of fitting grandeur for their saint. A crypt, on the scale of a small church in itself, was built over St Cedd's grave. Above this were built the magnificent choir, apse and transept. There have been alterations to the main body of the church since, but the crypt survives intact. With chancel, nave and aisles of its own, beneath a low vaulted roof supported on typical early Norman columns, it has an atmosphere redolent of ancient piety.

46. Marston Moor, Battlefield   8 G5
Between Long Marston and Tockwith, B1224. Site of an important battle of the Civil War, marking the turning point in favour of the Parliamentarians. Prince Rupert and his Royalist forces had successfully relieved the city of York, besieged by Parliamentary forces under the command of General Fairfax and their Scottish allies. Against all expectation, and much advice to the contrary, the Prince then decided to pursue his enemy and give battle. Had he attacked when the allied Parliamentary army was strung out in almost single file across the moor, early on 2nd of July, 1644, his success would have been assured. Instead, he allowed them time to take up position.
The Parliamentary army attacked at about half past four, taking the Royalists by surprise. Advantage swung first one way, and then another, even though the Royalists were outnumbered by about 3,000 men. Towards twilight a thunderstorm broke, accompanied by pouring rain, and with the gathering darkness chaos reigned with many leaders of both sides fleeing the battle. Prince Rupert himself hid in a nearby hayrick. It was Cromwell who finally broke through and destroyed the remnants of the Royalist army. Casualties were on a horrendous scale, estimated at between 8,000 and 12,000 dead, and many more wounded. For the Royalists it was a disaster, amounting to the ceding of the whole of the north to Parliament.

47. Middleham Castle   8 E3
Middleham. Built in the 12thC, in the 13thC it passed, by marriage, into the possession of the Neville family, the most powerful of the northern barons. Richard Neville, Earl of Warwick, known to posterity as the Kingmaker, used Middleham as his chief residence, extending it on a fittingly massive scale. The young King Edward IV was a frequent guest at Middleham. At first on the Yorkist side in the Wars of the Roses, Warwick proclaimed Edward IV king, but later changed sides and restored the Lancastrian Henry VI. Edward raised an army and met Warwick's forces at the Battle of Barnet in 1471. The Kingmaker was killed on the field and Edward regained his throne. Middleham then passed to the crown and became the home of Richard, Duke of Gloucester, the future Richard III. His only son was born and died at Middleham. Richard's death at Bosworth Field a year later brought an end to Middleham's dominance of English history, and an end to the 30-year Wars of the Roses.
Today Middleham is a massive, crumbling ruin, grey and brooding. Its great days can be recalled in the huge Norman keep, the ruin of past ambitions symbolised by the broken walls and decaying masonry.

48. Mount Grace Priory   8 F3
1½m E of East Harlsey, off A172. The best example in England of a Carthusian monastery. It was founded in 1397. The ground plan reflects the Carthusians' strict regime, with each monk living in a separate cell, 27ft square, off one of the two courts. Each cell had a small garden attached. In the front wall was a hatch through which food was passed – they only ate together on Saturdays. The monastery church lies between the two courts. After its Dissolution by Henry VIII, parts of the monastery's domestic buildings were converted to a private house. *Open most days*.

49. Newby Hall   8 F4
Skelton, 4m SE of Ripon. A fine, red-brick Queen Anne mansion with substantial additions and alterations made by Robert Adam in 1770. The interior is lavishly decorated and contains fine furniture, some by Adam, and superb tapestries by Gobelin. There's also a collection of Classical statuary made by its 18thC owner, William Weddell, and a collection of chamber pots. The lovely classical gardens were laid out this century. *Open most days, summer; gardens daily, summer*.

50. Nostell Priory   8 F7
4m SE of Wakefield, off A638. A grand 18thC mansion built on the site of a priory from which it takes its name. The house was begun in 1733 by James Paine, and completed by Robert Adam from 1765–80, illustrating the finest of his work. The result is a finely proportioned building with a splendidly decorated interior. Much of the furniture was made by Chippendale to designs by Adam. Chippendale was estate carpenter as a young apprentice, and a beautiful 18thC dolls' house, equipped with delightful miniature furniture, is attributed to him. Of the many

Nostell Priory

superb paintings there are works by Van Dyck, Breughel, Holbein and Lorraine, and there is also an excellent collection of Etruscan pottery.

The house is set in a beautiful park, providing pleasant walks, and contains a museum of veteran and vintage motorcycles. Also in the grounds is Wragby church which contains a collection of Swiss glass dating from 1514 to 1745, unequalled outside Zurich. It was collected by a local squire on a tour of Europe in the early 19thC. There are also fine monuments, one by John Flaxman. *Priory open most days, summer.*

51. Pickering   8 H3

A small market town distinguished by the ruin of its Norman castle and its church. Now considerably decayed, with only the outer wall and the lower parts of the shell keep remaining, Pickering Castle was host to Henry I, Richard II, King John and Edward II during the course of its history. The present fragments are of a 14thC rebuilding on the early Norman core. The parish church is Norman with later additions, and contains a remarkable set of wall-paintings depicting the lives of the saints. They date from c1450 and were uncovered and restored in the late 19thC.

52. Pontefract Castle   8 F7

Pontefract. Famous as the place of the imprisonment and murder of Richard II in 1399. Shakespeare called it 'bloody Pomfret', and small wonder when you recall that its owner in 1322, Thomas, Earl of Lancaster, was imprisoned here, as well as James I of Scotland and Charles, Duke of Orleans, and it was also a place of execution in the Wars of the Roses. The castle was rased by Parliamentarians in 1648, and the remains are disappointingly few – a single wall of the keep and traces of other buildings. The site has been made into a park and recreation ground.

53. Richmond   8 E3

Massively overseen by the cliff-top ruin of its castle, Richmond is one of Yorkshire's most attractive towns. The market place is one of the largest in Britain, and small, cobbled alleyways called 'wynds' lead off it to fine old houses. The town boasts one of the country's earliest unchanged theatres, *Friar's Wynd.* A small theatre built in 1788 by Samuel Butler, it has boxes named after the great English playwrights, decorated in elegant Georgian fashion. The theatre was restored and re-opened in 1963, after over 100 years of neglect.

Almost 300 years of the North Riding Regiment's history are displayed in medals, uniforms, documents, prints and photographs at the Green Howards Museum, *Trinity Sq, Market Place.* There's a special Victoria Cross exhibition. The history of the church is no less interesting. It has been used successively as a school, warehouse and assizes. It was rebuilt, for the second time, in 1745, and in the rebuilding a house and two shops somehow came between two halves of the building. Look out for Grey Friars tower, the elegant Perpendicular tower of the unfinished church of the Grey Friars monastery, founded in 1258. To complete the picture, there are attractive walks alongside the River Swale.

53. Richmond Castle   8 E3

A stupendous castle, built on a high, sheer cliff above the River Swale. It was founded in 1071 by Alan Rufus, making it one of the earliest stone built castles in England. The Scollard's Hall and Chapel of St Nicholas are completely of this date, as is the surrounding wall. The mighty 100ft-high keep was built on top of the Norman gatehouse at the end of the 12thC.

Through most of its history it was crown property, and never seriously attacked due to its isolated location. There's much to see, not least the town spread out like a map below, or the Swaledale countryside sweeping away for miles. Beneath the Great Court is the huge cockpit which was used for jousting contests. The Gold Hole Tower holds a fascinating legend. An old Richmond man, during the 16thC, found a tunnel in the tower that he'd never seen before. He followed it to discover the sleeping King Arthur, surrounded by his Knights and treasure. He was about to help himself to the riches when Arthur asked 'Is it Time?', whereon the man fled. No-one was ever able to discover the tunnel again.

54. Rievaulx Abbey   8 G3

One of the most extensive and romantic monastic remains in Yorkshire, beautifully situated in the wooded Rye Dale. It was the first Cistercian foundation in Yorkshire, founded in 1132. It quickly grew, and by the early 13thC had a staff of 140 monks and over 500 lay brothers, and the surviving buildings date from this time or earlier. They include the lower part of the nave and transepts of the church, and the striking Gothic choir, as well as some of the domestic buildings.

To experience the real breath-taking beauty of the place, the ruins and surrounding valley must be viewed from Rievaulx Terrace. The terrace, a half mile long, was landscaped in the 18thC for the earls of Feversham, owners of Duncombe Park. A rich Ionic temple was built at one end for hunting parties, and a small Doric one at the other for peace and solitude.

Rievaulx Abbey

55. Ripley   8 E5

4m N of Harrogate, A61. The village of Ripley was re-modelled in 1827 by the eccentric Sir William Ingilby, of Ripley Castle, to resemble a French village of the Alsace. The old thatched cottages were replaced by stone houses in the Gothic or Tudor style, the village hall was called the 'Hotel de Ville' and the inscription 'Parlez au Suisse' was placed above the gatehouse of his castle. Ripley church has bullet marks on the east wall where Royalist prisoners were shot after the Battle of Marston Moor. In the churchyard there's an interesting weeping cross, with niches at the base to kneel in and repent.

55. Ripley Castle   8 E5

Ripley. The home of the Ingilby family for over 600 years. The estate was granted them by Edward I after Thomas Ingilby saved the king from a charging boar, an event commemorated in the stone boar carved on the village fountain. A 16thC tower and 15thC gatehouse survive of an earlier building, while the main house was altered in the Classical style in 1780. There are fine panelled rooms, and good collections of armour and paintings. During the Civil War the Ingilbys were staunch Royalists. Sir William fought alongside his sister, Trooper Jane, at Marsden Moor. There is a famous story that when Cromwell arrived at Ripley Castle after the battle, demanding shelter in Sir William's absence, Sir William's wife greeted him with a loaded pistol in each hand. Cromwell was forced to sit up all night with the pistols trained on him. In the morning he was escorted off the premises, Lady Ingilby telling him: 'It is well that you behaved so peacefully, otherwise you would not have quitted Ripley Castle alive'. *Open most days, summer.*

Ripley Castle

56. Ripon   8 F4
An attractive, if somewhat austere, cathedral city on the River Skell. It has a large market square with a 90ft obelisk at its centre erected in 1781 by William Aislabie to celebrate his 60 years as Member of Parliament for Ripon. The town grew up around the Saxon cathedral founded by St Wilfrid cAD670.

56. Ripon Cathedral   8 F4
Kirkgate. A grey, sombre building containing parts from its Saxon origins, to early 16thC work. One of the oldest Christian buildings in Britain, the crypt of the Saxon church founded by St Wilfrid, a barrel vaulted cell 11ft by 8ft, survives intact. The main fabric of the building dates from the mid 12thC, and is notable for the width of the nave and aisles. The choir displays work of the three main periods of Gothic architecture, curiously interwoven to form a unified whole. The choir stalls and misericords have splendidly crafted, obscure 15thC carvings, among them allegories of the elephant and castle and the fox and the goose.

57. Roche Abbey   8 G8
2½m S of Maltby, off A634. Charmingly located in the wooded valley of the River Ryton, Roche was a 12thC Cistercian monastery. Only the tall grey and romantic walls of the transept and the 13thC gatehouse have survived the depredations of the Dissolution, and the years. Nearby are the landscaped grounds of Sandbeck Park.

58. Rotherham   8 F8
An industrial town of 'dark satanic mills', but containing a small glimpse of Jerusalem in its splendid Perpendicular Church of All Saints. It's built of red sandstone (beneath the grime) and has a central tower and spire rising to 180ft. Inside is some of the earliest fan vaulting in England, c1410, beneath the tower. The nave and chancel ceilings are panelled and have fine carved bosses, and there is intricate tracery on the stalls, dating from the 15thC. Rotherham's religious and industrial faces meet in Kirkstead Abbey Grange, *off Wortley Rd.* This is the archaeological site of four iron smelting forges, operated by monks in the 12thC.

59. Scarborough   8 J3
The north east coast's most popular seaside resort, centred around a rocky escarpment with a Norman castle on top. Its impregnable position attracted settlers from the Bronze Age onward, and it was an important Roman beacon station. Its popularity as a resort began with the discovery of a mineral spring in 1620. The 19thC boom in spas and resorts has left behind splendidly ostentatious hotels. The fishing harbour has remained busy but unspoilt.
A pre-Raphaelite paradise, the Church of St Martin-on-the-Hill, *South Cliff,* is a splendid 19thC Gothic church with a chancel roof by Morris, glass and murals by Burne-Jones and work by Rossetti and Ford Madox Brown. The Church of St Mary, *Castle Rd,* is 14thC, much damaged by bombing in the Civil War. There are some fine monuments, and Anne Bronte is buried in the adjacent churchyard.

59. Scarborough Castle   8 J3
Castle St. Perched imperiously 300ft above the sea, the present castle remains date from the 12thC. They comprise of a curtain wall and keep, built by Henry II. It suffered numerous sieges in the course of its history, two by Parliamentary forces during the Civil War. Between the castle and the cliff edge are the remains of the Roman signal station, built around AD370. It was part of a string of such defences built to detect the approach of Picts invading from the north.

60. Selby Abbey   8 G6
Market Sq. Despite a serious fire of 1906, Selby Abbey remains a splendid example of a medieval abbey church. The monastery at Selby was founded in 1068, probably by William the Conqueror. The original building was devastated by fire in 1096, and parts of the nave date from the first rebuilding. The nave is a beautiful construction: over 200ft long, with a triforium above the nave arches, and about this, a fine Early English clerestory. The choir is of a later period, richly carved throughout. The arresting great east Jesse window has profuse flamboyant tracery and in the west front is a splendid Norman doorway with five recessed arches. The whole interior is a tribute to remarkable and sensitive restoration early this century.

61. Sheffield   8 F8
Yorkshire's largest town, virtually synonymous with the production of steel and cutlery. The industry has long been established here – Chaucer's miller in the Canterbury Tales carried a 'Sheffield thwitel', or knife, in his stocking.
The Norman town had its castle, and Mary, Queen of Scots, was imprisoned there for 15 years. It was later destroyed by the Parliamentarians, and no traces remain.
By 1760 Sheffield was described, by Horace Walpole, as 'one of the foulest towns in England in the most charming situation'. The latter statement is still true, but the clean air act, and imaginative modern planning, have made it one of the sprucest and most attractive manufacturing cities in Europe.
The 15thC **Church of SS Peter and Paul**, *Church St,* was given cathedral status in 1914. The most noticeable features are the modern narthex and tower, grafted onto the old building. There are monuments to the earls of Shrewsbury in the chancel.
Abbeydale Industrial Hamlet, *4m SW of city centre, off A621,* is a preserved 18thC steel works, with the melting shop, forge, grinding shop and workers' cottages. The workshops are fully equipped and the warehouse contains displays showing the city's industrial development. Headquarters of the Company of Cutlers, founded in 1624 is the **Cutlers' Hall**, *Church St.* It contains a collection of silverware with at least one piece bearing a hallmark for every year from 1773. But an unmatched collection can be seen in the City Museum, *Weston Park.*

62. Skipton   8 D5
A characterful Dales market town, concentrated around the one wide, main street. Of many fine, old houses, the oldest, and most interesting, is the High Corn Mill, *Chapel St,* now the George Leatt Industrial and Folk Museum. It dates from the 13thC and recently has been restored to its original commercial use. The huge grindstones are powered by water-wheels. *Open certain days, or by arrangement.*
Skipton church stands by the castle, and is

Skipton Castle

mainly Perpendicular in period. Apart from the fine 16th and 17thC tombs of the Clifford family, it has a fine 13thC sedilia and 16thC screens.

62. Skipton Castle   8 D5
Off High St. Situated on a high rock with a sheer 100ft face on one side, Skipton Castle was the home of the Clifford family, earls of Cumberland, and their descendants from 1309 to 1955. The building dates in part from the early 14thC, with Tudor additions, and an extensive renovation in the 17thC after it had been slighted during the Civil War. During that time Skipton was the last northern stronghold of the Royalists.
Entrance to the castle is by the gatehouse with its four drum towers. The gatehouse battlements bear the enigmatic Clifford family motto, 'Desormais', meaning 'henceforth'. There's a picturesque main courtyard and other features are the grand banqueting hall and the 14thC kitchens and dungeons. The 'shell room' contains sea-shells and coral collected by the third Earl of Cumberland, one of Elizabeth I's admirals.

63. Spofforth Castle   8 F5
Spofforth. The ruins of the early 14thC fortified manor house of the Percy family. The Percys had been an influential baronial family since the Norman Conquest and, like many of the ancient Yorkshire families during the Wars of the Roses, were supporters of the Lancastrian cause. This was probably the birthplace of Harry Hotspur. Interesting features today are the hall with its 15thC windows and moulded doorway, and the undercroft, one wall of which is formed by the underlying rock, and which contained the castle's kitchen.

64. Stanwick Hill Fort   8 E2
4m SE of Caldwell. Huge Iron Age fort, the ramparts and ditches enclosing roughly 800 acres in all. It was built in the 1stC by King Venutius of the Brigantes, and became a major centre of resistance against the Romans in the north. The tribe later split into two factions, the pro-Roman one led by Venutius's wife, Cartimandua. The camp was captured in AD74 by the Ninth Roman Legion and marked the last serious battle against the conquering Romans.

65. Temple Newsam House   8 F6
Temple Newsam. An impressive red-brick mansion built in the early 17thC around three sides of a courtyard. Lord Darnley, the unfortunate second husband of Mary, Queen of Scots, was born here, in an earlier house, in 1545. The present house was considerably altered in the 18thC, and was bought in 1922 by Leeds Council for use as a museum and art gallery. The gallery, in the north wing, has a moulded ceiling with medallion portraits of George II, and splendid period furniture. There are also paintings of Venetian scenes by Guardi. Also notable are the Great Hall and Chinese Room with hand-painted Chinese wallpaper, and Chinese Chippendale furniture. *Open most days.*

66. Tickhill   8 G8
A South Yorkshire mining village with the scant remains of an important Norman castle and a beautiful Perpendicular church. The castle was only one of five in England licensed for royal jousting tournaments under Richard the Lionheart. Demolished by Cromwell, only part of the 12thC curtain wall and a gatehouse with an Elizabethan window, remain.
In the market place is an 18thC domed market cross standing on eight pillars, and in Northgate stands the timber-framed St Leonard's Hospital, dating from 1470. Also of interest is the fine 14thC friary, *Maltby Rd*, now a private house. The outstanding feature of St Mary's Church is its 124ft tower, beautifully proportioned, and embellished

with fine detail. The interior is delightfully pure and spacious.

67. Towton Battlefield   8 F6
2½m S of Tadcaster, A162. Towton was probably the most decisive battle of the Wars of the Roses. England was divided in allegiance between the newly crowned Edward IV and Henry VI, who had the Lancastrian support. The two armies, both about 40,000 strong, took up position on Towton Moor, marked today by a battle monument.
Battle was engaged in the morning of 29th March, 1461 – Palm Sunday. The struggle was savage and protracted, with 80,000 men locked in vicious hand-to-hand combat. At a critical moment the flagging Yorkists were given new strength by the arrival of the Duke of Norfolk and the tide of battle was turned. By late afternoon the Lancastrians were in flight, trying to make their escape over Cock Beck in Bloody Meadow. Such was the carnage at this point that the waters still ran red three miles downstream.
The Lancastrians had been dealt a crippling blow in the heartland of their support. Lords Neville, Clifford and Dacre and the earls of Northumberland and Devon lay among the 28,000 dead, while King Henry and his wife made good their escape to Scotland. It had been, and remains, the bloodiest encounter ever fought on British soil. Lord Dacre was buried upright on his horse in Saxton churchyard. His tomb is perhaps the best monument to the desperate heroism of the battle.

68. Victoria Cave   8 C4
2½m N of Settle. A treble cave, which contained, on its discovery on Queen Victoria's Coronation Day, 1838, remains of the animals and humans that had once occupied it. The skulls of a giant ox, a giant cave bear and hyena date from the last Ice Age. It seems that man moved in around 8,000BC, when the climate was becoming more hospitable. Discoveries show that the cave was briefly re-occupied at the time of the Romans. Some of the items found in the cave can be seen in the museum at Settle.

69. Wakefield   8 F7
A cloth-producing town since the Middle Ages, but few buildings remain to indicate its ancient heritage. Bridge Chapel, *S of Kirkgate*, dates from c1350, as does the bridge on which it stands. It's one of the few such bridge chapels to survive in England, although its appearance owes more to a 19thC restoration by Sir George Gilbert Scott than it does to the medieval architect. The Church of All Saints was given cathedral status in 1888, and its 247ft crocketed spire, the highest in Yorkshire, was a Victorian addition.
The Battle of Wakefield was fought south of the town, *nr Sandal Castle*, in 1460. The Duke of York was heavily outnumbered by the Lancastrians led by Queen Margaret. The Duke himself was killed and his head taken to be displayed from the town gate at York. Sandal Castle, the Duke's headquarters before the battle, was for a long while buried beneath an earthen mound. Recent excavations have uncovered the foundations and substantial portions of its walls. The whole layout, from great keep to kitchens, can be seen easily, in an attractive, grassy, archaeological site.

70. Whitby   8 J2
Busy fishing port and holiday resort, built on both banks of the River Esk. The town began with the founding of Whitby Abbey, a Saxon institution re-founded by Benedictine monks after the Norman Conquest. Captain Cook served as an apprentice in Grape Lane, and it was in a Whitby built ship, the Endeavour, that he made his first circumnavigation of the globe. Relics of Cook can be seen in Whitby

Museum, *Pannett Park*, along with model ships and local fossils.

70. Whitby Abbey 8 J2

Off Church St. Spectacularly poised on a high cliff 200ft above the sea, Whitby is one of the most exciting monastic ruins in England. It was founded originally in AD657 by St Hilda and both men and women lived in the early monastery. The famed poet, Caedmon, was one of the first of the many learned monks it produced. St Hilda's institution was destroyed by Danes in 867, and the monastery wasn't refounded until 1069. The present ruin dates from the late 12thC, with later 13thC work at the west end, which suffered from a naval bombardment in 1914. The splendid east and northern facades stand at their original height, and are both fine examples of the Early English style.

71. York 8 G5

York has been the stage for emperors, kings and princes, and King George VI rightly said of the city: 'the history of York, is the history of England'. One of the most historically important and interesting of English towns, the old walled city, with its stately Minster and narrow streets, is still substantially the medieval creation.

The Roman Ninth Legion founded a base here in AD71, and this soon became the colonia of Eboracum. It was here that Constantine the Great was proclaimed Emperor in AD306. Parts of the medieval city walls incorporate the Roman wall, and archaeologists have made important excavations. The most impressive is the **Multangular Tower**, *Museum St.*

In 867 the Vikings captured York and developed it as a port and trading centre. The city's present name is derived from the Danes' Jorvik, and many of the streets retain the typical 'gate' ending to their names. York remained a Danish colony until 944. The Normans refortified and extended the Roman town walls and in addition to founding the Minster and two castles, 40 churches and 16 hospitals, built nine guildhalls and four monasteries. After the Dissolution and the decline of the wool trade, York entered a period of stagnation but the 18thC saw a revival of the city's fortunes.

By far the best way to see York is on foot. Walk round the **city walls**, the complete circuit of which stretches about three miles. It takes an hour or two, but you're rewarded by magnificent views over the city. A marvellous example of medieval fortification, they date from the reign of Edward III, but incorporate the Roman wall in the north west section. There are four medieval 'bars' or gates: Monk, Bootham, Micklegate and Walmgate. Walmgate Bar is the only town gate in England to have retained its barbican. Monk Bar is the highest of the four and has its original portcullis in place. Micklegate Bar was where the heads of traitors were displayed, the most famous being that of Richard, Duke of York, after the Battle of Wakefield. The stretch between Monk Bar and Bootham Bar contains Roman brickwork, and offers fine views of York Minster.

York's oldest domestic houses are to be found in Lady's Row, *Goodramgate*, dating from the mid 14thC. Stonegate and The Shambles are among the best preserved medieval streets. In the mid 18thC **Stonegate** was the home of Laurence Sterne, the novelist, and Guy Fawkes was born in one of these houses in 1570. The overhanging upper storeys of **The Shambles**, once a street full of butcher's shops, are close enough for opposite neighbours to reach out and shake hands. The Shambles leads to the oddly named Whip-Ma-Whop-Ma Gate, where medieval malefactors were flogged.

The parish churches of York are famous for their medieval glass, as is the Minster. The **Church of All Saints**, *North St*, has some of the most beautiful in the city. In the north aisle is the window illustrating the 'Last 15 Days of the World', an allegory based on a 14thC poem by Richard Rolle 'The Prykke of Conscience', the text of which is incorporated in the design.

It's also worth stopping at **Mansion House**, *St Helen's Sq.* Early 18thC, it houses the city's silver, and is the home of the lord mayor. Behind it is the guildhall, originally built c1450, destroyed by bombs in 1942, and rebuilt on original lines in 1960. The **Merchant Adventurer's Hall**, *Fossgate*, is a magnificent hall of c1360. It's famed for its beautiful timberwork – huge oak tie beams supporting the roof, and fine panelling.

Of all the marvellous museums, the **National Railway Museum** is the most famous. York has been the centre of the railway network since the 19thC, and so it's appropriate that it has one of the largest railway museums in the country, opened in 1975. Apart from excellent mementoes, there are locomotives dating from the beginning of the railway age, and the record-breaking Mallard.

The **Treasurer's House**, containing 17th and 18thC furniture, is one of the city's loveliest buildings. It was built on 17thC foundations for the Treasurer of the Minster. But for an overall sense of the history of this beautiful city, go to the **Yorkshire Museum**, *Museum Gardens, Museum St.* A fine neo-Classical building of 1830, it houses an extensive collection of material from Roman York and the period of the Viking occupation. There's also a large collection of fossils and superb natural history exhibits. The museum gardens contain the ruins of St Mary's Abbey, a 12thC Benedictine foundation. The north wall of the nave and part of the west front of the abbey still stand and the original Norman church has been excavated.

71. York, Castle Museum 8 G5

Tower St. The main fabric of William the Conqueror's castle was replaced in the 18thC by an assize court and prison, built by the local architect John Carr. **Clifford's Tower**, the only remaining medieval building, dates from the 14thC, and occupies the site of the wooden keep burnt in 1190. Over 150 Jews had taken refuge there and perished in the fire. The museum contains notable reconstructions of 18th and 19thC street scenes, and period interiors from Jacobean to Victorian times. Dick Turpin spent his last days in the Debtor's Prison, which has been converted to display a collection of toys and weapons. Dick Turpin's grave can be seen in St George's Churchyard.

71. York Minster 8 G5

Minstergate. York Minster is the largest of the English cathedrals, and second in importance only to Canterbury in the church hierarchy. A wooden church founded by the first bishop, Paulinus, in AD625, first stood on this site, and was replaced by stone buildings. The present Minster was started by Archbishop Walter de Gray in the early 13thC.

The Minster contains England's greatest concentration of medieval stained glass. The finest feature of the exterior is the west facade, with its huge rose window commemorating the end of the Wars of the Roses, with alternating red and white roses. The 13thC Five Sisters window, with some of the earliest glass in England, is justly famous. The chapter house, a late 13thC building with a large vaulted span made possible by the use of wood, is the finest architectural feature. The glass in the traceried windows is among the best in the Minster. As part of recent restoration work, a new undercroft was created. Traces of Roman York beneath the Minster were uncovered and these can now be seen along with other archaeological finds and a display of the Minster's plate.

SCOTTISH LOWLANDS

The Lowlands of Scotland – Borders, Central, Dumfries and Galloway, Fife, Lothian and Strathclyde – are by no means the unvaried flat land the name suggests. Here you'll find some of the scenery most typically associated with Scotland: green hills sloping gently towards sapphire-coloured lochs, winding lands leading through curtains of trees, and isolated cottages standing exposed to the elements. Though lacking in the rugged grandeur of the Highlands, this area is more hilly than most parts of England and mid-winter conditions can be as bleak as any lonely village in the barren north.

Far from leading a quiet life free from Highland clan battles, the history of the counties neighbouring England has been more turbulent. The first shaggy mesolithic hunters followed the retreating ice sheet northwards from London as Scotland thawed 10,000 years ago. They lived off elk, deer, bear and wolf and eventually cleared land for farming in the friendlier, fertile soil of southern Scotland which had been squashed into plains by receding glaciers. Hill ridges like the Pentlands, Sidlaws and Ochills were coughed up by volcanoes, themselves crushed level by the ice. As the climate calmed, people arrived from Ireland, England and the Low Countries bringing new skills, thoughts and ways of life. They left behind more than 360 megalithic chamber tombs in Scotland, and later, earthworks, circles and vitrified forts.

Written history began with the Romans who belted Clyde to Forth with the Antonine Wall and had high, imperialist hopes of colonising the country. They couldn't, and kept the northern frontier of their empire further south at Hadrian's Wall.

During the Dark Ages, Scotland became a melting pot for wandering peoples of northern Europe. Battles raged between Celts, Picts, Scots, Angles and Britons until the terror of Norse invaders united the races and in 1018 Malcolm II won the important Battle of Carham, extending Scottish dominion to the Tweed.

For the next 500 years the south west was the setting for Scotland's struggle for independence from the English. In the late 13th and early 14thC, heroes Wallace and then Robert the Bruce took up banner against the English, culminating in the victory of the Scots at Bannockburn in 1314. Despite the demoralising defeat of the Scots by English forces at Flodden field in 1513, it was through the Lowlands that proud Mary, Queen of Scots, wound her way to claim her throne. Her magnetic but headstrong personality coupled with her insistent Catholicism conflicted with the Protestant zeal of John Knox, whose powerful doctrine contributed not only to Mary's ultimate downfall, but also to the Reformation of the Church in Scotland. Visible evidence of their influential lives can be seen at St Andrew's, Linlithgow Palace, and Edinburgh. It was Mary's son, James VI of Scotland and James I of England, whose reign at last brought about the union of the English and Scottish crowns. But the ultimate union of the nations didn't come about until 1707 when the Act of Union and the subsequent failure of the Jacobite rebellions put paid to Scotland's dreams of independence – at least until the recent move towards devolution.

Lowland Scots had other wars to contend with too – it was also an area torn by anarchy as the powerful families fought each other. The grim reminders of this strife are the castles at Caerlaverock and Threave. Like any buffer, the Border counties took the blows of this warfare and over the years the area became armoured with more strongholds per square mile than any other country. The scars remain today in assaulted castles, ruined abbeys and abandoned chapels.

Affluent even from the days when medieval monks husbanded the rich Lowland soil, southern Scotland found new prosperity centuries later in iron and coal, tweeds and linens, whisky and paper. It is still rich in farming and busy with sheep rearing. This area manages to support nearly all of Scotland's industry and two thirds of her population. Bustling Glasgow, one of Britain's finest Victorian cities, is the centre of the industrial belt which straddles the Clyde. The River Clyde was once a little salmon river, but by the 19thC Clydeside had become the greatest ship-building centre in the world. Classical Edinburgh, the country's capital and cultural centre, stands to the east wrapped in an eiderdown of hills. Proudly poised on its crags, and overlooked by a mountain-in-miniature, Arthur's Seat, the city still casts one of the most stirring silhouettes of any in Europe.

The Lowlands are the turning point where Scotland breaks away gradually from its neighbouring English counties and firmly establishes itself with these two great cities. The sparkling Tweed river enlivens the centre of the Lowlands, skirting the romantic ruined abbeys of Melrose and Dryburgh. The hills are gentle and often wooded and the true Scottish woollens come from Peebles, Hawick and Galashiels. Fife is flatter country, accommodating that great Scottish sport – golf. And let it not be forgotten that this now-peaceful land inspired many of the great historical novels of Sir Walter Scott, and the evocative verses of gentle Robert Burns, Scotland's national poet.

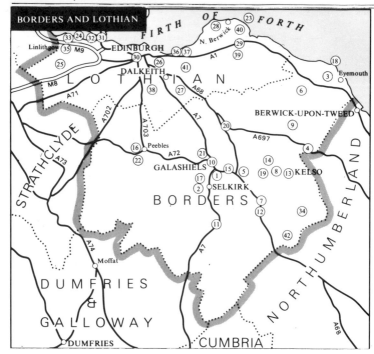

BORDERS AND LOTHIAN

BORDERS

1. Abbotsford House   10 M5
2½m SSE of Galashiels, A7. Sir Walter Scott watched avidly from the windows of a nearby cottage as the turrets of his romantic mansion above the Tweed rose, one by one. From 1817 to 1822, royalties from his books poured into the rebuilding of this architectural eccentricity which has since been called 'the first essay in Scottish Baronial style'. Being an enthusiastic, if unscientific, historian, Scott collected fragments and included them in the actual structure of his dream house, for instance, a 16thC lintel from the door of the old Edinburgh Tolbooth. The hall looks as though Scott tried to pack the whole of the Middle Ages into it. The armoury displays fine pistols and mementoes of Waterloo collected from the battlefield by Scott himself. Napoleon's pen case and leather-bound blotter can also be seen, along with Scott's study containing his desk and workmanlike chair, and a library of 9,000 books. Each literary success added another room to the house, and although Scott wrote himself to death in 1832 repaying debts, he left behind in Abbotsford – once a boggy meadow aptly named the Clarty Hole – a beautiful symbol of his passion for Borderland. *Open summer.*

Abbotsford House

2. Bowhill   10 M6
3m W of Selkirk, off A708. Conspicuous for its outstanding collection of pictures (Van Dyck, Reynolds, Gainsborough, Canaletto, Guardi, Claude Lorraine) and porcelain, this border home of the Scotts of Buccleuch dates from

1812 and is still furnished with many of its original silk brocades and hand-painted Chinese wallpapers. Much of the furniture on show was made in the famous workshops of André Boulle in Paris. Take a break from culture in the accompanying riding centre, garden, shops and nature trails. *Open summer.*

3. Coldingham Priory   10 P4
Coldingham, 3m NW of Eyemouth, off A1107. A female skeleton standing upright was discovered here built into the wall, and may confirm that this priory is indeed the site of a nunnery founded four centuries earlier by St Ebba. Apostate nuns were once buried alive in this position. Benedictines built the priory in 1098 and the external arcading between the buttresses is graceful late Norman. Note the leaf-form capitals and cross-slabs with design drawn in bare outline, with a plain Latin cross and sword. Like other houses, Coldingham suffered plunder and pillage – in 1216 by King John, and in 1544 by raiding invaders.

4. Coldstream   10 O5
General Monck founded the world famous regiment of guards in the 1650s. It was from here in 1660 that they set off for London and brought about the restoration of Charles II. Their original headquarters in Market Square now houses a small regimental museum. Ironically, the town has spent more time marrying runaway couples than fighting battles, and no fewer than three lord chancellors of England – Eldon, Erskine and Brougham – eloped into this first burgh over the Border. *Museum open summer.*

5. Dryburgh Abbey   10 N6
6m SE of Melrose, off A68. Cradled in a loop of the River Tweed, this beautiful abbey has survived 800 years of sack and outrage and today displays the most complete and characteristic range of conventual buildings in Scotland. One of the four great Border abbeys founded by Hugh de Morville, Constable of Scotland, Dryburgh stands serenely among

lawns and trees, visited and re-visited by pilgrims affected as much by its setting as its violent history or ruined splendour. Finches and pigeons perch on the 12th and 13thC transepts. Tourists wander the cloisters, refectory and chapter house with its stone bench where chilly-bottomed monks sat to hear the reading of their Rule. Traces of 12thC painted decoration adorn the barrel vault. Plundered four times in as many centuries, the last monk at Dryburgh died in 1600, pensioned off by the Reformers, but allowed to remain in the abbey buildings. Sir Walter Scott and Field Marshal Earl Haig, British Commander-in-Chief in France in 1915, are buried here: both lived nearby.

6. Edinshall Broch 10 O4
North east slope of Cockburn Law, 4m N of Duns, off A6112. Rare in Scottish lowlands, brochs generally belong to the north. But this one is the only broch within sight of England. It is exceptionally large and was built inside an earlier fort. Drystone walls survive to about 5ft and show superb construction. The site was occupied in Roman times.

7. Ferniehirst Castle 10 N6
2m N of Jedburgh. An ancient traditional Roxburghshire handball game is said to have gruesome origins at Ferniehirst where victorious Scots played football with the severed heads of their English opponents. Today, Ferniehirst is L-shaped with a 16thC stair tower attached to an elongated 17thC wing, and with some Renaissance detail round the doors and windows, plus a classically inspired gateway. The Kers owned it once – they were the 'Ker' or left-handed clan who carried their swords in their left hands.

8. Floors Castle 10 O5
2m NW of Kelso, B6089. Lurking behind formidable walls, this Vanbrugh and William Adam castle was greatly enlarged and 'Tudorised' by William Playfair in the 1840s. An abundance of capped turrets overlooks the park where a holly tree is said to mark the spot where James II was killed by a canon bursting during a siege of nearby Roxburgh Castle in 1460. Superbly placed to face across the Tweed and away to the Cheviots. *Open most days, summer.*

Floors Castle

9. Fogo Church 10 O5
3m SW of Duns, off B6460. Attractive church with outside staircase leading to private laird's loft which dates from 1671.

10. Galashiels 10 N5
Capital of Scotland's great woollen trade, this mill town spun the Gala Greys and Gala Tweeds that developed into the kind of fabric sought today by international fashion houses from New York to Rome. It seems ironic that the cloth began as solid, homely and hard-wearing, drawn from centuries of sheep breeding skills that started with the monks of Melrose Abbey. Around 1840, the old word 'tweel' became 'tweed' – perhaps because the River Tweed had flowed through the Waverley Novels into households nationwide. Today, the Scottish Woollen Technical College teaches the philosophy of design as well as techniques, and Old Gala House with its 17thC wing and 18thC drawing room is now an art centre.

11. Hawick 10 M6
Grey stone mills dominate this busy town which produces some of the best known knitwear in Britain. But once a year in June, Hawick forgets fashion to remember the Battle of Hornshole and celebrate it in the Common Riding. It happened a year after the disastrous Battle of Flodden when a party of English raiders snoring on the banks of the Teviot were massacred by a group of young lads from Hawick who rode home in triumph carrying the captured banner. The same banner streams proudly at the head of the Common Riding festivities.
On the western outskirts of Hawick is **Wilton Lodge Park**, ancestral home of the Langlands which contains an unrivalled collection of border relics, natural history, and paintings. *Open summer; most days, winter.*

12. Jedburgh Abbey 10 N6
High St, Jedburgh. Founded, like the other great Border abbeys, by David I, and ravaged by incessant border frays, this 12thC red sandstone church has a transitional nave unsurpassed in Scotland, and a fine rose window known as St Catherine's Wheel. There is also a richly carved Norman doorway. Standing in the path of so many invasions, the abbey was ransacked in 1297 by Edward I's army, burnt in 1523, and burnt again 11 years later: scorch marks can still be seen on the walls. Proof that the site itself was consecrated from very early times lies in the abbey museum which has a piece of sarcophagus dating from about AD700.

12. Jedburgh, Queen Mary's House 10 N6
Queen St. Passionate and rash, Mary, Queen of Scots, bequeathed a love story to this house. Holding assizes in Jedburgh in 1566, she heard that her beloved Bothwell was lying injured in Hermitage Castle, 25 miles away. Characteristically, she rode in drenching rain to his bedside, stayed two hours, and then rode home. Even for hardened mosstroopers, it was a tremendous journey. Tradition states she was thrown off her horse in the boggy area known as Queen's Mire, and in fact a lady's silver spur of antique design was found there some years ago. Exhausted and wet, Mary fell into a fever and nearly died. It was in this house, now a museum, that she was nursed back to health. On show here is a collection of her relics, ironically including a deathmask. Originally, the house was a minor seat of the Ker family – the Ker-handed clan who carried their swords in their left hands and whose staircases, like the one here, spiralled left accordingly. The house was adapted as a bastel or communal shelter for townsfolk during time of war or raid. *Open summer.*

13. Kelso Abbey 10 N5
Bridge St, Kelso. Slightly 'Continental' in tower and arch, this once-wealthy Benedictine abbey suffered more than its sister houses from the sword and cannon of repeated sacking. Shaped like a Greek cross, it survived from 1128 to 1545 when Hertford declared his determination to 'rase and deface this house of Kelso'. He did. But not without a fight. Led by 12 monks, 100 Scotsmen garrisoned the abbey as a fortress to repel the attack. Despite heavy gunning, they fought to the end – but were slaughtered. The tower is part of that original building. Kelso is the largest of the Border abbeys and was founded, like the others, by David I. Kelso itself was described by Sir Walter Scott as the most beautiful town in Scotland.

14. Mellerstain House 10 N5
8m NW of Kelso, off A6089. William Adam, father of Robert, returned from Italy heady with classicism. This elegant, 18thC mansion was his first Scottish commission after 10 years' successful work as a classicist in England. Poetess and heroine Lady Grizel Baillie hired Adam to build it for her and

today it is one of the most beautiful homes in the area. William built the wings in 1725 and his son Robert the central block in 1765. Inside are decorated plaster ceilings, Old Masters and much fine furniture. The library has a frieze of classical figures over the bookshelves, considered some of Adam's best work. Italianate in style, the terraced gardens with lake boast fine views. *Open most days, summer.*

15. Melrose Abbey   10 N5
Main Square, Melrose. Husbanding the soil as well as their souls occupied the early Cistercians brought to Melrose from Rievaulx in Yorkshire by David I in 1136. Farmers, gardeners, stockbreeders and millers, these busy monks soon established their abbey as one of the wealthiest in Scotland. Nearby Berwick bought much of their wool, and the abbey was close enough to the main Edinburgh–England road to receive many eminent visitors.

But like its sister abbeys Kelso, Jedburgh and Dryburgh, Melrose caught the cruelty of border warfare full-face. It suffered in the Wars of Independence in 1322, and in 1385 Richard II's troops sacked it so drastically, it had to be rebuilt. Splendidly reconstructed, it lasted till 1544 when it was destroyed by the Earl of Hertford. After that, it was plundered for building materials, but patched up enough to last as a parish church until 1810.

The ruins are considered the most beautiful in Scotland. Notable for its fine traceried stonework, this red sandstone abbey, plaided on its grassy setting, draws Northern English rather than Gallic inspiration for its solid shapeliness. Rivalled in scale by the Eildon summits, it's as if Melrose decided to concentrate on detail. Its clustered columns and carved capitals use rustic images of hedgerows and fields for their decoration, and on the roof there's a pig playing the bagpipes. In a country where 'graven images' were mostly cast down, Melrose hung on to a whole batch, including a girlish Virgin Mary whose face, unfortunately, needs more than cosmetic surgery after many centuries of border blizzards. Excavations have revealed the full spread of this remarkable settlement, but not unearthed the heart of Robert the Bruce, which, brought back from the Holy Land, is said to be buried here. A small museum contains pottery and floor tiles found there during the investigations.

Melrose Abbey

16. Neidpath Castle   10 L5
1m W of Peebles, A72. Strawberries are the unlikely emblem on the gateway keystone of this stern ruin, bedded on rock beside the Tweed. Neidpath was the former fortress of the Border Frasers – originally Norman Frasers who took their name from strawberries or 'fraises'. Parts of it are 13thC, and since then it has slipped from earls to marquesses, dukes to lords.

Cromwell knocked Neidpath about in 1650, removing most of the top storey, so the First Marquess of Tweeddale decided to restore it. It was sold at the end of the 17thC to the Duke of Queensberry. The 4th duke in that line died a bachelor in his eighties having cut down all the woods on the estate and generally ruined the property. Wordsworth was so outraged he exploded into a sonnet beginning: 'Degenerate Douglas! Oh, the unworthy

lord!' But Tweeddale's beautiful avenue of yews leading to the castle survived Queensberry's axe. Lowering your eyes from trees and headland views over the river, look at the steps leading from the drive to the garden. Called 'bow tell', they are typical of 17thC Scotland. Two of the windows retain their original bar protection – or yetts – and in places the walls are 11ft thick. *Open summer.*

17. Newark Castle   10 M6
4m W of Selkirk, off A708. Blood-curdling screams still haunt this five-storey Border keep tower built originally as a 15thC royal hunting lodge. Called Newark or 'new work' to distinguish it from Auldwark Castle that stood nearby, this stronghold saw and heard 100 Royalist prisoners from the terrible Battle of Philiphaugh shot by Covenanters in its courtyard. On a more romantic note, this is where the minstrel sang his famous lay to the Duchess of Buccleuch in Sir Walter Scott's 'The Lay of the Last Minstrel'.

18. St Abb's Head   10 O4
A porphyry fortress determined to resist the brutal waves, this 310ft cliff takes its name from Ebba who was shipwrecked off this coast in the 7thC and saved by what she considered a miracle. As a gesture of thanks, she founded a nunnery nearby and lived out her life as its abbess. Before it was destroyed by Danish marauders in AD870, St Ebba had welcomed many pilgrims – including the famous St Cuthbert in AD661 who allegedly spent the night in prayer standing in the sea up to his neck, nudged by playful seals. Coldingham Priory now stands on the site of her abbey, and a wide variety of seabirds nest in the rocky cliffs. Coldingham Bay is noted for its colourful pebbles.

19. Smailholm Tower   10 N5
7m W of Kelso, off B6404. Outcast on a bleak crop of volcanic rock, this 17thC border tower surveys a lush, Tweed valley of comfortable farms and villages. Well-preserved, roofed, but empty, this 57ft-high rectangle fascinated young Walter Scott who spent much of his boyhood at his grandfather's nearby farm. Later he wrote: 'I thought that shattered tower the mightiest work of human power,' and certainly, Smailholm is an outstanding example of a Border tower. A handsome chimney piece and stone window seats of what was once a hall are its most notable features.

20. Thirlestane Castle   10 N5
1m NE of Lauder, A697. Sumptuous and overpowering, this biggest of the Border castles was once the seat of Scotland's Chancellor, John Maitland, otherwise known as the Earl of Lauderdale – or 'L' in Charles II's notorious 'Cabal'. Intrigue and passion swirled round Thirlestane. Lauderdale's second wife was reputedly a rapacious and ruthless woman of overwhelming ambition, and it was she who nudged her husband into hiring William Bruce, the young Scots architect, to reconstruct and enlarge Thirlestane in the 17thC.

Although an admirer of Renaissance and Palladian work, Bruce retained the shell of the shabby old castle, but brought the whole thing together under a central tower crowned with an ogee (convex and concave) roof. Bruce employed Dutch craftsmen who executed the magnificent plaster ceiling. Lying on their backs on boards like Michelangelo, they worked hard and fast, calling for tobacco leaves, roses, thistles, hops and vines on which to model their motifs. This daring and spectacular plasterwork which took five years to complete, is probably unequalled in Scotland. Thirlestane's ballroom is its showpiece, and the Lauderdale eagle is well represented. *Open certain days, summer.*

21. Torwoodlee   10 N5
2m NW of Galashiels. This is one of 10 known

Iron Age walls probably destroyed by Roman soldiers: archaeologists found Roman pottery in the ditch here. Surviving only to 2ft, the wall marked a collision point between the Iron Age broch people and Roman outposts. A burial cist containing remains of a local woman was apparently interred with great care during the Roman demolition.

22. Traquair House 10 M5
8m ESE of Peebles, B709. Slake your thirst for ale or antiquity at this splendid mansion, an excellent example of Scots vernacular building. Originally a medieval hunting lodge, extensions were added throughout its long and romantic history. Since the 17thC, though, it has stayed unaltered and contains relics from the 13thC onwards: tapestries, glass, embroideries, silver and mementoes of Mary, Queen of Scots, and the Jacobite rebellions.

Apart from the 18thC library of rare books and intriguing priest's room with secret staircase, Traquair Ale is brewed by the present owner in the 18thC brewhouse, and

he has a licence to sell it. Refuelled, you can see the famous Bear Gates, locked in 1745 after Bonnie Prince Charlie had dropped in. The laird swore then never to open them until a Stuart sat on the throne again. Certainly, they have stayed shut ever since, but the tale itself may be doubtful.

As usual, Walter Scott fantasised madly about this history-drenched dwelling and possibly based his Tully-Veolan from Waverley on Traquair. Note the beautiful door-knocker, the ogee-roofed pavilion (ogee: using convex and concave curves), and the bed quilt reputed to have kept Mary, Queen of Scots, busy when she and Darnley stayed there in 1566. All this, plus woodland walks, craft shops and newly-planted maze. *Open summer.*

Traquair House

✤LOTHIAN✤

23. Bass Rock 10 N3
Off N Berwick. A paradise for ornithologists, this mile-wide crag hosts thousands upon thousands of gannets, or solan geese. Charles II once commented that there were two things he hated about Scotland – solan geese and the Solemn League and Covenant. Influenced, perhaps, by this distaste, he turned Bass into a gaol for Covenanters: they became known as the Martyrs of Bass. But the most extraordinary episode in its history was in 1691, when four young Jacobite prisoners hijacked the fortress by closing its gates against the entire garrison of 50, all of whom were down on the jetty loading coal. Amazingly, the young men held out for three years, aided by reinforcements and provisions from French ships. Eventually, their demands were honourably met.

Tide permitting, you can search for St Baldred's well, cradle and cobble (a rock, it's said, moved through telekinesis by the saint because it was dangerous to shipping). Bass was the last corner of Britain to recognise William of Orange as king, and yielded only when starved out by men-of-war.

24. Blackness 10 K3
4m NE of Linlithgow, B903. Few people seem drawn to this curiously faded area which was once a thriving trade centre with a harbour full of shipping important enough to be English fleet to burn in 1481. A few mercantile houses make Linlithgow worth looking at, but **Blackness Castle** is its main feature of interest. Jutting seawards in the shape of a ship, Blackness was once one of the most important fortresses in Scotland and under the 1707 Articles of Union had to be left fortified along with Edinburgh, Stirling and Dumbarton. Since then it has been a state prison, a powder magazine, and, for a while, a youth hostel.

25. Cairnpapple Hill 10 K3
3m N of Bathgate, off B792. Not much to see on this commanding hilltop except slight remains of a mound and ditch, some holes in the ground, and intoxicating views right over to the Firth of Forth six miles away. But these humps and bumps chronicle 1,000 years of primitive gods from neolithic times to the Bronze Age. Early farmers originally cleared the summit of oak and hazel – probably with axes hewn in the Lake District and North Wales – to make a sacred area, probably around 2,300BC. They erected three huge

stones which guarded cremation burials. Then, a few centuries later, the system was updated by enclosing the whole summit in a ditch cut from solid rock. Worshippers would have seen a circle of 26 standing stones sticking up like teeth. Finally, a great cairn 50ft in diameter was raised, then doubled in size. *Open summer; by arrangement, winter.*

26. Craigmillar Castle 10 M4
3¹/₂m SE of Edinburgh, A68. Housing estates impinge on this impressive ruin where Mary, Queen of Scots, fled to escape the intrigue of Holyrood, only to confront another 'bond of blood' – this time to murder her husband. Against this dramatic scenario, Craigmillar stands gauntly atop a green hill in the southern suburbs of Edinburgh. Originally an L-shaped 15thC tower, it was considerably enlarged 100 years later, and again in the 17thC. As well as strengthening its defences, more comfortable living quarters were added for the Queen. Many inside fittings have survived – stone window seats in the baronial hall, and the big open fireplace with its moulded canopy support and columns. This district is still known as Little France, from the members of Mary's French court who lodged here.

27. Crichton Castle 10 M4
7m SE of Dalkeith, B6367. Standing at the head of the River Tyne, you can't see Crichton until you're close enough to be apprehended, which shows how canny the old castle builders were when choosing their sites. The last inhabitant of Crichton was the wizard Francis Steward, a 'natural' grandson of James V who spent much of his time plaguing James VI. He once chased the King round Holyrood in his nightshirt, and on another occasion was caught sticking pins into an effigy of James. For this he was banished, and lived in Italy for many years 'improving' his art. Returning to Crichton, he embellished the courtyard to look like a palazzo in Ferrara. Although ruined, Crichton is worth visiting just for that.

28. Dirleton 10 M3
7m W of North Berwick, A198. A dovecote for 16thC doves and a yew-fringed green for 17thC bowlers are two of Dirleton's more idiosyncratic attractions. But basically, it was a great medieval castle built in the 13thC and a stronghold of the Norman family, De Vaux. Now it sports rather beautiful ruins with drum towers and 'clustered' donjon near the wide

village green of Dirleton. Called 'the most English village in Scotland', Dirleton looks wholesomely fertile. Beside its fragrant village, Castle Dirleton fought its last battle in 1650 when it fell against Cromwell's heavy artillery.

29. East Linton   10 N3
Sprightly village full of old world bonhomie. The parish kirk was built in 1733 and incorporates a 13thC chancel.
Preston Mill is the sole survivor of a score of mills that thrived beside the Tyne, and one of the smallest and oldest in Scotland. Grain has been milled on this site since the 12thC and a large part of the existing kiln, mill and outbuildings date from the 17thC. See how the miller worked – from drying the grain to its appearance as oatmeal from under the millstones, ready for bagging. Rank Hovis McDougall 'adopted' the mill in 1966, and now asks experienced millers reaching retirement to serve as custodians and keep the wheels turning.
Nearby **Phantassie Doocot** looks rather like a large, stone Dalek. It has 4ft-thick walls, shaped curiously into a horseshoe at the top, and nesting places for 500 birds. **Hailes Castle**. *2m SW of town*, is tumbledown, but worth a visit for the 16thC chapel, dungeon and water-gate. This manor-house pretending to be a castle is spotlessly maintained by the Department of the Environment on snooker-table-like tailored lawns. Bothwell brought Mary, Queen of Scots, here in 1567.

30. Edinburgh   10 L3
Plugging a vent in volcanic rock, Edinburgh Castle on Castle Rock was probably the site of an Iron Age fort rebuilt in the 7thC by King Edwin of Northumbria. By a quirk of language, his name mixed with 'Edinburgh' meaning fortress on a hill, and the town became Edwinesburg. Today battlements and bastions still tyrannise the city skyline. Historically, the castle is the core of this capital, and from it radiate buildings from almost every period of Scotland's passionate and violent past. From the 11thC St Margaret's Chapel, to Mons Meg, a massive 15thC cannon able to blast ironballs on foe a mile away, the city seethes with mansions, abbeys, cathedral, museums and inns. Walk the **Royal Mile** from the castle to Holyroodhouse and you walk a mile of history in stone.
Old Town Edinburgh spread from the original castle settlement into a maze of tall tenements with closes or wynds running between them. When elbow room got scarce in the 17th and 18thC, local citizens decided to drain stinking Nor' Loch and expand their city. **New Town** was the result: an orderly programme of classical architecture of crescents, avenues, leafy gardens, statuary – and taste! No surprise therefore that Edinburgh has some of the finest Georgian architecture in Britain. **The Georgian House**, *Charlotte Sq*, is furnished as it might have been by its first owners, showing domestic surroundings and reflecting the social conditions of that age.

Midlothian's papermaking has made Edinburgh famous for fine printing, and more books are printed here than almost anywhere in the world. Brewing and distilling are also important industries. Perhaps because of the world-famous Edinburgh Festival, the city has a name for culture. Museums and galleries abound – visit the **Royal Scottish**, *Chambers St*, the **National Museum of Antiquities**, *Queen St*, and the **National Gallery**, *The Mound*.
Princes Street is still one of the most celebrated thoroughfares in the world, despite an influx of chain stores. But escaping from mass production is easy in Edinburgh. **John Knox House** of 1490, *High St*, is complete with timbered galleries, and remains one of the most fascinating examples of late medieval Edinburgh. It contains relics and a splendid painted ceiling. **Gladstone's Land**, *Lawnmarket*, is furnished as a typical 17thC home and has excellent tempera painting on the walls and ceiling. Nearby **Lady Stair's House** is a museum with literary relics of Robert Burns, Sir Walter Scott and Robert Louis Stevenson.
The **High Kirk of St Giles** dates from the 14th and 15thC. Endowed with numerous memorials, it has endured a succession of enthusiastic over-restorations and alterations through the years. Although little remains of the original building, its square central tower of c1495 still raises unspoilt the famous Crown of St Giles. **Tron Church**, *High St*, of 1637, is so named because of the weighing beam, the tron, by which merchants' weights were checked, and which stood outside the church. **Parliament House**, *E of George IV Bridge*, dating from 1639, has a fine hammer-beam roof. This is where the Scottish Parliament met before the Union of 1707. Burns and Wordsworth supped ale at the White Hart Inn, and in Tanners Close in nearby West Port lived Burke and Hare, the murderers hanged in 1829 for selling the bodies of their victims for surgery. Visiting Edinburgh is like visiting other capitals. Drop your guard for a second, and you're likely to scoot off down some alley of history – only returning long after your holiday should have ended!

30. Edinburgh Castle   10 L3
Dominating Edinburgh, this sprawling castle crowns the huge rock 443ft above sea level. The oldest part still in use is St Margaret's Chapel of 1076. Wander through Mary, Queen of Scots's apartments, and the small room where her son, James VI was born. On the ceiling are his and Mary's initials surmounted by a crown. Her last letter, written before her execution, can be read at the National Library.

30. Edinburgh, Holyroodhouse   10 L3
E end of Canongate. Formal home of the Royal Family in Scotland, a historic royal palace in the 16thC. Above all, the building is associated with Mary, Queen of Scots. She lived and held court here from 1561 to 1567, and married Lord Darnley in the Old Abbey Chapel. Here, too, she watched as her husband and his fellow conspirators murdered her secretary, David Riccio. The present day palace was largely rebuilt by Sir William Bruce in the 17thC following its destruction during the Cromwellian occupation. The last Stuart to reside at Holyrood was Bonnie Prince Charlie: he briefly held court here before he was defeated at Culloden. The picture gallery and state apartments are outstanding. *Open most days*.

31. Forth Bridges   10 L3
Queensferry, 10m W of Edinburgh. For 800 years, travellers were ferried across the Firth of Forth that divides Dunfermline from Edinburgh. Queen Margaret, who regularly used this blowy route in the 11thC, gave her

Edinburgh

name to Queensferry. At North Queensferry peninsula, the opposite banks are only a mile apart and midway is the rocky islet of Inchgarvie. Each channel (north and south of the island) is 570 yds wide and 200ft deep. Daring engineers Sir John Fowler and Sir Benjamin Baker launched plans for a massive cantilever construction in 1882. Eight years later, it opened, having cost £3¼ million. Half a mile west is the Forth Road Bridge opened by the Queen in 1964 – the longest suspension bridge in Europe and costing £18 million.

Linlithgow Palace

32. Hopetoun House 10 L3
2m W of Queensferry. Parkland belonging to this estate drifts down to the sea not far from the Forth Bridges, and the grounds arc laid out in the style of Versailles. Sir William Bruce began building this enormous palace in 1699, and William Adam enlarged it. The east facade is entirely his, but his two sons Robert and John completed the extension some years later. The interior boasts splendid carving and plasterwork, plus portraits by Rubens, Van Dyck, Rembrandt and Canaletto. Deer and sheep roam the grounds, and there's a stables' museum featuring 'Horse and Man In Lowland Scotland'. *Open summer.*

33. House of the Binns 10 K3
4m E of Linlithgow, off A904. Binns is a corruption of 'ben', meaning hill, and in this Jacobean house of the hills overlooking the Firth of Forth, lived the notorious Sir Thomas Dalyell. On hearing of Charles I's execution, this eccentric Royalist vowed never again to cut his hair. And he didn't – even when beard and locks caused some embarrassment at the court of Charles II. During the Commonwealth, he travelled round Russia, served the Tsar, and came back for the Restoration to found a regiment now known as the Royal Scots Greys – the grey referring to white winter headgear copied from the Russians. Binns dates from 1478 and reflects the early 17thC transition in Scottish architecture from fortified stronghold to gracious mansion. See the magnificent plaster ceilings. *Open most days, summer.*

34. Hownam 10 O6
9½m SSE of Kelso. Excavations here in 1948 showed that Iron Age people chose this windswept hill to build a settlement of stone huts, platformed timber houses, stone broch towers and underground passages. Around 500BC, primitive re-developers put up a fort instead, with a massive, single rampart. Banks, ditches and gateways were added as general improvements until the Romans arrived. From then, an open settlement spread over the hill.

35. Linlithgow Palace 10 K3
S of the loch. More romantic than a castle on the Rhine – though looking rather like one from the banks of Loch Linlithgow – the history of this evocative ruin is closely bound to that of the Stuarts. James I began it, James V was born there, and so was Mary, Queen of Scots. In 1646, the last Scottish Parliament met there. Building started in the 15thC and continued till 1539. When the north quarter collapsed in 1607, it was rebuilt in Renaissance style. Star turns are the Great Hall, 100ft long, 35ft high and with a hammer-beam roof and fireplace extending the full width of the room. See the huge fireplace in the kitchens, too, and the royal apartments. A spiral staircase leads to Queen Margaret's Bower, a perfect little room with a fine view, from which the Queen is supposed to have watched anxiously for her husband's return from Flodden. Don't miss James V's fountain – Holyrood's is a copy of this. Adjacent to the palace is **St Michael's Church.** Fine Gothic with a Scottish accent, it's considered one of the loveliest parish churches in Britain. Controversy surrounds a

new gilt 'spire' – Sir Basil Spence's Crown of Thorns – many people feel it looks absurdly out of keeping with the rest of the Linlithgow 'complex'. Royal worshippers have knelt there under its columns and groins, and it was here that James IV had a premonition about the disaster at Flodden. Several sculptured slabs depict the Mockery of Christ and the Agony in the Garden.

36. Prestongrange Mining Museum and Historic Site 10 M4
Morrisons' Haven, 8m E of Edinburgh, B1348. Students of industrial archaeology can feast on an 1874 Cornish Beam Pumping Engine and its five-floor engine house here at this former colliery-turned-museum. Worked for over 800 years, the former power house is now an exhibition hall with many mining artefacts, plans, photographs and documents, plus two steam locos, a 100-year-old steam navvy, and a colliery winding engine. *Open summer; most days, winter.*

37. Prestonpans Battle Cairn 10 M3
E of Prestonpans, A198. An air, 'Hey, Johnnie Cope', sometimes sung in the folk clubs of Scotland, commemorates the Battle of Prestonpans on 21st September, 1745, when Bonnie Prince Charlie resoundingly beat the royal army under General John Cope. Planning to attack the Scots from the south, the English shipped from Aberdeen to Dunbar. But they put too much confidence in a bog between them and their foes, and at dawn the Scots came out of the mists with such surprise that in 15 minutes Cope's army was utterly routed. Today, a cairn marks the victory. Triumphantly, the army advanced into England as far as Derby. But they failed to pick up enough support, and had to fall back – defeated in the end at Culloden the following year.

38. Rosslyn Chapel 10 L4
7½m S of Edinburgh, off A703. Reckoned to be one of Scotland's most beautiful churches, this 15thC chapel is noted for its 13 different styles of florid Gothic arch. The exquisitely carved 'Prentice's Pillar' is said to have been finished by an apprentice during his master's absence. On his return, the man was so enraged by such youthful skill that he clouted the lad with a mallet, and killed him. The 14thC castle where the Scots defeated Edward I of England in his war with Robert the Bruce, is in ruins.

39. Traprain Law 10 N3
5m W of Dunbar, off A1. Archaeologists unearthed a pitful of silver on this 700ft whale-backed hill in 1919. Since the site was an Iron Age fort occupied continuously until the 11thC, they believe it was looted from the Romans and destined for the melting pot. The hoard is now in the Edinburgh National Museum of Antiquities.

40. Whitekirk 10 M3
5m SE of North Berwick, A198. Vatican records describe how this little church became famous because of a holy well that attracted more than 15,000 pilgrims in 1413. So impressed was a certain Aeneas Silvius Piccolomini that he walked barefoot there from Dunbar. Later, as a rheumatic Pope Pius II, he blamed the pilgrimage for his creaky joints. Others

claimed miracle cures, and James I honoured it with a new chapel. Suffragettes burned it down in 1914, but it has been well restored. The nearby two-storey barn, part 16thC, was once used by the monks of Holyrood to store grain.

41. Winton House 10 M4
6m SW of Haddington, B6355. Architects often refer whimsically to the 'Winton style' because it is such a gem of Scottish Renaissance, dating from about 1620. They rhapsodise about the ornamental stonework of the chimneys, Renaissance ballustrading, and Jacobean strapwork, but most of all, it is known for its splendid plaster ceilings. They were installed in honour of Charles I who visited the house in 1633. Winton so fascinated Sir Walter Scott that it is said he based Ravenwood Castle from 'The Bride of Lammermoor' on it. It also contains many fine pictures and furniture. *Open by arrangement.*

42. Woden Law 10 O6
4¹/2m S of Hownam. Roman roads connected the main forts of the day, and they can be traced over considerable distances. A good section of the road into Scotland, known as Dere Street, is visible next to Woden Law, the Iron Age fort. A centre for the Selgovae, it was abandoned after the Roman Conquest. The line of Roman siegeworks on the hill probably represents training manoeuvres, as the hill fort was unoccupied when they were built.

☙CENTRAL☙

Antonine Wall 10 K3
Bo'ness to Old Kilpatrick, best seen E of Bonnybridge, 12m S of Stirling, off A803. Dug by Roman legionnaires, it stretched 37 miles sea-to-sea across Scotland's 'waist', marking the chilly north westerly frontier of the Roman empire as well as the northern limits of Roman Britain. Despite its achievement, the wall was abandoned less than 50 years later, as the Romans needed their defences further south. Scotland, left to its own – in their eyes – uncouth habits, today bears few signs of the Romans' existence.
The wall was built in AD143 on the instructions of Emperor Antonius Pius – hence the name Antonine Wall. A stone-based turf rampart, it was garnished with 19 forts – one every two miles – probably with fortlets in between. Although it was built by legionnaires, auxiliaries of many different nationalities policed it. Distance slabs record the lengths of wall built by each unit, and some are on display at the Hunterian Museum in Glasgow. From archaeological finds like children's shoes, we can conclude that families lived with the soldiers on the wall. Unlike Hadrian's, this was an earthwork and as such sometimes needs careful observation to spot stretches of it that have been overgrown or levelled. One of the best sections is in the grounds of Callander House, *E of Falkirk,* and can be seen from the main road. Another chunk, *W of Falkirk on Bonnyhill–Camelon rd,* commands an impressive vista. Seabegs Wood, *1m W of Bonnybridge,* shows another angle. But Rough Castle, *6m W of Falkirk, B816,* is probably the best – a fort with a wall and ditches.

1. Bannockburn Battlefield 10 J3
2m S of Stirling, off M80. Bannockburn was one of the greatest battles in history; a crucial turning point in the Scottish wars of independence against England, it was the victory that fired Scotland's national identity. Brave and ambitious, Robert the Bruce had himself crowned King of Scotland and rallied the Scots under his royal leadership. On June 23rd, 1314, his army of 5,500 met an English force of 20,000 under Edward II on this 58 acre battlefield. A brilliant strategist, Bruce placed his troops on a height protected by Bannock Burn – a tidal and boggy stream still visible today. The Scots booby-trapped the bogs, and partly concealed themselves in scrub woodland. Edward confidently launched his heavy cavalry – the armoured fighting vehicles of medieval warfare – plus his foot and archers across Bannock Burn, and got trapped between bog and pikes. As Edward retreated, a reserve force of 2,000 'small folk' – Scots crofters and artisans – poured down from behind Gillies' Hill and turned defeat into rout.
The effects of this cunningly conceived and bravely fought battle were to last for 200 years, until the Battle of Flodden in 1513, when the English got their revenge and defeated King James IV. All the battle landmarks are there today, though you have to close your eyes to the housing estates and slag heaps of the nearby village of Bannockburn. To preserve this patch of momentous Scottish history, the National Trust bought the battlefield and built a rotunda where an audio visual programme, 'The Forging of a Nation' tells the story of those two summer days. Fragments of the Borestone, a boulder with a socket where Bruce is supposed to have set his standard, are preserved, and there is also a heroic bronze of Bruce in battle trappings. *Open summer.*

Bannockburn Monument

2. Castle Campbell 10 K2
Dollar Glen, 1m N of Dollar, off A91. Extraordinarily difficult to spot from anywhere in Dollar Glen, you eventually see this castle rearing above the trees and bracken. Optimist and politician, the first Earl of Argyll, bought it at the end of the 15thC because he needed somewhere to live near the King's court at Stirling. Not only was it called Castle Gloom before he changed its name, but it stood where the burns of Care and Sorrow flow down to the town of Dollar or dolour. Undismayed, he enlarged and embellished it in early Renaissance style so that today the courtyard, Great Hall and the huge barrel roof of the third floor are all worth seeing. Certainly not as depressing as its names suggest, this is an area of cataracts and chasms – Dollar may come from the Gaelic for 'dark place' meaning the glen woods. There's also a village nearby called Pool of Muckart!

3. Clackmannan Tower 10 K2
On hill W of Clackmannan, A907. A bastard line of Bruces related to the royal house acquired this tower in 1359. They stayed there until the end of the 18thC when the last Bruce heiress unofficially 'knighted' selected

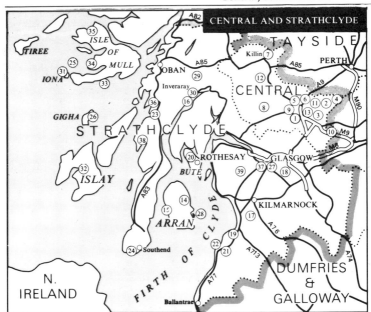

guests with her ancestor's great two-handed sword! One of these 'knights' was Robert Burns. The tower, which was built and altered between the late 14th and 17thC, is one of the best preserved keeps in Scotland and commands wide views over Forth country. In Clackmannan itself, see the Old Tolbooth or 'clack', the ancient Stone of Mannan, and the stepped Town Cross.

4. Devil's Mill and Cauldron Linn   10 K2
Off A823 at Rumbling Bridge. Roaring and cascading down 2,000ft in just 30 miles, the Devon River inspired Victorian travel-writers to new peaks of romantic enthusiasm. Devil's Mill and Cauldron Linn are the best known falls along this river with spectacular gorges. It is spanned here by two bridges: one built in 1713 and the other in 1816. Robert Burns is said to have turned away from Rumbling Bridge without comment. There's no accounting for poets!

5. Doune Castle   10 J2
Doune, off A84. Superb 14thC castle beside two rivers. Once a royal palace and once a state prison, it is now finely restored to show how people lived in those dramatic days of danger and intrigue. See the Baron's Hall, banqueting hall, kitchen and Queen Mary's Room. Lavatories, passageways and spiral stairs were built into the very thickness of the masonry, and you can see the fireplaces and ventilation louvres. There's even a secret room from which the laird could watch what was happening in the hall without being seen himself.
A motor museum houses Lord Doune's collection of vintage and post vintage cars including a unique 1938 Alfa Romeo coupé. The gardens include a pinetum dating from the 1860s with rare and exotic conifers. *Open summer.*

6. Dunblane Cathedral   10 J2
Dunblane, 6m N of Stirling, A9. Having suffered after the Reformation, this 13thC building was re-roofed in 1893 when the whole church was restored. The tower is Norman, and David I gave Dunblane its bishopric. The Dean's House, built in 1624, is worth seeing, as is the cathedral museum with its fine library.

7. Finlarig Castle   10 L1
Nr Killin, 22m WSW of Aberfeldy. A beheading

pit is the macabre feature of interest at this ivy-grown ruined stronghold among the trees by Loch Tay. Heads of the gentry rolled by means of a crude guillotine called The Maiden or, sometimes, The Widow, while common folk were hanged on a neighbouring oak tree. It's thought to be the only pit left in Scotland.

Forth/Clyde Canal   10 J3/K3
A monumental relic of the Industrial Revolution is this 38 mile canal which linked the industrial towns of western Scotland with the eastern coast at Grangemouth. Its summit is 156ft above sea level – which means 39 locks. It follows the Antonine Wall closely and was built between 1768 and 1790. Though sadly neglected, it provides excellent walks.

8. Inchmahome Priory   10 H2
On island in Lake Menteith, 4m E of Aberfoyle. Lake Mentieth has three islands in its square mile of water. Inchmahome – the Isle of Rest – is largest, and has the remains of a 13thC Augustinian priory. Parts of the nave and choir survive, and David II married his second wife, Margaret, here in 1362. There are several medieval tombs, too. As a little girl, Mary Stuart stayed in secrecy at the priory for nearly a year after the Battle of Pinkie in 1547. Before sailing for France, she is said to have busied herself with the garden, called Queen Mary's Bower.

9. Keir Gardens   10 J2
6m NW of Stirling, off B824. Chopin stayed in this flowery mansion in 1848 and might have composed a bar or two looking over rhododendrons. Azaleas, daffodils, a water garden and a yew tree house make Keir Gardens a delightful outing for the whole family. *Open certain days, summer.*

10. Kinneil House   10 K3
4m NW of Linlithgow, off A904. Experiments in the outhouse of this 17thC seat of the Dukes of Hamilton revolutionised industry. Around 1765, James Watt developed his invention of the steam engine here and erected it at a nearby colliery. He went on to revolutionise the propulsion of ships. Inside the house are decorated ceilings and a fine collection of paintings.

11. Menstrie Castle   10 K2
Menstrie, 5m NE of Stirling, A91. Scotland's

first imperialist, Sir William Alexander, was born here in 1567 and the Nova Scotia Room commemorates his efforts to found a Scots colony overseas. Cunning and far-seeing, Sir William planned to sell property and titles from the new colony to knights and gentlemen to raise money for the colonisation of Nova Scotia. A beautiful display of 107 shields bearing the arms of baronets of the Order created in 1625 is enough to convert anyone to heraldry in seconds.

In its day, Menstrie Castle was a lively manor house, but it decayed to a fragment which was almost demolished, until the National Trust for Scotland and the local authority agreed to save it. Today it is the focal point of an attractive housing estate, and contains four flats. *Open certain days, summer, or by arrangement.*

12. Rob Roy MacGregor's Grave   10 H1
Balquhidder churchyard, 14m NNW of Callender, off A84. Waterlogged mosses stretching eerily westwards from Stirling almost to Loch Lomond – this was red-headed Rob Roy's kingdom. He knew this strange marshland probably better than anyone: its hidden paths, causeways, fords and islands. Born second son of a Highland laird, he started a 'protection racket', and survived by stealing his southern neighbours' cattle if they refused to pay up. Herds disappeared into the watery wilderness of Flanders Moss and were never seen again. Yet he was a sort of Scottish Robin Hood, giving to the poor, fighting repressive authority, and staunchly loyal to the Stuarts in the Jacobite Rising. Despite his wild life, he died peacefully in bed, aged 64. Three flat stones enclosed by railings mark the graves of Rob, his wife, and two of his sons. The church itself contains the 8thC St Angus' Stone, a 17thC bell from the old church and old Gaelic bibles.

13. Stirling   10 J2
Well-mannered university town busily minding its own business in the shadows of its formidable castle, perched like some prehistoric skyscraper high on a rock. Scotland's major stronghold for centuries, Stirling was first occupied by the Romans, then the legendary King Arthur, and from the 12thC the sprawling castle was the favourite residence of the Scottish kings.

One of the most interesting of the many old buildings in the town is **Mar's Wark**, on the approach to Stirling Castle. The first Earl of Mar wanted to copy the castle's palace block. He failed, and today his unfinished palace still displays the extravagant carving with which he tried to impress his royal employers. The Mars stayed there until 1715 when the 6th Earl had to flee after heading the Jacobite Rising. The building became a barracks and then a workhouse (hence Mar's Wark or Work) and finally a ruin after its battering by Jacobite forces in 1746.

Opposite Mar's Wark is **Argyll's Lodging**, built in 1632 by Sir William Alexander of Menstrie, founder of Nova Scotia. It's reckoned to be the most perfect example of a private Renaissance town house in Scotland. Rich in Italianate sculpture and conical turrets, it could almost be a mini castle. Charles II slept there in 1650 as the guest of the Marquess of Argyll. Ten years later, Charles had Argyll beheaded. Damaged and defaced during its long years as a military hospital after 1791, the building is now a youth hostel.

The Church of the Holy Rude is the only church in Scotland still in use which has witnessed a coronation. In 1567, Mary, Queen of Scots' son, James VI, was crowned, then carried back to his castle nursery. John Knox officiated at the ceremony. In 1404 the entire town burned down and with it the parish church. The present one was started a

few years after that and in 1656 split into the East Kirk and the West Kirk. Not until 1935 were the halves reunited. This large Gothic church was quiet before the Reformation, presumably because most regal events took place in the castle's Chapel Royal. But afterwards, as a reformed kirk, its ministers were often militant and doughty: the head of the Reverend James Guthrie stayed spiked on the Netherbow Port in Edinburgh for 28 years for his Covenanting zeal.

An interesting few hours can be spent in the **Smith Art Gallery and Museum,** *Albert Place*. Thomas Stuart Smith was a benevolent, bewhiskered 19thC eccentric, passionately devoted to painting. Although Stirling-born, he hardly ever set foot in the town, but rather unexpectedly arranged for it to inherit his considerable fortune. This gave birth to the art gallery and museum. Stuart Smith's art collection may not be to today's taste, but the museum contains the remarkable Stirling Heads from the castle. Once adorning the ceiling of the king's presence chamber there, the 56 oak roundels were removed in the 18thC when one fell on a soldier and killed him. Most are dispersed, but the museum collection shows the liveliness of the king's master mason who carved them. Also on show is the oldest curling stone in Scotland (1511) and a 15thC measuring jug.

In Broad Street, see the Town House, Mercat Cross and Cowane's Hospital, built in 1637. Nearby is the Landmark Centre which brings alive the history of the town in a multi-screen audio visual show. Here you will also find crafts, books and a tea garden.

Stirling Castle

13. Stirling Castle   10 J2
Thrilled by Leonardo da Vinci's discoveries, a priest leapt from the battlements of this historic castle and tried to fly. Flapping wildly with his home-made wings, he plummeted to the ground, picked himself up, and tried again. Not surprisingly, he never succeeded, but survived with a few bruises, much disappointment, and tumultuous jeers from a nasty crowd. Airborne priests and the first nude sculptures in Scotland are just two of the historical quirks this worldly, gay, tragic and very human castle offers a visitor with imagination. And when you first peer cautiously over those battlements or see the walls rising like a continuation of the massive 250ft rock on which the castle stands, you feel flying might be quite easy after all.

Like Edinburgh, Stirling Castle is built on a volcanic plug of rock and has commanded the narrow point of the Firth of Forth – Gateway to the Highlands – since the Dark Ages. You approach it up the steep High Street lined with old houses, many recently restored and on the whole more authentic than those in Edinburgh's celebrated Royal Mile.

As one of the most strategic castles in Scotland, Stirling has been won and lost, lost and won, with bewildering frequency. Hard facts start around 1124 when Alexander I of Scotland is recorded as having died there: the castle was already centuries old then. A favourite royal residence of the Scottish kings, not much of the medieval building remains but there's plenty to see in the Parliament Hall, palace and Chapel Royal which are dazzling 15th and 16thC Renaissance. Mary, Queen of Scots, was crowned here as a baby and lived at the castle until she was five. The initials MR 1561 mark her look-out on the battlements. From here you can see seven battlefields – including the momentous Bannockburn. Jousts took place on the low ground to the south.

Housed in the castle is the **Argyll and Sutherland Highlanders' Museum**, a fine regimental museum with a notable medal collection. The officers' mess is also in the castle which has been used as a barracks for many years. The Royal chapel was once the regiment's dance hall, but is now a memorial to the regiment which garrisoned Stirling Castle for so long. Royal portraits and regimental banners adorn the walls. *Open summer.*

13. Stirling, Wallace Monument   10 J2
1¹/₂m NNE of Stirling, off A997. Truculent English governors had taken over every castle in Scotland, and William Wallace was livid. Born a humble laird, he gathered a few friends together and slew some soldiers at Lanark Castle. As a reprisal, the governor burned down Wallace's house and slaughtered his wife. That night a demented Wallace broke into the governor's bedroom and killed him. Then he and his friends attacked the soldiers and took over the town of Lanark.

By sheer bravery and skill, Wallace and his ever-growing band captured castle after castle. It took years, but eventually the English Governor General, the Earl of Surrey, gathered a mighty army at Stirling to defeat Wallace once and for all. He failed, and in 1297 at the Battle of Stirling Bridge, the English fled back over the border. Wallace

was made Guardian of Scotland and for a little while there was peace.

Edward retaliated and totally defeated Wallace at Falkirk in 1298. Wallace escaped, but was betrayed in 1305, taken to London and condemned to die a traitor's death. Half-hanged, then beheaded, his body was cut in pieces, his head put on a pole on London Bridge, and parts of him sent for public exhibition to Newcastle, Berwick, Stirling and Perth as an example to Scots who opposed the King.

This 220ft towering monument built in 1870 crowns Abbey Craig and commands a view equalled only by that from Stirling Castle. The little museum contains statues and relics, but most fascinating is a sword said to have been Wallace's. A chain-mailed Wallace surveys the scene of his victory.

The Trossachs   10 H2
Trossachs means 'bristly country' and it refers to the scenic pass between Loch Katrine and Loch Achray which is now part of the Queen Elizabeth National Forest Park. Sir Walter Scott and Wordsworth gaped in wonder as they rowed down Loch Katrine and saw it for the first time. Scott called Katrine 'Cateran' or 'robber' because the district was so wild and dangerous in the days before roads. Here inspiration was drawn for two of the best-loved poems in the English language: Scott's 'The Lady of the Lake' and Coleridge's 'The Solitary Reaper'. Today, 170 miles of track winds through the forest park, 40 of them waymarked and used by pony trekkers and ramblers.

❧STRATHCLYDE❧

Arran (Isle of)   10 E5
An attractive and unspoilt island, mountainous in the north and pastoral in the south, with sandy shores. For the best views, climb Goat Fell.

14. Arran, Brodick Castle and Gardens   10 E5
1¹/₂m N of Brodick pier. Goatfell mountain bodyguards this treasure-castle which is the oldest habitable house owned by the National Trust in Scotland. Parts of it go back to the 14thC, though most is 17th and mid 19thC. The Hamiltons owned the castle from 1503 and used it more as a retreat for hunting or avoiding the limelight than as a centre for affairs of state.

Unvisited for almost two centuries, two fortuitous marriages gave Brodick new life. The first emptied an amazing art collection into its rooms. The second gave a popular Scottish architect, James Gillespie Graham, a commission to double the size of Brodick with a new west wing. Today, the castle contains silver, porcelain, fine paintings, sporting pictures and trophies. Of the many beautifully-furnished apartments, the drawing room, with Italian marquetry, French gilt and ormulu pieces, a Chinese screen and Venetian mirrors, is the best. Outside is one of the finest rhododendron gardens in Britain. The climb to Goatfell, 2,866ft, starts at the south entrance to Brodick's grounds. *Open summer; gardens daily, all year.*

15. Arran, King's Cave   10 E6
W shore, 2m N of Blackwaterfoot. Caves gouge this stretch of coastline, and the largest one is said to be where Robert the Bruce and his followers lay in hiding for several months. King's Cave is one of the possible settings for the 'Bruce and spider' legend. Other caves are known as his Kitchen, Cellar, and Stable. There is also a tradition that Fingal used them. Carvings decorate the walls.

16. Auchindrain Museum   10 F2
5¹/₂m SW of Inverary, A83. A communal-tenancy farm with traditional dwellings and barns dating from the late 18th and early 19thC. Furnishings are on display, and the land is now farmed using traditional methods. Restaurant, craft shop and picnic places for not so traditional visitors. *Open summer; by arrangement, winter.*

17. Bachelors' Club   10 G6
Tarbolton, 7¹/₂m NE of Ayr, off A758. This thatched house of the 17thC gave Burns the chance to debate and philosophise with friends deep into the night. For eight years it was the focal point of his intellectual life. Now it's furnished as it might have been then, complete with old refectory table, country chairs and kitchen. Since 1971 when it was refurbished, a local Burns club has met there annually to celebrate the poet's birthday. *Open summer; by arrangement, winter.*

18. Bothwell Castle   10 J4
Uddingston, 7m SE of Glasgow, A74. Resolute and muscular, this great stone castle is picturesquely set above the Clyde valley. Built in the 13thC by William de Moravia, it is famous for its circular keep approached over a ditch and drawbridge. The ditch was cunningly used to drain the lavatories and send sewage through the outer walls down river. The castle was the principal base in western Scotland during the occupation. Today, we can see the roofless fortress – walls 60ft-high and 15ft-thick in places – and the great donjon.

19. Burns Cottage and Museum   10 G6
2m S of Ayr, B7024 at Alloway. Literary pilgrims swarm here to honour the thatched birthplace of their bard. They find it furnished as simply as it might have been when he first yowled his greeting to the world. Next door is a museum containing manuscripts, letters and

Robert Burns Cottage

other relics, and the gardens are pleasantly laid out. This is the beginning of the Burns' Heritage Trail which follows places hallowed by contact with the poet. *Open summer.*

20. Bute (Isle of)   **10 F4**
Popular holiday island with an ancient history, experienced nowhere better than **Rothesay Castle.** Stormed by Vikings in the 13thC, this spruced-up ruin is certainly one of the largest and finest medieval castles in Scotland. The Bute family cleared out its moat, filled it with water, and replaced the drawbridge and gatehouse before handing it over to the nation. And today, it is a favourite haunt of visitors to the Clyde resorts. Four round towers linked by a wall enclose a circular courtyard and keep – a design unique in Scotland. You can still see where Norsemen breached the walls.

21. Crossraguel Abbey   **10 G7**
2m SW of Maybole, A77. Benedictine monks lived here in this wild hill country as peacefully as history allowed, from 1244. In 1570 the Earl of Cassilis basted the abbot of this monastery in oil and roasted him over a slow fire until he signed away his ecclesiastical lands. The romantic well-preserved ruins of the monks' embattled settlement are worth visiting: gatehouse, keep tower, church and chapter house. The monks were here until 1592, and had the right to their own mint.

22. Culzean Castle and Country Park   **10 G7**
12m SSW of Ayr, A719. Commanding the cliff, Culzean (pronounced Cull-ain) challenges the elements with mighty elegance. Founded on a headland cheese-holed with smugglers' caves, the castle was designed by Robert Adam in the 1770s, and is one of the most complete examples of his genius. Working with the old Kennedy stronghold, he added wings and towers to create a great Gothic sham. Externally, the castle is rather un-Adam: presumably he adapted his style to the old fortress and its craggy setting. But inside it is one of his loveliest conceptions. Fine plasterwork, an exquisite oval staircase, and a round drawing room with furniture and carpet specially designed for it, are the star features. The gardens and exotic woodlands became Scotland's first country park, and today Culzean is among the National Trust's top six most visited properties. *Open summer.*

23. Dunadd Fort   **10 D2**
4m NNW of Lochgilphead, W of A816. The site of the ancient capital of the kingdom of Dalriada, from which the Celtic kingdom of Scotland sprang. This dynamic kingdom constantly harassed neighbouring Pictland, and Dunadd was skilfully fortified using natural rock outcrop and surrounding treacherous bog (now drained). From this settlement sprang Celtic Scotland. Near the summit – now protected by a glass frame – is a boar carved in the rock and the sign of a footprint. This is probably where early kings were invested with royal power. Nearby is an inscription in Ogham alphabet – an Irish script using vertical strokes along a horizontal bar for letters. Both boar and inscription are Pictish in style, which is surprising, and archaeologists think they might be the work of triumphant Pict raiders. Finds excavated at Dunadd tell us a lot about the early Scots. Clay moulds were used to cast bronze brooches and pins, and crucibles for melting bronze were unearthed. Brooch designs and pottery shards suggest links with Vikings and France. Tools found included saws, gouges, and querns for grain grinding.

24. Dunaverty Rock   **10 D7**
Southend. Known locally as 'Blood Rock' because of the 300 people slaughtered by Covenanters there in 1647, it was formerly the site of Dunverty Castle, a Macdonald stronghold.
St Columba, the gentle Irish monk, is supposed to have first set foot on Scottish soil west of Southend, at Keil. **St Columba's Footsteps** are imprinted on a flat-topped rock near the ruin of an old chapel.

25. Fingal's Cave   **10 B8**
Staffa, 8m off W coast of Mull. Seen by steamer and boat trips from Oban and Mull. The Gaelic name for this huge basaltic grotto is 'Uaimh Binn', or 'musical cave', and the booming echoes inspired Mendelssohn to compose his Hebrides overture. A majestic arch domes the entrance to the cave and rests of black, pillared walls: altogether, it's 227ft long and 66ft above sea level. It was discovered accidentally by Sir Joseph Banks who was blown into the Sound of Mull on his way to Iceland in 1772. Fingal, or Fion-na-Gael, was a great Gaelic hero.

26. Gigha (Isle of)   **10 C5**
Ferry from West Loch Tarbert and Tayinloan (no cars). A Hong Kong merchant banker recently bought this fertile blob off the west coast of Kintyre. It has a ruined church at Kilchattan and Achamore House gardens are famous for their semi-tropical plants.

27. Glasgow   **10 H4**
Glasgow is like a plain person who can talk away his face in five minutes. Always Edinburgh's ugly sister, Glasgow was once renowned as 'the second city of the Empire'. It is not that hard to understand why.
Medieval Glasgow takes a morning to see. Its beautiful cathedral is a fine example of Early English 13thC style and is dedicated to Glasgow's patron saint and founder, St Mungo.
The city's coat-of-arms shows, among other things, a robin (Mungo is supposed to have put the head back on a decapitated robin) and a salmon with a ring in its mouth. Legend tells that the King of Strathclyde gave his wife a ring, but she thought so little of him that she gave it to a boyfriend. By chance, the King spotted him wearing it. He wrenched it off his finger, flung it in the Clyde and then asked the Queen to produce it. She appealed to Mungo for help, and he told her to cast a line in the river – she actually caught a fish with the ring in its mouth!
Opposite Mungo's cathedral stands Glasgow's oldest house, Provand's Lordship, built in 1471 and with medieval furniture inside today. **Provan Hall** is also 15thC and said to be the most perfect example of a simple pre-Reformation house remaining in Scotland. Much architecture in Glasgow shows the influence of the Adam family. **Pollock House** was designed by William Adam in 1752 and contains a superb collection of Spanish paintings, glass, Oriental and Egyptian furniture, and some work by Blake. The Trades House in Glassford Street is by Robert Adam.
By the early 18thC, Glasgow had started lucrative trade with America, and her tobacco market became the greatest in Europe. The tobacco lords became the aristocracy and their mansions dotted the banks of the Clyde. From the Industrial Revolution, the town grew rapidly and today Glasgow is Scotland's largest city.
Glasgow's real architectural splendour is

Art Galleries, Glasgow

Victorian: she is the supreme surviving
Victorian city built of red sandstone. The
focus of this achievement is Kelvingrove Park,
by the river. The **Hunterian Museum** here
is probably the most interesting in Scotland.
Nearby, the spectacular municipal **Art
Gallery and Museum** contains the richest
collections of any galleries in Britain other
than London and Edinburgh. Other places to
visit are: the Museum of Transport (which
includes the oldest car in Scotland and a large
show of trams), the People's Palace (a local
history museum), and Haggs Castle, a
historical museum for children. See the
Egyptian Halls, *Union St*, remarkable for their
detached curtain walls of glass, and Gardner's
Warehouse, *Jamaica St* – a pioneering
example of iron frame and glass.

28. Holy Island (St Molaise)   10 F6
5m S of Brodick, off Arran. A discipline of St
Columba, St Molaise, is supposed to have
lived on this 1,000ft-high island – hence its
name. The Saint's Cave is 30ft above sea
level. Its roof and walls are covered with
inscriptions and carvings from different
periods, including a runic one in letters 1½ins
long. On the shore below the cave is a circular
well said to have been the saint's bathtub, and
a large block of sandstone, surrounded by
artificial recesses, is called the Saint's Chair.
For many centuries the well was thought to
have healing powers.

29. Inishail Chapel   10 F1
*10m N of Inverary on islet in Loch Awe. Boat
from Lochawe village, B840.* One of the islands
studding this large and beautiful loch is the
'isle of repose'. Once the site of a Cistercian
nunnery and for ages the burial ground of the
various chieftains who held sway in this part of
Argyllshire, Inishail's chapel was dedicated to
St Findoc in 1257. Lying on the ground are
two fine carved slabs from the 14th or 15thC.

30. Inverary   10 F2
Situated by the harbour at the head of Loch
Fyne, this is one of the most attractive towns
in Scotland. The old village, burnt by
Montrose in 1664, was demolished in 1743 by
the Duke of Argyll who had decided to
rebuild his castle and to replan the town.
Robert Milne designed the Town House in
1753 and the Palladian church in 1794. A
140ft granite tower houses the world's second
heaviest ring of 10 bells, whose melodious
peal regularly echoes over the loch. There are
excellent views from the tower.
From a distance, Inverary Castle looks almost
theatrical with its conical towers and fancy
crenellation – as if you could push over its
cardboard facade. Perhaps the trees round
here add to its Gothic fairytale atmosphere:

Inverary Castle

huge oaks, beech and ash, firs and limes by
the thousand. Roger Morris designed
Inverary along romantic and pseudo-medieval
lines for the Duke of Argyll in 1743. It has
pointed windows and arches, bridges across a
dry moat, and bits added upstairs as each
successive resident decided he wanted more
bedrooms. Apart from roomsfull of historic
relics, there are tapestries, Adam
chimney-pieces and portraits by
Gainsborough. The extensive damage caused
by fire in 1975 has now been impressively
restored. *Open summer.*

31. Iona (Isle of)   10 B1
*Off SW tip of Mull. A849 to Fionnphort, then
ferry. Also steamer trips from Oban.* In AD563 St
Columba stepped ashore this island with 12
followers and began the effective
Christianisation of Scotland. From the
monastery he founded, he and his monks went
out to preach the Word all over the mainland.
The monastery was often attacked by Norse
raiders and had to be replaced in 1203. Parts
of a nunnery remain along with the Street of
the Dead, leading from Martyrs' Bay to Reilig
Oran, which is thought to be the oldest
Christian burial-place in Scotland. Iona was a
popular burial ground for Royalty and other
eminent people, as a common belief held that
the island would be saved when all else sank.
Macbeth lies here, and three of the once 360
crosses are still standing.
Columba's monastery is now the home of the
Iona Community which was founded in 1938
by Dr George Macleod. It has handled much
restoration of the cathedral which has a
beautiful interior and interesting carvings. St
Oran's Chapel, c1080, is also restored.

Iona Abbey

32. Islay (Isle of)   10 B4
Islay distils whisky and also has a curious
circular building, Bowmere Round Church,
which was designed by a Frenchman in 1769.
It is said to be round so that no evil spirits –
bottled or otherwise – can hide in any corners.
Bowmore is a good example of an 18thC
countryside kirk.

Mull (Isle of)   11 C8
The third largest of the Hebridean islands,
sea lochs and creeks erode the west and south
coast in great Baroque swirls, while in the
north, Mull is bracken green with woods
flooding the sheltered valleys. The main town
is Tobermory, a polychrome wall of early
19thC houses jammed tight in a curve round
the harbour. In 1588 the Duque di Florencia,
a remnant of the Spanish Armada, sank in
Tobermory Bay with an alleged 3 million gold
doubloons on board. Only a few trinkets from
this legendary treasure trove have been found.
Also of interest are: 19thC Torosay Castle, *nr
Craignure*, a Scottish Baronial fairy-tale castle
by David Bryce; Duart Castle, an aggressive
13th–17thC monolith raised on a great
bastion of rock on the east point of Duart Bay;
Salen, a small village sheltering in a wooded
site; Mull Little Theatre, *Dervaig*, Scotland's
smallest professional theatre.

33. Mull, Carsaig Arches   11 C9
On shore 3m W of Carsaig. Remarkable
tunnels, the largest 150ft long and 60ft high,
formed by the sea in the basaltic rock. They
can only be reached at low tide after a three
mile walk. On the way is the curiously-carved
Nuns' Cave. It's said that nuns driven from
Iona during the Reformation sheltered here,
and that the carvings are the original designs

of the Iona Crosses. From here the freestone for Iona Cathedral was hewn, and it was sculptured in the cave.

34. Mull, The Burg 11 B8
5m W of track from B8085, N shore of Loch Scridain. Here you'll find MacCulloch's tree – a fossilised imprint possibly 50 million years old. You can reach it at low tide. This conifer embedded in upright rock, is one of the most famous fossil trees in the country. Cars are inadvisable beyond Tiroran, and the five mile walk is rough in places. En route over this National Trust terrain you might see golden eagles, harriers, peregrine, sparrow-hawk, buzzards, ravens or plovers. This area is also a haven for red deer, wild goats and otters.

35. Mull, The Old Byre Heritage Centre 11 B7
Dervaig. Winner of awards for its dramatic revival of crofting life. All the old passions and turbulence of the Highland Clearances are brought to life through a combination of theatre, tableaux and audio-dramatisation. Afterwards, enjoy a cuppa in the tea room. *Open summer.*

Old Byre Heritage Centre

36. Nether Largie Cairns 10 D2
1/2m SW of Kilmartin. By far the most impressive Bronze Age burial site in Scotland, this fine complex at Kilmartin stretches over three miles. Earliest is a neolithic chambered tomb, Nether Largie South, followed by six others containing stone coffins. People of this era were often buried with smart beakers which were probably beer mugs. Pottery

making had greatly improved, and the vessels were prized. Historically, the site is fascinating because linear cemeteries are unusual in Scotland, belonging mainly to the great Bronze Age culture of Wessex that produced Stonehenge.

37. Paisley Shawl Collection 10 H4
High St, Paisley. Whenever a bride was 'kirked' in Scotland (at church for the first time with her husband), she wore a Paisley shawl. Shawls are part of Scotland's culture, and this museum has the most complete collection of Paisley shawls in the world. These local shawls weren't original in design or concept, but clever mechanical imitations of the Turkish and Indian fabrics that flowed into Britain after the Napoleonic wars. Costly Kashmir shawls were favourites, and Paisley weavers copied them on the loom: the 'pine-pattern' typical of Paisley work is a direct pinch from Kashmir.

38. St Columba's Cave 10 D3
1m N of Ellary on W shore of Loch Killisport, 10m SW of Ardrishaig. Traditionally associated with St Columba's arrival in Scotland, the cave has a rock shelf with an altar. Above it are carved crosses. A large basin, possibly a Stone Age mortar, may have been used as a font. People occupied the cave from the Middle Stone Age, and traces of houses and a ruined 13thC chapel can be seen outside.

39. Weaver's Cottage 10 G4
Kilbarchan, 5m W of Paisley, off A761. This cosy little weaver's home was built in 1723 by the Bryden family: their initials are carved on the lintel above the front door. After them, successive generations of two families followed the same craft here and never found it necessary to alter the place. Called a 'cruck' cottage because of the curved timber supporting the roof, the walls were built of 'land gatherings' – boulders collected from the moor and roughly dressed. Handloom weavers worked and lived here until 1940, and this museum was inspired by the people of Kilbarchan who gave many items of local interest. Apart from a furnished parlour, there are tools, shoulder shawls, shirt patterns, some tartans, village silks, cambrics, muslins, woollens and linen. *Open most days, summer.*

🎭 DUMFRIES AND GALLOWAY 🎭

1. Castle of Park 10 F9
9m ESE of Stranraer, off A75 by Glenluce. A castle-cum-house begun in 1590 and recently restored. Still complete, this mansion was built by Thomas Hay of Park and it's a good example of how castles lost their aggressive appearance in the later 16th and 17thC as comfort became more important: windows got bigger and rooms were decorated with woodcarving, wrought iron work and painted plaster. Canvas or timber panels came into fashion at the expense of the militaristic parapets, turrets and gunloops.

2. Caerlaverock Castle 10 K9
9m S of Dumfries, off B725. Isolated in the middle of a coastal swamp, this shield-shaped castle of the Maxwells was built in 1220. Great double towers dominate the entrance, and it is triangular in plan. You can still see the grooves for portcullis and drawbridge machinery, and a loophole through which molten lead or quicklime was poured on foes. Edward's siege engines in 1300 devastated Caerlaverock in two days, but in 1638 it lasted 13 weeks against Covenanters. Over the gateway between the two towers is the Maxwell crest and motto. Nearby are the treacherous Solway mudflats which must have protected the castle to some extent against

heavily armed knights. The interior was reconstructed in the 17thC as a Renaissance mansion with fine carving, and the whole place has a fairy-tale charm.

3. Cardoness Castle 10 H9
1m SW of Gatehouse-of-Fleet, on A75. Ruined home of the McCullochs of Galloway, this 15thC tower house is four storeys high with a vaulted basement. Built on a rocky hill by the Water of Fleet, it is a good example of the way tower houses became more comfortable. Finding it inconvenient to have four floors each of just one room and approached by a circular or turnpike stair, residents divided up each large room into smaller ones. Cardoness has a maze of chambers, an original stairway, stone benches and elaborate fireplaces.

4. Drumlanrig Castle 10 K7
3m N of Thornhill, Dumfriesshire, off A76. A white elephant in pink sandstone is one way of looking at this heap of stately Renaissance splendour with pepper-pot turrets. It cost the first Duke of Queensberry so much to build that he spent only one night in it and went off to Sanquhar Castle nursing his accounts. Ironically, Drumlanrig is now one of the grandest and richest homes in Scotland with a priceless art collection, furniture, and rooms of intriguing 'objets'. Treasures overflow:

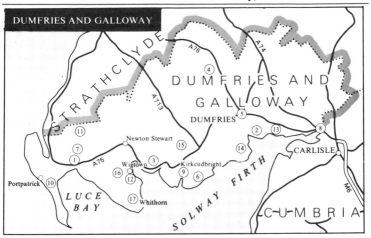

Louis XIV furniture, paintings by Rembrandt and Murillo, traditional family portraits, tapestries, porcelain, wood carvings, and a 1680 silver chandelier weighing nine stones. Set in parkland and ringed by the wild Dumfriesshire hills, this 'courtyard' chateau has spiral staircases that rise the full height of the castle, and the main entrance is at first floor level. Charming Victorian summer-houses and one of the oldest Douglas Firs in Britain – now 132ft high – stand in the grounds. Here is also the country's biggest sycamore, estimated to drink 180 tons of water annually. *Open most days, summer.*

5. Dumfries   10 K8
Dumfries is said to derive from 'fort of the Friesians', whom the Romans released from duty on Hadrian's Wall. Factories and housing estates swelled the settlement to a busy industrial town. The Old Bridge across the River Nith is the only remaining medieval structure, though a number of 18thC buildings survive. The Midsteeple of 1707 is the tolbooth which was used as a courtyard and prison until 1867. In 1745, Bonnie Prince Charlie held the town to ransom for three days. Unable to muster up support, he left the town taking with him £2,000 – and the Provost as a hostage.
Robert Burns lived his last five years here, and the town remembers its 'Shakespeare' with as much energy and devotion as Stratford its bard: he was more than a poet to the Scots – he was their voice after centuries of silence. Before coming to Dumfries, he made a last attempt at farming. It failed and he took a job as an exciseman in Dumfries for £50 a year. **Burns House,** *Burns St,* the 18thC house where he died, is furnished as it was when he lived there, and many relics can be seen. Down a narrow passage off the High Street is Burns's favourite pub, The Globe Inn. His chair, an inscribed window pane and other relics are on display – along with a convivial atmosphere of the sort Burns would have relished. He and his family are buried in St Michael's churchyard.
A well-stocked regional museum recently refurbished, **Dumfries Burgh Museum,** *Church St,* is based on an 18thC windmill, used as an observatory, and has a camera obscura. Among many relics there associated with the town of Dumfries is a bell from St Michael's Church dated 1443 – one of the oldest bells in Scotland. Another is the celebrated Dumfries Siller Gun, presented in 1617 by James VI.

6. Dundrennan Abbey   10 J10
7m SE of Kirkcudbright, A711. Ruined it may be, but this Cistercian house, open to the sky,

has enough spirit left to spring many surprises. Like so many other Lowland abbeys, it was founded by David I in 1142 and colonised by monks from Rievaulx. Note the startling contrast between Norman exterior and Gothic-arched interior. The abbey contains two of the most fascinating ecclesiastical sculptures in Scotland. One is a 13thC abbot – reckoned by some to be the oldest sculptural representation of a Cistercian in Britain. Over 7ft tall and injured by a dagger in his chest, he is standing on the slain body of a kilted man with hideous wounds from which the bowels ooze. Another portrays a monk who lived here in the 15thC. Mary, Queen of Scots, is said to have spent her last night in Scotland at this house. Guided to the wilds of Galloway after 11 months' captivity in Lochleven Castle, search parties were after her and she hid in glens and caves. The story goes that lonely, weary and disturbed by the horrors of the past few years' she asked that a child might be allowed to sleep with her so she could cuddle him. Near the abbey at Port Mary is a big stone washed by the tide where Mary probably embarked onto a fishing boat for England.

Galloway Forest Park   10 G8
10m NW of Newton Stuart, off A714. Covering 150,000 acres of hills, forests, trails and lochs, this abundant area is where Robert the Bruce wandered as a fugitive in the early 14thC, hunted by Scots and English. **The Bruce Monument,** *E side of Loch Trool, off A714,* celebrates his incredible escape from five separate forces of archers, horsemen, and Highlanders – totalling about 2,500 men. Trailed by a bloodhound, the chase became so hot that Bruce and his companion were actually seen, and five Highlanders were sent ahead to slay them. They failed, and Bruce and his friend escaped by wading upstream.

Galloway Highlands

7. Glenluce Abbey   10 F9
2m N of Glenluce, off A75. Cistercian monks from Melrose worked and prayed in this

now-ruined 12thC abbey near the sand dunes of Luce Bay. Only the 15thC vaulted chapter house remains intact, but Glenluce survived unbruised longer than many of her sister houses – the building was recorded as complete in 1646.

8. Gretna Green 10 M9
At English border, off A74. Passionate couples and livid parents once hurtled over the border to Gretna Green to take advantage of Scotland's laxer marriage laws – or to stop them before they did! Scottish law recognised as man and wife a couple who had made a plain declaration before witnesses. Things were made more difficult after 1856, when various laws were passed, but it's still possible to get married after the age of 16 without parental consent. Gretna's runaway 'ceremonies' took place at the Sark Toll Bar, a few yards over the border (now by-passed by the A74), and the well-known smithy where curios are now preserved. Interestingly, Joseph Paisley who began the marriage business in the mid 18thC, was never the village blacksmith and probably knew more about public relations than anvils!

But Gretna had a history of 'law-breaking' in other ways when it was part of the Debatable Land. This area between Sark and Esk belonged neither to Scotland nor England, and numerous Robin Hood type gangs grew up there. A large boulder near the farm of old Gretna called the Clochmaben Stone marks a place where commissioners for England and Scotland met secretly to discuss border disputes.

9. Kirkcudbright 10 J10
Far from being a backwater, Kirkcudbright (pronounced Kirkcoobry) is one of the most ancient ports in Scotland. Healthily set on the River Dee, it was among the first six ports in Scotland, and is the capital of Galloway. Philip of Spain planned to land his Armada there to cadge Scottish help. Now an artists' colony, it also has an ancient burgh wassail-bowl of walnut wood hooped with iron, which holds 10 gallons! Kirkcudbright obviously took its wassails very seriously. Perhaps that's why the artists are there. See the Stewarty Museum which has objects connected with Galloway and a good natural history section. *Open most days, summer.*
In the centre of the town is **Broughton House**, a charming Georgian building which belonged to the late 19thC artist E. A. Hornel. Today, it contains a display of his paintings, antique furniture, a large library and attractive garden. *Open summer; certain days, winter.*
A bulky skeleton, **MacLellan's Castle**, *off High St*, is a handsome, castellated mansion overlooking the harbour and dating from 1582. Castle is the wrong word for Sir Thomas MacLellan's house because it's far more civic in appearance and attitude than aggressive or military. He used stones from the old convent estate to build it – on the L-plan, but with an extra bit in one corner, and a network of staircases. A little room off the first floor landing has a tiny opening into the back of a huge inglenook chimneypiece; it was probably for spying on activities in the hall. Although ruined in 1752, the house has many fine architectural details – plus good corbels, a fake cannon, and a falsely blocked window showing the arms of the builder and his wife.

Kirkcudbright

10. Kirkmadrine Stones 10 E10
8m S of Stranraer, off A716. Glass-cased outside the church are three of the earliest Christian monuments in Britain – stones inscribed from the 5thC. The first is a gravemarker in good Roman lettering: *hic iacent scti et praecipvi sacerdotes ides viventivs et mavorivs* (here lies the holy and principal priests Ides, Viventius and Mavorius). Above it is a chi-rho symbol – the first two letters of Christ's name in the form of a monogram. Praecipui sacerdotes, meaning 'bishops', is especially interesting because it shows that 5thC Galloway had a sort of diocese. The second stone's inscription is incomplete, but the third says: *initivm et finis* (the beginning and the end), a quote from Revelations.

11. Laggangairn Standing Stones 10 F9
9m N of Glenluce on Barrhill Rd. Ignored, vandalised, ridiculed, misunderstood, standing stones have recently attracted serious research and if you're a devotee of these eerie, powerful presences, you won't mind the three mile hike to Laggangairn – or Hollow of the Cairns. The crosses of these two grey stones date from the Dark Ages, and a slab with a simple Latin cross leans against a wall by the ruined farmhouse. You won't get further into the back of beyond than here.

12. Martyrs' Monument 10 G9
Nr Wigtown, A714. This monument commemorates two Margarets, aged 18 and 63, who were tied to stakes and drowned by the tide in 1685 for their religious beliefs. Three men were also hanged without trial. Certainly, Wigtown had a reputation for demonic detection. Even the vicar of Kirkmaiden called in the services of a 'weird woman of Wigtown' who was reputedly able to identify a witch or warlock on sight. His only problem was that she identified nearly everyone in Kirkmaiden as a necromancer!

13. Ruthwell Cross 10 K9
Ruthwell church, B724. A major monument of Dark Age Europe, this 18ft cross is spotlighted and behind railings in a 'well' built to hold it. Defiantly, it has survived many attempts to destroy it. Broken in two and partly defaced in 1640, the buried pieces were dug up from beneath the church floor in the late 18thC. Other fragments had broken off. As it stands today, the side arms are modern. The rest is crawling with figures, birds, beasts, and the text of that beautiful Old English poem 'Dream of the Rood', inscribed in runes. The cross was probably set up after the Synod of Whitby in AD664, to commemorate the ascendancy of the Roman over the Celtic church.

14. Sweetheart Abbey 10 K9
New Abbey, A710. Beautiful and renowned, Devorgilla of Galloway was so much in love

Sweetheart Abbey

with her husband, John de Balliol (a Norman English lord) that when he died she founded this Cistercian abbey. Although she buried him at her home at Barnard Castle, she embalmed his heart in a casket 'of evorie' and carried it with her wherever she went. When

Devorgilla died, aged 80, the casket was laid upon her breast and the high altar of the great abbey erected over them both. It has been known as Dulce Cor, or Sweetheart, ever since. Today, the abbey feels remarkably whole despite being roofless. Most of the original (1273) wall of enormous granite boulders survives, there's a 90ft-high central tower and a rose window in the choir.

15. Threave Castle 10 J9
1½m W of Castle Douglas, N of A75. Fearsome stronghold of the Black Douglases, lords of Galloway, this four storey tower on an island in the Dee was built by the blackest of the lot – Archibald the Grim. Dark and ugly, Archibald ruled his island fortress with gloomy brutality. A granite knob projecting from the castle's front is known as the 'Gallows Knob'. Archibald used to boast gleefully that it 'never lacked a tassel'. A small mound on the west side of the loch is supposed to have been a pit where skeletons were thrown after rotting on the knob. Archibald got his come-uppance when James II besieged Threave with Mons Meg, the great bombard now in Edinburgh Castle, and Threave promptly became royal property. Today, Archibald's tower rises darkly 70ft from its marshy island and gives the ferry-born visitor a sharp taste of life in the Middle Ages.
Threave House is now a school of practical gardening and the gardens themselves – acres of naturalised daffodils, peat, rock and water gardens – are open to the public. **Threave Wildfowl Refuge** nearby is a roosting and feeding place for many species of wild geese and ducks on the River Dee.

16. Torhousekie Stone Circle 10 G10
3½m W of Wigtown, off B733. This perfect circle of 19 boulders, about 60ft in diameter and standing on a low mound, is probably Bronze Age. Each monolith is about 5ft high.

17. Whithorn Priory and Museum 10 H10
Whithorn. Calculated to have worshipped Christ uninterrupted for 1,500 years, this Whithorn peninsula near St Ninian established the first Christian church in Scotland in AD397 affects many visitors with a sense of peace and history. During the Middle Ages, pilgrims journeyed here from all over Britain and Europe. Border wars were no obstacle, either: safe conduct was guaranteed to all strangers who were on their way to St Ninian's shrine. The present priory is 12thC, built on the site of an 8thC Celtic one. The most impressive remaining part is a Norman doorway.
Whithorn may have been the place to go for a bad conscience, but by all accounts you didn't have to rough it with bare feet and hair shirts. Queen Mary, wife of James II, made the pilgrimage with six ladies of her bedchamber – all in new gowns. James IV made a point of visiting Whithorn at least once a year, and often twice. He put an iron girdle of penance round his waist which he wore till death at Flodden. James V continued the habit and eventually the Reformed Kirk protested against such Popish practices, and pilgrimages to Whithorn were declared illegal by the Scots Parliament in 1581. Many defied the ruling – testament, perhaps, to Whithorn's magnetism. Early Christian crosses are on show in the museum.
The Isle of Whithorn, *3m SE of Whithorn*, is no longer an island, but ruins of a 13thC chapel mark the spot where St Ninian landed in AD395. There are also remains of an Iron Age fort and a 17thC tower.

FIFE

1. Aberdour Castle 11 L3
Aberdour, 10m E of Dunfermline, A92. No-one is quite sure that 'castle' is the right name for this Scottish house. Certainly there's the ruined nucleus of a medieval castle – a tower dating back to the 14thC – but domestic buildings were added in the late 16thC very similar to other houses along this bit of Fife coast. See the fine circular or 'beehive' dovecote and the bowling green outside. Cross to Incholm Island from Aberdour.

2. Alexander III Monument 11 L3
S of Kinghorn at Pettycur Promontory, A92. Superstition surrounds the death of Alexander III who, on a dark, stormy night in 1286, fell from his horse on the cliffs here and died. Only the year before, he'd married a French aristocrat – Ioland de Dreux – at Jedburgh Abbey with much revelry and pageantry. In the middle, say the chroniclers, the figure of Death mingled in the masque and there was foreboding because the bride had been destined for a convent. Within months, Alexander was dead, and the 300 years' war with England began.

3. Anstruther 11 N2
Hugging the harbour that once brought it prosperous trade with the Low Countries and Baltic, Anstruther recently attracted money from the National Trust for Scotland's Little House Improvement Scheme. Like other Fife village ports, Anstruther has a collection of beautiful 17th and 18thC buildings which the Trust wanted to rescue. They bought a group of old houses and sheds on St Ayles Land, and local initiative prompted the start of the **Scottish Fisheries Museum** there. Set around a cobbled courtyard, the buildings illustrate a Scottish fisherman's life at sea and

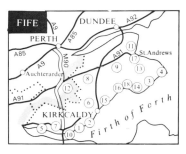

at home. There are fishing boats and gear, and it also contains a marine aquarium. *Open summer; most days, winter.*

Scottish Fisheries Museum

4. Crail 11 N9
Comely and clustering, this oldest of the Fife royal burghs is cherished by the National Trust for Scotland who have worked hard

preserving its sea-blown 17thC streets and houses. In Marketgate, Rumford and Shoregate are groups of traditional 17th and 18thC houses with crow-stepped gables and red-tiled roofs. Tolbooth Tower is early 16thC and shows a fish weather-vane. A Dutch bell of 1520 hangs in the Town House, and the Church of St Mary where Knox thundered one of his most violent sermons, dates back to the 13thC.

5. Culross   11 K3
Half-close your eyes in this 16thC royal burgh, and you could easily slip back among the weavers and salt panners, miners and merchants jostling and jabbering up and down its cobbled streets. Nurtured lovingly by the National Trust for Scotland who took over many of the town's small buildings, Culross has kept its character – in detail and layout. A model of a 17thC burgh, it grew prosperous from coal and salt. James VI even went down one of its mines in 1588.
Of interest is the Town House of 1626, rebuilt with a tower in 1783, and now the National Trust headquarters. Miscreants and debtors were detained in it, councils met under its painted ceiling, and witches were watched from its garret. Outside was a weighing post for checking and controlling the sale of goods. Bessie Bar's Hall once belonged to a widow who sold malt and left her name to the Hall, a well and a footpath called Bessie Bar's Hagg. The Study – so called because of the small room at the top of its tower – is an L-plan building from the 17thC. Other 17thC buildings include The Ark, The Nunnery, Bishop Leighton's House and The Butcher's House. A spectacular alabaster monument in the parish church is worth seeing, and nearby Parleyhill House is otherwise called The House with the Evil Eyes because of its oeil de boeuf windows.

5. Culross Palace   11 K3
Industrialist George Bruce built this town house between 1597 and 1611 with cash from his coal mines and salt pans. Bruce added stables and kitchens to the house during his lifetime and today it stands as one of the most vivid expressions of lairdly town life in Scotland. His grandson and great grandson lived there and in about 1700 it passed to a Colonel John Erskine – popularly called the 'Black Col' because of his vitriolic outbursts in the local church.
Bruce marked the architecture with his personality and way of life. Past the business room and through an iron door is his counting house or strong-room which is stone vaulted, fireproof and burglar-proof, with extra safes sunk into the walls plus a fireplace, and windows for light and comfort during calculations. An outstanding painted ceiling, wall decoration, kitchen and terraced garden all add interest to this most human of 'palaces'.

Culross Palace

6. Dogton Stone   11 L10
5m NW of Kirkcaldy, off B922. A weathered and ancient Celtic cross with animal and figure sculpture, and key pattern ornament.

7. Dunfermline   11 L10
A thousand years ago, Dunfermline was Scotland's capital. Today, it is second in county-size to Kirkcaldy and seems at first glance just a busy, terylene-producing town. Balladed as a 'toun wib bluid-red wine', it expresses its rich and royal past most poignantly in splendid, ruined **Dunfermline Abbey.** This great Benedictine house was founded by Queen Margaret in the 11thC. The foundations of her modest church can be seen through grating in the floor of the existing nave, which is only 50 years older than Margaret's original chapel. Considered one of the finest Romanesque monuments in Scotland, its pillars are oddly fluted with zig-zags so that they seem to decrease in thickness from top or bottom, according to where you stand to look at them. Durham has similar spirals, and the same masons may have been hired for both jobs.
Margaret and her husband, Malcolm, are buried here along with Robert the Bruce, whose body was disinterred in the 19thC. He was re-buried and his grave is marked by modern brass. Dunfermline Abbey is the 'Westminster' of Scotland – five other Scottish kings lie buried here. A list of them hangs on the front of the royal pew of James VI, which is itself fixed to a wall in the modern church. Note the beautiful sculptures of Dean Stanley's wife and other members of the Elgin family.

A Victorian villa houses **Dunfermline Museum,** *Viewfield Terrace,* with its interesting local collection. It specialises in weaving and the linen damask articles that made the town famous. Lint mills grew up all over Fife, but Dunfermline's linens and damasks were supremely fine. *Open most days.* Dunfermline is well-known for being the home of philanthropist Andrew Carnegie. He left his humble weaver's cottage, now **Andrew Carnegie Birthplace,** *junction of Moodie St and Priory Lane,* to emigrate to Pittsburgh during the 1850s. Steel and railways made him extremely wealthy, and he showered benefits not only on his home town but the whole of Scotland. Recognising the power of education, he started public libraries all over the country (and all over the world) before many local authorities had thought of doing so. It cost him over £8 million. **Pittencrieff House and Park** were bought by Carnegie in 1902, and he presented it to the town. Set in 60 acres of beautiful glen, this 17thC mansion built for the lairds of Pittencrieff now displays local history, costume and an art gallery. Apart from tea room and culture, there's a paddling pool for children. The great educational trusts left by this Dunfermline lad who made multi millions in America, are still administered from offices in Dunfermline. *Open most days, summer.*

8. Falkland Palace and Gardens   11 L9
11m N of Kirkcaldy, A912. Elegantly settled at the foot of the Lomond Hills, Falkland was a hunting palace and recreation ground for the Stuart kings, and may mean 'falcon-land'. Treason and revenge dropped it into royal hands in 1437 and James IV decided to rebuild it using the Great Hall as the nucleus of his new palace. Completely at odds with the usual style of lairdly tower houses, the whole design is Renaissance, or what has been called

Falkland Palace

the 'Court School' – that is, expressing status and prestige in a flurry of Italianate columns and sculpture. Cromwell's troops billeted there in 1654 and fire destroyed much of the palace. Tragically, only the south wing is intact. Now you can see painted ceilings, 17thC Flemish tapestries, a chapel, and the 16thC royal tennis court. James V built it in 1539 eight years after Henry VIII devised his at Hampton Court. It is still played on from time to time. *Open summer.*

9. Hill of Tarvit 11 L9
2m S of Cupar, A916. A shrine of Edwardian taste and atmosphere, this 70-year-old mansion was built by a Mr Sharp to house his collection of furniture and pictures as gracefully as possible. The National Trust for Scotland calls this house 'a lesson in urbane good manners' and points out that the value of Tarvit is the way its contents fit the house. To see: two Flemish 16thC tapestries, the 18thC French drawing room, portraits and pictures. Part of the building has been converted into self-contained flats. *House open most days, summer; gardens daily, all year.*

10. Incholm Abbey 11 L3
Incholm Island, Firth of Forth. Boats from Aberdour. Imagine as you wander round this drafty Augustian monastery what life was like for the 12thC monks who prayed, ate and contemplated here on this elemental island known as 'the Iona of East Scotland'. In 1123, an early religious recluse is said to have entertained Alexander I here on a nourishing diet of shellfish and milk after he'd been shipwrecked. The king was so grateful that he vowed to found a monastery. And he did. Incholm became well-endowed and even owned property on the mainland. Isolation has preserved it amazingly intact so that a whole layout remains. Admittedly, much of it was rebuilt later, but fragments of mural painting on the south wall of the 13thC choir can be seen. They show a funeral procession, and style dates them as 12thC. The octagonal chapter house and cloistral buildings are more complete than those of any other Scottish monastery. Discover a small vault to the west of the main buildings with a 'Celtic' style door, and peer inside at the hermit's cell.

11. Leuchars Norman Church 11 M1
5½m NW of St Andrews, A919. Undoubtedly one of the purest Norman specimens in Scotland, this modern church is built onto a magnificent 12thC chancel and apse. Architects rhapsodise over its shafted arcading. The marks of the axes used to dress the stones can be seen easily. The 17thC tower looks exactly like a lantern hanging by a chain – which probably accounts for its descriptive name of lantern tower!

12. Loch Leven Castle 11 L2
Castle Island, Kinross. Ferry from lochside. A desperate scenario enacted here in 1568 by Mary, Queen of Scots, her gaoler and rescuers gives this castle more historic charisma than its ruins really warrant. Standing ruggedly on a loch island near Kinross, here the Queen was brought after her surrender at Carberry in 1567. Several rescue attempts failed. Then young William Douglas, her gaoler, got hold of the castle keys, helped his pretty prisoner to safety, locked the castle doors behind her and threw the keys in the loch. Ever since, anglers have trawled the slimy depths for those keys and come up with plump pink trout instead. *Open summer.*

13. Lochty Private Railway 11 M10
Lochty, B940 (Cupar/Crail road), 7m W of Crail. Steam enthusiasts might enjoy this one-and-a-half mile trip on a steam-hauled passenger train. There are locomotives, shunter and passenger coaches to see. All privately owned. *Open certain days, summer.*

14. Pittenweem 11 M10
A painter's paradise, trade gave this windswept village the status of a royal burgh in 1542, and it flourished for at least another 200 years. Out went cargoes of salt, malt and fish, and in from the Continent came pine, wine and silks. Several houses and streets reflect this atmosphere even today: Kellie Lodging, The Gyles, Gyles House, and No 18 East Shore.

Pittenweem (Pictish for Place of the Cave) got its name from **St Fillan's Cave**, *Cove Wynd*. In the 12thC, Augustinian monks sailed over from the Isle of May and founded a priory above the cave. They cut through the rock from the garden to the holy cave-shrine below. It was restored and rededicated in 1935. St Fillan was the son of an 8thC Irish princess and he roved about Scotland starting religious settlements.

Close to Pittenweem is **Kellie Castle and Gardens**. Originally a tower owned by Macbeth's contemporaries, it passed from one family to another and ended up with the Oliphants, who built another tower 50ft east of the old one. A new block containing a hall, dining room, bedrooms and cellars bridged the gap between the two towers, and Kellie Castle was born. Civil war interrupted progress on the plasterwork, and 70 years later the beautiful plasterwork and panelling were installed. But again, events forced neglect on the castle and in 1875 Prof. James Lorimer found the roof leaky, windows broken and gutters choked. What we see today is the result of a marvellous rescue operation undertaken by this one man and his family, with masterpieces like the elaborate vine ceiling and coats of arms surviving intact. *Open most days, summer.*

15. Ravenscraig Castle 11 L10
On rocky promontory between Dysart and Kirkcaldy. An uninhabited ruin, gaunt and thwarted on the clifftop. James II built this blackened 15thC fortress as part of a chain of strong-points protecting the Firth against hostile men-of-war. This was the first castle in Britain specifically designed for defence by and against firearms. Ironically, the only onslaught Ravenscraig has ever felt is from caustic seawinds and nearby coal mines. During the American War of Independence when a squadron threatened the Forth towns, the vicar of Kirkcaldy cheated it by using un-military defences. He knelt on the wet sands below Ravenscraig and prayed. At once the wind veered west and blew the privateers back to open sea!

16. Robinson Crusoe Statue 11 M10
Lower Largo. Fifer and sailor, Alexander Selkirk, was born at Largo in 1676. A wild youth, he ran away to sea and on a privateering expedition in 1703 quarrelled with his captain who marooned him on the uninhabited island of Juan Fernandez off the west coast of South America. He survived there nearly five years before being picked up by another ship, and became the prototype for Defoe's Robinson Crusoe.

17. St Andrews 11 M9
Old grey town wrapped comfortably in its 17th and 18thC gentility, the buildings reflecting the once-prosperous trade between Fife and the Low Countries. It's perhaps most famous for its connections with golf, and the St Andrews Royal and Ancient Golf Club became the mecca of the golfing world. A fine personal collection of golfing relics, photographs, clubs and balls going back to golf's very beginnings, is housed in **Auchterlonie's Golf Museum**. *Open summer.* **St Andrew's Cathedral**, founded in 1160, was once the country's largest church. Now a pious skeleton, this seaside cathedral fell out of use after the Reformation and became a quarry for local townsfolk: many of its stones

St Andrew's Cathedral

can be seen built into local houses. Even so, its dignity survives, and you can piece together evidence of its stormy history from what remains. Edward I robbed the nave of its lead for his siege-engines in 1304, and a century later, gales brought down the gable of the south transept. During a four-day Reformation clean-up, much was destroyed. One casualty of mob zeal was the beautiful head of a bishop (now in the cathedral museum) which, though damaged, shows the sensitivity and power of Egyptian royal sculpture. A piece of 9thC stone sarcophagus showing an exotic hunting scene with lions and apes is one of the most interesting cathedral 'finds'.

St Andrews University is the oldest in Scotland, but it's still 190 years younger than the oldest parts of Oxford and Cambridge. Founded in 1412, it had three colleges – St Mary's, St Salvator's and St Leonard's. The last two united in 1747. St Salvator still has its ancient chapel buildings, and the university has an unrivalled collection of silver maces, or verges, which anyone with an eye for medieval craftsmanship should see. They are the oldest pieces of their kind in Britain. The university library dates from 1612 and has over 500,000 books plus many rare manuscripts. Mary, Queen of Scots, is said to have planted a hawthorn in the courtyard.

17. St Andrews Castle   11 M9
Stumps survive to tell the bloody tale of those early Protestant reformers burned at the stake by the archbishops of St Andrews episcopal castle. Doubting the rule of Rome, they met their end here at the hands of men like Cardinal David Beaton who hounded heretics ferociously to stake or dungeon. Today you can see the infamous 'bottle dungeon' (so-called because of its shape) where reformers were thrown, and from which no-one ever escaped. Beaton was a focus for Catholicism and Henry VIII plotted his murder. Less than three months after watching the last St Andrews martyr roast, Beaton himself was thrown into the bottle dungeon and pickled with salt 'to keep him from stinking' by a band of reforming sympathisers. The following year, a French fleet took the castle. Today, you can see where the besiegers drove a mine to get inside the castle, and the counter-mine by the besieged which foiled the attempt.

18. St Monans   11 M10
12m S of St Andrews, A917. The epitome of the small Fife seaside town, with colour-washed houses standing shoulder to shoulder. The town has relied on the fishing industry for its survival, and scars of the post-war struggle to survive are evident. But the town has fought to preserve its identity and with help from the National Trust for Scotland, they have restored several groups of 18th and 19thC buildings. St Monans also has one of the best of the little towered kirks – a real fisherman's church licked by spray from south-easterly gales. David II built it in the 14thC as a thank-you for his recovery from a wound at the tomb of St Moinenn. An octagonal steeple sits atop a squat tower with little belfry windows, there are beautiful windows and a fine groined roof. It was well restored in 1828.

Dangerous and flaking remnants of an old castle stand on the cliffs near St Monans. Near them is a dovecote that matches the castle complete with its rings of pigeon holes. In Jacobean times there were more than 300 dovecotes in Fife and James VI, being superstitious, made it illegal to pull them down. Over 100 are still listed.

SCOTTISH HIGHLANDS

Round the great fault where Highland Scotland hangs by a geological thread from the rest of mainland Britain, earthquake trembles are still sometimes felt. Crumpled and melted, crushed and tilted by violent upheavals, mountains and glens beyond are formed of the most ancient rocks in Britain. This is the most remote part of the British Isles, a land full of the secret signs of vanished races, frequently invaded by the Norsemen and the Vikings who have left remnants of their culture in silent stone tombs and the Gaelic language.

Bones and shells found in caves at Sutherland, Oronsay and Oban tell us that people lived in this craggy, misty, forested country 10,000 years ago, at the close of the Ice Age. As weather improved, they met and mated with short, dark newcomers from the south who brought with them Mediterranean customs – building stone monuments was one of them. Later a taller race, probably from the Rhineland, arrived, who spoke a language similar to Welsh. The Bronze Age peoples, who started arriving from about 2,000BC, made improvements in the arts, modified burial traditions and began to build vast stone circles and fortified villages. They were followed by Iron Age peoples, who built brochs (fortified towers).

It was frozen Romans probing the chilly north who first labelled these people 'Picts' – the name means 'painted people' – and routed them at Mons Graupius in AD60. Grampian is named after it. But Rome never got the better of the Picts and gave up just before the Scots crossed the sea from Ireland, singing Gaelic and preaching Christianity. Enemies at first, Scots and Picts gradually united to fight off Norse attacks, which began in the early 9thC. By AD875 they had virtually destroyed the Picts, and what was left of their kingdom was taken over by the first Scottish/Pictish monarch – Kenneth MacAlpine.

Wild and mountainous country always made communications difficult, and each clan had its own territory which it protected with fierce blood loyalty. Loyalty to the clan leader was often stronger than loyalty to the King. Clan feuds were frequent, and came to a bloody climax at the massacre of Glen Coe when, in 1691, Campbells of Glenlyon seized the opportunity to destroy the MacDonalds of Glen Coe after they delayed signing the Oath of Allegiance to William and Mary. Though Scottish and English families intermarried, there was always an underlying enmity between the two countries. As English influence fingered northwards, Gaelic was dropped as the official language, and major settlements were moved further and further south. To the north, Celts (Gaels) kept their ways and tongue. National survival, symbolised by the Jacobite rebellions, the second of which was led by romantic hero Bonnie Prince Charlie, climaxed in the 18thC when England decided to crush Highland resistance for good.

Clearances nothing short of genocide wiped out a large proportion of Highlanders as room was made for large-scale sheep farming. Crofters had always been at the mercy of their landowners and when the clan system disintegrated after the Battle of Culloden, a rift was caused. As the demand for wool was high and the profits fat, the lairds discovered the advantages of using the land for sheep grazing, and between 1820 and 1840 the crofters were evicted. Some eked out a meagre living on the wastelands and thousands emigrated.

Today, although the Highlands and islands cover one-sixth of Britain, their total population is less than a suburb of London or Glasgow. Maps of the area look sparse, bare of towns and villages. The distant islands – the Orkneys, Shetlands and far Hebrides – depend on the sea and the sparse landscape for their livelihood. For centuries the Orkneys and Shetlands were Viking strongholds and their people and buildings are still more Norse than Scottish, whereas the old Gaelic way of life survives in the Outer Hebrides, in its music, crafts and language. Of even greater significance is the lonely, barren island of Iona. It was here that Christian Scotland first began as in AD563, St Columba established a monastery that was to become the cradle of Christianity in Scotland.

Much of the agricultural land of the northern part of the Highlands is reclaimed peat bog. Here you find the shaggy, horned cattle and watch for wandering sheep in the path of your car on the narrow, winding roads. Fishing is the other occupation of these areas. The Highlands has its towns – the industrial centre is Aberdeen, the 'Granite City' and booming oil capital. Fort Augustus, hard and forbidding, is the key to Loch Ness which stretches the distance to Inverness, a town full of gun shops and all the gear you need to go deer-stalking. You can't escape the sea on the hundreds of miles of coastline, and in a good summer you can wander and swim from the deserted, white, sandy beaches on the west coast with only the seals for company. If man is largely absent, wildlife is not. The remote Highlands are the last refuge of many birds and mammals found nowhere else in Britain. This richly beautiful area offers most to the naturalist, the fisherman, the bird-watcher, the climber and the lover of outdoor life. You need stamina, good maps and stout shoes to explore the glens, crags and islands – and a dram of whisky to ward off the nip in the air.

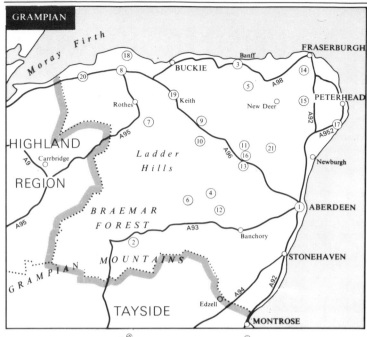

GRAMPIAN

GRAMPIAN

1. Aberdeen   11 O4
Bounded by the Rivers Don and Dee,
Aberdeen is a remarkable mixture of culture
and commerce, beaches and banking, soil and
oil, tourism and fishing. Trade and craft
guilds patterned the city and have left their
mark on it like a silversmith's punch.
Noted for its cleanliness, Aberdeen's pale,
silvery, granite buildings are scrubbed by wind
and sun until they shine. The town is
world-famous for the granite of which it is
built. When the linen industry failed abruptly
in the mid 19thC, Aberdeen continued to
supply the world with pavements and
tombstones: Londoners, Americans and
Australians walk on Aberdeen granite. It is
quarried from Rubislaw, which is probably the
largest man-made hole in the world – a pit
465ft deep at the bottom of which men and
machines move like dinky toys.
Built as a quadrangle in 1494 **Kings College**,
High St, has a chapel comparable to King's
College Chapel in Cambridge. No soaring
Gothic splendour here, but beautiful medieval
woodcarving in ceiling, stalls and screens,
rarely found in Scotland. See, too, the 'crown'
tower and treasure-filled library.
'Wedding cake architecture' is a term often
applied to the spires and pinnacles of
buildings like **Marischal College**. But they
present a stunning Gothic face to Broad
Street and together with Mitchell Tower and
Greyfriars church form one of the finest
complexes of granite buildings in the country.
Excellent anthropological museum: mummies
and Beaker people, carved jade and classical
vases.

Aberdeen

Along the street is **Provost Skene's House**, a
striking 17thC town house owned by George
Skene, one time merchant and Provost of
Aberdeen. A coved ceiling covered with
tempera paintings of religious topics is its
main feature, though the house is now a
museum of old town life. Skene was an
entrepreneur of his day who helped forge
trade links between Aberdeen, the Baltic and
Low Countries, and through that influenced
Aberdeen's whole way of life.
St Machar's Cathedral, *Chasonry*, is the only
granite cathedral in Britain. It was founded in
1157 on the site of a primitive church built by
St Machar, on instructions from St Columba.
Today's remains are 15th and 16thC, and
most striking is the oak ceiling of the nave
decorated with 48 shields of arms to declare –
merrily, judging by the colours – the universal
embrace of Christianity. The nave is now used
as a parish church.

2. Balmoral   11 L5
8m W of Ballater, A93. Summer home of the
Royal Family for over 100 years, this white
granite castle was built between 1853 and
1856 and looks so fresh today that it's hard to
believe it has survived a century of Highland

Balmoral

weather. Prince Albert spotted the estate in
1848 and bought it for £31,000. Although he
died soon afterwards, he and Victoria spent
long enough there together for her to feel a
deep attachment to it.
Architectural snobs often sneer at the Scottish
baronial style complete with odd proportions,
pompous exteriors, chilly stone passages and
cavernous kitchens – but they are pure
Victorian and valuable for that. Along with the
procession of princes and politicians,

princesses and premiers who have stayed at Balmoral, thousands of tourists throng the gardens every year to see Queen Victoria's garden cottage, Queen Mary's sunken garden, the beautiful birches – and just breathe the pure Braemar air. *Open weekdays, summer.*

3. Banff 11 N1
This delightful country town of old-fashioned charm has 20 distilleries and a one-time thriving ship-building industry. The museum concentrates on birds and local history. **Duff House** is a superb mansion designed by William Adam for the first Earl of Fife. Unfortunately it was never completed due to a quarrel between the Earl and Adam over a crack in the central block. They became so embittered that the Earl refused ever to live in the house. However, this mansion, modelled on the Villa Borghese, still ranks as among the finest works of Georgian architecture in Scotland. *Open summer.*

4. Craigievar Castle 11 M4
7m S of Alford, N of junction of A974 and A980. Situated in secluded, hilly country, Craigievar Castle contains all the ingredients its fairy-tale exterior promises. Four-posters, curtained baths, an underground prison, secret stairways – all these are here to explore, plus cultural features like magnificent decorated plaster ceilings. Built in 1626 by William Forbes, a successful Aberdeen merchant trading with Scandinavia, it has been occupied by the family ever since. William would probably still recognise his home today because very little has changed. First and foremost it was a family home; then an architectural extravaganza. Even its turrets wear caps. Forbes tartan is everywhere, and upstairs a room (reputedly haunted) displays the Forbes motto: 'Do not vaiken sleiping dogs'. *House open most days, summer; gardens daily, all year.*

5. Craigston Castle 11 O2
10m SE of Banff, B9105. A library on the top floor of this lovely castle home belonged to Sir Thomas Urquhart, the delicious eccentric who translated Rabelais, invented a universal language, traced the Urquharts back to Adam, and gave the world a precise age. Craigston was built in 1604 by his grandfather, and sports an arc de triomphe over the front entrance as well as some playful carvings of knights, a piper, and animal gargoyles. The grounds were laid out by Capability Brown and the pretty dovecote has been restored and reinhabited by doves. *Open by arrangement.*

6. Culsh Earth House 11 M4
Nr Tarland, 13m NE of Ballater, B9119. Nowhere in this peculiar, almost circular dwelling – if dwelling it was – is the passage or chamber more than 5ft high. Although they were considerably shorter than us, it still must have been very uncomfortable for the Iron Age people who built it. Roofslabs are still intact and as you crouch you get a good idea of what it must have felt like to live here. Earth houses like this are still an archaeological mystery because even winter shelter would have been easier to build above ground. It might have been a secure hiding-place from raiders, or a primitive refuge.

7. Dufftown 11 L3
Planned in 1817 by an enlightened landowner named, predictably, Duff, this little town should be in perpetual stupor because it's surrounded by distilleries and right in the middle of the Glenlivet and Glen Fiddich whisky-producing area. The museum, *The Tower, The Square*, acknowledges this with displays of whisky-making plus local photographs and civic regalia. Nearby is 13thC Mortlach church, still used, and standing on the site of a Celtic monastery founded in the 6thC. *Museum open, summer.*

Bare to the weather for nearly 250 years, **Balvenie Castle**, *1m N of Dufftown*, is one of the earliest stone castles in Scotland. It still has parts which were built in the 13thC, and larger, better-preserved bits dating from the 16th and 17thC. The remarkable massive curtain wall is built from banded rubble which masons quarried from the formidable rock-hewn ditch surrounding the castle. It was visited by Edward I in 1304 and Mary, Queen of Scots, in 1562.

7. Dufftown, Glenfiddich and Balvenie Distilleries 11 L2
Just N of centre. Malting, mashing, fermenting, distilling and bottling of malt whisky are shown here in this prime whisky-making area of the world. This region lends itself to the industry because of the unusual amount of sunshine compared with the rest of the country. The soil is extolled for grain growing, especially barley. Add magnificent water flowing from the high granite Cairngorms and you have – top quality Scotch. Though international now, whisky has always been a local trade too, with naughty scatterings of illicit stills.

8. Elgin 11 L1
Picturesque buildings play hide-and-seek along Elgin's long, curving High Street which links old castle hill with the low-lying cathedral meadows. Keep an eye out for Braco's Banking House, a 17thC arcaded house with a characteristic courtyard behind. Anderson's Institution is a domed presence in Greek Revival style at the eastern end of the town. Gray's Hospital wears another dome, and pigeons wheedle round the belfry of St Giles 19thC kirk. Make time for the museum, *Nr Braco's*, because it contains fascinating work by the Pictish stone carvers who cut masterpieces used in fertility rites.

8. Elgin Cathedral 11 L1
North College St. Known as 'The Lantern of the North', this 13thC building was probably the finest of the Scottish cathedrals. It was inspired by political as well as religious motives: Bishop Andrew de Moray had been at Lincoln and probably wanted as fine a church in the north, Alexander II gave money for its construction, and, particularly as there was trouble from rebels in this area, it was regarded as a unifying force.
One century after its completion, the 'Wolf of Badenoch', brother of Robert III, burned down part of it in revenge for being excommunicated by the Bishop for his misdeeds. Slowly, it was restored over the next 100 years, and what remains is mainly 13th and 15thC. Suffering at the Dissolution, in 1567 lead was stripped from the roof to pay soldiers, rafters blew down, the great tower collapsed and it gradually became a complete ruin.
In the 19thC it was decided to preserve Elgin Cathedral and a ne'er-do-well shoemaker was appointed as its custodian. Responsibility rehabilitated him, and he cleared the site of rubble barrow by barrow with his own hands.

9. Huntly Castle 11 M3
Castle St, Huntly. Home of the 'gay Gordons', a ferocious and power-hungry family who dominated the north east until well into the 16thC. Though ruined and pot-bellied, the building is striking – chateau-like with four storeys, big round tower, and mock window. This idea was borrowed from France where palaces often had fake windows with fake servants and other figures leaning out of them. Contrary to the sound of their name, the Gordons were a Norman/French family who settled at Gordon in Berwickshire and took their name from the property. Their influence spread until they absorbed many smaller clans and grew strong enough to affect affairs of state. The existing castle is 17thC and was rebuilt on the site of medieval Strathbogie

Huntly Castle

Castle which was destroyed in 1452, rebuilt in 1551 and burned again 40 years later. See the beautiful heraldic adornments on the walls, the richly-decorated fireplaces, and wander round wooded parkland cavorting that famous dance.

10. Leith Hall   11 M3
7m S of Huntly, B9002. Family life in a Scottish country house through three centuries is followed here in architecture, keepsakes, pictures, needlework, glass and porcelain. The Jacobite relics are particularly interesting. Started in 1650, parts were added to the building by each generation and each Leith seems to have contributed his or her own personality to the house. Today it's a gracious rather than dramatic mixture of turrets, courtyard, pavilions and stables. The grounds are attractive with a particularly fine rock garden. *House open summer; gardens daily, all year.*

11. Loanhead Stone Circle   11 N3
Daviot, 5m NNW of Inverurie, off B9001. With at least three stone circles, this stretch of wild and beautiful countryside obviously attracted Ancient Man. This funeral monument or ring cairn is known archaeologically as a recumbent stone circle because of the large slab lying horizontal between two uprights. A burial cairn is usually found in the centre of the circle. This one is the best-known of the north east group.

12. Lumphanan, Macbeth's Cairn 11 M4
11m NW of Banchory, A980. This is meant to be the site of Macbeth's death at the hand of Macduff after fleeing from Dunsinane. Tradition states that he made his last stand here at the medieval peel castle which is now reduced to little but a bank 18ft high, eaten away here and there by cattle to reveal chunks of old castle stone.

13. Maiden Stone   11 N3
Chapel of Garioch, 6m WNW of Inverurie, off A96. Pictish symbol stones are open to all sorts of interpretations. This beautiful 10ft high pillar of red granite is associated with primitive rites of the early church and has symbols of a centaur, mirror and comb. Its meaning has never been satisfactorily explained.
Not surprisingly, the stone has a number of stories to its name. One goes that a beautiful maiden baking cakes for her wedding the next day is persuaded by a handsome stranger to wager her heart he can lay a stone causeway right up to Mither Tap of Bennachie (a local hilltop) before they are cooked. Laughing, she agrees. That evening, she sees the stone causeway. Horrified, she flees to woods and as he comes to claim her, calls on heavenly powers to come to her aid. They do – virgo intactus – by turning her to stone. In fact, there *are* traces of an ancient stone causeway up the hillside!

14. Memsie Burial Cairn   11 O1
Nr village, 3m SSW of Fraserburgh. A fine example of a large stone-built cairn or tomb dating from around 1500BC.

15. Old Deer   11 O2
12m W of Peterhead, off A950. Old Deer has a history of religious fervour and notoriety. The celebrated Book of Deer, a manuscript now in Cambridge University Library, is the oldest surviving document written in Scots Gaelic and dates from the 9thC. This is the sole relic of a 7thC monastery founded by St Drostan. In 1711, bloody fighting broke out in and around Deer church between Stewart supporters and the new Presbyterian vicar who had to call in help from Aberdeen to defend himself. The incident is known as The Rabble of Deer. Remains of Deer Abbey, a 13thC Cistercian monastery, can be seen, including the 14thC refectory and the abbot's lodge. *Open summer.*

16. Pitcaple Castle   11 N3
4m NW of Inverurie, A96. One of the best and earliest examples of the Z-plan, this fine 15thC castle has been a family home for over 500 years. Mary, Queen of Scots, James IV and Charles II were entertained here and the Marquess of Montrose lodged in one of the rooms en route to his execution in Edinburgh. The castle is now a family museum. *Open most days, summer.*

17. Slains Castle   11 P3
7m SSW of Peterhead, off A975. Visiting the castle with Boswell in 1773, Johnson declared that it looked 'only a continuation of the perpendicular rock'. Perhaps he was awestruck by the savagery of the coast round here, battered into chasms and tunnels by the violent sea. Weathered ruins of the castle, which was the seat of the Hays of Erroll for almost three centuries, date from 1664. On the headland are two cannons from the 'Santa Caterina', the Spanish galleon wrecked in 1594.
One cavern near the castle is called Hell's Lum. It is 200ft deep with branching tunnels surging with sea.

18. Spynie Palace   11 L1
2m N of Elgin, off A941. A hubblebubble of witches was said to fly across the sky on All-Hallows Eve making straight for this 15thC residence of the Bishops of Moray. This massive stronghold – its original tower was six storeys high – proved a good defence, and a considerable ecclesiastical empire was founded here. Just before the Reformation, the bishops grew a reputation for having pacts with the Evil One. If you're sceptical, wander down the lonely road in a summer gloaming . . . *View from outside only.*

19. Strathisla Distillery   11 M2
Keith. Oldest established distillery in Scotland dating from 1786 and typical of the small, old-fashioned sort once scattered through this north east region. *Open summer.*

20. Sueno's Stone   11 K2
8m W of Elgin towards Forres, A96. Baffling to archaeologists and arresting to look at, this 23ft-high stone shows elaborate battle scenes that no-one seems able to identify. Chained captives and headless corpses possibly recall the lipsmacking tale of Sigurd the Powerful (Earl of Orkney) and Maelbrigd (of the single protruding tooth) who contested for power in Moray around AD900. They agreed to fight with 40 picked horsemen on either side, but dastardly Sigurd put two men on each horse – and won. Triumphantly hanging Maelbrigd's ghastly head over his saddle, Sigurd scratched his leg on the protruding tooth and died three days later.

21. Tolquhon Castle   11 O3
7m ENE of Oldmeldrum, off B999. Jolly faces peer down at you from the sculpture of this quaint, hollow ruin so carefully preserved by the Department of the Environment. Beautifully set in its wooded dell, it began as a 15thC rectangular tower, then converted into a bakehouse when a mansion was added a century later by William Forbes. Note the gatehouse and the remarkable variety of ornate gun-loops.

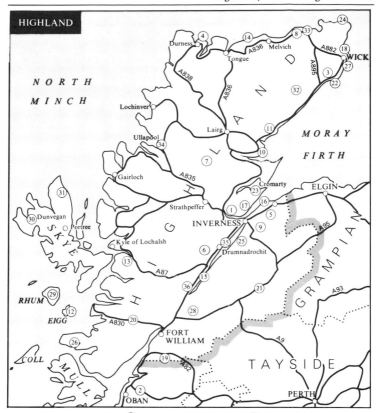

❦ HIGHLAND ❦

1. Beauly Priory　　　　12 J8
Beauly, 12m W of Inverness. In this 'beau lieu'
or 'beautiful place', a fertile vale with
oysterbeds in the nearby firth, stand the ruins
of a 13thC priory built by French monks. A
solitary stone crusader now guards this gentle
red-stone haven.

2. Bonawe Iron Furnace　　　11 E8
Bonawe, 12m E of Oban, off A85. These
restored remains of a charcoal furnace for
iron smelting are probably the first monument
of their kind in Scotland. Started in 1730 by
an Irish company, the venture ended tragically
when one partner stabbed the other in a pub
fight. New owners bought woods from all the
local lairds for fuel and the furnace operated
successfully until 1874. The sites and pits
where charcoal makers worked can still be
seen here and there, especially on the Loch
Etive side. The whole site, with its furnace
workers' houses, is more complete than any
other elsewhere. *View from outside only.*

Caledonian Canal
A straight line linking all the lochs in the great
fault which nearly made Scotland an island
millions of years ago. The Caledonian Canal
basically links the west coast with the east
coast and runs across some of Scotland's most
dramatic scenery. Of its length of 60 miles, 22
are man-made, and 38 go through natural
lochs.
Thomas Telford was hired to build the canal
in 1800 to open up the Highlands for trade
and commerce. Politicians of the day thought
it would increase trade with the Baltic and
West Indies and save the difficult journey
round Pentland Firth. Ironically, the
government also thought it would check the
alarming emigration from the Highlands that

had continued since the Clearances.
Some east coast fishing boats continue to use
the canal to travel to and from west coast
fishing grounds.

3. Camster, Grey Cairns　　12 M6
6m N of Lybster on Watten rd, off A9. Neolithic
stone tombs with their passages and chambers
were built over a period of 22 centuries –
longer than Christianity has yet lasted. These
two on bleak Caithness moorland are
excellent examples. Camster Long has parts
from several periods and was built over two
smaller tombs. One of them had a strange,
many-sided chamber, and the other a
chamber divided into 'stalls' by big stone
slabs. The enclosing cairn formed courtyards
at either end. Funeral rites may have been
held in them. You can crawl down a
passageway into the very heart of the mound.

4. Cave of Smoo　　　　12 H2
1½m E of Durness, A838. Walter Scott, the
novelist, explored this triple-cavern at great
risk to himself and his party because he was
beguiled by its drama and mystery. You
scramble down a cliff path and find a large
cavern yawning blackly like the entrance to an
aircraft hangar. Cavern One is 200ft by 110ft
and leads to Cavern Two, 70ft by 30ft. An
80ft waterfall plunges through a hole in the
roof there, into a lake. Cavern Three is more
of a huge cleft filled with brown stalactites,
and you reach it with difficulty via the
subterranean lake. The word 'smoo' comes
from 'smjuga' meaning a cleft.

5. Cawdor Castle　　　　12 K8
Cawdor, 5m SW of Nairn, B9090. Shakespeare
probably misspelt this home of the thanes of
Calder (Cawdor is lowland pronunciation of

Calder) and lodged Macbeth in our imagination as Thane of Cawdor. Today, this spine-chilling castle boasts the oldest original drawbridge in Scotland, and has a central tower of 1372 surrounded by 16thC buildings. Down in the dungeon depths of the tower stands a decayed tree trunk. Here, says the legend, William Calder's ass halted and thus chose the site for his master. Calders, then Cawdors, have lived here 600 years – and still do. Their family records are remarkably complete and even the contents of the house listed in old documents can still be seen in many of the rooms. Note especially the decorated lintel of the great fireplace. *Open summer.*

Cawdor Castle

6. Corrimony Cairn 11 G3
Glen Urquhart, 8m W of Drumnadrochit, Loch Ness. A signpost points you in the right direction for this kraal-shaped cairn made of stone by neolithic people who often chose fertile spots near water for living – and dying. This one is sheltered from harsh weather and possible attack from the surrounding hills. The entrance is 3ft by 4ft leading to a tunnel 15ft long. A circular chamber inside is about 9ft wide and 7ft high and outside are 10 standing stones in a circle round it.

7. Croick Church 12 H6
10m W of Ardgay, up Strathcarron. Telford built this small Highland church, and it has remarkable inscriptions on the windows by crofters evicted during the Clearances in 1845.

8. Crosskirk, St Mary's Chapel 12 L5
6½m WNW of Thurso, off A836. Rudely-constructed chapel with very low doors narrowing at the top in Irish style. Probably 12thC, it's unusual enough to warrant a diversion if you're in the area.

9. Culloden Moor Battlefield 12 J8
5m E of Inverness, B9006. Culloden was the last great battle fought in Britain. With it died Prince Charlie's cause – the Stuart claim to the throne – and a system of loyalties Scotland had known for centuries.
Ironically, the battle itself lasted less than one hour. Prince Charlie's army was ragged and hungry after a winter-weather retreat from Derby and on April 16, 1746, the battle day, the army was diminished as sections of the force had been dispatched to find food and others were sent to garrison strategic spots elsewhere in the Highlands. Prince Charlie had wanted to surprise the Duke of Cumberland's birthday party at the English camp in Nairn, but failed to make it in time – so the weary Jacobites had no sleep before battle either. Many clansmen and commanders told the Prince that Culloden was the wrong place and the time mistaken. He ignored them, and 1,000 Jacobites died. After the fight, Cumberland butchered prisoners, women and children, burned homes, fired crops and drove off cattle: his brief was to reduce the Highlands to wilderness. A ransom of £30,000 was offered for Charlie, but although he hid in Scotland for five months, no-one betrayed him.

Like most battlefields, nothing much remains except the lie of the land where it all happened. Modern features of interest at Culloden are the Graves of the Clans, the great memorial cairn, the Well of the Dead, and Old Leanach Farmhouse now restored as a battle museum. The Cumberland Stone still stands where 'Butcher' Cumberland is said to have eaten his lunch after the battle. The Culloden Centre has a historical display and lecture room with an audio-visual show.

10. Dornoch Cathedral 12 K6
Dornoch. Feuding clans burned down this little cathedral in 1570 and it wasn't until 1835 that restoration was complete. Today, the cathedral is a parish church and its origins trace back to the 13thC. Part of the Bishop of Sutherland's palace is now the Dornoch Castle Hotel. Unfortunately, the church restoration was clumsy and many fine features were obliterated: the organ has been described as: 'Victorian plumbing on a grand scale'. More seriously, spare a glance for the 13thC stonework.

11. Dunrobin Castle 12 K5
12½m NNE of Dornoch, off A9. Ever popular with tourists, this all-minarets-and-turrets seat of the earls and dukes of Sutherland is the northernmost stately home open to the public in Britain. Although Dunrobin has been claimed as the oldest inhabited house in the kingdom, the present mansion is only mid 19thC. Originally a 13thC keep, it was built by Robert, second Earl of Sutherland, and named after him. In 1856 it was extended. As English absentee landlords, the Sutherlands have always had bad publicity for their eviction of crofters from Highland estates during the late 18th and early 19thC. Magnificently set in a great park overlooking the sea, Dunrobin's collection of paintings, furniture and museum items provide an excellent occupation for a rainy afternoon. Exhibits are often oddly eccentric: iguanas, hankies, socks, whales, rare stones, alligators and there is even a test tube filled with grey matter and labelled 'mud from the Nile'. *Open summer.*

12. Eigg (Isle of) 11 B5
Ferry from Mallaig and Arisaig. This fertile, basalt blob, five miles by two and a half miles, is home to 40 people. Called Eigg from the Gaelic word for 'hollow', the island's highest peak is the Scuir of Eigg (1,289ft) which contains fossilised driftwood.
Eigg's township is Cleadale and its principal residence is a colonial-style house with palm trees and rare shrubs built by the Runciman brothers who owned Eigg for many years. Sir Steven Runciman, the historian, and his shipowning brother were benevolent and creative, and still remembered affectionately by the island's inhabitants. A cave near the south east shore of the island was the tragic scene of a 16thC clan feud when 200 Macdonalds hiding there were suffocated by smoke from a fire lit at the entrance.

13. Eilean Donan Castle 11 E3
9m E of Kyle of Lochalsh, off A87. Most photographed stronghold in Scotland, this replica 13thC castle commands a rocky tidal islet at the meeting of three fiords and its setting is stunning.
Recent excavation revealed evidence of a Pictish fort on the site. Alexander II probably saw it when he chose this spot for a springboard fort from which to attack the Norse kingdom of the Isles and ward off Danish invaders. For the next five centuries his castle figured in many famous raids and sieges and certainly it is well-known in the Highlands for its eventful life. However, doom lurked when Jacobite troops occupied it in 1719. English frigates shelled and destroyed it, and the ruins gathered moss for another two centuries. In 1912, Lt Col John

MacRae-Gilstrap of Bailliemore came to the rescue and reconstructed the castle at the huge cost of £¼ million. All architectural features are modern, but authentically reproduced. *Open summer.*

Eilean Donan Castle

14. Farr Stone 12 K2
22m W of Thurso, A836. Fine example of Celtic art standing 7ft tall. The long shaft of the cross has characteristic 'armpits' and is enclosed in a halo. Spirals coil everywhere, even into two birds with their long necks entwined. It has lasted remarkably unweathered since AD900 – probably because it is carved in hard Highland schist.

15. Fort Augustus Abbey 11 G4
S end of Loch Ness, A82. Ironic that this fort-turned-abbey was named after 'Butcher' Cumberland (William Augustus) who slaughtered so many after the Battle of Culloden. General Wade built it in the 1720s as one of a chain of three frontier posts to subdue the Highlanders. The other two are Fort William to the south and Fort George beyond Inverness.
In 1876, the fort was handed over to Benedictines who enlarged it with a series of graceful buildings. The school and tower were designed by the inventor of the Hansom cab, Joseph Hansom. On the south side of the school runs Wade's road over the Corrieyarrick Pass: Prince Charlie's army marched this way to Edinburgh.

16. Fort George 11 J2
8m W of Nairn, B9039. Textbook example of an 18thC garrison fortress and one of the finest in Europe. Jacobites blew up the original, but this one was built in 1748 as a symbol of English victory after Culloden. It has a protective ditch and drawbridges – and there's no better place to study 18thC theories of defence. The Queen's Own Highlanders have their regimental museum here.

17. Fortrose Cathedral 12 J7
Fortrose, 8m SSW of Cromarty. Dreamy ruins of the old 14thC red sandstone cathedral set on a green and surrounded by mellow old houses. Cromwell is said to have used the stones to build his fort at Inverness. Note the vaulting and fine detail.

18. Girnigoe and Sinclair Castles 12 M5
3m N of Wick, airport rd towards Noss Head lighthouse. Side by side above the sea like two old comrades, it is difficult to tell where one castle begins and the other ends. Oddly, Sinclair which was built in the 17thC is a total ruin while Girnigoe, 100 years older, still stands stoutly at five storeys high. At least one poor prisoner is known to have starved to death in Girnigoe's dismal dungeon on a waterless diet of salted meat. A noisy place of heaving rollers, spume-splashed walls, and gulls shrieking in the whistling wind.

19. Glen Coe and Dalness 11 F7
10m N of Tyndrum, A82, runs through glen. Spectacular but gloomy, Glen Coe was scene of a miserable massacre on 13th February 1692 and the fierce, bleak mountains seem to bear a grudge even today.
The Macdonalds of Glencoe were notorious cattle rustlers and thoroughly unpopular with their neighbours. So when Alexander Macdonald failed to take the oath of allegiance to King William on time – through administrative error rather than disobedience – the government saw a chance to bump off the clan. But they used the sacred virtue of hospitality to do it. A detachment of Campbells marched into Glencoe and asked the Macdonalds to put them up as there was no room at Fort William. The Macdonalds entertained the Campbells for two weeks in their own homes. At 5am on the day arranged, the massacre began: out of about 200 occupants, 40 were slain and several died of exposure after fleeing to the hills. The whole episode was hidden under an unofficial secrets pact.

20. Glenfinnan Monument 11 D6
18½m W of Fort William, A830. Addressing the expanse of Loch Shiel like an orator, this tower commemorates the raising of Prince Charlie's standard at Glenfinnan in 1745. This beautiful and romantic spot was a rallying point for the clans in the '45 Rising. Today, a spiral staircase inside the tower climbs to a battlemented platform 65ft above the ground on which stands a statue of a kilted Highlander. Angus, 12th Chieftain of Glenaladale, raised the tower to mark 'the generous zeal, the undaunted bravery and inviolable fidelity' of his ancestors who 'fought and bled in that arduous and unfortunate enterprise'. The National Trust centre there tells the story of the Prince's campaign from Glenfinnan to Derby and back to the final defeat at Culloden.

21. Highland Folk Museum 12 K10
Nr Kincraig, 12m SW of Aviemore. A woman historian saved a miscellany of 'humble' things from remote Highland farms and homesteads that would otherwise have been thrown away or destroyed. Gradually, she built up a collection and thanks to her forethought this museum is now grandly administered by four Scottish universities. She originally christened it The Shelter, but the name has been dropped. To be seen are: an 18thC shooting lodge, a Black House, a clack mill, a barn, a dairy, a stable, Highland tinker relics, weapons, costume, musical instruments and furniture.

22. Hill o' Many Stanes 12 M6
3¼m ENE of Lybster. Strange neolithic or Bronze Age site with almost 200 stones – none particularly large – set out in 22 parallel rows.

23. Hugh Miller's Cottage 12 K7
Church St Cromarty. Scandal or accident – no-one knew why Hugh Miller shot himself at the age of 54. He died in 1856 as a renowned geologist, journalist and theologian, leaving behind many books and relics of his energetic searching – both inner and outer. He's also bequeathed a strong sense of his own personality to this beautiful thatched cottage in the ancient burgh of Cromarty. His ancestor, John Fiddes, built it in 1711 and his initials flank the date on the mantel with those of his bride.
Hugh was born in a room on the right at the top of the stairs. His scrubbed-wood nursing chair is still there, and a shepherd tartan plaid he wore rather conspicuously round Edinburgh as editor of 'The Witness'. A collection of his letters includes correspondence from Darwin and Carlyle.

24. John o' Groats 12 M5
Caithness. Like Land's End, this bit of coast has deteriorated into souvenirs and hot-dogs. Popular as the most northerly point of the British mainland, this distinction correctly belongs to Dunnet Head.
Three Dutch brothers, the de Groots, came to Caithness in 1496 to work a ferry to the Orkneys. By the mid 16thC the family had increased to eight and they had an argument about who was head of the household. So John de Groot built an octagonal house with eight doors and windows and an octagonal table. Each therefore had his own entrance and place at table. Unfortunately, the house

no longer exists but the site is marked by a flagpole on a mound. The nearby beach is famous for 'Groatie Buckies', small corrie shells once the basis of many prehistoric ornaments found in the area.

25. Loch Ness 11 H3

Po-faced sceptics won't enjoy this stupendous loch nearly as much as visitors with minds and eyes open to monster possibilities. Nearly 22 miles long and 754ft deep, Loch Ness holds the greatest volume of fresh water in Britain. The loch's bottom is estimated at about 700ft below sea level but in places is much deeper. For several centuries there has been speculation about the coming-and-going of some sea creatures. In the 7thC an 'aquatilis bestia' was reported by an abbot of Iona. In 1975 great controversy raged over the findings of a team of American scientists which were supported by Sir Peter Scott. Nessie was honoured with the magnificent title 'Nessiteras rhombopteryx' which, translated, means 'Loch Ness marvel with a diamond-shaped fin', and members of Parliament were given a private viewing of the photographic evidence. It took an astute member of the public to point out that this impressive-sounding name was, in fact, an anagram for 'monster hoax by Sir Peter S'! But don't be disheartened – hundreds of people claim to have seen something, and an organised party maintains dawn-to-dusk observation on the loch during summer months. The records of their sightings are enough to shake even the crustiest cynic.

Loch Ness

26. Mingary Castle 11 B7

2m from Kilchoan on the Ardnamurchan peninsula W of Fort William, B8007. Care is needed when exploring this 13thC ruin built to guard the entrance to Loch Sunart and the Sound of Mull. Although tumbledown and mossy, you can still see the inner 15thC buildings. A laird of Mull besieged it in 1588 and collared 100 Spaniards off a doomed Armada ship to help him. The bay is still known as Port nan Spainneach. In 1495 James IV visited the castle, when he received the submission of the island chiefs.

27. Old Wick Castle 12 M6

1½m S of Wick, off A9. Seablown ruin perched on a spectacular rocky promontory above a deep cleft in the cliff where ancient sailors sheltered their longboats. Known also as the Old Man of Wick it is a windowless square tower which dates from the 14thC. *Open most days.*

28. Parallel Roads of Glen Gloy and Glen Roy 11 F6

Near Spean Bridge, 9m NE of Fort William. These gigantic terraces several miles long and at precisely the same levels on opposite sides of the glen are a striking sight. In the past it was thought they were the hunting roads of Celtic heroes along which Fingal and Co drove their deer herds. Today they are considered the scars of a receded lake once dammed in the glen by a glacier. At Mulroy, Roy Bridge, the last of the great

clan battles took place in 1688, between the MacIntoshes and the MacDonells of Keppoch. The MacDonells won, and it is said that this battle marked the last use of bows and arrows by the Highlanders.

29. Rum (Isle of) 11 B5

An outstanding area for geological and botanical research, but tourists will be more interested in **Kinloch Castle**. Opulent and outrageous, this transplant from Belgravia was built at the turn of the century for Sir George Bullough, son of a wealthy mill owner. George thought big. He hired the architects who designed the Admiralty in Whitehall and they presented him with a turreted mansion surrounded by an open cloister which he could perambulate on rainy days: a sensible idea as Rum's rainfall can be 100 ins a year. He crammed this amazing castle with deer heads, organs, sea-chairs made of slate, gongs, eagle eggs and decadent bathrooms. Shooting parties luxuriated there. Rum became a nature reserve in 1957 on condition that Kinloch Castle remained unaltered. It has. You can still see the Castle's old laundry, woodland, and the monolithic mausoleum George built for his father. *Open most days.*

30. Skye (Isle of) 12 B8

To many people this is the most beautiful of the Scottish Isles, and it's certainly one of the most popular. Of chief interest here is **Dunvegan Castle**. For 700 years the Macleods have lairded it at Dunvegan, and this is the oldest continuously-inhabited castle in Scotland. The family can trace their tree from Norse times through 30 generations. Parts of the building are said to date back to the 9thC, but the main body of the work was executed between the 15th and 19thC. Today it has a fairy-tale, breath-of-the-past appeal with its 15thC dungeon and tartan and treasures and relics and manuscripts, not to mention the famous 'fairy flag' and 12thC drinking horn. There is a boat-trip from the castle jetty to the seal colony. *Open weekdays, summer.*

Dunvegan Castle

31. Skye, Quiraing 11 B1

19m N of Portree, A855. Cattle were driven up during raids into this extraordinary mass of rocky towers and pinnacles. A rough track zigzags up to The Needle – an obelisk 120ft high – and beyond that is a grassy amphitheatre called The Table.

32. Strath Kildonan Gold-field 12 K4

20m S of Melvich, off A897. Records of the Kildonan gold field date back to 1868 and cover about two years. During the Kildonan Gold Rush it is said that £12,000 worth of gold was extracted by 400 freelance miners before mining permission was withdrawn. Although geologists have recently confirmed that gold exists in these marshes, it's doubtful whether there is enough of it to make extraction worth while. Someone recently suggested making the area a pan-for-gold tourist attraction!

33. Thurso 12 L5

Caithness, off A836. Important in medieval

times as the chief port for Scandinavian trade, Thurso is the most northerly town on the British mainland. Its name derives from the Norse Thor's-a, meaning 'river of the god Thor'. It declined in importance only to be resurrected as a boom town by nuclear power at Dounreay. Its great trade in 'Caithness flags' has waned, though these splendid natural flagstones once bore feet and traffic as far off as Paris and Australia. The last of the paving is disappearing even from Thurso and a Flagstone Preservation Society was founded in 1972!

Architecturally, Thurso falls into three periods – 18th and 17thC main streets, the older fishertown, and modern Swedish-style suburbs. The Folk Museum has agricultural and domestic displays, trades and crafts, plus a room showing an old Caithness cottage. The ruins of the 17thC castle, ancestral home to the earls of Sinclair, stand sentinel over the small harbour. Apparently the castle was so close to the sea that it was possible to fish from the windows. *View from outside only.*

34. Ullapool   12 G5
Sad emigrants sailed from the Highlands to America, Canada, Australia and New Zealand from this port in the late 18th and early 19thC following the eviction of crofters from their land and homes. Not surprisingly, perhaps, the road from Lochinver to Ullapool is known as Destitution Road. Today Ullapool is a rather beautiful 18thC white fishing village with a resemblance to the Côte d'Azur on a fine day.

35. Urquhart Castle   12 J9
2m SE of Drumnadrochit on W shore of Loch Ness. Sentinel and commanding, this awesome castle thrusts out on a promontory at a spot where the Loch is three miles wide. Most of its surviving parts are 16thC, but there was probably a fortress on this site from c1200. It was once one of the largest castles in Scotland and played a great part in Scottish history from the invasion of Edward I to the Jacobite rising of 1689. Sadly, in 1692 it was blown up to prevent the Jacobites occupying it. Legend states that in one vault treasure is concealed and in another the plague is somehow miraculously contained.

Urquhart Castle

36. Well of Seven Heads   12 H10
W shore of Loch Oich, off A82. Curious monument inscribed in Gaelic, Latin, French and English and topped by seven men's heads. It stands above a spring and recalls the gloomy story of seven brothers executed for the murder of a 17thC chieftain's two sons.

ORKNEY ISLANDS

1. Barony Mill   12 M2
NW tip of Mainland, off A967. A large commercial mill of the type built by wealthy landowners. Tenants brought their grain there and left it as rent. This one started in 1873 and is the last Orkney mill to remain in commercial operation, milling both home and imported grain. A few fields nearby grow bere, which ripens before other grains in this northern climate, and beremeal is exported to Shetland and the Hebrides. *Open by arrangement.*

2. Brough of Birsay   12 M2
Birsay, 11m N of Stromness. A sharp eye for tides is essential when visiting this 50 acre island accessible only by a causeway at low water; when the tide is rising, the path covers remarkably quickly. But once on the island you have a clear head, too, for sorting out the complicated archaeology successive cultures have left behind.

Of major interest are the ruins of a medieval chapel and the extensive remains of a Viking settlement. The chapel, now known as St Peter's, has stone benches along the nave walls. It stands on the site of an older Celtic church and to the north are foundations of a monastery.

The celebrated Birsay Stone, a large memorial slab of red sandstone showing incised figures of three bare-headed warriors, was found here in 1935. Above the figures are Pictish symbols of a mirror, a V-shaped rod and crescent, an elephant and an eagle. The stone is conclusive proof that the earlier chapel was 6th or 7thC and it now lies in the National Museum in Edinburgh. Also of interest are remains of houses – 12 or more rooms with hearths and stables – and Earl Thorfinn's hall which had heating and a bath house.

3. Broch of Gurness   12 M2
11m NNW of Kirkwall, off A966. This 12ft stump which once commanded the Eynhallow

Broch of Gurness

Sound is no less a mystery than other Scottish brochs. An official pamphlet and site plan help explain the jumble of walls and partitions. The block itself was built cAD100. A century later in more settled times other 'rooms' were added – there was even a foundary. People stayed on the site till Viking

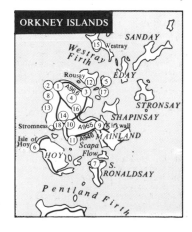

times when several long-houses were added. Examples of these have been disentangled from the ruins and rebuilt clear of the broch. A well of fresh water still bubbles in the centre of the broch.

4. Click Mill   12 M2
2m NE of Dounby, off B9057. Only working example of the many small water-mills once a common feature on local landlords' properties. Built drystone in 1800 with a turf roof, the mill represents a type centuries old which spread through many parts of Europe. Almost identical mills in west Norway were put to use again during the Second World War when commercial flour became scarce.

5. Egilsay (Isle of)   12 N2
Dominating the island is the Church of St Magnus, whose remarkable 50ft-tall round tower can be seen from the main road on the mainland. Experts think the church is 12thC, but it is difficult to date from architecture alone. It is dedicated to a young Earl Magnus, slain nearby.
The church is roofless and its rectangular nave is about 30ft long and 15ft wide with a narrower chancel 15ft long. The stone walls are very thick, especially at the base of the tower. The chancel is barrel vaulted and there is an apartment known as the 'grief' house – the word comes from Old Norse for 'sanctuary'. The tower is one of two built in Orkney. The other at Stenness is long since demolished. Some people have mistakenly compared the tower to those of East Anglia but, in fact, it has Irish connections.

6. Hoy (Isle of)   12 M3
Nr Bay of Rackwick. Sunk in a wilderness of steep, sulky hills is the **Dwarfie Stone**, a strange rock-hewn tomb of neolithic date. Measuring 28ft by 14ft, it has a passage and two cells cut in it. Nearby lies a large stone that once sealed its entrance. The top is open, though no-one knows how or why it came to be so. 16thC speculators held that a giant carved it for his pregnant wife and put her in the larger of the cells. If so, she must have been a mini giantess because the cell is only 5ft long!

7. Italian Chapel   12 N3
St Margaret's Hope, Lamb Holm. Homesick Italian prisoners-of-war built this attractive Catholic chapel in 1943 from a Nissen hut, using scrap metal, concrete, general debris – and a great deal of skill. There were 550 Italians in Orkney captured during Gen Wavell's victory in the western desert of north Africa. They helped build the Churchill Barrier across eastern Scapa Flow – and, say the stories, felt the cold miserably!

8. Kitchener Memorial   12 M2
Marwick Head, SW of Birsay Bay. Nightfall, on June 5th, 1916, Lord Kitchener left Scapa Flow where he had lunched with Admiral Jellicoe aboard the Iron Duke. He was on his way to Russia to confer with the Tsar, and boarded the cruiser Hampshire which was to take him there. Two hours later it sank off Marwick Head: it had struck a mine, laid the week before by a German submarine. Lord Kitchener and all but six of the 700 men aboard her drowned. This tower was unveiled in 1925 'on that corner of his country, which he served so faithfully, nearest to the place where he died on duty'.

9. Kirkwall
Busy town with narrow, twisting streets, which has been the capital of Orkney for many centuries.
Bishop's Palace, *Palace Road*, is the old home of King Hakon Hakonsson of Norway. This 12thC palace was rebuilt in the 16thC and little of the ruin is older than the 15thC. The most conspicuous feature is the five storey round tower, raised by Bishop Reid, the founder of Edinburgh University.

Just along the road is **Earl Patrick's Palace**, hailed as 'not only the finest secular building in Orkney, but possibly the most mature and accomplished piece of Renaissance architecture left in Scotland'. This palace boasts a Great Hall which was warmed by a magnificent fireplace 14ft wide. It was here that dastardly Earl Patrick toasted his toes of a stormy night. How ironic that a man so ill-remembered by Orkadians should leave behind so beautiful a monument of tall windows, graceful turrets, store-rooms, guard-rooms and kitchens! Until rescued by the government, this site and Bishop's Palace were weed-choked rubbish dumps.

Earl Patrick's Palace, Kirkwall

Vikings started building the rose-red **St Magnus Cathedral**, *Broad Street*, of local stone, in 1137. Compared with other cathedrals, it's small, but so skilfully proportioned that gazing round inside it you get an impression of height and space, especially with the seven massive columns on either side of the nave. It was built by masons from Durham and is regarded as an example of some of the finest Norman architecture in Scotland.
In 1919, human bones, including a skull, were found in a wooden case by one of the southern columns, and were identified as those of the martyred St Magnus. Other bones found by a corresponding northern column had already been accepted as those of Magnus's nephew, who established the church. Work continued on the building for 300 years and today it is still in regular use as the parish church. There are splendid views from the cathedral tower.
The charming **Tankerness House**, *Broad St*, is now a museum which follows Orkney life through 4,000 years. Its square courtyard, gardens and arched gateway are a testament to an urbane, rather stylish mode of life which was maintained in the centre of the Orkneys at a time when many rural folk were dying of hunger. Other affluent houses can be seen in Shore Street, Bridge Street and Watergate Street.
Grain Earth House, *Hatson*, is a bean-shaped Iron Age souterrain with an entrance stair leading to an underground passage and chamber. *Key from nearby factory.*

10. Maeshowe   12 M3
10m W of Kirkwall, off A965. This enormous, 30-centuries-old and 115ft in diameter burial mound is the finest megalithic tomb of its kind in western Europe. And graffiti left by Norse marauders who raided it in the 12thC makes it even more interesting: they wrote their names and accounts of their activities in 24 runes, 22 of which have been deciphered. From the inscriptions, we can see that Maeshowe has been used for more than just burial. One inscribed: 'She was bedded. Helgi says so'; another 'Ingigeld is the best of them all'; and a third, 'many a woman has had to stoop to get in here'. Apart from the obvious, this refers to the fact that to enter Maeshowe you have to

Maeshore

stoop in a passage 36ft long and 4ft high. On three sides of the chamber are cells where bodies were laid, knees folded, inside 3½ft compartments.

11. Orphir Church   12 M3
6m SW of Kirkwall, A964. A round, medieval church unique in Scotland, built by Earl Hakon c1116 as a penance for the murder of St Magnus. All that remains is the apse and outline of the circular nave because it was pulled down in the 18thC to make room for a new parish church. This newer church, which was built against the apse of the old one, has itself been demolished.

The church stands near the Earl's great drinking hall, of which nothing remains except some of its foundations, including the base of a south wall more than 100ft long and 4ft thick.

12. Rousay (Isle of)   12 N2
Pre-history hangs heavy on this little-visited relic-ridden island. Excavation of **Midhowe Broch and Tombs** begun in 1938, uncovered a hutted settlement of the wandering Beaker Folk who arrived in Britain around 1800BC, when megalithic nomads from the Mediterranean were burying their dead in elaborate tombs or cairns.

Resident laird of Rousay between the wars was Walter Grant (of whisky fame) who acquired an eye for antiquity as well as distilling. He found and opened the great 'cowstall cairn' of Midhowe – 106ft long, 42ft wide with walls 18ft thick. Stones on the outer wall are tilted to make an ornamental herring-bone pattern. Inside, 25 skeletons were assembled: 17 adults, six adolescents, two young children – plus sheep and cattle bones, deer antlers, a heap of limpet shells and pottery shards. Unlike other cairns on the island, this one is too huge to line with concrete for the safety of visitors, so you have to see it from catwalks under a barnlike construction.

Other ancient sites include **Blackhammer Cairn**, *S coast, N of B9064,* a long cairn bounded by a well-preserved wall and containing a burial chamber divided into seven compartments or 'stalls'. Nearby is **Yarso**, a small, stalled cairn which yielded the bones of 21 people when excavated. Oddly, the skulls were of neolithic date, but pottery fragments suggested connections with the later Bronze Age. Reckoned to be one of the most remarkable neolithic tombs in Orkney, **Taiverso Tuick**, *nr Trumland House,* is a two-storeyed double cairn and has two entrances. Little remains of the upper storey. The tomb was accidentally discovered in 1898 when the proprietor of Trumland House decided to build a look-out seat on this very spot. Bones and some pottery have been unearthed.

13. Skara Brae   12 M2
7½m N of Stromness. A vicious storm blew up in the winter of 1850 and raged across the Bay of Skaill stripping grass and whirling up sand from sand dunes. Next morning, the laird of Skaill found the stone walls of some ancient dwellings laid bare. To this day, Skara Brae neolithic village of 10 one-roomed houses is the best-preserved settlement of the period in Europe.

Having no wood, the community had to build everything of stone which is why we know so much about how these people lived. Several covered passages link houses to each other, and although you walk on grass mounds covering these passages, the huts lie exposed showing their stone furnishings, beds, cupboards, fireplaces, clay-lined larders, and an elaborate drainage system running under the buildings. There's even a paved open courtyard where communal problems were probably discussed. Determined to keep warm, they not only built thick walls, but used their own rubbish as insulation.

You don't have to be archaeologically-minded to really appreciate Skara Brae; it has a touching domesticity similar to Pompeii. This village seems to have been overwhelmed by a violent sandstorm and, like Pompeii, evacuated in panic. One woman in her haste to squeeze through a narrow passageway broke her necklace and strewed beads on the floor where they were found centuries later. *Open by arrangement.*

Skara Brae

14. Stenness, Ring of Brodgar   12 M3
Between Loch of Harray and Loch Stenness, 5m NE of Stromness. A moonlit walk through this magnificent circle of 27 stones is bound to give you the jitters because this whole area of the Orkneys is dotted with Bronze Age remains, and a sense of mystery exudes from every rock. No-one knows why this patch of moorland has been so honoured. Originally, there were probably 60 stones. Some now lie prone or stumped, but several are preserved in situ unlike many other prehistoric sites where stones have been moved over the years. For scenic beauty, the Ring of Brodgar rivals the most splendid circles.

Not quite as striking but also of great significance are the **Standing Stones of Stenness**. Originally there had been 12 stones set out with geometric accuracy round the inside of a ditch 12ft wide and 7ft deep – now only four large, upright stones remain of this Bronze Age circle. Cremated bones, pottery shards, charred grain and a fragment of a stone implement have been found on the site.

15. Westray (Isle of)   12 N1
Its main claim to fame is **Notland Castle**. Menacing and vast, this Orkadian fort has been said by many to look more like a man o' war than a castle. Gun-loops pierce the walls instead of windows, and it was clearly never a house for living in. However, it contains one of the most beautiful staircases in Scotland and many pages of prose have waxed enthusiastic about its strength, proportion and source of inspiration. Although the castle was built originally in 1420 by the governor of Westray, Thomas de Tulloch, it fell into the hands of the dubious Gilbert Balfour, Master of the Household to Mary, Queen of Scots, during the 16thC and it is from then that most of the building dates. Gilbert spent most of his life plotting and conniving and was eventually

Notland Castle, Westray

executed in Sweden in 1576 where he was conspiring against the King.
Pierowall Church has a ruined nave and chancel, out of alignment, with finely lettered tombstones nearby. The Viking graves are interesting.

16. Winksetter   12 M2
Harray Hills, off A986. This could be the oldest surviving house in Orkney from the Norse period – no-one really knows because at the moment the building is being used as a byre (its roof has fallen in) and bits have been added and subtracted. But several experts certainly think it is. Note especially the stone cupboards and shelves, the level flagged floor and the gun-loop windows – all reminiscent of Icelandic houses in the 14thC or earlier.

17. Wyre (Isle of)   12 N2
A mighty Norwegian called Kolbein built Wyre Castle with 8ft-thick walls, in the 12thC. A square keep with a deep ditch are all that remain of the famous stronghold which was recorded in sagas as 'a very unhandy place to attack'. A water tank is cut into the stone floor, and all the stonework is very skilled. The keep had a door at first floor level from which a ladder was lowered to admit welcome visitors only.
North of the castle is a farm called Bu of Wyre. The name shows it belonged to the 'first' family on the island and may have been Kolbein's farm. Further east is a small roofless 12thC church probably built by Kolbein's son. The poet Edwin Muir recalls life on Wyre, where he was born, in his autobiography.

18. Unston Chambered Tomb   12 M3
2m NE of Stromness, A965. Pots found in large numbers in this chambered tomb have given the name Unston Ware to similar pottery found elsewhere in Orkney. The tomb is divided into cells by large stone slabs over 6ft high.

SHETLAND ISLANDS

1. Bressay (Isle of)   12 P9
Apart from having the most northerly nine-hole golf course in Britain, this six-by-two mile slab yielded the interesting Bressay Stone found at Cullinsburgh. Carved with sea monsters, this relic is now in Edinburgh's National Museum of Antiquities. The northern shore of the island was settled in very early times and there are many mounds and standing stones. In the 19thC, the Marquess of Londonderry ran a pony farm on the island; mares were pastured on Bressay and stallions on next door Noss. They were sold profitably as pit ponies to Durham collieries for £25 each, and Shelties are now exported to America as children's pets. Seafarers have known Bressay Sound for centuries and Norsemen often anchored their longships there.

2. Fair Isle   12 O8
Half way between Orkney and Shetland. Acquired by the National Trust for Scotland from the ornithologist George Waterston, Fair Isle has survived more buoyantly than many other islands which gradually lost their inhabitants. Birds and knitwear now draw visitors. The traditional woollen designs, made with home-spun and home-dyed wool, are said to have originated with Spanish sailors who were wrecked after the Great Armada, but it is more likely that the patterns are Norse.

SHETLAND ISLANDS

Fair Isle also has the largest Bronze Age mound in Shetland. There are 200 altogether and this one is 122ft by 88ft and stands 10ft high. These grass-covered, unnatural looking heaps are composed entirely of fist-sized stones broken and discoloured by heat. Their origin and purpose remain a mystery.

3. Croft House   12 O10
Dunrossness, 25m S of Lerwick, E of A970. A thatched croft complex of mid 19thC croft house and steading – carefully restored and authentically furnished. Dunrossness is a long peninsula descriptively named 'dyn-rastr-ness' or 'headland of the dinning rost'. Even on calm days waves can be heard breaking off Sumburgh Head. Shetland crofts were generally five to 10 acres of arable land with pasture rights in the hills. Isolated crofts were rare; people grouped together and the little villages lived from cultivating land and the Scattald, or common grazing, which a century ago was the only source of fuel. Croft houses often face the sea and above high water is a 'naust' or shelter for a small boat. Shetland crofters made use of everything on the island: sea gave food; arable land gave crops; hills gave fuel and roofs. Twisted heather ropes weighted with stones held down the roof in winter gales. Each croft had a kiln and floors were only trodden earth. Families slept in box beds according to sex and status and their little lamps burned fish liver oil. Cabbage, potatoes, beremeal and oats were staple foods, and seabird eggs, fish, cheese and lamb were also on the menu. Crofters probably ate better than families elsewhere in Britain, but they were always vulnerable to famine from crop failure, loss of livestock and war. *Open most days, summer.*

4. Jarlshof   12 O10
Sumburgh Head, 28m S of Lerwick. Three thousand years of human life have been unearthed at this remarkable three acre archaeological site south of the airport. Excavation started at the turn of the century, and the oldest building uncovered was a Stone Age hut. In the Bronze Age a village was built on top of it and newcomers added iron implements, circular huts and souterrains or weems (underground earth houses). Later, Iron Age folk raised a massive broch on the growing pile. By AD200, the 'wheel house' people had arrived, and after them, around AD800, the Norsemen. The Viking settlement spread and was obviously peaceful enough for fond parents to fashion little soapstone toys for their children. During the

Middle Ages, a farmstead was built and in the 16thC, a hall.

Jarlshof has yielded many fascinating finds from its human quarry. It shows the earliest evidence for stalling cattle in Britain. A channel was found to carry cattle urine into a special tank and one of the excavators also detected a stain from a manure heap. A whale's vertebra set into the wall of the house had been used as a tethering post. Also found by that excavator was a Bronze Age smithy, complete with a sandfilled casting pit in which the clay moulds rested while molten metal was poured in. Broken moulds show that the smith made socketed axes, knives, swords and 'sunflower' pins. Seven Norse houses have been dug up and personal belongings such as bone needles and combs, glass beads, lamps, whorls for spinning and even stone gaming boards were unearthed. One Jarlshof artist left drawings scratched on slate of Viking ships with dragonhead prows and two portraits. Some archaeologists regard this as the most interesting site in Britain because of the way each culture superimposed itself on the next. Today, you can step into the Bronze Age houses, still surviving to more or less roof height, wander into wheel-houses, and imagine the people who sat by the still-reddened hearths.

5. Lerwick   12 O9
The fishing industry brought countryfolk to Lerwick in the 16thC: they sold their produce to Dutch fishermen anchored in the sheltered Bressay Sound. Produce wasn't all they sold – in 1625 the court at Scalloway ordered the erring village to be demolished for immoral goings-on! Next to anchor there was the English fleet, fighting against the Dutch. After the wars, Dutch nets were cast again and Lerwick grew from their trade and recreation. Naval vessels brought more activity and the herring industry established Lerwick once and for all as 'capital' of the Shetlands. In the 19thC, smuggling and whaling became prosperous. The oldest streets and buildings can be seen along the shore – the storehouses reach out into the sea. Subterranean passages are still discovered during building work, and twisting Commercial Street, cosmopolitan as ever, displays signs in Norwegian as well as English.

In January, Lerwick forgets the 20thC and welcomes the return of the sun in the fire festival of 'Up-Helly-Aa'. For this Viking ceremony, a Norse 30ft longship is built and a crew wearing winged helmets voyage through torchlit streets. The Guiser Jarl leads his horned men brandishing broadswords and battleaxes to Clickhimin loch, 10 minutes from town. There the galley is set on fire – echo of an old Viking funeral rite – to mark the death of winter. Afterwards, Jarl and the crew have to visit every gathering that night – including the sick in hospital. The following day is always a holiday for sleeping off the after-effects.

'Up Helly Aa Festival', Lerwick

People of the Iron Age secured the site of **Clickhimin Broch**, *1m SW of centre*, with a stone fort when it was a rocky islet in a fresh-water loch. Now it's a promontory reached by a causeway over marshes. Clickhimin is an excellent example of a broch. You enter it through a massive wall surrounding the islet and find it standing 17ft tall. Two other

openings in the wall at higher levels are unusual in design and puzzle archaeologists. The oldest building in Lerwick after Clickhimin Broch is **Fort Charlotte**. It was begun in 1655 by Cromwell to protect the Sound of Bressay from the Dutch. The fort is five sided with high walls and gunpoints leering seawards. When Cromwell left in 1658, he took the cannon with him. Five years later the Dutch landed at Lerwick, and burned the barracks and several of the best houses in town. Today, the fort is rather obscured by buildings on three sides but, standing on a clifftop, it overlooks the harbour and occupies two acres of ground. The first real road in Shetland was a gun-track from Fort Charlotte to the Knab headland.

The **Shetland Museum**, *Lower Hillhead*, follows the development of man in Shetland from pre-history to the present. Galleries are devoted to archaeology, art and textiles, folk life and shipping. The collection is entirely local.

6. Scalloway   12 O9
Baned 'skalavagr' – Norse for 'bay of the skali or hall' – this fishing and fish processing settlement is the second largest town in the Shetlands and was formerly the capital During World War II, Scalloway was a base for operations by Norwegian patriots sent on sabotage missions to Nazi-occupied Norway. They sailed in wooden fishing boats across the North Sea, landing ammunition and returning with refugees. Scalloway undoubtedly maintained morale among many Norwegians, and coined the phrase: 'to take the Shetland bus' meaning to escape.

Mocked by incontinent gulls, the medieval **Scalloway Castle** was built by the tyrannical Earl Patrick Stewart – known locally for his cruelty as Black Pate – in 1600. He drove his Shetland subjects to quarry and hump stone and lime for this new stronghold and legend states that warriors' blood and maidens' hair were used as cement. Keen to dilute all Norse influence, Patrick moved the ancient Alting (supreme court) from Tingwall to Scalloway. There, the udallers (landowners under udal or Norse law) had to acknowledge the earl's supremacy. However, he got his just dues – Patrick was executed at Edinburgh for treason, and by 1700, slates were falling off the castle roof and the timbers were rotting. Today the castle still shows a gaunt grace with interesting, intimate details in the fireplaces, circular privies and single rooms.

7. Tingwall   12 O9
3m N of Scalloway. The word 'ting' in Norse meant law court: they were the basis of Norse government and each district had one, hence the surviving names of Delting, Lunnasting and Aithsting. Tingwall was the meeting-place of the supreme court, or alting, of the Shetlands, and here on this green headland the earliest kind of democracy or 'parliament' in Britain took place. It is thought to have been held on a little island in Tingwall loch reached in those days by stepping stones. Since Norse times, the loch level has lowered and the islet is now a promontory on the north shore. Here, people brought complaints, petitions and appeals, and criminals were tried. All freemen were obliged to attend, and new legislation was passed there. A simple, undated standing stone can be seen from the Tingwall valley road.

Tingwall Valley Agricultural Museum is a private collection of tools and equipment used by Shetland crafters. It is housed in a mid 18thC granary, stables and bothy. *Open most days, summer; or by arrangement.*

8. Staneydale Temple   12 N8
3m ENE of Walls. Malta and Gozo are the only other places with buildings like this neolithic 65ft by 54ft 'temple'. There is nothing like it on the Orkneys, and Shetland seems to have

its own kind of cairn or tomb – horseshoe shaped with three inner chambers. Twenty eight have been discovered, but none as huge as Staneydale which has 12ft-thick walls. Perhaps settlers voyaged on Kon-tiki rafts from the south, when the climate was kinder and sea crossings calmer.

9. Mousa (Isle of)   12 O10
Island of sheep and plump, dark ponies, whose main claim to fame is **Mousa Broch.** The best preserved broch in Britain, this 40ft tall ruin stands on a cliff-edge, exuding mystery. No-one really knows who built brochs, though archaeologists believe that they are Iron Age. There are 500 of them all over northern Scotland, 95 in Shetland. These circular 'fortresses' were built drystone and are reckoned to be the highest development of drystone building in western Europe.
Commonly known as 'Picts houses', brochs are defensive rather than offensive. The walls, skilfully composed of small, locally quarried stones, are unscalable and their sites are generally strategic, such as headlands or hills. Bell-shaped brochs have walls up to 20ft thick at base. Higher up they hollow, and contain a series of galleries with stairs running round and up the tower. How their builders kept the inner walls so straight is unknown, but Viking shipbuilders worked by eye alone, and Iron Age masons probably developed a similar feel for their material. Broch speculation is endless. But their distribution implies a well-organised people pushed to northern extremes of the country: during the Iron Age the weather deteriorated, wetter, stormier conditions spoiling agricultural land. Both the resulting land hunger in western Europe and the news of Roman advances caused widespread migration. *Open summer.*

10. Papa Stour (Isle of)   12 N8
'Lepers' were once isolated in a colony on this small island one mile off Mainland's western coast. Victims were, in fact, suffering from a degenerate kind of scurvy – rife in Scotland during the 17th and 18thC. It wasn't contagious, but many sufferers elsewhere died alone in little stone huts in the hills isolated from the rest of the community.
The island was named by Norsemen after the Papae, or Scottish–Irish priest who established monastic settlements all over Shetland (Papa ey Storr means big island of the priests). Depopulation in the last 100 years has been a problem for this fertile island. In 1841 there were 382 inhabitants and

today there are only 30. From this island stems the Papa Stour sword dance which is one of the most ancient dances in Scotland: with a Scandinavian tune, it is performed by seven men representing the seven saints of Christendom.

11. St Ninian's (Isle of)   12 O10
Off W coast of Mainland. A schoolboy helping archaeology students from Aberdeen with a dig on this tiny tidal island in 1958, struck something firm under a thin slab of stone. It was a box of rotted larch filled with one of the most amazing treasure finds in Britain – second only to Sutton Hoo. This priceless silver, known as the St Ninian's Treasure, included: bowls, brooches, a spoon with a dog's head, a fork-like implement with one prong, a sword pommel and various other items of uncertain use. As larch wasn't planted in Britain until the 18thC, it was concluded that the box must have been Norse. But who buried it upside-down and never came back for it, no-one knows.
The students had been excavating the site of a 12thC chapel on the island. They opened up the apse, altar and nave, and found stones inscribed with Pictish symbols and a skeleton of a man 6ft tall, possibly the bones of St Ninian himself, who preached the gospel to Picts more than 100 years before Columba came to Iona. Later, 17thC Catholics used the chapel ruins for candlelit worshipping, when disapproved of by the new official Presbyterian church of Scotland.
The St Ninian treasure is now in the National Museum of Antiquities in Edinburgh. The University of Aberdeen fought hard to keep it north, either in Shetland or Aberdeen, but they lost a savage legal battle with the Crown. St Ninian's is not strictly an island, but a spit jutting out into the sea, known locally as an ayre. The stretch of white sand which joins it to the mainland is one of the most beautiful in the world. St Ninian's well brims with clear water – throw in a coin and have a wish.

12. Unst (Isle of)   12 P6
Most northerly castle in Britain, the late 16thC ruin of **Muness Castle** stands on the south eastern tip of Unst and still boasts a fair display of towers and turrets. It was built by Laurence Bruce, half-brother of the unpopular and callous Robert Stewart who bled Shetlanders of their money and treated them more harshly than they had ever known under Norse thumbs. Having acquired lands on Unst, Laurence bought Muness to defend them.

TAYSIDE

1. Aberlemno Sculptured Stones   11 M7
Aberlemno, 5m NE of Forfar, B9134. These stones, like many other beautiful stones in the area, were sculpted by Picts. Their strange, undeciphered symbols with figures of animals and warriors riding horses, adorn the upright cross slab in the churchyard. Three other stones stand beside the road. Many consider that the skill of the carving, before it was weathered, would have compared with the best relief work in the world.

2. Arbroath Abbey   11 N8
Arbroath. Thomas a Becket is remembered here in this prosperous 12thC Benedictine abbey. The great rose window known as the Arbroath 'O' is said to have been illuminated as a guide to ships and contrived beautiful light effects. Only the cloisters remain intact, and an abbot's house has been converted to a museum.
Scotland's Declaration of Independence, acclaimed as one of the greatest

pronouncements of freedom in the history of Europe, was signed here in 1320. In a letter to the Pope, the Scottish barons acknowledged Robert Bruce as their king and affirmed their determination to maintain Scottish independence. It also stated that the Scottish people had the right to cast out their king should he betray the cause for freedom.

3. Ardoch Roman Camp   11 J9
10m S of Crieff, A822 at Braco. Agricola and his legions once tramped this ground scanning the horizon for lurking Caledonians. They settled here, and this is now considered to be the most impressive Roman fort in Scotland. It is thought that the Romans called the fort Alanus after the River Allan close by.
Among the extraordinary maze of ridges and ditches, post holes and charcoal have been found. Early wood houses were later replaced with stone. Forts like this were permanent army bases and built as rectangles with curved corners: you recognise them by their

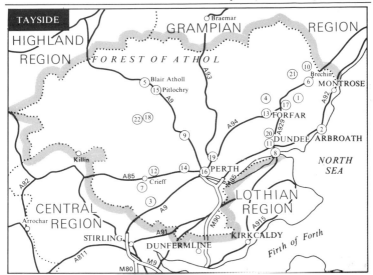

defensive banks and ditches and by their two entrances, one long and one short.
Long after the Romans left, local legends simmered about buried treasure here. A criminal was even pardoned by the court on condition that he descend a deep hole near the camp to look for it. He did, and came up with a batch of Roman helmets and weapons. On his second descent for the elusive treasure, he unfortunately suffocated.

4. Barrie's Birthplace   11 M7
Brechin Rd, Kirriemuir. American fans of this Scottish playwright nearly succeeded in removing his cottage stone by stone and setting it down across the Atlantic as a Barrie museum. Other enthusiasts wanted to take it down to Kensington Gardens in London to join Peter Pan. Fortunately, it was bought soon after Barrie's death and given to the National Trust for Scotland and today it stands where Barrie left it – a modest, slate-roofed, two-storeyed house of local stone.
The wash house in the yard was Barrie's first 'theatre'. Furnished by his mother, it contains possessions and paraphenalia belonging to her writer son: desk, couch and settle from his Adelphi Terrace flat, manuscripts, letters, photographs and press cuttings. Barrie used material from Kirriemuir in much of his work. *Open summer, or by arrangement.*

5. Blair Castle   11 J6
6m NNW of Pitlochry, A9. Changing like an architectural chameleon with the needs and styles of the day, Blair is now a phoney but appealing white turreted baronial castle containing many fascinating features and objects. It originated as Cumming's Tower in 1269, grew to a 15thC castle and is the seat of the Duke of Atholl, or chief of Clan Murray.

Blair Castle

Blair saw violent times in the 17th and 18thC. Garrisoned by Montrose in 1644, it was captured by Cromwell in 1652 and held for eight years until the Restoration. Later, the castle was occupied by the Jacobites. Blair was the last castle in Britain to be besieged. Because of the damage suffered from the Jacobite attack, the castle was remodelled in the mid 18thC in the Georgian, classical style, but with the return of the Gothic fashion in the 19thC, it was re-baronialised by the 7th duke.
See the splendid 'picture staircase' (panelled and lined with portraits), a variety of gruesome broadswords and other Highland weapons: Blair is best known as a museum of Highland relics. *Open summer.*

6. Brechin Round Tower   11 N7
Brechin. This impressive 106ft-high tower with 'foreign' looking Celtic styles, is one of only two of its kind in Scotland (the other is at Abernethy). Very similar to the round towers of Ireland built as refuges for the clergy in times of invasion, this one shows the strength of the influence of the Irish. Windows and doors have sloping sides (typically Celtic) and the legs of Christ in the crucifixion above the door hang uncrossed in the Irish way. Two weird beasts guarding the door are also thoroughly Irish.

7. Drummond Castle Gardens   11 J9
2½m S of Crieff, A8022. A graceful, Italian garden designed in the reign of Charles II is the showpiece of this Drummond family settlement. Queen Victoria prompted its restoration in the late 19thC when she decided to visit, and a garden banquet was spread in her honour. After the last war it was once more revived. A multiple sundial dating from 1630 tells the time in all the major cities of Europe and the 15thC tower is now an armoury. The little lake in the fields marks the place where government troops camped during the '45 rebellion. The Duchess of Perth, a Jacobite fanatic, was so appalled by this that afterwards she had the area flooded to erase their memory.
Drummond Castle was partly rebuilt during the Restoration having been bombarded by Cromwell, and was much modified in Victorian times. The family built another mansion alongside in which to live. *Gardens open certain days, summer.*

8. Dundee   11 M8
Historically fascinating, but not visibly so, Dundee is a city of fine views and jam

factories, memories of whaling days and jute jaunts to Calcutta. Dundee was and is the centre of the jute-spinning industry in Britain. Jute is used in matting, sacking and lino backing. For generations, Dundee businessmen spent time in India and returned wealthy to build the great 'colonial' houses which are now hotels, flats and institutions.

The Old Steeple, *Kirkstile, Nethergate*, 156ft high and considered one of the finest steeples in Scotland, peers over the city square proud of its 15thC Gothic. Originally it was part of four churches called the City Churches, but they were burned down in the 19thC and rebuilt. Displays of bell-ringing, stained glass and local history are staged in the tower.

The Unicorn, *Victoria Dock*, a 46-gun wooden frigate, is the oldest in Britain and recently has been restored. Launched in 1824 at Chatham, she now tells on board the history of shipbuilding, the Royal Navy – and herself. *Open summer.*

9. Dunkeld 11 K8
15m NNW of Perth. Gently snoozing beside the River Tay, Dunkeld remembers stormier times when Jacobites burned down the town after the Battle of Killiecrankie in 1689. Its beautiful little houses date from the years just after that, and they have been charmingly restored by the National Trust and Perth County Council. Ordinary people live in them, so you can only view from the outside. But there's a visitor's centre which gives information and audio/visual shows about the town.
Meaning 'fort of the Culdees', Dunkeld became a major religious centre for the Celtic church when St Columba's relics were transferred here from Iona which was threatened by Norse invasion. It became the mother-church of Scotland and despite its secluded position was frequently attacked by the Vikings. A remarkable larch in the grounds of Dunkeld House Hotel is said to be the first tree of its kind ever planted in Britain.

9. Dunkeld Cathedral 11 K8
High Street, Dunkeld. Described as the most beautifully-situated cathedral in Britain, this ruined church ponders peacefully among trees and lawns by the River Tay. Founded in the 9thC, many benefactors have paid to restore damage made over the centuries. Parts are 13thC, but after the Reformation it lay in ruins for 40 years. Because there was no road to it, mortar for repairs was carried there in baskets and stones on horseback. By 1691, a local family had re-roofed the choir, and final restoration was completed in 1908. Look out for two special tombs: the Wolf of Badenoch, an outlaw who ran wild over the Highlands in the 14thC, is buried here, and 15thC Bishop Cardeny is in St Ninian's chapel.

10. Edzell Gardens and Castle 11 N6
6m N of Brechin, off B966. A delightful Renaissance garden created by Lord Lindsay in the 17thC with help from foreign experts. Enclosed within warm red walls are a vaulted summer-house, part of a bath-house and lawns outlined in low hedges cut to form family mottos. The armorial wall of stone sculptures, heraldry and panels has recesses filled with summer-blooming blue and white lobelia which team up with the red of the wall to make the laird's colours. The 'big walls' round old gardens in Scotland sometimes had a greenhouse effect that ripened peaches and nurtured exotic blooms.
The castle keep of the Lindsays is an impressive ruin. It was once the most magnificent castle in Angus, and the oldest part, which is preserved, dates from the 16thC. In 1562 Edzell was visited by Mary, Queen of Scots, and her bower is in the main Stirling Tower.

11. Fowlis Easter Kirk 11 M8
4m NNW of Dundee, A923. The only church in Scotland still decorated with pre-Reformation paintings – and no-one knows how they survived. Records show that in 1610 the synod said they should be 'obliterated with green colour'. Three centuries later they are still here. The paintings depict a Crucifixion, the Virgin Mary, St John the Baptist, and St Catherine. Though many Flemish artists sailed over to Firth and Tay shores seeking work about this time, they are naive enough to have been painted locally.
The first church was built on this site c1150 but the oldest part of the church as it now stands, is 15thC. Note the bronze alms-dish, dated 1487, which is one of the finest in the country and the tabernacle with a sculpture of the Annunciation.

12. Fowlis Wester Sculptured Stone and St Bean's Church 11 J9
5m NE of Crieff, off A85. A Pictish stone from the 8thC with unusually clear carvings stands 10ft high within a railing in the village. Opposite is St Bean's church which has a finely carved Pictish cross in it. Though the church itself is 13thC, it was restored in 1927.

13. Glamis Castle 11 M7
5m SW of Forfar, A928. Aptly associated with Shakespeare's 'Macbeth', this forest of towers and turrets is one of the most theatrical-looking in Scotland. Inside, there are all sorts of things to see: a medieval hall, a crypt, spiral staircases and huge fireplaces. Rumour has it that there's a secret chamber known only to each heir.
The castle dates mainly from 1675, but portions of the tower with walls 15ft thick are much older. Crowning glory of the medieval hall is its plaster ceiling, and there is china, tapestry, and furniture to admire, too. Don't miss the massive sundial in the grounds. The Queen Mother spent her childhood here (you can see her rooms) and Princess Margaret was born here. *Open most days, summer.*

Glamis Castle

14. Huntingtower Castle 11 K8
3m WNW of Perth, off A85. The space between the two towers is known as 'Maiden's leap' after the story that a daughter of the first Earl caught with her lover had to jump from one tower of this fortified manor to another across a drop of 60ft to escape discovery.
Leaping lovers aren't all this castle has witnessed in its four centuries. The so-called Raid of Ruthven (as it was then) was when the Gowries, who lived here during the 16thC, held captive the boy King James VI. Shakespeare may have based the plotting and conspiracy of Macbeth on this situation. But James escaped, and lured the entire Gowrie clan to their death four years later. Ruthven was then re-named Huntingtower. Murals, plasterwork and fine, painted,wooden ceilings are its most famous features inside.

15. Pass of Killiecrankie 11 K7
2½m N of Pitlochry, off A9. A wooded gorge once a nightmare to any traveller en route from Perth to Inverness. Until General Wade built his military road here, nothing but a narrow track ran above the river. This was the bloody site where, in 1689, Jacobites, led by

Bonnie Dundee, routed William III's army under General MacKay. Although the Jacobites 'won', victory was fleeting. Dundee died of his wounds in the moment of victory and within a year Jacobite resistance had collapsed. A steep footpath descends to Soldier's Leap, where one fleeing redcoat evaded capture by leaping from rock to rock over the river. A National Trust information centre features the battle, natural history and ranger services.

16. Perth   11 K9

Once Scotland's capital, many of its older buildings were pulled down by 16thC religious fanatics or 19thC city councils. Excavation round the Mercat Cross in the 1950s showed signs of prehistoric habitation. A wattle hut on a rough timber platform was found, with a kitchen rubbish dump for shellfish nearby. It has been dated c4,000BC. Roman legions reaching this gateway to the Highlands on the Tay are supposed to have exclaimed in wonder: 'Ecce, Tiber!'
John Knox thundered forth his momentous sermon on 'idolatory' in St John's Kirk, *St John's St*, in 1559 and incited a riot of Reformers who rampaged through church and town. Apart from being a noble, 15thC cruciform church, St John's has a priceless collection of pre-Reformation silver plate. The 16thC baptismal basin is particularly fine and there is also some excellent modern stained glass. For many years three separate congregations worshipped here and it was only this century that the partitions were removed.
North Inch is a spacious green sward sporting golf course and recreation ground – but in 1396 the scene of a notorious clan combat between the Chattans and the Kays. Thirty men on each side fought to the death before Robert III and thousands of spectators to settle a squabble. Only 11 Chattans survived and all the Kays died. Witches were burned on South Inch.
Headquarters of the famous Black Watch Highland regiment, Balhousie Castle, *facing North Inch Park*, houses their musuem, too, with displays from 1740 to the present.

17. Restenneth Priory   11 M7

1½m ENE of Forfar, off B9113. An epoch-making story lies behind the stones of this 13thC Augustinian priory and its 8thC chapel ruin. King Nechtan of the Picts (who built the chapel) asked an abbot friend to send him a list of the differences between the Roman church and his own Irish church. The abbot sent St Boniface to explain, and this chapel may be the first in Scotland – or Britain – to take up 'Roman' Christianity. The tower could be 8thC – which certainly fits the story. The fine chancel, in its beautiful surroundings, is 13thC.

18. St Mary's Church   11 K7

Grandtully, Pitcairn Farm, 2m ENE of Aberfeldy. A 16thC church with a painted ceiling well worth the squint to work out all its heraldic and symbolic themes.

19. Scone Palace   11 K8

2m N of Perth, off A93. Drama and magic surround the Stone of Destiny or Stone of Scone, an oblong block of red sandstone brought here in the 9thC by Kenneth MacAlpine. Legend says that Jacob rested his head on the stone when he had his vision. Somehow it got to Spain, then Ireland, and Kenneth picked it up in Argyll and brought it to Scone where he defeated the Picts. Edward I sacked Scone for it in 1296 and put it in Westminster Abbey as part of the 'chair' used in coronation ceremonies, where it rests today.
The present palace was built as recently as 1803, but on the site of an ancient abbey and palace dating back to the earliest days of Scottish history when Scone was the capital of the Pictish kingdom. A religious centre for over 1,000 years, Scottish kings were crowned at Scone until the 16thC.
Treasures in the state rooms include: 18thC clocks, 16thC needlework, ivories, French furniture, porcelain, and 16thC needlework, including bed hangings worked by Mary, Queen of Scots. See the grounds and pinetum which has one of the finest collections of rare conifers in the country. *Open summer*.

Scone Palace

20. Tealing Earth House and Dovecote   11 M8

5m N of Dundee, off A929. Investigate this souterrain or earth house and hazard a guess at its function for our Iron Age ancestors who crouched in its inner chambers, passage and long, curved gallery. Nearby is a lovely 16thC dovecote.

21. The Caterthuns   11 M6

5m NW of Brechin. Iron Age people must have worked hard to raise these forts that now stand on hills either side of the road from Balrownie to Pitmudie beyond Little Brechin. Brown Caterthun has four concentric ramparts and ditches. White Caterthun is well-preserved with a massive stone rampart, defensive ditch and outer earthworks. Walk across to Lundie Hill and you'll find similar earthworks.

22. Wade's Bridge   11 J7

N of Aberfeldy, B846. Wade may have failed to quell the Jacobite unrest, but he opened up almost impenetrable country, leaving his mark all over the central Highlands. Altogether, he built 250 miles of metalled road and 40 bridges. Most were so soundly devised that we use them today, and this one carries heavy motor traffic without any strengthening.

WESTERN ISLES

1. Barra (Isle of)   12 A9

St Barr gave his name to the island on which **Cille Barra** and the restored chapel of St Mary, *Eoligarry, N end*, stand. They were once part of a medieval monastery. Four gravestones thought to have come from Iona are preserved here.
But Barra's main centre of interest is **Kisimul Castle** *by Castlebay*. Pirates galore harried the coasts of 16thC Scotland and one of them – MacNeil of Barra – took refuge here in his

islet castle home whenever the going got hot. MacNeil the Turbulent, as he was known, was outlawed, and so enraged Queen Elizabeth with his outrageous exploits that she demanded his head. MacKenzie of Kintail was set to trap him. He did, and MacNeil was shipped to Edinburgh where the court was astonished to find this fiend of the seas a friendly old man with a long grey beard. MacNeil used his head to save his head. He won James over by pointing out that his

WESTERN ISLES

ST. KILDA IS.

OUTER HEBRIDES

ISLE OF LEWIS

B857

Stornoway

B859

Tarbert

LITTLE MINCH

N. UIST

S. UIST

Castlebay

ISLAND OF SKYE

INNER HEBRIDES

'piracies' were the Queen's just toll. She, after all, had executed James's mother, Mary Stewart. James released him.

Despite his eccentricity, this laird of Kisimul 'fathered' his people: he found wives for widowers and husbands for widows; if tenants lost cattle by misfortune, MacNeil replaced them; when they grew too old to farm, MacNeil fed and sheltered them.

Castle Kisimul stands 150 yds offshore and was restored by Robert MacNeil, an American whose forebears thought so highly of themselves that after dinner their trumpeter mounted the battlements to announce that since MacNeil himself had dined, the rest could now do likewise! *Open certain days, summer.*

Barra

2. Eriskay (Isle of) 12 A8

Famous for its yearning love lilt (often misleadingly pronounced 'a risky love lilt'), this three-by-one-and-a-half mile isle lacks soil, and its 200 people live by selling prawn, herring and lobster. The women knit gossamer shawls and fishermen's jerseys in traditional patterns unique to Eriskay: sails, waves and harbour steps.

Prince Charlie first set foot in Scotland here on a silver beach, in 1745. A pink flower near it is said to grow nowhere else in Scotland, and some people believe the seeds fell from his pocket. More recently, the 12,000 ton Politician went aground one February night in 1941 spilling 20,300 cases of whisky, en route to New York. When news leaked, boozing expeditions arrived from as far away as Stornaway and Oban. Even the hens on

Eriskay were drunk for a week, and women poured finest Scotch on their fires to flame the peat. Most hotels in the area can still offer you a souvenir of the Politician – but polluted with oil and seawater.

3. Harris (Isle of) 12 C4

When the Earl of Dunmore bought the island in 1834, his wife promoted the sale of the first Harris tweeds in London. The crofters' skill had long been famous, but they wove cloth only for themselves or local markets. Her public relations campaign developed the industry and it spread to South Uist, Barra, Lewis and the West Coast. Modern mills mushroomed, and by the 1960s, annual production was six million yards worth £4 million. America bought three quarters of it. Other weavers began to take the Harris name and a court case in 1964 decided the issue once and for all. A tweed has the distinctive Harris trade mark only if: 'It's made from pure wool produced in Scotland, spun, dyed and finished in the Outer Hebrides, and handwoven by islanders in their own homes . . .'. A glance at the label guarantees the genuine product.

St Clement's, *Rodel*, is a 16thC cruciform church. No-one knows who St Clement was though informed guesses say an early chief of the MacLeods is most likely as the clan has long been buried at Rodel. In fact, this simple church is more famous for its three tombs than its own charm. Each tomb shows a recumbent warrior chief sculpted in jet black schist, glittering with quartz granules. The church's south wall has a sheel-na-gig, a roughly-hewn little fertility figure. Celtic churches in Ireland have at least 30 of these, but the only other one in Scotland (at Iona's nunnery) has recently disappeared. The chips knocked off this otherwise excellent example were caused by the Countess of Dunmore who ordered her gillie to fire his gun at it.

Lewis (Isle of) 12 D1

An exciting landscape of peaty moorlands with a menacing outcrop of grey rock and sheer cliffs forming sandy bays and numerous lochs. Over the years the crofters have improved the pastures, now rich with wild flowers, and have cultivated oats and potatoes. The traditional black houses are being replaced with modern buildings. This is the most prosperous of the islands in the Outer Hebrides, partly due to the importance of Stornoway, a 'proper' town and a major port.

4. Lewis Black House 12 D1

Arnol, 15m NW of Stornoway. A 'little Ice Age', officially known as the second post-glacial oscillation, hit Scotland between 1550 and 1700 and prompted hardy islanders to cosy themselves in new 'black houses' of which this one at Arnol is an excellent example.

Designed to withstand terrible gales, the gap between the double walls was filled with peat or rubble. The thatched roof rested on the inner wall which swept wind blasts up clear of the roof edge and gave a platform for rethatching work. Hebridean families kept warm round a continuously-burning peat fire in the centre of the house which belched murky smoke through a hole in the roof. A big iron pot hung above it, and light came in through the door or from seal oil lamps. Opinions of the origin of the name black house vary; it could refer to soot-blackened rafters and thatch or the drystone walls which looked darker than cemented walls of ordinary houses.

5. Lewis, Dun Carloway Broch 12 C2

15m WNW of Stornoway, A858.

Broch-spotters will want to visit this excellent example of Iron Age masonry preserved to a height of 30ft. Brochs are peculiar to Scotland and come from the Gaelic word 'bradh' meaning 'round'. Their double walls were usually built to 50ft from a base diameter of 60ft. Galleries rose to the top of the broch inside these double walls which were 15ft thick, the stones of which were too closely laid even for one toe-hold. Some of these surfaces have remained unbroken by weather for 2,000 years.

6. Lewis, Shawbost Folk Museum 12 D1
19m NW of Stornoway, A858. See how a Norse water-mill worked at this lively folk museum which also conveys how a Hebridean black house really felt. Although other cottages on the mainland and inner isles call themselves 'black', they aren't. Black houses have a checklist of four definite characteristics: drystone walls, double walls, thatch roof, and roof set on the inner wall. This museum was created under the Highland Village Competition in 1970. *Open weekdays.*

7. Lewis, Standing Stones of Callanish 12 C2
Callanish, 16m W of Stornoway, off A858. Decoding Callanish has absorbed scientists since the site was first excavated by Sir James Matheson in 1857. The stones seem to be astronomically lined up for sun, moon and star sightings. The central pillar, for instance, casts its shadow exactly along the line of the grave and passage at sunset on the day of the equinox.
Callanish is considered by some as the most impressive stone circle in Britain. It isn't a henge like Stonehenge (from Old English 'hengen' meaning 'to hang' which refers to the lintel stones across the tall standing stones), but an avenue of 19 monoliths leading to a circle of 13 stones with rows of stones fanning out from it. Part of the complex is a chambered cairn or tomb with a long entrance passage and human bone has been found there. The estimated date is c1600BC which would mean Callanish was built 200 years later than the great lintelled circle of Stonehenge.

8. Lewis, The Trushel Stone 12 D1
Ballantrushel, 13m NW of Stornoway, off A857. Isles people hardly notice the single standing stones and circles dotted about the Hebrides. So old in age and memory, they are part of the landscape itself. Many stones and circles have sunk into the peat and will probably never be found. But this 19ft monolith probably raised around 1600BC is especially impressive. It is 6ft wide, 4ft thick and the tallest in Scotland. Other stones nearby at Steinacleit suggest that it was part of a group.

9. North Uist (Isle of) 12 A6
Ruins of a medieval college and monastery, known as **Trinity Temple,** *8m SW of Lochmaddy, off A865,* are said to have been founded by Beathag, daughter of the warrior king Somerled, in 1200. It's the most famous ecclesiastical building in North Uist and Duns Scotus, one of the great medieval philosophers, studied here. Close by is the Field of Blood – site of a gruesome clan battle between the MacLeods of Harris and MacDonalds of Uist in 1601. Look out for some cup and ring marks.

10. St Kilda Islands 12 A4
St Kilda isn't one island, but a mountainous archipelago of four islands and five great rock stacks far out in the Atlantic. A small, primitive, patriarchial society subsisted here for centuries in damp gales. The last 36 people left in 1930 because life had become insupportable. Today, the National Trust for Scotland takes boat-loads of volunteers over to Hirta, the main island, for summer restoration work on the cottages, dykes and church of St Kilda's only village.
St Kildans lived mainly off wild fowl and elementary crofting. Sometimes they fished, or ran cattle and ponies. Aristocratic tourists travelled here during the 18th and 19thC to 'view the human menagerie'. So much remains of the St Kildans themselves that its desertion seems especially sad. Sixteen new cottages were built there in 1860 and they are still standing. So is the manse, school, factor's house and the church where the religious islanders spent 10 hours on a Sunday. Even the black houses survive. Cleits or stone beehive cells were built as larders, wardrobes or storerooms and more than a 1,000 dot the hill-slopes. Wind whistling through them preserved seafowl for food and kept clothes aired.
Earlier settlements have yet to be explored: a fort site at Dun and three ecclesiastical sites on Hirta.
Alexander Thom, emeritus Professor of Engineering at Oxford, published in 1967 a revolutionary report on 500 stone circles and standing stones in all parts of Britain which he had surveyed. From this he drew conclusions about prehistoric British mathematics. One of his surveys involved four standing stones in the St Kilda group of isles, known as **Boreray Stone Alignment.** The stones are: Clack Mhic Leoid on the headland of Harris above the Sound of Taransay; a stone on Benbecula west of Beinn Rueval; An Carra on South Uist west of Beinn Mhor; and Clach an t-Saggirt on North Uist. From these stones, the sun setting behind Boreray gives all kinds of calendar information.

11. South Uist (Isle of) 12 A8
A wee green island with the ruins of 13thC **Calvay Island Castle,** *N of Lochboisdale,* where Bonnie Prince Charlie hid in 1746.

Croft House, South Uist

Ideal Home to islanders of AD200 were wheelhouses divided into 'stalls' like the spokes of a wheel. **Kilpheder Wheelhouse,** *2m W of A865,* is a classic example of that strange, but efficient, design. Sunk in flat ground between dune hills, it looks like an open pit, 7ft deep and 30ft in diameter. Pillars supported a thatch and timber roof, and a 24ft entrance passage runs in from the east away from the chilly shore wind. People lived in these circular houses until the 4thC (and possibly until the 7thC) and borrowed the design from round broch towers. Few wheelhouses have been excavated and many may have been buried by sand drifts.

INDEX

Oswestry, Shrops. 164
Outwood Mill, Surrey. 103
Overbury Court, Tewkesbury, Glos. 156
Owen, Robert. 152
Owletts, Cobham, Kent. 95
Oxburgh Hall, Oxborough, Norfolk. 183, 197
Oxford. 77, 87, 193
Oxford Canal. 87
Oxford Street, London. 119
Oxford University. 46, 54, 86, 87
Oxfordshire, 77, 85–9
Oxwich. W Glam. 141
Oystermouth, W Glam. 141

Padstow, Cornwall. 44
Paine, Thomas. 109, 198
Paisley Shawl Collection, Paisley, Strath. 250
Pakenham Mills, Suffolk. 201
Pall Mall, London. 119
Palmerston, Lord. 72, 73, 74, 185
Pangbourne, Berks. 84
Papa Stour (Isle of), Shetland. 270
Papplewick, Notts. 178
Paradise, Glos. 155
Parc-y-Meirch, Clwyd. 131
Parham House, Storrington, Sussex. 111
Parliament House, Edinburgh, Lothian. 242
Parliaments. 86, 163, 164, 269
Parnell, James. 188
Parnham House, Dorset. 61
Parr, Queen Catherine. 156, 216
Paston letters. 194
Patrington, Humber. 228
Paxton's Tower, Dyfed. 136
Peak Cavern, Castleton, Derbs. 173
Peasants' Revolt. 123, 189, 202
Peckover House, Wisbech, Cambs. 187
Peel, Sir Robert. 209
Peel Tower, Holcombe, Gtr Manchester. 209
Pembroke, Dyfed. 136
Pembroke Castle, Pembroke, Dyfed. 136
Pembroke College, Cambridge. 185
Pendennis Castle, Falmouth, Cornwall. 42
Penmon Priory, Gwynedd. 148
Penn, William. 54–5
Pennard Castle, Swansea, W Glam. 141
Pennine Way. 171
Pennines. 174, 221
Penpont Water, Cornwall. 40
Penrhyn Castle, Gwynedd. 149
Penshurst Place, Kent. 97
Pentre Ifan Burial Chamber, Dyfed. 136
Penzance, Cornwall. 43, 44–5
Pepys, Samuel. 67, 80, 186
Pepysian Library, Magdalene College, Cambridge. 185
Perranporth, Cornwall. 45
Pershore, Here & Worcs. 157
Perth, Tay. 273
Peterborough, Cambs. 186, 187
Peterborough Cathedral, Cambs. 187
Peterhouse College, Cambridge. 185
Petworth House, Sussex. 109
Pevensey Castle, Sussex. 93, 109
Peveril Castle, Castleton, Derbs. 173
Phantassie Doocot, East Linton, Lothian. 242
Piccadilly, London. 119
Pickering, Yorks. 233
Piddlehinton & Piddletrenthide, Dorset. 61
Pierowall Church, Isle of Westray, Orkney. 268
Pilgrim Fathers. 50, 73, 191
Pilgrimages. 95, 101, 103, 124, 196
Pilgrims' Way. 93, 103
Pilkington Glass Museum, Mersey. 213–4
Pilleth Hill, Presteigne, Powys. 152

Pinkworthy Pond, Exmoor, Som. 53
Pitcaple Castle, Grampian. 260
Pitt, William. 99
Pittencrieff House & Park, Dunfermline, Fife. 254
Pittenweem, Fife. 255
Plague. 115, 161, 174, 208–9, 265
Plas Newydd, Gwynedd. 149
Pleshey Castle, Essex. 189
Plush, Dorset. 61
Plymouth, Devon. 50–1
Plympton, Devon. 51
Polesden Lacey, Surrey. 103
Pollock House, Glasgow, Strath. 248
Polperro, Cornwall. 45
Pontardulais, W Glam. 141
Pontcysyllte Aqueduct, Clwyd. 131
Pontefract Castle, Yorks. 233
Pontypool, Gwent. 143
Poole, Dorset. 57, 61–2
Pope, Alexander. 77, 82, 87, 125, 193
Porlock, Som. 54
Port Mary, Dumf & Gall. 251
Port Sunlight, Wirral, Mersey. 214
Porthmadog, Gwynedd. 146, 149
Portland, Isle of, Dorset. 57, 62
Portmeirion, Gwynedd. 149
Portsmouth, Hants. 57, 72
Portsmouth Cathedral, Portsmouth, Hants. 72
Potter, Beatrix. 215
Potteries. 171, 181–2
Potterne, Wilts. 67
Potter's Museum and Exhibition of Humerous Taxidermy, Nr Steyning, Sussex. 111
Powderham Castle, Devon. 51
Powis Castle, Welshpool, Powys. 152
Powys. 150–2
Presteigne, Powys. 152
Preston, Lancs. 211
Preston, Battle of. 210, 211
Preston Manor, Sussex. 110
Preston Mill, East Linton, Lothian. 242
Preston Tower, Northd. 220
Prestongrange Mining Museum and Historic Site, Morrison's Haven, Lothian. 243
Prestonpans Battle Cairn, Preston, Lothian. 243
Prideaux Place, Padstow, Cornwall. 44
Priest's Holes. 87, 94, 148, 153, 166, 198
Prince Regent. See George IV, King
Princes Risborough, Bucks. 91
Princetown, Devon. 49
Prinknash Abbey, Nr Paradise, Glos. 155
Prior's Dean, Hants. 72
Priory Church of St Mary, Lancaster, Lancs. 211
Priory Museum, Reigate, Surrey. 103
Probus, Cornwall. 45
Provan Hall, Glasgow, Strath. 248
Provost Skene's House, Aberdeen, Grampian. 258
Pugin, Augustus. 117, 125
Pulborough, Sussex. 110
Purbeck, Isle of. 57, 59, 62

Quarry Bank Mill, Styal, Ches. 207
Quebec House, Westerham, Kent. 99
Queen Anne's Gate, London. 119
Queen Mary's House, Jedburgh, Borders. 239
Queens' College, Cambridge. 185
Queen's Own Highlanders Regimental Museum, Fort George, Highland. 263
Queen's Picture Gallery, Buckingham Palace, London. 115
Quenby Hall, Leics. 161
Quiraing, Skye, Highland. 264

Raby Castle, Durham. 224

Radipole Lake, Dorset. 64
Radnor, Powys. 151
Raglan Castle, Gwent. 42, 143–4
Ragley Hall, Alcester, Warw. 167
Raleigh, Sir Walter. 42, 44, 49, 63, 74, 81; 122
Ravenglass, Cumbria. 216
Ravenscraig Castle, Fife. 255
Reading, Berks. 84
Rebecca Riots. 129, 141
Reculver Roman Fort, Kent. 98
Redditch, Here & Worcs. 158
Reepham, Norfolk. 198
Reform Act 1832. 67, 178
Regent St, London. 119
Regent's Canal, London. 127, 128
Regent's Park, London. 119
Reigate, Surrey. 103
Rennie, Sir John. 50, 83, 117, 142, 195
Restenneth Priory, Nr Forfar, Tay. 273
Restormel Castle, Nr Lostwithiel, Cornwall. 44
Reynolds, Sir Joshua. 117, 124
Rhuddlan Castle, Clwyd. 131
Ribchester Museum and Fort, Lancs. 211
Richard I, King. 117, 162, 235
Richard II, King. 69, 81, 117, 147, 164, 189, 195, 232, 233, 240
Richard III, King. 92, 145, 159, 160, 162, 191, 223, 232
Richborough Castle and Fort, Nr Sandwich, Kent. 98
Richmond, London. 124
Richmond, Yorks. 233
Richmond Castle, Yorks. 233
Rickmansworth, Herts. 81
Ridgeway Path. 155
Rievaulx Abbey, Yorks. 221, 233, 251
Ring of Brodgar, Stenness, Orkney. 267
Ring Hill, Audley End, Essex. 188
Ripley, Yorks. 233
Ripley Castle, Ripley, Yorks. 233
Ripon, Yorks. 234
Ripon Cathedral, Ripon, Yorks. 234
Rob Roy MacGregor's Grave, Balquihidder Churchyard, Central Scot. 246
Robert III, King. 273
Robin Hood. 171, 178
Robinson Crusoe Statue, Lower Largo, Fife. 255
Roche Abbey, Yorks. 234
Roche Rock Chapel, Nr St Austell, Cornwall. 45
Rochester, Kent. 98
Rockingham, Northants. 162
Rollright Stones, Oxon. 87–8, 167
Rolvenden, Kent. 98
Roman Baths. 55, 56, 142, 151, 160, 165, 203, 219
Roman Museum, Bath, Avon. 56
Roman Museum, Wroxeter, Shrops. 165
Roman Roads. 58, 77, 82, 92, 93, 95, 98, 101, 110, 119, 153, 155, 160, 162, 163, 165, 176, 177, 183, 190, 203, 228
Roman Villas. 65, 74, 75, 95, 105, 107, 154–5, 161
Romney, Hythe & Dymchurch Railway, New Romney, Kent. 98
Romsey, Hants. 72, 73
Romsey Abbey, Romsey, Hants. 72
Ross-on-Wye, Here & Worcs. 158
Rosslyn Chapel, Lothian. 243
Rotherhithe, London. 123
Rotherham, Yorks. 234
Rothesay Castle, Isle of Bute, Strath. 248
The Rothschild Family. 77, 82, 91, 92
Rougemont Castle, Exeter, Devon. 49
Rough Castle, Antonine Wall, Central Scot. 244
Round Church, Cambridge. 185